About the cover

View of Boston and the South Boston Bridge, 1829

The cover image presents a portion of the larger print that appears below. When they explore American histories, scholars consider many different aspects of America's past and connect them for a rich, fresh synthesis. While American images of Boston are plentiful, this one was originally drawn by the French naturalist Jacques Milbert, who toured the northern United States from 1815 to 1823, and later it was reproduced as a lithograph by an unknown French artist. The larger picture thus captures the early fascination of naturalists and of the French with the young American nation.

50°N 120°W   110°W   100°W

Columbia River

Seattle
● Olympia
★ WASHINGTON
▲ Mt. Rainier
(14,411 ft.; 4,392 m)
Mt. St. Helens
(8,366 ft.; 2,550 m) ▲
MTS.

Columbia River

Portland
★ Salem
Eugene ●
CASCADE
OREGON

COAST

RANGES

Helena
★ MONTANA
● Billings

Missouri River
Yellowstone River

NORTH
DAKOTA
Bismarck ★

BADLANDS

SOUTH
DAKOTA
Pierre ★
Sioux
Falls

Boise ●
IDAHO

Snake River

ROCKY

WYOMING
GREAT
DIVIDE
BASIN

Cheyenne ★

BLACK
HILLS

GREAT

NEBRASKA

Platte River

PLAINS

40°N

SIERRA

Carson ●
City
★ Sacramento
San ●
Francisco
● Oakland
San Jose ●

Sacramento River

NEVADA

San Joaquin
River

Fresno ●
▲
Mt. Whitney
(14,494 ft.; 4,418 m)
CALIFORNIA

GREAT
SALT
LAKE

Great
Salt
Lake

Salt Lake
● City

GREAT
BASIN

NEVADA

UTAH

Las
Vegas
●

MOJAVE
DESERT

Colorado River

COLORADO
Mt. Elbert
(14,433 ft.; 4,399 m) ▲
Pikes Peak ▲
(14,110 ft.; 4,301 m)

★ Denver
Colorado
Springs ●

MOUNTAINS

KANSAS
Wichita ●

Arkansas River

Los Angeles ●

San Diego ●

ARIZONA

Phoenix ★

Tucson ●

Santa Fe
★
Albuquerque ●
NEW
MEXICO

El Paso ●

Pecos River

OKLAHOMA

Oklahoma ★
City

Lubbock ●
LLANO
ESTACADO

Red River

Fort Worth ●
TEXAS

Colorado River

PACIFIC
OCEAN

EDWARDS
PLATEAU
Austin ★
San Antonio ●

Rio Grande

M E X I C O

ARCTIC OCEAN
170°W   130°W

RUSSIA

BROOKS RANGE

ALASKA

70°N

Arctic Circle

Mt. McKinley
(20,320 ft.; 6,194 m)
▲
ALASKA
RANGE

CANADA

Yukon River

60°N

Anchorage ●

Bering
Sea

Gulf of Alaska

Juneau ★

ALEUTIAN
ISLANDS

0   250   500 miles
0   250   500 kilometers

160°W   150°W   140°W

Kauai

Niihau

Oahu
Honolulu ★ Molokai
Lanai   Maui
Kahoolawe

HAWAII 22°N

PACIFIC
OCEAN

Hawaii 20°N

0   50   100 miles
0   50   100 kilometers

160°W   158°W   156°W

CANADA

MINNESOTA

WISCONSIN

MICHIGAN

IOWA

MISSOURI

ILLINOIS

INDIANA

OHIO

KENTUCKY

TENNESSEE

ARKANSAS

MISSISSIPPI

ALABAMA

LOUISIANA

GEORGIA

FLORIDA

VERMONT

MAINE

NEW
YORK

NEW
HAMPSHIRE

MASS.

R.I.

CONNECTICUT

PENNSYLVANIA

NEW JERSEY

DELAWARE

WASHINGTON, D.C.

MARYLAND

W. VA.

VIRGINIA

NORTH CAROLINA

SOUTH CAROLINA

TIDEWATER

APPALACHIAN MTS.

CENTRAL
LOWLAND

*Mt. Washington
(6,288 ft.; 1,917 m)*

*Mt. Mitchell
(6,684 ft.; 2,037 m)*

Lake Superior

Lake Huron

Lake Michigan

Lake Ontario

Lake Erie

St. Lawrence River

Hudson River

Potomac River

Chesapeake Bay

Ohio River

Cumberland River

Tennessee River

Mississippi River

Missouri River

Alabama River

Lake Okeechobee

St. Paul
Minneapolis
Milwaukee
Madison
Lansing
Detroit
Chicago
Des Moines
Omaha
Lincoln
Springfield
Indianapolis
Cincinnati
Columbus
Cleveland
Pittsburgh
Wheeling
Charleston
Frankfort
Louisville
Kansas City
St. Louis
Topeka
Jefferson
City
Tulsa
Little
Rock
Memphis
Nashville
Knoxville
Birmingham
Atlanta
Jackson
Montgomery
Baton Rouge
New Orleans
Houston
Dallas
Tallahassee
Jacksonville
Orlando
Miami
Charlotte
Columbia
Charleston
Raleigh
Richmond
Norfolk
Baltimore
Annapolis
Dover
Harrisburg
Trenton
Philadelphia
New York
Hartford
Providence
Boston
Albany
Manchester
Concord
Portland
Augusta
Montpelier
Burlington
Buffalo

ATLANTIC
OCEAN

*Gulf
of
Mexico*

BAHAMAS

CUBA

THE
UNITED STATES

Elevation

Feet	Meters
Over 13,001	Over 3,001
6,561–13,000	2,001–3,000
3,281–6,560	1,001–2,000
1,641–3,280	501–1,000
661–1,640	201–500
0–660	0–200
Below sea level	Below sea level

N
W   E
S

| 0 | 150 | 300 miles |

| 0 | 150 | 300 kilometers |

ATLANTIC OCEAN

**PUERTO
RICO**

San Juan

VIRGIN
ISLANDS

Caribbean Sea

67°W   65°W
18°N

| 0 | 50 | 100 miles |

| 0 | 50 | 100 kilometers |

90°W   80°W   70°W

EXPLORING AMERICAN HISTORIES

EXPLORING AMERICAN HISTORIES

A BRIEF SURVEY WITH SOURCES

Volume 1: To 1877

Nancy A. Hewitt
Rutgers University

Steven F. Lawson
Rutgers University

Bedford/St. Martin's
Boston • New York

To Mary and Charles Takacs, Florence and Hiram Hewitt,
Sarah and Abraham Parker, Lena and Ben Lawson,
who made our American histories possible.

For Bedford/St. Martin's

Publisher for History: Mary V. Dougherty
Senior Executive Editor for History: William J. Lombardo
Director of Development for History: Jane Knetzger
Senior Developmental Editor: Sara Wise
Senior Production Editor: Christina M. Horn
Senior Production Supervisor: Jennifer Peterson
Senior Marketing Manager for U.S. History: Amy Whitaker
Associate Editor: Jennifer Jovin
Editorial Assistant: Arrin Kaplan
Production Assistant: Elise Keller
Copy Editor: Linda McLatchie
Map Editor: Charlotte Miller
Indexer: Leoni McVey
Cartography: Mapping Specialists, Ltd.
Photo Researcher: Naomi Kornhauser
Permissions Manager: Kalina K. Ingham
Senior Art Director: Anna Palchik

Text Designer: Jerilyn Bockorick
Cover Designer: Billy Boardman
Cover Art: View of Boston and the South Boston Bridge (color litho), based on a painting by Jacques Milbert (1766–1840). © Collection of the New-York Historical Society, USA/The Bridgeman Library.
Composition: Cenveo Publisher Services
Printing and Binding: RR Donnelley and Sons

President, Bedford/St. Martin's: Denise B. Wydra
Presidents, Macmillan Higher Education: Joan E. Feinberg and Tom Scotty
Director of Marketing: Karen R. Soeltz
Production Director: Susan W. Brown
Associate Production Director: Elise S. Kaiser
Managing Editor: Elizabeth M. Schaaf

Manufactured in the United States of America.

7   6   5   4
f   e   d   c

For information, write: Bedford/St. Martin's, 75 Arlington Street, Boston, MA 02116   (617-399-4000)

ISBN 978-0-312-40998-2 (Combined Edition)
ISBN 978-1-4576-4194-7 (Loose-leaf Edition)
ISBN 978-0-312-41000-1 (Volume 1)
ISBN 978-1-4576-4195-4 (Loose-leaf Edition, Volume 1)
ISBN 978-0-312-41001-8 (Volume 2)
ISBN 978-1-4576-4196-1 (Loose-leaf Edition, Volume 2)

Exploring American Histories is a new kind of U.S. history survey text. Unique among textbooks, its innovative format makes a broad and diverse American history accessible to a new generation of students and instructors interested in a more active learning and teaching style. To accomplish this, our book joins an inclusive yet brief narrative text with an integrated documents reader; together, these two elements create unsurpassed opportunities for exploring American history in ways best suited for the twenty-first-century classroom.

Format

Our extensive experience teaching American history in a wide variety of classrooms has led us to conclude that students learn history most effectively when they read historical narrative in conjunction with primary sources. Sources bring the past to life in ways that narrative alone cannot, while narrative offers the necessary framework, context, and chronology that documents by themselves do not typically provide. We believe that the most engaging entry to the past starts with individuals and how people in their daily lives connect to larger political, economic, cultural, and international developments. This approach makes the history relevant and memorable. The available textbooks left us unsatisfied, compelling us to assign additional books, readers, and documents we found on the Web. However, these supplementary texts raised costs for our students, and too often students had difficulty seeing how the different readings related to one another. Simply remembering what materials to bring to class became too unwieldy. So we decided to write our own book.

For *Exploring American Histories*, we sought to reconceive the relationship of the textbook and reader to create a mutually supportive set of course materials designed to help our students appreciate the diversity of America's history, to help instructors teach that primary sources are the building blocks of historical interpretation, and to encourage students to see that every past event can and should be considered from multiple perspectives. The people of the past experienced the events of their lifetimes in a variety of ways and from multiple vantage points, and historians debate continually among themselves and the general public about what actually happened and why it matters for us today. Consequently, there is no one story about the past; there are many stories, and so we wanted to emphasize these plural *Histories* in the book's title. Indeed, on the last day of our own survey classes, we measure our success by how well our students can demonstrate that they understand this rich complexity that is central to the discipline, and whether they can put the multiple stories they have come to understand into the context of the larger whole. Instructors at all types of schools share our goal, and we hope that *Exploring American Histories* will help them enrich their students' understanding of events of the past.

For *Exploring American Histories*, we have selected an extensive and diverse array of primary-source materials that highlight multiple perspectives, and we have integrated them at key points as teaching moments within the narrative text. Each chapter contains numerous featured primary sources with a distinctive pedagogy designed to help students make connections between the documents and the text's big themes. Every document is clearly cross-referenced within the narrative so that students can easily incorporate them into their reading as well as reflect on our interpretation. A specially selected set of interrelated documents placed at the end of each chapter addresses an important historical question related to the chapter.

Exploring American Histories also opens up a new dimension to the familiar textbook format by expanding beyond its printed pages to grant students and teachers access to a wealth of online tools and resources built specifically for our text to enhance reading comprehension and promote in-depth study. Of special note, every chapter includes an additional document set that instructors can order packaged with the book; each set of documents focuses on a particular theme and is available only online. Many of these projects incorporate multimedia sources such as audio and video files that until recently were unavailable to work with in class. In addition, *Exploring American Histories* features LearningCurve, an easy-to-assign adaptive learning tool that helps students rehearse the material in the narrative so that they come to class better prepared. Students receive access to LearningCurve, described more fully below, when they purchase a new copy of the book. And because textbook prices are a big concern, our "two-in-one" survey text—a combination of brief narrative plus reader—offers attractive cost savings for students.

Approach

During the last thirty years, scholarship in history has transformed our vision of the past, most notably by dramatically increasing the range of people historians study, and thus deepening and complicating traditional understandings of change over time. Creating a story of the past was easier to do when it was limited to the study of great white men engaged in national politics and high-level diplomacy, but it was also stunted in its explanatory power and disconnected from the life experiences of nearly all our students. Over the last several decades, the historical profession itself has made huge strides in becoming more inclusive in membership, with teachers and scholars increasingly reflecting the diverse face of America. The range of new research has been vast, with a special focus on gender, race, ethnicity, and class, and historians have produced landmark work in women's history, African American history, American Indian history, and labor history.

All of these changes in the historical profession have greatly influenced how the American history survey course is taught in two fundamental ways. First, many instructors now try to help their students see that ordinary people, from all walks of life, can and do affect the course of historical change. Second, many historians have become increasingly transparent about their methodology and have a strong desire to teach their students that history is an interpretive discipline and open to multiple perspectives. Since the 1970s, survey textbooks have changed in coverage, organization, and pedagogy, but they have struggled to get it right—becoming overwhelming in their scope, difficult to read, and losing the sense of story that makes the past accessible, engaging, and comprehensible. As more instructors have embraced teaching with documents, they have come to see these shortcomings in the available survey textbooks. Along with many of our colleagues, we came to the same conclusion ourselves. Many current texts are too long, so we've made ours brief. *Exploring American Histories* is comprehensive, but with a carefully selected amount of detail that is more in tune with what instructors can realistically expect their students to remember. Many texts include some documents, but the balance between narrative (too much) and primary sources (too few) was off-kilter, so we have included more documents and integrated them in creative ways that help students make the necessary connections and that spur them to think critically. But the most innovative aspect of *Exploring American Histories*, and what makes it a true alternative, is that its format introduces a unique textbook structure organized around the broad theme of *diversity.*

Diversity as a theme works in *Exploring American Histories* in several ways. First, diversity supports our presentation of an inclusive historical narrative, one that recognizes the American past as a series of interwoven stories made by a multiplicity of historical actors. We do this within a strong national framework that allows our readers to see how the various stories fit together and to understand why they matter. Our narrative is complemented by a wide variety of documents that challenge students to consider multiple points of view. In chapter 4, students hear from both a woman accused of witchcraft and a minister who defended the Salem witch trials. In chapter 25, we ask our readers to contrast an idyllic, inviting depiction of 1950s suburbia with a racially restrictive covenant of the same period.

Second, our theme of diversity allows us to foreground the role of individual agency as we push readers to consider the reasons behind historical change. Each chapter opens with a pair of **American Histories**, biographies that showcase individuals who experienced and influenced events in a particular period, and then returns to them throughout the chapter to strengthen the connections and highlight their place in the bigger picture. These biographies cover both well-known Americans—such as Daniel Shays, Frederick Douglass, Andrew Carnegie, and Eleanor Roosevelt—and those who never gained fame or fortune—such as the activist Amy Kirby Post, organizer Luisa Moreno, and World War II internee Fred Korematsu. Introducing such a broad range of biographical subjects illuminates the many ways that individuals shaped and were shaped by historical events. This strategy also works to make visible throughout the chapter the intersections where history from the top down meets history from the bottom up and to connect social and political histories to their relationships with economic, cultural, and diplomatic developments. We work to show that events at the national level, shaped by elite political and economic leaders, have a direct impact on the lives of ordinary people; at the same time, we demonstrate that actions at the local level often have a significant influence on decisions made at the centers of national government and commerce. The discussions of the interrelationship among international, national, and local theaters and actors incorporate the pathbreaking scholarship of the last three decades, which has focused on gender, race, class, and ethnicity in North America and the United States, and on colonization, empire, and globalization in the larger world.

Primary Sources

The heart of *Exploring American Histories* is its primary sources, and in every chapter we supply students with numerous and carefully selected documents from which they can evaluate the text's interpretations and construct their own versions of history. These firsthand accounts include maps, drawings, material artifacts, paintings, speeches, sermons, letters, diaries, memoirs, newspaper articles, political cartoons, laws, wills, court cases, petitions, advertisements, photographs, and blogs. In selecting documents, we have provided multiple perspectives on critical issues, including both well-known sources and those that are less familiar. But our choices were also influenced by the kinds of primary sources that exist. For some periods of American history and some topics, the available primary sources are limited and fragmentary.

For other eras and issues, the sources are varied and abundant, indeed sometimes overwhelming, especially as we move into the twentieth century. In all time periods, some groups of Americans are far better represented in primary sources than others. Those who were wealthy, well educated, and politically powerful produced and preserved many sources about their lives. And their voices are well represented in this textbook. But we have also provided documents by American Indians, enslaved Africans, colonial women, rural residents, immigrants, working people, and young people. Moreover, the lives of those who left few sources of their own can often be illuminated by reading documents written by elites to see what information they yield, intentionally or unintentionally, about less well-documented groups.

Individual documents are embedded throughout every chapter and connected to the narrative text with **Explore** prompts, and within each chapter these documents are treated in the following three ways:

- Each chapter has one annotated textual or visual source, with questions in the margins to help students consider a specific phrase or feature and analyze the source as a whole. These questions and annotations are intended to train students in historical habits of mind. A **Put It in Context** question prompts students to consider the source in terms of the broad themes of the chapter.
- Each chapter contains **Two Views**, a paired set of documents that show contrasting perspectives. Two Views documents are introduced by a single headnote and are followed by **Interpret the Evidence** and **Put It in Context** questions that prompt students to analyze and compare both items and place them in a larger historical framework.
- Each chapter also presents one or more additional documents consisting of excerpts or images of classic or lesser-known sources. These are provided to encourage more practice working with sources and to offer additional perspectives to compare with the narrative. These documents are accompanied by informative headnotes and conclude with **Interpret the Evidence** and **Put It in Context** questions.

A **Document Project** at the end of every chapter is the capstone of our integrated primary-sources approach. Each Document Project is a collection of five or six documents focused on a critical issue central to that chapter. It is introduced by a brief overview and ends with interpretive questions that ask students to draw conclusions based on what they have learned in the chapter and read in the sources.

We understand that the instructor's role is crucial in teaching students how to analyze primary-source materials and develop interpretations. Teachers can use the documents to encourage critical thinking and also to measure students' understanding and assess their progress. The integration of the documents in the narrative should prompt students to read more closely than they usually do, as they will see more clearly the direct connection between the two. We have organized the documents to give instructors the flexibility to use them in many different ways—as in-class discussion prompts, for take-home writing assignments, and even as the basis for exam questions—and also in different combinations, as the documents throughout the chapter can be compared and contrasted with one another. An instructor's manual for *Exploring American Histories* provides a wealth of creative suggestions for using the documents program effectively (see the Versions and Supplements description on pages xv–xviii for more information on all the available instructor resources).

More Help for Students

We know that students often need help making sense of their reading. As instructors, all of us have had students complain that they cannot figure out what's important in the textbooks we assign. For many of our students, especially those just out of high school, their college history survey textbook is likely the most difficult book they have ever encountered. We understand the challenges that our students face, so in addition to the extensive document program, we have included the following pedagogical features designed to aid student learning:

- **Review and Relate** questions help students focus on main themes and concepts presented in each major section of the chapter.
- **Key terms** in boldface highlight important content. All terms are defined in a glossary at the end of the book.
- Clear **conclusions** help students summarize what they've read.
- A full-page **Chapter Review** lets students review key terms, important concepts, and notable events.

In addition, the book includes access to **LearningCurve**, an online adaptive learning tool that promotes engaged reading and focused review. Cross-references at the end of every major section and chapter in the text prompt students to log in and rehearse their understanding of the material they have just read. Students move at their own pace and accumulate points as they go, giving the interaction a game-like feel. Feedback for incorrect responses explains why the answer is incorrect and directs students back to the text to review before they attempt to answer the question again. The end result is a better understanding of the key elements of the text. See the inside front cover for more details.

We imagine *Exploring American Histories* as a new kind of American history textbook, one that not only offers a strong, concise narrative but also challenges students to construct their own interpretations through primary-source analysis. We are thrilled that our hopes have come to fruition, and we believe that our textbook will provide a thought-provoking and highly useful foundation for every U.S. history survey course and will benefit students and faculty alike. The numerous opportunities provided for active learning will allow teachers to engage students in stimulating ways and help them experience the past in closer connection to the present. After all, active learning is the basis for active citizenship, and teaching the survey course is our chance as historians, whose work is highly specialized, to reach the greatest number of undergraduates. We hope not only to inspire the historical imaginations of those who will create the next generation of American histories but also to spur them to consider the issues of today in light of the stories of yesterday.

Acknowledgments

We wish to thank the talented scholars and teachers who were kind enough to give their time and knowledge to review the manuscript:

Benjamin Allen, *South Texas College*
Christine Anderson, *Xavier University*
Uzoamaka Melissa C. Anyiwo, *Curry College*
Anthony A. Ball, *Housatonic Community College*
Terry A. Barnhart, *Eastern Illinois University*
Edwin Benson, *North Harford High School*
Paul Berk, *Christian Brothers University*
Deborah L. Blackwell, *Texas A&M International University*
Thomas Born, *Blinn College*
Margaret Bramlett, *St. Andrews Episcopal High School*
Lauren K. Bristow, *Collin College*
Tsekani Browne, *Duquesne University*
Jon L. Brudvig, *Dickinson State University*
Dave Bush, *Shasta College*
Barbara Calluori, *Montclair State University*
Julia Schiavone Camacho, *The University of Texas at El Paso*
Jacqueline Glass Campbell, *Francis Marion University*
Amy E. Canfield, *Lewis-Clark State College*
Dominic Carrillo, *Grossmont College*
Mark R. Cheathem, *Cumberland University*
Laurel A. Clark, *University of Hartford*
Myles L. Clowers, *San Diego City College*
Hamilton Cravens, *Iowa State University*
Audrey Crawford, *Houston Community College*
John Crum, *University of Delaware*
Alex G. Cummins, *St. Johns River State College*
Susanne Deberry-Cole, *Morgan State University*
Julian J. DelGaudio, *Long Beach City College*

Patricia Norred Derr, *Kutztown University*
John Donoghue, *Loyola University Chicago*
Timothy Draper, *Waubonsee Community College*
David Dzurec, *University of Scranton*
Keith Edgerton, *Montana State University Billings*
Blake Ellis, *Lone Star College*
Christine Erickson, *Indiana University–Purdue University Fort Wayne*
Todd Estes, *Oakland University*
Gabrielle Everett, *Jefferson College*
Julie Fairchild, *Sinclair Community College*
Randy Finley, *Georgia Perimeter College*
Kirsten Fischer, *University of Minnesota*
Michelle Fishman-Cross, *College of Staten Island*
Jeffrey Forret, *Lamar University*
Kristen Foster, *Marquette University*
Susan Freeman, *Western Michigan University*
Nancy Gabin, *Purdue University*
Kevin Gannon, *Grand View University*
Benton Gates, *Indiana University–Purdue University Fort Wayne*
Bruce Geelhoed, *Ball State University*
Mark Gelfand, *Boston College*
Jason George, *The Bryn Mawr School*
Judith A. Giesberg, *Villanova University*
Sherry Ann Gray, *Mid-South Community College*
Patrick Griffin, *University of Notre Dame*
Aaron Gulyas, *Mott Community College*
Scott Gurman, *Northern Illinois University*
Melanie Gustafson, *University of Vermont*
Brian Hart, *Del Mar College*
Paul Hart, *Texas State University*
Paul Harvey, *University of Colorado Colorado Springs*
Woody Holton, *University of Richmond*
Vilja Hulden, *University of Arizona*
Colette A. Hyman, *Winona State University*
Brenda Jackson-Abernathy, *Belmont University*
Troy R. Johnson, *California State University–Long Beach*
Shelli Jordan-Zirkle, *Shoreline Community College*
Jennifer Kelly, *The University of Texas at Austin*
Kelly Kennington, *Auburn University*
Andrew E. Kersten, *University of Wisconsin–Green Bay*
Janilyn M. Kocher, *Richland Community College*
Max Krochmal, *Duke University*
Peggy Lambert, *Lone Star College*
Jennifer R. Lang, *Delgado Community College*
John S. Leiby, *Paradise Valley Community College*
Mitchell Lerner, *The Ohio State University*
Matthew Loayza, *Minnesota State University, Mankato*
Gabriel J. Loiacono, *University of Wisconsin Oshkosh*
John F. Lyons, *Joliet Junior College*
Lorie Maltby, *Henderson Community College*

Christopher Manning, *Loyola University Chicago*
Marty D. Matthews, *North Carolina State University*
Eric Mayer, *Victor Valley College*
Suzanne K. McCormack, *Community College of Rhode Island*
David McDaniel, *Marquette University*
J. Kent McGaughy, *Houston Community College, Northwest*
Alan McPherson, *Howard University*
Sarah Hand Meacham, *Virginia Commonwealth University*
Brian Craig Miller, *Emporia State University*
Brett Mizelle, *California State University Long Beach*
Mark Moser, *The University of North Carolina at Greensboro*
Jennifer Murray, *Coastal Carolina University*
Peter C. Murray, *Methodist University*
Steven E. Nash, *East Tennessee State University*
Chris Newman, *Elgin Community College*
David Noon, *University of Alaska Southeast*
Richard H. Owens, *West Liberty University*
David J. Peavler, *Towson University*
Laura A. Perry, *University of Memphis*
Wesley Phelps, *University of St. Thomas*
Merline Pitre, *Texas Southern University*
Eunice G. Pollack, *University of North Texas*
Kimberly Porter, *University of North Dakota*
Cynthia Prescott, *University of North Dakota*
Gene Preuss, *University of Houston*
Sandra Pryor, *Old Dominion University*
Rhonda Ragsdale, *Lone Star College*
Michaela Reaves, *California Lutheran University*
Peggy Renner, *Glendale Community College*
Steven D. Reschly, *Truman State University*
Barney J. Rickman, *Valdosta State University*
Pamela Riney-Kehrberg, *Iowa State University*
Paul Ringel, *High Point University*
Timothy Roberts, *Western Illinois University*
Glenn Robins, *Georgia Southwestern State University*
Alicia E. Rodriquez, *California State University Bakersfield*
Mark Roehrs, *Lincoln Land Community College*
Patricia Roessner, *Marple Newtown High School*
John G. Roush, *St. Petersburg College*
James Russell, *St. Thomas Aquinas College*
Eric Schlereth, *The University of Texas at Dallas*
Ronald Schultz, *University of Wyoming*
Stanley K. Schultz, *University of Wisconsin–Madison*
Sharon Shackelford, *Erie Community College*
Donald R. Shaffer, *American Public University System*
David J. Silverman, *The George Washington University*
Andrea Smalley, *Northern Illinois University*
Molly Smith, *Friends School of Baltimore*
David L. Snead, *Liberty University*
David Snyder, *Delaware Valley College*
Jodie Steeley, *Merced College*
Bryan E. Stone, *Del Mar College*

Emily Straus, *SUNY Fredonia*
Jean Stuntz, *West Texas A&M University*
Nikki M. Taylor, *University of Cincinnati*
Heather Ann Thompson, *Temple University*
Timothy Thurber, *Virginia Commonwealth University*
T. J. Tomlin, *University of Northern Colorado*
Laura Trauth, *Community College of Baltimore County–Essex*
Russell M. Tremayne, *College of Southern Idaho*
Laura Tuennerman-Kaplan, *California University of Pennsylvania*
Vincent Vinikas, *The University of Arkansas at Little Rock*
David Voelker, *University of Wisconsin–Green Bay*
Ed Wehrle, *Eastern Illinois University*
Gregory Wilson, *University of Akron*
Maria Cristina Zaccarini, *Adelphi University*
Nancy Zens, *Central Oregon Community College*
Jean Hansen Zuckweiler, *University of Northern Colorado*

We also appreciate the help the following scholars and students gave us in providing the information we needed at critical points in the writing of this text: Leslie Brown, Andrew Buchanan, Gillian Carroll, Susan J. Carroll, Paul Clemens, Dorothy Sue Cobble, Jane Coleman-Harbison, Alison Cronk, Elisabeth Eittreim, Phyllis Hunter, Tera Hunter, William Link, James Livingston, Julia Livingston, Gilda Morales, Vicki L. Ruiz, Susan Schrepfer, Bonnie Smith, Melissa Stein, Margaret Sumner, Jessica Unger, and Anne Valk. Jacqueline Castledine and Julia Sandy-Bailey worked closely with us in finding documents and creating the Document Projects. Without them, this would not be a docutext.

We would particularly like to applaud the many hardworking and creative people at Bedford/St. Martin's who guided us through the labyrinthine process of writing a textbook from scratch. No one was more important to us than the indefatigable and unflappable Sara Wise, our developmental editor. We are also deeply grateful to Patricia Rossi, who first persuaded us to undertake this project. Joan Feinberg had the vision that guided us through every page of this book. We could not have had a better team than Denise Wydra, Mary Dougherty, William Lombardo, Jane Knetzger, Christina Horn, Jennifer Jovin, Katherine Bates, Amy Whitaker, Jenna Bookin Barry, Daniel McDonough, and Arrin Kaplan. They also enlisted Naomi Kornhauser, Charlotte Miller, Linda McLatchie, Heidi Hood, Rob Heinrich, Shannon Hunt, John Reisbord, and Michelle McSweeney to provide invaluable service. Finally, we would like to thank our friends and family who have been asking us these past years, "When will you be finished?" We are very pleased to be able to respond, "The time is now."

Nancy A. Hewitt and Steven F. Lawson

Adopters of **Exploring American Histories** and their students have access to abundant resources, including documents, presentation and testing materials, volumes in the acclaimed Bedford Series in History and Culture, and much more. For more information on the offerings described below, visit the book's catalog site at bedfordstmartins.com/hewittlawson/catalog, or contact your local Bedford/St. Martin's sales representative.

Get the Right Version for Your Class

To accommodate different course lengths and course budgets, *Exploring American Histories* is available in several different formats, including three-hole punched loose-leaf Budget books versions and e-books, which are available at a substantial discount.

- Combined edition (chapters 1–29)—available in paperback, loose-leaf, and e-book formats
- Volume 1: To 1877 (chapters 1–14)—available in paperback, loose-leaf, and e-book formats
- Volume 2: Since 1865 (chapters 14–29)—available in paperback, loose-leaf, and e-book formats

Assign the online, interactive Bedford x-Book. With all the content of the print book—plus integrated LearningCurve and the 29 extra Document Projects, some with audio or video—the *x-Book for Exploring American Histories* features a robust search engine, navigation tools, easy ways to take and share notes, and interactive exercises. And with fast ways to rearrange chapters and add new pages, sections, or links, it lets teachers build just the right book for their course.

Let students choose their e-book format. Students can purchase the downloadable *Bedford e-Book to Go for Exploring American Histories* from our Web site or find other PDF versions of the e-book at our publishing partners' sites: CourseSmart, Barnes & Noble NookStudy; Kno; CafeScribe; or Chegg.

Assign LearningCurve So That Your Students Come to Class Prepared

As described in the preface and on the inside front cover, students purchasing new books receive access to Learning Curve for *Exploring American Histories*, an online learning tool designed to help students rehearse content at their own pace in a nonthreatening, game-like environment. The feedback for wrong answers provides instructional coaching and sends students back to the book for review. Students answer as many questions as necessary to reach a target score, with repeated chances to revisit material they haven't mastered. Assigning LearningCurve is easy for instructors, and the reporting features help instructors track overall class trends and spot topics that are giving students trouble.

Send Students to Free Online Resources

The book's companion site at bedfordstmartins.com/hewittlawson gives students a way to read, write, and study by providing plentiful quizzes and activities, study aids, and history research and writing help.

FREE Online Study Guide. Available at the companion site, this popular resource provides students with quizzes and activities for each chapter, including multiple-choice self-tests that focus on important concepts; flash cards that test students' knowledge of key terms; timeline activities that emphasize causal relationships; and map quizzes intended to strengthen students' geography skills. Instructors can monitor students' progress through an online Quiz Gradebook or receive email updates.

FREE Research, Writing, and Anti-plagiarism Advice. Available at the companion site, Bedford's **History Research and Writing Help** includes **History Research and Reference Sources**, with links to history-related databases, indexes, and journals; **More Sources and How to Format a History Paper**, with clear advice on how to integrate primary and secondary sources into research papers and how to cite and format sources correctly; **Build a Bibliography**, a simple Web-based tool known as The Bedford Bibliographer that generates bibliographies in four commonly used documentation styles; and **Tips on Avoiding Plagiarism**, an online tutorial that reviews the consequences of plagiarism and features exercises to help students practice integrating sources and recognize acceptable summaries.

Take Advantage of Instructor Resources

Bedford/St. Martin's has developed a rich array of teaching resources for this book and for this course. They range from lecture and presentation materials and assessment tools to course management options. Most can be downloaded or ordered at bedfordstmartins.com/hewittlawson/catalog.

***HistoryClass* for *Exploring American Histories*.** *History-Class*, a Bedford/St. Martin's Online Course Space, puts the online resources available with this textbook in one convenient and completely customizable course space. There you and your students can access the interactive x-book; video clips, maps, images, documents, and links; chapter review quizzes; and research and writing help. In *HistoryClass* you can get all our premium content and tools, which you can assign, rearrange, and mix with your own resources. *HistoryClass* also includes LearningCurve, Bedford/St. Martin's adaptive tool for quizzing to learn, and the additional Document Project for each chapter. For more information, visit yourhistoryclass.com.

Instructor's Resource Manual. The instructor's manual offers both experienced and first-time instructors tools for preparing lectures and running discussions. It includes chapter-review material, teaching strategies, and a guide to chapter-specific supplements available for the text, plus suggestions on how to get the most out of LearningCurve.

Computerized Test Bank. The test bank includes a mix of carefully crafted multiple-choice, short-answer, and essay questions for each chapter. It also contains the Interpret the Evidence and Put It in Context questions from the text-book and model answers for each. All questions appear in Microsoft Word format and in easy-to-use test bank soft-ware that allows instructors to add, edit, re-sequence, and print questions and answers. Instructors can also export questions into a variety of formats, including WebCT and Blackboard.

***The Bedford Lecture Kit*: PowerPoint Maps, Images, Lecture Outlines, and i>clicker Content.** Look good and save time with *The Bedford Lecture Kit*. These presentation materials are downloadable individually from the Instructor Resources tab at bedfordstmartins.com/hewittlawson/catalog and are available on *The Bedford Lecture Kit* **Instructor's Resource CD-ROM**. They provide ready-made and fully customizable PowerPoint multimedia presentations that include lecture outlines with embedded maps, figures, and selected images from the textbook and extra background for instructors. Also available are maps and selected images in JPEG and PowerPoint formats; content for i>clicker, a classroom response system, in Microsoft Word and PowerPoint formats; the Instructor's Resource Manual in Microsoft Word format; and outline maps in

PDF format for quizzing or handing out. All files are suit-able for copying onto transparency acetates.

***Make History*—Free Documents, Maps, Images, and Web Sites.** *Make History* combines the best Web resources with hundreds of maps and images, to make it simple to find the source material you need. Browse the collection of thousands of resources by course or by topic, date, and type. Each item has been carefully chosen and helpfully annotated to make it easy to find exactly what you need. Available at bedfordstmartins.com/makehistory.

***America in Motion*: Video Clips for U.S. History.** Set history in motion with *America in Motion,* an instructor DVD containing dozens of short digital movie files of events in twentieth-century American history. From the wreckage of the battleship *Maine*, to FDR's fireside chats, to Oliver North testifying before Congress, *America in Motion* engages students with dynamic scenes from key events and challenges them to think critically. All files are classroom-ready, edited for brevity, and easily inte-grated with PowerPoint or other presentation software for electronic lectures or assignments. An accompanying guide provides each clip's historical context, ideas for use, and suggested questions.

Videos and Multimedia. A wide assortment of videos and multimedia CD-ROMs on various topics in U.S. history is available to qualified adopters through your Bedford/St. Martin's sales representative.

Package and Save Your Students Money

For information on free packages and discounts up to 50%, visit bedfordstmartins.com/hewittlawson/catalog or contact your local Bedford/St. Martin's sales representative.

Online Document Projects for *Exploring American Histories*. A complete set of additional 29 Document Projects—one per chapter—is available to provide students with more opportunities to work with primary sources. Each set mirrors the pedagogy in the text with overviews, headnotes, and Interpret the Evidence and Put It in Context questions, and many sets include audio and video sources. Topics include loyalists in the American Revolution, abolitionist debates, women's liberation, and the Reagan Revolution. Automatically available online to all students who purchase the x-Book or *HistoryClass* and free when packaged with the text.

The Bedford Series in History and Culture. More than 150 titles in this highly praised series combine first-rate scholarship, historical narrative, and important primary documents for undergraduate courses. Each book is brief, inexpensive, and focused on a specific topic or period. For a complete list of titles, visit bedfordstmartins.com/history/series. Package discounts are available.

Rand McNally Historical Atlas of American History. This collection of more than 84 full-color maps illustrates key events and eras, from early exploration, settlement, expansion, and immigration to U.S. involvement in wars abroad and on U.S. soil. Introductory pages for each section include a brief overview, timelines, graphs, and photographs to quickly establish a historical context. Available for $3.00 when packaged with the print text.

Maps in Context: A Workbook for American History. Written by historical cartography expert Gerald A. Danzer (University of Illinois at Chicago), this skill-building workbook helps students comprehend essential connections between geographic literacy and historical understanding. Organized to correspond to the typical U.S. survey course, *Maps in Context* presents a wealth of map-centered projects and convenient pop quizzes that give students hands-on experience working with maps. Available free when packaged with the print text.

The Bedford Glossary for U.S. History. This handy supplement for the survey course gives students historically contextualized definitions for hundreds of terms—from *abolitionism* to *zoot suit*—that they will encounter in lectures, reading, and exams. Available free when packaged with the print text.

U.S. History Matters: A Student Guide to U.S. History Online. This resource, written by Kelly Schrum, Alan Gevinson, and the late Roy Rosenzweig (all of George Mason University), provides an illustrated and annotated guide to 250 of the most useful Web sites for student research in U.S. history as well as advice on evaluating and using Internet sources. This essential guide is based on the acclaimed "History Matters" Web site developed by the American Social History Project and the Center for History and New Media. Available free when packaged with the print text.

Trade Books. Titles published by sister companies Hill and Wang; Farrar, Straus and Giroux; Henry Holt and Company; St. Martin's Press; Picador; and Palgrave Macmillan are available at a 50% discount when packaged with Bedford/St. Martin's textbooks. For more information, visit bedfordstmartins.com/tradeup.

A Pocket Guide to Writing in History. This portable and affordable reference tool by Mary Lynn Rampolla, now also available as a searchable e-book, provides reading, writing, and research advice useful to students in all history courses. Concise yet comprehensive advice on approaching typical history assignments, developing critical-reading skills, writing effective history papers, conducting research, using and documenting sources, and avoiding plagiarism—enhanced with practical tips and examples throughout—have made this slim reference a best seller. Package discounts are available.

A Student's Guide to History. This complete guide to success in any history course provides the practical help students need to be effective. In addition to introducing students to the nature of the discipline, author Jules Benjamin teaches a wide range of skills from preparing for exams to approaching common writing assignments, and he explains the research and documentation process with plentiful examples. Package discounts are available.

Going to the Source: The Bedford Reader in American History. Developed by Victoria Bissell Brown and Timothy J. Shannon, this reader's strong pedagogical framework helps students learn how to ask fruitful questions in order to evaluate documents effectively and develop critical-reading skills. The reader's wide variety of chapter topics that complement the survey course and its rich diversity of sources—from personal letters to political cartoons—provoke students' interest as it teaches them the skills they need to successfully interrogate historical sources. Package discounts are available.

America Firsthand. With its distinctive focus on ordinary people, this primary documents reader, by Anthony Marcus, John M. Giggie, and David Burner, offers a remarkable range of perspectives on American history from those who lived it. Popular Points of View sections expose students to different perspectives on a specific event or topic, and Visual Portfolios invite analysis of the visual record. Package discounts are available.

Explore Other Docutexts from Bedford/St. Martin's

Bedford/St. Martin's has been a leader in pioneering new ways to bring primary sources into the undergraduate classroom, beginning with the Bedford Series in History and

Culture, described above. The "docutext" format of *Exploring American Histories,* which combines a brief narrative with themed collections of written and visual sources, represents another innovation in making documents accessible for students. Docutexts authored by leading historians are now available from Bedford for a variety of history courses.

World History Survey. Find out about *Ways of the World: A Brief Global History with Sources,* by Robert W. Strayer, at bedfordstmartins.com/strayersources/catalog.

African American History. Find out about *Freedom on My Mind: A History of African Americans, with Documents,* by Deborah Gray White, Mia Bay, and Waldo E. Martin Jr., at bedfordstmartins.com/graywhite/catalog.

U.S. Women's History. Find out about *Through Women's Eyes: An American History with Documents,* by Ellen Carol DuBois and Lynn Dumenil, at bedfordstmartins.com/duboisdumenil/catalog.

Native American History. Find out about *First Peoples: A Documentary Survey of American Indian History,* by Colin G. Calloway, at bedfordstmartins.com/calloway/catalog.

Twentieth-Century European History. Find out about *Europe in the Contemporary World, 1900 to the Present: A Narrative History with Documents,* by Bonnie G. Smith, at bedfordstmartins.com/smitheurope/catalog.

Brief Contents

Contents

3
Global Changes Reshape Colonial America
1680–1750   64

4
Religious Strife and Social Upheavals
1680–1750   96

5
Wars and Empires
1750–1774   128

6
Revolutions
1775–1783   160

7

Political Cultures
1783–1800   192

AMERICAN HISTORIES
Daniel Shays and Alexander Hamilton   193

8

New Frontiers
1790–1820   226

AMERICAN HISTORIES
Parker Cleaveland and Sacagawea   227

9

**Defending and
Redefining the Nation**

1809–1832   258

AMERICAN HISTORIES
Dolley Madison and John Ross   259

10

**Slavery Expands
South and West**

1830–1850   292

AMERICAN HISTORIES
James Henry Hammond and Solomon Northrup   293

11
Social and Cultural Ferment in the North
1820–1850   326

14
Emancipations and Reconstructions
1863–1877 424

Maps, Figures, and Tables

Maps

How to Use This Book

Start by reading the narrative and using the chapter tools to help you focus on what's important.

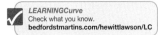

LEARNINGCurve
Check what you know.
bedfordstmartins.com/hewittlawson/LC

Scan the **chapter outline** for a preview of the chapter's big topics and themes.

The Granger Collection, New York

Sawmill in Terraville, South Dakota, 1888.

The Granger Collection, New York

Shoe-factory worker in Lynn, Massachusetts, 1895.

As you read, pay attention to the **boldfaced key terms**, which highlight important concepts you'll likely see on an exam. All terms are defined in the glossary of Key Terms at the end of the book.

oslavery document. Some Garrisonians a
work of the **underground railroad**, a se
ivists who assisted fugitives fleeing ensla
In 1835 Sarah and Angelina Grimké j
d soon began lecturing for the organiza
rominent South Carolina planter, they
iladelphia and converted to Quakerism

new leisure pursuits. Many joined colleagues at restaurants, the theater, or sporting events. They also attended plays and lectures with their wives, visited museums, and took their children to the circus.

REVIEW & RELATE

At the end of each major section, answer the **Review & Relate** questions to check your understanding of key concepts.

Why did American cities become larger and more diverse in the first half of the nineteenth century?

What values and beliefs did the emerging American middle class embrace?

LEARNINGCurve bedfordstmartins.com/hewittlawson/LC

Then log on to **LearningCurve** to review the section you've just read. LearningCurve lets you move at your own pace and earn points as you go.

Use the Chapter Review to draw connections across all the sections of the narrative and identify significant historical developments.

Return to **LearningCurve** to review chapter material.

Test your knowledge of important concepts from the **Key Terms** list. See if you can not only define each term but also describe its significance.

LEARNINGCurve
Check what you know.
bedfordstmartins.com/hewittlawson/LC

Chapter Review

Online Study Guide ▶ bedfordstmartins.com/hewittlawson

KEY TERMS

separate spheres (p. 331)
deskilling (p. 333)
nativists (p. 337)
Second Great Awakening (p. 339)
temperance (p. 340)
transcendentalism (p. 341)
utopian societies (p. 344)
Appeal . . . to the Colored Citizens (p. 346)

Answer the **Review & Relate** questions, which repeat the chapter's end-of-section comprehension prompts.

iety (AASS) (p. 346)
46)
(p. 348)

REVIEW & RELATE

1. Why did American cities become larger and more diverse in the first half of the nineteenth century?

2. What values and beliefs did the emerging American middle class embrace?

3. How and why did American manufacturing change over the course of the first half of the nineteenth century?

4. How did Northerners respond to the hard times that followed the panic of 1837? How did responses to the crisis vary by class, ethnicity, and religion?

5. What impact did the Second Great Awakening have in the North?

6. What new religious organizations and viewpoints emerged in the first half of the nineteenth century, *outside* of Protestant evangelical denominations?

7. How did the temperance movement reflect the range of tactics and participants involved in reform during the 1830s and 1840s?

8. What connections can you identify between utopian communities and mainstream reform movements in the first half of the nineteenth century?

9. How did the American Anti-Slavery Society differ from earlier abolitionist organizations?

10. How did conflicts over gender and race shape the development of the abolitionist movement in the 1830s and 1840s?

TIMELINE OF EVENTS

1820–1850	Size, number, and diversity of northern cities grow; immigration surges
1823	Textile factory town built in Lowell, Massachusetts
1826	American Temperance Society founded
1827	First workingmen's political party founded
1829	David Walker publishes *Appeal . . . to the Colored Citizens*
1830	Joseph Smith publishes *The Book of Mormon*
September 1830	Charles Grandison Finney brings Second Great Awakening to Rochester, New York
1833	William Lloyd Garrison founds American Anti-Slavery Society (AASS)
1837–1842	Panic of 1837
1839	American Anti-Slavery Society splits over the role of women in the society
1840	Liberty Party formed
	World Anti-Slavery Convention, L
1842	Amy Post helps found the Wester Anti-Slavery Society
1843	William Miller predicts Second Coming of Christ
1844	Congress funds construction of the first telegraph line
May 1844	Anti-immigrant violence rocks Philadelphia
1845	Frederick Douglass publishes *Narrative of the Life of Frederick Douglass*
	Margaret Fuller publishes *Woman in the Nineteenth Century*
1845–1846	Irish potato famine
1846	Henry David Thoreau publishes *Civil Disobedience*

Review the **Timeline of Events**, which shows the relationship among chapter events.

Visit the **free Online Study Guide**, which provides more quizzes and activities to help you master the chapter content.

Apply these principles to your analysis of the chapter's primary sources.

What will they be able to say about the author? How will they interpret the meaning of these sentences? Will they understand the abbreviations that have become a part of our everyday language?

A tweet—like a blog, a speech on YouTube, or a video of a protest—is a primary source, an original document or artifact created at or near the time of an event by people participating in or observing it. Different types of primary sources exist from different periods of history. In the seventeenth century and earlier, drawings, paintings, stone carvings, and relics were as plentiful as written sources are today. Printed texts and handwritten letters became more available from the eighteenth century on, while photographs, newspapers, typewritten letters, and recordings are widely available from the mid-nineteenth century through the twentieth and twenty-first centuries.

Many primary sources are produced by official institutions, while others are created by ordinary people who wrote and kept diaries and letters, took pictures, participated in oral interviews, or sent e-mails. Some documents such as newspapers provide information from official sources alongside letters, interviews, articles, and opinions offered by editors and political cartoonists. As with future historians who try to decode Twitter, historians have always had to make sense of documents filled with abbreviations and peculiarities of language and to decipher handwriting styles as puzzling as digital shorthand.

Historians use a wealth of primary sources to build an interpretation of the past and to set that interpretation alongside the work of other scholars. History refers to both the uncovering of facts about the past and interpretations of it. Besides presenting facts, then, this textbook provides interpretations of American history constructed by the book's authors that are based on their own primary research as well as the work of other historians. But it also offers a large array of primary sources, described on the next several pages, from which you can create your own interpretations and compare them with those offered by the authors.

To guide your analysis, begin by asking several basic questions that can be succinctly thought of as the five Ws: Who? What? Where? When? Why?

- **Who** is the author of the document and who is the intended audience?
- **What** kind of source is it—written, visual, official, unofficial—and what are the main ideas or opinions presented?
- **Where** was it created and how might that shape its meaning?
- **When** was it produced and how close to the event being recorded?
- **Why** was it created and how does that influence your interpretation of it?

Because history is interpretive, the kind of questions you ask will help shape the answers you come up with. The more questions you explore, the richer the history you produce will be.

Keep in mind that this book's narrative text and documents work together, each reinforcing the other. While the narrative helps place the documents in a larger context, the documents provide for more active engagement with an event or issue. Rather than merely receiving a collection of information, you will be able to participate in shaping an account of the past. If you consider all the primary sources in a chapter together, including those in the Document Project, you can begin to understand how historians assess and piece together diverse sources of evidence to forge a larger narrative about American history. The next pages introduce you to the types of documents you will be working with in this book.

Get to work exploring the documents.

Individual documents are easy to find and well integrated into every chapter.

> Red **Explore** boxes tell you where to find the source and where to return to the text to continue the story.

the issue opposing the measure. John C. Calhoun, a proslavery senator from South Carolina, refused to support any compromise that allowed Congress to decide the fate of slavery in the western territories. Meanwhile William H. Seward, an antislavery Whig senator from New York, proclaimed that in all good conscience he could not support a compromise that forced Northerners to help hunt down fugitives from slavery. Daniel Webster, a Massachusetts Whig and an elder statesman, appealed to his fellow senators to support the compromise in order to preserve the Union, but Congress adjourned with the fate of California undecided.

Explore

See Document 12.2 for Calhoun's final attempt to reject a compromise.

Before the Senate reconvened in the fall of 1850, however, the political landscape changed in unexpected ways. Henry Clay retired in the spring of 1850, leaving the Capitol with his last great legislative effort unfinished. On March 31, Calhoun died; his absence from the Senate made compromise more likely. In July, President Taylor died unexpectedly, and his vice president, Millard Fillmore of Buffalo, New York, was elevated to the presidency. Fillmore then appointed Webster as secretary of state, removing him from the Senate as well.

In September 1850, with President Fillmore's support, a younger cohort of senators and representatives steered the **Compromise of 1850** through Congress, one clause at a time, thereby allowing legislators to support only those parts of the compromise they found palatable. In the end, all the provisions passed, and Fillmore quickly signed the bills into law. California entered the Union as a free state, and John C. Frémont entered Congress as one of that state's first two senators. The Compromise of 1850, like the Missouri Compromise thirty years earlier, fended off a sectional crisis, but it also signaled future problems. Would popular sovereignty prevail when later territories sought admission to the Union, and would Northerners abide by a fugitive slave law that called on them to aid directly in the capture of runaway slaves?

The Fugitive Slave Act Inspires Northern Protest

The fugitive slave laws of 1793 and 1824 mandated that all states aid in apprehending and returning runaway slaves to their owners. The **Fugitive Slave Act of 1850** was different in two important respects. First, it eliminated jury trials for alleged fugitives. Second, the law required individual citizens, not just state officials, to help return runaways or

DOCUMENT 12.2

John C. Calhoun | On the Compromise of 1850, 1850

California's application for statehood in 1849 prompted another crisis over slavery. Southerners feared that admitting California as a free state would tip the balance in Congress against them. Senator Henry Clay tried to broker a compromise that would admit California as a free state but toughen the fugitive slave law. Amid vigorous congressional debate, South Carolina senator John C. Calhoun insisted that slavery be preserved. A colleague read Calhoun's address for the aging and ill senator. Calhoun's death a few weeks later helped pave the way for final passage of the Compromise of 1850.

Explore

How can the Union be saved? To this I answer, there is but one way by which it can be, and that is, by adopting such measures as will satisfy the States belonging to the Southern section that they can remain in the Union consistently with their honor and their safety. . . .

. . . The South asks for justice, simple justice, and less she ought not to take. She has no compromise to offer but the Constitution, and no concession or surrender to make. She has already surrendered so much that she has little left to surrender. Such a settlement would go to the root of the evil, and remove all cause of discontent, by satisfying the South that she could remain honorably and safely in the Union, and thereby restore the harmony and fraternal feelings between the sections which existed anterior to the Missouri agitation. . . .

But can this be done? Yes, easily; not by the weaker party, for it can of itself do nothing—not even protect itself—but by the stronger. The North has only to will it to accomplish it—to do justice by conceding to the South an equal right in the acquired territory, and to do her duty by causing the stipulations relative to fugitive slaves to be faithfully fulfilled—to cease the agitation of the slave question, and to provide for the insertion of a provision in the Constitution, by an amendment, which will restore to the South in substance the power she possessed of protecting herself, before the equilibrium between the sections was destroyed by the action of this Government. There will be no difficulty in devising such a provision—one that will protect the South, and which at the same time will improve and strengthen the Government, instead of impairing and weakening it.

Source: *The Congressional Globe*, 31st Cong., 2nd Sess. (1850), 453, 455.

Interpret the Evidence

- Calhoun objects to the Compromise of 1850 because it does not sufficiently protect southern rights. Which rights does he think need protection, and why does he think those rights are in jeopardy?
- Calhoun wants to regain the "harmony and fraternal feelings" between the sections that existed before "the Missouri agitation." Why does he pinpoint the Missouri Compromise as the moment when sectional divisions took hold?

Put It in Context

What developments in the 1840s led Calhoun and other southern leaders to fear that the South was becoming weaker, at least politically, compared to the North? Would northern senators have agreed?

else risk being fined or imprisoned. The act angered many Northerners who believed that the federal government had gone too far in protecting the rights of slaveholders and thereby aroused sympathy for the abolitionist cause.

Before 1850, the most well-known individuals aiding fugitives were free blacks such as David Ruggles in New

York City; Jermaine Loguen in Syracuse, New York; and, after his own successful escape, Frederick Douglass in Rochester, New York. Their main allies in this work were white Quakers such as Amy and Isaac Post in Rochester; Thomas Garrett in Chester County, Pennsylvania; and Levi and Catherine Coffin in Newport, Indiana. The work was

> Two **Interpret the Evidence** questions help you analyze the source.

> A **Put It in Context** question helps you connect the primary source to the larger historical narrative.

Annotated documents help you examine sources closely by breaking them down into smaller components.

Annotations direct you to points of interest—either specific text passages or visual details—to help you analyze the document and to model what to look for when you approach similar types of documents on your own.

Drunkard's Home, 1850

Temperance societies undertook a variety of activities to publiciz[e] and parades were popular venues, as were newspapers and boo[ks] *Temperance Offering*, an 1850 publication of the Sons of Temper[ance] 1842, the Sons of Temperance was one of the oldest temperance [societies] mutual aid society that offered members life insurance, funeral b[enefits]

Explore

How does the father's drinking seem to affect the family's economic situation?

In this illustration, what is the source of the father's violence?

How [...] me[...]

The National Temperance Offering, and Sons and Daughters of Temperance Gift (PS1265.N3 1850), University of Virginia Library

Put It in Context
What moral arguments did members of the temperance movement use to support their cause?

Sharecropping Agreement, 1870

Because Congress did not generally provide freedpeople with land, African Americans lacked the capital to start their own farms. At the same time, plantation owners needed labor to plant and harvest their crops for market. Out of mutual necessity, white plantation owners entered into sharecropping contracts with blacks to work their farms in exchange for a portion of the crop, such as the following contract between Willis P. Bocock and several of his former slaves. Bocock owned Waldwick Plantation in Marengo County, Alabama.

Explore

What are the farmers' responsibilities?

Why would Bocock want to clarify that his laborers would work equally hard throughout the year?

How might putting a lien on crops for debts owed create difficulties for the black farmer?

Contract made the 3rd day of January in the year 1870 between us the free people who have signed this paper of one part, and our employer, Willis P. Bocock, of the other part. We agree to take charge of and cultivate for the year 1870, a portion of land, say [left blank] acres or thereabouts, to be laid off to us by our employer on his plantation, and to tend the same well in the usual crops, in such proportions as we and he may agree upon. We are to furnish the necessary labor, say an average hand to every 15 acres in the crops, making in all average hands; and are to have all proper work done, ditching, fencing, repairing, etc., as well as cultivating and saving the crops of all kinds, so as to put and keep the land we occupy and tend in good order for cropping, and to make a good crop ourselves; and to do our fair share of job work about the place. . . . We are to be responsible for the good conduct of ourselves, our hands, and families, and agree that all shall be respectful to employer, owners, and manager, honest, industrious, and careful about every thing, and shall not interrupt any thing about the place, working as industriously the last part of the year as the first; and then our employer agrees that he and his manager shall treat us kindly, and help us to study our interest and do our duty. If any hand or family proves to be of bad character, or dishonest, or lazy, or disobedient, or any way unsuitable our employer or manager has the right, and we have the right, to have such turned off. . . .

For the labor and services of ourselves and hands rendered as above stated, we are to have one third part of all the crops, or their net-proceeds, made and secured, or prepared for market by our force. . . .

We are to be furnished by our employer through his manager with provisions if we call for them: not over one peck of meal or corn, and $3\frac{1}{2}$ pounds of meat or its equivalent per week, for every 15 acres of land or average hand, to be charged to us at fair market prices.

And whatever may be due by us, or our hands to our employer for provisions or any thing else, during the year, is to be a lien on our share of the crops, and is to be retained by him out of the same before we receive our part.

Source: Waldwick Plantation Records, 1834–1971, LPR174, box 1, folder 9, Alabama Department of Archives and History.

Put It in Context
Why would free blacks and poor whites be willing to enter into such a contract?

All annotated documents conclude with **Put It in Context** questions that ask you to figure out how the document fits in—or doesn't fit in—with the narrative you're reading.

"Two Views" comparison documents present contrasting or complementary perspectives on a single topic so that you can form your own interpretation.

Life in the Mills: Two Views

In the 1820s, the textile mills of Lowell, Massachusetts, provided the daughters of local farmers a way to contribute to their family incomes and experience some adventure. Soon, however, a slowing economy led to reduced wages, longer hours, and demands for increased productivity. The Lowell workers organized to protest these changes and went on strike several times during the late 1820s and the 1830s. The first selection below is from an 1844 edition of *The Lowell Offering*, a magazine to which mill workers contributed stories and poems. Factory owners controlled the content of the magazine to ensure an idealized vision of life in the mills. Still, the letter from "Susan" below does highlight the physical toll of industrial labor. Susan was a pseudonym for Harriet Farley, a weaver and the editor of *The Lowell Offering*. The selection at right is by Harriet Robinson, who entered the mills at age ten in 1834. She published a memoir in 1898 in which she recalls the growing dissatisfaction of the women workers and her critical role in a strike in 1836.

Explore

11.1 Letter from a Lowell Factory Worker, 1844

It makes my feet ache and swell to stand so much, but I suppose I shall get accustomed to that too. The girls generally wear old shoes about their work, and you know nothing is easier; but they almost all say that when they have worked here a year or two they have to procure shoes a size or two larger than before they came. The right hand, which is the one used in stopping and starting the loom, becomes larger than the left; but in other respects the factory is not detrimental to a young girl's appearance. Here they look delicate, but not sickly; they laugh at those who are much exposed, and get pretty brown; but I, for one, had rather be brown than pure white. I never saw so many pretty looking girls as there are

here. Though the number of men is small in proportion there are many marriages here, and a great deal of courting. I will tell you of this last sometime. . . .

You ask if the work is not disagreeable. Not when one is accustomed to it. It tried my patience sadly at first, and does now when it does not run well; but, in general, I like it very much. It is easy to do, and does not require very violent exertion, as much of our farm work does.

You also ask how I get along with the girls here. Very well indeed.

and workingmen started joining forces throughout the North to advocate for principles of liberty and equality. Self-educated artisans like Thomas Skidmore of New York City argued for the redistribution of property and the abolition of inheritance to equalize wealth in the nation. However, most workingmen's parties focused on more practical proposals: government distribution of free land in the West, the abolition of compulsory militia service and imprisonment for debt, public funding for education, and the regulation of banks and corporations. Although the

Explore

11.2 Harriet Robinson | Reflections on the 1836 Lowell Mills Strike, 1898

My own recollection of this first strike (or "turn out" as it was called) is very vivid. I worked in a lower room, where I had heard the proposed strike fully, if not vehemently, discussed; I had been an ardent listener to what was said against this attempt at "oppression" on the part of the corporation, and naturally I took sides with the strikers. When the day came on which the girls were to turn out, those in the upper rooms started first, and so many of them left that our mill was at once shut down. Then, when the girls in my room stood irresolute, uncertain what to do, asking each other, "Would you?" or "Shall we turn out?" and not one of them having the courage to lead off, *I*, who began to think they would not go out, after all their talk, became impatient, and started on ahead, saying, with childish bravado, "I don't care what you do, I am going to turn out, whether any one else does or not"; and I marched out, and was followed by the others.

As I looked back at the long line that followed me, I was more proud than I have ever been since at any success I may have achieved, and more proud than I shall ever be again until my own beloved State gives to its women citizens the right of suffrage.

The agent of the corporation where I then worked took some small revenges on the supposed ringleaders; on the principle of sending the weaker to the wall, my mother [a landlady] was turned away from her boarding-house, that functionary saying, "Mrs. Hanson, you could not prevent the older girls from turning out, but your daughter is a child, and *her* you could control."

It is hardly necessary to say that so far as results were concerned this strike did no good. The dissatisfaction of the operatives subsided, or burned itself out, and though the authorities did not accede to their demands, the majority returned to their work, and the corporation went on cutting down the wages.

Source: Harriet H. Robinson, *Loom and Spindle; or, Life among the Early Mill Girls* (New York: Thomas Y. Crowell, 1898), 84–86.

Interpret the Evidence questions help you analyze the sources.

Interpret the Evidence

- How did life on the farm differ from life in the factory? How does "Susan" describe her own adjustment to industrial work?
- What connections does Robinson make between the strike and the larger social and political context of 1830s Massachusetts? How does she see herself and her actions?

Put It in Context

Were "Susan" and Robinson typical factory workers in this period? Why or why not?

Trades Union was established later that year, with delegates representing more than twenty-five thousand workers across the North. These organizations aided skilled workers but refused admission to women and unskilled men.

panic of 1837, the common plight of workers became clearer. But the economic crisis made unified action nearly impossible as individuals sought to hold on to what little they had by any means available.

A **Document Project** concludes each chapter.

Each project provides multiple perspectives on a particular issue or development along with an **introduction** and **questions** to guide you through the process of interpretation. The chapter itself offers the background material for your interpretation.

and grasses that would have kept the earth from eroding and turning into dust. Instead, dust storms brought life to a grinding halt, blocking out the midday sun. **See Document Project 22: The Depression in Rural America, page 712.**

As the storms continued through the 1930s, most residents—approximately 75 percent—remained on

Red **cross-references** at the relevant point in the chapter direct you to the chapter's Document Project.

DOCUMENT 22.6
The Life of a White Sharecropper, 1938

In 1936 workers in the WPA's Federal Writers Project began the Folklore Project. Interviewers spoke with thousands of ordinary individuals to document their home lives, education, occupations, political and religious views, and the impact of the Great Depression on their families. Folklore Project worker Claude Dunnagan collected the following story from a white sharecropping family in Longtown, North Carolina.

I guess we been hard luck renters all our lives—me and Morrison both. They was ten young'uns in my family, and I was next to the youngest. We had it awful hard. . . . We went to Yadkin County and rented an old rundown farm for a share of what we could raise. The crops wasn't any good that year, the landlord came and got what we had raised and had the auctioneers come and sell our tools and furniture. They was a bunch of people at the sale that day from all around. I was standin' there watchin' the man sell the things when I saw a good lookin' man in overalls lookin' toward me. He watched me all durin' the sale and I knew what he was thinkin'. That was the first time I ever saw Allison. I reckon he fell in love with me right off, for we was married a few days later. Allison didn't have no true father. His mother wasn't married, and he was raised up by his kin folks. Then we moved to a little farm near Longtown, about ten miles away. The owner said we could have three-fourths of what we raised. The first two years the crops turned out pretty good so we could pay off the landlord and buy a little furniture . . . a bed and table and some chairs. Then the first baby came on. That was Hildreth. He's out in the field workin' now, suckerin' [removing sprouts] tobacco. . . . By that time, we was able to get a cow, and that came in good, for the baby was awful thin and weak. . . .

Hildreth was only six, but he could help a lot, pullin' and tyin' the tobacco, and helpin' hang it in the barn. We got out more tobacco that year than any other, but when we took it to market in Winston, they wasn't payin' but about twelve cents a pound for the best grade, so when we give the landlord his share and paid the fertilizer bill, we didn't have enough left to pay the doctor and store bill. We didn't know what we was goin' to do durin' the winter. Allison had raised a few vegetables and apples, so we canned what we could and traded the rest for some cotton cloth up at the store so the children would have something to wear that winter. Allison got a job helpin' build a barn for a neighbor, but it didn't last but two days. The neighbor gave him two second hand pairs of overalls for the work. . . .

Things are a lot better for the renter today than in the past. It used to be we couldn't get enough to eat and wear. Now we got a cow, a hog, and some chickens. Allison bought a second-hand car and every Sunday afternoon we ride somewhere. It's the only time we ever get away from home.

The landlord gives us five-sixths of what we raise, so we get along pretty good when the crops are fair. Of course we have to furnish the fertilizer and livestock. This year we had seven barns of tobacco and four acres of corn. Wheat turned out pretty good, too. We raised forty-three bushels, and I hear the price is going to be fair at the roller mill. I canned about all our extra fruits and vegetables. I reckon we still got about a hundred cans in the pantry.

Source: Library of Congress, Manuscript Division, WPA Federal Writers Project Collection.

DOCUMENT PROJECT 22

The Depression in Rural America

During the 1930s, rural Americans' lives were devastated by the twin disasters of the Great Depression and, in the Great Plains, the most sustained drought in American history. But both problems only deepened the already difficult lives of many farmers. Agriculture in the South had long been dominated by sharecropping, a system that hampered crop diversification and left many African American tenant farmers vulnerable to exploitation by white landowners. In the Midwest, farmers had spent decades overgrazing pastures and exhausting the soil through overproduction. Prices dropped dramatically throughout the 1920s, and farmers were the only group whose incomes fell during that decade.

When the depression hit, many farmers did not have the resources to stay on their land, and farm foreclosures tripled in the early 1930s. Sharecroppers, tenant farmers, and former farm owners left their homes to find better opportunities, and a million people left the Great Plains alone. Most ended up as migrant agricultural laborers in farms and orchards on the West Coast. Feeling overrun by refugees, California passed a law in 1937 making it a misdemeanor to bring into California any indigent person who was not a state resident. This law remained in effect until 1941.

Under the New Deal, the federal government acted in a number of ways to relieve the plight of farmers around the country. The Agricultural Adjustment Act attempted to raise crop prices and stabilize agricultural incomes by encouraging farmers to cut production. The Farm Credit Act helped some farmers refinance mortgages at a lower rate, the Rural Electrification Administration brought electricity to farm areas previously without it, and the Soil Conservation Service advised farmers on how to properly cultivate their hillsides. The report of the Great Plains Committee (Document 22.10), another Roosevelt creation, details additional recommendations for helping the agricultural economy in the Midwest.

The following documents on the lives of farmers, sharecroppers, migrants, and labor organizers during the 1930s shed light on many aspects of the Great Depression. Consider what they reveal about the challenges faced by rural Americans and how different individuals and groups responded to those problems.

DOCUMENT 22.5
Ann Marie Low | Dust Bowl Diary, 1934

When massive dust storms swept through the Midwest beginning in the early 1930s, they blew away the topsoil of a once productive farm region and created hazardous living conditions. Residents needed to clean and wash repetitively to perform even simple daily tasks. Ann Marie Low, a young woman living with her family in southeastern North Dakota, describes in her diary the monotony and difficulty of life in the Dust Bowl.

May 21, 1934, Monday . . .
Saturday Dad, Bud, and I planted an acre of potatoes. There was so much dirt in the air I couldn't see Bud only a few feet in front of me. Even the air in the house was just a haze. In the evening the wind died down, and Cap came to take me to the movie. We joked about how hard it is to get cleaned up enough to go anywhere.

The newspapers report that on May 10 there was such a strong wind the experts in Chicago estimated 12,000,000 tons of Plains soil was dumped on that city. By the next day the sun was obscured in Washington, D.C., and ships 300 miles out at sea reported dust settling on their decks.

Sunday the dust wasn't so bad. Dad and I drove cattle to the Big Pasture. Then I churned butter and baked a ham, bread, and cookies for the men, as no telling when Mama will be back.

May 30, 1934, Wednesday
Ethel got along fine, so Mama left her at the hospital and came to Jamestown by train Friday. Dad took us both home.

The mess was incredible! Dirt had blown into the house all week and lay inches deep on everything. Every towel and curtain was just black. There wasn't a clean dish or cooking utensil. There was no food. Oh, there were eggs and milk and one loaf left of the bread I baked the weekend before. I looked in the cooler box down the well (our refrigerator) and found a little ham and butter. It was late, so Mama and I cooked some ham and eggs for the men's supper because that was all we could fix in a hurry. It turned out they had been living on ham and eggs for two days.

Mama was very tired. After she had fixed starter for bread, I insisted she go to bed and I'd do all the dishes. It took until 10 o'clock to wash all the dirty dishes. That's not wiping them—just washing them. The cupboards had to be washed out to have a clean place to put them.

Saturday was a busy day. Before starting breakfast I had to sweep and wash all the dirt off the kitchen and dining room floors, wash the stove, pancake griddle, and dining room table and chairs. There was cooking, baking, and churning to be done for those hungry men. Dad is 6 feet 4 inches tall, with a big frame. Bud is 6 feet 3 inches and almost as big-boned as Dad. We say feeding them is like filling a silo.

Mama couldn't make bread until I carried water to wash the bread mixer. I couldn't churn until the churn was washed and scalded. We just couldn't do anything until something was washed first. Every room had to have dirt almost shoveled out of it before we could wash floors and furniture.

We had no time to wash clothes, but it was necessary. I had to wash out the boiler, wash tubs, and the washing machine before we could use them. Then every towel, curtain, piece of bedding, and garment had to be taken outdoors to have as much dust as possible shaken out before washing. The cistern is dry, so I had to carry all the water we needed from the well.

Source: Ann Marie Low, *Dust Bowl Diary* (Lincoln: University of Nebraska Press, 1984), 96–97.

DOCUMENT 22.7

Sharecropping Family in Washington County, Arkansas, 1935

The Resettlement Administration (later the Farm Security Administration) documented the plight of migrant farmworkers and sharecroppers in numerous photographs. The following photo, taken by the noted photojournalist Arthur Rothstein, depicts a sharecropper's wife and daughters in Washington County, Arkansas, in 1935.

DOCUMENT 22.9

Frank Stokes | Let the Mexicans Organize, 1936

While union organizers made some gains in the industrial sector, they made little headway in the agricultural fields of California. Frank Stokes was a citrus grower who broke with his fellow farmers to support migrant labor organizing. In the following selection, Stokes argues in favor of unionization among migrant Mexican farmworkers.

The Mexican is to agricultural California what the Negro is to the medieval South. His treatment by the vegetable growers of the Imperial Valley is well known. What has happened to him in the San Joaquin has likewise been told. But for a time at least it appeared that the "citrus belt" was different. Then came the strike of the Mexican fruit pickers in Orange County. In its wake came the vigilantes, the night riders, the strike-breakers, the reporters whose job it was to "slant" all the stories in favor of the packers and grove owners. There followed the State Motor Patrol, which for the first time in the history of strike disorders in California set up a portable radio broadcasting station "in a secret place" in the strike area "to direct law-and-order activities." And special deputy badges blossomed as thick as Roosevelt buttons in the recent campaign.

Sheriff Jackson declared bravely: "It was the strikers themselves who drew first blood so from now on we will meet them on that basis." "This is no fight," said he, "between orchardists and pickers. It is a fight between the entire population of Orange County and a bunch of Communists." However, dozens and dozens of non-Communist Mexican fruit pickers were jailed; 116 were arrested en masse while traveling in automobiles along the highway. They were charged with riot and placed under bail of $500 each. . . . After fifteen days in jail the hearing was finally held—and the state's witnesses were able to identify only one person as having taken part in the trouble. . . . Judge Ames of the Superior Court ordered the release of all but one identified prisoner and severely criticized the authorities for holding the Mexicans in jail for so long a time when they must have known it would not be possible to identify even a small portion of the prisoners.

For weeks during the strike newspaper stories described the brave stand taken by "law-abiding citizens." These stories were adorned with such headlines as "Vigilantes Battle Citrus Strikers in War on Reds." During all this time, so far as I know, only one paper—the Los Angeles *Evening News*—defended the fruit pickers. . . .

These Mexicans were asking for a well-deserved wage increase and free transportation to and from the widely scattered groves; they also asked that tools be furnished by the employers. Finally they asked recognition of their newly formed union. Recognition of the Mexican laboring man's union, his cooperative organization formed in order that he might obtain a little more for his commodity, which is labor—here was the crucial point. The growers and packers agreed to furnish tools; they agreed to furnish transportation to and from the groves. They even agreed to a slight wage increase, which still left the workers underpaid. But recognition of the Mexican workers' union? Never! . . .

Not only in the fields are the Mexican people exploited. Not only as earners but as buyers they are looked upon as legitimate prey—for old washing machines that will not clean clothes, for old automobiles that wheeze and let down, for woolen blankets made of cotton, for last season's shop-worn wearing apparel. Gathered in villages composed of rough board shanties or drifting with the seasons from vegetable fields of the Imperial Valley to the grape vineyards of the San Joaquin, wherever they go it is the same old, pathetic story. Cheap labor!

Source: Frank Stokes, "Let the Mexicans Organize," *The Nation*, December 19, 1936, 731–32.

DOCUMENT 22.10

Report of the Great Plains Committee, 1937

In 1936 President Roosevelt established the Great Plains Committee to investigate the causes of the Dust Bowl and possible solutions for the region. The committee's report, submitted the following year, outlined how federal, state, and local government agencies could work together to restore the Great Plains to economic health. One of the witnesses the committee called to testify was Otis Nation, an organizer for the Oklahoma Tenant Farmers' Union, whose testimony follows.

Much has been written of our droughts here in Oklahoma, and how they have driven the farmers from the land. But little has been said of the other tentacles that choke off the livelihood of the small owner and the tenant. We do not wish to minimize the seriousness of these droughts and their effects on the farming population. But droughts alone would not have permanently displaced these farmers. The great majority of migrants had already become share-tenants and sharecroppers. The droughts hastened a process that had already begun. We submit the following as the cases for migratory agricultural workers:

1. *High interest rates.* Often a farmer borrows money for periods of 10 months and is charged an interest rate of 10 percent. These rates are charged when crops are good and when they fail. Through such practices the farmer loses his ownership; he becomes a tenant, then a sharecropper, then a migrant.
2. *The tenant and sharecropping system.* When share tenants are charged 33⅓ percent of all corn or feed crops and 25 percent or more on cotton, plus 10 percent on all money borrowed at the bank, when sharecroppers are charged 50 to 75 percent of all he produces to the landlords, plus 10 percent for the bank's share on money invested; when these robbing practices are carried on in a community or a State, is it surprising that 33,241 farm families have left Oklahoma in the past 5 years?
3. *Land exhaustion, droughts, soil erosion, and the one-crop system of farming.* Lacking capital and equipment, small farmers have been unable to terrace their land or conduct other soil-conservation practices. The tenant and sharecropping system is chiefly responsible for the one-crop system. The landlord dictates what crops are to be planted—invariably cotton—and the tenant either plants it or gets off.
4. *Unstable markets.* Approximately a month and a half before the wheat harvest this year the price for this product was 93 cents here in Oklahoma City. But at harvest time the farmer sold his wheat for 46 cents to 60 cents per bushel, depending on the grade. . . . Kaffir [a grain sorghum] was selling for $1.30 one month ago, and yesterday we sold some for 85 cents per hundred. . . .

It is obvious to all of us that farm prices are set by speculators. The farmer's losses at the market have contributed in no small part to the farmer losing his place on the land. Higher prices for farm products are quoted when the farmer has nothing to sell.

5. *Tractor farming.* In Creek County, Okla., we have the record of one land-owner purchasing 3 tractors and forcing 31 of his 34 tenants and croppers from the land. Most of these families left the State when neither jobs nor relief could be secured. This is over 10 families per machine, 10 families who must quit their profession and seek employment in an unfriendly, industrialized farming section of Arizona or California. Many of these families were even unable to become "Joads" [the fictional family in *The Grapes of Wrath*] in these other States, and had to seek relief from an unfriendly national administration and a more unfriendly State administration. . . .

At this hearing we will have all kinds of statistical material presented and arguments based on this material. But I am one of those who is more interested in the people, my people, than in mere figures. I do not agree with those who say "the no-good must always be weeded out." I say that all of these people, casually referred to in statistical sums, are 100-percent Americans. There are no more important problems facing us than the problem of stopping this human erosion and rehabilitating those unfortunates who have already been thrown off the land. Certainly it is un-American for Americans to be starved and dispossessed of their homes in our land of plenty. Those who seek to exploit and harass these American refugees, the migratory workers, are against our principles of democracy.

Source: U.S. Congress, House Select Committee to Investigate the Interstate Migration of Destitute Citizens (Washington: Government Printing Office, 1940–1941), 2102.

Interpret the Evidence

1. What does Ann Marie Low's description of a typical day suggest about the particular challenges women faced during the Dust Bowl era (Document 22.5)?
2. Compare the living conditions described by a white southern sharecropper (Document 22.6) to those of the migrant family described by John Steinbeck (Document 22.8). How does the poverty of the two families differ? How would you explain the differences you note?
3. Compare the sharecropper's story (Document 22.6) with the photograph of the Arkansas family (Document 22.7). Do the subjects seem to react to the Great Depression in the same way? Do they seem hopeful or hopeless?
4. According to Frank Stokes, how did the fruit packers and grove owners characterize their conflict with the Mexican farmworkers (Document 22.9)? In what ways did their characterization draw on more general conservative criticisms of the New Deal?
5. According to the Great Plains Committee testimony (Document 22.10), what role did human-caused factors play in producing the misery that accompanied the dust storms of the early 1930s?

Put It in Context

- What do these documents tell us about expectations regarding government help during the Great Depression?

EXPLORING AMERICAN HISTORIES

Service Historique de la Marine, Vincennes, France/Giraudon/The Bridgeman Art Library

Biblioteca Medicea-Laurenziana, Florence, Italy/The Bridgeman Art Library

A map showing the arrival of the English in Virginia, 1585–1588.

Aztec feather artisans at work, from the Florentine Codex, c. 1540–1585.

1
Mapping Global Frontiers
to 1585

Meeting of Hernán Cortés and Montezuma, from the Duran Codex, 1579.

AMERICAN HISTORIES

In 1519 a young Indian woman named Malintzin was thrust into the center of dramatic events that transformed not only her world but also the world at large. As a young girl, Malintzin, whose birth name is lost to history, lived in the rural area of Coatzacoalcos on the frontier between the expanding kingdom of the Mexica and the declining Mayan states of the Yucatán peninsula. Raised in a noble household, Malintzin was fluent in Nahuatl, the language of the Mexica.

In 1515 or 1516, when she was between the ages of eight and twelve, Malintzin was taken by or given to Mexica merchants, perhaps as a peace offering to stave off military attacks. She then entered a well-established trade in slaves, consisting mostly of women and girls, who were sent eastward to work in the expanding cotton fields. Malintzin was apparently sold to a Chontal Mayan village along the Tabasco River near the Gulf of Mexico. As a slave, Malintzin was among thousands of workers who planted, watered, weeded, and harvested the cotton or beat and carded the raw fibers into thread and spun and dyed the yarn. She may also have been forced into a sexual relationship as the concubine of a landowner. Whatever her situation, Malintzin learned the Mayan language during her captivity.

In 1517 Mayan villagers sighted Spanish adventurers along local rivers and drove them off. But in 1519 the Spaniards returned. Well armed and sailing huge boats, they traveled up the Tabasco River and attacked local villages. The Maya's cotton armor and wooden arrows were no match for the invaders' steel swords, guns, and horses. Forced to surrender, the Maya offered the Spaniards food, gold, and twenty enslaved women, including Malintzin. The Spanish leader, Hernán Cortés, baptized the enslaved women as Christians, though they neither understood nor consented to the ritual. He assigned each of them Christian names, including Marina, which was later changed to Malintzin. Cortés then divided the women among his senior officers, giving Malintzin to the highest-ranking noble.

Already fluent in Nahuatl and Mayan, Malintzin soon learned Spanish. Within a matter of months, she became the chief translator between the Spaniards and native peoples. As Cortés moved into territories ruled by the Mexica (whom the Spaniards called Aztecs), his success depended on his ability to understand Aztec ways of thinking and to convince subjugated groups to fight against their despotic rulers. Malintzin thus accompanied Cortés at every step, including his triumphant conquest of the Aztec capital in the fall of 1521.

At the same time that Malintzin played a key role in the conquest of the Aztecs, Martin Waldseemüller sought to map the frontiers along which these conflicts erupted. Born in present-day Germany in the early 1470s, Waldseemüller enrolled at the University of Fribourg in 1490, where he probably studied theology. He would gain fame, however, not as a cleric but as a cartographer, or mapmaker.

In 1507 Waldseemüller and Mathias Ringmann produced a map of the world, a small globe, and a Latin translation of the four voyages of the Italian explorer Amerigo Vespucci. The map and the globe, entitled *Universalis Cosmographia*, depict the "known" world as well as the "new" worlds recently discovered by European explorers. The latter include an elongated territory labeled America, set between the continents of Africa and Asia. A thousand copies of the map were produced, each consisting of twelve sections engraved on wood and covering some 36 square feet. The map offered a view of the world never before attempted.

In 1513 Waldseemüller and Ringmann published the world's first atlas, which included a Latin edition of the works of Ptolemy, the Greco-Egyptian mathematician and astronomer. Three years later, Waldseemüller produced an updated map of the world, the *Carta Marina*. Apparently in response to challenges regarding Vespucci's role in discovering new territories, he substituted the term *Terra Incognita* ("unknown land") for the region he had earlier labeled America. But the 1507 map had already circulated widely, and *America* became part of the European lexicon. •

THE PERSONAL HISTORIES of Malintzin and Martin Waldseemüller were both shaped by the profound consequences of contact between the peoples of Europe and those of the Americas. Both Malintzin and Waldseemüller helped to map the frontiers of an increasingly global society. **See Document Project 1: Mapping America, page 27**. It took much longer in the sixteenth century than today to travel from continent to continent and to communicate across such vast distances. Nonetheless, animals, plants, goods, ideas, and people began circulating regularly among Asia, Africa, Europe, and the Americas during the sixteenth century. Malintzin and Waldseemüller, in their very different ways, were part of these dramatic transformations.

Native Peoples in the Americas

It is likely that the first migrants to the Americas were northeast Asians who arrived some 13,000 to 15,000 years ago. By the time Malintzin participated in the Spanish conquest of the Aztecs in the early sixteenth century, the Americas probably had a population of 60 million to 70 million people. The Nahuatl- and Mayan-speaking groups whose lands bordered the Gulf of Mexico were among hundreds of native societies that covered this vast landmass. Most lived within a few hundred miles of the equator, while only about 6 million to 7 million people likely lived in present-day North America. Despite its isolation, the Americas, like other regions of the world, were home to diverse and dynamic societies, ranging from nomadic hunter-gatherers to large and sophisticated city-centered empires.

Native Peoples Develop Diverse Cultures

Much of what we know as the Americas was probably first settled by peoples from northeast Asia. Between about 16,000 and 14,000 B.C.E., the growth of glaciers during the Wisconsin period led to a dramatic drop in sea levels and created a land bridge in the Bering Straits, between present-day Siberia and Alaska. Early settlers probably traveled over this bridge, known as **Beringia**, following herds of mammoths, musk oxen, and woolly rhinoceroses.

While most of these groups settled along the coast or gradually pushed inland, others probably used boats, hugging the shore and landing at various points along the Pacific coastline. Whether on foot or by boat, most groups traveled southward, skirting melting glaciers and seeking better hunting grounds and more abundant plant life. The mammoths and other large game disappeared about 10,000 years ago, and many groups then depended on smaller game, fish, roots, berries, and other plant foods to survive. At the same time, migrations continued across the Bering Straits, with Inuit and Aleut peoples arriving in present-day Alaska about 5,000 years ago (Map 1.1).

About 3,000 years ago, some communities in the Americas began establishing agricultural systems that encouraged more stable settlements, population growth, and the accumulation of possessions. In the Americas, **horticulture**—a form of agriculture in which people work small plots of land with simple tools—first developed in present-day Mexico. There men and women developed strains of maize (or Indian corn) with larger kernels and higher yields than those that grew in the wild. They also cultivated beans, squash, tomatoes, potatoes, and manioc (a root vegetable), providing rich sources of protein. The combination of beans, squash, and corn offered an especially nutritious diet while maintaining the fertility of the soil. Moreover, high yields produced surplus food that could be stored or traded to neighboring communities.

By 500 C.E., complex societies, rooted in intensive agriculture, began to thrive in the equatorial region. Between 500 and 1500 C.E., thousands of separate societies and cultures speaking hundreds of distinct languages developed in the Americas. Small bands of hunters and gatherers continued to thrive in deserts and forests while impressive civilizations marked by gigantic stone statuary, complex irrigation systems, and ornate gold and silver ornaments arose on swamplands and in the mountains.

The Aztecs, the Maya, and the Incas

Three significant civilizations had developed by the early sixteenth century: Aztec and Mayan societies in the equatorial region and the Inca society along the Pacific coast in present-day Peru. Technologically advanced and with knowledge of mathematics and astronomy, these societies were characterized by vast mineral wealth, large urban centers, highly ritualized religions, and complex political systems. Unlike their counterparts in Europe, Asia, and Africa, they did not develop the wheel to aid in transportation, nor did they have steel tools and weapons. Since most of their commerce was carried out over land or along rivers and coastlines, they did not build large boats. They also lacked horses, which had disappeared from the region thousands of years earlier. Still, the Aztecs, Maya, and Incas established grand cities and civilizations that rivaled those of the most sophisticated societies in the world.

Around 1325 C.E., the **Aztecs**, who called themselves Mexica, built their capital, Tenochtitlán, on the site of present-day Mexico City. As seminomadic warriors who had invaded and then settled in the region, the Aztecs drew on local residents' knowledge of irrigation and cultivation and adopted their written language. Aztec commoners,

Figure Whistle, Peru, 3rd–7th Century

This figure whistle made of hammered gold was produced by the Moche (pre-Inca) civilization in northern Peru. The man pictured here is a warrior and once held an object in his right hand. Moche people used figure whistles to communicate with their ancestors when a human offering was made.   Image © Metropolitan Museum of Art/Art Resource, NY

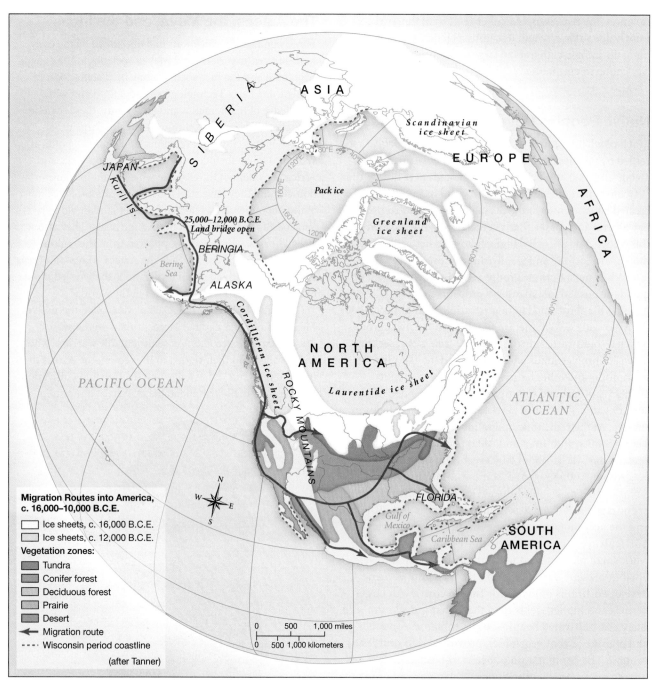

MAP 1.1   The Wisconsin Glaciation and the Settling of the Americas

In roughly 16,000 B.C.E., ice covered most of North America. Its presence lowered the depth of the world's oceans, creating a land bridge called Beringia between Siberia and Alaska. Asian peoples likely migrated to North America across this bridge, hunting woolly mammoths and other game, and then slowly moved south and east as the ice retreated over the next four thousand years.

who tilled communally owned lands, were ruled over by priests and nobles. The nobles formed a warrior class and owned vast estates on which they employed both serfs and slaves captured from non-Aztec communities in the region. Priests promised fertility—for the land and its people—but demanded human sacrifices, including thousands of men and women from captured tribes. To sustain their society, Aztecs extended their trade networks into surrounding areas. Aztec artisans produced valuable trade goods like pottery, cloth, and leather goods that were exchanged for textiles, food items, and obsidian (the volcanic rock used to make sharp-edged tools) as well as bird feathers, tortoiseshells, and other luxury goods. As Malintzin's story illustrates, Aztecs also traded in slaves.

When Malintzin was sold to a Chontal Mayan village by Aztec merchants, she was being traded from one grand civilization to another. The **Maya** had slowly settled the Yucatán peninsula and the rain forests of present-day Guatemala between roughly 900 B.C.E. and 300 C.E. They established large cities that were home to skilled artisans and developed elaborate systems for irrigation and water storage. Farmers worked the fields and labored to build huge stone temples and palaces for rulers who claimed to be descended from the gods. Learned men developed mathematical calculations, hieroglyphic writing, and a calendar. Mayan astronomers also developed an amazingly accurate system for predicting eclipses of the sun and the moon.

Yet the Mayan civilization began to decline around 800 C.E. An economic crisis, likely the result of a drought and exacerbated by heavy taxation, probably drove peasant families into the interior. Many towns and religious sites were abandoned. Yet some communities survived the crisis and reemerged as thriving city-states. By the early sixteenth century, they traded with the Aztecs.

The **Incas** developed an equally impressive civilization in the Andes Mountains along the Pacific coast. The Inca empire, like the Aztec empire, was built on the accomplishments of earlier societies. At the height of their power, in the fifteenth century, the Incas controlled some sixteen million people spread over 350,000 square miles. They constructed an expansive system of roads and garrisons to ensure the flow of food, trade goods, and soldiers from their capital at Cuzco through the surrounding mountains and valleys. Pack trains of llamas hauled tribute from conquered tribes to provincial centers and then on to Cuzco.

The key to Inca success was the cultivation of fertile mountain valleys. Cuzco, some eleven thousand feet above sea level, lay in the center of the Inca empire, with the Huaylas and Titicaca valleys on either side. Here residents cut timber from dense forests and cultivated potatoes and other crops on terraces watered by an elaborate irrigation system. Some artisans crafted gold and silver from the rich mountains into jewelry and decorative items, while others excelled at stone carving, pottery, and weaving. Thousands of laborers constructed elaborate palaces and temples. And like the Aztecs, Inca priests sacrificed humans to the gods to stave off natural disasters and military defeat.

Native Cultures to the North

To the north of these grand civilizations, smaller societies with less elaborate cultures thrived. In present-day Arizona and New Mexico, the Mogollon and Hohokam established communities around 500 C.E. The Mogollon were expert potters while the Hohokam developed extensive irrigation systems. Farther north, in present-day Utah and Colorado, the ancient Pueblo people built adobe and masonry homes cut into cliffs around 750 C.E. The homes clustered around a sunken ceremonial room, the kiva. A century later, the center of this culture moved south to the San Juan River Basin, where the Pueblo constructed large buildings that housed the people and their rulers along with administrative offices, religious centers, and craft shops. When a prolonged drought settled on the region in the early twelfth century, many Pueblo moved back north into cliff dwellings that offered greater protection from invaders as well as from the heat and sun. By 1300 these areas, too, were gripped by drought, and the residents appear to have dispersed into smaller groups.

Farther north on the plains that stretched from present-day Colorado into Canada, hunting societies developed around herds of bison. A weighted spear-throwing device, called an *atlatl*, allowed hunters to capture smaller game, while nets, hooks, and snares allowed them to catch birds, fish, and small animals. For many such groups, hunting was supplemented by the gathering of berries, roots, and other edible plants. These Plains societies generally remained small and widely scattered since they needed a large expanse of territory to ensure their survival as they traveled to follow migrating animals or seasonal plant sources.

Hunting-gathering societies also emerged along the Pacific coast, but the abundance of fish, small game, and plant life there provided the resources to develop permanent settlements. The Chumash Indians, near present-day Santa Barbara, California, harvested resources from the land and the ocean. Women gathered acorns and pine nuts, while men fished along the coastal waters and in rivers and hunted deer and smaller animals. The Chumash, whose villages sometimes held a thousand inhabitants, participated in regional exchange networks up and down the coast. As many as 300,000 people may have lived along the Pacific in a diverse array of societies before the arrival of Europeans.

Even larger societies with more elaborate social, religious, and political systems developed near the Mississippi River. A group that came to be called the **Hopewell people** established a thriving culture there in the early centuries C.E. The river and its surrounding lands provided fertile fields and easy access to distant communities. Centered in present-day southern Ohio and western Illinois, the Hopewell constructed towns of four thousand to six thousand people. Artifacts from their burial sites reflect extensive trading networks that stretched from the Missouri River to Lake Superior, and from the Rocky Mountains to the Appalachian region and Florida.

Serpent Mound

This mound was most likely constructed sometime between 950 and 1200 C.E. by the Mississippian society found in present-day southern Ohio. A sun-worshipping culture, the Mississippians aligned the head of the serpent with the sunset of the summer solstice (June 20 or 21). Goods found at such sites indicate that Hopewell networks were further extended by the Mississippians.   Mark C. Burnett/Photo Researchers

Beginning around 500 C.E., the Hopewell culture gave birth to larger and more complex societies that flourished in the Mississippi River valley and to the south and east. As bows and arrows spread into the region, people hunted more game in the thick forests. But Mississippian groups also learned to cultivate corn. The development of corn as a staple crop allowed the population to expand dramatically, and more complex political and religious systems developed in which elite rulers gained greater control over the labor of farmers and hunters.

Mississippian peoples created massive earthworks sculpted in the shape of serpents, birds, and other creatures. Still visible in present-day north Georgia, eastern Oklahoma, and southern Ohio and at Cahokia Creek near modern East St. Louis, Illinois, some earthen sculptures stood over 70 feet high and stretched more than 1,300 feet in length. Mississippians also constructed huge temple mounds that could cover nearly 16 acres.

By about 1100 C.E., the community around Cahokia Creek had grown to some fifteen thousand inhabitants. Powerful chieftains extended their trade networks, conquered smaller villages, and created a centralized government. But the rulers proved too weak to maintain their control over numerous scattered towns. To the south, near present-day Tuscaloosa, Alabama, more than twenty flat-topped mounds formed an important ceremonial center in the thirteenth century. By 1400, however, the Mississippians began to lose power there as well. Over the next century, this once-flourishing culture declined, leaving behind vast temple mounds and stunning earthen sculptures.

REVIEW & RELATE

• Compare and contrast the Aztecs, Incas, and Maya. What similarities and differences do you note?

• How did the societies of North America differ from those of the equatorial zone and the Andes?

✔ *LEARNINGCurve* **bedfordstmartins.com/hewittlawson/LC**

Europe Expands Its Reach

The complex societies that emerged in the Americas were made possible by an agricultural revolution that included the establishment of crop systems, the domestication of animals, and the development of tools. These developments had occurred 4000–3000 B.C.E. in the Fertile Crescent (see Map 1.2) in southwest Asia and in China. The increased productivity in these areas ensured population growth and allowed attention to science, trade, politics, religion, and the arts. Over millennia, knowledge from these civilizations made its way northward and westward into Europe, and at the height of the Roman empire in the early centuries C.E., Europe was part of dense global trade networks that connected the peoples of Europe, Africa, and Asia. With the decline of Roman power in western Europe, however, those connections broke down, and Europeans turned inward. It would take many centuries for European societies to recover. When they did, motivated by a desire to gain access to the riches of the East, they began to search for ways to regain their connections to the larger world.

The Mediterranean World

For several centuries before 1500, Islam proved one of the most dynamic cultural, political, and military forces in the world. By the ninth century, Islamic (also known as Muslim) regimes controlled most of southwest Asia and North Africa and conquered parts of the Iberian peninsula. The Muslims' greatest competitors were the Ottoman Turks, not European Catholics (Map 1.2). Still, in the eleventh and twelfth centuries, Catholic leaders launched several military and religious campaigns to reclaim the Holy Land for the church. Later known as the **Crusades**, these campaigns largely failed in establishing Christian settlements in the East and exacerbated conflicts with Greek Orthodox and Jewish communities. But they enhanced the roles of Italian merchants, who profited from both outfitting Crusaders and opening new trade routes to the East.

Moreover, these campaigns inspired explorers and adventurers throughout Europe.

Medieval European elites were first introduced to goods and ideas from the East by merchant adventurers such as Marco Polo. He traveled to Cathay (his name for China) during the 1270s and published his *Travels* in 1292. Describing his adventures along the Silk Road, Polo introduced Europeans to "burning rocks" (coal), spices that preserved meat, and other wonders of the Far East.

Europeans also learned of successful civilizations in the Middle East, where inhabitants had managed to survive droughts and other ecological crises, largely because of their productive economic systems. In the Mediterranean world, this productivity depended on technological advances in irrigation and navigation and on adequate labor in the form of slavery. Earlier European societies as well as the Aztecs, Incas, and Maya had put

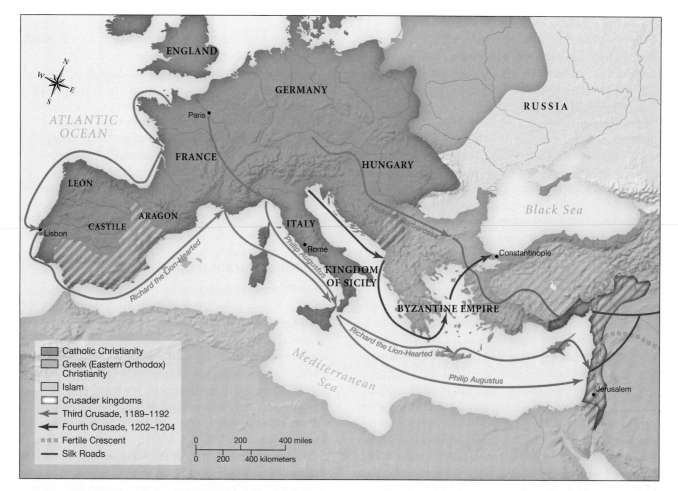

MAP 1.2   The Mediterranean World, c. 1150–1300

The Mediterranean Sea sat at the center of dynamic religious, political, and commercial networks. Crusaders traveled from Europe to Turkey, Arabia, and Persia, hoping to spread Christianity among Islamic peoples. In the thirteenth century, Marco Polo and other adventurers followed the Silk Road deeper into Asia, returning with goods, technologies, and diseases from the eastern Mediterranean, India, and China.

conquered peoples to work as slaves, but none compared to the vast network of slave-trading centers that fueled agricultural development in the Middle East. And it was the productivity of agriculture—developed centuries earlier than in Europe or America—that allowed societies along the southern Mediterranean, in northern Africa, and in southwest Asia to excel in astronomy, mathematics, architecture, and the arts.

Medieval European states proved far less adept at staving off human and environmental disasters than their counterparts to the south. Besieged by drought and disease as well as wars and peasant rebellions, rulers across the continent expended most of their resources on trying to sustain their population and protect their borders. Even launching trade with Asia led to disaster: In the 1340s, the bubonic plague was carried from Central Asia to Middle Eastern and European seaports by rats stowed away on ships. Sailors who contracted the disease at sea also spread the infection far and wide. From the 1340s to the early fifteenth century, the plague—later called the **Black Death**—periodically ravaged European cities and towns. During the initial outbreak between 1346 and 1350, about 36 million people—half of Europe's population—perished. At the same time, France and England engaged in a century-long war that added to the death and destruction.

By the early fifteenth century, the plague had retreated from much of Europe, and the climate had improved. Only then were European peoples able to benefit significantly from the riches of the East. Smaller populations led to an improved standard of living. Then rising birthrates and increased productivity, beginning in Italian city-states, fueled a resurgence of trade with other parts of the world. The profits from agriculture and commerce allowed the wealthy and powerful to begin investing in painting, sculpture, music, and literature and to pay jewelers, potters, and other craftsmen for their wares. Indeed, a cultural **Renaissance** (from the French word for "rebirth") flourished in the Italian city-states and then spread to France, Spain, the Low Countries, and central Europe.

The cultural rebirth went hand in hand with political unification as more powerful rulers extended their control over smaller city-states and principalities. In 1469, for example, the marriage of Isabella of Castile and Ferdinand II of Aragon led to the unification of Spain. By 1492 their combined forces expelled the last Muslim conquerors from the Iberian peninsula. Promoting Catholicism to create a more unified national identity, Isabella and Ferdinand also launched a brutal Inquisition against supposed heretics and executed or expelled Jews and Muslims. This reconquest of

Comparing Chinese and European Sailing Ships

The lateen sail used by the Chinese in the early fifteenth century marked a considerable improvement over the square sails used by Europeans such as Columbus, illustrated in the lower right corner by a contemporary artist. The lateen sail was developed as early as the sixth century C.E. by Byzantine shipbuilders in the Mediterranean region.   © Dugald Stermer

the Iberian peninsula fueled the revival of trade with North Africa, India, and other Asian lands.

Yet Italy controlled the most important routes through the Mediterranean, so leaders in Spain and Portugal sought alternate paths to riches. Their efforts were aided by explorers, missionaries, and merchants who traveled to Morocco, Turkey, India, and other distant lands. They brought back trade goods and knowledge of astronomy, shipbuilding, mapmaking, and navigation that allowed Iberians to venture farther south along the Atlantic coast of Africa and, eventually, west into the uncharted Atlantic Ocean.

Portugal Pursues Long-Distance Trade

Cut off from the Mediterranean by Italian city-states and Muslim forces in North Africa, Portugal looked toward the Atlantic. Motivated by dreams of wealth and a desire to challenge Muslim power, Portuguese rulers sought another route to India and the Far East. Although a tiny nation, Portugal benefited from the leadership of its young prince, Henry (1394–1460), who launched an effort to explore the African coast and find a passage to India via the Atlantic Ocean. Prince Henry—known as Henry the Navigator— gathered information from astronomers, geographers, mapmakers, and craftsmen in the Arab world and recruited Italian cartographers and navigators along with Portuguese scholars, sailors, and captains. He then launched a systematic campaign of exploration, observation, shipbuilding, and long-distance trade that revolutionized Europe and shaped developments in Africa and the Americas.

Prince Henry and his colleagues developed ships known as caravels—vessels with narrow hulls and triangular sails that were especially effective for navigating the coast of West Africa. His staff also created state-of-the-art maritime charts, maps, and astronomical tables; perfected navigational instruments; and mastered the complex wind and sea currents along the African coast. Soon Portugal was trading in gold, ivory, and slaves from West Africa. By the time Prince Henry died in 1460, his ships had ventured as far east as the Canary Islands and Cape Verde and as far south as Sierra Leone.

In 1482 Portugal built Elmina Castle, a trading post and fort on the Gold Coast (present-day Ghana). The castle served as a launching point for further expeditions and as protection against Spanish competitors. Five years later, a fleet led by Bartolomeu Dias rounded the Cape of Good Hope, on the southernmost tip of Africa, demonstrating the possibility of sailing directly from the Atlantic to the Indian Ocean. Vasco da Gama followed this route to India in 1497, returning to Portugal in 1499, his ships laden with cinnamon and pepper.

By the early sixteenth century, Portuguese traders wrested control of the India trade from Arab fleets. They established fortified trading posts at key locations on the Indian Ocean and extended their expeditions to Indonesia, China, and Japan. Within a decade, the Portuguese had become the leaders in international trade. Spain, England, France, and the Netherlands competed for a share of this newfound wealth by developing long-distance markets that brought spices, ivory, silks, cotton cloth, and other luxury goods to Europe.

With expanding populations and greater agricultural productivity, European nations developed more efficient systems of taxation, built larger military forces, and adapted gunpowder to new kinds of weapons. The surge in population provided the men to labor on merchant vessels, staff forts, and protect trade routes. More people began to settle in cities like London, Bristol, Amsterdam, and Venice, which became important commercial centers. Slowly, a form of capitalism based on market exchange, private ownership, and capital accumulation and reinvestment developed across much of Europe.

African slaves were among the most lucrative goods traded by European merchants. Slavery had been practiced in Europe and other parts of the world, including Africa, for centuries. But in most times and places, slaves were

Elmina Castle, 1603
This engraving by Johann Theodor de Bry depicts the fortress of São Jorge da Mina, known as Elmina Castle, on the African Gold Coast. Built in 1482 at the order of King John II of Portugal, the fort served as a supply base for Portuguese navigators and housed thousands of Africans bound for slavery in the Americas.   The Granger Collection, New York

captives of war or individuals sold in payment for deaths or injuries to conquering enemies. Under such circumstances, slaves generally retained some legal rights, and bondage was rarely permanent and almost never inheritable. With the advent of large-scale European participation in the African slave trade, however, the system of bondage began to change, transforming Europe and Africa and eventually the Americas.

European Encounters with West Africa

In the 1440s, Portuguese ships began to trade along the West African (or Guinea) coast. The Portuguese established bases in port cities like Benin to collect trade goods, including slaves, for sale in Europe. The slave trade expanded with the building of Elmina Castle and by the early sixteenth century had increased significantly. Initially, Africans were viewed as "exotic" objects and were often put on display at courts or for popular entertainment. Increasingly, however, African slaves were put to work in households and shops or on large estates.

Still, Europeans were most familiar with North Africa, a region deeply influenced by Islam and characterized by large kingdoms, well-developed cities, and an extensive network of trading centers. In northeast Africa, including Egypt, city-states flourished, with ties to India, the Middle East, and China. In northwest Africa, Timbuktu linked North Africa to empires south of the Great Desert as well as to Europe. Here African slaves labored for wealthier Africans in a system of bound labor long familiar to Europeans.

As trade with western Africa increased, however, Europeans learned more about communities that lived by hunting and subsistence agriculture. By the mid-sixteenth century, European nations established competing forts along the African coast from the Gold Coast and Senegambia in the north to the Bight of Biafra and West Central Africa farther south. The men and women shipped from these forts to Europe generally came from communities that had been raided or conquered by more powerful groups. They arrived at the coast exhausted, hungry, dirty, and with few clothes. They worshipped gods unfamiliar to Europeans, and their cultural customs and social practices seemed strange and often frightening. Over time, it was the image of the captured West African slave that came to dominate European visions of the entire continent.

As traders from Portugal, Spain, Holland, and England brought back more stories and more African slaves, these negative portraits took deeper hold. Woodcuts and prints circulated in Europe that showed half-naked Africans who looked more like apes than humans. These images resonated with biblical stories like that of Ham, who sinned against his father, Noah. Noah then cursed Ham's son Canaan to a life of slavery. Increasingly, European Christians considered Africans the "sons of Ham," infidels rightly assigned by God to a life of bondage. This self-serving idea then justified the enslavement of black men, women, and children.

Explore

For one English captain's impression of Africans during this period, see Document 1.1.

Of course, these images of West Africa failed to capture the diverse peoples who lived in the area's tropical rain forests, plains, and savannas. By the fourteenth century, agricultural productivity in the region fueled population growth and the rise of both city-states and trade networks. The Yoruba people developed walled towns ruled by *obas*, many of whom were women, who served as religious and political leaders. To the south lay the highly centralized kingdom of Benin. Its warrior king, Euware, had conquered some two hundred villages to create his kingdom and then used his power and wealth to promote trade and patronize the arts. Nearby the Igbo people rejected kingships in favor of title societies composed of wealthy men, women's associations tied to kinship, and hereditary organizations that created cohesion among competing groups. Despite their political and social differences, the Yoruba, Beni, and Igbo traded with one another and with more distant African kingdoms.

In addition to these powerful kingdoms, smaller societies based on farming or herding existed across western and central Africa. These communities were sometimes conquered by expanding kingdoms and their members sold as slaves within Africa. But once trade developed with Portugal, Spain, and other nations, these communities were increasingly raided to provide slaves for European markets. As the slave trade expanded in the sixteenth and seventeenth centuries, it destabilized large areas of western and central Africa, with smaller societies decimated by raids and even larger kingdoms damaged by the extensive commerce in human beings. As early as 1526, Afonso, the king of the Kongo people and a convert to Christianity, begged the Portuguese to end the slave trade: "Merchants are taking everyday our natives, sons of the land and the sons of our noblemen and vassals and our relatives."

Still, rulers of the most powerful African societies helped shape the slave trade. For instance, because women were more highly valued by Muslim traders in North Africa and Asia, African traders steered women to these profitable markets. At the same time, African societies organized along matrilineal lines—where goods and political power passed through the mother's line—often tried to protect

DOCUMENT 1.1

John Lok | The Second Voyage to Guinea, 1554

By the mid-fifteenth century, Europeans had developed a lucrative trading relationship with Africa, which included gold, ivory, and slaves. African slaves were first seen as exotic oddities, but increasingly they were bought as laborers to work in shops or on agricultural estates. As the slave trade increased, Europeans developed a vision of Africans as heathen, savage, and vastly inferior to themselves. The following passage, taken from the descriptions of John Lok, the captain of an English expedition to Africa in 1554, represents common European depictions of Africans in the sixteenth century.

Explore

It is to be understood, that the people which now inhabite the regions of the coast of Guinea, and the midle parts of Africa, as Libya the inner, and Nubia, with divers other great and large regions about the same, were in old time called Æthiopes and Nigritæ, which we now call Moores, Moorens, or Negroes, a people of beastly living, without a God, lawe, religion, or common wealth, and so scorched and vexed with the heat of the sunne, that in many places they curse it when it riseth. . . .

There are also other people of Libya called Garamantes, whose women are common: for they contract no matrimonie, neither have respect to chastitie.

Source: "The Second Voyage of M. John Lok to Guinea, Anno 1554," in Richard Hakluyt, *The Principal Navigations, Voyages, Traffiques & Discoveries of the English Nation* (Glasgow: James MacLehose and Sons, 1904), 6:167–68.

Interpret the Evidence

- What characteristics does the author associate with Africans? To what extent, if any, does the author differentiate among African peoples?
- Do Lok's characterizations seem to be based on firsthand observation? Why or why not?

Put It in Context

How did descriptions such as these justify African enslavement?

---

women against enslavement. Other groups sought to limit the sale of men.

Ultimately, men, women, and children were captured by African as well as Portuguese, Spanish, Dutch, and English traders. Still, Europeans did not institute a system of perpetual slavery, in which enslavement was inherited from one generation to the next. Instead, Africans formed another class of bound labor, alongside peasants, indentured servants, criminals, and apprentices. Slavic-speaking workers imported from areas around the Black Sea were especially prominent on sugar plantations in the Mediterranean region. Indeed, the term *Slav* became the basis for the word *slave*. When the Ottoman Turks cut off access to Slavic laborers, Europeans increased their slave trade with Africa.

Distinctions among bound laborers on the basis of race had not yet fully developed. Thus affluent Europeans condemned pagan rituals, sexual licentiousness, and ignorance among both Slavic and African laborers. They also considered such traits common among their own peasants. When the English entered the African slave trade in the 1560s, via the privateer John Hawkins, they quickly put their own spin on such comparisons. In the sixteenth century, they viewed both Africans and the conquered Irish as "rude, beastly, ignorant, cruel, and unruly infidels."

REVIEW & RELATE

How and why did Europeans expand their connections with Africa and the Middle East in the fifteenth century?

How did early European encounters with West Africans lay the foundation for later race-based slavery?

Worlds Collide

In the 1520s and 1530s, Spain and Portugal chartered traders to ship enslaved Africans to the Caribbean, Brazil, Mexico, and Peru. The success of this trade relied heavily on the efforts of European cartographers, who began to chart the coastlines, rivers, and inland territories of the Western Hemisphere described by explorers and adventurers. Their maps illustrated the growing connections among Europe, Africa, and the Americas even as they also reflected the continued dominance of the Mediterranean region, the Middle East, India, and China in European visions of the world. Yet that world was changing rapidly as Europeans introduced guns, horses, and new diseases to the Americas and came in contact with previously unknown flora and fauna. The resulting exchange of plants, animals, and germs transformed the two continents as well as the wider world.

Europeans Cross the Atlantic

The first Europeans to discover lands in the western Atlantic were Norsemen. In the early ninth century, Scandinavians colonized Ireland, and in the 870s they settled Iceland. A little more than a century later, seafarers led by Erik the Red reached Greenland. Sailing still farther west, Erik's son Leif led a party that discovered an area that they called Vinland, near the Gulf of St. Lawrence. The Norse established a small settlement there around 1000 C.E., and people from Greenland continued to visit Vinland for centuries. By 1450, however, the Greenland settlements had disappeared.

Nearly a half century after Norse settlers abandoned Greenland, a Genoese navigator named Christopher Columbus visited the Spanish court of Ferdinand and Isabella and proposed an **Enterprise of the Indies**. He planned to sail west across the Atlantic to Cipangu (Japan) and Cathay (China). Because Italian city-states controlled the Mediterranean and Portugal dominated the routes around Africa, Spain sought a third path to the rich Eastern trade. Columbus claimed he could find it.

Columbus's 1492 proposal was timely. Having just expelled the last Muslims from Granada and imposed Christian orthodoxy on a now-unified nation, the Spanish monarchs sought to expand their empire. Queen Isabella, ignoring the advice of two royal committees that had rejected Columbus's plan, decided to fund his initial venture. With her support, the Genoese captain headed off in three small ships with ninety men. They stopped briefly at the Canary Islands and then headed due west on September 6, 1492.

Columbus had calculated the distance to Cipangu based on Ptolemy's division of the world into 360 degrees of north-south lines of longitude. But in making his calculations, Columbus made a number of errors that led him to believe that it was possible to sail from Spain to Asia in about a month. The miscalculations nearly led to mutiny when Columbus's crew had not sighted land after more than four weeks at sea. Disaster was averted, however, when on October 12 a lookout spotted a small island. Columbus named the island San Salvador and made contact with local residents, whom he named Indians in the belief that he had found the East Indies. These "Indians" offered the newcomers food, drinks, and gifts. Columbus was impressed with their warm welcome and viewed their gold jewelry as a sign of greater riches in the region.

Although the native inhabitants and Columbus's men did not speak a common language, they communicated sufficiently to explore San Salvador as well as a larger island nearby, present-day Cuba. The crew then sailed on to an island they named Hispaniola. Nothing they saw resembled contemporary descriptions of China or the East Indies, but Columbus was convinced he had reached his destination. Leaving a small number of men behind, he sailed for Spain with samples of gold jewelry and tales of more wonders to come.

> **Explore**
>
> Read part of Columbus's account of his first encounter with native people in Hispaniola in Document 1.2.

Columbus and his crew were welcomed as heroes when they returned to Spain in March 1493. Their discovery of islands seemingly unclaimed by any known power led the pope to confer Spanish sovereignty over all lands already claimed or to be claimed 100 leagues west of the Cape Verde Islands. A protest by Portugal soon led to a treaty that moved the line 270 leagues farther west, resulting ultimately in Portugal's control of Brazil and Spain's control of the rest of what would become known as South America.

Europeans Explore the Americas

Columbus made two more voyages to the Caribbean to claim land for Spain and sought to convince those who accompanied him to build houses, plant crops, and cut logs for forts. But the men had come for gold, and when the Indians stopped trading willingly, the Spaniards used force to claim their riches. Columbus sought to impose a more rigid discipline but failed. On his final voyage, he was forced to introduce a system of *encomiendas*, by which leading men received land and the labor of all Indians

DOCUMENT 1.2

Christopher Columbus | Reaching the West Indies, 1492

On October 12, 1492, five weeks after heading into the Atlantic Ocean, Christopher Columbus landed on an island in the West Indies that he named San Salvador. The exact location and name of the island where Columbus first made landfall is in dispute, but we do know that it is in the Bahamas, although Columbus believed it to be India. Columbus spent five days exploring the area where he and his men first encountered native people and kept a detailed journal of his experiences. Although the original journal was lost, large parts of it had been copied by the Catholic friar Bartolomé de Las Casas, including the following journal entry.

Explore

What motivates Columbus to give gifts to the people he meets?

Why does Columbus think the people he encounters are very poor?

Why does Columbus think the people that he meets will be good servants?

October 12, 1492

I, . . . that we might form great friendship, for I knew that they were a people who could be more easily freed and converted to our holy faith by love than by force, gave to some of them red caps, and glass beads to put round their necks, and many other things of little value, which gave them great pleasure, and made them so much our friends that it was a marvel to see. They afterwards came to the ship's boats where we were, swimming and bringing us parrots, cotton threads in skeins, darts, and many other things; and we exchanged them for other things that we gave them, such as glass beads and small bells. In fine [In short], they took all, and gave what they had with good will. It appeared to me to be a race of people very poor in everything. They go as naked as when their mothers bore them, and so do the women, although I did not see more than one young girl. . . . They have no iron, their darts being wands without iron, some of them having a fish's tooth at the end. . . . They should be good servants and intelligent, for I observed that they quickly took in what was said to them, and I believe that they would easily be made Christians, as it appeared to me that they had no religion. I, our Lord being pleased, will take hence, at the time of my departure, six natives for your Highnesses, that they may learn to speak.

Source: *The Journal of Christopher Columbus (during His First Voyage, 1492–93) and Documents Relating to the Voyages of John Cabot and Gaspar Corte Real* (London: Hakluyt Society, 1893), 37–38.

Put It in Context

How might Columbus's journal entry, which was circulated among clerics and officials, have shaped Spanish views about native peoples?

residing on it. Although he boasted to the Spanish crown that he had "placed under their Highnesses' sovereignty more land than there is in Africa and Europe," Columbus had lost the support of the Spanish authorities by the time he died in 1506. The islands he discovered were quickly dissolving into chaos as traders and adventurers fought with Indians and one another over the spoils of conquest.

By then, no one believed that he had discovered a route to China, and few people understood the revolutionary importance of the lands he had found.

Nonetheless, Columbus's voyages inspired others to head across the Atlantic (Map 1.3). In 1497 another Genoese navigator, John Cabot (or Caboto), sailing under the English flag, headed into the northern Atlantic in a tiny

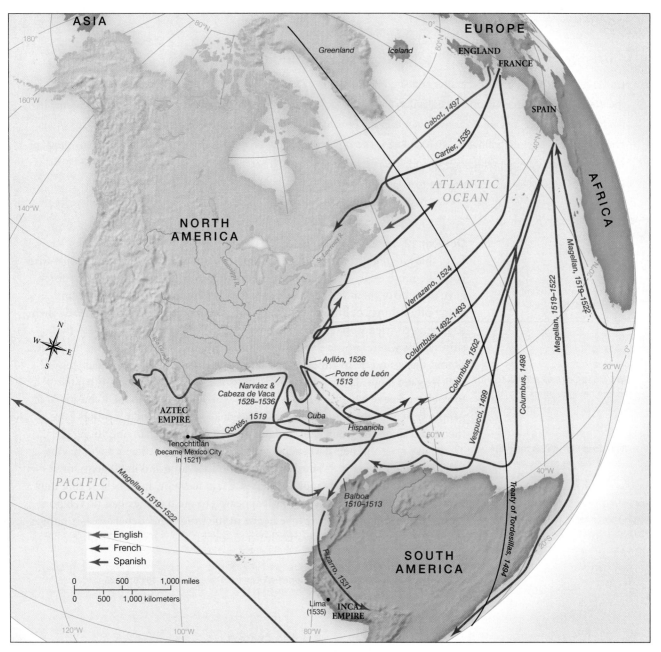

MAP 1.3 European Explorations in the Americas, 1492–1536

Early explorers, funded by Spain, sought trade routes to Asia or gold, silver, and other riches in the Americas. The success of these voyages encouraged adventurous Spaniards to travel throughout the West Indies and across South America and southern North America. It also inspired the first expeditions by the French and the English, who sought treasures farther north.

ship with only eighteen men. He reached an island off Cape Breton, where he discovered good cod fishing but met no local inhabitants. Over the next several years, Cabot and his son Sebastian made more trips to North American shores, but England failed to follow up on their discoveries.

More important at the time, Portuguese and Spanish mariners continued to explore the western edges of the Caribbean. Amerigo Vespucci, a Florentine merchant, joined one such voyage in 1499. It was Vespucci's account of his journey that led Martin Waldseemüller to identify the new continent he charted on his 1507 *Universalis Cosmographia* as "America." Meanwhile, Spanish explorers subdued tribes like the Arawak and Taino in the Caribbean and headed toward the mainland. In 1513 Vasco Nuñez de

Balboa traveled across the Isthmus of Darien (now Panama) and became the first European to see the Pacific Ocean. That same year, Juan Ponce de León launched a search for gold and slaves along a peninsula to the north. Although he did not find riches there, he named the region Florida, meaning "flowery land," and claimed it for Spain.

Ferdinand Magellan launched an even more impressive expedition in August 1519 when he, with the support of Charles V of Spain, sought a passageway through South America to Asia. In the first fifteen months, Magellan faced bad weather, disappointments, hostile Indians, and open mutiny. But he managed to maintain his authority, and in October 1520 his crew discovered a strait at the southernmost tip of South America that connected the Atlantic and Pacific Oceans. Ill with scurvy and near starvation, the crew reached Guam and then the Philippines in March 1521. Magellan died there a month later, but one of his five ships and eighteen of the original crew finally made it back to Seville in September 1522, having successfully circumnavigated the globe. Despite the enormous loss of life and equipment, Magellan's lone ship was loaded with valuable spices, his venture allowed Spain to claim the Philippine Islands, and his journals provided cartographers with vast amounts of knowledge about the world's oceans and landmasses.

Mapmaking and Printing

Waldseemüller's 1507 map reflected the expanding contacts among Europe, Africa, and the Americas. Over the following decades, as ships from Europe sailed back and forth across the Atlantic, cartographers charted newly discovered islands, traced coastlines and bays, and situated each new piece of data in relation to lands already known.

The dissemination of geographical knowledge was greatly facilitated by advances in information technology. The Chinese had developed a form of printing with wood blocks in the tenth century, and woodcut pictures appeared in Europe in the fifteenth century. In the 1440s, German craftsmen invented a form of movable metal type in which each letter was created in a separate mold. This allowed printers to rearrange the type for each page and create multiple copies of a single manuscript more quickly and more cheaply than ever before. Between 1452 and 1455, Johannes Gutenberg, a German goldsmith, printed some 180 copies of the Bible with movable type. Although this was not the first book printed using the new system, Gutenberg's Bible marked a revolutionary change in the production and circulation of written texts.

Innovations in printing helped publicize Portuguese and Spanish explorations, the travels of European adventurers, and the atlases created by Waldseemüller and other cartographers. Italian craftsmen contributed by manufacturing paper

Printing Press

This woodcut of a printing press from Leipzig, Germany, in 1520 illustrates typical printing equipment of the sixteenth century. A craftsman applies inked type to the paper using a screw press, and a second worker gathers and stacks the printed pages. This process accelerated the publication and distribution of books and pamphlets throughout early modern Europe. © Mary Evans Picture Library/The Image Works

that was thinner and cheaper than traditional vellum and parchment. Books were still expensive, and they could be read only by the small minority of Europeans who were literate. Still, mechanical printing rapidly increased the speed with which knowledge was circulated, allowing a German mapmaker like Waldseemüller to read the journals of the Italian mariner Vespucci. Of course, not everything that was printed was accurate, but the ability to exchange ideas encouraged their expression and ensured the flow of information among scholars and rulers across Europe.

The peoples of the Americas had their own ways of charting land, waterways, and boundary lines and for circulating information. The Maya, for instance, developed a system of glyphs—images that represented prefixes, suffixes, numbers, people, or words. Scribes carved glyphs

The Aztec City of Tenochtitlán

German geographers drew this map of Tenochtitlán in 1524 based on Aztec sources. At its peak, the city contained some 100,000 people, and at its center stood temples, a marketplace, schools, the palace of the Aztec chief Montezuma, and a ball-game court. The Aztecs viewed Tenochtitlán as the intersection of the secular and divine worlds.
Bildarchiv Preussischer Kulturbesitz/Dietmar Katz/Art Resource, NY

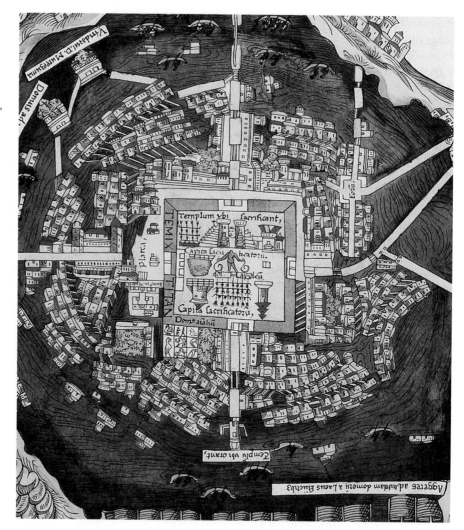

into large flat stones, or *stela*, providing local residents with histories of important events. In settled farming villages, this system communicated information to a large portion of the population. But it could not serve, as printed pages did, to disseminate ideas more widely. Similarly, the extant maps created by the Maya, Aztecs, and other native groups tended to focus on specific locales. Still, we know that these groups traded across long distances, so they must have had some means of tracing rivers, mountains, and villages beyond their own communities.

The Columbian Exchange

Even as maps documented Europeans' expanded knowledge of the Americas, they could not capture the experience of contact between peoples separated for centuries by the Atlantic Ocean. Most important, the Spaniards were aided in their conquest of the Americas as much by germs as by maps, guns, or horses. Because native peoples in the Western Hemisphere had had almost no contact with the rest of the world for millennia, they lacked immunity to most germs

carried by Europeans. Disease along with warfare first eradicated the Arawak and Taino on Hispaniola, wiping out some 300,000 people. In the Inca empire, the population plummeted from about 9 million in 1530 to less than half a million by 1630. Among the Aztecs, the Maya, and their neighbors, the population collapsed from some 40 million people around 1500 to about 3 million a century and a half later. The germs spread northward as well, leading to catastrophic epidemics among the Pueblo peoples of the Southwest and the Mississippian cultures of the Southeast.

These demographic disasters—far more devastating even than the bubonic plague in Europe—were part of what historians call the **Columbian exchange**. But this exchange also involved animals, plants, and seeds and affected Africa and Asia as well as Europe and the Americas. The transfer of flora and fauna and the spread of diseases transformed the economies and environments of all four continents. Initially, however, it was the catastrophic decline in Indian populations that ensured the victory of Spain and other European powers over American populations, facilitating their subsequent exploitation of American land, labor, and resources.

The diseases that swept across the Americas came from Africa as well as Europe. Indeed, it was Africans' partial immunity to malaria and yellow fever that made them so attractive to European traders seeking laborers for Caribbean islands after the native population was decimated. African coconuts and bananas had already been introduced to Europe, while European traders had provided their African counterparts with iron and pigs. Asia also participated in the exchange, introducing Europe and Africa not only to the bubonic plague but also to sugar, rice, tea, and highly coveted spices.

America provided Europeans with high-yielding, nutrient-rich foods like maize and potatoes, as well as new indulgences like tobacco and cacao. The conquered Inca and Aztec empires also provided vast quantities of gold and silver, making Spain the treasure-house of Europe and ensuring its dominance on the continent for several decades. Sugar was first developed in the East Indies, but once it took root in the West Indies, it, too, became a source of enormous profits and, when mixed with cacao, created an addictive drink known as chocolate.

In exchange for products that America offered to Europe and Africa, these continents sent rice, wheat, rye, lemons, and oranges as well as horses, cattle, pigs, chickens, and honeybees to the Western Hemisphere (Map 1.4). The grain crops transformed the American landscape, particularly in North America, where wheat became a major food source. Cattle and pigs, meanwhile, changed native diets, while horses inspired new methods of farming, transportation, and warfare throughout the Americas.

The Columbian exchange benefited Europe far more than the Americas. Initially, it also benefited Africa, providing new crops with high yields and rich nutrients. Ultimately, however, the spread of sugar and rice to the West Indies and European cravings for tobacco and cacao increased the demand for labor, which could not be met by the declining population of Indians. This situation ensured the expansion of the African slave trade. The consequences of the Columbian exchange were thus monumental for the peoples of all three continents.

REVIEW & RELATE

What were the short-term consequences in both Europe and the Americas of Columbus's voyages?

How did the Columbian exchange transform both the Americas and Europe?

LEARNINGCurve **bedfordstmartins.com/hewittlawson/LC**

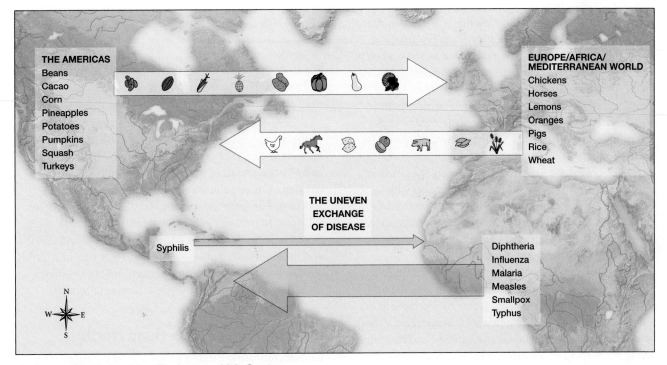

MAP 1.4   The Columbian Exchange, 16th Century

When Europeans made contact with Africa and the Americas, they initiated an exchange of plants, animals, and germs that transformed all three continents. The contact among these previously isolated ecosystems caused dramatic transformations in food, labor, and mortality. American crops changed eating habits across Europe, while foreign grains and domesticated animals thrived in the Americas even as diseases devastated native populations.

Europeans Make Claims to North America

With the help of native translators, warriors, and laborers, Spanish soldiers called **conquistadors** conquered some of the richest and most populous lands in South America in the early sixteenth century. Others then headed north, hoping to find gold in the southern regions of North America or develop new routes to Asia. At the same time, rulers of other European nations, jealous of Spanish wealth, began to fund expeditions to North America. However, both France and England were ruled by weak monarchs and divided both religiously and politically. Consequently, their early efforts met with little success. By the late sixteenth century, Spanish supremacy in the Americas and the wealth acquired there transformed the European economy. But conquest also raised critical questions about Spanish responsibilities to God and humanity.

Spaniards Conquer Indian Empires

Although rulers in Spain supposedly set the agenda for American ventures, it was difficult to control the campaigns of their emissaries at such a distance. The Spanish crown held the power to grant successful leaders vast amounts of land and Indian labor, expanding the encomienda system introduced by Columbus. But the leaders themselves then divided up their prizes to reward those who served under them, giving them in effect an authority that they sometimes lacked in law. This dynamic helped make Cortés's conquest of the Aztecs possible.

Diego de Velásquez, a Spanish nobleman appointed the governor of Cuba, granted Cortés the right to explore and trade along the coast of South America. He gave him no authority, however, to attack native peoples in the region or claim land for himself. But seeing the possibility for gaining great riches, Cortés forged alliances with local rulers willing to join the attack against the Aztec chief, Montezuma. From the perspective of local Indian communities, Cortés's presence offered an opportunity to strike back against the brutal Aztec regime.

Despite their assumption of cultural superiority, many Spaniards who accompanied Cortés were astonished by Aztec cities, canals, and temples, which rivaled those in Europe. Bernal Díaz, a young foot soldier, marveled, "These great towns and cues [pyramid-like temples] and buildings rising from the water, all made of stone, seemed like an enchanted vision. . . . Indeed, some of our soldiers asked if it were not all a dream." Seeing these architectural wonders may have given some soldiers pause about trying to conquer the Indian kingdom. But when Montezuma presented Cortés with large quantities of precious objects, including gold-encrusted jewelry, as a peace offering, he alerted Spaniards to the vast wealth awaiting them in the Aztec capital.

When Cortés and his men marched to Tenochtitlán in 1519, Montezuma was indecisive in his response. After an early effort to ambush the Spaniards failed, the Aztec leader allowed Cortés to march his men into the capital city, where the Spanish conquistador took Montezuma hostage. In response, Aztec warriors attacked the Spaniards, but Cortés and his men managed to fight their way out of Tenochtitlán. They suffered heavy losses and might have been crushed by their Aztec foes but for the alliances they had made among native groups in the surrounding area. Given time to regroup, the remaining Spanish soldiers and their allies attacked the Aztecs with superior steel weapons, horses, and attack dogs and gained a final victory.

The Spanish victory was also aided by the germs that soldiers carried with them. The invaders unintentionally introduced smallpox to the local population, which led to a staggering epidemic. It swept through Tenochtitlán in 1521, killing thousands and leaving Montezuma's army dramatically weakened. This human catastrophe as much as military resources and strategies allowed Cortés to conquer the capital. He then claimed the entire region as New Spain, asserting Spanish authority over the native groups that had allied with him. The Spanish conquistador then settled in Tenochtitlán while his men constructed the new capital of Mexico City around him.

Explore

For an illustration of the devastating effects of smallpox on an Aztec victim, see Document 1.3.

As news of Cortés's victory spread, other Spanish conquistadors sought gold and glory in the Americas. Most important, in 1524 Francisco Pizarro, with only 168 men and 67 horses, conquered the vast Inca empire in present-day Peru. Once again, the Spaniards were aided by the spread of European diseases and conflicts among peoples subjected to Inca rule. This victory ensured Spanish access to vast supplies of silver in Potosí (in present-day Bolivia) and the surrounding mountains. Spain was now in control of the most densely populated regions of South America, areas that also contained the greatest mineral wealth.

Spanish Adventurers Head North

In 1526, following Pizarro's conquest of the Incas, a company of Spanish women and men traveled from the West Indies as far north as the Santee River in present-day South Carolina. They planned to settle in the region and then search for gold and other valuables. The effort failed, but two years later Pánfilo de Narváez—one of the survivors—led four hundred soldiers from Cuba to Florida's Tampa Bay. Seeking precious metals, the party instead confronted hunger, disease, and hostile Indians. The ragtag group continued to journey along the Gulf coast, until only four men, led by Álvar Núñez Cabeza de Vaca, made their way from Galveston Bay back to Mexico City.

A decade later, in 1539, a survivor of Narváez's ill-fated venture—a North African named Esteban—led a party of

---

DOCUMENT 1.3

Aztec Smallpox Victim, 1540

Between 1519 and 1521, the Spanish explorer Hernán Cortés led a war of conquest against the Aztecs. His eventual victory was greatly aided by advanced military technology, native allies, and the unintended introduction of European diseases into the Aztec population. Spanish contact spread smallpox to the region, killing thousands and weakening a once-powerful Aztec military. The image below, from a treatise written by a Franciscan missionary, shows the different stages suffered by a smallpox victim.

Explore

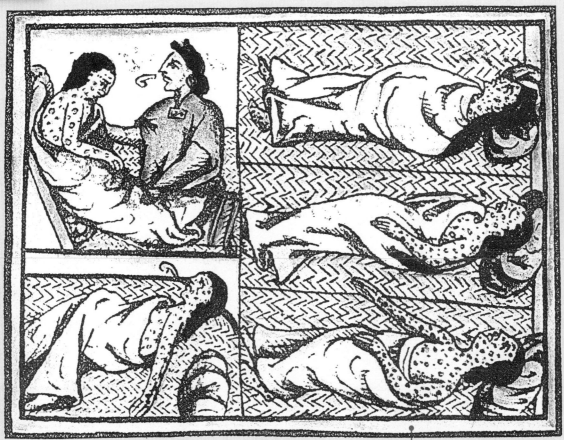

The Granger Collection, New York

Interpret the Evidence

- What does this image tell us about the role of the Aztec healer, standing before one of the victims, in the face of a smallpox epidemic?
- What does this group of five panels imply about the way that smallpox victims experienced the disease?

Put It in Context

What message do you think Bernardino de Sahagun, the Franciscan missionary, meant to convey in using this image in his history of New Spain?

Spaniards from Mexico back north. Lured by tales of Seven Golden Cities, the party instead encountered Zuñi Indians, who attacked the Spaniards and killed Esteban. Still, the men who returned to Mexico passed on stories about an extensive system of pueblos, where many Spaniards believed mountains of gold were hidden. Hoping to find fame and fortune, Francisco Vásquez de Coronado launched a grand expedition northward in 1540. Angered when they discovered that the fabled "Seven Cities are seven little villages," Coronado and his men terrorized the region, burning towns and stealing food and other goods before returning to Mexico.

Hernando de Soto headed a fourth effort to find wealth in North America. He had first sailed to America in 1514 and participated in conquests around present-day Panama. There he achieved a reputation for brutality and gained wealth through the Indian slave trade and by looting native treasures. Then in 1539 de Soto received royal authority to explore Florida, and that spring he established a village near Tampa Bay with more than six hundred Spanish, Indian, and African men, a few women, and more than two

hundred horses. A few months later, de Soto and the bulk of his company traveled up the west Florida coast with Juan Ortiz. Ortiz, a member of the Narváez expedition, was an especially useful guide and interpreter. That winter, the expedition traveled into present-day Georgia and the Carolinas in an unsuccessful search for riches (Map 1.5).

On their return trip, de Soto's men engaged in a brutal battle with local Indians led by Chief Tuskaloosa. Although the Spaniards claimed victory, they lost a significant number of men and horses and most of their equipment. Fearing that word of the disaster would reach Spain, de Soto steered his men away from supply ships in the Gulf of Mexico and headed back north. The group continued through parts of present-day Tennessee, Arkansas, Oklahoma, and Texas, and in May 1541 they became the first Europeans to report seeing the vast Mississippi River. By the winter of 1542, the expedition had lost more men and supplies to Indians, and de Soto had died. The remaining members finally returned to Spanish territory in the summer of 1543.

The lengthy journey of de Soto and his men brought European diseases into new areas, leading to epidemics

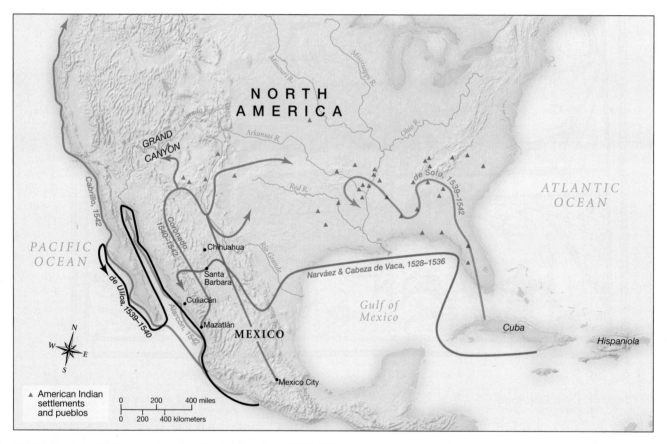

MAP 1.5   Spanish Explorations in North America, 1528–1542

Spanish explorers in North America hoped to find gold and other treasures. Instead, they encountered difficult terrain and native peoples hostile to Spanish intrusions. Many Spaniards died on these expeditions, and they failed to discover new sources of wealth. But they laid the foundations for Spanish settlements in Florida, northern Mexico, and California, in part by devastating local Indian populations.

and the depopulation of once-substantial native communities. At the same time, the Spaniards left horses and pigs behind, creating new sources of food and transportation for native peoples. Although most Spaniards considered de Soto's journey a failure, the Spanish crown claimed vast new territories. Two decades later, in 1565, Pedro Menéndez de Avilés established a mission settlement on the northeast coast of Florida, named St. Augustine. It became the first permanent European settlement in North America and served as a model for missions later founded by Spaniards in Santa Fe, New Mexico, and in California.

Europeans Compete in North America

Spain's early ventures in North America helped inspire French and English explorers to establish their own footholds on the continent. The French entered the race for empire in 1524, when an Italian navigator named Giovanni da Verrazano led a French company along the coast of North America. Landing initially near Cape Fear on the Carolina coast, the expedition headed north, sailing into what would become New York harbor. Verrazano then continued north, claiming lands all along the coast for France.

A decade later, in 1534, the Frenchman Jacques Cartier sailed to the Gulf of St. Lawrence and traded for furs with the Micmac Indians. In two subsequent expeditions, Cartier pushed deeper into the territory known as Canada. Although he failed to discover precious metals or the elusive passage to the Pacific Ocean, Cartier's adventures inspired a French nobleman, the Sieur de Roberval, and several hundred followers to attempt a permanent settlement at Quebec in 1542. But the project was abandoned within a year because of harsh weather, disease, and high mortality.

English interest in North America was ignited by Spanish and French challenges to claims Cabot had made along the North Atlantic coast in the 1490s. To secure these rights, the English needed to colonize the disputed lands. Since the English crown did not have funds to support settlement, the earliest ventures were financed by minor noblemen who hoped to gain both wealth and the crown's favor. But early efforts failed. In 1583 inadequate financing doomed Sir Humphrey Gilbert's effort to plant a colony in Newfoundland, and inadequate supplies along with the harsh climate undercut Sir Ferdinando Gorge's settlement on the Maine coast the next year.

The most promising effort to secure an English foothold in North America was organized by Sir Walter Raleigh, a half-brother of Humphrey Gilbert. Claiming all the land north of Florida for England, Raleigh called the vast territory Virginia (after Elizabeth I, "the Virgin Queen"). Although he did not set foot in North America himself, in 1585 Raleigh sent a group of soldiers to found a colony on Roanoke Island, off the coast of present-day North Carolina. The colony would establish England's claims and serve as a launching point for raids against Spanish ships laden with valuables. This venture lasted less than a year before the company returned to England. But in 1587 Raleigh tried again to colonize the area, sending a group of 117 men, women, and children to Roanoke. When supply ships came to fortify the settlement in 1590, no trace of the English settlers remained.

By 1590, then, nearly a century after Columbus's initial voyage, only Spain had established permanent colonies in the Americas, mostly in the West Indies, Mexico, and South America. St. Augustine remained the only European outpost in North America. The French and the English, despite numerous efforts, had not sustained a single ongoing settlement by the end of the sixteenth century. Yet neither nation gave up hope of benefiting from the wealth of the Americas.

Spain Seeks Dominion in Europe and the Americas

The continued desire of European nations to gain colonies in the Americas resulted from the enormous wealth garnered by Spanish conquests. That wealth transformed economies throughout Europe. Between 1500 and 1650, Spanish ships carried home more than 180 tons of gold and 16,000 tons of silver from Mexico and Potosí. About one-fifth of this amount was taken by the Spanish crown for taxes; the rest was spent on goods imported from the Americas, Asia, or other European nations. Very little of this wealth was invested in improving conditions at home. Instead, the elite displayed their wealth in ostentatious ways: elaborate silver candelabras, dresses drenched in jewels, and lavish tapestries imported from Asia. Meanwhile the rapid infusion of gold and silver fueled inflation, making it harder for ordinary people to afford the necessities of life.

In one area, however, employment for the poor expanded rapidly. King Philip II, who ruled Spain from 1556 to 1598, used American gold and silver to fund a variety of military campaigns, ensuring an endless demand for soldiers and sailors. The king, a devout Catholic, claimed to be doing God's work as Spain conquered Italy and Portugal, including the latter's colonies in Africa, and tightened its grip on the Netherlands, which had been acquired by Spain through marriage in the early sixteenth century. In response, the English aristocrat Sir Walter Raleigh warned, "It is his [Philip's] Indian Gold that . . . endangereth and disturbeth all the nations of Europe."

Despite the obvious material benefits, the Spaniards were not blind to the enormous human costs of colonization, and the conquest of the Americas inspired heated debates within Spain. Roman Catholic bishops and priests, royal officials, and colonial leaders disagreed vehemently about whether Spanish conquerors could simply acquire riches from foreign lands or were required to Christianize those they conquered for the glory of God. While Catholic leaders believed that the conversion of native peoples was critical to Spanish success in the Americas, most royal officials and colonial agents viewed the extraction of precious metals as far more important. They argued that cheap labor was essential to creating wealth. Yet brutal conditions led to the death of huge numbers of Indians, and many church officials insisted that such conditions made it nearly impossible to gain new converts to Catholicism.

By 1550, tales of the widespread torture and enslavement of Indians convinced the Spanish king Carlos V to gather a group of theologians, jurists, and philosophers at Valladolid to discuss the moral and legal implications of conquest. From Mexico, Hernán Cortés sent the king a message, insisting that there was no need to consider the natives' views since they "must obey the royal orders of Your Majesty, whatever their nature." But not all the participants at Valladolid agreed. Bartolomé de Las Casas, a former conquistador and Dominican friar, spent many years preaching to Indians in America. He asked, "And so what man of sound mind will approve a war against men who are harmless, ignorant, gentle, temperate, unarmed, and destitute of every human defense?" Las Casas reasoned that even if Spain defeated the Indians, the souls of those killed would be lost to God, while among the survivors "hatred and loathing of the Christian religion" would prevail. He even suggested replacing Indian labor with African labor, apparently less concerned with the souls of black people.

Juan Ginés de Sepúlveda, the royal historian, attacked Las Casas's arguments. Although he had never set foot in America, he read reports of cannibalism and other violations of "natural law" among native peoples. Since the Indians were savages, the civilized Spaniards were obligated to "destroy barbarism and educate these people to a more humane and virtuous life." If they refused such help, Spanish rule "can be imposed upon them by force of arms." Like Ginés de Sepúlveda, Theodor de Bry, the well-known illustrator of Documents 1.4 and 1.5, never visited the Americas, yet his depictions of the region shaped European impressions. Although Ginés de Sepúlveda spoke for the majority at Valladolid, Las Casas and his supporters continued to press their case as Spain expanded its reach into North America.

Explore

> To examine two European depictions of interactions between Spanish and native peoples, see Documents 1.4 and 1.5.

At the same time, American riches increasingly flowed beyond Spain's borders. The Netherlands was a key beneficiary of this wealth, becoming a center for Spanish shipbuilding and trade. Still, the Dutch were never completely under Spanish control, and they traded independently with their European neighbors. Thus gold, silver, and other items made their way to France, England, and elsewhere. Goods also followed older routes across the Mediterranean to the Ottoman empire, where traders could make huge profits on exotic items from the Americas. Thus, while some Europeans suffered under Spanish power, others benefited from the riches brought to the continent. By the late sixteenth century, the desire for a greater share of those riches revitalized imperial dreams among the French and English as well as the Dutch.

REVIEW & RELATE

What motives were behind the Spanish conquest and colonization of the Americas?

What were the consequences in Europe of Spain's acquisition of an American empire?

✔ **LEARNING***Curve* bedfordstmartins.com/hewittlawson/LC

Conclusion: A New America

When Spanish explorers happened upon the Americas, they brought Europeans into contact with native peoples who had inhabited the two continents for thousands of years. But these explorations and the conquests that followed did transform North and South America in dramatic ways. Martin Waldseemüller died in 1521 or 1522, so he was not able to incorporate into his maps the coastlines, waterways, and mountains reported by Magellan, Balboa, Cortés, Coronado, de Soto, Cartier, and other European adventurers. He would no doubt have been amazed to see the increasingly detailed maps that cartographers created of the elongated continent he first named America.

While mapmakers benefited from Europeans pushing deeper and deeper into the Americas, native residents were rarely asked if they wanted the plants, animals, goods, and germs offered by these invaders. Even Europeans seeking permanent settlements and peaceful trade relations with the Indians brought diseases that devastated local populations along with plants and animals that transformed their landscape, diet, and traditional ways of life.

Malintzin saw these changes firsthand. She watched as disease ravaged not only rural villages but even the capital city of Tenochtitlán. She encountered horses, pigs, attack dogs, and other European animals. She ate the foods and

DOCUMENTS 1.4 AND 1.5

European Depictions of the Americas: Two Views

In the late 1500s, the engraver Theodor de Bry and his sons began creating a series of copperplate illustrations depicting the exploration of the Americas. Because de Bry had never visited the New World, his illustrations came from descriptions and pictures by explorers. He got a number of cultural facts wrong, but his scenes were detailed and graphic and enormously popular. The de Bry family created hundreds of illustrations, which were used in their own books and those of others, including Bartolomé de Las Casas. These scenes figured into discussions about the legitimacy of Spanish actions in the Americas, as well as popular views of native populations. The first illustration below depicts Spanish cruelty against Indians; the second one shows Indian torture of Spanish explorers.

Explore

1.4 Theodor de Bry | Engraving of the Black Legend, 1598

Beinecke Rare Book and Manuscript Library, Yale University

1.5 Theodor de Bry | Indians Torturing Spaniards, 1594

Beinecke Rare Book and Manuscript Library, Yale University

Interpret the Evidence

- What do these images tell us about public perceptions of Indians and Spanish explorers?
- What details reveal that de Bry never went to the Americas?

Put It in Context

Who would have used these images in debates over Spanish exploration in the Americas and for what purpose?

---

wore the clothes that her Spanish captors provided. Malintzin accompanied Cortés and his men as they conquered the Aztecs, and she watched as more Spaniards, including the first women, settled in New Spain. In 1522 she gave birth to Cortés's son; two years later, she served as interpreter when he ventured north from Mexico City to conquer more territory. In 1526 or 1527, however, she married a Spanish soldier, Juan Jaramillo, and settled in Mexico City. She soon had a daughter, Maria, and in 1528

Jaramillo and "his wife, doña Marina" were granted lands for an orchard and a farm. We do not know how long Malintzin lived or what she thought of her life as the wife of a Spanish gentleman. But her children would grow up in a world that was very different from the one in which their mother was raised. In the century to come, the contacts and conflicts between native peoples and Europeans escalated, especially in North America. So, too, did conflicts among European nations seeking to gain control of North American lands.

LEARNINGCurve
Check what you know.
bedfordstmartins.com/hewittlawson/LC

Chapter Review

Online Study Guide ▶ bedfordstmartins.com/hewittlawson

KEY TERMS

Beringia (p. 5)
horticulture (p. 5)
Aztecs (p. 5)
Maya (p. 7)
Incas (p. 7)
Hopewell people (p. 7)
Crusades (p. 9)
Black Death (p. 10)
Renaissance (p. 10)
Enterprise of the Indies (p. 14)
encomiendas (p. 14)
Columbian exchange (p. 18)
conquistadors (p. 20)

REVIEW & RELATE

1. Compare and contrast the Aztecs, Incas, and Maya. What similarities and differences do you note?

2. How did the societies of North America differ from those of the equatorial zone and the Andes?

3. How and why did Europeans expand their connections with Africa and the Middle East in the fifteenth century?

4. How did early European encounters with West Africans lay the foundation for later race-based slavery?

5. What were the short-term consequences in both Europe and the Americas of Columbus's voyages?

6. How did the Columbian exchange transform both the Americas and Europe?

7. What motives were behind the Spanish conquest and colonization of the Americas?

8. What were the consequences in Europe of Spain's acquisition of an American empire?

TIMELINE OF EVENTS

13,000–11,000 B.C.E.	First northeast Asians migrate to the Americas
1000 B.C.E.	Agriculture develops in some parts of the Americas
900 B.C.E.–300 C.E.	Maya settle Yucatán peninsula
500 C.E.	Mogollon and Hohokam communities established in present-day Arizona and New Mexico
500–1400	Mississippian people establish complex societies centered on towns and massive earthworks
800	Mayan civilization begins to decline
1000	Norse establish small settlement in North America
1292	Marco Polo publishes his *Travels*
1325	Aztecs build Tenochtitlán
1340s	Bubonic plague arrives in Europe from Asia
1400–1500	Inca empire reaches the height of its power
1440s	Portuguese begin to trade along the coast of West Africa
1452–1455	Johannes Gutenberg uses movable type to produce 180 copies of the Bible
1469	Marriage of Isabella of Castile and Ferdinand II of Aragon leads to unification of Spain
1482	Portugal builds Elmina Castle on the Gold Coast of West Africa
1487	Bartolomeu Dias rounds the Cape of Good Hope
1492	Isabella and Ferdinand expel last Muslim conquerors from the Iberian peninsula
	Columbus launches Enterprise of the Indies
1497	Vasco da Gama reaches India by sailing around Africa
1507	Martin Waldseemüller and Mathias Ringmann publish *Universalis Cosmographia*
1519	Malintzin captured by Spaniards
1519–1521	Spanish and Indian army led by Cortés conquers the Aztecs
1519–1522	Fleet led by Ferdinand Magellan circumnavigates the globe sailing west
1524	Francisco Pizarro conquers the Incas
1587	English colony of Roanoke established in North America

Mapping America

As Europeans expanded their trade and exploration in the fifteenth century, they gathered information about navigational routes and the regions they encountered. Cartographers used this information to create increasingly accurate maps of the known world. One of the leading efforts in mapmaking was conducted under the leadership of Prince Henry of Portugal. His assemblage of cartographers, geographers, astronomers, and explorers helped revolutionize European understandings of the western coast of Africa and nearby islands in the Atlantic. The 1513 Piri Reis map (Document 1.8), in particular, used Portuguese maps to chart Africa and the Atlantic.

Columbus's discovery of the Western Hemisphere in 1492 redrew the map of the world. Although he believed he had found a route to Asia, by 1507 when the *Universalis Cosmographia* (Document 1.7) appeared, cartographers understood this as an entirely new region. Throughout the early sixteenth century, maps of the Americas continued to expand and modify knowledge of what was termed the "New World," whose territory would be claimed by Spain, Portugal, England, France, and other European powers. Of course, the Western Hemisphere was not a "new" world but instead one inhabited by millions of indigenous peoples with complex societies of their own. Document 1.10 is an example of a map created by indigenous people in what is now Mexico; they often used maps not only to depict an area but also to record developments in that region that had occurred over decades or even centuries.

The following maps depict changing understandings of Europe, Africa, and the Americas from 1490 to the mid-sixteenth century, as well as the increasing interconnectedness of these regions. They represent not only attempts to chart territory and navigational routes but also cultural beliefs about the world and the people encountered by Europeans. As you examine them, think about what their creators chose to include, what they left out, and how these maps helped shape European attitudes toward Africa and the Western Hemisphere.

DOCUMENT 1.6

Christopher and Bartolomeo Columbus |
Map of Europe and North Africa, c. 1490

While Christopher Columbus's discovery of the Americas is well known, his younger brother, Bartolomeo, also played a part in the early discovery and exploration of the Western Hemisphere. Bartolomeo was a cartographer and navigator who accompanied Christopher on several explorations. This map is believed to have been produced in the Lisbon workshop of Christopher and Bartolomeo Columbus in 1490, two years before Columbus set sail on his first voyage. It depicts Europe and North Africa and also includes a circular world map on the left.

DOCUMENT 1.7

Martin Waldseemüller and Mathias Ringmann | *Universalis Cosmographia*, 1507

In 1507 German cartographers Martin Waldseemüller and Mathias Ringmann produced a map of the "known" world, which included those areas in the Western Hemisphere recently discovered by European explorers. They were the first to use the term *America*, and their *Universalis Cosmographia* was also the first map to show the Americas as separate from Asia. The map was printed from wood engravings and produced in twelve sections.

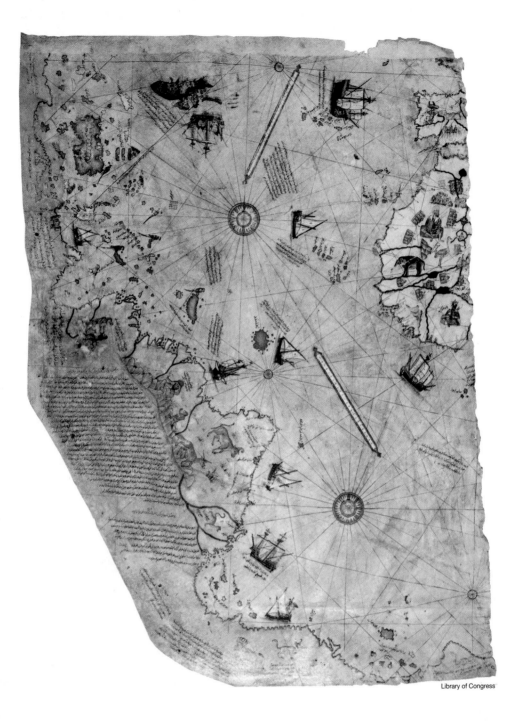

Library of Congress

DOCUMENT 1.8

Piri Reis Map, 1513

The Turkish admiral and cartographer Piri Reis produced another early-sixteenth-century map. While much of the map does not survive, the remaining part includes the western coasts of Europe and North Africa, the eastern coast of South America, and the northern coast of Antarctica. Reis used Portuguese, Ptolemaic, and Arabic maps to produce his version of the world, and the illustrations are detailed and reasonably accurate.

DOCUMENT 1.9

Dauphin Map of Canada, c. 1543

Although Jacques Cartier was not the first European to explore present-day Canada, he was the first to penetrate into the eastern interior, aided by two Iroquois guides whom he had kidnapped. The French explorer claimed the region for France in the 1530s, and over the next decade he completed three voyages to explore and map the Gulf of St. Lawrence region. He also sought what he believed were great riches at a legendary Indian kingdom named Saguenay. The map shown here, known as the Dauphin Map of Canada and based on Cartier's explorations, includes French Canada and the entire east coast of North America. Created in 1543, this map includes the largest Indian settlements (Hochelaga and Stadaconna) but also names and claims numerous rivers, inlets, harbors, and the lands surrounding them for the French. Finally, it also illustrates some of the land claims of England and Spain in the region.

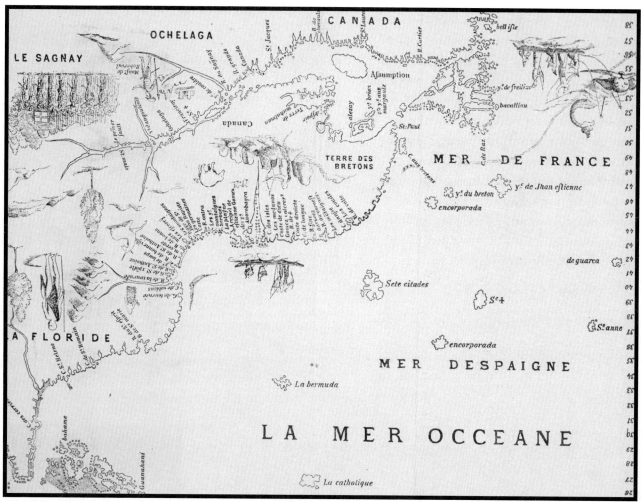

DOCUMENT 1.10

Map of Cuauhtinchan, 1550

The *Historia Tolteca-Chichimeca* is a series of Nahuatl-language annals written in the mid-sixteenth century. Covering the history of the Cuauhtinchan region (in present-day Mexico) during the previous four hundred years, the text focuses mainly on the area's social and political history. Most of the narrative deals with events that occurred before, or were unrelated to, Spanish activity in the region. Illustrations accompanied the text, including the map shown here. This map, covered with some seven hundred glyphs, depicts how the Toltec-Chichimeca peoples of the Puebla valley left their seven-chambered cave of Chicomoztoc, conquered their enemies, and established their new home at Cuauhtinchan in 1183 C.E. Like many native maps, it combines myth and history with geography and tells a story across time and space. Yet this territorial map was considered so reliable that it was used as evidence in Spanish colonial courts in the sixteenth century.

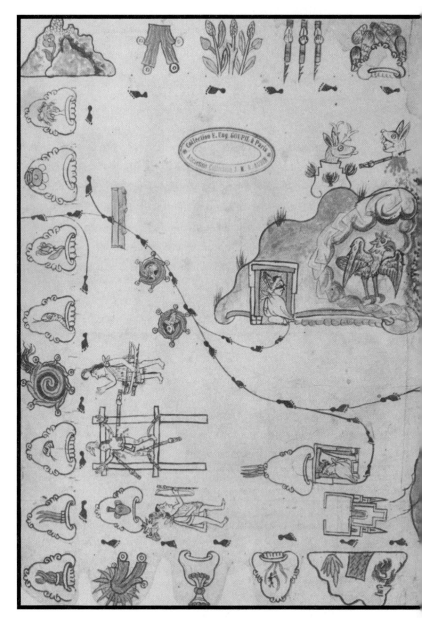

Nettie Lee Benson Latin American Collection, University of Texas Libraries, The University of Texas at Austin

Interpret the Evidence

1. How did the mapmakers in Documents 1.7, 1.8, and 1.9 represent the lands being discovered and claimed by various European nations?

2. What were the different purposes of the various maps included here?

3. What elements other than geographical features appear on these maps, and what were they intended to symbolize?

4. Compare the Cuauhtinchan map (Document 1.10) with those created by Europeans. What are the major differences? What do you think these differences reveal about the cultures of the mapmakers?

Put It in Context

- What are the strengths and weaknesses of modern mapmaking compared with older mapmaking?

- What is gained and what is lost in the transition from one to the other?

HIP/Art Resource, NY

© Burstein Collection/CORBIS

English Captain Bartholomew Gosnold trading with Indians, Virginia, 1634.

Portrait of Elizabeth Paddy Wensley by unknown artist, c. 1670–1680.

2
Colonization and Conflicts
1550–1680

HIP/Art Resource, NY

Village of Pomeiooc, Virginia, 1618.

AMERICAN HISTORIES

Born in 1580 to a yeoman farm family in Lincolnshire, the adventurer John Smith left England as a young man "to learne the life of a Souldier." After fighting and traveling in Europe, the Mediterranean, and North Africa for several years, Captain Smith returned to England around 1605. There he joined the Virginia Company, whose investors planned to establish a private settlement on mainland North America. In December 1606, Captain Smith sailed with a contingent of 104 men, arriving in Chesapeake Bay the following April. The group founded Jamestown, named in honor of King James I. In doing so, they claimed the land for themselves and their country. However, whatever abstract claims Captain Smith and his comrades believed they were making to the region, their settlement was located in an area already controlled by a powerful leader, Chief Powhatan, who headed a confederation of local tribes.

In December 1607, when Powhatan's younger brother discovered Smith and two of his Jamestown comrades in the chief's territory, the Indians executed the two comrades but eventually released Smith. It is likely that before sending him back to Jamestown, Powhatan performed an adoption ceremony in an effort to bring Smith and the English under his authority. A typical ceremony would have involved Powhatan sending out one of his daughters—in this case, Pocahontas, who was about twelve years old—to indicate that the captive was spared. But Smith either did not understand or refused to accept his new status. He later claimed that

35

**John Smith
and Anne Hutchinson**

Pocahontas saved him out of love. At the time, however, he simply returned to Jamestown and urged the residents to build fortifications to enhance their strength and security.

The following fall, the colonists elected Smith president of the Jamestown council. Holding the power of a colonial governor, he argued that intimidating the Indians was the way to win Powhatan's respect. He also demanded that the English labor on farms and fortifications six hours a day. Many colonists resisted. Like Smith himself, most of the men were adventurers; they had little skill—and even less interest—in farming. They came to America not to settle down but to gain wealth and glory. Despite improvements in conditions in the colony under Smith's regime, the Virginia Company soon replaced him with a new set of leaders. In October 1609, angry and bitter, Smith returned to England.

Captain Smith criticized Virginia Company policies on a number of fronts, publishing his views in 1612, which brought him widespread attention. Smith then set out to map the northern Atlantic coast, and in 1616 he published a tract that emphasized the similarity of the area's climate and terrain to the British Isles, calling it New England. He argued that colonies there could be made commercially viable but that success depended on recruiting settlers with the necessary skills and offering them land and a say in the colony's management.

English men and women settled New England in the 1620s, but they did not invite Smith to join them. The first colonists to the region sought religious sanctuary, not commercial success or military dominance. Yet they, too, suffered schisms in their ranks. Anne Hutchinson, a forty-five-year-old wife and mother, was at the center of one such division. Also born in Lincolnshire, England, in 1591, about a decade after Smith, Anne was well educated by her father, a minister in the Church of England.

In 1612 she married William Hutchinson, a merchant, and over the next twenty years she gave birth to thirteen children. The Hutchinsons began attending Puritan sermons and by 1630 had embraced the new faith. Four years later, they followed the Reverend John Cotton to Massachusetts Bay.

The Reverend Cotton was soon urging Anne Hutchinson to use her exceptional knowledge of the Bible to hold prayer meetings in her home on Sundays for pregnant and nursing women who could not attend regular services. Hutchinson, like Cotton, preached a covenant of grace, by which individuals must rely solely on God's grace and could play no part in their own salvation.

By contrast, mainstream Puritan leaders claimed that a man or woman could cooperate with God's grace by leading a saintly life and performing good works.

Hutchinson began challenging Puritan ministers who opposed a pure covenant of grace, charging that they posed a threat to their congregations. She soon attracted a loyal following that included men as well as women. The growing size of her Sunday meetings helped convince Puritan leaders to call the first synod of their Congregational Church in August 1637. The synod denounced Hutchinson's views and condemned her Sunday meetings. When she refused to recant, she was put on trial. Standing alone to face a panel of forty-nine powerful men in November 1637, Hutchinson defended herself against charges that she presumed to teach men and failed to honor the ministers of the colony. Unmoved by her defense, the Puritan judges convicted her of heresy and banished her from Massachusetts Bay. Hutchinson, her husband, and their six youngest children, along with dozens of followers, then settled in the recently established colony of Rhode Island. ●

bottom photo: Schlesinger Library, Radcliffe Institute, Harvard University/The Bridgeman Art Library

THE AMERICAN HISTORIES of John Smith and Anne Hutchinson illustrate the diversity of motives that drew English men and women to North America in the seventeenth century. Smith led a group of soldiers and adventurers seeking wealth and glory, both for themselves and for their king. In many ways, their efforts to colonize Virginia were an extension of a larger competition between European states. The roots of Hutchinson's journey to North America can be traced to the Protestant Reformation of the sixteenth century, a massive religious upheaval that divided Europe into rival religious factions. The Puritan faith that was so central to her life was an outgrowth of the Reformation. Yet as different as these two people and their motives were, both worked to further English settlement in North America even as they generated conflict within their own communities. At the same time, those communities confronted the needs and desires of diverse native peoples as well as the colonial aspirations of other Europeans. These contending forces reshaped the landscape of North America between 1550 and 1680.

Religious and Imperial Transformations

The Puritans were part of a relatively new religious movement known as **Protestantism** that had emerged around 1520. Protestants challenged Catholic policies and practices but did not form a single church of their own. Instead, a number of theologians, including Martin Luther and John Calvin, formed distinct denominations in various regions of Europe, especially the German states, Switzerland, France, England, and the Netherlands. Catholics sought to counter their claims by revitalizing their faith and reasserting control. These religious conflicts shaped developments in North America as groups with competing visions worked to claim lands and sometimes souls.

The Protestant Reformation

Critiques of the Catholic Church multiplied in the early sixteenth century, driven by papal involvement in conflicts among monarchs and corruption among church officials. But the most vocal critics focused on immorality, ignorance, and absenteeism among clergy. These anticlerical views appeared in popular songs and printed images as well as in learned texts by theologians such as Martin Luther.

Luther, a professor of theology in Germany, believed that faith alone led to salvation, which could be granted only by God. He challenged the claims of Pope Leo X and his bishop in Germany that individuals could achieve salvation by buying indulgences, which were documents that absolved the buyer of sin. The church profited enormously from these sales, but they suggested that God's grace could be purchased. In 1517 Luther wrote an extended argument against indulgences and sent it to the local bishop. Although intended for learned clerics and academics, his writings soon gained a wider audience.

Luther's followers, who protested Catholic practices, became known as Protestants. His teachings circulated widely through sermons and printed texts, and his claim that ordinary people should read and reflect on the Scriptures appealed to the literate middle classes. Meanwhile his attacks on indulgences and corruption attracted those who resented the church's wealth and priests' lack of attention to their flock. In Switzerland, John Calvin developed a version of Protestantism in which civil magistrates and reformed ministers ruled over a Christian society. According to Calvinist beliefs, God was all-knowing and absolutely sovereign, while man was weak and sinful. Calvin argued that God had decided at the beginning of time who was saved and who was damned. Calvin's idea, known as predestination, energized Protestants who understood salvation as a gift from an all-knowing God in which human "works" played no part.

The Protestant Reformation quickly spread through central and northern Europe. England, too, came under the influence of Protestantism in the 1530s, although for different reasons. When the pope refused to annul the marriage of King Henry VIII and Catherine of Aragon, Henry denounced papal authority and established the **Church of England**, or Anglicanism, with himself as "defender of the faith." Despite the king's conversion to Protestantism, the Church of England retained many Catholic practices.

In countries like Spain and France with strong central governments and powerful ties to the Catholic Church, a strong Catholic Counter-Reformation largely quashed Protestantism. At the same time, Catholic leaders initiated reforms to counter their critics. In 1545 Pope Paul II called together a commission of cardinals, known as the Council of Trent (1545–1563), to address contentious issues such as corrupt bishops and priests, indulgences, and other financial abuses. The council initiated reforms, such as the founding of seminaries to train priests and the return of monastic orders to their spiritual foundations.

Religious upheavals in Europe contributed significantly to empire building in North America. Protestant and Catholic leaders urged followers to spread their faith across the Atlantic, while religious minorities sought a safe haven in North America. Just as important, political struggles erupted between Catholic and Protestant rulers in Europe following the Reformation. The politicization of religious divisions resulted in peasant unrest, economic crises, and military conflicts that pushed (or forced) people to seek new opportunities in the Americas. Thus in a variety of ways, religious transformations in Europe fueled the construction of empires in America.

Spain's Global Empire Declines

As religious conflicts escalated in Europe, the Spaniards in America continued to push north from Florida and Mexico in hopes of expanding their empire. At times, they confronted Protestants seeking to gain a foothold in the New World. For example, French Protestants, known as Huguenots, settled in Florida in the 1550s. By 1565, Spanish soldiers had constructed a fort at St. Augustine and massacred some three hundred Huguenots. The fort's main purpose, however, was to limit raids on Spanish ships by French and English privateers seeking to enrich themselves and their monarchs.

Yet as a result of the Council of Trent and the Catholic Counter-Reformation, Spain increasingly emphasized its religious mission. Thus Spanish authorities decided in 1573 that missionaries rather than soldiers should direct all new settlements. Franciscan priests began founding missions on the margins of Pueblo villages north of Mexico. They named the area Nuevo México (New Mexico), and many learned Indian languages. Over the following decades, as many as twenty thousand Pueblos officially converted to Catholicism, although many still retained traditional beliefs and practices. Thus they continued to practice religious ceremonies at sacred shrines known as kivas. Missionaries periodically destroyed the shrines and flogged Pueblo ceremonial leaders, but to no avail.

At the same time, the Franciscans tried to force the Pueblo people to adopt European ways. They insisted that men rather than women farm the land and that the Pueblos speak, cook, and dress like the Spaniards. Yet the missionaries largely ignored Spanish laws intended to protect Indians from coerced labor. Indeed, the Franciscans forced the Pueblos to build churches, provide the missions with food, and carry their goods to market. Wealthy landowners who followed the missionaries into New Mexico also demanded tribute in the form of goods and labor.

Then in 1598 Juan de Oñate, a member of a wealthy mining family, established a trading post and fort in the upper Rio Grande valley. The 500 soldiers who accompanied him seized corn and clothing from Pueblo villages and murdered or raped those who resisted. When the Spanish force was confronted by Indians at the Acoma pueblo, 11 soldiers were killed. The Spanish retaliated, slaughtering 500 men and 300 women and children. But fearing reprisals

San Esteban del Rey Mission

Opened in 1644 after fourteen years of construction, this Spanish mission in present-day New Mexico provided instruction in Christianity and Hispanic customs for the Acoma (Pueblo) people. To this end, Spanish missionaries prohibited traditional Pueblo practices such as dances and wearing masks. The mission was one of the few to survive Pueblo revolts in the late seventeenth century.
© age fotostock/SuperStock

from outraged Indians, most Spanish settlers withdrew from the region.

In 1610 the Spanish returned, founded Santa Fe, and established a network of missions and estates owned by *encomenderos*, Spanish elites granted land and the right to exploit local Indian labor. The Pueblo people largely accepted the new situation. In part, they feared military reprisals if they challenged Spanish authorities. But they were also faced with droughts and disease, as well as raids by hostile Apache and Navajo tribes. The Pueblos hoped to gain protection from Spanish soldiers and priests. Yet their faith in the Franciscans' spiritual power soon began to fade when conditions did not improve. Although Spain maintained a firm hold on Florida and its colonies in the West Indies, it began focusing most of its efforts on staving off growing resistance among the Pueblo people. Thus as other European powers expanded their reach into North America, the Spaniards were left with few resources to protect their eastern frontier.

France Enters the Race for Empire

In the late sixteenth century, French, Dutch, and English investors became increasingly interested in gaining a foothold in North America. But until Catholic Spain's grip on the Atlantic world was broken, other nations could not hope to compete for an American empire. It was the Protestant Reformation that helped shape the alliances that shattered Spain's American monopoly. As head of the Church of England, King Henry VIII and then his daughter Queen Elizabeth I sought closer political and commercial ties with Protestant nations like the Netherlands. At the same time, the queen assented to, and benefited from, Francis Drake's raids on Spanish ships. She rewarded him with a knighthood for services to the crown. In 1588 King Philip II of Spain decided to punish England for its attacks against Spanish shipping and intervention in the Netherlands and sent a massive armada to spearhead the invasion of England. Instead, the English, aided by Dutch ships that were smaller and more mobile, defeated the armada and ensured that other nations could compete for riches and colonies in North America.

Although French rulers shared Spain's Catholic faith, the two nations were rivals, and the defeat of the armada provided them as well as the Dutch and English with greater access to North American colonies. Moreover, once in North America, the French adopted attitudes and policies that were significantly different from those of Spain. This was due in part to their greater interest in trade than in conquest. They needed to develop alliances with local inhabitants who could supply them with fish and furs to be sold in Europe. The French had fished the North Atlantic since the mid-sixteenth century, but in the 1580s

they built stations along the Newfoundland coast for drying codfish. French traders then established relations with local Indians and eagerly exchanged iron kettles, which the native peoples desired, for beaver skins, which were highly prized in Europe.

By the early seventeenth century, France's King Henry IV sought to profit more directly from the resources in North America. With the Edict of Nantes (1598), the king ended decades of religious wars by granting political rights and limited toleration to French Protestants, the Huguenots. Now he could focus on developing the increasingly lucrative trade in American fish and furs. Samuel de Champlain, an experienced soldier and sailor, founded the first permanent French settlement in North America in 1608 at Quebec. Accompanied by several dozen of his men, Champlain joined a Huron raid on the Iroquois, who resided south of the Great Lakes. Using guns, which had rarely been seen in the region, the French helped ensure a Huron victory and a powerful ally for the French. But the battle also fueled lasting bitterness among the Iroquois.

Trade relations flourished between the French and their Indian allies, but relatively few French men and even fewer French women settled in North America in the seventeenth century. Government policies discouraged mass migration, and peasants were also concerned by reports of short growing seasons and severe winters in Canada. Cardinal Richelieu, the king's powerful chief minister, urged priests and nuns to migrate to New France and establish missions among the Indians, but he barred Huguenots from emigrating, which further limited colonization. Thus into the 1630s, French settlements in North America consisted largely of fishermen, fur traders, and Catholic missionaries.

Fur traders were critical to sustaining the French presence and warding off encroachment by the English. They journeyed along lakes and rivers throughout eastern Canada, aided by the Huron tribe. Some Frenchmen took Indian wives, who provided them with both domestic labor and kinship ties to powerful trading partners. These marriages also helped forge a middle ground in the Great Lakes region as French traders pushed westward and gained new Indian allies among the Ojibwe and Dakota tribes. The middle ground was a space in which shared economic interest motivated a remarkable degree of cultural exchange and mutual adaptation. Some French learned native languages and recognized the incredible value of canoes to their trade. They also came to appreciate Indian women's importance in gathering and preparing food, scraping beaver pelts, and weaving. At the same time, Indian communities adopted iron cooking pots and needles and European cloth. Jesuit missionaries, who entered New France in 1625, frowned on these marriages and the cultural exchanges they fostered. Nonetheless, they followed the path set out by fur traders and established missions among the Hurons and later the Ojibwes.

Explore

In Documents 2.1 and 2.2, compare a Huron woman's concerns about the Jesuits' presence in New France with a French priest's speech on the Jesuits' motivations.

In their ongoing search for new sources of furs, the French established a fortified trading post at Montreal in 1643, and over the next three decades they continued to push farther west. However, in extending the fur trade beyond the St. Lawrence River valley, the French left their Huron allies open to attacks from the Iroquois. The Iroquois suffered from the same diseases that decimated other tribes, and they also wanted to keep the Huron tribe from trading their high-quality furs to the Dutch. With guns supplied by Dutch merchants, the Iroquois could fend off economic competition and secure captives to restore their population. The result was a series of devastating assaults on Huron villages in which dozens of Jesuits died alongside the Indians they had converted.

The ongoing wars among native rivals limited the ability of France to capitalize on its North American colonies. Indeed, the only hope of maintaining profits from the fur trade was to continue to move westward. But in doing so, the French carried European diseases into new areas, ignited warfare among more native groups, and stretched their always small population of settlers ever thinner. Still, French explorers, traders, and priests extended their reach across Canada and by 1681 moved southward along the Mississippi to a territory they named Louisiana in honor of King Louis XIV. There they would find themselves face-to-face with Spanish adventurers heading east from New Mexico.

The conflicts between commerce and conversion so evident in Spanish America were far less severe in New France. Not only did French traders rely on Indian allies, but French missionaries also sought to build on native beliefs and to learn their language and customs. Although the Jesuits assumed that their own religious beliefs and cultural values were superior to those of the Indians, they did seek to engage Indians on their own terms. Thus one French Jesuit employed the Huron belief that "our souls have desires which are inborn and concealed" to explain Christian doctrines of sin and salvation to potential converts. Still, French traders and missionaries carried deadly germs, and Catholics sought conversion, not mutual adaptation. Thus while Indians clearly benefited from their alliances with the French in the short term, the long-term costs were devastating.

The Dutch Expand into North America

The Dutch, who eagerly embraced the Protestant Reformation at home, made no pretense of bringing religion to Indians in America. From the beginning, their goals were primarily economic. As Spain's shipbuilding center, the Netherlands benefited from the wealth pouring in from South America. The affluent merchant class that emerged among the Dutch promoted the arts, and artists like Salomon van Ruysdael and Johannes Vermeer in turn captured the importance of trade in their work. But the Dutch also embraced Calvinism and sought to separate themselves from Catholic Spain. In 1581 the Netherlands declared its independence from King Philip II, although Spain refused to recognize the new status for several decades. Still, by 1600 the Netherlands was both a Protestant haven and the trading hub of Europe. Indeed, the Dutch East India Company controlled trade routes to much of Asia and parts of Africa.

With the technology and skills developed under Spanish control, the Dutch decided to acquire their own American colonies. In 1609 the Dutch established a trading center on the Hudson River in present-day New York, where they could trade with Iroquois to the west as well as with Indians who gathered beaver skins along Lake Champlain and farther north. The small number of Dutch traders developed especially friendly relations with the powerful Mohawk nation, and in 1614 the trading post was relocated to Fort Orange, near present-day Albany.

In 1624, to fend off French and English raids on ships sent downriver from Fort Orange, the Dutch established New Amsterdam on Manhattan Island, which they purchased from the Lenape Indians. The new settlement was organized by the Dutch West Indies Company, which had been chartered three years earlier. New Amsterdam was the centerpiece of the larger New Netherland colony and attracted a diverse community of traders, fishermen, and farmers. It was noted for its representative government and religious toleration, which ensured that religious differences did not get in the way of making money.

The European settlers of New Netherland may have gotten along with one another, but the same could not be said for the settlers and the local Indian populations. Tensions increased as Dutch colonists carved out farms north of New Amsterdam where larger communities of Algonquian Indians lived and where European pigs and cattle foraged in Indian cornfields. Algonquians in turn killed and ate Dutch livestock. In 1639 conflict escalated when Governor William Kieft demanded an annual tribute in wampum or grain. Local Algonquians resisted, raiding Dutch farms on the frontier and killing at least two colonists. Then in 1643 Kieft launched a surprise attack on an

Indians and Jesuit Missionaries in New France: Two Views

The arrival of Jesuit missionaries further exposed the cultural differences between Indians and Europeans in New France. In Document 2.1, an elder Huron woman advises her village to reject the Jesuits' preaching and suggests that the Black Robes, as the missionaries were called, be put to death. Although her sentiments were relayed by a third party to a French nun, Marie de L'Incarnation, who then quoted them in a letter sent to France, they seem to accurately reflect the views of many Indians in New France. Document 2.2 indicates that, despite Indian resistance, French Jesuits continued to proselytize in New France. In 1656 Father Pierre Chaumont spoke to a group of Iroquois assembled on the shores of Lake Onondaga. Like many Jesuits, he had learned several Indian languages and spoke to the assembled Iroquois in their own language.

Explore

2.1 Statement from a Huron Woman, 1640

It is the Black Robes that make us die by their spells. Harken to me. I am proving it by arguments you will know to be true. They lodged in a certain village where everyone was well. As soon as they were established there, everyone was dead except for three or four persons. They went elsewhere and the same thing happened. They visited the cabins in other villages and only those they did not enter were free of mortality and sickness. Do you not see that when they move their lips—what they call prayers—those are spells that come from their mouths? It is the same way when they read in their books. Besides, in their cabins they have big pieces of wood [those are guns] with which they make a great noise and spread their magic everywhere. If they are not promptly put to death, they will finally ruin the country so that neither small nor great will remain.

Source: Joyce Marshall, ed. and trans., *Word from New France: The Selected Letters of Marie de L'Incarnation* (Toronto: Oxford University Press, 1967), 82.

Explore

2.2 Father Pierre Chaumont | Speech to the Iroquois, 1656

For the Faith, we have departed from our country; for the Faith, we have abandoned our relatives and our friends; for the Faith, we have crossed the Ocean; for the Faith, we have left behind the great ships of the French to set off on your small canoes; for the Faith, we have relinquished our fine houses to live in your bark cabins; for the Faith, we have deprived ourselves of our natural nourishment and the delicious foods that we could have enjoyed in France to eat your boiled meal and your other victuals, which the animals of our country would hardly touch.

Source: Natalie Zemon Davis, *Women on the Margins: Three Seventeenth Century Lives* (Cambridge, MA: Harvard University Press, 1995), 94.

Interpret the Evidence

- According to the Huron woman, why should Native Americans reject the efforts of Jesuit missionaries?
- How does Father Pierre Chaumont characterize the lives of Jesuit missionaries?

Put It in Context

What do these documents reveal about how Native Americans and Jesuit missionaries perceived each other? How do these perceptions compare with Indian-European relations in English and Spanish colonies?

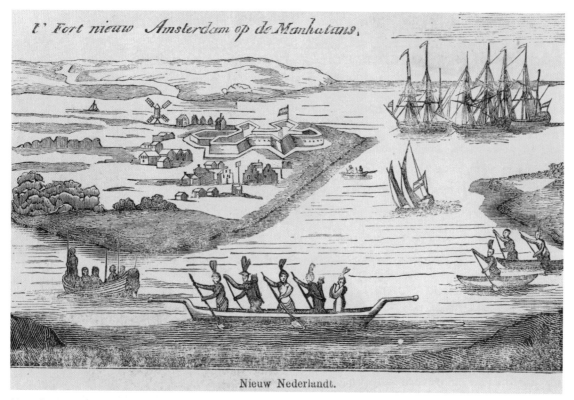

Nieuw Nederlandt.

New Amsterdam

This engraving from the 1620s provides the oldest view of the Dutch colony of New Amsterdam. Located at the tip of present-day Manhattan, the Dutch settlement consisted mainly of a fort and trading post. The ships suggest the importance of commerce, and the Indians, from whom the island was purchased, demonstrate their significant presence in the region.   Culver Pictures/The Art Archive at Art Resource, NY

Indian encampment on Manhattan Island, murdering eighty people, mostly women and children. Outraged Algonquians burned and looted homes north of the city, killed livestock, and murdered settlers. For two decades, sporadic warfare continued, but eventually the Algonquians were defeated.

At the same time, the Dutch eagerly traded for furs with Mohawk Indians along the upper Hudson River. The Mohawks were a powerful tribe that had the backing of the even more powerful Iroquois Confederacy. Their ties to Indian nations farther west allowed them to provide beaver skins to Dutch traders long after beavers had died out in the Hudson valley. Still, the Mohawk people did not deceive themselves. As one chief proclaimed in 1659, "The Dutch say we are brothers and that we are joined together with chains, but that lasts only so long as we have beavers."

Meanwhile reports of atrocities by both Indians and the Dutch circulated in the Netherlands. These damaged New Amsterdam's reputation and slowed migration dramatically. Exhausted by the unrelenting conflicts, the Dutch surrendered New Amsterdam to the English without a fight when the latter sent a convoy to oust their former allies in 1664.

REVIEW & RELATE

How did the Protestant Reformation shape the course of European expansion in the Americas?

How did the French and Dutch colonies in North America differ from the Spanish empire to the south?

LEARNINGCurve bedfordstmartins.com/hewittlawson/LC

The English Seek an Empire

The English, like the French and the Dutch, entered the race for an American empire late. England's failed efforts to colonize North America in the sixteenth century had left them without a permanent settlement until the founding of **Jamestown** on the Chesapeake River in 1607. In the 1620s, the English also established settlements in the West Indies, which quickly became the economic engine of English colonization. Expansion into these areas demanded new modes of labor to ensure a return on investment. Beginning in the mid-sixteenth century, large numbers of European indentured servants and growing numbers of African men and women crossed the Atlantic, some voluntarily, many involuntarily.

The English Establish Jamestown

England's success in colonizing North America depended in part on a new economic model in which investors sold shares in joint-stock companies and sought royal support for their venture. In 1606 a group of London merchants formed the Virginia Company, and King James I granted them the right to settle a vast area of North America, from present-day New York to North Carolina. The proprietors promised to "propagate the *Christian* religion" among native inhabitants in the region, but they were far more interested in turning a profit.

Most of the men that the Virginia Company recruited as colonists were, like John Smith, adventurers who hoped to get rich through the discovery of precious metals. Arriving on the coast of North America in April 1607 after a four-month voyage, the weary colonists established Jamestown on a site they chose for its easy defense. Although bothered by the settlement's mosquito-infested environment, the colonists focused their energies on the search for gold and silver.

The Englishmen also made contact with the Indian chief Powhatan, who presided over a confederation of some 14,000 Algonquian-speaking Indians from 25 to 30 tribes. The **Powhatan Confederacy** was far more powerful than its English neighbors, and, indeed, for the first two years the settlers depended on the Indians to survive. Although the Jamestown settlers were often hungry, few of them engaged in farming. Moreover, the nearby water was tainted by salt from the ocean, and diseases that festered in the low-lying area ensured a high death toll. Nine months after arriving in Virginia, only 38 of the original 105 settlers remained alive.

Despite the Englishmen's aggressive posture and inability to feed themselves, Powhatan initially assisted the settlers in hopes they could provide him with English cloth, iron hatchets, and even guns. His capture and subsequent release of John Smith in 1607 suggests his interest in developing trade relations with the newcomers even as he sought to subordinate them. But leaders like Captain Smith considered Powhatan and his warriors a threat rather than an asset. Although Jamestown residents could not afford to engage in open hostilities with local natives, they did raid villages for corn and other food, making Powhatan increasingly wary. The settlers' decision to construct a fort under Smith's direction only increased the Indians' concern.

Meanwhile the Virginia Company devised a new plan to stave off the collapse of its colony. It started selling seven-year joint-stock options to raise funds and recruited new settlers to produce staple crops—grapes, sugar, cotton, or tobacco—for export since the search for precious metals had failed. Interested individuals who could not afford to invest cash could sign on for service in Virginia. After seven years, these colonists would receive a hundred acres of land. In June 1609, a new contingent of colonists attracted by this plan—five hundred men and a hundred women—sailed for Jamestown (Map 2.1).

The new arrivals, however, had not brought enough supplies to sustain the colony through the winter. Powhatan did offer some aid, but a severe dry spell meant that the Indians, too, suffered from shortages in the winter of 1609–1610. A "starving time" settled on Jamestown. By the spring of 1610, seven of every eight settlers who had arrived in Jamestown since 1607 were dead. One colonist noted that settlers "were destroyed by cruell diseases, as Swellings, Fluxes, [and] Burning Fevers," though most "died of mere famine."

That June, the sixty survivors decided to abandon Jamestown and sail for home. But in the harbor, they met three English ships loaded with supplies and three hundred more settlers. Fresh supplies and a larger population inspired the English to take a much more confrontational

MAP 2.1   Jamestown, c. 1615

After eight years, the English settlement at Jamestown was finally expanding. Most important for the future, John Rolfe's experiments with tobacco promised a profitable cash crop. Still, English colonists remained a small minority huddled along the James River. Numerous Indian tribes, many of them members of the Powhatan Confederacy, surrounded them on all sides.

approach. Jamestown's new leaders adopted an aggressive military posture, attacking native villages, burning crops, killing many Indians, and taking others captive. They believed that such brutality would horrify neighboring tribes and convince them to obey English demands for food and labor.

Tobacco Fuels Growth in Virginia

It was not, however, military aggression but the discovery of a viable cash crop that saved the colony. Orinoco tobacco, a sweet-flavored leaf grown in the West Indies and South America, sold well in England and Europe. One Virginia colonist, John Rolfe, began to experiment with its growth in 1612. Within two years, it was clear that Orinoco tobacco prospered in Virginia soil. Production of the leaf soared as eager investors poured seeds, supplies, and labor into Jamestown. Exports multiplied rapidly, from 2,000 pounds in 1615 to 40,000 five years later and an incredible 1.5 million pounds by 1629. Although high taxes and overproduction led to declining prices in the 1630s, tobacco remained the most profitable cash crop on mainland North America throughout the seventeenth century.

Tobacco cultivation transformed relations between the English and the Indians. Farmers could increase their profits only by obtaining more land and more laborers. The Virginia Company sought to supply the laborers by offering those who could pay their own way land for themselves and their families. Those who could not afford passage could labor for landowners for seven years and then gain their independence and perhaps land of their own. Yet the land the Virginia Company so generously offered would-be colonists was, in most cases, already settled by members of the Powhatan Confederacy. Thus the rapid increase in tobacco cultivation intensified competition for land between colonists and Indians.

As circumstances began to change, Powhatan tried one last time to create an alliance between his confederacy and the English settlers. In 1614 he agreed to allow his daughter Pocahontas to marry John Rolfe. Pocahontas converted to Christianity, took the name Rebecca, and two years later traveled to England with Rolfe and their infant son. Rebecca was treated royally, but she fell ill and died in 1617. After her death, Rolfe returned to Virginia and continued to develop successful strains of tobacco. Soon after his return, Powhatan died, and his younger brother Opechancanough took over as chief.

Explore

To examine the only image of Pocahontas drawn from life, see Document 2.3.

In 1619 the English crown granted Virginia the right to establish a local governing body, the **House of Burgesses**. Its members could make laws and levy taxes, although the English governor or the company council in London held veto power. At the same time, the Virginia Company resolved to recruit more female settlers as a way to increase the colony's population so that it "may spread into generations." Other young women and men arrived as **indentured servants**, working in the fields and homes of more affluent Englishmen for a set period of time, often seven years, in exchange for the price of passage to America. The first boatload of twenty Africans also arrived in Jamestown aboard a Dutch ship in 1619, bound as indentured servants to farmers desperate for labor.

Although the English colony still hugged the Atlantic coast, its expansion increased conflict with native inhabitants. In March 1622, after repeated English incursions on land cleared and farmed by Indians, Chief Opechancanough mobilized area tribes for a surprise attack on English settlements. The Indians killed nearly a third of the colonists. In retaliation, Englishmen assaulted native villages, killed inhabitants, burned cornfields, and sold captives into slavery.

Announcing victory in 1623, the English claimed they owned the land "by right of Warre." But hostilities continued for nearly a decade. In 1624, in the midst of the crisis, King James annulled the Virginia Company charter and took control of the colony. He appointed the governor and a small advisory council, required that legislation passed by the House of Burgesses be ratified by the Privy Council, and demanded that property owners pay taxes to support the Church of England. These regulations became the model for royal colonies throughout North America. Still, royal proclamations could not halt Indian opposition. In 1644 Opechancanough launched a second uprising against the English, in which some five hundred colonists were killed. However, after two years of bitter warfare, the Powhatan chief was finally captured and then killed. With the English population now too large to eradicate, the Chesapeake Indians finally submitted to English authority in 1646, paying tribute to remain on lands they had lived on for generations.

Expansion, Rebellion, and the Emergence of Slavery

By the 1630s, despite continued conflicts with Indians, Virginia was well on its way to commercial success. The most successful tobacco planters utilized indentured servants, including some Africans as well as thousands of English and Irish immigrants. Between 1640 and 1670, some 40,000 to 50,000 of these migrants settled in Virginia and neighboring Maryland (Map 2.2). Maryland was

DOCUMENT 2.3

Simon van de Passe | Engraving of Pocahontas, 1616

Simon van de Passe created this portrait of Pocahontas during her visit to England in 1616. The engraving was commissioned by the Virginia Company as a way to market settlement in Jamestown. It was the only depiction of Pocahontas drawn from life because she died in London the following year. This engraving was copied, though not always accurately, many times during the eighteenth and nineteenth centuries.

Explore

While most portraits of English women from this period show the women looking down or to the side, Pocahontas looks directly at the viewer. Why might Simon van de Passe have portrayed Pocahontas in this way?

What does the elaborate clothing suggest about the parallels Simon van de Passe intends to draw between Indian royalty and English royalty?

What possible messages did the Virginia Company hope to promote with this image and its caption?

Library of Congress

Put It in Context

This image suggests both the possibility for establishing a long-term alliance between the Powhatan Indians and the English and the Virginia Company's desire to promote further English settlement in the Chesapeake. What is the relationship between the two messages offered by Pocahontas's portrait?

founded in 1632 when King Charles I, the successor to James I, granted most of the territory north of Chesapeake Bay and the title of Lord Baltimore to Cecilius Calvert. Calvert was among the minority of English who remained a Catholic, and he planned to create Maryland as a refuge for his persecuted coworshippers. Appointing his brother Leonard Calvert as governor, he carefully prepared for the first settlement. The Calverts recruited skilled artisans and farmers (mainly Protestant) as well as wealthy merchants and aristocrats (mostly Catholic) to establish St. Mary's City on the mouth of the Potomac River. Although conflict continued to fester between the Catholic elite and the Protestant majority, Governor Calvert convinced the Maryland assembly to pass the Act of Religious Toleration in 1649, granting religious freedom to all Christians.

Taken together, Maryland and Virginia formed the Chesapeake region of the English empire. Both colonies relied on tobacco to produce the wealth that fueled their growth, and both introduced African labor to complement the supply of white indentured servants. This proved especially important from 1650 on, as improved economic conditions in England meant fewer English men and women were willing to gamble on a better life in North America. Although the number of African laborers remained small until late in the century, there was a growing effort on the part of colonial leaders to increase their control over this segment of the workforce. Thus in 1660 the House of Burgesses passed an act that allowed African laborers to be enslaved. In 1664 Maryland followed suit. A slow if unsteady march toward full-blown racial slavery had begun.

> **Explore**
>
> See Document 2.4 for the Virginia law that made slavery an inherited condition passed from mother to child.

In legalizing human bondage, Virginia legislators followed a model established in Barbados, where the booming sugar industry spurred the development of plantation slavery. By 1660 Barbados had become the first English colony with a black majority population. Twenty years later, there were seventeen slaves for every white indentured servant on Barbados. The growth of slavery on the island depended almost wholly on imports from Africa since slaves there died faster than they could reproduce themselves. In the context of high death rates, brutal working conditions, and massive imports, Barbados systematized its slave code, defining enslaved Africans as chattel—that is, as mere property more akin to livestock than to human beings. Slaves existed to enrich their masters, and masters could do with them as they liked.

While African slaves would, in time, become a crucial component of the Chesapeake labor force, indentured servants made up the majority of bound workers in Virginia and Maryland for most of the seventeenth century. They labored under harsh conditions, and punishment for even minor infractions could be severe. Servants had holes bored in their tongues for complaining against their masters; they were beaten, whipped, and branded for a variety of "crimes"; and female servants who became pregnant had two years added to their contracts. Some white servants made common cause with black laborers who worked side by side with them on tobacco plantations. They ran away together, stole goods from their masters, and planned uprisings and rebellions.

By the 1660s and 1670s, the population of former servants who had become free formed a growing and increasingly unhappy class. Most were struggling economically, working as common laborers or tenants on large estates. Those who managed to move west and claim land on the frontier were confronted by hostile Indians like the Susquehannock. Virginia governor Sir William Berkeley had little patience with the complaints of these colonists. The labor demands of wealthy tobacco planters needed to be met, and

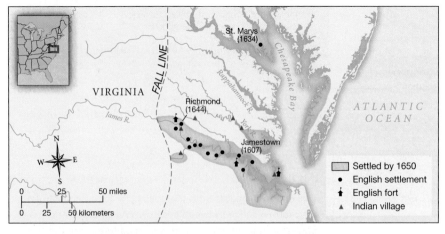

MAP 2.2   The Growth of English Settlement in the Chesapeake, c. 1650

With the success of tobacco, English plantations and forts spread along the James River and north to St. Mary's. By 1650 most Chesapeake Indian tribes had been vanquished or forced to move north and west. While the fall line, which marked the limit of navigable waterways, kept English settlements close to the Atlantic coast, it also ensured easy shipment of goods.

DOCUMENT 2.4

Virginia Slave Law, 1662

When the flow of white indentured servants to the Virginia colony slowed at midcentury, tobacco planters imported Africans to fill their labor needs. Anxious to define the status of these new workers, in the 1660s Virginia legislators passed a series of slave-related laws, such as the 1662 legislation that defined slavery as an inherited position, thus ensuring the perpetual enslavement of Africans and therefore a steady supply of workers. The act differed significantly from English common law, in which legal status and inheritance passed through the father.

Explore

Whereas some doubts have arisen whether children got by any Englishman upon a Negro woman should be slave or free, *Be it therefore enacted and declared by this present grand assembly*, that all children born in this country shall be held bond or free only according to the condition of the mother; and that if any Christian shall commit fornication with a Negro man or woman, he or she so offending shall pay double the fines imposed by the former act.

Source: William W. Hening, ed., *The Statutes at Large; Being a Collection of All Laws of Virginia, from the First Session of the Legislature in the Year 1619* (New York and Philadelphia, 1819–1823), 2:170.

Interpret the Evidence

- Why would the Virginia General Assembly make slavery an inheritable condition passed down through the mother instead of the father?
- What might explain the Assembly's decision to double the fine for fornication between a "Christian" and an African American?

Put It in Context

How did such laws create clearer distinctions between white indentured servants and enslaved Africans and African Americans?

frontier settlers' call for an aggressive Indian policy would hurt the profitable deerskin trade with the Algonquian Indians. Adopting a defensive strategy, Berkeley maintained a system of nine forts along the frontier that was supported by taxes, providing another aggravation for poorer colonists.

In late 1675, conflict erupted when frontier settlers attacked not the Susquehannock nation but rather Indian communities allied with the English since 1646. An even larger force of Virginia militiamen then surrounded a Susquehannock village and murdered five chiefs who tried to negotiate for peace. Susquehannock warriors retaliated with deadly raids on frontier farms. Despite the outbreak of open warfare, Governor Berkeley still refused to send troops, so disgruntled farmers turned to Nathaniel Bacon. Bacon, only twenty-nine years old and a newcomer to Virginia, came from a wealthy family and was related to Berkeley by marriage. But he defied the governor's authority and called up an army to attack all of the region's Indians, whether Susquehannocks or English allies. **Bacon's Rebellion** had begun. Frontier farmers formed an important part of Bacon's coalition. But affluent planters who had been left out of Berkeley's inner circle also joined Bacon in hopes of gaining access to power and profits. And bound laborers, black and white, assumed that anyone who opposed the governor was on their side.

In the summer of 1676, Governor Berkeley declared Bacon guilty of treason. Rather than waiting to be captured, Bacon led his army toward Jamestown. Berkeley then arranged a hastily called election to undercut the rebellion. Even though Berkeley had rescinded the right of men without property to vote, Bacon's supporters won control of the House of Burgesses, and Bacon won new adherents. These included "news wives," lower-class women who spread information (and rumors) about oppressive conditions, thereby aiding the rebels. As Bacon and his followers marched across Virginia, his men plundered the plantations of Berkeley supporters and captured Berkeley's estate at Green Spring. In September they reached Jamestown after the governor and his administration fled across Chesapeake Bay. The rebels burned the capital to the ground, victory seemingly theirs.

Only a month later, however, Bacon died of dysentery, and the movement he formed unraveled. Governor Berkeley, with the aid of armed ships from England, quickly reclaimed power. Outraged by the rebellion, he hanged twenty-three rebel leaders and incited his followers to plunder the estates of planters who had supported Bacon. But he could not undo the damage to Indian relations on the Virginia frontier. Bacon's army had killed or enslaved hundreds of once-friendly Indians and left behind a tragic and bitter legacy.

An even more important consequence of the rebellion was that wealthy planters and investors realized the depth of frustration among poor white men and women who were willing to make common cause with their black counterparts. Having regained power, the planter elite worked to crush any such interracial alliance. They promised most white rebels who put down arms the right to return home peacefully, and most complied. Virginia legislators then began to improve the conditions and rights of poorer white settlers while imposing new restrictions on blacks. At nearly the same time, in an effort to meet the growing demand for labor in the West Indies and the Chesapeake, King Charles II chartered the Royal African Company in 1672 to carry enslaved women and men from Africa to North America.

The English Compete for West Indies Possessions

While tobacco held great promise in Virginia, investors were eager to find other lucrative exports. Some turned their sights on the West Indies, where the English, the French, and the Dutch had all established bases on small islands during the sixteenth century. In the 1620s, the English developed more permanent settlements on St. Christopher, Barbados, and Nevis. Barbados quickly became the most attractive of these West Indies colonies. English migrants settled Barbados in growing numbers, clearing land and bringing in indentured servants from England, Ireland, and Scotland to cultivate tobacco and cotton and raise livestock.

The Dutch and the French also began establishing more permanent settlements in the West Indies. The Dutch colonized St. Martin and Curaçao, while the French settled Guadalupe, Martinique, and later Saint Domingue. The Dutch, however, profited mainly from carrying trade goods for other nations, while the French faced significant resistance from Carib Indians who resided on their island colonies. Thus neither developed their West Indies outposts to the same extent as the English. But even the English faced economic stagnation on Barbados as tobacco prices fell in the 1630s.

A few forward-looking planters were already considering another avenue to wealth: sugarcane. English and European consumers absorbed as much of the sweet gold as the market could provide, but producing sugar required

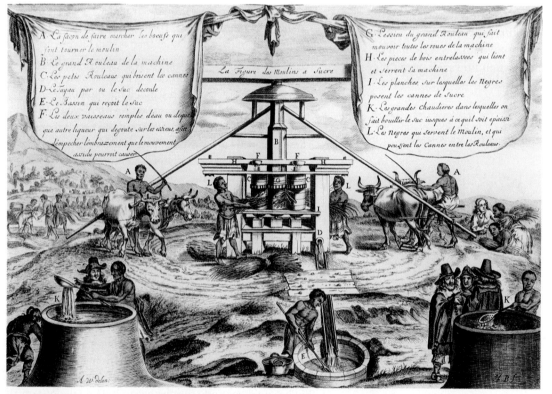

Sugar Manufacturing in the West Indies
This 1665 engraving depicts the use of slave labor in the production of sugar in the Antilles (West Indies). As shown in the illustration, the Dutch and English used slaves to plant sugarcane and then cut, press, and boil it to produce molasses. The molasses was turned into rum and refined sugar, which were among America's most profitable exports.   Private Collection/The Bridgeman Art Library

expensive equipment and technical know-how as well as a large number of laborers. In addition, the sugar that was sent from America needed further refinement in Europe before being sold to consumers. The Dutch had learned the secrets of sugar cultivation from the Portuguese in Brazil, and they built the best refineries in Europe. But their small West Indies colonies could not supply sufficient raw material. By 1640 they decided to form a partnership with English planters, offering them the knowledge and financing to establish sugar plantations and mills on Barbados. That decision would reshape the economic and political landscape of North America and intensify competition for both land and labor.

REVIEW & RELATE

- How did the Virginia colony change and evolve between 1607 and the 1670s?
- How did the growth of the English colonies on the mainland and in the West Indies shape conflicts in Virginia and demands for labor throughout North America?

✓ *LEARNINGCurve* bedfordstmartins.com/hewittlawson/LC

Pilgrims and Puritans Settle New England

Along with merchants, planters, and indentured servants, religious dissenters also traveled to North America. Critics of the Church of England formed a number of congregations in the early seventeenth century, and some sought refuge in New England. One such group, the Pilgrims (also known as Separatists), landed on the Massachusetts coast in 1620 and established a permanent settlement at Plymouth. Their goal was to establish a religious community wholly separate from the Anglican Church. The Puritans, who hoped to purify rather than separate from the Church of England, arrived a decade later with plans to develop their own colony. Over the next two decades, New England colonists prospered, but they also confronted internal dissent and conflicts with local Indians.

Pilgrims Arrive in Massachusetts

In the 1610s, to raise capital, the Virginia Company began offering legal charters to groups of private investors, who were promised their own tract of land in the Virginia colony with minimal oversight by the governor or the company council. One such charter was purchased by a group of English **Pilgrims** who wanted to form a separate church and community in a land untainted by

Catholicism, Anglicanism, or European cosmopolitanism. Thirty-five Pilgrims from Leiden in the Dutch Republic and several dozen from England signed on to the venture and set sail on the *Mayflower* from Plymouth, England, in September 1620.

Battered by storms, the ship veered off course, landing at Cape Cod in present-day Massachusetts in early December. With winter closing in, the exhausted passengers decided to disembark. Before leaving the ship, the settlers, led by William Bradford, signed a solemn pact, which they considered necessary because they were settling in a region where they had no legal authority. The Pilgrims agreed to "combine ourselves together into a civill body politick." The **Mayflower Compact** was the first written constitution adopted in North America. It followed the Separatist model of a self-governing religious congregation.

After several forays along the coast, the Pilgrims located an uninhabited village surrounded by cornfields where they established their new home, Plymouth. Uncertain of native intentions, the Pilgrims were unsettled by sightings of Indians near their hastily built fort. They did not realize that a smallpox epidemic in the area only two years earlier had killed nearly 90 percent of the local Wampanoag population, leaving them too weak to launch an assault on the Pilgrims. Indeed, fevers and other diseases proved far more deadly to the settlers than did Indians. By the spring of 1621, only half of the 102 Pilgrims remained alive.

Desperate to find food, the survivors were stunned when two English-speaking Indians—Samoset and Squanto—appeared at Plymouth that March. Both had been captured as young boys by English explorers, and they now negotiated a fragile peace between the Pilgrims and Massasoit, chief of the Wampanoag tribe. Although concerned by the power of English guns, Massasoit hoped to create an alliance that would assist him against his traditional native enemies. The Wampanoags supplied the English with seeds, fishing gear, and other goods that allowed them to take advantage of the short growing season and the abundant fish and wildlife in the region. The surviving Pilgrims soon regained their health.

In the summer of 1621, reinforcements arrived from England, and the next year the Pilgrims received a charter granting them rights to Plymouth Plantation and a degree of self-government. The region's cold climate turned out to be a boon as well, minimizing the spread of disease. These developments encouraged the Pilgrims to take a more aggressive stance toward Indians, like the Massachusetts tribe, who posed a threat to them. In 1623 Captain Miles Standish led an attack on a Massachusetts village after kidnapping and killing the chief and his younger brother. The survivors fled north and west, alerting other Indians to the Pilgrims' presence. Although Separatist leaders in

Leiden were appalled that their brethren were assaulting rather than converting Indians, Standish's strategy ensured that Massasoit, the colonists' Wampanoag ally, was now the most powerful chief in the region.

The Puritan Migration

As the Pilgrims gradually expanded their colony during the 1620s, a new group of English dissenters, the **Puritans**, made plans to develop their own settlement. As religious dissenters, Puritans faced persecution in England. However, persecution was only one reason the Puritans chose to leave England. They believed that their country's church and government had grown corrupt and was being chastened by an all-powerful God. During the early seventeenth century, the English population boomed but harvests failed, the poor suffered from famine and rising prices, the number of beggars multiplied, and crime and taxes rose.

The enclosure movement, in which landlords fenced in fields and hired a few laborers and tenants to replace a large number of peasant farmers, increased the number of landless vagrants. At the same time, the English cloth industry nearly collapsed under the weight of competition from abroad. In the Puritans' view, all of these problems were divine punishments for the nation's sins.

Thus, from the Puritans' perspective, New England was a safe haven from God's wrath. Puritan lawyer John Winthrop claimed that God offered New England as "a refuge for manye, whom he meant to save out of the general destruction." Consequently, under his leadership a group of affluent Puritans sought and received a royal charter for the Massachusetts Bay Company. To the Puritans, however, New England was more than just a place of safety. Unlike the Pilgrims, they believed that England and the Anglican Church could be redeemed. By prospering spiritually and materially in America, they could establish a model "City

Map of New England in 1614

This engraving by the Dutchman Simon van de Passe in 1616 is based on a map drawn by the English explorer John Smith two years earlier. After leaving Jamestown, Smith, who is pictured in the upper left corner, sailed along the Atlantic coast of North America, a region he named New England.　Beinecke Rare Book and Manuscript Library, Yale University

upon a Hill" that would then inspire reform among residents of the mother country.

About one-third of English Puritans chose to leave their homeland for North America. They were better supplied, more prosperous, and more numerous than either their Pilgrim or Jamestown predecessors. Arriving in an armada of seventeen ships, the settlers included ministers, merchants, craftsmen, and farmers. Many Puritans sailed with entire families in tow, ensuring the rapid growth of the colony. Having seen the risks of settling in unhealthy or unknown locales, they studied John Smith's map of the New England coast to select the best site for their community.

The first Puritan settlers arrived on the coast north of Plymouth in 1630 and named their community Boston, after the port city in England from which they had departed. Once established, they relocated the Massachusetts Bay Company's capital and records to New England, thereby converting their commercial charter into the founding document of a self-governing colony. They instituted a new kind of polity in which all adult males participated in the election of a governor (John Winthrop), deputy governor, and legislature. Although the Puritans suffered a difficult first winter, they quickly recovered and soon cultivated sufficient crops to feed themselves and a steady stream of new migrants. During the 1630s, some eighteen thousand Puritans migrated to New England, fourteen thousand of those to Massachusetts. Even without a cash crop like tobacco or sugar, the Puritan colony flourished.

Eager to take advantage of the abundant land, the close-knit community spread quickly beyond its original boundaries. The legislature, known as the General Court, was thus forced early on to develop policies for establishing townships with governing bodies that supported a local church and school. By the time the migration of Puritans slowed around 1640, the settlers had turned their colony into a thriving commercial center. They shipped codfish, lumber, wheat, rye, oats, pork, cheese, and other agricultural products to England in exchange for cloth, iron pots, and other manufactured goods and to the West Indies for rum and molasses. This trade, along with the healthy climate, relatively egalitarian distribution of property, and more equal ratio of women to men, ensured a stable and prosperous colony.

Puritans also sought friendly relations with some local natives; in their case it was with the neighboring Massachusetts tribe, who were longtime enemies of the

Thomas Smith, Self-Portrait

This self-portrait of the Massachusetts painter Thomas Smith, dating from around 1680, remains both the earliest seventeenth-century New England painting attributed to a specific person and the only surviving self-portrait from that period. Little is known about Smith, but the battle scene in the background hints that he may once have been a naval officer.   Worcester Art Museum, Worcester, Massachusetts

Pilgrims' allies, the Wampanoags. Many Puritans hoped that their Indian neighbors could be converted to Christianity. Such efforts were made easier by the death of many of the Massachusetts tribe's religious leaders in the Pilgrim attack of 1623. Puritan missionaries taught their pupils how to read the Bible, and a few students attended Harvard College, founded in 1636. In an effort to wean converts from their traditional customs and beliefs, missionary John Eliot created "praying towns." There Christian Indians could live among others who shared their faith while being protected from English settlers seeking to exploit them. Yet most "praying Indians" continued to embrace traditional rituals and beliefs alongside Christian practices.

The Puritan Worldview

Opposed to the lavish rituals and hierarchy of the Church of England and believing that few Anglicans truly felt the grace of God, Puritans set out to establish a simpler form of worship. They focused on their inner lives and on the purity of their church and community. Puritans followed Calvin, believing in an all-knowing God who had seen his flock wander away from his most basic teachings. The true Word of God was presented in the Bible, not in the Anglican Book of Common Prayer or hymns written by modern composers. The biblically sanctioned church was a congregation formed by a group of believers who made a covenant with God. Only a small minority of people, known as Saints, were granted God's grace, and Puritans believed (or at least hoped) that their churches were filled with Saints.

Saints were granted God's grace even though all humans since the fall of Adam were deserving of perpetual damnation. Whether one was a Saint and thereby saved was predetermined by and known only to God. Yet Puritans believed that those who were chosen led a godly life. Visible signs included individuals' passionate response to the preaching of God's Word, their sense of doubt and despair over their own soul, and that wonderful sense of reassurance that came with God's "saving grace." Saints were also expected to be virtuous, neighborly, benevolent, and successful.

Puritans, like most Christians at the time, believed that signs of God's hand in the world were everywhere. They appeared in natural phenomena like comets, eclipses, and deformed births as well as in "remarkable providences" that eased believers' way. Thus when a smallpox epidemic killed several thousand Massachusetts Indians in 1633–1634, a Puritan town council observed: "Without this remarkable and terrible stroke of God upon the native, we would with much more difficulty have found room, and at a far greater charge have obtained and purchased land." Clearly God was shining his light on the Puritans, rather than on the Massachusetts.

Shared religious beliefs helped forge a unified community where faith guided civil as well as spiritual decisions. Most political leaders were devout Puritans. Indeed, ministers often served as members of the General Court or presided over town meetings. Puritan leaders determined who got land, how much, and where; they also served as judge and jury for those accused of crimes or sins. Their leadership was largely successful. Even if colonists differed over who should get the most fertile strip of land, they agreed on basic principles. Still, almost from the beginning, certain Puritans challenged some of the community's fundamental beliefs, and in the process, the community itself.

Dissenters Challenge Puritan Authority

In the early 1630s, Roger Williams, a Salem minister, criticized Puritan leaders for not being sufficiently pure in their rejection of the Church of England and the English

monarchy. He preached that not all the Puritan leaders were Saints and that some were bound for damnation. Despite admonitions from the Massachusetts Bay authorities, Williams continued to rail against what he saw as deviations from the one true faith. By 1635 he was forced out of Salem and moved south with his followers to found Providence in the area that became Rhode Island. Believing that there were very few Saints in the world, Williams and his followers accepted that one must live among those who were not saved. Thus unlike Massachusetts Bay, Williams welcomed Quakers, Baptists, and Jews to the community, and his followers insisted on a strict separation of church and state. Williams also forged alliances with the Narragansetts, the most powerful Indian nation in the region, trading with them and securing land for a growing number of English settlers.

A year later, Anne Hutchinson and her followers joined Williams's Rhode Island colony. When put on trial in November 1637, Hutchinson was initially accused of sedition, or trying to overthrow the government by challenging colonial leaders, such as Governor John Winthrop, who were devout Puritans. An eloquent orator,

Anne Hutchinson
This drawing of Anne Hutchinson is based on a 1620 portrait made while she still lived in England. Here she appears as a proper matron, but sixteen years later she would be tried for heresy by Puritan leaders in Massachusetts Bay and banished from the colony.   Schlesinger Library, Radcliffe Institute, Harvard University/The Bridgeman Art Library

Hutchinson ultimately claimed that her authority to challenge the Puritan leadership came from "an immediate revelation" from God, "the voice of his own spirit to my soul." Since Puritans believed that God spoke only through the intermediary of properly appointed male ministers, her claim was condemned as heretical.

Hutchinson was seen as a threat not only because of her religious beliefs but also because she was a woman. The Reverend Hugh Peter, for example, reprimanded her at trial: "You have stept out of your place, you have rather bine a Husband than a Wife and a preacher than a Hearer; and a Magistrate than a Subject." Thus the accusations against her were rooted as much in her challenge to gender hierarchies as to Puritan authority, although her accusers no doubt viewed these as synonymous.

Wars in Old and New England

As Anne Hutchinson and Roger Williams confronted the religious hierarchy, Puritans and Pilgrims faced another serious threat from the Pequot nation. Among the most powerful tribes in New England, the Pequots had been allies of the English for several years. Yet some Puritans feared that the Pequots, who opposed the colonists' continued expansion, "would cause all the Indians in the country to join to root out all the English." Using the death of two Englishmen in 1636 to justify a military expedition against the Pequots, the colonists went on the attack. The Narragansetts, whom Roger Williams had befriended, fought with the English in the **Pequot War**. After months of bloody conflict, the English and their Indian allies launched a brutal attack on a Pequot fort in May 1637 that left some four hundred men, women, and children dead. The English saw the victory as a sign of God's grace, and the Narragansetts saw it as the defeat of a powerful rival.

Explore

To examine an illustration of an attack on the Pequots as depicted by the English captain who led the assault, see Document 2.5.

Puritans in England were soon engaged in armed conflict as well, but this time against other Englishmen. Differences over issues of religion, taxation, and royal authority had strained relations between Parliament and the crown for decades, as James I (r. 1603–1625) and his son Charles I (r. 1625–1649) sought to consolidate their own power at Parliament's expense. In 1642 the relationship between Parliament and King Charles I broke down completely, and the country descended into civil war. Oliver Cromwell, a Puritan, emerged as the leader of the Protestant parliamentary forces, and after several years of fighting, he claimed victory. Charles I was executed,

Parliament established a republican commonwealth, and bishops and elaborate rituals were banished from the Church of England. Cromwell ruled England as a military dictator until his death in 1658. By then, much of England had tired of religious conflict and Puritan rule, so Charles I's son, Charles II (r. 1660–1685), was invited to return from exile on the continent and restore the monarchy and the Church of England. In 1660, when Charles II acceded to the throne, the Puritans recognized that their only hope for building a godly republic lay in North America.

During the civil war of the 1640s, English settlements had quickly spread throughout Connecticut, Massachusetts, and Rhode Island, as well as into Maine and what became New Hampshire. The English king and Parliament, embroiled in war, paid little attention to events in North America, allowing these New England colonies to develop with little oversight. In 1664, after the restoration of the monarchy, the English wrested control of New Amsterdam from the Dutch and renamed it New York. Although it would be another decade before they fully subordinated the Dutch to their rule, by 1674 the English could claim dominance—in population, trade, and politics—over the other European powers vying for empires along the northern Atlantic coast.

The spread of English control was, however, still contested by various Indian groups. In New England, only 15,000 to 16,000 native people remained by 1670, a loss of about 80 percent over fifty years. Meanwhile the English population soared from a few hundred to more than 50,000, with settlers expanding into new territories and encroaching on native hunting grounds. In 1671 the English demanded that the Wampanoags, who had been their allies since the 1620s, surrender their guns and be ruled by English law. Instead, many Indians hid their weapons and, over the next several years, raided frontier farms and killed several settlers. English authorities responded by hanging three Wampanoag men.

By 1675 the Wampanoag chief Metacom, called King Philip by the English, came to believe that Europeans had to be forced out of New England if Indians were going to survive. As conflict escalated between the English and the Wampanoags, Metacom gained the support of the Narragansett and Nipmuck Indians. Together warriors from the three tribes attacked white settlements throughout the region. Armed with hundreds of guns as well as more traditional knives, hatchets, and arrows, Indians terrorized frontier communities. They burned fields, killed male settlers, and took women and children captive.

Initially, the English were convinced they could win an easy victory over their Indian foes, but the war dragged on and became increasingly brutal on both sides. Some 1,000 English settlers were killed and dozens were taken captive

DOCUMENT 2.5

Captain John Underhill | Attack at Mystic, Connecticut, 1638

Determined to expand westward, the English went to war with the Pequot Indians. The Pequot War culminated when the English and their Narragansett allies brutally attacked a Pequot fort at Mystic, Connecticut, in 1637. John Underhill, an English captain who helped lead the raid, claimed that four hundred Pequots were killed during the short but bloody battle. By the end of the war, most Pequots had either died, been sold into slavery, or fled the region. The following image, an engraving created by Underhill himself, gives the English perspective on the attack.

Explore

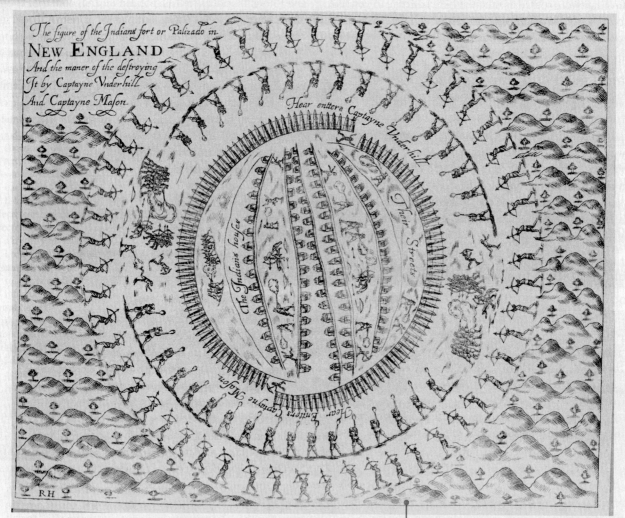

Library of Congress

Interpret the Evidence

- According to this image, how did the English defeat the Pequots, and what role did their Narragansett allies play?
- How had the Pequots attempted to defend themselves and their community?

Put It in Context

How might this image support the English view of the Pequots as a threat to English expansion that needed to be contained?

during the war. Eighteen New England towns were destroyed, almost 1,200 homes were burned, and 8,000 cattle were slaughtered. Metacom's forces attacked Plymouth and Providence and marched within twenty miles of Boston. The English meanwhile made an alliance with Mohawks, Pequots, Mohegans, and praying Indians (mostly Christian Wampanoags) in the region, who ambushed Narragansett forces. The English also attacked enemy villages, killing hundreds of Indians and selling hundreds more into slavery in the West Indies, including Metacom's wife and son. Indian losses were catastrophic on both sides of the conflict, as food shortages and disease combined with military deaths to kill as many as 4,500 men, women, and children. About a quarter of the remaining Indian population of New England died in 1675–1676.

The war, called **King Philip's War** by the English, finally ended when Wampanoag, Narragansett, and Nipmuck forces ran short of guns and powder and the Mohawks ambushed and killed Metacom. **See Document Project 2: King Philip's War, page 57**. The remaining Algonquian-speaking Indians moved north and gradually intermarried with tribes allied with the French. As the carnage of the war spilled into New York, Iroquois leaders and colonists met at Albany in 1677. There they formed an alliance, the Covenant Chain, in hopes of forestalling future conflict so that they could continue their profitable fur trade. In the following decades, furs and land would continue to define the complex relations between Indians and Europeans across the northern regions of North America.

REVIEW & RELATE

How did the Puritans' religious views shape New England's development?

Why did conflict between New England settlers and the region's Indians escalate over the course of the seventeenth century?

✓ *LEARNINGCurve* bedfordstmartins.com/hewittlawson/LC

Conclusion: European Empires in North America

When John Smith died in 1631, the English were just beginning to establish colonies in North America. Despite Smith's love of adventure, he realized early on that a successful empire in Virginia required a different approach than the Spanish had taken in Mexico and Peru. North American colonies demanded permanent settlement,

long-term investment, and hard work. Liberal land policies, self-government, and trade formed the touchstones of colonies along the north Atlantic coast.

Yet as European colonists found different ways to prosper in Virginia, Massachusetts Bay, Quebec, and New Amsterdam, they faced daunting choices. Most important, should they create alliances with local Indians for sustenance and trade, or should they seek to dominate them and take what they needed? Smith, Miles Standish, and many other early settlers supported an aggressive policy, much like that of Spain. In Virginia this policy ended persistent threats from the Powhatan Confederacy by the 1640s. But many Europeans, especially in New England, New Amsterdam, and Canada, advocated a different approach. Some, like French Jesuit priests and Puritan missionaries, focused on the spiritual and material benefits of conversion. Far more argued that building alliances was the most effective means of advancing trade and gaining land, furs, and other goods valued by Europeans.

Throughout the early and mid-seventeenth century, English, Dutch, and French colonists profited from trade relations and military alliances with Indian nations. Nonetheless, European demands for land fueled repeated conflicts with tribes like the Pequots in the 1630s and the Wampanoags and Narragansetts in the 1670s. The exhaustion of furs along the Atlantic coast only increased the vulnerability of those Indians who could no longer provide this valuable trade item. Already devastated by European-borne diseases, their very survival was at stake. Indians in New Amsterdam as well as New England resisted the loss of their land and livelihood, often with violence. It was such violence that led to the death of Anne Hutchinson. In 1642 she and her six youngest children moved to the outskirts of New Netherland after the death of her husband. They lived on an isolated farm on what is now Pelham Bay in the Bronx. A year later, Anne and all but one of her children were massacred by Indians outraged by Dutch governor William Kieft's 1643 slaughter of peaceful Indians on Manhattan Island.

Still, as European settlements reached deeper into North America in the late seventeenth century and early eighteenth century, their prosperity continued to depend on trade goods and land that were often in Indian hands. At the same time, a growing demand for labor led wealthier settlers to seek an increased supply of indentured servants from Europe and enslaved workers from Africa. Over the next half century, relations between wealthy and poor settlers, between whites and blacks, between settlers and Indians, and among the European nations that vied for empire would only grow more complicated.

LEARNINGCurve
Check what you know.
bedfordstmartins.com/hewittlawson/LC

Chapter Review

Online Study Guide ▶ bedfordstmartins.com/hewittlawson

KEY TERMS

Protestantism (p. 37)
Church of England (p. 37)
Jamestown (p. 42)
Powhatan Confederacy (p. 43)
House of Burgesses (p. 44)
indentured servants (p. 44)
Bacon's Rebellion (p. 47)
Pilgrims (p. 49)
Mayflower Compact (p. 49)
Puritans (p. 50)
Pequot War (p. 53)
King Philip's War (p. 55)

REVIEW & RELATE

1. How did the Protestant Reformation shape the course of European expansion in the Americas?

2. How did the French and Dutch colonies in North America differ from the Spanish empire to the south?

3. How did the Virginia colony change and evolve between 1607 and the 1670s?

4. How did the growth of the English colonies on the mainland and in the West Indies shape conflicts in Virginia and demands for labor throughout North America?

5. How did the Puritans' religious views shape New England's development?

6. Why did conflict between New England settlers and the region's Indians escalate over the course of the seventeenth century?

TIMELINE OF EVENTS

1517	Martin Luther denounces indulgences, sparking the Protestant Reformation
1530s	England breaks with the Roman Catholic Church
1545–1563	Council of Trent (Catholic Church)
1598	Acoma pueblo uprising in New Mexico
	Edict of Nantes (France)
1607	Jamestown founded under leadership of Captain John Smith
1608	First permanent French settlement in North America founded at Quebec
1609	Dutch traders establish a settlement on the Hudson River
1612	John Rolfe experiments with tobacco cultivation in Virginia
1619	House of Burgesses established in Virginia
	First Africans arrive in Virginia
1620	Pilgrims found Plymouth settlement in Massachusetts
1624	Dutch establish New Amsterdam on Manhattan Island
1630	Puritans found Massachusetts Bay colony
1632	Maryland founded
1635	Roger Williams moves with followers to Rhode Island
1636–1637	Pequot War
1637	Anne Hutchinson banished from Massachusetts Bay colony
1642–1649	English civil war
1660	Monarchy restored in England
1660–1664	House of Burgesses passes acts that allow enslavement of African laborers
1664	Dutch surrender New Amsterdam to the English
1675–1676	King Philip's War
1676	Bacon's Rebellion

DOCUMENT PROJECT 2

King Philip's War

King Philip's War was proportionally one of the bloodiest conflicts in American history. Although Indians and whites had lived in relative peace for nearly forty years, tensions escalated during the mid-seventeenth century due to a steady decline in Indian population, territory, and cultural integrity. Metacom, whom the colonists called King Philip, became grand sachem of the Wampanoag Confederacy in 1662 after the death of his brother. Troubled by English encroachments on native lands and hunting grounds, King Philip negotiated an alliance with two-thirds of the region's Indian population, including the Narragansett and Nipmuck tribes. They began coordinating attacks on white settlements in New England, burning fields, taking captives, and killing male colonists.

In 1675 Indian attacks on New England towns escalated. In Document 2.10, Mary Rowlandson describes her experiences when she was taken captive during an Indian raid on Lancaster, Massachusetts, in February of that year. As relations between settlers and Indians deteriorated, the Rhode Island colony sent representatives to meet with King Philip in June (Document 2.6). The colonists were hoping for a diplomatic solution, but the meeting was unsuccessful, and Indian attacks increased throughout the summer. The New England Confederation declared war in September, and fighting continued for a year, with one thousand whites and more than four thousand Indians killed in the conflict. The English, who had forged alliances with the surviving Pequots and powerful Mohawks, finally gained the upper hand in August 1676 when King Philip was ambushed in a swamp near Bristol, Rhode Island, by soldiers led by Captain Benjamin Church. Philip was shot and killed by John Alderman, an Indian ally of the colonists, which signaled the end of the war in southern New England.

Because there are fewer Indian written sources, historians have struggled to develop a balanced picture of the war. William Nahaton (Document 2.9) learned firsthand that the English would go to great lengths to infiltrate Indian communities, Christian or otherwise. Which other documents provide information about Indian perceptions of the war? What do disagreements among Englishmen reveal about English-Indian relations?

DOCUMENT 2.6

John Easton | A Relation of the Indian War, 1675

As relations between English settlers and Indians grew more tense, a meeting was arranged for June 1675 between King Philip and John Easton, attorney general of the Rhode Island colony. At this meeting, Philip related the Indians' many complaints, which included the sale of liquor to Indians, the destruction of their crops, and their mistreatment under the colonial justice system. This meeting was unsuccessful in preventing further violence, however, and by the end of the month King Philip's War began.

Another Grievance was, when their King sold Land, the English would say, it was more than they agreed to, and a Writing must be prove against all them, and some of their Kings had dun Rong [done wrong] to sell so much. He left his Peopell [people] none, and some being given to Drunknes the English made them drunk and then cheated them in Bargains, but now their Kings were forewarned not for to part with Land, for nothing in Comparison to the Value thereof. Now home [some] the English had owned for King or Queen, they would disinherit, and make another King that would give or sell them these Lands; that now they had no Hopes left to keep any Land. Another Grievance, the English Catell [cattle] and Horses still increased; that when they removed 30 Miles from where English had any thing to do, they could not keep their Corn from being spoiled, they never being used to fence, and thought when the English bought Land of them they would have kept their Catell upon their owne Land. Another Grievance, the English were so eager to sell the Indians Lickers [liquor], that most of the Indians spent all in Drunknes, and then ravened upon the sober Indians, and they did believe often did hurt the English Cattel, and their King could not prevent it.

Source: John Easton, "A Relation of the Indian War," in *A Narrative of the Causes Which Led to Philip's Indian War, of 1675 and 1676* (Albany: J. Munsell, 1858), 13–15.

DOCUMENT 2.7

Benjamin Church | Passages Relating to Philip's War, 1716

Benjamin Church was an aide to Plymouth governor Josiah Winslow. But Church was also viewed as a fair man by local Indian leaders. Thus in June 1675, before the outbreak of war, Awashonks, the sachem of the Sakonnet Indians, invited Church to meet with her. He offered his advice on how best to secure the protection of her people. Despite his advice, the Sakonnets initially allied with King Philip but later switched to the English side. Meanwhile, as captain in the Plymouth colony militia, Church adopted Indian fighting tactics, and his unit conducted successful raids against King Philip and his allies. In 1716 Church's son, Thomas, published an account of the war from his father's notes. The following passage recalls his visit with Awashonks.

The next Spring advancing, while Mr. Church was diligently settling his new Farm, stocking, leasing, and disposing of his Affairs, and had a fine prospect of doing no small things; and hoping that his good success would be inviting unto other good Men to become his Neighbours; Behold! the rumor of a War between the English and the Natives gave check to his projects. People began to be very jealous of the Indians, and indeed they had no small reason to suspect that they had form'd a design of War upon the English. Mr. Church had it daily suggested to him that the Indians were plotting a bloody design. That Philip the great Mount-hope Sachem was leader therein: and so it prov'd, he was sending his Messengers to all the Neighbouring Sachems, to ingage them in a Confederacy with him in the War.

Among the rest he sent Six Men to Awashonks Squaw-Sachem of the Sogkonate [Sakonnet] Indians, to engage her in his Interests: Awashonks so far listened unto them as to call her Subjects together, to make a great Dance, which is the custom of that Nation when they advise about Momentous Affairs. But what does Awashonks do, but sends away two of her Men that well understood the English Language . . . to invite Mr. Church to the Dance. Mr. Church upon the Invitation, immediately takes with him Charles Hazelton his Tennants Son, who well understood the Indian Language, and rid [rode] down to the Place appointed: Where they found hundreds of Indians gathered together from all Parts of her Dominion. Awashonks her self in a foaming Sweat was leading the Dance. But she was no sooner sensible of Mr. Churches arrival, but she broke off, sat down, calls her Nobles round her, orders Mr. Church to be invited into her presence. Complements being past, and each one taking Seats. She told him, King Philip had sent Six Men of his with two of her People that had been over at Mount-hope, to draw her into a confederacy with him in a War with the English. . . .

Then Mr. Church turn'd to Awashonks, and told her, if Philip were resolv'd to make War, her best way would be to knock those Six Mount-hopes on the head, and shelter her self under the Protection of the English: upon which the Mount-hopes were for the present Dumb. . . .

Then he told Awashonks he thought it might be most advisable for her to send to the Governour of Plymouth, and shelter her self, and People under his Protection. She lik'd his advice, and desired him to go on her behalf to the Plymouth Government, which he consented to: And at parting advised her what ever she did, not to desert the English Interest, to joyn with her Neighbours in a Rebellion which would certainly prove fatal to her. He mov'd none of his Goods from his House that there might not be the least umbrage from such an Action. She thank'd him for his advice, and sent two of her Men to guard him to his House; which when they came there, urged him to take care to secure his Goods, which he refused for the reasons before mentioned. But desired the Indians that if what they feared should happen, they would take care of what he left, and directed them to a Place in the woods where they should dispose them; which they faithfully observed.

Source: Benjamin Church, *The History of King Philip's War* (Boston: John Kimball Wiggin, 1865), 5–11.

DOCUMENT 2.8

Edward Randolph | Report on the War, 1676

Edward Randolph was an English customs official sent to the colonies to investigate colonial compliance with English laws. He criticized the Puritan colonies for pursuing political autonomy, like coining money and administering their own oath of allegiance, and called for greater control by Parliament. Randolph's reports to his superiors in London also described the outbreak of violence. He reported on what he saw as the causes of the war, criticizing the actions of both colonists and Indians.

Various are the reports and conjectures of the causes of the late Indian wars. Some impute it to an imprudent zeal in the magistrates of Boston to Christianize those heathens, before they were civilized, and enjoining them to the strict observation of their laws, which, to people so rude and licentious hath proved even intolerable; and that the more, for while the magistrates, for their profit, severely put the laws in execution against the Indians, the people on the other side, for lucre [money] and gain, intice and provoke the Indians to the breach thereof, especially to drunkenness, to which these people are so generally addicted, that they will strip themselves to the skin to have their fill of rum and brandy.

The Massachusetts government having made a law that every Indian being drunk should pay ten shillings or be whipped, according to the discretion of the magistrate, many of these poor people willingly offered their backs to the lash, to save their money. Upon the magistrate finding much trouble and no profit to arise to the government by whipping, did change that punishment of the whip into ten days' work, for such as would not or could not pay the fine of ten shillings; which did highly incense the Indians. . . .

Others impute the cause to arise from some injuries offered to the Sachem Philip; for he being possessed of a tract of land called Mount Hope, a very fertile, pleasant and rich soil, some English had a mind to dispossess him thereof, who, never wanting some pretence or other to attain their ends, complained of injuries done by Philip and his Indians to their stock and cattle. Whereupon the Sachem [King] Philip was often summoned to appear before the magistrates, sometimes imprisoned, and never released but upon parting with a considerable part of his lands.

But the government of the Massachusetts . . . do declare [the following acts] are the great and provoking evils which God hath given the barbarous heathen commission to rise against them: . . .

For men wearing long hair and perriwigs made of women's hair.

For women wearing borders of hair and cutting, curling and laying out their hair and disguising themselves by following strange fashions in their apparel.

For profaneness of the people in not frequenting their [church] meetings, and others going away before the blessing is pronounced.

For suffering the Quakers to dwell among them, and to set up their thresholds by God's thresholds, contrary to their old laws and resolutions, with many such reasons.

But whatever was the cause, the English have contributed very much to their misfortunes, for they first taught the Indians the use of arms and admitted them to be present at all their musters and trainings, and showed them how to handle, mend and fix their muskets, and have been constantly furnished with all sorts of arms by permission of the government, so that the Indians are become excellent fire-men.

Source: John Norris McClintock, *History of New Hampshire* (Boston: B. B. Russell, 1888), 79–80.

DOCUMENT 2.9

William Nahaton | Petition to Free an Indian Slave, 1675

The English sold a number of Indians into slavery during King Philip's War. Many English colonists petitioned the government of Massachusetts Bay to stop this practice. As the following document indicates, Indians also tried to find recourse through petitions. William Nahaton, an Indian who had embraced Christianity, sent this petition to convince colonial leaders to release a relative who was about to be sold into slavery in the West Indies.

To the honored counsel now siting at boston to the humble petition of william [n]ahaton hee humbly sheweth.

I have seing a woman taken by the mohegins and now brought to boston which woman although she did belong to [King] phillip his Company yet shee is a kinn to me and all so to john huntar as severall of the indians of punkapoag do know[.] my humble and right request there fore to the Renowned Counsel is that if it may stand with there plesure and with out futur inconvenience her Life may be spared and her Liberty granted under such conditions as the honored Counsel see most fit: shee being a woman whatever her mind hath been it is very probable she hath not dun much mischefe and if the honored counsel shall plese so grant me that favor I shall understand to leve her at punkapoag[.] . . . I shall obtaine so much favor from the honored counsel which will further oblige him who is your honored to command william [n]ahaton.

Source: Jill Lepore, *Encounters in the New World: A History in Documents* (New York: Oxford University Press, 2000), 154–55.

pon a *Friday*, a little after noon we came to this River. When all the company was come up, and were gathered together, I thought to count the number of them, but they were so many, and being somewhat in motion, it was beyond my skil. In this travel, because of my wound, I was somewhat favored in my load; I carried only my knitting work and two quarts of parched meal: Being very faint I asked my mistriss to give me one spoonfull of the meal, but she would not give me a taste. They quickly fell to cutting dry trees, to make Rafts to carry them over the river: and soon my turn came to go over: By the advantage of some brush which they had laid upon the Raft to sit upon, I did not wet my foot (which many of themselves at the other end were mid-leg deep) which cannot but be acknowledged as a favour of God to my weakened body, it being a very cold time. I was not before acquainted with such kind of doings or dangers. *When thou passeth through the waters I will be with thee, and through the rivers they shall not overflow thee*, Isai. 43.2. A certain number of us got over the River that night, but it was the night after the Sabbath before all the company was got over. On the *Saturday* they boyled [boiled] an old Horses leg which they had got, and so we drank of the broth, as soon as they thought it was ready, and when it was almost all gone, they filled it up again.

The first week of my being among them, I hardly ate any thing; the second week, I found my stomach grow very faint for want of something; and yet it was very hard to get down their filthy trash: but the third week, though I could think how formerly my stomach would turn against this or that, and I could starve or die before I could eat such things, yet they were sweet and savory to my taste. I was at this time knitting a pair of white cotton stockins for my mistriss: and had not yet wrought upon a Sabbath day; when the Sabbath came they bade me go to work; I told them it was the Sabbath-day, and desired them to let me rest, and told them I would do as much more tomorrow; to which they answered me, they would break my face. And here I cannot but take notice of the strange providence of God in preserving the heathen: They were many

DOCUMENT 2.10

Mary Rowlandson | Narrative of Captivity, 1682

In February 1675, the Wampanoags and their allies attacked Lancaster, Massachusetts, setting fire to the town and killing many residents. Mary Rowlandson and her three children were captured and forced to flee with the Indians as they tried to outrun colonial forces. Mary's six-year-old daughter Sarah died, but she and her other children survived and were sold for ransom after eleven weeks and reunited with her husband, Joseph. After the war, she published an account of her captivity that highlighted the ways in which her Puritan faith helped her survive the ordeal. The book became one of the most popular publications of its era.

hundreds, old and young, some sick, and some lame, many had *Papooses* [infants] at their backs, the greatest number at this time with us, were *Squaws*, and they travelled with all they had, bag and baggage, and yet they got over this River aforesaid; and on *Munday* they set their *Wigwams* on fire, and away they went: On that very day came the *English* Army after them to this River, and saw the smoak of their *Wigwams*, and yet this River put a stop to them. God did not give them courage or activity to go over after us; we were not ready for so great a mercy as victory and deliverance; if we had been, God would have found out a way for the *English* to have passed this River, as well as for the *Indians* with their *Squaws* and *Children*, and all their Luggage. . . .

On Munday *(as I said) they set their* Wigwams *on fire, and went away.* It was a cold morning, and before us there was a great Brook with ice on it; some waded through it, up to the knees & higher, but others went till they came to a Beaver dam, and I amongst them, where through the good providence of God, I did not wet my foot. I went along that day mourning and lamenting, leaving farther my own Country, and travelling into the vast and howling *Wilderness,* and I understood something of *Lot's* Wife's Temptation, *when she looked back.* We came that day to a great Swamp, by the side of which we took up our lodging that night. When I came to the brow of the hill, that looked toward the Swamp, I thought we had been come to a great *Indian* Town (though there were none but our own Company). The *Indians* were as thick as the trees: it seemed as if there had been a thousand Hatchets going at once: if one looked before one, there was nothing but *Indians,* and behind one, nothing but *Indians,* and so on either hand, I my self in the midst, and no Christian soul near me, *and yet how hath the Lord preserved me in safety! Oh the experience that I have had of the goodness of God, to me and mine!*

Source: Henry S. Nourse, ed., *The Narrative of the Captivity and the Restoration of Mrs. Mary Rowlandson* (Lancaster, MA, 1903), 17–20.

Interpret the Evidence

1. What types of complaints did the Wampanoags have against the English (Documents 2.6 and 2.8)? Which seem the most grievous to the Indians? What do these complaints reveal about how the colonists viewed the Wampanoags?

2. What does Edward Randolph's description of the causes of the war (Document 2.8) reveal about how this war might be viewed by Englishmen who were not colonists?

3. What does Benjamin Church's meeting with Awashonks (Document 2.7) suggest about the difficult choices faced by some Indians and some colonists as war approached?

4. In what ways did the English disagree among themselves over the causes of war? What do these differences tell us about the era and the war?

5. What does William Nahaton's petition (Document 2.9) reveal about English leaders' main goal when dealing with the Indians? Do you think the English differentiated between Christian and non-Christian Indians?

6. How does Mary Rowlandson employ religion to explain the events that happen to her during her captivity? What does the enormous popularity of her book indicate about the place of religion in New England in the 1680s?

Put It in Context

• King Philip's War was one of the bloodiest in American history. From these documents, what do you think accounts for its ferociousness?

background photos: pages 58 and 61, HIP/Art Resouce, NY

Bibliothèque Nationale, Paris, France/Giraudon/The Bridgeman Art Library

Virginia Historical Society, Richmond, Virginia, USA/The Bridgeman Art Library

• View of Boston Town Hall, 18th century.

• Tobacco label showing two Native Americans with pipes, 18th century.

3

Global Changes Reshape Colonial America

1680–1750

© Pictorial Press Ltd./Alamy

English cartoon of industrious American colonists, mid-18th century.

AMERICAN HISTORIES

In 1729, at age thirty, William Moraley Jr. signed an indenture to serve a five-year term as a "bound servant" in the "American Plantations." This was not what his parents had imagined for him. The only child of a journeyman watchmaker and his wife, Moraley received a good education and was offered a clerkship with a London lawyer. But Moraley preferred London's pleasures to legal training. At age nineteen, out of money, he was forced to return home and become an apprentice watchmaker for his father. Moraley's apprenticeship went no better than his clerkship, and in 1725, fed up with his son's lack of enterprise, Moraley's father rewrote his will, leaving him just 20 shillings. When Moraley's father died unexpectedly, his wife gave her son 20 pounds, and in 1728 Moraley headed back to London.

But London was in the midst of a prolonged economic crisis, and Moraley failed to find work. By May 1729, he was imprisoned for debt. Three months later, he sold his labor for five years in return for passage to America. Moraley sailed for Philadelphia in September and was indentured in January to a Quaker clockmaker in Burlington, New Jersey. Eventually, he tired of this situation as well, and he ran away. But when he was caught, he was not punished by having his contract extended, as happened to most fugitive servants. Instead, he was released before his indenture was up, after serving only three years.

Moraley spent the next twenty months traveling the northern colonies, but found no steady employment. Hounded by creditors, he boarded a ship in Philadelphia bound for Ireland. He returned to his mother's home, penniless and unemployed. In 1743, hoping to cash in on popular interest in adventure tales, he published an account of his travels. In the book, entitled *The Infortunate, the Voyage and Adventures of William Moraley, an Indentured Servant,* he offered a poor man's view of eighteenth-century North America. Like so much else in Moraley's life, the book was not a success.

In 1738, while Moraley was back in England trying to carve out a career as a writer, sixteen-year-old Eliza Lucas, the eldest daughter of a career British military officer, arrived in South Carolina. Her father, Colonel George Lucas, had inherited a 600-acre plantation, called Wappoo, six miles south of Charles Town (later Charleston), and moved his family there in hopes that the climate would improve his wife's health. Eliza had been born on Antigua, where her father served with the British army and owned a sugar plantation. Although the move north did not benefit his wife, it created an unusual opportunity for his daughter, who was left in charge of the estate when Colonel Lucas was called back to Antigua in May 1739.

For the next five years, Eliza Lucas managed Wappoo and two other Carolina plantations owned by her father. Rising each day at 5 a.m., she checked on the fields and the enslaved laborers who worked them, balanced the books, nursed her mother, taught her younger sister to read, and wrote to her younger brothers at school in England. In a large bound book, she kept the accounts; copies of her letters to family, friends, commercial agents, and fellow planters; and information on legal affairs.

She also embarked on plans to improve her family estates. With her father's enthusiastic support, Lucas began experimenting with new crops, particularly indigo. The indigo plant, which was first imported to Europe from India in the seventeenth century, produced a blue dye popular for coloring textiles. When her experiments proved successful, Lucas encouraged other planters to follow her lead, and with financial aid from the colonial legislature and Parliament, indigo became a profitable export from South Carolina, second only to rice. •

THE AMERICAN HISTORIES of William Moraley and Eliza Lucas were shaped by a profound shift in global trading patterns that resulted in the circulation of labor and goods among Asia, Africa, Europe, and the Americas. Between 1680 and 1750, indentured servants, enslaved Africans, planters, soldiers, merchants, and artisans traveled along these new trade networks. So, too, did sugar, rum, tobacco, indigo, cloth, and a host of other items. As England, France, and Spain expanded their empires, colonists developed new crops for export and increased the demand for manufactured goods from home. Yet the vibrant, increasingly global economy was fraught with peril. Economic crises, the uncertainties of maritime navigation, and outbreaks of war caused constant disruptions. For some, the opportunities offered by colonization outweighed the dangers; for others, fortune was less kind, and the results were disappointing, even disastrous.

Europeans Expand Their Claims

Beginning with the restoration of Charles II to the throne in 1660, English monarchs began granting North American land and commercial rights to men who were loyal to the crown. Shaped in part by rebellions at home and abroad, the policies of English monarchs aimed to expand England's imperial reach at the lowest possible cost. France and Spain also expanded their empires in North America, frequently coming into conflict with each other in the late seventeenth and early eighteenth centuries. At the same time, American Indians challenged various European efforts to displace them from their homelands. A Pueblo rebellion against Spanish authorities in New Mexico provided other Indian nations with access to guns and horses. In Florida, Indian-Spanish conflicts allowed England to gain native allies.

English Colonies Grow and Multiply

To repay the men who helped him return to power, Charles II granted them land and commercial rights in North America (see chapter 2). The king rewarded his most important allies with positions on the newly formed Councils for Trade and Plantations. Many of the appointees also gained other benefits: partnerships in the Royal African Company, vast lands along the South Atlantic coast, or charters for territory in Canada. In addition, he gave his brother James, the Duke of York, control over all the lands between the Delaware and Connecticut Rivers, once known as New Netherland, but now known as New York. He then conveyed the adjacent lands to investors who established the colonies of East and West Jersey. Finally, Charles II repaid debts to Admiral Sir William Penn by granting his son huge tracts of land in the Middle Atlantic region. Six years later, William Penn Jr. left the Church of England and joined the Society of Friends, or Quakers. This radical Protestant sect was severely persecuted in England, so the twenty-two-year-old Penn turned his holdings into a Quaker refuge named Pennsylvania.

Between 1660 and 1685, Penn and other English gentlemen were established as the proprietors of a string of **proprietary colonies** from Carolina to New York. These powerful aristocrats could govern largely as they wished as long as they conformed broadly to English traditions. Most envisioned a manorial system in which they and other gentry presided over workers producing goods for export. In practice, however, local conditions dictated what was possible, and by the 1680s a range of labor relationships had emerged. Following Bacon's Rebellion in Virginia (see chapter 2), small farmers and laborers in northern Carolina rose up and forced proprietors there to offer land at reasonable prices and a semblance of self-government. In the southern part of Carolina, however, English West Indian planters dominated. They created a mainland version of Barbados by introducing enslaved Africans as laborers, carving plantations out of coastal swamps, and trading with the West Indies.

William Penn provided a more progressive model of colonial rule. He established friendly relations with the local Lenni-Lenape Indians and drew up a Frame of Government in 1681 that recognized religious freedom for all Christians. It also allowed all property-owning men to vote and hold office. Under Penn's leadership, Pennsylvania attracted thousands of middling farm families, most of them Quakers, as well as artisans and merchants. By the time Charles II died in 1685, Pennsylvania was the most successful of his proprietary colonies.

Charles's death marked an abrupt shift in crown-colony relations. Charles's successor, James II, instituted a more authoritarian regime both at home and abroad. He consolidated the colonies in the Northeast and established tighter controls. His royal officials banned town meetings, challenged land titles granted under the original colonial charters, and imposed new taxes. Fortunately for the colonists, the Catholic James II alienated his subjects in England as well as in the colonies, inspiring a bloodless coup in 1688. His Protestant daughter Mary and her husband William of Orange (r. 1689–1702) then ascended the throne, introducing more democratic systems of governance in England and the colonies. This so-called **Glorious Revolution** inspired John Locke to write his famous treatise justifying the changes made by William and Mary. Locke challenged the divine right of monarchs and insisted that government depended on the consent of the governed.

> **Explore**
>
> For Locke's thoughts on property and the rule of law, see Document 3.1.

Eager to restore political order and create a commercially profitable empire, William and Mary established the new colony of Massachusetts (which included Plymouth, Massachusetts Bay, and Maine) and restored town meetings and an elected assembly. But the 1692 charter also granted the English crown the right to appoint a royal governor and officials to enforce customs regulations. It ensured religious freedom to members of the Church of England and allowed all male property owners (not just Puritans) to be elected to the assembly. In Maryland, too, the crown imposed a royal governor and replaced the Catholic Church with the Church of England as the established religion. And in New York, wealthy English merchants won the backing of the newly appointed royal governor, who instituted a representative assembly and supported a merchant-dominated Board of Aldermen. Thus, taken as a whole, William and Mary's policies asserted royal authority at the same time that they sought to create a partnership between England and colonial elites by allowing colonists to retain long-standing local governmental institutions (Table 3.1).

In the early eighteenth century, England's North American colonies took the form that they would retain until the revolution in 1776. In 1702 East and West Jersey united into the colony of New Jersey. Delaware separated from Pennsylvania in 1704. By 1710 North Carolina became fully independent of South Carolina, forming its own assembly and receiving its own charter. Finally, in 1732, the colony of Georgia was established as a buffer between Spanish Florida and the increasingly lucrative plantations of South Carolina. At the same time, settlers pushed back the frontier in all directions. Wealthy Englishmen like Robert Livingston bought up land on the upper Hudson River and

DOCUMENT 3.1

John Locke | On the State of Nature, 1690

John Locke was an English physician and philosopher whose ideas influenced England's Glorious Revolution, as well as the development of Enlightenment thought. In the late eighteenth century, revolutionaries such as Thomas Jefferson and Benjamin Franklin incorporated his ideas into their justifications for revolution and, especially, the Declaration of Independence. The following selection is from "Of the Ends of Political Society and Government."

Explore

Section 123. If man in the state of nature be so free, as has been said; if he be absolute lord of his own person and possessions, equal to the greatest, and subject to nobody, why will he part with his freedom? why will he give up his empire, and subject himself to the dominion and control of any other power? To which it is obvious to answer, that though in the state of nature he hath such a right, yet the enjoyment of it is very uncertain, and constantly exposed to the invasion of others; for all being kings as much as he, every man his equal, and the greater part no strict observers of equity and justice, the enjoyment of the property he has in this state is very unsafe, very unsecure. This makes him willing to quit a condition, which, however free, is full of fears and continual dangers; and it is not without reason, that he seeks out, and is willing to join in society with others, who are already united, or have a mind to unite, for the mutual preservation of their lives,

liberties, and estates, which I call by the general name, property.

Section 124. The great and chief end, therefore, of men's uniting into commonwealths, and putting themselves under government, is the preservation of their property. To which in the state of nature there are many things wanting.

First, There wants an established, settled, known law, received and allowed by common consent to be the standard of right and wrong, and the common measure to decide all controversies between them: for though the law of nature be plain and intelligible to all rational creatures; yet men being biassed by their interest, as well as ignorant for want of studying it, are not apt to allow of it as a law binding to them in the application of it to their particular cases.

Source: John Locke, *Two Treatises on Government* (London: C. and J. Rivington, 1824), 203–4.

Interpret the Evidence

- According to Locke, why would man leave the state of nature?
- By leaving the state of nature, what does man gain? What does he give up?

Put It in Context

How did Locke's theories strengthen calls for greater autonomy among British colonists in America?

---

joined Dutch *patroons* who had earlier established vast estates in the region. Meanwhile families in Massachusetts carved out farms and villages on the New Hampshire and Maine frontier, while migrants and immigrants pushed the boundaries of Pennsylvania, Virginia, and the Carolinas westward.

France Seeks Lands and Control

When James II became king of England, he modeled himself after Louis XIV of France. Like Louis, James saw

himself as ruling by divine right and with absolute power, but the French king was far more successful in establishing and sustaining his authority. During his long reign from 1661 to 1715, Louis XIV dominated European affairs and oversaw an expansion of North American possessions. Still, in 1680 New France comprised only ten thousand inhabitants, and one potential source of settlers—Protestant Huguenots—was denied the right to emigrate.

The French government thus extended the boundaries of its North American colonies more through exploration and trade than through settlement. In 1682 French

TABLE 3.1   English Colonies Established in North America, 1607–1750

Colony	Date	Original Colony Type	Religion	Status in 1750	Economic Activity
Virginia	1624	Proprietary	Church of England	Royal	Tobacco, wheat
Massachusetts	1630	Proprietary	Congregationalist	Royal	Fishing, mixed farming, shipbuilding materials, shipping
Maryland	1632	Royal	Catholic	Royal	Tobacco, wheat
Carolina	1663	Proprietary	Church of England	Royal	
North	1691				Shipbuilding materials, farming
South	1691				Rice, indigo
New Jersey	1664	Proprietary	Church of England	Royal	Wheat
New York	1664	Proprietary	Church of England	Royal	Furs, naval stores, mixed farming, shipping
Pennsylvania	1681	Proprietary	Quaker	Proprietary	Wheat
Delaware	1704	Proprietary	Lutheran/Quaker	Proprietary	Furs, farming, shipping
Georgia	1732	Trustees	Church of England	Royal	Rice
New Hampshire (separated from Massachusetts)	1741	Royal	Congregationalist	Royal	Mixed farming, lumber, shipbuilding materials

adventurers and their Indian allies journeyed down the lower Mississippi River. Led by René-Robert Cavelier, Sieur de La Salle, the party traveled to the Gulf of Mexico and claimed all the land drained by its tributaries for Louis XIV. The new territory of Louisiana (named for the king) promised great wealth, but its development stalled when La Salle failed in his attempt to establish a colony.

Still eager for a southern outlet for furs, the French did not give up. After several more attempts at colonization in the early eighteenth century, French settlers maintained a toehold along Louisiana's Gulf coast. Most important, Pierre LeMoyne d'Iberville, a Canadian military officer, and his brother established forts at Biloxi and Mobile bays, where they traded with local Choctaw Indians. They recruited settlers from Canada and France, and the small outpost survived despite conflicts among settlers, pressure from the English, a wave of epidemics, and a lack of supplies from France. Still, Louisiana counted only three hundred French settlers by 1715.

Continuing to promote commercial relations with diverse Indian nations, the French built a string of missions and forts along the upper Mississippi and Illinois Rivers. These outposts in the continent's interior allowed France to challenge both English and Spanish claims to North America. And extensive trade with a range of Indian nations ensured that French power was far greater than the small number of French settlers would suggest.

The Pueblo Revolt and Spain's Fragile Empire

As New France pushed westward and southward, Spain continued to oversee an empire that was spread dangerously thin on its northern reaches. In New Mexico, tensions between Spanish missionaries and *encomenderos* and the Pueblo nation had simmered for decades (see chapter 2). Relations worsened in the 1670s when a drought led to famine among many area Indians and brought a revival of Indian rituals that the Spaniards viewed as a threat to Christianity. In addition, Spanish forces failed to protect the Pueblos against devastating raids by Apache and Navajo warriors. Finally, Catholic prayers proved unable to stop Pueblo deaths in a 1671 epidemic. When some of the Pueblos returned to their traditional priests, Spanish officials hanged three Indian leaders for idolatry and whipped and incarcerated forty-three others. Among those punished was Popé, a militant Pueblo who upon his release began planning a broad-based revolt.

On August 10, 1680, seventeen thousand Pueblo Indians initiated a coordinated assault on numerous Spanish missions and forts. They destroyed buildings and farms, burned crops and houses, and smeared excrement on Christian altars. The Spaniards retreated to Mexico without launching any significant counterattack.

Yet the Spaniards returned in the 1690s and recon-quered parts of New Mexico, aided by growing internal

Battling the Spaniards

After the Pueblo revolt in 1680 drove out the Spaniards, the Pueblos established close contact with the Navajo people. In 1692 Spain reconquered the region, and skirmishes continued. This Navajo petroglyph (rock engraving) in One Crow Canyon near Farmington, New Mexico, records one such battle, with Spanish soldiers on horseback wielding swords.   Photograph © George Oxford Miller

conflict among the Pueblos and fierce Apache raids. The governor general of New Spain worked hard to subdue the province and in 1696 crushed the rebels and opened new lands for settlement. Meanwhile Franciscan missionaries established better relations with the Pueblos by allowing them to retain more indigenous practices and built new missions in the region.

Yet despite the Spanish reconquest, in the long run the **Pueblo revolt** limited Spanish expansion by strengthening other indigenous peoples in the region. In the aftermath of the revolt, some Pueblo refugees moved north and taught the Navajos how to grow corn, raise sheep, and ride horses. Through the Navajos, the Ute and Comanche peoples also gained access to horses. By the 1730s, the Comanches, who had become a fully equestrian society, launched mounted bison hunts and traded over vast areas. One key trading center formed at Taos in northern New Mexico, where Spanish control was weak. There Comanches sold captives as slaves and gained more horses, metal tools, and guns. Thus the Pueblos provided other Indian nations with the means to support larger populations, wider commercial networks, and more warriors. These nations would continue to contest Spanish rule.

At the same time, Spain sought to reinforce its claims to Texas (named after the Tejas Indians) in response to French settlements in the lower Mississippi valley. Thus, in the early

eighteenth century, Spanish missions and forts appeared along the route from San Juan Batista to the border of present-day Louisiana. Although small and scattered, these outposts were meant to ensure Spain's claim to Texas. But the presence of large and powerful Indian nations, including the Caddo and the Apache, forced Spanish residents to accept many native customs in order to maintain their presence in the region.

Spain also faced challenges to its authority in Florida, where Indians resisted the spread of cattle ranching in the 1670s. Authorities imposed harsh punishments on those killing cows or raiding herds and forced hundreds of Indians to construct a stone fortress, San Marcos, at St. Augustine. Meanwhile the English wooed Florida natives by exchanging European goods for deerskins. Some Indians then moved their settlements north to the Carolina border. The growing tensions along this Anglo-Spanish border would turn violent when Europe itself erupted into war.

REVIEW & RELATE

What role did the crown play in the expansion of the English North American colonies in the second half of the seventeenth century?

How did the development of the Spanish and French colonies in the late seventeenth century differ from that of the English colonies?

European Wars and American Consequences

Developments in North America in the late seventeenth and early eighteenth centuries were driven as much by events in Europe as by those in the colonies. From 1689 until 1713, Europe was in an almost constant state of war, with continental conflicts spilling over into colonial possessions in North America. The result was increased tensions between colonists of different nationalities, Indians and colonists, and colonists and their home countries.

Colonial Conflicts and Indian Alliances

France was at the center of much of the European warfare of the period. Louis XIV hoped to expand France's borders and gain supremacy in Europe. To this end, he built a powerful professional army under state authority. By 1689 more than 300,000 well-trained troops had been outfitted with standardized uniforms and weapons. Having gained victories in the Spanish Netherlands, Flanders, Strasbourg, and Lorraine, the French army seemed invincible.

In the 1690s, France and England fought their first sustained war in North America, **King William's War** (1689–1697). The war began over conflicting French and English interests on the European continent, but it soon spread to the American frontier when English and Iroquois forces attacked French and Huron settlements around Montreal and northern New York. English and Iroquois forces captured Fort Royal in Acadia (present-day Nova Scotia), while the French destroyed Schenectady, New York, and attacked settlers in Maine and New Hampshire.

Although neither side had gained significant territory when peace was declared in 1697, the war had important consequences. Many colonists serving in the English army died of battle wounds, smallpox, and inadequate rations. Those who survived resented their treatment and the unnecessary deaths of so many comrades. The Iroquois fared even worse. Their fur trade was devastated, and hundreds of Mohawks and Oneidas were forced to flee from France's Indian allies along the eastern Great Lakes. "French Indians" and Iroquois continued to attack each other after the peace settlement, but in 1701 the Iroquois agreed to end the raids and remain neutral in all future European conflicts. Wary of further European entanglements, Iroquois leaders focused on rebuilding their tattered confederacy.

A second protracted conflict, known as the **War of the Spanish Succession** (1702–1713) or Queen Anne's War, had even more devastating effects on North America. The conflict erupted in Europe when Charles II of Spain died without an heir, launching a contest for the Spanish

kingdom and its colonies. France and Spain squared off against England, the Netherlands, Austria, and Prussia. In North America, however, it was England alone that faced France and Spain, with each nation hoping to gain additional territory. Both sides recruited Indian allies.

After more than a decade of savage fighting, Queen Anne's War ended in 1713 with the Treaty of Utrecht, which sought to secure a prolonged peace by balancing the interests of the great powers in Europe and their colonial possessions. Yet England benefited the most in North America even as it consolidated power at home by incorporating Scotland into Great Britain through the 1707 Act of Union. Just six years later, France surrendered Newfoundland, Nova Scotia, and the Hudson Bay Territory to England, while Spain granted England control of St. Kitts in the West Indies, Gibraltar, and Minorca as well as the right to sell African slaves in its American colonies. Yet neither the treaty nor Britain's consolidation forestalled further conflict. Indeed, Spain, France, and Britain all strengthened fortifications along their North American borders (Map 3.1).

Indians Resist European Encroachment

The European conflicts in North America put incredible pressure on Indian peoples to choose sides. It was increasingly difficult for native peoples in colonized areas to remain autonomous, yet Indian nations were not simply pawns of European powers. Some sought European allies against their native enemies, and most improved their situation by gaining cloth, metal tools, guns, or horses from their European trading partners. However, many Indian nations suffered growing internal conflicts as war, trade, and colonial expansion increased the power of male warriors. In societies like the Cherokee and Iroquois, in which older women had long held significant economic and political authority, the rising power of young men threatened traditional gender and generational relations. In addition, struggles between the English and the French often fostered conflict among Indian peoples, reinforcing grievances that existed before European settlement.

The tensions among Indians escalated during the late seventeenth century as southern tribes like the Tuscarora, Yamasee, Creek, Cherokee, Caddo, and Choctaw gained European goods, including guns. As deer disappeared from the Carolinas and the lower Mississippi valley, the most precious commodity for trade became Indian captives sold as slaves. Indians had always taken captives in war, but some of those captives had been adopted into the victorious nation. Now, however, war was almost constant in some areas, and captives were more valuable for sale as slaves than as adopted tribesmen. Moreover, slave raiding occurred outside formal conflicts, intensifying hostilities across the southern region.

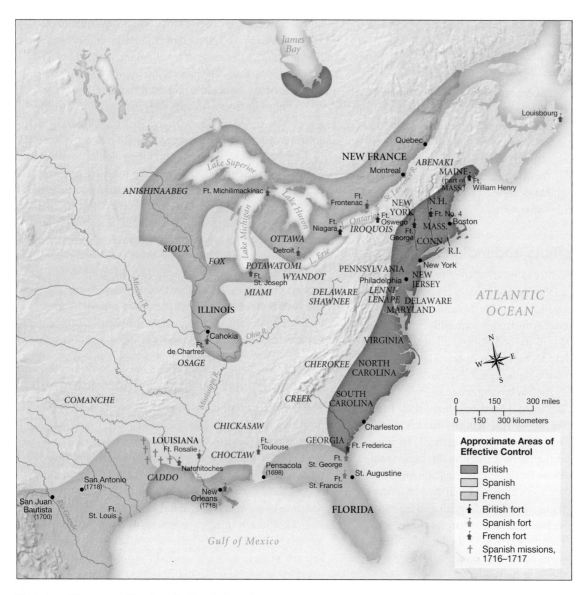

MAP 3.1   European Empires in North America, 1715–1750

France, Great Britain, and Spain competed with one another and with numerous Indian nations for control of vast areas of North America. Although European wars repeatedly spilled over into North America in the early to mid-eighteenth century, this map shows the general outlines of the empires claimed by each European nation in this period and the key forts established to maintain those claims.

Still, during the 1710s, some southern Indians tried to develop a pan-Indian alliance similar to that forged by New England Indians in the 1670s (see chapter 2). First, a group of Tuscarora warriors, hoping to gain support from other tribes, launched an attack on North Carolina settlements in September 1711. Over the next several months, hundreds of settlers were killed and hundreds more fled. However, South Carolina colonists came to the aid of their North Carolina countrymen and persuaded Indian allies among the Yamasee, Catawba, and Cherokee nations to join forces against the Tuscaroras. Although some of these allies had

traditionally been enemies, they now cooperated. Meanwhile political leaders in North Carolina convinced a competing group of Tuscaroras to ally with the colonists. By 1713 the war was largely over, and in 1715 the Tuscaroras signed a peace treaty and forfeited their lands. Many then migrated north and were accepted as the sixth nation of the Iroquois Confederacy.

> **Explore**
>
> See Document 3.2 to read a Tuscarora appeal to British colonial officials.

DOCUMENT 3.2

The Tuscarora Appeal to the Pennsylvania Government, 1710

Shortly before the outbreak of the Tuscarora War, a delegation of Tuscaroras traveled to Pennsylvania to negotiate with British colonial officials and representatives of the Iroquois Confederacy. These representatives included Iwaagenst Terrutawanaren and Teonnottein. Although summarized by two white officials, John French and Henry Worley, the following document clearly presents the views of the Tuscarora Indians. The Pennsylvania government subsequently denied their requests, but the meeting did produce one important benefit for the Tuscaroras. When the war ended in 1715, members of the tribe moved to New York and became the sixth nation of the Iroquois Confederacy.

Explore

At Conestogo, June 8th, 1710.

The Indians were told that according to their request we were come from the Govr. and Govmt. to hear what proposals they had to make anent [about] a peace, according to the purport of their Embassy from their own People.

They signified to us by a Belt of Wampum, which was sent from their old Women, that those Implored their friendship of the Christians & Indians of this Govmt., that without danger or trouble they might fetch wood & Water.

The second Belt was sent from their Children born, & those yet in the womb, Requesting that Room to sport & Play without danger of Slavery, might be allowed them.

The third Belt was sent from their young men fitt to Hunt, that privilege to leave their Towns, & seek provision for their aged, might be granted to them without fear of Death or Slavery.

The fourth was sent from the men of age, Requesting that the Wood, by a happy peace, might be as safe for them as their forts.

The fifth was sent from the whole nation, requesting peace, that thereby they might have Liberty to visit their Neighbours.

The sixth was sent from their Kings and Chiefs, Desiring a lasting peace with the Christians & Indians of this Govmt., that thereby they might be secured against those fearful apprehensions they have for these several years felt. . . .

These Belts (they say) are only sent as an Introduction, & in order to break off hostilities till next Spring, for then their Kings will come and sue for the peace they so much Desire.

We acquainted them that . . . if they intend to settle & live amiably here, . . . to Confirm the sincerity of their past Carriage towards the English, & to raise in us a good opinion of them, it would be very necessary to procure a Certificate from the Govmt. they leave, to this, of their Good behaviour, & then they might be assured of a favourable reception.

Source: Sherman Day, *Historical Collections of the State of Pennsylvania* (Philadelphia: George W. Gorton, 1853), 391–92.

Interpret the Evidence

- What gifts did the Tuscarora delegation present to the Pennsylvania officials? What did the gifts symbolize?
- What did French and Worley require of the Tuscaroras before allowing them to move to Pennsylvania?

Put It in Context

Why was it important for many American Indian nations to negotiate with both Europeans and other Indian tribes simultaneously?

The end of the war did not mean peace in the Carolinas, however. For the next two years, fierce battles erupted between a Yamasee-led coalition and the South Carolina militia. The Yamasee people remained deeply in debt to British merchants even as the trade in deerskins and slaves moved farther west. They thus secured allies among the Creeks and launched an all-out effort to force the British out. The Yamasee War marked the Indians' most serious challenge to European dominance. Indeed, it was even bloodier than King Philip's War. The British gained victory only after the Cherokees switched their allegiance to the colonists in early 1716 and thus ended the possibility of a major Creek offensive. The final Indian nations withdrew from the conflict in 1717, and a fragile peace followed.

The Yamasee War did not oust the British, but it did transform the political landscape of native North America. In its aftermath, the Creek and Catawba tribes emerged as powerful new confederations, the Cherokees became the major trading partner of the British, and the Yamasee nation was seriously weakened. And as the Cherokees allied with the British, the Creek and the Caddo tribes strengthened their alliance with the French. Meanwhile many Yamasees migrated to Spanish Florida, joining the Seminole nation.

Despite the British victory, colonists on the Carolina frontier faced raids on their settlements for decades to come. In the 1720s and 1730s, settlers in the Middle Atlantic colonies also experienced fierce resistance to their westward expansion. And attacks on New Englanders along the Canadian frontier periodically disrupted settlement there. Still, many Indian tribes were pushed out of their homelands. As they resettled in new regions, they alternately allied and fought with native peoples already living there. At the same time, the trade in Indian slaves expanded in the west as the French and the Spanish competed for economic partners and military allies.

Global Conflicts on the Southern Frontier

Indians were not the only people to have their world shaken by war. By 1720 years of warfare and upheaval had transformed the mind-set of many colonists, from New England to the Carolinas. Although most considered themselves loyal British subjects, many believed that British proprietors remained largely unconcerned with the colonies' welfare. Others resented the British army's treatment of colonial militia and Parliament's unwillingness to aid settlers against Indian attacks. Moreover, the growing numbers of settlers who arrived from other parts of Europe had little investment in British authority.

The impact of Britain's ongoing conflicts with Spain during the 1730s and 1740s on southern colonists illustrates this development. Following the Yamasee War, South

Carolina became a royal colony, and its profitable rice and indigo plantations spread southward. Then, in 1732, Parliament established Georgia (named after King George II) on lands north of Florida as a buffer between Carolina colonists and their longtime Spanish foes. The colony was initiated by social reformers like James Oglethorpe who hoped to provide small farms for Britain's poor. Initially slavery was outlawed, and land grants usually consisted of 50 to 100 acres.

Despite the noble intentions of Georgia's founders, Spanish authorities were furious at this expansion of British territorial claims. Thus in August 1739, a Spanish naval ship captured an English ship captain who was trading illegally in the Spanish West Indies and severed his ear. In response, Great Britain attacked St. Augustine and Cartagena (in present-day Colombia), but its troops were repulsed. In 1742 Spain sent troops into Georgia, but Oglethorpe's militia pushed back the attack. By then, the American war had become part of a more general European conflict. Once again France and Spain joined forces while Great Britain supported Germany in Europe. When the war ended in 1748, Britain had ensured the future of Georgia and reaffirmed its military superiority. Once again, however, victory had come at the cost of the lives of many colonial settlers and soldiers, a fact that was not lost on the colonists, some of whom began to wonder if their interests and those of the British government were truly the same.

Southern Indians were also caught up in ongoing disputes among Europeans. While both French and Spanish forces attacked the British along the Atlantic coast, they sought to outflank each other in the lower Mississippi River valley and Texas. With the French relying on Caddo, Choctaw, and other Indian allies for trade goods and defense, the Spaniards needed to expand their alliances beyond the Tejas. Initially, however, Apache raids on Spanish missions led Spanish settlers to sell captured Apache women and children into slavery in Mexico. In 1749, however, Father Santa Ana convinced a Spanish general to send two Apache women and a man back to their village with a peace proposal. Shortly afterward, in an elaborate ceremony at the mission, the two sides literally buried their differences in a large pit and negotiated peace.

The British meanwhile became increasingly dependent on European immigrants to defend colonial frontiers against the French, Spaniards, and Indians. Certainly many Anglo-Americans moved westward as coastal areas became overcrowded, but frontier regions also attracted immigrants from Scotland and Germany who sought refuge and economic opportunity in the colonies. Many headed to the Virginia and Carolina frontier and to Georgia in the 1730s and 1740s. Meanwhile South

Carolina officials recruited Swiss, German, and French Huguenot as well as Scots-Irish immigrants in the 1740s to settle along the Pee Dee River and other inland waterways. Small communities of Jews settled in Charleston as well. Gradually many of these immigrants moved south into Georgia, seeking more and cheaper land. Thus when Spanish, French, or Indian forces attacked the British colonial frontier, they were as likely to face Scots-Irish and German immigrants as Englishmen.

REVIEW & RELATE

How did the European wars of the late seventeenth and early eighteenth centuries impact relations between colonists and England?

How and why were Indians pulled into the wars between European powers fought in North America?

✓ *LEARNINGCurve* bedfordstmartins.com/hewittlawson/LC

The Benefits and Costs of Empire

The combined forces of global trade and international warfare altered the political and economic calculations of imperial powers. This was especially true for British North America, where colonists settled as families and created towns that provided key markets for Britain's commercial expansion. Over the course of the eighteenth century, British colonists became increasingly avid consumers of products from around the world. Meanwhile the king and Parliament, determined to reap the benefits of their costly empire, sought greater control over these far-flung commercial networks.

Colonial Traders Join Global Networks

In the late seventeenth and early eighteenth centuries, trade became truly global. Not only did goods from China, India, the Middle East, Africa, and North America gain currency in England and the rest of Europe, but the tastes of European consumers also helped shape goods produced in other parts of the world. For instance, wealthy Englishmen had long desired fine porcelain from China, and by the early eighteenth century the Chinese were making teapots and bowls specifically

for that market. The trade in cloth, tea, and sugar was similarly influenced by European tastes. The exploitation of African laborers contributed significantly to this global commerce. They were a crucial item of trade in their own right, and their labor in the Americas ensured steady supplies of sugar, rice, tobacco, indigo, and other goods for the world market.

By the early eighteenth century, both the volume and the diversity of goods multiplied. Silk, calico, porcelain, olive oil, wine, and other goods were carried from the East to Europe and the American colonies, while cod, mackerel, shingles, pine boards, barrel staves, rum, sugar, rice, and indigo filled ships returning west. A healthy trade also grew up within North America as New England fishermen, New York and Charleston merchants, and Caribbean planters met one another's needs. Salted cod and mackerel flowed to the Caribbean, and rum, molasses, and slaves flowed back to the mainland. This commerce required ships, barrels, docks, warehouses, and wharves, all of which ensured a lively trade in lumber, tar, pitch, and rosin. The volume of trade originating in British North America was impressive. Between April and December 1720, for example, some 425 ships sailed in and out of Boston harbor alone (Map 3.2).

The flow of information was critical to the flow of goods and credit. By the early eighteenth century, coffeehouses flourished in port cities around the Atlantic, providing access to the latest news. Merchants, ship captains, and traders met in

London Coffeehouse, 1725

This London coffeehouse, situated in the courtyard of the Royal Exchange (bank), was one among many such establishments in port cities on both sides of the Atlantic. In this setting, patrons conducted business related to overseas trade. They read the *Spectator* and *London Times* among other newspapers and swapped stories about politics, business, and other events of the day.
© The Trustees of the British Museum/Art Resource, NY

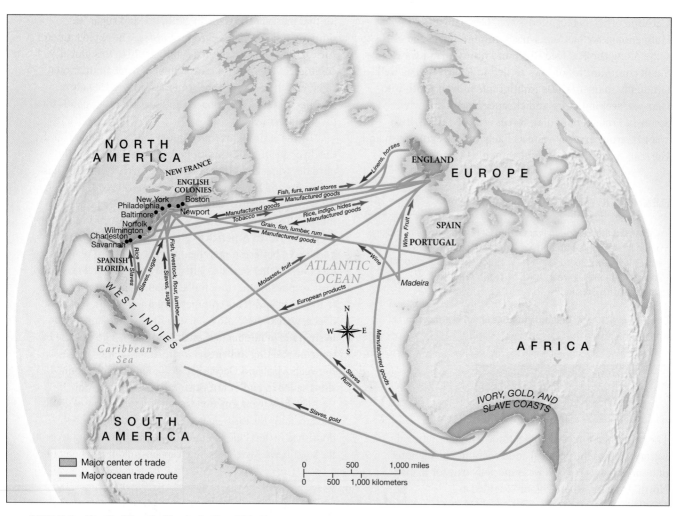

MAP 3.2   North Atlantic Trade in the 18th Century

North Atlantic trade provided various parts of the British empire with raw materials, manufactured goods, and labor. Many ships traveled between only two regions because they were equipped to carry particular kinds of goods—slaves, grains, or manufactured goods. Ultimately, however, people and goods were exchanged among four key points: the West Indies, mainland North America, West Africa, and Great Britain.

person to discuss new ventures and to keep apprised of recent developments. British and American periodicals reported on parliamentary legislation, commodity prices in India and Great Britain, the state of trading houses in China, the outbreak of disease in foreign ports, and stock ventures in London. Thus colonists from Boston to Charleston could follow the South Seas Bubble in 1720, when shares in the British South Seas Company rose to astronomical heights and then collapsed. William Moraley's father was among the thousands of British investors who lost a great deal of money in this venture. But colonists could also track the rising price of wheat.

Imperial Policies Focus on Profits

In the midst of this growing international trade, European sovereigns worked to ensure that colonial possessions benefited their own treasuries. In the late seventeenth century, both Louis XIV and his English rivals embraced a system known as **mercantilism**, which centered on the maintenance of a favorable balance of trade, with more gold and silver flowing into the home country than flowed out. In France, finance minister Jean-Baptiste Colbert honed the system. Beginning in the 1660s, he taxed foreign imports while removing all barriers to trade within French territories. Colonies like New France provided valuable raw materials— furs, fish, lumber—that could be used to produce manufactured items for sale to foreign nations and to colonists.

While France's mercantile system was limited by the size of its empire, England benefited more fully from such policies. The English crown had access to a far wider array of natural resources and a larger market for its manufactured goods. As early as 1660, Parliament passed a

Navigation Act that required merchants to conduct trade with the colonies only in English-owned ships. In addition, certain items imported from foreign ports—salt, wine, and oil, for instance—had to be carried in English ships or in ships with predominantly English crews. Finally, a list of "enumerated articles"—from tobacco and cotton to sugar and indigo—had to be shipped from the colonies to England before being re-exported to foreign ports. Thus the crown benefited directly or indirectly from nearly all commerce conducted by its colonies. But colonies, too, often benefited, as when Parliament helped subsidize the development of indigo in South Carolina. **See Document Project 3: The Production of Indigo, page 90**.

In 1663 Parliament expanded its imperial reach by requiring that goods sent from Europe to English colonies also pass through its ports. And a decade later, ship captains had to pay a duty or post bond before carrying enumerated articles between colonial ports. Despite the Great Plague of 1665 and the London fire of 1666, England's overseas colonies fueled an economic upsurge. Indeed, when London was rebuilt after the fire, its wide boulevards, massive mercantile houses, crowded wharves, and bustling coffee shops marked it as the hub of an expanding commercial empire. Beginning in 1673, England sent customs officials to the colonies to enforce the various parliamentary acts. And by 1680, London, Bristol, and Liverpool all thrived as barrels of sugar, cases of indigo, and stacks of deerskin were unloaded and bolts of dyed cloth and cartons of felt hats were put on board for the return voyage. At the same time, the transformation of New Amsterdam into New York allowed England to incorporate the diverse commercial ventures that thrived in the Dutch colony into its imperial network.

Parliament then sought to quash nascent manufacturing in the colonies by prohibiting the sale of products such as American-made textiles (1699), hats (1732), and iron goods (1750). In addition, Parliament worked to restrict trade among the North American colonies. Settlers in the British West Indies had begun selling surplus fish, flour, and meat arriving from the mainland to their French neighbors. Meanwhile mainland colonists bought growing quantities of molasses, which they made into rum, from those same French islands at a much lower price than British West Indians could offer. Fearing French planters would dominate the sugar and molasses trade, Parliament passed the 1733 Molasses Act, which allowed mainland merchants to export fish and agricultural goods directly to the French West Indies but required them to pay a high import tariff on French molasses. The law might have crippled the American distilling industry, but mainland colonists instead began smuggling cheap French molasses into their ports and bribing customs officials to look the other way.

Despite the increasing regulation, American colonists could own British ships and transport goods produced in the colonies. Indeed, by the mid-eighteenth century, North American merchants oversaw 75 percent of the trade in manufactures sent from Bristol and London to the colonies and 95 percent of the trade with the West Indies. Ironically, then, a system established to benefit Great Britain ended up creating a mercantile elite in British North America. Most of those merchants traded in goods, but some traded in human cargo.

The Atlantic Slave Trade

Parliament chartered the Royal African Company in 1672, and England slowly expanded its role in the slave trade as the Dutch commercial empire waned. In 1713, when the British gained the right to sell slaves to Spanish colonies, that nation became a major player in the horrific trade in human cargo. Between 1700 and 1808, some 3 million captive Africans were carried on British and Anglo-American ships, about 40 percent of the total of those sold in the Americas in this period (Figure 3.1). Half a million Africans died on the voyage across the Atlantic. Huge numbers also died in Africa, while being marched to the coast or held in forts waiting to be forced aboard ships. Yet despite this astounding death rate, the slave trade yielded enormous profits and had far-reaching consequences: The Africans that British traders bought and sold transformed labor systems in the colonies, fueled international trade, and enriched merchants, planters, and their families and partners.

European traders worked closely with African merchants to gain their human cargo. Where once they had traded textiles and alcohol for gold and ivory, Europeans now traded muskets, metalware, and linen for men, women, and children. Originally many of those sold into slavery were war captives. But by the time British and Anglo-American merchants became central to this notorious trade, their contacts in Africa were procuring labor in any way they could. The cargo included war captives, servants, and people snatched in raids specifically to secure slaves. Over time, African traders moved farther inland to fill the demand, devastating large areas of West Africa, particularly the Congo-Angola region, which supplied some 40 percent of all Atlantic slaves.

The trip across the Atlantic, known as the **Middle Passage**, was a brutal and often deadly experience for Africans. Exhausted and undernourished by the time they boarded the large oceangoing vessels, the captives were placed in dark and crowded holds. Most had been poked and prodded by slave traders, and some had been branded to ensure that a trader received the exact individuals he

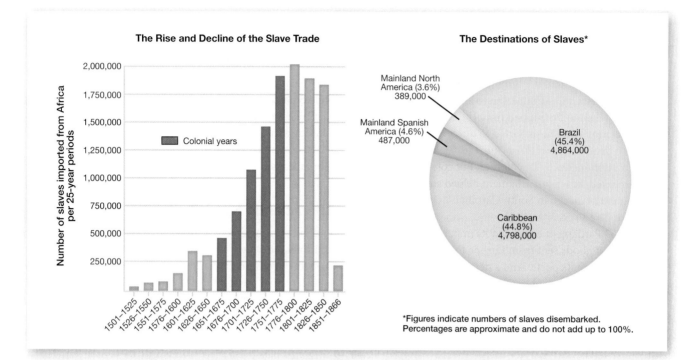

The Rise and Decline of the Slave Trade

The Destinations of Slaves*

Mainland North America (3.6%) 389,000

Mainland Spanish America (4.6%) 487,000

Brazil (45.4%) 4,864,000

Caribbean (44.8%) 4,798,000

*Figures indicate numbers of slaves disembarked. Percentages are approximate and do not add up to 100%.

FIGURE 3.1   The Slave Trade in Numbers, 1501–1866

Extraordinary numbers of Africans were shipped as slaves to other parts of the world from the sixteenth to the nineteenth century. These shipments increased dramatically during North America's colonial era (1601–1775). Although the slave trade transformed mainland North America, the vast majority of enslaved Africans were sent to Brazil and the West Indies.

Source: Trans-Atlantic Slave Trade Database, http://www.slavevoyages.org/tast/assessment/estimates.faces.

had purchased. Once in the hold, they might wait for weeks before the ship finally set sail. By that time, the foul-smelling and crowded hold became a nightmare of disease and despair. There was never sufficient food or fresh water for the captives, and women especially were subject to sexual abuse and rape by crew members. Many captives could not communicate with each other since they spoke different languages, and none of them knew exactly where they were going or what would happen when they arrived.

Explore

See Document 3.3 for a look inside a slave ship.

Those who survived the voyage were likely to find themselves in the slave markets of Barbados or Jamaica, where they were put on display for potential buyers. Once purchased, the slaves went through a period of **seasoning** as they regained their strength, became accustomed to their new environment, and learned commands in a new language. In this period of acculturation, enslaved laborers

also confronted strange foods, new diseases, and unfamiliar tasks. Most were also given new names. Some did not survive seasoning, falling prey to malnutrition and disease or committing suicide. Others adapted to the new circumstances and adopted enough European or British ways to carry on even as they sought means to resist the shocking and oppressive conditions.

More than half of the slaves imported to the Lower South entered the mainland at Charleston, South Carolina. Beginning around 1700, enslaved Africans were shipped directly to Charleston rather than transshipped from the West Indies. Successful planters like Eliza Lucas likely had first choice of the new arrivals, sending agents to the wharves to buy Africans.

Seaport Cities and Consumer Cultures

The same trade in human cargo that brought misery to millions of Africans provided traders, investors, and plantation owners with huge profits that helped turn America's seaport cities into centers of culture and consumption. When Eliza Lucas arrived in Charleston in 1738, she

DOCUMENT 3.3

Plan of a Slave Ship, 1789

To increase the profitability of the slave trade, cargo ships by the mid-eighteenth century had been replaced by ships built specifically to transport African slaves. Designed to hold as many people as possible in the lower decks, these ships were scenes of horror, disease, and death for Africans during the Middle Passage. This image of the slave ship *Brookes* vividly portrays the business of transporting human cargo. It was widely used by British abolitionists in their campaign against slavery and the slave trade.

Explore

Would this visual representation of enslaved Africans have been more or less effective than written descriptions of the Middle Passage? Why or why not?

Why did the artist include the insurrection? What purpose does it serve?

How might this image make viewers identify and sympathize with captured Africans?

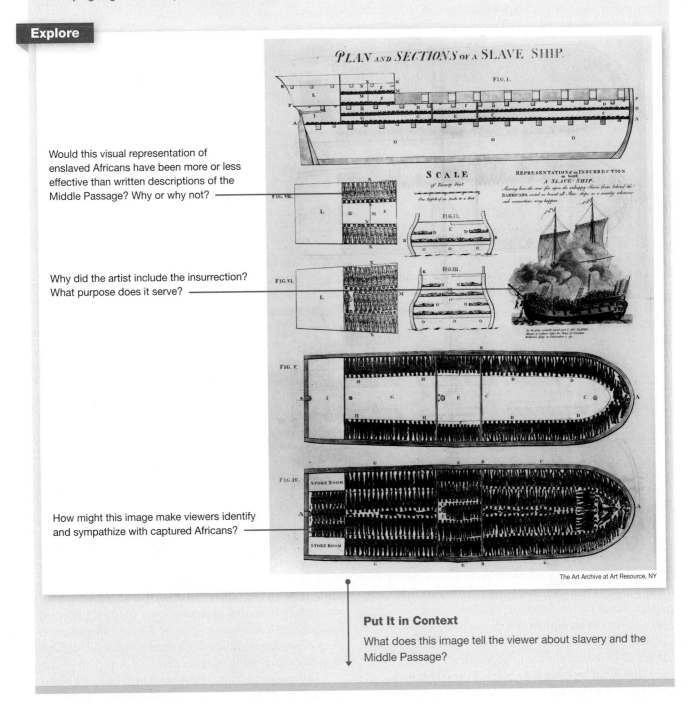

The Art Archive at Art Resource, NY

Put It in Context

What does this image tell the viewer about slavery and the Middle Passage?

Charleston, 1739

This 1739 engraving offers a view of Charleston harbor from the Battery, where heavy rocks fortified the banks of the Cooper River and artillery later was placed in the American Civil War. Some of the ships in this scene carried slaves and consumer goods that made Charleston one of the great commercial centers in the South.   The Granger Collection, New York

noted that "the Metropolis is a neat pretty place. The inhabitants [are] polite and live in a very gentile [genteel] manner." Throughout British North America, seaports, with their elegant homes, fine shops, and lively social seasons, captured the most dynamic aspects of colonial life. Although cities like New York, Boston, Philadelphia, Baltimore, and Charleston contained less than 10 percent of the colonial population, they served as focal points of economic, political, social, and cultural activity.

Many affluent urban families shed the religious strictures or financial constraints that shaped the lives of their colonial forebearers and created a consumer revolution in North America. Changing patterns of consumption challenged traditional definitions of status. Less tied to birth and family pedigree, status in the colonies became more closely linked to financial success and a genteel lifestyle. Successful men of humble origins and even those of Dutch, Scottish, French, and Jewish heritage might join the British-dominated colonial gentry.

Of those who made the leap in the early eighteenth century, Benjamin Franklin was the most notable. He might have taken the path of the "infortunate" William Moraley Jr., but Franklin was apprenticed to his brother, a printer, an occupation that matched his interest in books, reading, and politics. At age sixteen, Franklin published (anonymously) his first essays in his brother's paper, the *New England Courant.* Two years later, a family dispute led Franklin to try his luck in New York and then Philadelphia. His fortunes were fragile, but hard work, a quick wit, good luck, and political connections led to success. In 1729 Franklin

purchased the *Pennsylvania Gazette* and became the colony's official printer.

While Franklin worried about the concentration of wealth in too few hands, most colonial elites happily displayed their profits. Thus in the early eighteenth century, leading merchants in Boston, Salem, New York, and Philadelphia emulated British styles and built fine two- and three-story brick homes that had separate rooms for sleeping, eating, and entertaining guests. Mercantile elites also redesigned the urban landscape in the early eighteenth century. They donated money for brick churches and stately town halls. They constructed new roads, wharves, and warehouses to facilitate trade, and they invested in bowling greens and public gardens that beckoned affluent families on a Sunday afternoon.

Many Anglo-American elites used their knowledge of London fashions to reassert their British identity. Tea drinking was especially important in this regard, and families who could afford the finest furnishings and the time for extended social rituals made teatime a daily event. Yet the tea served at the home of Boston merchant Anthony Stoddard was imported from East Asia; the cups, saucers, and teapot were from China; and a handsome bowl held sugar from the West Indies. Stoddard decorated his home with heavily lacquered "japanned" boxes, French-patterned wallpaper, Indian calico bedding, and Italian silk curtains— all of which demonstrated that he was a successful merchant as well as a fashionable British citizen.

The spread of international commerce created a lively cultural life and great affluence in colonial cities. But it also created deep divisions between rich and poor. Wealthy merchants and professionals congregated in urban areas along with a middling group of artisans and shopkeepers and a growing class of unskilled laborers, widows, orphans, the elderly, the disabled, and the unemployed. The frequent wars of the late seventeenth and early eighteenth centuries contributed to these divisions by boosting the profits of merchants, shipbuilders, and artisans. They also improved the wages of seamen temporarily. But in their aftermath, rising prices, falling wages, and a lack of jobs led to the concentration of wealth in fewer hands.

REVIEW & RELATE

What place did North American colonists occupy in the eighteenth-century global trade network?

How did the British government seek to maintain control over the colonial economy and ensure that its colonies served Britain's economic and political interests?

LEARNINGCurve bedfordstmartins.com/hewittlawson/LC

Labor in North America

What brought the poor and the wealthy together was the demand for labor. Labor was sorely needed in the colonies, but this did not mean that it was easy to find steady, high-paying employment. Many would-be laborers had few skills and faced fierce competition from other workers for limited, seasonal manual labor. Moreover, a majority of immigrants, both European and African, arrived in America with significant limits on their freedom.

Finding Work in the Colonies

The demand for labor did not necessarily help free laborers find work. Many employers preferred indentured servants, apprentices, or others who came cheap and were bound by contract. Others employed criminals or purchased slaves, who would provide years of service for a set price. Free laborers who sought a decent wage and steady employment needed to match their desire to work with skills that were in demand.

When William Moraley ended his indenture and sought work, he discovered that far fewer colonists than Englishmen owned timepieces, leaving him without a useful trade. So he tramped the countryside, selling his labor when he could, but found no consistent employment. Returning to New York and Philadelphia, William begged lodging from friends, considered marrying an elderly widow, was imprisoned for

minor offenses, and accepted Quaker charity. But he fell ever deeper in debt. Thousands of other men and women, most without Moraley's education or skills, also found themselves at the mercy of unrelenting economic forces.

Many poor men and women found jobs building homes, loading ships, or spinning yarn. But they were usually employed for only a few months a year. The rest of the time they scrounged for bread and beer, begged in the streets, or stole what they needed. Most lived in ramshackle buildings filled with cramped and unsanitary rooms. Freezing in winter and sweltering in summer, these quarters served as breeding grounds for smallpox, scarlet fever, and other diseases. Children born into such squalid circumstances were lucky to survive their first year. Those who survived could watch ships sail into port and earn a few pence running errands for captains or sailors, but they would never have access to the bounteous goods intended for those who lived in stately mansions.

By the early eighteenth century, older systems of labor, like indentured servitude, began to decline in many areas. In some parts of the North and across the South, white servants were gradually replaced by African slaves. At the same time, farm families who could not usefully employ all their children began to bind out sons and daughters to more prosperous neighbors. Apprentices, too, competed for positions. Unlike most servants, apprentices contracted to learn a trade. They trained under the supervision of a craftsman, who gained cheap labor by promising to teach a young man (and most apprentices were men) his trade. But master craftsmen limited the number of apprentices they accepted to maintain the value of their skills.

Another category of laborers emerged in the 1720s. A population explosion in Europe and the rising price of wheat and other items convinced many people to seek passage to America. Shipping agents offered them loans that were repaid when the immigrants found a colonial employer who would redeem (that is, repay) the original loan. In turn, these **redemptioners** labored for the employer for a set number of years, though they could live independently with their own family. The redemption system was popular in the Middle Atlantic colonies, especially among German immigrants who hoped to establish farms on the Pennsylvania frontier. While many succeeded, their circumstances could be extremely difficult.

Explore

Read two immigrants' descriptions of their varying experiences in Documents 3.4 and 3.5.

Large numbers of convicts, too, entered the British colonies in the eighteenth century. Jailers in charge of Britain's overcrowded prisons offered inmates the option of transportation to the colonies. Hundreds were thus bound out each year to American employers. The combination of indentured servants, redemptioners, apprentices, and convicts ensured that as late as 1750 the majority of white workers—men and women—were bound to some sort of contract.

Sometimes white urban workers also competed with slaves, especially in the northern colonies. Africans and African Americans formed only a small percentage of the northern population, just 5 percent from Pennsylvania to New Hampshire in 1750. In the colony of New York, however, blacks formed about 14 percent of inhabitants.

While some enslaved blacks worked on agricultural estates in the Hudson River valley and New Jersey, even more labored as household servants, dockworkers, seamen, and blacksmiths in New York City alongside British colonists and European immigrants (Figure 3.2). Considered a status symbol by many wealthy merchants, urban slaves were usually discouraged from marrying or bearing large numbers of children. However, some masters allowed their slaves to marry and set up independent households or to hire themselves out to other employers, as long as their wages were paid to their owners.

DOCUMENTS 3.4 AND 3.5

Pennsylvania as Promised Land? Two Views

German colonists began moving to Pennsylvania in the late seventeenth century, encouraged by reports of rich land and religious freedom. Francis Pastorius was an agent for the Frankfort Land Company who successfully promoted German settlement in the colony. In Document 3.4, he describes life in Pennsylvania as lush and prosperous. Document 3.5, published more than fifty years later, offers a very different depiction of life for German settlers. Gottlieb Mittelberger left his home in Germany to move to Pennsylvania in 1750. When he returned to Germany in 1754, he wrote a book (published two years later) warning others against settling in the American colonies. Although Mittelberger was not an indentured servant, his book focused on the hardships brought about by this practice.

Explore

3.4 Francis Pastorius | Description of Pennsylvania, 1700

Inasmuch as this region lies in the same degree of latitude as Montpelier and Naples, but has a much richer soil, and that better watered by its many springs and rivulets, it is but reasonable to suppose that such a country must be well calculated to produce all kinds of fruit. The air is pure and serene, the summer is longer and warmer than it is in Germany, and we are cultivating many kinds of fruits and vegetables, and our labors meet with rich reward.

Of cattle we have a great abundance, but for want of proper accommodation they roam at large for the present. . . .

Although this far-distant land was a dense wilderness—and it is only quite recently that it has come under the cultivation of the Christians—there is much cause of wonder and admiration how rapidly it has already, under the blessing of God, advanced, and is still advancing, day by day. The first part of the time we were obliged to obtain our provisions from the Jerseys for money, and at a high price; but now we not only have enough for ourselves, but a considerable surplus to dispose of among our neighboring colonies. Of the most needful mechanics we have enough now; but day-laborers are very scarce, and of them we stand in great need. . . .

Our surplus of grain and cattle we trade to Barbados for rum, syrup, sugar, and salt. The furs, however, we export to England for other manufactured goods.

Source: Francis Daniel Pastorius, *A Particular Geographical Description of the Lately Discovered Province of Pennsylvania*, trans. Lewis H. Weiss (1700), reprinted in *Old South Leaflets*, No. 95 (Boston, 1898), 8–9.

Coping with Economic Distress

White workers who were bound by contracts might have felt common cause with slaves, but most recognized that eventually they would be free. Despite the challenges faced by white workers who migrated to British North America in the early eighteenth century, many still improved their lives. Most servants, apprentices, redemptioners, and convicts hoped one day to purchase land, open a shop, or earn a decent wage. Yet gaining freedom did not promise economic success.

Several challenges confronted those looking to succeed. First, white women and men who gained their freedom from indentures or other contracts had to compete for jobs with a steady supply of redemptioners, convicts, and apprentices as well as other free laborers. Second, by the early eighteenth century, many areas along the Atlantic coast faced a land shortage that threatened the fortunes even of long-settled families. Finally, a population boom in Britain's North American colonies produced growing numbers of young people seeking land and employment. Thus many free laborers migrated from town to town and from country to

Explore

3.5 Gottlieb Mittelberger | Journey to Pennsylvania, 1756

Our Europeans, who are purchased [indentured servants and redemptioners], must always work hard, for new fields are constantly laid out; and so they learn that stumps of oak-trees are in America certainly as hard as in Germany. In this hot land they fully experience in their own persons what God has imposed on man for his sin and disobedience; for in Genesis we read the words: In the sweat of thy brow shalt thou eat bread. Who therefore wishes to earn his bread in a Christian and honest way, and cannot earn it in his fatherland otherwise than by the work of his hands, let him do so in his own country, and not in America; for he will not fare better in America. However hard he may be compelled to work in his fatherland, he will surely find it quite as hard, if not harder, in the new country. Besides, there is not only the long and arduous journey lasting half a year, during which he has to suffer, more than with the hardest work; he has also spent about 200 florins which no one will refund to him. If he has so much money, it will slip out of his hands; if he has it not, he must work his debt off as a slave and poor serf. Therefore let every one stay in his own country and support himself and his family honestly. Besides I say that those who suffer themselves to be persuaded and enticed away by the man-thieves, are very foolish if they believe that roasted pigeons will fly into their mouths in America or Pennsylvania without their working for them.

Source: Gottlieb Mittelberger, *Gottlieb Mittelberger's Journey to Pennsylvania in the Year 1750 and Return to Germany in the Year 1754*, trans. Carl Theo. Eben (Philadelphia: John Jos. McVey, 1898), 30–31.

Interpret the Evidence

- What might Pastorius's readers have found most appealing about the land he describes? How did his description differ from the experience of the average agricultural worker in Germany?
- What myths about America did Mittelberger try to dispel?
- How would you account for the differences between Pastorius's and Mittelberger's accounts of Pennsylvania?

Put It in Context

What do these accounts tell us about the experiences of colonial settlers in the early and mid-eighteenth century?

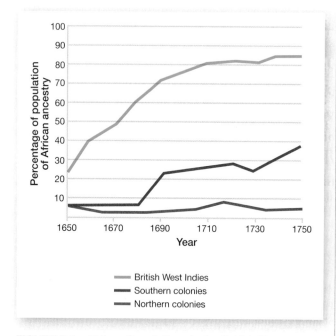

FIGURE 3.2 African Populations in the British West Indies, Northern Colonies, and Southern Colonies, 1650–1750

In 1650 the African population in the British West Indies already far exceeded that in mainland North America. Over the next century, the number of Africans and African Americans increased significantly on the mainland. But the growth was far greater in the southern than in the northern colonies, reaching 40 percent in the Chesapeake and Lower South colonies by the mid-eighteenth century.
Source: Data from Robert William Fogel and Stanley L. Engerman, *Time on the Cross: The Economics of American Negro Slavery.*

city seeking work. They hoped to find farmers who needed extra hands for planting and harvesting or ship captains and contractors who would hire them to load or unload cargo or assist in the construction of homes and churches. The Royal Army and Navy also periodically sought colonial recruits, though mostly in times of war. Women meanwhile hoped for employment spinning yarn or working as cooks, laundresses, or nursemaids.

Seasonal and temporary demands for labor created a corps of transient workers. Many New England towns developed systems to "warn out" those who were not official residents. Modeled after the British system, warning-out was meant to ensure that strangers did not become public dependents. Still, being warned did not mean immediate removal. Sometimes transients were simply warned that they were not eligible for poor relief. At other times, constables returned them to an earlier place of residence. In many ways, warning-out served as an early registration system, allowing authorities to encourage the flow of labor, keep residents under surveillance, and protect the town's coffers. But it rarely aided those in need of work.

Residents who were eligible for public assistance might be given food and clothing or boarded with a local family.

Many towns began appointing Overseers of the Poor to deal with the growing problem of poverty. By 1750 every seaport city had constructed an almshouse that sheltered residents without other means of support. In 1723 the Bridewell prison was added to Boston Almshouse, built in 1696. Then in 1739 a workhouse was opened on the same site to employ the "able-bodied" poor in hopes that profits from it would help fund the almshouse and prison. Overseers in each city believed that a workhouse would "simultaneously correct the idle poor and instill in them a habit of industry by obliging them to work to earn their keep." Still, these efforts at relief fell far short of the need, especially in hard economic times.

Rural Americans Face Changing Conditions

While seaport cities and larger towns fostered a growing cohort of individuals who lived outside traditional households, families remained the central unit of economic organization in rural areas, where the vast majority of Americans lived. Yet even farms were affected by the transatlantic circulation of goods and people.

In areas along the Atlantic coast, rural families were drawn into commercial networks in a variety of ways. Towns and cities needed large supplies of vegetables, meat, butter, barley, wheat, and yarn. Farm families sold produce or homemade goods to residents and bought sugar, tea, and other imported items that diversified their diet. Few rural families purchased ornamental or luxury items, but cloth or cheese bought in town saved hours of labor at home. Just as important, coastal communities like Salem, Massachusetts, and Wilmington, Delaware, that were once largely rural became thriving commercial centers in the late seventeenth century.

In New England, the land available for farming shrank as the population soared. In the original Puritan colonies, the population rose from 100,000 in 1700 to 400,000 in 1750, and many parents were unable to provide their children with sufficient land for profitable farms. The result was increased migration to the frontier, where families were more dependent on their own labor and a small circle of neighbors. And even this option was not accessible to all. Before 1700, servants who survived their indenture had a good chance of securing land, but by the mid-eighteenth century only two of every ten were likely to become landowners.

In the Middle Atlantic region, the population surged from 50,000 in 1700 to 250,000 in 1750. The increase was due in part to the rapid rise in wheat prices, which leaped by more than 50 percent in Europe. Hoping to take advantage of this boon, Anglo-Americans, Germans, Scots-Irish, and other non-English groups flooded into western Pennsylvania, New

York's Mohawk River valley, and the Shenandoah valley of Virginia in the early eighteenth century. By the 1740s, German families had created self-contained communities in these areas. They worshiped in German churches, read German newspapers, and preserved German traditions. Meanwhile Scots-Irish immigrants, most of them Presbyterians, established churches and communities in New Jersey, central Pennsylvania, and western Maryland and Virginia (Map 3.3).

In the South, immigrants could acquire land more easily, but their chances for economic autonomy were increasingly influenced by the spread of slavery. As hundreds and then thousands of Africans were imported into the Carolinas in the 1720s and 1730s, economic and political power became more entrenched in the hands of planters and merchants. Increasingly, they controlled the markets, wrote the laws, and set the terms by which white as well as black families lived. Farms along inland waterways and on the frontier were crucial in providing food and other items for urban residents and for planters with large labor forces. But farm families depended on commercial and planter elites to market their goods and help defend their communities against hostile Indians or Spaniards.

Slavery Takes Hold in the South

The rise of slavery reshaped the South in numerous ways. The shift from white indentured servants to black slaves began in Virginia after 1676 (see chapter 2) and soon spread across the Chesapeake. The Carolinas, meanwhile, developed as a slave society from the start. Slavery in turn allowed for the expanded cultivation of cash crops like tobacco, rice, and indigo, which promised high profits for planters as well as merchants. But these developments also made southern elites more dependent on the global market and limited opportunities for poorer whites and all blacks. They also ensured that Indians and many whites were pushed farther west as planters sought more land for their ventures.

In the 1660s, the Virginia Assembly passed a series of laws that made slavery a status inherited through the mother, denied that the status could be changed by converting to Christianity, and granted masters the right to kill slaves who resisted their authority (see chapter 2). In 1680 the Assembly made it illegal for "any negro or other slave to carry or arme himself with any club, staffe, gunn, sword, or

any other weapon of defence or offence." Nor could slaves leave their master's premises without a certificate of permission. Those who disobeyed were whipped or branded. Increasingly harsh laws in Virginia and Maryland, modeled on those in Barbados, coincided with a rise in the number of slaves imported to the colony. The statutes also ensured the decline of the free black population in the Chesapeake. In 1668 one-third of all Africans and African Americans in Virginia and Maryland were still free, but the numbers dwindled year by year. Once the Royal African Company started supplying the Chesapeake with slaves directly from Africa in the 1680s, the pace of change quickened. By 1750, 150,000 blacks resided in the Chesapeake, and only about 5 percent remained free.

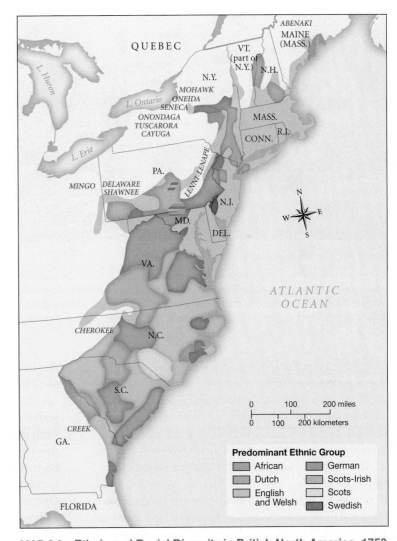

MAP 3.3 Ethnic and Racial Diversity in British North America, 1750

By 1750 British North America was a far more diverse region than it had been fifty years earlier. In 1700 the English dominated most regions, while the Dutch controlled towns and estates in the Hudson River valley. By 1750, however, growing numbers of African Americans, German and Scots-Irish immigrants, and smaller communities of other ethnic groups predominated in various regions.

Black Slaves Working on a Tobacco Plantation

This eighteenth-century engraving shows slaves laboring on a tobacco plantation. The bare-chested slaves have brought tobacco leaves from the fields and are packing them in barrels while well-dressed whites oversee their work. The head of the Indian displayed in the banner at the top is a reminder of the people who introduced tobacco to the English colonists. Peter Newark American Pictures/The Bridgeman Art Library

Direct importation from Africa had other negative consequences on slave life. Far more men than women were imported, skewing the sex ratio in a population that was just beginning to form families and communities. Women like men performed heavy field work, and few bore more than one or two children. When these conditions sparked resistance by the enslaved, fearful whites imposed even stricter regulations. In 1705 the Virginia Assembly passed an omnibus "Negro Act" that incorporated earlier provisions and made absolutely clear the special legal status of the enslaved. For instance, while mistreated white servants could sue in court, black slaves could not. And a slave who ran away and was captured could be tortured and dismembered in hopes of "terrifying others from the like practices."

While slavery in the Carolinas was influenced by developments in the Chesapeake, it was shaped even more

directly by practices in the British West Indies. Many wealthy families from Barbados, Antigua, and other sugar islands—including that of Colonel Lucas—established plantations in the Carolinas. At first, they brought slaves from the West Indies to oversee cattle and pigs and assist in the slaughter of livestock and curing of meat for shipment back to the West Indies. Some of the slaves grew rice, using techniques learned in West Africa, to supplement their diet. Owners soon realized that rice might prove very profitable. Although not widely eaten in Europe, rice could provide cheap and nutritious food for sailors, orphans, convicts, and peasants. Relying initially on Africans' knowledge, planters began cultivating rice for export.

The need for African rice-growing skills and the fear of attacks by Spaniards and Indians led Carolina owners to grant slaves rights unheard of in the Chesapeake or the West

Indies. Initially slaves were allowed to carry guns and serve in the militia. For those who nonetheless ran for freedom, Spanish and Indian territories offered refuge. Still, most stayed, depending for support on bonds they had developed in the West Indies. The frequent absence of owners also offered Carolina slaves greater autonomy.

As rice cultivation expanded, however, slavery in the Carolinas turned more brutal. The Assembly enacted harsher and harsher slave codes to ensure control of the growing labor force. No longer could slaves carry guns, join militias, meet in groups, or travel without a pass. As planters began to import more slaves directly from Africa, sex ratios, already male dominated, became even more heavily skewed. In addition, older community networks from the West Indies were disrupted. Military patrols by whites were initiated to enforce laws and labor practices. Some plantations along the Carolina coast turned into virtual labor camps, where thousands of slaves worked under harsh conditions with no hope of improvement.

By 1720 blacks outnumbered whites in the Carolinas, and fears of slave rebellions inspired South Carolina officials to impose even harsher laws and more brutal enforcement measures. When indigo joined rice as a cash crop in the 1740s, the demand for slave labor increased further. Although far fewer slaves—about 40,000 by 1750—resided in South Carolina than in the Chesapeake, they constituted more than 60 percent of the colony's total population.

Africans Resist Their Enslavement

Enslaved laborers in British North America resisted their subjugation in a variety of ways. They sought to retain customs, foods, belief systems, and languages from their homelands. They tried to incorporate work patterns passed down from one generation to the next into new environments. They challenged masters and overseers by refusing to work, breaking tools, feigning illness, and other means of disputing whites' authority. Some ran for freedom, others fought back in the face of punishment, and still others used arson, poison, or other means to defy owners. A few planned revolts.

The consequences for resisting were severe, from whipping, mutilation, and branding to summary execution. Because whites were so fearful of rebellion, they often punished people falsely accused of planning revolts. Yet some slaves did plot ways to rise up against their owners or whites in general. Southern whites, living amid large numbers of blacks, were most deeply concerned about resistance and rebellion. But even in the North, whites did not doubt slaves' desire for freedom. As more slaves were imported directly from Africa, both the fear and the reality of rebellion increased.

In New York City in 1712, several dozen enslaved Africans and Indians set fire to a building. When whites rushed to the scene, the insurgents attacked them with clubs, pistols, axes, and staves, killing 8 and injuring many more. The rebels were soon defeated by the militia, however. Authorities executed 18 insurgents, burning several at the stake as a warning to others, while 6 of those imprisoned committed suicide. In 1741 a series of suspicious fires in the city led to accusations against a white couple who owned an alehouse where blacks gathered to drink. To protect herself from prosecution, an Irish indentured servant testified that she had overheard discussions of an elaborate plot involving black and white conspirators. Frightened of any hint that poor whites and blacks might make common cause, authorities immediately arrested suspects and eventually executed 34 people, including 4 whites. They also banished 72 blacks from the city. Among those executed was Cuffee, a slave who claimed that "a great many people have too much, and others too little."

The most serious slave revolt, however, erupted in South Carolina, just a few miles from Wappoo, the Lucas plantation. A group of recently imported Africans led the **Stono rebellion** in 1739. On Sunday, September 9, a group of enslaved men stole weapons from a country store and killed the owners. They then marched south, along the Stono River, beating drums and recruiting others to join them. Torching plantations and killing whites along the route, they had gathered more than fifty insurgents when armed whites overtook them. In the ensuing battle, dozens of rebels died. The militia, along with Indians hired to assist them, killed another twenty over the next two days and then captured a group of forty, who were executed without trial.

This revolt reverberated widely in a colony where blacks outnumbered whites nearly two to one, direct importation from Africa was at an all-time high, and Spanish authorities in Florida promised freedom to runaway slaves. In 1738 the Spanish governor formed a black militia company, and he allowed thirty-eight fugitive families to settle north of St. Augustine and build Fort Mose for their protection. When warfare erupted between Spain and Britain over commercial rivalries in 1739, Carolina slaves may have seen their chance to gain freedom en masse. But as with other rebellions, this one failed, and the price of failure was death.

REVIEW & RELATE

- What were the sources of economic inequality in North America in the early eighteenth century?

- Under what kinds of contracts and conditions did poor people, both white and black, work?

Conclusion: Changing Fortunes in British North America

Global commerce, international wars, and immigration reshaped the economy and geography of North America between 1680 and 1750. Many colonists thrived, initiating a consumer revolution that transformed daily life and ensured the growth of seaport cities. Others found greater opportunities by pushing inland and establishing farms and communities along new frontiers. But many failed to benefit from either land or trade. White workers caught in a downward economic spiral, enslaved Africans, and Indians on the wrong side of a war—all became victims of international trade and imperial conflicts.

The development of manufacturing in England shaped the lives of working people on both sides of the Atlantic Ocean. William Moraley Jr., for example, lived out his life in Newcastle-upon-Tyne, making and repairing watches at a time when cheap watches were being turned out in large numbers. While master craftsmen and shop owners could make a good living, those with less skill and fewer funds commanded far lower wages. When Moraley died in January 1762, his only claim to fame was his "adventures" in the American colonies. Yet the nascent industrial revolution had far more positive effects for

some colonists. The mechanization of cloth production in England demanded vast amounts of raw material from the English countryside and the colonies. It ensured, for example, the profitability of indigo. This crop benefited many South Carolina planters, including Eliza Lucas and—after her marriage in 1744—her husband, Charles Pinckney, a successful planter himself. Still, profits from indigo could be gained only through the labor of hundreds of slaves.

Eliza Pinckney's sons became important leaders in the colony, and despite their English education and the benefits they gained through British trade, both developed a strong belief in the rights of the colonies to control their own destinies. Like many American colonists, they were spurred by the consumer revolution, geographical expansion, growing religious and ethnic diversity, and conflicts with Indian and European enemies to develop a mind-set that differed significantly from their counterparts back home. As the fortunes of colonists rose or fell with the changing dynamics of global trade and as they grappled with the claims of Indians and the growth of slavery, some reimagined their relationships not only to production and consumption, agriculture and commerce, but also to the religious and political beliefs that had sustained them for generations.

LEARNINGCurve
Check what you know.
bedfordstmartins.com/hewittlawson/LC

Chapter Review

Online Study Guide ▶ bedfordstmartins.com/hewittlawson

KEY TERMS

proprietary colonies (p. 67)
Glorious Revolution (p. 67)
Pueblo revolt (p. 70)
King William's War (p. 71)
War of the Spanish Succession (p. 71)
mercantilism (p. 76)
Middle Passage (p. 77)
seasoning (p. 78)
redemptioners (p. 81)
Stono rebellion (p. 87)

REVIEW & RELATE

1. What role did the crown play in the expansion of the English North American colonies in the second half of the seventeenth century?

2. How did the development of the Spanish and French colonies in the late seventeenth century differ from that of the English colonies?

3. How did the European wars of the late seventeenth and early eighteenth centuries impact relations between colonists and England?

4. How and why were Indians pulled into the wars between European powers fought in North America?

5. What place did North American colonists occupy in the eighteenth-century global trade network?

6. How did the British government seek to maintain control over the colonial economy and ensure that its colonies served Britain's economic and political interests?

7. What were the sources of economic inequality in North America in the early eighteenth century?

8. Under what kinds of contracts and conditions did poor people, both white and black, work?

TIMELINE OF EVENTS

1660	Monarchy restored in England
	Parliament passes first of a series of Navigation Acts to regulate colonial commerce
1660–1685	Charles II rewards his most important allies with proprietorships in North America
1672	Royal African Company chartered
1680	Pueblo revolt against Spanish rule in New Mexico
1688	Glorious Revolution
1689–1697	King William's War
1692	New colony of Massachusetts established
1700–1750	New England colonial population increases from 100,000 to 400,000
	Middle Atlantic colonial population increases from 50,000 to 250,000
1700–1808	British and Anglo-American ships transport 3 million African slaves to the Americas
1702	East and West Jersey unite into colony of New Jersey
1702–1713	War of the Spanish Succession
1704	Delaware separates from Pennsylvania
1705	Virginia passes "Negro Act" consolidating and tightening earlier slave laws
1710	North Carolina becomes fully independent of South Carolina
1711–1715	Tuscaroras lead pan-Indian war against settlers in the Carolinas
1715–1717	Yamasee War
1729	Benjamin Franklin becomes Pennsylvania's official printer
1732	Colony of Georgia established
1739	Eliza Lucas takes charge of her father's South Carolina estates
	Stono rebellion
1743	William Moraley publishes an account of his time in America
1749	Spanish settlers in Texas make peace with the Apaches

The Production of Indigo

Indigo dye was a very popular commodity in seventeenth-century Europe, but it was notoriously difficult to produce and indigo plants grew only in tropical climates. Most European nations, therefore, relied on their colonies to produce indigo, with the British government even paying subsidies to indigo planters. While British colonies in the West Indies took advantage of this financial incentive, those in North America were slow to develop the product. Attempts in the early eighteenth century produced poor yields, and most planters switched to the ease and profitability of rice as an export crop.

Those who attempted to grow indigo faced many obstacles. First, indigo plants were fragile, and their cultivation required a significant capital investment, including money to purchase and clear land, create irrigation systems, and build processing vats and drying sheds. Second, the work was extremely labor intensive. It was rendered even more unpleasant, even dangerous, by the sickening fumes that emanated from fermenting indigo and attracted hordes of flies and other insects (see Document 3.7). As a result, planters would invest in indigo only if they could be assured the use of slave labor. In fact, some slaves from Africa or the West Indies brought with them prior knowledge about how to grow and process indigo.

In the early 1740s, Eliza Lucas Pinckney produced the first successful crop in South Carolina (see Document 3.6). She donated seeds to other planters in the area, and South Carolina indigo became extremely popular in Great Britain. By 1755 the colony's annual indigo exports exceeded 200,000 pounds, making it the second most exported crop behind rice. In addition, the cycle of indigo planting, harvesting, and production could be integrated with the cycles of rice cultivation, ensuring the optimum use of enslaved labor year-round (see Document 3.9). Georgia planters also grew and exported indigo, although far less than those in South Carolina (see Document 3.10).

The following documents explore the history of indigo production in the American colonies. They highlight the challenges that planters and laborers encountered and the benefits of indigo for local economies (see Documents 3.7 and 3.8). Although no slave left us a direct description of cultivating the crop, consider what these documents tell us about the role of slave labor in producing indigo.

DOCUMENT 3.6

Eliza Lucas Pinckney | Letter to Charles Cotesworth Pinckney, 1785

In the early 1740s, Eliza Lucas was looking for a cash crop to grow on her family's South Carolina plantation. Her father, then the lieutenant governor of Antigua, sent her various seeds to try, including indigo. Her first few attempts were unsuccessful, but she continued her efforts and hired an expert in indigo production from Montserrat. After marrying Charles Pinckney, Eliza expanded her cultivation of indigo to his plantations as well. In the following letter, Eliza Lucas Pinckney recalls for her son some of the difficulties she encountered in her first few attempts to produce a successful indigo crop. Among her problems was the sabotage of her crop by her hired expert, Mr. Cromwell.

September 10, 1785

My Dear Child,

You wish me to inform you what I recollect of the introducing and culture of indigo in this country. You have heard me say I was very early fond of the vegetable world, my father was pleased with it and encouraged it, he told me the turn I had for those amusements might produce something of real and public utility, if I could bring to perfection the plants of other countries which he would procure me. Accordingly when he went to the West Indies he sent me a variety of seeds, among them the indigo. I was ignorant both of the proper season for sowing it, and the soil best adapted to it. To the best of my recollection I first try'd it in March 1741, or 1742; it was destroyed (I think by a frost). The next time in April, and it was cut down by a worm; I persevered to a third planting and succeeded, and when I informed my father it bore seed and the seed ripened, he sent a man from the Island of Monserat by the name of Cromweel [Cromwell] who had been accustomed to making indigo there, and gave him high wages; he made some brick vats on my fathers plantation on Wappo Creek and then made the first indigo; it was very indifferent, and he made a great mistery of it, said he repented coming as he should ruin his own country by it, for my father had engaged him to let me see the whole process. I observed him as carefully as I could and informed Mr. Deveaux an old gentleman a neighbour of ours of the little knowledge I had gain'd and gave him notice when the indigo was to be beat; he saw and afterwards improved upon it, not withstanding the churlishness of Cromwell, who wished to deceive him, and threw in so large a quantity of lime water as to spoil the colour. In the year 1744 I married, and my father made Mr. Pinckney a present of all the indigo then upon the ground as the fruit of my industry. The whole was saved for seed, and your father gave part of it away in small quantities to a great number of people that year, the rest he planted the next year at Ashipo for seed, which he sold, as did some of the gentlemen to whom he had given it the year before; by this means there soon became plenty in the country. Your father gained all the information he could from the French prisoners brought in here, and used every other means of information, which he published in the Gazette for the information of the people at large.

The next year Mr. Cattle sent me a present of a couple of large plants of the wild indigo which he had just discovered. Experiments were afterwards made upon his sort, which proved to be good indigo, but it did not produce so large a quantity as the cultivated sort.

I am your truly affectionate mother,

Eliza Pinckney

Source: "A Letter from Eliza Lucas Pinckney, 1785," in *The Colonial South Carolina Scene: Contemporary Views, 1697–1774*, ed. H. Roy Merrens (Columbia: University of South Carolina Press, 1977), 145–46.

George Milligen-Johnston | A Description of South Carolina, 1770

Colonial officials encouraged planters to invest in indigo production by providing subsidies and assurances that it would be a lucrative venture. Harvesting and processing a successful crop, however, required skill and tremendous physical labor. In the following passage, George Milligen-Johnston, a Scottish-born physician who immigrated to South Carolina as a young man, explains the processes required to ferment and dry indigo. His description indicates some of the challenges that indigo planters faced and the work required of their slaves, though he does not state who is performing the tasks he describes.

In Carolina we generally begin to plant about the beginning of April, in the following manner: The ground being well prepared, furrows are made with a drill-plough, or hoe, two inches deep, and eighteen inches distant from each other, to receive the seed, which is sown regularly, and not very thick, after which it is covered lightly with earth. A bushel of seeds will sow four English acres. If the weather proves warm and serene, the plant will appear above ground in ten or fourteen days. After the plant appears, the ground, though not grassy, should be hoed to loosen the earth about it, which otherwise would much hinder its growth. In good seasons it grows very fast, and must all the while be kept perfectly clean of weeds. Whenever the plant is in full bloom it must be cut down, without paying any regard to its height, as its leaves are then thick and full of juice, and this commonly happens in about four months after planting. . . . When everything is ready, the weed must be cut and laid regularly in the steeper [vat] with the stalk upward, which will hasten the fermentation; then long rails must be laid the length of the vat, at eighteen inches distance from one another, and wedged down to the weed, to prevent its buoying up when the water is pumped into the steeper. For this purpose the softest water answers best, and the quantity of it necessary must be just sufficient to cover all the weed. In this situation it is left to ferment, which will begin sooner or later in proportion to the heat of the weather and the ripeness of the plant, but for the most part takes twelve or fifteen hours. After the water is loaded with the salts and substance of the weed, it must be let out of the steeper into the battery, there to be beat; in order to perform which operation, many different machines have been invented; but for this purpose any instrument that will agitate the water with great violence may be used. When the water has been violently agitated for fifteen or twenty minutes in the battery, by taking a little of the liquor up in a plate it will appear full of small grain or curdled; then you are to let in a quantity of lime-water kept in a vat for the purpose, to augment and precipitate the fæculæ [starch], still continuing to stir and beat vehemently the indigo water, till it becomes of a strong purple colour, and the grain hardly perceptible. Then it must be left to settle, which it will do in eight or ten hours. After which the water must be gently drawn out of the battery through plug-holes contrived for that purpose, so that the fæculæ may remain at the bottom of the vat. It must then be taken up, and carefully strained through a horsehair sieve, to render the indigo perfectly clean, and put into bags . . . and suspended for six hours, to drain the water out of it. After which the mouths of these bags being well fastened, it must be put into a press to be entirely freed from any remains of water, which would otherwise greatly hurt the quality of the indigo. The press commonly used for this purpose is a box of five feet in length, two and a half wide, and two deep, with holes at one end to let out the water. In this box the bags must be laid, one upon another, until it is full, upon which a plank must be laid, fitted to go within the box, and upon all a sufficient number of weights to squeeze out the water entirely by a constant and gradual pressure so that the indigo may become a fine stiff paste; which is then taken out and cut into small pieces, each about two inches square, and laid out to dry. A house made of logs must be prepared on purpose for drying it, and so constructed that it may receive all the advantages of an open and free air, without being exposed to the sun, which is very pernicious to the dye. For here indigo placed in the sun in a few hours will be burnt up to a perfect cinder. While the indigo remains in the drying house, it must be carefully turned three or four times in a day, to prevent its rotting. Flies should likewise be carefully kept from it, which at this season of the year are hatched in millions, and infest an indigo plantation like the plague. After all, great care must also be taken, that the indigo be sufficiently dry before it is packed, lest after it is headed up in barrels it should sweat, which will certainly spoil and rot it.

Source: B. R. Carroll, *Historical Collections of South Carolina* (New York: Harper and Brothers, 1836), 1:387–89.

DOCUMENT 3.8

Pamphlet on Cultivating Indigo, 1746

Promoters of indigo highlighted the profits to be gained by producing the crop, and some detailed the steps in its cultivation and the problems posed for planters. But almost none of them described the intensive labor demanded of the slaves who produced the crop or the putrid smell of the fermented plant and the swarms of flies it attracted. However, in this pamphlet, dedicated to "A Friend to Carolina," the author briefly describes the backbreaking labor required for planting and the dangers of imbibing indigo dust in the drying process.

They [the slaves] weed and cleanse the Ground where they intend to plant the Indigo-seed, five times over. They sometimes carry their Neatness to such a Pitch, that they sweep the Piece of Ground, as they do a Room. After that, they make the Holes or Pits, wherein the Seeds are to be put; for this Purpose, the Slaves . . . range themselves in the same Line . . . and going backwards, they make little Pits of the Breadth of their Hough, of the Depth of three or four Inches, at about a Foot Distance every Way, and as much as possible in a strait Line. When they are come to the End of the Ground, each furnishes himself with a little Bag of Seeds, and returning that Way they came, they put eleven or thirteen Seeds into each of the Holes. . . .

This Work is the most toilsom of any in the Manufacture of Indigo; for those who plant it, must be always stooping, without riseing up, till the planting of the whole Length of the Piece is ended; so that, when that is large, (which almost always happens) they are obliged to remain two Hours, and often more, in this Posture. . . .

[*The indigo is then soaked, fermented, and dried.*]

. . . M. Tavernier observes, in his Book, Page 242, that the Indigo Dust is so subtile [subtle], and so penetrating, that those who sift it are obliged to have their Faces covered, and drink Whey very often: And to confirm this, and make good the Penetration of the Indigo-Powder, he says, having put several Times an Egg, in the Morning, near the Sifters of Indigo, and at Night breaking it, the Inside should be all stained thro' with a blue Colour.

Source: "Observations Concerning Indigo and Cochineal" (London, 1746), 7–8, 21–22.

DOCUMENT 3.9

Laboring for Indigo, 1773

Henry Mouzon Jr. was born in 1741 on his family's South Carolina plantation. Sent to France for his education, Mouzon returned to the colonies and became an important civil engineer and surveyor. In 1771 he was commissioned to survey the boundaries of North and South Carolina. As was the custom at the time, Mouzon's map contained visual depictions of local society. This image from his map shows slaves working on a South Carolina indigo plantation.

Courtesy David M. Rubenstein Rare Book & Manuscript Library, Duke University, Durham, North Carolina

DOCUMENT 3.10

James Habersham | Letter to Benjamin Martyn, June 13, 1751

In 1738 James Habersham accompanied the Reverend George Whitefield to Georgia, agreeing to help establish an orphanage at Bethesda. He soon became a leading merchant and by the 1750s was active in Georgia's colonial government. He was also instrumental in establishing slavery in the colony. The following selection is from a letter Habersham wrote to Benjamin Martyn, secretary to the Trustees of Georgia, in which he discusses his hopes for the production of indigo by Georgia planters.

Before the Conclusion of the late War, when Rice [was] a very low Price, the Planters in the neighbouring Province were very Sanguine in raising of Indicoe [indigo], and several made very good, which answered their Expectations in England, but most rather endeavouring to make a large Quantity, than a good Quality brought it into Disrepute, some being sold so low in England as Eight Pence per Pound, and a great deal from one to two Shillings per Pound, which struck almost a universal Damp on it; and [after] riseing in Price after the Conclusion of the Peace, most People dropt planting Indicoe, and employed their Strength in raising Rice, which is indeed a most usefull Commodity to the Planter, as their greatest Staple, as well as Fodder are produced by one Expence; and its said Indicoe very much impoverishes Land, and its certain affords nothing for the Subsistance of any living Creature about a Plantation; however I now hear several are renewing their former Industry in producing this Article, having had extraordinary Accounts of the Sale of the last in England—I don't hear of but only one of our Planters . . . who have attempted to make any this Year, and He purposes employing his few Hands (except planting Provisions for his Family) in this Produce and Silk, for which he has got a fine Quantity of young Mulberry Trees. It seems highly necessary that People should turn their Thoughts on different Cultures, and what their Genius's leads them to, and I could wish more would go upon Indicoe (as it will prevent our depending so much on the French for it) but there is no forcing them to do, what they don't see to be their Interest, however I hope the Production of this Article will in Time appear so, as well as that of Silk which now seems to engage the Attention of our Planters.

Source: *The Colonial Records of the State of Georgia, 1750–1752* (Atlanta, 1916), 26:235–36.

Interpret the Evidence

1. What seem to be the biggest challenges that indigo planters faced, and how did they overcome those challenges?

2. What advantages did indigo production have for planters and for the American colonies?

3. How would you compare the descriptions of growing indigo by Eliza Lucas Pinckney (Document 3.6), George Milligen-Johnston (Document 3.7), and the London pamphleteer (Document 3.8)? What different insights do you gain about the importance of slave labor in these three documents, and why does only the London pamphleteer mention slave labor directly?

4. On what grounds does James Habersham (Document 3.10) promote the introduction of indigo into Georgia?

5. What does the image of slaves working on an indigo plantation (Document 3.9) convey about indigo's production and about the experience of slaves? How would you compare it with the written descriptions in Documents 3.7 and 3.8?

Put It in Context

- How did the initiative of North American planters in developing new crops for export shape the development of the southern colonies and the economic relations between the colonies and Great Britain?

- How did planters respond to their vital need for more labor, and how did enslaved laborers respond to the harsh demands of cultivating cash crops like rice and indigo?

Gianni Dagli Orti/The Art Archive at Art Resource, NY

Private Collection/Peter Newark American Pictures/The Bridgeman Art Library

Niagara Falls, 18th century.

The New Dutch Reformed Church, New York City, 1731.

4

Religious Strife and Social Upheavals

1680–1750

Image copyright © The Metropolitan Museum of Art. Image source: Art Resource, NY

Linen embroidered with wool and silk thread, 1750s.

AMERICAN HISTORIES

In the 1730s Gilbert Tennent, a leading preacher in the American colonies, outraged more traditional ministers with his evangelical zeal. The son of a Scots-Irish clergyman, Gilbert Tennent was born in Vinecash, Ireland, in 1703 and at age fifteen moved with his family to Philadelphia. After receiving an M.A. from Yale College in 1725, Gilbert was ordained a Presbyterian minister in New Brunswick, New Jersey, with little indication of the role he would play in a major denominational schism.

Tennent entered the ministry at a critical moment, when leaders of a number of denominations had become convinced that the colonies were descending into spiritual apathy. Tennent dedicated himself to sparking a rebirth of Christian commitment, and by the mid-1730s the pastor had gained fame as a revival preacher. At the end of the decade, he journeyed through the middle colonies with Englishman George Whitefield, an Anglican preacher known for igniting powerful revivals. Then in the fall of 1740, following the death of his wife, Tennent launched his own evangelical "awakenings."

Revivals inspired thousands of religious conversions across denominations, but they also fueled conflicts within established churches. Presbyterians in Britain and America disagreed about whether only those who had had a powerful, personal conversion experience were qualified to be ministers. Tennent made his opinion clear by denouncing unconverted ministers in his sermons, a position that led to his expulsion from the Presbyterian Church in 1741. But many local churches sought converted preachers, and four years later a group of ejected pastors formed a rival synod that trained its own evangelical ministers. During these upheavals, Tennent married a widow with children and became pastor of the New Building of Philadelphia, a church founded by Whitefield supporters. But he proved too moderate for many of the more enthusiastic congregants, who left to join the Baptist Church.

While ministers debated the proper means of saving sinners, ordinary women and men searched their souls. In Pomfret, Connecticut, Sarah Grosvenor certainly feared for hers in the summer of 1742 when the unmarried nineteen-year-old realized she was pregnant. Her situation was complicated by her status in the community. She was the daughter of Leicester Grosvenor, an important local landowner and town official, and Sarah's family regularly attended Pomfret's Congregational church.

The pew next to Sarah and her family was occupied by Nathaniel Sessions and his sons, including the twenty-six-year-old Amasa, who had impregnated Sarah. Many other young women became pregnant out of wedlock in the 1740s, but families accepted the fact as long as the couple married before the child was born. In Sarah's case, however, Amasa refused to marry her and suggested instead that she have an abortion.

For centuries, women had sought to end unwanted pregnancies by using herbal potions. Although Sarah was reluctant to follow this path, Amasa insisted. When the herbs failed to induce a miscarriage, he introduced Sarah to John Hallowell, a doctor who claimed he could remove the fetus with forceps, a recently developed instrument to aid in delivery. After admitting her agonizing situation to her older sister Zerviah and her cousin Hannah, Sarah allowed Hallowell to proceed. He finally induced a miscarriage, but Sarah soon grew feverish, suffered convulsions, and died ten days later.

Apparently Sarah's and Amasa's parents were unaware of the events leading to her demise. Then in 1745, a powerful religious revival swept through the region, and Zerviah and Hannah suffered great spiritual anguish. We are not sure whether they finally confessed their part in the affair, but that year officials finally brought charges against Sessions and Hallowell for Sarah's death. At the resulting trial, Zerviah and Hannah testified about their roles and those of Sessions and Hallowell. Still, their spiritual anguish did not lead to earthly justice. Hallowell was found guilty but escaped punishment by fleeing to Rhode Island. Sessions was acquitted and remained in Pomfret, where he married and became a prosperous farmer. •

THE AMERICAN HISTORIES of Gilbert Tennent and Sarah Grosvenor were shaped by powerful religious forces—later called the Great Awakening—that swept through the colonies in the early eighteenth century. Those forces are best understood in the context of larger economic and political changes. Many young people became more independent of their parents and developed tighter bonds with siblings, cousins, and neighbors their own age. Towns and cities developed clearer hierarchies by class and status, which could protect wealthier individuals from being punished for their misdeeds. A double standard of sexual behavior became more entrenched as well, with women subject to greater scrutiny than men for their sexual behavior. Of course, most young women did not meet the fate of Sarah Grosvenor. Still, pastors like Gilbert Tennent feared precisely such consequences if the colonies—growing ever larger and more diverse—did not reclaim their religious foundations.

An Ungodly Society?

The upheavals that marked the lives of Gilbert Tennent and Sarah Grosvenor were shaped in part by economic and political changes that began several decades earlier. As American colonists became more engaged in international and domestic commerce, spiritual commitments appeared to wane. In New England, Congregational ministers condemned the apparent triumph of worldly ambition over religiosity. Nonetheless, some ministers saw economic success as a reward for godly behavior even as they worried that wealth and power opened the door to sin. In the late seventeenth century, these anxieties deepened when accusations of witchcraft erupted across southern New England.

The Rise of Religious Anxieties

In 1686 the Puritan minister Samuel Sewell railed against the behavior of Boston mercantile elites, many of whom spent more time at the counting house than the house of worship. Citing examples of their depravity in his diary, including drunkenness and cursing, he claimed that such "high-handed wickedness has hardly been heard of before." Sewell was outraged as well by popular practices such as donning powdered wigs in place of God-given hair, wearing scarlet and gold jackets rather than simple black cloth, and offering toasts rather than prayers.

While Sewell spoke for many Puritans concerned with the consequences of commercial success, other religious leaders tried to meld old and new. The Reverend Cotton Mather bemoaned the declining number of colonists who participated in public fast days and their greater interest in the latest fashions than in the state of their souls. Yet he was attracted by the luxuries available to colonists and hoped to make his son "a more finished Gentleman." Mather was also fascinated by new scientific endeavors and supported inoculations for smallpox, which others viewed as challenging God's power.

Certainly news of the Glorious Revolution in England (1688) offered Puritans hope of regaining their customary authority (see chapter 3). But the outbreak of King William's War in 1689 quickly ended any notion of an easy return to peace and prosperity. Instead, continued conflicts and renewed fears of Indian attacks on rural settlements heightened the sense that Satan was at work in the region. Soon, accusations of witchcraft joined outcries against other forms of ungodly behavior.

Cries of Witchcraft

Belief in witchcraft had been widespread in Europe and England for centuries. It was part of a general belief in supernatural causes for events that could not otherwise be explained—severe storms, a suspicious fire, a rash of deaths among livestock. God sent signs through nature, but so, too, did Satan. Thus people searched babies for deformities, scheduled important events using astrological charts, and feared eclipses of the sun. When a community began to suspect witchcraft, they often pointed to individuals who challenged cultural norms. Women who were quarrelsome, eccentric, or poor were especially easy to imagine as cavorting with evil spirits and invisible demons.

Witchcraft accusations tended to be most common in times of change and uncertainty. Over the course of the seventeenth century, colonists had begun to spread into new areas seeking more land and greater economic opportunities. But expansion brought with it confrontations with Indians, exposure to new dangers, and greater vulnerability to a harsh and unforgiving environment. As the stress of expansion mounted, witchcraft accusations emerged. Some 160 individuals, mostly women, were accused of witchcraft in Massachusetts and Connecticut between 1647 and 1692, although only 15 were put to death. They were linked to ruined crops, sickened neighbors, and the death of cattle. Many of the accused were poor, childless, or disgruntled women, but widows who inherited property also came under suspicion, especially if they fought for control against male relatives and neighbors.

The social and economic complexities of witchcraft accusations are well illustrated by the most famous of American witch-hunts, the Salem witch trials of the early 1690s. In 1692 Salem confronted conflicts between long-settled farmers and newer mercantile families, political uncertainties following the Glorious Revolution, ongoing fear of threats from Indians, and local quarrels over the choice of a new minister. These tensions were brought to a head when the Reverend Samuel Parris's daughter and niece learned voodoo lore and exotic dances from the household's West Indian slave, Tituba. The daughters and servants of neighboring families also became entranced by Tituba's tales and began to tell fortunes, speak in gibberish, and contort their bodies into painful positions. When the girls were questioned about their strange behavior, they pointed not only to Tituba but also to other people in the community. They first accused an elderly female pauper and a homeless widow of bewitching them, but soon they singled out respectable churchwomen as well as a minister, a wealthy merchant, and a four-year-old child.

Within weeks, more than one hundred individuals, 80 percent of them women, stood accused of witchcraft. When the new governor, William Phips, took office in May 1692, he set up a special court to handle the cases and appointed eight Puritan leaders, including Samuel Sewell, to preside. Twenty-seven of the accused came to trial, and twenty were found guilty based on testimony from the girls and on **spectral evidence**—whereby the girls were seen writhing, shaking, and crying out in pain when they came in contact with invisible spirits sent by the accused. Nineteen people were hanged, and one was pressed to death with stones.

But when accusations reached into prominent Salem and Boston families, Governor Phips stepped in. He ended the proceedings and released the remaining suspects. In the following months, leading ministers and colonial officials condemned the use of spectral evidence, and some of the young accusers recanted their testimony. Witch-hunts in North America were small affairs compared to those in Europe, rarely occurred outside New England, and died out by 1700. Yet for those caught up in the trials, the consequences were severe.

> **Explore**
>
> Compare the statement of an accused woman and one minister's defense of the trials in Documents 4.1 and 4.2.

The Salem trials illuminate far more than beliefs in witchcraft, however. The trials pitted the daughters and servants of prosperous farmers against the wives and widows of recently arrived merchants. The accusers

---

DOCUMENTS 4.1 AND 4.2

The Devil's Work: Two Views

Abigail Faulkner, the daughter of a minister and the wife of a large landowner, was among those accused of witchcraft during the frenzied hysteria that occurred in Salem, Massachusetts, in 1692. Although she maintained her innocence, Faulkner was declared guilty, entirely on the basis of coerced confessions and spectral evidence. Because she was pregnant, however, her execution was postponed, and she petitioned Governor Phips to be released (Document 4.1). Faulkner was released, but only after Massachusetts officials stepped in and ended the trials. Still, the belief in witches

Explore

4.1 Petition of Abigail Faulkner, 1692

The humblee Petition of Abigall: Falkner unto his Excellencye S'r W'm Phipps knight and Govern'r of their Majestyes Dominions in America: humbly sheweth

That your poor and humble Petitioner having been this four monthes in Salem Prison and condemned to die having had no other evidences against me but the Spectre Evidences and the Confessors w'ch Confessors have lately since I was condemned owned to my selfe and others and doe still own that they wronged me and what they had said against me was false: and that they would not that I should have been put to death for a thousand worldes for they never should have enjoyed themselves againe in this world; w'ch undoubtedly I shoulod have been put to death had it not pleased the Lord I had been with child. Thankes be to the Lord I know my selfe altogether Innocent & Ignorant of the crime of witchcraft w'ch is layd to my charge: as will appeare at the great day of Judgment (May it please yo'r Excellencye) my husband about five yeares a goe was taken w'th fitts

w'ch did very much impaire his memory and understanding but w'th the blessing of the Lord upon my Endeavors did recover of them againe but now through greife and sorrow they are returned to him againe as bad as Ever they were: I having six children and having little or nothing to subsist on being in a manner without a head [husband] to doe any thinge for my selfe or them and being closely confined can see no otherwayes but we shall all perish Therfore may it please your Excellencye your poor and humble petition'r doe humbly begge and Implore of yo'r Excellencye to take it into yo'r pious and Judicious consideration that some speedy Course may be taken w'th me for my releasement that I and my children perish not through meanes of my close confinement here w'ch undoubtedly we shall if the Lord does not mightily prevent and yo'r poor petitioner shall for ever pray for your health and happinesse in this life and eternall felicity in the world to come.

Source: Paul Boyer and Stephen Nissenbaum, eds., *The Salem Witchcraft Papers, Verbatim Transcripts of the Legal Documents of the Salem Witchcraft Outbreak of 1692* (New York: Da Capo Press, 1977), 1:333–34.

included young women like nineteen-year-old Mercy Lewis, who was bound out as a servant when her parents were killed by Indians. Fear of attack from hostile Indians, hostile officials in England, or hostile neighbors fostered anxieties in Salem, as it did in many colonial communities. Other anxieties also haunted the accusers. A shortage of land led many New England men to seek their fortune farther west, leaving young women with few eligible bachelors to choose from. Marriage prospects were affected as well by battles over inheritance. Thomas Putnam Jr., who housed three of the accusers, was in the midst of one such battle, which left his three sisters—the accusers' aunts—in limbo as they awaited legacies that could enhance their marriage prospects. As young women in Salem forged tight bonds in the face of such uncertainties, they turned their anger not against men, but instead persisted. Cotton Mather, a prominent Puritan minister, defended the trials and his role in them in *Wonders of the Invisible World*, published the following year (Document 4.2). His justifications for the trials and their outcome reveal some awareness of the problems associated with the evidence used against the accused. Nonetheless, his writings indicate his belief that Satan was actively working to undermine colonial communities and that godly Christians needed to take extreme measures to save their communities.

Explore

4.2 Cotton Mather | *The Wonders of the Invisible World,* 1693

These our poor afflicted neighbours, quickly after they become infected and infested with these dæmons, arrive to a capacity of discerning those which they conceive the shapes of their troublers; and notwithstanding the great and just suspicion, that the dæmons might impose the shapes of innocent persons in their spectral exhibitions upon the sufferers (which may perhaps prove no small part of the witch-plot in the issue), yet many of the persons thus represented, being examined, several of them have been convicted of a very damnable witchcraft: yea, more than one twenty have confessed, that they have signed unto a book, which the devil show'd them, and engaged in his hellish design of bewitching, and ruining our land. We know not, at least I know not, how far the delusions of Satan may be interwoven into some circumstances of the confessions; but one would think, all the rules of understanding humane affairs are at an end, if after so many most voluntary harmonious confessions, made by intelligent persons of all ages, in sundry towns, at several times, we must not believe the main strokes wherein those confessions all agree: especially when we have a thousand preternatural things every day before our eyes, wherein the confessors do acknowledge their concernment, and give demonstration of their being so concerned. If the devils now can strike the minds of men with any poisons of so fine a composition and operation, that scores of innocent people shall unite, in confessions of a crime, which we see actually committed, it is a thing prodigious, beyond the wonders of the former ages, and it threatens no less than a sort of a dissolution upon the world.

Source: Cotton Mather, *The Wonders of the Invisible World: Being an Account of the Tryals of Several Witches Lately Executed in New-England* (London: John Russell Smith, 1862), 15–16.

Interpret the Evidence

- On what grounds did Abigail Faulkner defend herself?
- How does Mather both defend and question the events in Salem, including the use of spectral evidence?

Put It in Context

What circumstances might have convinced innocent people to confess to witchcraft?

against older women, including respectable "goodwives" like Abigail Faulkner.

REVIEW & RELATE

| What factors led to a rise in tensions within colonial communities in the early 1700s? | How did social, economic, and political tensions contribute to an increase in accusations of witchcraft? |

☑ *LEARNINGCurve* bedfordstmartins.com/hewittlawson/LC

Family and Household Dynamics

Concerns about marriage, property, and inheritance were not limited to Salem or to New England. As the American colonies became more populous and the numbers of women and men more balanced, husbands gained greater control over the behavior of household members, and the legal and economic rewards available to most women declined. Colonial women with wealth, education, or special skills like midwifery or beer brewing might hold some power in their household and community. But those saddled with abusive husbands or masters quickly discovered that their rights and resources were severely limited.

Women's Changing Status

In most early American colonies, the scarcity of women and workers ensured that many white women gained economic and legal leverage. In the first decades of settlement in the Chesapeake, where women were in especially short supply and mortality was high, young women who arrived as indentured servants and completed their term might marry older men of property. If the husbands died first, widows often took control of the estate and passed on the property to their children. Even in New England, where the numbers of men and women were more balanced from the beginning, the crucial labor of wives in the early years of settlement was sometimes recognized by their control of family property after a husband's death.

By the late seventeenth century, however, as the sex ratio in the Chesapeake evened out, women lost the opportunity to marry "above their class" (Table 4.1). And across the colonies, widows lost control of family estates. Even though women still performed vital labor, the spread of indentured servitude and slavery lessened the recognition of their contributions, while in urban areas the rise of commerce highlighted their role as consumers rather than as producers. As a result, most wives and daughters of white settlers were assigned primarily domestic roles. While domestic chores involved hard physical labor, many women welcomed the change from the more arduous tasks performed by their mothers and grandmothers. Yet they also found their legal and economic rights restricted to those accorded their female counterparts in Great Britain.

According to English common law, a wife's status was defined as *feme covert*, which meant that she was legally covered over by (or hidden behind) her husband. The husband controlled his wife's labor, the house in which she lived, the property she brought into the marriage, and any wages she earned. He was also the legal guardian of their children, and through the instrument of a will he could continue to control the household after his death. In many ways, a wife's legal status was that of a child, with her husband acting in this context as her father.

With the growth and diversity of colonial towns and cities, the **patriarchal family**—a model in which fathers have absolute authority over wives, children, and servants—came to be seen as a crucial bulwark against disorder. Families with wealth were especially eager to control the behavior of their sons and daughters as they sought to build commercial and political alliances. The refusal of Amasa Sessions to marry Sarah Grosvenor, for instance, may have resulted from his belief that his father expected a better match. Although a few women escaped the worst strictures of patriarchal households, most were expected to comply with the wishes of their fathers and then their husbands. Even as widows, many found their finances and daily life shaped by a husband's will and its implementation by male executors.

TABLE 4.1   Sex Ratios in the White Population for Selected Colonies, 1624–1755

Date	Colony	White Male Population	White Female Population	Females per 100 Males
1624–1625	Virginia	873	222	25
1660	Maryland	c. 600	c. 190	32
1704	Maryland	11,026	7,136	65
1698	New York	5,066	4,677	92
1726	New Jersey	15,737	14,124	90
1755	Rhode Island	17,860	17,979	101

Explore

Read the will of a New York farmer in Document 4.3.

Working Families

For most colonial women and men, daily rounds of labor shaped their lives more powerfully than legal statutes or inheritance rights. Whatever their official status, husbands and wives depended on each other to support the family. By the early eighteenth century, many colonial writers promoted the idea of marriage as a partnership, even if the wife remained the junior partner. In 1712 Benjamin Wadsworth published his advice for *The Well-Ordered Family*, in which he urged couples to "delight in each other's company," "be helpful to each other," and "bear one another's burdens."

This concept of marriage as a partnership took practical form in communities across the colonies. In

---

DOCUMENT 4.3

Will of Edmund Titus, Oyster Bay, New York, 1754

The treatment of widows indicates the limited rights that colonial women held by the mid-eighteenth century. Wills provide detailed examples of wives' lack of control over property, even after the death of their husbands. Instead of directly inheriting land, houses, and goods, widows were often placed under the legal protection (and control) of male relatives, whose decisions would regulate their finances and daily lives. The will of New York farmer Edmund Titus shows the customary arrangements of the era.

Explore

How does Titus view the ownership of his family's property and possessions?

In what ways will Titus's wife and daughters have power over their own lives after his death?

Who is left in charge of Titus's estate, and what does this choice tell you about gender relations in mid-eighteenth-century New York?

"I, EDMUND TITUS, of Wheatly, in the bounds of Oyster Bay, in Queens County, yeoman, being this 5 day of the 3d month, called March, in the year 1754, in a feeble condition of body, and willing to set my house in order before my final change." I leave to my wife Sarah one of the choicest of my beds, with full furniture, and one of the choicest of my horses, and her riding saddle, and my cupboard and oval table, and my Great Bible, and all bed linnen. I will that all my lands and meadows, both divided and undivided, lying in the Town of Hempstead, be sold by my executors, and the money to go towards payment of debts. My executors are to set apart so much of my household goods and utensils of husbandry [farming] as they shall find expedient for my wife and family to keep house with, and the rest to be sold. My will and desire is that my wife is to have liberty to carry on farming for the support of herself and family so long as my wife shall think it profitable, and my executors may sell lands at discretion. My 4 daughters, Sarah, Martha, Mary, and Hannah, shall each have so much money as to be equal to what I have given to my eldest daughter, Phebe Pryer, and when my youngest daughter is of age or married, then the estate to be divided between my wife and my 5 daughters. I make my brother in law, Jacob Titus, and my cousin, Samuel Willis, of Jericho, and Thomas Seaman, of Westbury, executors.

Source: "Abstracts of Wills on File in the Surrogate's Office, City of New York. Vol. V 1754–1760," in *Collections of the New-York Historical Society for the Year 1896* (New York: New-York Historical Society, 1897), 30–31.

Put It in Context

What does Edmund Titus's will indicate about the lifestyle and the gender and generational relations within middling farm families?

towns, the wives of artisans often learned aspects of their husband's craft and assisted their husbands in a variety of ways. Given the overlap between homes and workplaces in the eighteenth century, women often cared for apprentices, journeymen, and laborers as well as their own children. Husbands meanwhile labored alongside their subordinates and represented their family's interests to the larger community. Both spouses were expected to provide models of godliness and to encourage prayer and regular church attendance among household members.

On farms, where the vast majority of colonists lived, women and men played crucial if distinct roles. In general, wives and daughters labored inside the home as well as in the surrounding yard with its kitchen garden, milk house, chicken coop, dairy, or washhouse. Husbands and sons worked the fields, kept the livestock, and managed the orchards. However, we should not imagine such farm families as self-sufficient units. Many families supplemented their own labor with that of servants, slaves, or hired field hands. And surplus crops—from corn to apples to eggs—and manufactured goods, such as cloth, sausage, or nails, were exchanged with neighbors or sold at market, creating a linked economic community of small producers.

Indeed, in the late seventeenth and early eighteenth centuries, many farm families in long-settled areas participated in a household mode of production. Men lent each other tools and draft animals and shared grazing land, while women gathered together to spin, sew, and quilt.

Farm Life

This colorful piece of needlework embroidered by Mehitable Starkey of Boston around 1760 portrays three farmers harvesting grain. A woman at the center holds up a sickle, while a man at her right cuts the wheat and a man at her left bundles it. The frontier environment is suggested by the wild game running about the field at the bottom.   Image copyright © The Metropolitan Museum of Art. Image source: Art Resource, NY

Individuals with special skills like midwifery or blacksmithing assisted neighbors, adding farm produce or credit to the family ledger. Surplus corn, wheat, beef, or wool might be exchanged for sugar and tea from traveling salesmen or for an extra hand from neighbors during the harvest. One woman's cheese might be bartered for another woman's jam. A family that owned the necessary equipment might brew barley and malt into beer, while a neighbor with a loom would turn yarn into cloth. The system of exchange, managed largely through barter, allowed individual households to function even as they became more specialized in what they produced.

Reproduction and Women's Roles

Maintaining a farm required the work of both women and men, which made marriage an economic as well as a social and religious institution. In the early eighteenth century, more than 90 percent of white women married. And as mortality declined in the South and remained low in the North, most wives spent the first twenty years of marriage bearing and rearing children. By 1700 a New England wife who married at age twenty and survived to forty-five bore an average of eight children, most of whom lived to adulthood. In the Chesapeake, where mortality rates remained higher and the sex ratio still favored men, marriage and birth rates were slightly lower and infant mortality higher. Still, by the 1720s, southern white women nearly matched the reproductive rates of their northern counterparts.

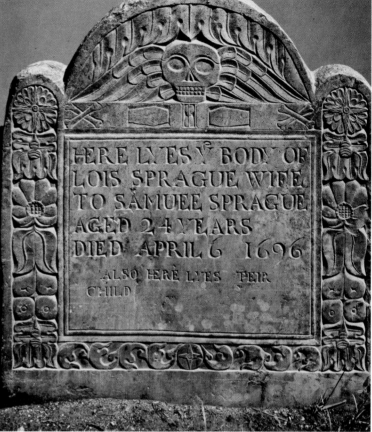

The Perils of Maternal Health

Women often died in childbirth in the late seventeenth century. In this instance, neither mother nor newborn survived. Lois Sprague, twenty-four years old, and her unnamed infant died on April 6, 1696. The skull with wings at the top of the gravestone was a typical symbol of death and heavenly ascension.   Courtesy American Antiquarian Society

Fertility rates among enslaved Africans and African Americans were much lower than those among whites in the early eighteenth century, and fewer infants survived to adulthood. It was not until the 1740s that the majority of slaves were born in the colonies rather than imported. But slowly some slave owners began to realize that encouraging reproduction made good economic sense. Still, enslaved women, most of whom worked in the fields, gained only minimal relief from their labors during pregnancy. Female slaves who lived in seaport cities were more likely to work in homes or shops, a healthier environment than the fields. But owners in already-crowded urban households often discouraged marriage and childbearing.

Immigrants from Scotland, Ireland, and Europe, many of whom lived in the Middle Atlantic colonies, often bore large numbers of children. Quakers, German Mennonites, Scots-Irish Presbyterians, and other groups flowed into New Jersey, Pennsylvania, and Delaware. Some settled in New York City and Philadelphia, but even more spread into rural areas, filling the interior of New Jersey and populating the Pennsylvania frontier. As they pushed westward, growing families replicated the experiences of early colonists, depending on their own resources and those of their immediate neighbors to carve farms and communities out of the wilderness.

Wherever they settled, mothers combined childbearing and child rearing with a great deal of other work. While some affluent families could afford wet nurses and nannies, most colonial women fended for themselves or hired temporary help for particular tasks. Mothers with babies on hip and children under foot hauled water, fed chickens, collected eggs, picked vegetables, prepared meals, spun thread, and manufactured soap and candles. Children were at constant risk of disease and injury, but physicians were rare in many rural areas. Still, farm families were spared from the overcrowding, raw sewage, and foul water that marked most urban neighborhoods.

Colonists feared the deaths of mothers as well as of infants. In 1700 roughly one out of thirty births ended in the mother's death. Women who bore six to eight children thus faced death on a regular basis. Many prayed intensely before and during labor, hoping to survive the ordeal. One minister urged pregnant women to prepare their souls, claiming, "For ought you to know your Death has entered into you."

When a mother died when her children were still young, her husband was likely to remarry soon afterward in order to maintain the family and his farm or business. Even though fathers held legal guardianship over their children, there was little doubt that child rearing, especially for young children and for daughters, was women's work. Many husbands acknowledged this role, prayed for their wife while in labor, and sought to ease her domestic burdens near the end of a pregnancy. But some women received only hostility and abuse from their husbands. In these cases, wives and mothers had few means to protect their children or themselves.

The Limits of Patriarchal Order

Sermons against fornication; ads for runaway spouses, servants, and slaves; reports of domestic violence; poems about domineering wives; petitions for divorce; and legal suits charging rape, seduction, or breach of contract—all of these make clear that ideals of patriarchal authority did not always match the reality. It is impossible to quantify precisely the frequency with which women experienced or resisted abuse at the hands of men. Still, a variety of evidence points to increasing tensions in the early eighteenth century around issues of control—by husbands over wives, fathers over children, and men over women.

Women's claims about men's misbehavior were often demeaned as gossip, but gossip could be an important weapon for those who had little chance of legal redress. In colonial communities, credit and thus trust were central to networks of exchange, so damaging a man's reputation could be a serious matter. Still, gossip was not as powerful as legal sanctions. Thus in cases in which a woman bore an illegitimate child, suffered physical and sexual abuse, or was left penniless by a husband who drank and gambled, she or her family might seek assistance from the courts.

Divorce was as rare in the colonies as it was in England. In New England, colonial law allowed for divorce, but few were granted and almost none to women before 1750. In other colonies, divorce could be obtained only by an act of the colonial assembly and was therefore confined to the wealthy and powerful. If a divorce was granted, the wife usually received "maintenance," an allowance that provided her with funds to feed and clothe herself. Yet without independent financial resources, she nearly always had to live with relatives. Custody of any children was awarded to the father because he had the economic means to support them, although infants or young girls might be assigned to

Advertising a Married Couple's Separation

Although it was difficult to obtain a legal divorce, husbands and wives sometimes abandoned each other or agreed to separate. In this November 1768 notice in the *Boston-Gazette and County Journal*, John Crede notified merchants and other creditors that he would not pay debts contracted by his wife Elizabeth, from whom he claimed to have been separated for twenty years.   Library of Congress

live with the mother. Some couples were granted a separation of bed and board, which meant they lived apart but could not remarry. Here, too, the wife remained dependent on her estranged husband or on family members for economic support. A quicker and cheaper means of ending an unsatisfactory marriage was to abandon one's spouse. Again wives were at a disadvantage since they had few means to support themselves or their children. Colonial divorce petitions citing desertion and newspaper ads for runaway spouses suggest that husbands fled in at least two-thirds of such cases.

In the rare instances when women did obtain a divorce, they had to bring multiple charges against their husband. Domestic violence, adultery, or abandonment alone was insufficient to gain redress. Indeed, ministers and relatives were likely to counsel abused wives to change their behavior or suffer in silence since by Scripture and law a wife was subject to her husband's will. Even evidence of brutal assaults on a wife rarely led to legal redress. Because husbands had the legal right to "correct" their wives and children and because physical punishment was widely accepted, it was difficult to distinguish between "correction" and abuse.

Single women also faced barriers in seeking legal redress. By the late seventeenth century, church and civil courts in New England gave up on coercing sexually active couples to marry. Judges, however, continued to hear complaints of seduction or breach of contract brought by the fathers of single women who were pregnant but unmarried. Had Sarah Grosvenor survived the abortion, her family could have sued Amasa Sessions on the grounds that he gained "carnal knowledge" of her through "promises of marriage." If the plaintiffs won, the result was no longer marriage, however, but financial support for the child. In 1730 the Court of Common Pleas in Concord, Massachusetts, heard testimony from Susanna Holding that a local farmer, Joseph Bright, who was accused of fathering her illegitimate child, had "ruined her Reputation and Fortunes." When Bright protested his innocence, Holding found townsmen to testify that the farmer, "in his courting of her . . . had designed to make her his Wife." In this case, the abandoned mother mobilized members of the community, including men, to uphold popular understandings of patriarchal responsibilities. Without such support, women were less likely to win their case. Still, towns were eager to make errant men support their offspring so that the children did not become a public burden. And at least in Connecticut, a growing number of women initiated civil suits from 1740 on, demanding that men face their financial and moral obligations.

Women who were raped faced even greater legal obstacles than those who were seduced and abandoned. In most colonies, rape was a capital crime, punishable by death, and all-male juries were reluctant to find men guilty. In addition, men were assumed to be the aggressor in sexual encounters. Although bawdy women were certainly a part of colonial lore, it was assumed that most women needed persuading to engage in sex. Precisely when persuasion turned to coercion was less clear. Unlikely to win and fearing humiliation in court, few women charged men with rape. Yet more did so than the records might show since judges and justices of the peace sometimes downgraded rape charges to simple assault or fornication, that is, sex outside of marriage (Table 4.2).

TABLE 4.2 Sexual Coercion Cases Downgraded in Chester County, Pennsylvania, 1731–1739

Date	Defendant/Victim	Charge on Indictment in Testimony	Charge in Docket
1731	Lawrence MacGinnis/Alice Yarnal	Assault with attempt to rape	None
1731	Thomas Culling/Martha Claypool	Assault with attempt to rape	Assault
1734	Abraham Richardson/Mary Smith	Attempted rape	Assault
1734	Thomas Beckett/Mindwell Fulfourd	Theft (testimony of attempted rape)	Theft
1734	Unknown/Christeen Pauper	(Fornication charge against Christeen)	None
1735	Daniel Patterson/Hannah Tanner	Violent assault to ravish	Assault
1736	James White/Hannah McCradle	Attempted rape/adultery	Assault
1737	Robert Mills/Catherine Parry	Rape	None
1738	John West/Isabella Gibson	Attempt to ravish/assault	Fornication
1739	Thomas Halladay/Mary Mouks	Assault with intent to ravish	None

Source: Sharon Block, *Rape and Sexual Power in Early America* (Chapel Hill: University of North Carolina Press). Data from Chester County Quarter Sessions Docket Books and File Papers, 1730–1739.

White women from respectable families had the best chance of gaining support from local authorities, courts, and neighbors when faced with seduction, breach of contract, or rape. Yet such support depended on young people confiding in their elders. By the mid-eighteenth century, however, children were seeking more control over their sexual behavior and marriage prospects, and certain behaviors—for example, sons settling in towns distant from the parental home, younger daughters marrying before their older sisters, and single women finding themselves pregnant—increased noticeably. In part, these trends were natural consequences of colonial growth and mobility. The bonds that once held families and communities together began to loosen. But in the process, young women's chances of protecting themselves against errant men diminished. Just as important, even when they faced desperate situations, young women like Sarah Grosvenor increasingly turned to sisters and friends rather than fathers or ministers.

If women in respectable families found it difficult to redress abuse from suitors or husbands, the poor and those who labored as servants or slaves had even fewer options. Slaves in particular had little hope of prevailing against brutal owners. Even servants faced tremendous obstacles in obtaining legal independence from masters or mistresses who beat or sexually assaulted them. Colonial judges and juries generally refused to declare a man who was wealthy enough to support servants guilty of criminal acts against them. Moreover, female servants and slaves were regularly depicted in popular culture as lusty and immoral, making it even less likely that they would gain the sympathy of white male judges or juries. Thus for most servants and slaves, running away was their sole hope for escape from abuse; however, if they were caught, their situation would likely worsen. Even poor whites who lived independently had little chance of addressing issues of domestic violence, seduction, or rape through the courts. For unhappy couples beyond the help or reach of the law, abandonment was no doubt the most likely option. And as the colonies grew and diversified, leaving a wife and children or an abusive husband or master behind may have become a bit easier than it was in the small and isolated communities of earlier periods.

REVIEW & RELATE

Why and how did the legal and economic status of colonial women decline between 1650 and 1750?	How did patriarchal ideals of family and community shape life and work in colonial America? What happened when men failed to live up to those ideals?

LEARNINGCurve bedfordstmartins.com/hewittlawson/LC

Diversity and Competition in Colonial Society

As the English colonies in North America expanded, divisions increased between established families living in long-settled regions—whether on rural farmsteads or in urban homesteads—and the growing population of women and men with few resources. Although most colonists still hoped to own their own land and establish themselves as farmers, artisans, or shopkeepers, fewer were likely to succeed than in the past. By 1760 half of all white men in North America were propertyless. This growing class cleavage was accompanied by increasing racial, national, and religious diversity.

Population Growth and Economic Competition

After 1700, the population grew rapidly across the colonies. In 1700 about 250,000 people lived in England's North American colonies. By 1725 that number had doubled, and fifty years later it had reached 2.5 million. Much of the increase was due to natural reproduction, but in addition nearly 250,000 immigrants and Africans arrived in the colonies between 1700 and 1750.

Because more women and children arrived than in earlier decades, higher birthrates and a more youthful population resulted. At the same time, most North American colonists enjoyed a better diet than their counterparts in Europe and had access to more abundant timber, furs, fish, and other resources. Thus colonists in the eighteenth century began living longer, with more adults surviving to watch their children and grandchildren grow up.

As the population soared, the chance for individuals to obtain land or start a business of their own diminished. Even those with land did not always thrive: Farmers living in New England where the soil was exhausted or in swampy frontier regions or in areas already claimed by Indian, French, or Spanish settlers found that owning land did not automatically lead to prosperity. In the South Carolina backcountry, a visitor in the mid-eighteenth century noted that many residents "have nought but a Gourd to drink out of, nor a Plate, Knive or Spoon, a Glass, Cup, or anything." In the Carolinas and along the Hudson River, many farmers rented land from large landowners, thus ensuring limited profits even in years of relative abundance.

In prosperous parts of Middle Atlantic colonies like Pennsylvania, many landless laborers abandoned rural life and searched for urban opportunities. They moved to Philadelphia or other towns and cities in the region, seeking jobs as dockworkers, street vendors, or servants, or as apprentices in one of the skilled trades. But newcomers found the job market flooded and the chances for advancement growing slim (Figure 4.1).

In the South, too, divisions between rich and poor became more pronounced in the early decades of the eighteenth century. Tobacco was the most valuable product in the Chesapeake, and the largest tobacco planters lived in relative luxury. Families with extensive landholdings and large numbers of slaves grew rich. They developed mercantile contacts in seaport cities on the Atlantic coast and in the Caribbean and imported luxury goods from Europe. They also began training some of their slaves as domestic workers to relieve wives and daughters of the strain of household labor.

The profits from tobacco allowed a larger percentage of southern than northern whites to own land. In 1750 two-thirds of white families farmed their own land in Virginia, and an even higher percentage did so in the Carolinas. Yet small farmers became increasingly dependent on large landowners, who controlled markets, political authority, and the courts. Many artisans, too, depended on wealthy planters for their livelihood, working either for them directly or for the shipping companies and merchants that relied on plantation orders. And the growing number of tenant farmers relied completely on large landowners for their sustenance.

Some southerners fared far worse. One-fifth of all white southerners owned little more than the clothes on their backs in the mid-eighteenth century. Thus those with small plots of land could easily imagine what their future would be if they suffered a bad season, a fall in tobacco prices, or the death of a father or husband. At the same time, free blacks in the South found their opportunities for landownership and economic independence increasingly curtailed, while enslaved blacks had little hope of gaining their freedom and held no property of their own.

Increasing Diversity

Population growth and economic divisions were accompanied by increased diversity in the North American colonies. Indentured servants arrived from Ireland and Scotland as well as England. Africans were imported in growing numbers and entered a more highly structured system of slavery, whether laboring on southern farms, on northern estates, or in seaport cities. In addition, free families and redemptioners from Ireland, Scotland, the German states, and Sweden came in ever-larger numbers and developed their own communities and cultural institutions. There were also more colonists who had spent time in the Caribbean before settling on the mainland, and the frontiers of British North America were filled with American Indians and French and Spanish settlers as well as European immigrants.

As the booming population increased the demand for land in the colonies, diverse groups of colonists pushed westward to find territory that either was not claimed by others or could be purchased. In Pennsylvania in the early eighteenth century, Moravian and Scots-Irish immigrants settled in areas like Shamokin that were dotted with Iroquois, Algonquian, and Siouan towns, negotiating with Indians to obtain farmland. At the same time, Delaware and Shawnee groups moved into Pennsylvania from New Jersey and the Ohio River valley and negotiated with colonists and the colonial government to establish communities for themselves. All along the Pennsylvania

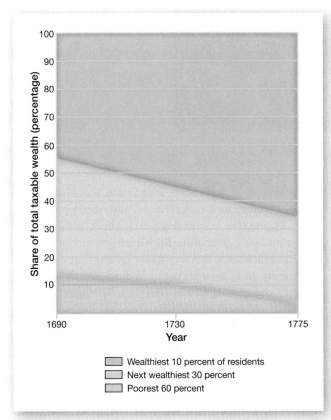

FIGURE 4.1 Wealth Inequality in Northern Cities, 1690–1775

During the eighteenth century, the wealth of merchants rose much faster than that of artisans and laborers. By 1750 the wealthiest 10 percent of the taxable residents of major northern cities owned 60 percent of the taxable wealth, while the poorest 60 percent owned less than 10 percent. This gap between rich and poor only increased over the next quarter century.

Source: Gary B. Nash, *The Urban Crucible: Social Change, Political Consciousness, and the Origins of the American Revolution* (Cambridge, MA: Harvard University Press, 1979).

Fraktur Birth and Baptismal Certificate

Frakturs were an elaborate form of German folk art and style of lettering adapted by the Pennsylvania Dutch (from *Deutsch*, meaning "German"). They were first used in North America in the 1740s to commemorate births, baptisms, weddings, and other life events. This birth and baptismal certificate for Eva Eissenhaer from around 1773 likely shows the infant's parents in their finest dress.   Used by permission of the Rare Book Department, Free Library of Philadelphia

frontier, the lines between Indian and immigrant settlements blurred, and neither Indian chiefs nor colonial authorities seemed able to demarcate clear boundaries. Still, many communities prospered in the region, with white settlers exchanging European and colonial trade goods for access to Indian-controlled orchards, waterways, and lands (Map 4.1).

In the 1720s and 1730s, however, a flood of Scots-Irish settlers arrived in Pennsylvania when bad harvests and high rents caused them to flee oppressive conditions back home. The new immigrants overwhelmed native communities that had welcomed earlier settlers. The death of William Penn in 1718 exacerbated the situation as his sons and closest advisers struggled to gain political and economic control over the colony, but this did not halt the flow of white settlers into the region. Indeed, as Indians were pushed to the margins, more diverse groups of European settlers moved into frontier territories.

Expansion and Conflict

As more and more colonists sought economic opportunities on the frontier, conflicts erupted regularly between earlier British and newer immigrant settlers as well as among immigrant groups. In Pennsylvania, Dutch, Scots-Irish, and German colonists took each other to court, sued land surveyors, and even burned down cabins built by their immigrant foes. For longtime British settlers, such acts only reinforced their sense that recent immigrants were a threat to their society. In 1728 James Logan, William Penn's longtime secretary, complained that the "Palatines [Germans] crowd in upon us and the Irish yet faster." For Logan, these difficulties were exacerbated by what he considered the "idle," "worthless," and "indigent" habits of Scots-Irish and other recent arrivals.

Despite their disparagement of others, Anglo-Americans hardly set high standards themselves, especially when negotiating with Indians. Even in Pennsylvania, where William Penn had established a reputation for (relatively) fair dealing, the desire for Indian land led to dishonesty and trickery. Colonial leaders' success in prying more territory from Indians, however, also resulted from conflicts within the Iroquois Confederacy. Hoping to assert their authority over the independent-minded Delaware Indians, Iroquois chiefs negotiated with Pennsylvania officials in the 1720s, claiming they held rights to much of the Pennsylvania territory. Colonial authorities then produced a questionable treaty supposedly drafted by

0 25 50 miles
0 25 50 kilometers

NEW YORK

PENNSYLVANIA

▲ Tioga (Iroquois)

Susquehanna R.

Delaware R.

▲ Ostonwakin

▲ Great Island

▲ Wyoming

Pechoquealing (Shawnee) ▲

▲ Wapwallopen (Delaware)

Hunter ● Settlement

▲ Nescopeck (Delaware)

▲ Buchkabuchka

▲ Clistowackin (Delaware)

▲ Shamokin

Hockendauqua ▲

▲ Easton

McKee's ● Trading Post

Craig's Settlement ●

NEW JERSEY

Bethlehem ●

Tulpewihacki ▲

▲ Tulpehocken

▲ Clistowackin (Delaware)

Conodogwinet (Shawnee) ▲

Harris's Ferry ● (Paxton)

Manatawny (Delaware) ▲

Schuylkill R.

Delaware R.

Susquehanna R.

● Lancaster

Philadelphia ●

N
W E
S

Conestoga ▲

MARYLAND

DEL.

▲ Indian town
● White settlement

MAP 4.1 Frontier Settlements and Indian Towns in Pennsylvania, 1700–1740

German and Scots-Irish immigrants to Pennsylvania mingled with Indian settlements in the early eighteenth century as Delaware and Shawnee groups pushed east from New Jersey. In the 1720s and 1730s, however, European migration escalated dramatically in the fertile river valleys. In response, once-independent Indian tribes joined the Delaware and Shawnee nations to strengthen their position against the influx of colonists.

Source: Jane T. Merritt, *At the Crossroads: Indians & Empires on a Mid-Atlantic Frontier, 1700–1763* (Chapel Hill: University of North Carolina Press, 2003), 35.

Penn in 1686 to claim that large portions of that territory had already been ceded to settlers. James Logan "discovered" a copy of the treaty deed that allowed the English to control an area that could be walked off in a day and a half. The Iroquois finally agreed to this **Walking Purchase**, giving Pennsylvania officials the leverage they needed to persuade the Delawares to allow them to walk off the boundaries. By the time the Delawares acquiesced in the fall of 1737, Pennsylvania surveyors had already marked off the "shortest and best course," which allowed them to extend the boundaries by at least thirty miles beyond those set in the original, and questionable, treaty.

While extending colonial boundaries provided more land for hungry settlers, the rapid expansion of the colonial population ensured that conflicts would continue to erupt. Indian and British authorities repeatedly argued over treaty rights, boundary lines, and the power to cede or purchase land. Meanwhile migrants and immigrants on the Anglo-American frontier claimed land simply by taking control of it, building houses, and planting crops. This led to conflicts with local Indian communities that still considered the territory their own, with English officials who demanded legal contracts and deeds, and among immigrants who settled in the same area.

Immigrants also introduced greater religious diversity into the British colonies. But in Pennsylvania, several religious groups sought friendly relations with local Indians in order to secure land and trade goods. Some early immigrants, such as William Penn's Quakers, accepted Indian land claims and tried to pursue honest and fair negotiations. German Moravians who settled in eastern Pennsylvania in the 1740s also developed good trade relations with area tribes, shared in burial rituals, and acquiesced when the local Iroquois chief demanded the services of a blacksmith to make and repair guns. Meanwhile Scots-Irish Presbyterians settled along the western frontier and established alliances with Delaware and Shawnee groups there. These alliances were rooted less in religious principles, however, than in the hope of profiting from the fur trade when area Indians pursued new commercial partners after their former French allies became too demanding.

As tensions escalated between English and French authorities in the region, conflicts intensified among the various immigrant and religious communities and with Indians. Although colonists had disagreed many times before over policies toward native people, the dramatically different visions of Indian-settler relations rooted in distinct religious traditions magnified these differences and made it more difficult to find common ground. Growing religious diversity also created sharper boundaries within and between colonial communities. German Moravians and Scots-Irish Presbyterians in Pennsylvania established churches and schools separate from their Quaker neighbors, while Puritan New Englanders remained suspicious of Quakers as well as other Protestant sects. Moravians and other German sects also flourished in Georgia and the Carolinas, and nearly all sought to isolate themselves from the influences of other religious and ethnic groups.

Some religious groups were isolated as much by force as by choice. While most early Irish immigrants were Protestant, by the early eighteenth century more Irish Catholics began to arrive. Then in 1745 some forty thousand Scots who had supported the Catholic monarchs in England prior to the Glorious Revolution (see chapter 3) were shipped to the Carolinas after a failed rebellion. As traitors to the crown, they were doubly marginalized. But even long-settled Catholics, like those in Maryland, were looked on with suspicion by many Protestants. Jewish families also multiplied, founding the first American synagogues in Newport, Rhode Island; Savannah; Charleston; and Philadelphia. Although only a few hundred Jewish families resided in the colonies by 1750, they formed small but enduring communities in a number of seaport cities, where they developed a variety of mercantile ventures and practiced their faith.

Africans, too, brought new ideas and practices to North America. Transported by force to an unknown land, they may have found religious faith particularly important. Enslaved blacks included some Catholics from regions long held by the Portuguese and a few thousand Muslims, but many Africans embraced religions that were largely unknown to their Anglo-American masters. Even those planters who allowed Protestants to minister to their slaves discovered that many Africans and African Americans retained beliefs and rituals handed down across generations.

As religious affiliations in the colonies multiplied, they reinforced existing concerns about spiritual decline. Moreover, spiritual differences often exacerbated cleavages rooted in nationality and class. And they heightened concerns among many well-established families over the future of British culture and institutions in North America.

REVIEW & RELATE

How and why did economic inequality in the colonies increase in the first half of the eighteenth century?

How did population growth and increasing diversity contribute to conflict among and anxieties about the various groups inhabiting British North America?

✔ *LEARNINGCurve* bedfordstmartins.com/hewittlawson/LC

Religious Awakenings

Whether rooted in fears that worldly concerns were overshadowing spiritual devotion or that growing religious diversity was undermining the power of the church, Protestant ministers lamented the state of faith in eighteenth-century America. Many church leaders in Britain and the rest of Europe shared their fears. Ministers eager to address this crisis of faith—identified in the colonies as **New Light clergy**—worked together to re-energize the faithful and were initially welcomed, or at least tolerated, by more traditional **Old Light clergy**. But by the 1740s, fears that revivalists had gone too far led to a backlash. Still, for a time, the religious awakenings of the

early eighteenth century created a powerful sense of common cause among Protestant colonists of different faiths, nationalities, and classes and promised a rebirth of commitment to both spiritual values and the larger society.

The Roots of the Great Awakening

The European religious landscape had grown remarkably more diverse in the two hundred years following the Reformation as Presbyterians, Lutherans, Methodists, Baptists, Quakers, and a variety of smaller sects competed for followers. Another current also had an impact: By the eighteenth century, the **Enlightenment**, a cultural movement that emphasized rational and scientific thinking over traditional religion and superstition, had taken root, particularly among elites. As North American colonies attracted settlers from new denominations and as more and more colonists were influenced by Enlightenment thought, the colonists as a whole became more accepting of religious diversity.

There were, however, countervailing forces. The German **Pietists** in particular challenged Enlightenment ideas that had influenced many Congregational and Anglican leaders in Europe and the colonies. Pietists not only decried the power of established churches but also urged individuals to follow their heart rather than their head in spiritual matters. Only by restoring intensity and emotion to worship, they believed, could spiritual life be revived. Persecuted in Germany, Pietists migrated to Great Britain and North America, where their ideas influenced Scots-Irish Presbyterians, French Huguenots, and members of the Church of England. John Wesley, the founder of Methodism and a professor of theology at Oxford University, taught Pietist ideas to his students. George Whitefield was inspired by Wesley. Like the German Pietists whose ideas he embraced, Whitefield believed that the North American colonies offered an important opportunity to implement these ideas.

But not all colonists waited for Whitefield or the German Pietists to rethink their religious commitments. By 1700 both laymen and ministers voiced growing concern with the state of colonial religion. Preachers educated in England or at the few colleges established in the colonies, like Harvard College (1636) and the College of William and Mary (1693), often emphasized learned discourse over passion. At the same time, there were too few clergy to meet the demands of the rapidly growing population in North America. Many rural parishes covered vast areas, and residents grew discouraged at the lack of ministerial attention. Meanwhile urban churches increasingly reflected the class divisions of the larger society. In many meetinghouses, wealthier members paid substantial rents to seat their families in the front pews. Small farmers and shopkeepers rented the cheaper pews in the middle of the church, while the poorest congregants—including landless laborers, servants, and slaves—sat on free benches at the very back or in the gallery. Educated clergy might impress the richest parishioners with their learned sermons, but they did little to move the spirits of the congregation at large.

In 1719 the Reverend Theodorus Freylinghuysen, a Dutch Reformed minister in New Brunswick, New Jersey, began emphasizing parishioners' emotional investment in Christ. The Reverend William Tennent arrived in neighboring Pennsylvania with his family about the same time. He despaired that Presbyterian ministers were too few in number to reach the growing population and, like Freylinghuysen, feared that their approach was too didactic and cold. Tennent soon established his own academy—one room in a log cabin—to train his four sons and other young men for the ministry. Though disparaged by Presbyterian authorities, the school attracted devout students. A decade later, in 1734–1735, Jonathan Edwards, a Congregational minister in Northampton, Massachusetts, made clear the value of religious appeals that emphasized emotion over logic. Proclaiming that "our people do not so much need to have their heads stored [with knowledge] as to have their hearts touched," he initiated a local revival that reached hundreds of colonists.

Like Edwards, William Tennent's son Gilbert urged colonists to embrace "a true living faith in Jesus Christ." Assigned a church in New Brunswick in 1726, Tennent met Freylinghuysen, who viewed conversion as a three-step process: Individuals must be convinced of their sinful nature, experience a spiritual rebirth, and then behave piously as evidence of their conversion. Tennent embraced these measures, believing they could lance the "boil" of an unsaved heart and apply the "balsam" of grace and righteousness. Then in 1739 Tennent met Whitefield, who launched a wave of revivals that revitalized and transformed religion across the colonies.

A North-West Prospect of Nassau-Hall, with a Front View of the Presidents House, in New Jersey.

The College of New Jersey

The College of New Jersey, which later became Princeton University, developed out of the Reverend William Tennent's Log Cabin College and was established to train New Light ministers. This engraving by Henry Dawkins shows the campus in 1764 and is based on drawings by William Tennent Jr., the minister's son. © Corbis

An Outburst of Revivals

Whitefield was perfectly situated to initiate the series of revivals that scholars later called the **Great Awakening**. Gifted with a powerful voice, he understood that the expanding networks of communication and travel—developed to promote commerce—could also be used to promote religion. Advertising in newspapers and broadsides and traveling by ship, coach, and horseback, Whitefield made seven trips to the North American colonies during his career, beginning in 1738. He reached audiences from Georgia to New England to the Pennsylvania backcountry and inspired ministers in the colonies to extend his efforts.

In 1739 Whitefield launched a fifteen-month preaching tour that reached tens of thousands of colonists. Like Edwards, Freylinghuysen, and Tennent, he asked individuals to invest less in material goods and more in spiritual devotion. **See Document Project 4: Awakening Religious Tensions, page 122**. If they admitted their depraved and sinful state and truly repented, God would hear their prayers. The droughts and locusts that plagued farmers and the epidemics and fires that threatened city folk were signs of God's anger at the moral decay that marked colonial life. Whitefield danced across the platform, shouted and raged, and gestured dramatically, drawing huge crowds everywhere he went. And he went everywhere, preaching on 350 separate occasions in 1739–1740. He attracted 20,000 people to individual events, at a time when the entire city of Boston counted just 17,000 residents.

> **Explore**
>
> Read one follower's impression of Whitefield in Document 4.4.

Whitefield encouraged local ministers like Tennent to join him in his efforts to revitalize Protestantism. Less concerned with denominational affiliation than with core beliefs and passionate preaching, Whitefield hailed his fellow revivalists as "burning and shining lights" and embraced the vitality (and disruption) that followed in their wake. New Light ministers carried on Whitefield's work throughout the 1740s, honing their methods and appeal. They denounced urbane and educated clergy, used extemporaneous oratorical styles and outdoor venues to attract crowds, and invited colonists from all walks of life to build a common Christian community. Some became itinerant preachers, preferring the freedom to carry their message throughout the colonies to the security of a traditional pulpit.

New Light clergy brought young people to religion by the thousands. In addition, thousands of colonists who were already church members were "born again," recommitting themselves to their faith. Poor parishioners who felt little connection to preaching when they sat on the back benches eagerly joined the crowds at outdoor revivals, where they could stand as close to the pulpit as a rich merchant. Indeed, Tennent appealed especially to poor and single women and girls when he preached with Whitefield in Boston. Enthusiastic parishioners from a wide range of denominations formed new churches. Some, like the New Building of Philadelphia, sought interdenominational communion, but most expanded the reach of particular denominations, whether Presbyterian, Congregational, Methodist, Baptist, or Anglican.

Religious Dissension

Initially, the Great Awakening drew support from large numbers of ministers because it increased religious enthusiasm and church attendance throughout the colonies. After decades of decline, religion once again took center stage. But the early embrace by Old Light clergy diminished as revivals spread farther afield, as critiques of educated clergy became more pointed, and as New Light clergy began carrying parts of older congregations into new churches. A growing number of ministers and other colonial leaders began to fear that revivalists were providing lower-class whites, free blacks, and even women and slaves with compelling critiques of those in power. As the Great Awakening peaked in 1742, a backlash developed among more settled ministers and their congregations.

Itinerant preachers traveling across the South seemed especially threatening as they invited blacks and whites to attend revivals together and proclaimed their equality before God. Although it was rare that New Light clergy directly attacked slavery—indeed, many preached that worldly status was irrelevant to salvation—they implicitly challenged racial hierarchies. New Light preachers also gained more adherents among African Americans and American Indians than had earlier clergy by emphasizing communal singing and emotional expressions of the spirit, both of which echoed traditional African and Indian practices. Combined with their recruitment of young, poor, and female converts, such a broad appeal came to seem more dangerous than beneficial.

In the North, too, Old Light ministers and local officials began to question New Light techniques and influences. One of the most radical New Light preachers, James Davenport, attracted huge crowds when he preached in Boston in the early 1740s. Drawing thousands of colonists to Boston Common day after day, Davenport declared that the people "should drink rat poison rather than listen to corrupt, unconverted clergy." Claiming that Davenport's followers were "idle or ignorant Persons, [and] those of the Lowest

DOCUMENT 4.4

Nathan Cole | On George Whitefield Coming to Connecticut, 1740

The evangelical religious movement known as the Great Awakening swept through British North America in the 1730s and 1740s. Thousands flocked to revivals led by traveling ministers, especially George Whitefield, an evangelical Anglican whose religious ideas were shaped by the teachings of John Wesley. Whitefield launched an extensive speaking tour of the colonies in 1739. In the following passage, Nathan Cole, a Connecticut farmer, describes the crowd assembled at Wethersfield to hear Whitefield preach.

Explore

We went down in the Stream; I heard no man speak a word all the way three mile but every one pressing forward in great haste and when we got down to the old meeting house there was a great multitude; it was said to be 3 or 4000 of people assembled together. We got off from our horses and shook off the dust and the ministers were then coming to the meeting house. I turned and looked toward the great river and saw the ferry boats running swift forward and backward bringing over loads of people; the oars rowed nimble and quick. Every thing men horses and boats all seemed to be struggling for life; the land and the banks over the river looked black with people and horses all along the 12 miles. I see no man at work in his field but all seemed to be gone—when I saw Mr. Whitefield come upon the Scaffold [platform] he looked almost angelical, a young slim slender youth before some thousands of people and with a bold undaunted countenance, and my hearing how God was with him every where as he came along it solemnized my mind and put me in a trembling fear before he began to preach; for he looked as if he was clothed with authority from the great God, and a sweet solemn solemnity sat upon his brow. And my hearing him preach gave me a heart wound; by God's blessing my old foundation was broken up and I saw that my righteousness would not save me; then I was convinced of the doctrine of Election and went right to quarreling with God about it because all that I could do would not save me; and he had decreed from Eternity who should be saved and who not.

Source: George Leon Walker, *Some Aspects of the Religious Life of New England* (New York: Silver, Burnett, 1897), 91–92.

Interpret the Evidence

- How does Cole describe Whitefield, and what does this description tell us about Whitefield's popularity among the colonists?
- What messages does Cole take away from Whitefield's sermon?

Put It in Context

How might colonists' religious experience have been affected by hearing Whitefield and others preach to such a large audience?

Rank," Boston officials finally called a grand jury into session to silence him "on the charge of having said that Boston's ministers were leading the people blindfold to hell."

Although Davenport was unusual in directly linking corrupt clergy to a corrupt social order, he suggested to authorities the dangers of allowing revivalists to go unanswered. The extremes to which a few revivalists went also disturbed some New Light ministers, including Tennent, who eventually sought to reunite the Presbyterian Church he had helped to divide. From the beginning, he had celebrated Christian love and fellowship. In 1757 Tennent wrote a sacramental sermon entitled "Love to Christ" that emphasized pietistic communion. He then worked earnestly to reunite the New York and Philadelphia synods, and his efforts succeeded a year later.

Not all churches reconciled their differences so easily, however. Revivals continued throughout the 1740s, as the awakening in Pomfret, Connecticut, indicates. Yet over time, they lessened in intensity as churches and parishioners settled back into a more ordered religious life. Moreover, the central tenets of revivalist preaching—criticisms of educated clergy, itinerancy, and extemporaneous preaching—worked against the movement's institutionalization. The Great Awakening echoed across the colonies for at least another generation, but its influence was felt more often in attitudes and practices than in institutions.

For example, when, in 1750, King George II threatened to appoint an Anglican bishop for the North American colonies, many North American ministers, both Old Light and New, resisted the appointment. Most colonists had become used to religious diversity and toleration, at least for Protestants, and had little desire to add church officials to the existing hierarchies of colonial authorities. In various ways, revivalists also highlighted the democratic tendencies in the Bible, particularly in the New Testament. Thus even as they proclaimed God's wrath against sinners, they also preached that a lack of wealth and power did not diminish a person in God's eyes. Indeed, it was often the well educated, the wealthy, and the powerful who had the most to fear from the righteous. And revivalists honed a style of passionate and popular preaching that would shape American religion and politics for centuries to come. This mode of communication had immediate application as colonists mobilized to resist what they saw as tyrannical actions by colonial officials and others in authority.

REVIEW & RELATE

What groups were most attracted to the religious revivals of the early eighteenth century? Why?

What were the legacies of the Great Awakening for American religious and social life?

LEARNINGCurve bedfordstmartins.com/hewittlawson/LC

Political Awakenings

The effects of eighteenth-century religious awakenings rippled out from churches and revivals to influence social and political relations. In various areas of life, colonists began to question the right of those in power to impose their will on the community as a whole. Similar issues had surfaced before the revivals, but New Light clergy gave greater weight to political and social challenges, allowing colonists to view their resistance to traditional authorities as part of their larger effort to create a better and more just world.

Changing Political Relations

The settlements of the seventeenth century could be regulated with a small number of officials, and in most colonies male settlers agreed on who should rule. However, with geographical expansion, population growth, and commercial development, colonial officials—whether appointed by the crown or selected by local residents—found themselves confronted with a more complex, and more contentious, situation. Most officials were educated men who held property and had family ties to other colonial elites. Although they made decisions locally, ultimate political authority—or sovereignty—rested with the king and Parliament. The crown appointed governors, judges, and other royal officials and approved those elected locally. The king and Parliament held veto power over colonial legislation and made all decisions about war and peace. Finally, they set policy for the colonies in such critical areas as taxes and duties and military service.

While ultimate political sovereignty rested with authorities in England, the king and Parliament were too distant to have a hand in the daily workings of colonial life. Even royal officials appointed to carry out official policies often discovered that what sounded good in London was not practicable in North America. Another factor that weakened the power of royal officials was the tradition of town meetings and representative bodies, like the Virginia House of Burgesses, that had emerged within the colonies, giving colonists a stake in their own governance. Officials in England and the colonies assumed that most people would defer to those in authority, and they minimized resistance by holding public elections in which freemen cast ballots by voice vote. Not surprisingly, those with wealth and power, who often treated voters with food and drink on election days, continued to win office.

Still, evidence throughout the colonial period indicates that deference to authority was not always sufficient to maintain order. Roger Williams and Anne Hutchinson, Bacon's Rebellion, the Stono rebellion, the Salem witchcraft trials, and the radical preaching of James Davenport make clear that not everyone willingly supported their supposed superiors. These episodes of dissent and protest were widely scattered across time and place. But as the ideas disseminated by New Light clergy converged with changing political relations, resistance to established authority became more frequent and more collective.

Dissent and Protest

Protests against colonial elites multiplied from the 1730s on. The issues and methods varied, but they indicate a growing sense of political and economic autonomy among

Virginia House of Burgesses

This engraving depicts the Virginia House of Burgesses as it looked around 1740. Established in 1619, this legislature was the oldest institution of self-government in British North America. White men over the age of seventeen who owned land could vote for its members. After 1699, the House of Burgesses met in Williamsburg, where it remained throughout the colonial period.　The Granger Collection, New York

North American colonists. Some protests focused on royal officials like governors and Royal Navy captains; others focused on local authorities, merchants, or large landowners. Whatever the target of resistance, protests demonstrated colonists' belief that they had rights that were worth protecting, even against those who held legitimate authority. Just as importantly, dissenters included the poor, women, and African Americans as well as property-owning white men.

Access to reasonably priced food, especially bread, inspired regular protests in the eighteenth century. During the 1730s, the price of bread—a critical staple in colonial diets—rose despite falling wheat prices and a recession in seaport cities. Bread rioters attacked grain warehouses, bakeries, and shops, demanding more bread at lower prices. Like similar protests in Europe, these riots were often successful in the short run, though eventually prices began to rise again. They were often led by women, who were

responsible for putting bread on the table; thus when grievances involved domestic or consumer issues, women felt they had the right to make their voices heard.

Public markets were another site where struggles over food led to collective protests. In 1737, for instance, Boston officials decided to construct a public market and charge fees to farmers who sold their goods there. Small farmers, who were used to selling produce from the roadside for free, clashed with officials and with larger merchants over the venture. Many Boston residents supported the protesters because the market fees would lessen competition and raise prices for consumers. When petitions to city officials had no effect, opponents demolished the market building and stalls in the middle of the night. Local authorities could find no witnesses to the crime. Like bread riots, the success of this protest was short-lived. Officials built another market; nonetheless, the protest had demonstrated the collective power of those with limited resources.

Access to land was also a critical issue in the colonies. Beginning in the 1740s, protests erupted on estates in New Jersey and along the Hudson River in New York over the leasing policies of landlords as well as the amount of land controlled by speculators. When tenants and squatters petitioned colonial officials and received no response, they took collective action. They formed groups, targeted specific landlords, and then burned barns, attacked livestock, and emptied houses and farm buildings of furniture and tools. Eventually, they established regional committees to hear grievances and formed "popular" militia companies and courts to mete out justice to those who refused to renegotiate rental agreements and prices. When landlords and colonial officials called out local militia to arrest the perpetrators, they failed to consider that militia members were often the same poor men whose protests they ignored.

In seaport cities, a frequent source of conflict was the **impressment** of colonial men who were forcibly drafted into service in the Royal Navy. British officials, caught up in nearly continuous warfare in Europe, periodically raided portside communities in order to fill their complement of sailors. Not only sailors but also dockworkers and men drinking at taverns along the shore might find themselves suddenly inducted into military service. Facing high mortality rates, bad food, rampant disease, and harsh discipline on navy ships, these impressed men were unwilling to wait while colonial officials complained to the British government about the labor shortages that impressment caused. Instead, they fought back. In 1747 in Boston, a general impressment led to three days of rioting. An observer noted that "Negros, servants, and hundreds of seamen seized a naval lieutenant, assaulted a sheriff, and put his deputy in stocks, surrounded the governor's house, and stormed the Town House (city hall)." Such riots did not end the system of impressment, but they showed that colonists would battle those who sought to deprive them of their liberty.

The religious upheavals and economic uncertainties of the 1730s and 1740s led colonists to challenge colonial and British officials with greater frequency than in earlier decades. But most protests also accentuated class lines as the poor, small farmers, and craftsmen fought against merchants, landowners, and local officials. Still, the resistance to impressment proved that colonists could mobilize across economic differences when British policies affected diverse groups of colonial subjects.

Transforming Urban Politics

The development of cross-class alliances in the 1730s and 1740s was also visible in the more formal arena of colonial politics. Beginning in the 1730s, some affluent political leaders in cities like New York and Philadelphia began to seek support from a wider constituency. In most cases, it was conflicts among the elite that led to these appeals to the "popular" will. In 1731, for instance, a new royal charter confirmed New York City's existence as a "corporation" and stipulated the rights of freemen (residents who could vote in local elections after paying a small fee) and freeholders (individuals, whether residents or not, who held property worth £40 and could vote on that basis). A large number of artisans, shopkeepers, and laborers acquired the necessary means to vote, and shopkeepers and master craftsmen now sat alongside wealthier men on the Common Council. Yet most laboring men did not participate actively in elections until 1733, when local elites led by Lewis Morris sought to mobilize the mass of voters against royal officials, like Governor William Cosby, appointed in London.

Morris, a wealthy man and a judge, joined other colonial elites in believing that the royal officials recently appointed to govern New York were tied to ministerial corruption in England. Morris thus presented himself as the voice of the common man when he ran against a candidate approved by Cosby. On election day, hundreds of his supporters marched across the town green of Eastchester behind "two Trumpeters and 3 Violines." His opponent also mustered followers on horseback, escorted by royal officials, including the "high sheriff." But the voters chose Morris. The Morrisites then helped launch a newspaper, published by John Peter Zenger, a printer, to mobilize laborers, shopkeepers, and artisans on their behalf.

In his *New-York Weekly Journal*, Zenger leaped into the political fray, accusing Governor Cosby and his cronies of corruption, incompetence, election fraud, and tyranny. The vitriolic attacks led to Zenger's indictment for seditious libel and his imprisonment in November 1734. At the time, libel related only to whether published material undermined government authority, not whether it was true or false. But Zenger's lead attorney, Andrew Hamilton of Philadelphia, argued that truth must be recognized as a defense against charges of libel. Appealing to a jury of Zenger's peers, Hamilton proclaimed, "It is not the cause of a poor printer, nor of New York alone, which you are now trying. . . . It is the best cause. It is the cause of liberty." In response, jurors ignored the law as written and acquitted Zenger. A pamphlet about the case, authored by one of his lawyers and printed by Zenger in 1736, gained a wide readership in Britain and America.

> **Explore**
>
> See part of Hamilton's defense of Zenger in Document 4.5.

Although the decision in the Zenger case did not lead to a change in British libel laws, it did signal the willingness of colonial juries to side with fellow colonists against king and

DOCUMENT 4.5

The Trial of John Peter Zenger, 1736

In 1734 John Peter Zenger, the publisher of the *New-York Weekly Journal*, was arrested for printing articles accusing New York's colonial governor of corruption and fraud. Colonists widely protested Zenger's arrest and followed his trial closely. Zenger's attorney, Andrew Hamilton, argued that his client's accusations against the governor were true and therefore not libel. Since English common law defined libel as a statement undermining government authority, regardless of whether or not it was truthful, Hamilton's successful defense of Zenger signaled an important moment in the history of free speech and the press.

Explore

Mr. Hamilton. May it please Your Honour; I agree with Mr. Attorney, that Government is a sacred Thing, but I differ very widely from him when he would insinuate, that the just Complaints of a Number of Men, who suffer under a bad Administration, is libelling that Administration. Had I believed that to be Law, I should not have given the Court the Trouble of hearing any Thing that I could say in this cause. . . . What strange Doctrine is it, to press every Thing for Law here which is so in England? I believe we should not think it a Favour, at present at least, to establish this Practice. In England so great a Regard and Reverence is had to the Judges, that if any man strike another in Westminster Hall, while the Judges are sitting, he shall lose his Right Hand, and forfeit his Land and Goods, for so doing. And tho' the Judges here claim all the Powers and Authorities within this Government, that a Court of King's Bench has in England, yet I believe Mr. Attorney will scarcely say, that such a Punishment could be legally inflicted on a Man for committing such an Offence, in the Presence of the Judges sitting in any Court within the Province of New-York. The Reason is obvious; a Quarrel or Riot in New-York cannot possibly be attended with those dangerous Consequences that it might in Westminster Hall; nor (I hope) will it be alledged, that any Misbehaviour to a Governor in the Plantations will, or ought to be, judged of or punished, as a like Undutifulness would be to Our Sovereign.

Source: Livingston Rutherfurd, ed., *John Peter Zenger, His Press, His Trial, and a Bibliography of Zenger Imprints* (New York: Dodd, Mead, 1904), 74, 77.

Interpret the Evidence

- What do Hamilton's arguments tell us about colonial perceptions of government?
- What argument is Hamilton making about the relationship between the colonies and Britain?

Put It in Context

Why were jurors willing to ignore English common law in finding Zenger innocent and to thereby set a novel legal precedent?

Parliament, at least when it came to their right to censure public officials. Building on their success, Morris and his followers continued to gain popular support. In 1737 his son, Lewis Morris Jr., was appointed speaker of the new Assembly, and the Assembly appointed Zenger as its official printer. But soon after this victory, the group fell into disarray when royal officials offered political prizes to a few of their leaders. Indeed, the elder Morris accepted appointment as royal governor of New Jersey, after which he switched allegiances and became an advocate of executive authority. Nonetheless, the political movement he led had aroused ordinary freemen to participate in elections, and newspapers and pamphlets now readily attacked corrupt officials and threats to the rightful liberties of British colonists.

Even as freemen gained a greater voice in urban politics, they could challenge the power of economic and political leaders only when the elite were divided. Moreover, the rewards they gained sometimes served to reinforce class divisions. Thus many city workers had benefited when the elder Morris used his influence to ensure the building of the city's first permanent almshouse in 1736. The two-year project employed large numbers of artisans and laborers in a period of economic contraction. Once built, however, the almshouse became a symbol of the growing gap between rich and poor in the city and in the colonies more generally. Its existence was also used by future city councils as a justification to eliminate other forms of relief, leaving the poor in worse shape than before.

Conclusion: A Divided Society

By 1750 religious and political awakenings had transformed colonists' sense of their relation to spiritual and secular authorities. Both Gilbert Tennent and Sarah Grosvenor were caught up in these transitions. Like most colonists, they did not conceive of themselves as part of a united body politic but rather identified most deeply with their family, town, or church. Indeed, most colonists thought of themselves as English, or Scots-Irish, or German, rather than American. At best, they claimed identity as residents of Massachusetts, New Jersey, or South Carolina rather than British North America. By 1750 the diversity and divisions among colonists were greater than ever as class, racial, religious, and regional differences multiplied across the colonies. Still, by midcentury, religious leaders had gained renewed respect, colonial assemblies had wrested more autonomy from royal hands, freemen participated more avidly in political contests and debates, printers and lawyers insisted on the rights and liberties of colonists, and local communities defended those rights in a variety of ways. When military conflicts brought British officials into more direct contact with their colonial subjects in the following decade, they sought to check these trends, with dramatic consequences.

REVIEW & RELATE

How did ordinary colonists, both men and women, black and white, express their political opinions and preferences in the first half of the eighteenth century?

How did politics bring colonists together across economic lines in the first half of the eighteenth century? How did politics highlight and reinforce class divisions?

LEARNINGCurve bedfordstmartins.com/hewittlawson/LC

LEARNINGCurve
Check what you know.
bedfordstmartins.com/hewittlawson/LC

Chapter Review

Online Study Guide ▸ bedfordstmartins.com/hewittlawson

KEY TERMS

spectral evidence (p. 99)
patriarchal family (p. 102)
Walking Purchase (p. 111)
New Light clergy (p. 112)
Old Light clergy (p. 112)
Enlightenment (p. 112)
Pietists (p. 112)
Great Awakening (p. 114)
impressment (p. 118)

REVIEW & RELATE

1. What factors led to a rise in tensions within colonial communities in the early 1700s?

2. How did social, economic, and political tensions contribute to an increase in accusations of witchcraft?

3. Why and how did the legal and economic status of colonial women decline between 1650 and 1750?

4. How did patriarchal ideals of family and community shape life and work in colonial America? What happened when men failed to live up to those ideals?

5. How and why did economic inequality in the colonies increase in the first half of the eighteenth century?

6. How did population growth and increasing diversity contribute to conflict among and anxieties about the various groups inhabiting British North America?

7. What groups were most attracted to the religious revivals of the early eighteenth century? Why?

8. What were the legacies of the Great Awakening for American religious and social life?

9. How did ordinary colonists, both men and women, black and white, express their political opinions and preferences in the first half of the eighteenth century?

10. How did politics bring colonists together across economic lines in the first half of the eighteenth century? How did politics highlight and reinforce class divisions?

TIMELINE OF EVENTS

1636	Harvard College established
1647–1692	Some 160 individuals tried for witchcraft in Massachusetts and Connecticut
1688	Glorious Revolution
1692	Salem witch trials
1693	College of William and Mary established
1700–1750	250,000 immigrants and Africans arrive in the colonies
1700–1775	Population of British North America grows from 250,000 to 2.5 million
1712	Benjamin Wadsworth publishes *The Well-Ordered Family*
1720–1740	Large numbers of Scots-Irish arrive in Pennsylvania
1734	John Peter Zenger acquitted of libel in New York City
1736	First permanent almshouse built in New York City
1737	Delaware Indians acquiesce to Walking Purchase
	Protest against public market in Boston
1739	George Whitefield launches fifteen-month preaching tour of the colonies
1741	Gilbert Tennent expelled from the Presbyterian Church
1742	Sarah Grosvenor dies as a result of a botched abortion
1745	40,000 Scottish Catholics shipped to the Carolinas after a failed rebellion
1747	Impressment leads to three days of rioting in Boston
1750	American colonists resist appointment of an Anglican bishop for the North American colonies
1757	George Tennent initiates effort to reunite the Presbyterian Church

DOCUMENT PROJECT 4

Awakening Religious Tensions

The Great Awakening reveals many of the tensions present in British North America in the mid-eighteenth century. Many upper-class and educated Americans embraced the Enlightenment and deism, which viewed God as a kind of rational "watchmaker" who had set the world in motion but did not directly intervene in its daily workings. Other colonists rejected this intellectual approach in favor of the emotional connections they found in evangelical revivals. The Great Awakening challenged the authority of legally established churches and their ministers, whose congregations began flocking to New Light preachers. These "separatist" groups criticized state-sponsored churches and proposed, instead, that churches be supported through voluntary contributions by church members. Some denominations, such as the Presbyterian Church, split over the controversies engendered by the religious revivals in their midst. The Great Awakening also threw established relations of class and social status into question. Women and men, old and young, upper and lower classes, and even blacks and whites mingled together at revivals, where religious instruction blended with sometimes pointed critiques of colonial power structures. (See Document 4.4 on page 115 for one participant's description of a revival.)

At first, established clergy, known as the Old Lights, embraced the Awakening as a way to promote church attendance and religious practices. However, as revivalist preachers grew more popular, Old Lights became increasingly uneasy about their messages (Documents 4.9 and 4.10). The powerful preaching of George Whitefield of England initiated a wave of revivals across the colonies (Document 4.6). New Light minister Gilbert Tennent, for example, argued that a minister's authority rested on his conversion experience, not his education and training (Document 4.7). By 1742 the controversial actions of itinerant preachers such as James Davenport (Document 4.8) led to a backlash from Old Light ministers and their congregations. The following selections reflect the competing religious views of the Old Lights and the New Lights. As you read, consider the issues at stake in the Great Awakening. Why was the conversion experience espoused by New Lights embraced by some but rejected by others? How do these documents reveal the religious, social, and economic tensions that were a part of eighteenth-century colonial society?

DOCUMENT 4.6

George Whitefield | Marks of a True Conversion, 1739

When George Whitefield was first ordained as a minister in the Anglican Church, he began open-air preaching in parks and fields to reach those who did not regularly attend church. Whitefield used dramatic gestures, a commanding speaking voice, and personal charisma to inspire an emotional response from his audiences. In 1738 he brought his revivals to the American colonies, attracting audiences by the tens of thousands. "Marks of a True Conversion," excerpted here, was one of his most famous sermons.

If a person is what the world calls an honest moral man, if he does justly, and, what the world calls, loves a little mercy, is now and then good-natured, reacheth out his hand to the poor, receives the sacrament once or twice a year, and is outwardly sober and honest; the world looks upon such a one as a Christian indeed, and doubtless we are to judge charitably of every such person. There are many likewise who go on in a round of duties, a model of performances, that think they shall go to heaven; but if you examine them, though they have a Christ in their heads, they have no Christ in their hearts.

The Lord Jesus Christ knew this full well; he knew how desperately wicked and deceitful men's hearts were; he knew very well how many would go to hell even by the very gates of heaven, how many would climb up even to the door, and go so near as to knock at it, and yet after all be dismissed with a "Verily, I know thee not." The Lord, therefore, plainly tells us, what great change must be wrought in us, and what must be done for us, before we can have any well-grounded hopes of entering into the kingdom of heaven. Hence, he tells Nicodemus, "that unless a man be born again, and from above, and unless a man be born of water and of the Spirit, he cannot enter into the kingdom of God." And of all the solemn declarations of our Lord, I mean with respect to this, perhaps, the words of the text are one of the most solemn, "Except, (says Christ) ye be converted, and become as little children, ye shall not enter into the kingdom of heaven." The words, if you look back to the context, are plainly directed to the disciples; for we are told, "that at the same time came the disciples unto Jesus." And I think it is plain from many parts of scripture, that these disciples, to whom our Lord addressed himself at this time, were in some degree converted before. If we take the words strictly, they are applicable only to those, that have already gotten some, though but weak, faith in Christ. Our Lord means, that though they had already tasted the grace of God, yet there was so much of the old man, so much indwelling sin, and corruption, yet remaining in their hearts, that unless they were more converted than they were, unless a greater change past upon their souls, and sanctification was still carried on, they could give but very little evidence of their belonging to his kingdom, which was not to be set up in outward grandeur, as they supposed, but was to be a spiritual kingdom, begun here, but completed in the kingdom of God hereafter.

Source: George Whitefield, *Sermons on Important Subjects* (London: Henry Fisher, Son, and P. Jackson, 1832), 269.

DOCUMENT 4.7

Gilbert Tennent | The Danger of an Unconverted Ministry, 1739

Gilbert Tennent, one of the most important New Light ministers of the Great Awakening, underwent a religious conversion at the age of twenty. Tennent became convinced that all true believers—especially ministers—needed to undergo the same type of conversion experience. His attacks on the intellectualism of Old Light ministers, highlighted in his famous sermon "The Danger of an Unconverted Ministry," contributed to the division of the Presbyterian Church into the Old Lights and the New Lights. Tennent eventually tried to heal this divide and helped to reunite the New York and Philadelphia synods in 1758.

And let gracious Souls be exhorted, to express the most tender Pity over such as have none but Pharisee-Teachers; and that in the Manner before described: To which let the Example of our LORD in the Text before us, be an inducing and effectual Incitement; as well as the gracious and immense Rewards, which follow upon so generous and noble a Charity, in this and the next State.

And let those who live under the Ministry of dead Men, whether they have got the Form of Religion or not, repair to the Living, where they may be edified. Let who will, oppose it. What famous Mr. Jenner observes upon this Head, is most just, "That if there be any godly Souls, or any that desires the Salvation of his Soul, and lives under a blind Guide, he cannot go out (of his Parish) without giving very great Offence; it will be tho't a Giddiness, and a Slighting of his own Minister at home. When People came out of every Parish round about, to John [The Baptist], no Question but this bred Heart-burning against John, ay, and Ill-will against those People, that would not be satisfied with that Teaching they had in their own Synagogues." . . . But tho' your Neighbors growl against you, and reproach you for doing your Duty, in seeking your Souls Good; bear their unjust Censures with Christian Meekness, and persevere; as knowing that Suffering is the Lot of Christ's Followers, and that spiritual Benefits do infinitely overbalance all temporal Difficulties.

And O! that vacant Congregations would take due Care in the Choice of their Ministers! Here indeed they should hasten slowly. The Church of Ephesus . . . is commended, for Trying them which said they were Apostles, and were not; and for finding them Liars. Hypocrits are against all Knowing of others, and Judging, in order to hide their own Filthiness; like Thieves they flee a Search, because of their stolen Goods. But the more they endeavour to hide, the more they expose their Shame.

Source: Gilbert Tennent, *The Danger of an Unconverted Ministry Considered in a Sermon on Mark VI. 34* (Philadelphia: Benjamin Franklin, 1740).

DOCUMENT 4.8
Newspaper Report on James Davenport, 1743

James Davenport, whose popular sermons denounced Old Light clergy as corrupt and worldly, was one of the more controversial New Light ministers. Throughout the early 1740s, his behavior became increasingly erratic, culminating in a public book burning in New London, Connecticut, in 1743. After leading his audience in the burning of what he termed "immoral books," Davenport then urged them to throw luxury items and clothing into the fire. In the excitement of the event, Davenport even took off his own pants and threw them into the fire. His actions, and the ensuing controversy, caused even New Light ministers to turn against Davenport, and by 1744 he issued a public apology for his extreme behavior. The following selection from a Boston newspaper describes the incident in New London.

Multitudes hasten'd toward the Place of Rendezvous, directing themselves by the Clamor and Shouting, which together, with the ascending Smoak [smoke] bro't them to one of the most public Places in the Town, and there found these good People encompassing a Fire which they had built up in the Street, into which they were casting Numbers of Books, principally on Divinity, and those that were well-approved by Protestant Divines, viz. . . . Mr. Russel's Seven Sermons, one of Dr. Colman's, and one of Dr. Chauncy's Books, and many others. Nothing can be more astonishing than their insolent Behaviour was during the Time of their Sacrifice, as 'tis said they call'd it; whilst the Books were in the Flames they cry'd out, *Thus the Souls of the Authors of those Books, those of them that are dad [dead], are roasting in the Flames of Hell;* and that *the Fate of those surviving, would be the same, unless speedy Repentance prevented*: On the next Day they had at the same Place a second Bonfire of the like Materials, and manag'd in the same manner. Having given this fatal Stroke to Heresy, they made ready to attack Idolatry, and sought for Direction, as in the Case before; and then Mr. [Davenport] told them to look at Home first, and that they themselves were guilty of idolizing their Apparel, and should therefore divest themselves of those Things especially which were for Ornament, and let them be burnt: Some of them in the heighth of their Zeal, conferred not with Flesh and Blood, but fell to stripping and cast their Cloaths [clothes] down at their Apostle's Feet; one or two hesitated about the Matter, and were so bold as to tell him they had nothing on which they idoliz'd: He reply'd, that such and such a Thing was an Offence to him; and they must down with them. One of these being a Gentleman of Learning and Parts ventur'd to tell Mr. [Davenport], that he could scarce see how his disliking the Night-Gown that he had on his Back, should render him guilty of Idolatry. However, This carnal Reasoning avail'd nothing; strip he must, and strip he did. . . . Next Mr. [Davenport] pray'd himself; and now the Oracle spake clear to the Point, without Ambiguity, and utter'd that *the Things must be burnt*; and to confirm the Truth of the Revelation, took his wearing Breeches, and hove them with Violence into the Pile, saying, *Go you with the Rest.*

Source: "Religious Excess at New London," *The Boston Weekly Post-Boy,* March 28, 1743, in *The Great Awakening: Documents on the Revival of Religion, 1740–1745*, ed. Richard L. Bushman (New York: Institute of Early American History and Culture, 1970), 51–52.

DOCUMENT 4.9

Charles Chauncy | Letter to Scottish Minister George Wishart, 1742

As the Great Awakening gained strength, it was increasingly attacked by Old Light ministers. The leader of the Old Lights was Charles Chauncy, a Harvard-educated minister who led the First Church of Boston for more than sixty years. Chauncy detested the emotionalism of the Great Awakening, preferring instead a rationalist and intellectual approach to faith. The following selection is from a letter he wrote to a Scottish minister describing George Whitefield's reception in the colonies.

The minds of people in this part of the world had been greatly prepossessed in favor of Mr. Whitefield, from the accounts transmitted of him, from time to time, as a wonder of piety, a man of God, so as no one was like him. Accordingly, when he came to town, about two years since, he was received as though he had been an angel of God; yea, a god come down in the likeness of man. He was strangely flocked after by all sorts of persons, and much admired by the vulgar, both great and small. The ministers had him in veneration, at least in appearance, as much as the people; encouraged his preaching, attended it themselves every day in the week, and mostly twice a day. The grand subject of conversation was Mr. Whitefield, and the whole business of the town to run from place to place to hear him preach. And as he preached under such uncommon advantages, being high in the opinion of the people and having the body of the ministers hanging on his lips, he soon insinuated himself still further into the affections of multitudes, insomuch that it became dangerous to mention his name without saying something in commendation of him. . . .

I deny not but there might be here and there a person stopped from going on in a course of sin; and some might be made really better. But so far as I could judge upon the nicest observation, the town, in general, was not much mended in those things wherein a reformation was greatly needed. I could not discern myself, nor many others whom I have talked with and challenged on this head, but that there was the same pride and vanity, the same luxury and intemperance, the same lying and tricking and cheating as before this gentleman came among us.

There was certainly no remarkable difference as to these things, and 'tis vain in any to pretend there was. This I am sure of, there was raised such a spirit of bitter, censorious, uncharitable judging as was not known before; and is, wherever it reigns, a scandal to all who call themselves Christians. Nor was it ever evident to me but that the greatest friends to Mr. Whitefield were as much puffed up with conceit and pride as any of their neighbors; and as to some of them, and the more eminent too, I verily believe they possess a worse spirit than before they heard of his name, and it had been as well for them if they had never seen his face.

Source: "A Letter from a Gentleman in Boston to Mr. George Wishart," in *The Clarendon Historical Society's Reprints*, Series 1 (Edinburgh: Clarendon Historical Society, 1883), 5–7.

DOCUMENT 4.10

Dr. Squintum's Exaltation or the Reformation, 1763

The engraving shown here satirizes George Whitefield and his followers, with the title highlighting an eye disease that left Whitefield cross-eyed. The image shows an imp and "Fame" hovering on either side of Whitefield's head, while the Devil rakes in money below his podium. On the left, Whitefield's followers are seen with a prostitute, while other followers are shown shoving a mother and child and taking food from a poor woman.

Library of Congress

Interpret the Evidence

1. How do these documents reflect debates over emotionalism and intellectualism in religious life?
2. What are Tennent's accusations against Old Light ministers in his sermon "The Danger of an Unconverted Ministry" (Document 4.7)?
3. What aspects of the Great Awakening did Old Light ministers find threatening?
4. How do Chauncy's letter (Document 4.9) and the engraving of Dr. Squintum (Document 4.10) criticize Whitefield? How are his followers portrayed?
5. Why did James Davenport (Document 4.8) encourage his followers to burn religious books by traditional ministers like Chauncy, and how did the Boston newspaper respond to the resulting bonfires?

Put It in Context

● How do these documents help explain the appeal of the Great Awakening to American colonists, particularly non-elites? What legacies—ideas or practices—remained after the revivals ended?

background photo: page 124, Private Collection/Peter Newark American Pictures/The Bridgeman Art Library

Private Collection/Phillips, Fine Art Auctioneers, New York, USA/The Bridgeman Art Library

The Granger Collection, New York

The death of General James Wolfe, commander of British forces against the French at Quebec in 1759.

Paul Revere's engraving of British troops in Boston Harbor, 1774.

5
Wars and Empires
1750–1774

Sketch of Boston Tea Party, 1773.

The Granger Collection, New York

AMERICAN HISTORIES

Although best known as the founding father of the United States, George Washington grew to adulthood as a loyal British subject. He was born in 1732 to a prosperous farm family in eastern Virginia. When George's father died in 1743, he became the ward of his half-brother Lawrence and moved to Lawrence's Mount Vernon estate. Lawrence's father-in-law, William Fairfax, was an agent for Lord Fairfax, one of the chief proprietors of the colony. When George was sixteen, William hired him as an assistant to a party surveying Lord Fairfax's land on Virginia's western frontier.

Although less well educated and less well positioned than the sons of Virginia's largest planters, George shared their ambitions. As a surveyor, he journeyed west, coming into contact with Indians, both friendly and hostile, as well as other colonists seeking land. George himself began investing in western properties. But when Lawrence Washington died in 1752, twenty-year-old George suddenly became head of a large estate. He gradually expanded Mount Vernon's boundaries and increased its profitability, in part by adding to Mount Vernon's enslaved workforce. He now had the resources to speculate more heavily in western lands.

George was soon appointed an officer in the Virginia militia, and in the fall of 1753 Virginia's governor sent him to warn the French stationed near Lake Erie against encroaching on British territory in the Ohio River valley. The French commander rebuffed Washington and within six months gained control of a British post near present-day Pittsburgh, Pennsylvania, and named it Fort Duquesne. With help from Indians hostile to the French, Lieutenant Colonel Washington launched a surprise attack on Fort Duquesne in May 1754. The initial attack was successful and led the governors of Virginia and North Carolina to send in more troops under the command of the newly promoted Colonel Washington. The French then responded with a much larger force that repelled the British troops, and Washington was forced to surrender.

Colonel Washington gained valuable experience through both successful surveying expeditions and failed military ventures. As a landowner in Virginia and on the western frontier, he had also gained property to defend. Washington's fortunes and his family increased when he married the wealthy widow Martha Dandridge Custis in 1759 and became stepfather to her two children. An increasingly successful planter, Washington sought to extend Britain's North American empire westward as a way to create opportunities for an expanding population as well as a protective buffer against European and Indian foes.

Like Washington, Herman Husband hoped to improve his lot through hard work and the opportunities offered by the frontier. Born to a modest farm family in Maryland in 1724, he was swept up by the Great Awakening in the early 1740s. He became a New Light Presbyterian but later joined the Society of Friends, or Quakers. In 1754, as Washington headed to the Ohio valley, Husband explored prospects on the North Carolina frontier and decided to settle with his family at Sandy Creek.

Husband proved a successful farmer, but he denounced wealthy landowners and speculators who made it difficult for small farmers to obtain sufficient land. He also challenged established leaders in the Quaker meeting and was among a number of worshippers disowned from the Cane Creek Friends Meeting in 1764. Disputes within radical Protestant congregations were not unusual in this period as members with deep religious convictions chose the liberty of their individual conscience over church authority.

In 1766 a number of Quaker and Baptist farmers joined Husband in organizing the Sandy Creek Association. The group hoped to increase farmers' political clout as a way to combat corruption among local officials. The association disbanded after two years, but its ideas lived on in a group called the Regulation, which brought together frontier farmers who sought to "regulate" government abuse. Husband quickly emerged as one of the organization's chief spokesmen. The Regulators first tried to achieve reform through legal means. They petitioned the North Carolina Assembly and Royal Governor William Tryon, demanding legislative reforms and suing local officials for extorting labor, land, or money from poorer residents.

Husband wrote pamphlets articulating the demands of the Regulators and wielding religious principles to justify resistance to existing laws and customs. In certain ways, his ideas echoed those of colonial leaders like Governor Tryon, who had launched protests in 1765 against British efforts to impose taxes on the colonies. Tryon, however, viewed the Regulators as political foes who threatened the colony's peace and order. In 1768 he had Husband and other Regulators arrested, which confirmed the Regulators' belief that they could not receive fair treatment at the hands of colonial officials. They then turned to extralegal methods to assert their rights, such as taking over courthouses so that legal proceedings against debt-ridden farmers could not proceed. This led the Regulators into open conflict with colonial officials. •

THE AMERICAN HISTORIES of Washington and Husband were shaped by both opportunities and conflicts. Mid-eighteenth-century colonial America offered greater opportunities for social advancement and personal expression than anywhere in Europe, but the efforts of individuals to take advantage of these opportunities often led to tension and discord. The conflicts on the frontiers of Virginia, Pennsylvania, and North Carolina foreshadowed a broader struggle for land and power within the American colonies. Religious and economic as well as political discord intensified in the mid-eighteenth century as conflicts within the colonies increasingly occurred alongside challenges to

British authority. Individual men and women made difficult choices about where their loyalties lay. Whatever their grievances, most worked hard to reform systems they considered unfair or abusive before resorting to more radical means of instituting change. Some, such as Washington, became revered leaders. Others, like Husband, gained local support but were viewed by those in authority as extremists who threatened to subvert the religious, economic, and political order.

A War for Empire, 1754–1763

The war that erupted in the Ohio valley in 1754 sparked an enormous shift in political and economic relations in colonial North America. What began as a small-scale, regional conflict expanded into a brutal and lengthy global war. Known as the French and Indian War in North America and the Seven Years' War in Great Britain and Europe, the conflict led to a dramatic expansion of British territory in North America, but also to increasing demands from American colonists for more control over their own lives.

The Opening Battles

Even before Washington and his troops were defeated in July 1754, the British sought to protect the colonies against threats from the French and the Indians. To limit such threats, the British were especially interested in cementing an alliance with the powerful Iroquois Confederacy, composed of six northeastern tribes. Thus the British invited an official delegation from the Iroquois to a meeting in June 1754 in Albany, New York, with representatives from the New England colonies, New York, Pennsylvania, and Maryland. Benjamin Franklin of Philadelphia had drawn up a Plan of Union that would establish a council of representatives from the various colonial assemblies to debate issues of frontier defense, trade, and territorial expansion and to recommend terms mutually agreeable to colonists and Indians. Their deliberations were to be overseen by a president-general appointed and supported by the British crown.

The **Albany Congress** created new bonds among a small circle of colonial leaders, but it failed to establish a firmer alliance with the Iroquois or resolve problems of colonial governance. The British government worried that the proposed council would prove too powerful, undermining the authority of the royal government. At the same time, the individual colonies were unwilling to give up any of their autonomy in military, trade, and political matters to some centralized body. Moreover, excluded from Franklin's Plan of Union, the Iroquois delegates at the Albany Congress broke off talks with the British in early July. The Iroquois became more suspicious and resentful when colonial land agents and fur traders used the Albany meeting as an opportunity to make side deals with individual Indian leaders.

Yet if war was going to erupt between the British and the French, the Iroquois and other Indian tribes could not afford to have the outcome decided by imperial powers alone. For most Indians, contests among European nations for land and power offered them the best chance of survival in the eighteenth century. They gained leverage as long as various imperial powers needed their trade items, military support, and political alliances. This leverage would be far more limited if one European nation controlled most of North America.

The various Indian tribes adopted different strategies. The Delaware, Huron, Miami, and Shawnee nations, for example, allied themselves with the French, hoping that a French victory would stop the far more numerous British colonists from invading their settlements in the Ohio valley.

Join, or Die
Benjamin Franklin created the first political cartoon in American history to accompany an editorial he wrote in the *Pennsylvania Gazette* in 1754. Franklin's cartoon urged the mainland British colonies to unite politically during the French and Indian War. Legend had it that a snake could come back to life if its severed sections were attached before dusk.   Library of Congress

Members of the Iroquois Confederacy, on the other hand, tried to play one power against the other, hoping to win concessions from the British in return for their military support. The Creek, Choctaw, and Cherokee nations also sought to perpetuate the existing stalemate among European powers by bargaining alternately with the British in Georgia and the Carolinas, the French in Louisiana, and the Spaniards in Florida.

Faced with incursions into their lands, some Indian tribes launched preemptive attacks on colonial settlements. Along the northern border of Massachusetts, for example, in present-day New Hampshire, Abenaki Indians attacked British settlements in August 1754, taking settlers captive and marching them north to Canada. There they traded them to the French, who later held the colonists for ransom or exchanged them for their own prisoners of war with the British.

Colonel George Washington

This 1772 oil painting by Charles Willson Peale portrays George Washington as a colonel in the Virginia militia. Washington commanded this militia during the French and Indian War following the death of General Braddock. After the war, Washington prospered as a planter and land speculator.   The Granger Collection, New York

The British government soon decided it had to send additional troops to defend its American colonies against attacks from Indians and intrusions from the French. General Edward Braddock and two regiments arrived in 1755 to expel the French from Fort Duquesne. At the same time, colonial militia units were sent to battle the French and their Indian allies along the New York and New England frontiers. Colonel Washington joined Braddock as his personal aide-de-camp. Within months, however, Braddock's forces were ambushed, bludgeoned by French and Indian forces, and Braddock was killed. Washington was appointed commander of the Virginia troops, but with limited forces and meager financial support from the Virginia legislature, he had little hope of victory.

Other British forces fared little better during the next three years. Despite having far fewer colonists in North America than the British, the French had established extensive trade networks that helped them sustain a protracted war with support from numerous Indian nations. They also benefited from the help of European and Canadian soldiers as well as Irish conscripts who happily fought their British conquerors. Alternating guerrilla tactics with conventional warfare, the French captured several important forts, built a new one on Lake Champlain, and moved troops deep into British territory. The ineffectiveness of the British and colonial armies also encouraged Indian tribes along the New England and Appalachian frontiers to reclaim land from colonists. Bloody raids devastated many outlying settlements, leading to the death and capture of hundreds of Britain's colonial subjects.

A Shift to Global War

As the British faced defeat after defeat in North America, European nations began to contest imperial claims elsewhere in the world. In 1756 France and Great Britain officially declared war against each other. Eventually Austria, Russia, Sweden, most of the German states, and Spain allied with France, while Portugal and Prussia sided with Great Britain. Naval warfare erupted in the Mediterranean Sea and the Atlantic and Indian Oceans. Battles were also fought in Europe, the West Indies, India, and the Philippines. By the end of 1757, Britain and its allies had been defeated in nearly every part of the globe. The war appeared to be nearing its end, with France in control.

Then in the summer of 1757, William Pitt took charge of the British war effort and transformed the political and military landscape. A man of formidable talents and grand vision, Pitt redirected British efforts toward victory in North America, while Prussian forces held the line in Europe. Pouring more soldiers and arms into the North

American campaign along with young and ambitious officers, Pitt energized colonial and British troops.

By the summer of 1758, the tide began to turn. In July, British generals recaptured the fort at Louisbourg on Cape Breton Island, a key to France's defense of Canada. Then British troops with George Washington's aid seized Fort Duquesne, which was renamed Pittsburgh. Other British forces captured Fort Frontenac along the St. Lawrence River, while Prussia defeated French, Austrian, and Russian forces in Europe and Britain gained key victories in India (Map 5.1). In 1759 General Jeffrey Amherst captured Forts Ticonderoga and Crown Point on Lake Champlain. Then General James Wolfe, with only four thousand men, attacked a much larger French force in Quebec. Despite heavy casualties, including Wolfe himself, the British won Quebec and control of Canada.

The Costs of Victory

Despite Wolfe's dramatic victory, the war dragged on in North America, Europe, India, and the West Indies for three more years. By then, however, King George III had tired of Pitt's grand, and expensive, strategy and dismissed him. He then opened peace negotiations with France and agreed to give up a number of conquered territories in order to finalize the **Peace of Paris** in 1763. Other countries

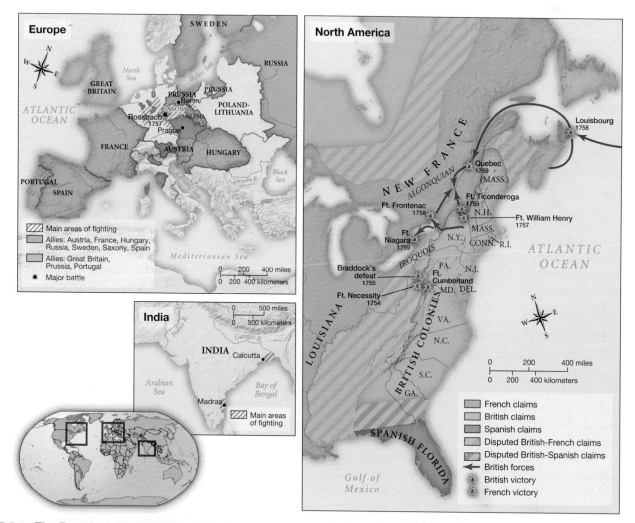

MAP 5.1 The French and Indian War, 1754–1763

Clashes between colonial militia units and French and Indian forces erupted in North America in 1754. The conflict helped launch a wider war that engulfed Europe as well as the West Indies and India. In the aftermath of this first global war, Britain gained control of present-day Canada and India, but France retained its West Indies colonies.

were ready to negotiate as well. To regain control of Cuba and the Philippines, Spain ceded Florida to Great Britain. Meanwhile France rewarded Spain for its support by granting it Louisiana and all French lands west of the Mississippi River. Despite these concessions, the British empire reigned supreme, regaining control of India as well as North America east of the Mississippi, all of Canada, and a number of Caribbean islands.

The wars that erupted between 1754 and 1763 reshaped European empires, transformed patterns of global trade, and initially seemed to tighten bonds between North American residents and the mother country. English colonists in North America as well as their Scottish, Irish, German, and Dutch neighbors celebrated the British victory. Yet the Peace of Paris did not resolve many of the problems that had plagued the colonies before the war, and it created new ones as well.

The incredible cost of the war raised particularly difficult problems. Over the course of the war, the national debt of Great Britain had more than doubled. At the same time, as the North American colonies grew and conflicts erupted along their frontiers, the costs of administering these colonies increased fivefold. With an empire that stretched around the globe, the British crown and Parliament were forced to consider how to pay off war debts, raise funds to administer old and new territories, and keep sufficient currency in circulation for expanding international trade. Just as important, the Peace of Paris ignored the claims of the Iroquois, Shawnee, Creek, and other Indian tribes to the territories that France and Spain turned over to Great Britain. Nor did the treaty settle contested claims among the colonies themselves over lands in the Ohio valley and elsewhere along British North America's new frontiers.

Battles and Boundaries on the Frontier

The sweeping character of the British victory encouraged thousands of colonists to move farther west, into lands once controlled by France. This exacerbated tensions on the southern and western frontiers of British North America, tensions that escalated in the final years of the war and continued long after the Peace of Paris was signed.

In late 1759, for example, the Cherokee nation, reacting to repeated incursions on their hunting grounds, dissolved their long-term trade agreement with South Carolina. Cherokee warriors attacked backcountry farms and homes, leading to counterattacks by British troops. The fighting continued into 1761, when Cherokees on the Virginia frontier launched raids on colonists there. General Jeffrey Amherst then sent 2,800 troops to invade Cherokee territory and end the conflict. The soldiers sacked fifteen villages; killed men, women, and children; and burned acres of fields.

Although British raids diminished the Cherokees' ability to mount a substantial attack, sporadic assaults on frontier settlements continued for years. These conflicts fueled resentments among backcountry settlers against political leaders in more settled regions of the colonies who rarely provided sufficient funds or soldiers for frontier defense. The raids also intensified hostility toward Indians.

A more serious conflict erupted in the Ohio valley when Indians there realized the consequences of Britain's victory in Quebec. As the British took over French forts along the Great Lakes and in the Ohio valley in 1760, they immediately antagonized local Indian groups by hunting and fishing on tribal lands and depriving villages of much-needed food. British traders also defrauded Indians on numerous occasions and ignored traditional obligations of gift giving. They refused to provide kettles, gunpowder, or weapons to the Indians and thereby caused near starvation among many tribes that depended on hunting and trade.

The harsh realities of the British regime led some Indians to seek a return to ways of life that preceded the arrival of white men. An Indian visionary named Neolin, known to the British as the Delaware Prophet, preached that Indians had been corrupted by contact with Europeans and urged them to purify themselves by returning to their ancient traditions, abandoning white ways, and reclaiming their lands. Neolin was a prophet, not a warrior, but his message inspired others, including an Ottawa leader named Pontiac.

When news arrived in early 1763 that France was about to cede all of its North American lands to Britain and Spain, Pontiac convened a council of more than four hundred Ottawa, Potawatomi, and Huron leaders near Fort Detroit. Drawing on Neolin's vision, he mobilized support to drive out the British. In May 1763, Pontiac's forces laid siege to Detroit and soon gained the support of eighteen Indian nations. They then attacked Fort Pitt and other British frontier outposts and attacked white settlements along the Virginia and Pennsylvania frontier.

> **Explore**
>
> Read part of Pontiac's speech to a council of Indian tribes in Document 5.1.

Accounts of violent encounters with Indians on the frontier circulated throughout the colonies and sparked resentment among local colonists as well as British troops. Many colonists did not bother to distinguish between friendly and hostile Indians, and General Amherst claimed that all Indians deserved extermination "for the good of

DOCUMENT 5.1

Pontiac | Speech to Ottawa, Potawatomi, and Huron Leaders, 1763

Following Great Britain's victory in the French and Indian War, many American Indian leaders grew discontented with British settlements in the former French territories. In the Great Lakes region, this dissatisfaction turned to open rebellion when Pontiac, an Ottawa leader, convened a council of local tribes who then laid siege to Fort Detroit. Pontiac's speech at that council is excerpted here. Though the siege was ultimately unsuccessful, Pontiac's uprising soon spread beyond the Detroit region and lasted until the summer of 1766, when the British negotiated a peace with Pontiac and other Indian leaders.

Explore

It is important, my brothers, that we should exterminate from our land this nation, whose only object is our death. You must be all sensible, as well as myself, that we can no longer supply our wants in the way we were accustomed to do with our Fathers the French. They [the English] sell us their goods at double the price that the French made us pay, and yet their merchandise is good for nothing; for no sooner have we bought a blanket or other thing to cover us than it is necessary to procure others against the time of departing for our wintering ground. Neither will they let us have them on credit, as our brothers the French used to do. When I visit the English chief, and inform him of the death of any of our comrades, instead of lamenting, as our brothers the French used to do, they make game of us. If I ask him for any thing for our sick, he refuses, and tells us he does not want us, from which it is apparent he seeks our death. We must therefore, in return, destroy them without delay; there is nothing to prevent us: there are but few of them, and we shall easily overcome them—why should we not attack them? Are we not men? Have I not shown you the belts [beaded belts symbolizing a treaty] I received from our Great Father the King of France? He tells us to strike—why should we not listen to his words? What do you fear? The time has arrived.

Source: Francis Parkman, *The Conspiracy of Pontiac and the Indian Wars after the Conquest of Canada* (Boston: Little, Brown, 1884), 330.

Interpret the Evidence

- How would you explain Chief Pontiac's decision to emphasize the differences between the French and the British?
- What action against the British does he advocate, and why?

Put It in Context

How does Pontiac's speech reflect larger tensions between British officials and colonists and various Indian nations?

---

mankind." A group of men from Paxton Creek, Pennsylvania, agreed. In December 1763, they raided families of peaceful, Christian Conestoga Indians near Lancaster, killing thirty. Protests from eastern colonists infuriated the Paxton Boys, who then marched on Philadelphia demanding protection from "savages" on the frontier.

Although violence on the frontier slowly subsided, neither side had achieved victory. Without French support, Pontiac and his followers ran out of guns and ammunition and had to retreat. About the same time, Benjamin Franklin negotiated a truce between the Paxton Boys and the Pennsylvania authorities, but it did not settle the

fundamental issues over protection of western settlers. These conflicts convinced the British that the government could not endure further costly frontier clashes. So in October 1763, the crown issued a proclamation forbidding colonial settlement west of a line running down the Appalachian Mountains to create a buffer between Indians and colonists (Map 5.2).

The **Proclamation Line of 1763** denied colonists the right to settle west of the Appalachian Mountains. Instituted just months after the Peace of Paris was signed, the Proclamation Line frustrated colonists who sought the economic benefits won by a long and bloody war. Small

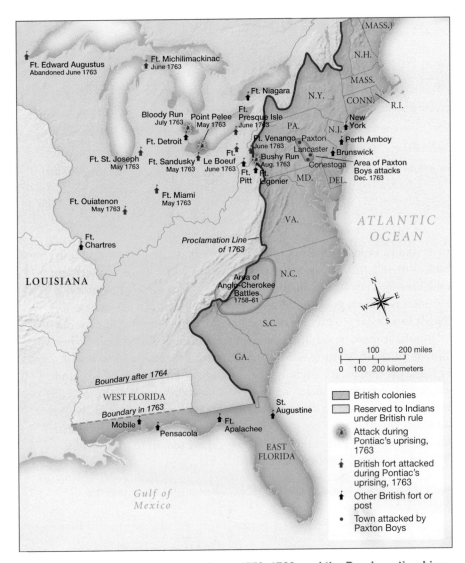

MAP 5.2 British Conflicts with Indians, 1758–1763, and the Proclamation Line
The entrance of British troops into former French territory in the Ohio River valley following the French and Indian War fueled conflicts with Indian nations. Colonists in Pennsylvania and the Carolinas also battled with Indians, including tribes who were allies or remained neutral during the war. Parliament established the Proclamation Line to limit westward expansion and thereby diminish such hostilities.

before the war, and these struggles continued into the 1760s. New clashes also occurred in the Carolinas as pioneer settlers like Herman Husband clashed with landlords and speculators there.

Even before the French and Indian War ended, the owners of large estates along the Hudson River in New York State raised rents and reduced the rights of tenants. These enormous estates had been granted in two periods. In 1629 the Dutch government established a patroon system by which men who provided fifty adult settlers to New Amsterdam were granted vast estates. Then in the early 1680s, the newly installed English governor Thomas Dongan granted lands to a select group of Englishmen. Some of these estates encompassed nearly 400 square miles, far larger than the island of Manhattan. In the early eighteenth century, the titles to some of these estates were challenged by small landowners and tenants, but even where legitimate titles existed, tenants declared a moral right to own the land they had long farmed. The manors and estates of the Hudson valley, they claimed, were more appropriate to a feudal government than to an enlightened empire.

Farmers in neighboring New Hampshire were drawn into battles over land when the king's Privy Council in London decided in 1764 that the Green Mountains belonged to New York rather than New Hampshire. Landlords along the Hudson River hoped to expand eastward into this region, but the farmers already living there claimed they had bought the land in good faith and deserved to keep it.

Following the Privy Council's decision, groups of farmers in New Hampshire waged guerrilla warfare against New York authorities, large landowners, and New York farmers who now claimed land that others had already cleared and settled. These Green Mountain Boys,

farmers, backcountry settlers, and squatters had hoped to improve their lot by acquiring rich farmlands, and wealthy land speculators like Washington had staked claims to property no longer threatened by the French or their Indian allies. Now both groups were told to stay put.

Conflicts over Land and Labor Escalate

Conflicts among colonists and with Britain were not confined to frontier regions. Land riots directed against the leasing policies of landlords and the greed of speculators had plagued New York's Hudson valley and New Jersey

Catamount Tavern

This nineteenth-century photograph shows the Catamount Tavern, located in present-day Bennington, Vermont. Here Ethan Allen founded the Green Mountain Boys and used the tavern as a meeting place. After British authorities ruled that the Green Mountains belonged to New York rather than New Hampshire, Allen and his troops battled outsiders seeking land, a struggle that lasted through the American Revolution. Courtesy, Vermont Historical Society

led by Ethan Allen, refused to recognize New York authorities as legitimate in the region and established their own local governments and popular courts.

Inspired by the Green Mountain Boys and earlier uprisings in New Jersey, tenants in the Hudson valley banded together in 1765–1766. Under the leadership of William Prendergast, a group of tenants calling themselves Levellers refused to pay rent and instead claimed freehold title to the land they farmed. New York tenants petitioned the colonial assembly and sought redress in a variety of ways. But landowners refused to negotiate, and Prendergast concluded that "there was no law for poor men."

In many ways, the beliefs of Allen, Prendergast, and their followers echoed those of Herman Husband and the North Carolina **Regulators**. All of these groups developed visible, well-organized networks of supporters, targeted specific landlords, sought redress first through colonial courts and assemblies, and then established popular militias and other institutions to govern themselves and to challenge those in authority. These challenges included attacks on property: Burning barns, attacking livestock, and pulling down fences were common practices among irate farmers.

Conflicts in North Carolina escalated when the colonial assembly, dominated by the eastern slaveholding elite, passed a measure to build a stately mansion for Governor Tryon with public funds. Outraged frontier farmers, many already in debt and paying high taxes, withheld their taxes, took over courthouses, and harassed corrupt local officials. By the spring of 1771, faced with what he viewed as open rebellion on his western frontier, Governor Tryon recruited a thousand militiamen to

confront the Regulators. In May, armed conflict erupted. The Regulators were defeated, and half a dozen leaders were publicly hanged. Herman Husband managed to escape and headed to the Pennsylvania frontier to establish a new homestead for his family. There, too, he met frontier farmers angered by their lack of political representation, economic opportunity, and protection from Indians.

REVIEW & RELATE

How did the French and Indian War and the subsequent peace treaty affect relations between Britain and its North American subjects?

How did the French and Indian War and the increasing power of large landowners contribute to conflict between average colonists and colonial elites?

LEARNINGCurve bedfordstmartins.com/hewittlawson/LC

Postwar British Policies and Colonial Unity

Throughout the 1750s and 1760s, ordinary colonists challenged the authority of economic and political elites to impose their will on local communities and individual residents. Before and during the French and Indian War, most of these challenges involved conflicts among colonists themselves. Yet in the decade following the war, from

1764 to 1774, common grievances against Britain united colonists on the frontier and along the eastern seaboard, allowing them to launch effective protests against the British government. British policies, like the Proclamation Line of 1763, inspired widespread dissent as poor farmers, large landowners, and speculators sought to expand westward. A second policy, impressment, by which the Royal Navy forced young colonial men into military service, also aroused anger across regions and classes. At the same time, the Great Awakening, for all the upheaval it had engendered, provided colonists with shared ideas about moral principles and new techniques for mass communication. Finally, Britain's efforts to repay its war debts by taxing colonists and its plan to continue quartering troops in North America led colonists to forge intercolonial protest movements.

Common Grievances

Like the Proclamation Line, which denied all colonists the right to settle beyond the Appalachian Mountains,

the policy of impressment affected port city residents of all classes. British agents, desperate for seamen during the extended European wars of the eighteenth century, periodically impressed sailors and other poor men from British ports around the world, including seaboard cities in North America, and from merchant ships at sea. Impressment had been employed for decades by the time of the French and Indian War. Increasingly, however, merchants and other well-to-do American colonists joined common folk in demanding an end to this practice.

Seamen and dockworkers had good reason to fight off impressment agents. Men in the Royal Navy faced low wages, bad food, harsh punishment, rampant disease, and high mortality. As the practice escalated with each new war, the efforts of British naval officers and impressment agents to capture new "recruits" met violent resistance, especially in the North American colonies. At times, whole communities joined in the battle—relatives and friends, blacks and whites, women and men.

In 1757, in the midst of the French and Indian War, some 3,000 British soldiers cordoned off New York City

Impressment by the British
This eighteenth-century engraving depicts the harsh impressment of men into the British navy. Set in England, this illustration shows that impressment was widely practiced at home. Thus the British government did not single out colonists for special mistreatment.   © Mary Evans/The Image Works

and visited "the Taverns and other houses, where sailors usually resorted." According to printer Hugh Gaines, "All kinds of Tradesmen and Negroes" were hauled in by British press gangs. Local residents rioted along the docks the next day, but of the 800 men picked up the night before, some 400 were "retained in the service." With impressment robbing colonial seaports of much-needed laborers, some merchants and colonial officials began to petition Parliament for redress. But Parliament, seeing no reason why the British in America should avoid the fate of their counterparts in Great Britain, ignored the petitions.

In the aftermath of the French and Indian War, more serious impressment riots erupted in Boston, New York City, and Newport, Rhode Island. Increasingly, poor colonial seamen and dockworkers made common cause with owners of merchant ships and mercantile houses in protesting British policy. Colonial officials—mayors, governors, and custom agents—were caught in the middle. Some insisted on upholding the Royal Navy's right of impressment; others tried to placate both naval officers and local residents; and still others resisted what they saw as an oppressive imposition on the rights of colonists. Both those who resisted British authority and those who sought a compromise had to gain the support of the lower and middling classes to succeed.

Employers and politicians who opposed impressment gained an important advantage if they could direct the anger of colonists away from themselves and toward British officials and policies. The decision of British officials to continue quartering troops in the colonies gave local leaders another opportunity to join forces with ordinary colonists. Colonial towns and cities were required to quarter (that is, house and support) British troops even after the Peace of Paris was signed. While the troops were intended to protect the colonies against disgruntled Indians and French on their borders, they also provided reinforcements for impressment agents and surveillance over other illegal activities like smuggling and domestic manufacturing. Thus a range of issues and policies began to bind colonists together through common grievances against the British Parliament.

Forging Ties across the Colonies

The ties forged between poorer and wealthier colonists over issues of westward expansion, impressment, and quartering grew stronger in the 1760s, but they tended to be localized in seaport cities or in specific areas of the frontier. Creating bonds across the colonies required considerably more effort in a period when communication and transportation beyond local areas were limited. The Albany Congress of 1754 had been one of the first attempts to develop

intercolonial bonds, but it had not been very successful. Means had to be found to disseminate information and create a sense of common purpose if the colonists were going to persuade Parliament to take their complaints seriously. One important model for such intercolonial communication was the Great Awakening.

By the 1750s, the Great Awakening seemed to be marked more by dissension than by unity as new denominations continued to split from traditional churches. For example, in the Sandy Creek region of North Carolina, home to Herman Husband, radical Protestants formed the Separate Baptists (named for their separation from traditional Baptists) in order to proclaim a message of absolute spiritual equality. From the late 1750s through the 1770s, Separate Baptists converted thousands of small farmers, poor whites, and enslaved women and men and established churches throughout Virginia, Georgia, and the Carolinas.

Methodists, Dunkards, Moravians, and Quakers joined Separate Baptists in offering southern residents religious experiences that highlighted spiritual equality. Appealing to blacks and whites, women and men, they challenged the social order, especially in frontier regions that were beyond the reach of many established institutions. Some dissenting preachers invited slaves and free blacks to attend their services alongside local white farmers and laborers. Slaveholders and other elite southerners considered such practices outrageous and a challenge to the political as well as the social order.

Most women and men who converted to Separate Baptism, Methodism, or other forms of radical Protestantism did not link their religious conversion directly to politics. Those who did, including many Regulators, suggested that religion was a force for division rather than unity in the colonies. But as more and more ordinary colonists and colonial leaders voiced their anger at offensive British policies, evangelical techniques used to rouse the masses to salvation became important for mobilizing colonists to protest.

Thus even though the Great Awakening had spent its religious passion in most parts of North America by the 1760s, the techniques of mass communication and critiques of opulence and corruption it initiated provided emotional and practical ways of forging ties among widely dispersed colonists. Many evangelical preachers had condemned the lavish lifestyles of colonial elites and the spiritual corruption of local officials who failed to consider the needs of their less well-to-do neighbors. Now in the context of conflicts with Great Britain, colonial leaders could turn such rhetoric against new targets of resentment by painting Parliament and British officials as aristocrats with little faith and less compassion.

During the Great Awakening, preachers also honed techniques of popular appeal that proved useful in uniting colonists to voice opposition to British policies. The public sermons and mass rallies meant to inspire loyalty to a greater moral cause could all be translated into forms applicable to political protest. These techniques challenged established forms of authority, which certainly gave pause to some colonial leaders. Nonetheless, casting aside deference to king and Parliament was necessary if colonists were going to gain rights within the British empire that met the needs of elites and laborers alike. The efforts of Great Britain to assert greater control over its North American colonies provided colonial dissidents an opportunity to test out these new ways to forge intercolonial ties.

Great Britain Seeks Greater Control

Until the French and Indian War, British officials and their colonial subjects coexisted in relative harmony. Economic growth led Britain to ignore much of the smuggling and domestic manufacturing that took place in the colonies. Although the system of mercantilism (see chapter 3) assumed that the colonies supplied raw materials and the mother country manufactured goods, a bit of manufacturing for local needs did not significantly disrupt British industry. Similarly, although the king and Parliament held ultimate political sovereignty, or final authority, over the American colonies, it was easier to allow some local government control over decisions, given the communication challenges created by distance.

This pattern of **benign** (or "salutary") **neglect** led some American colonists to view themselves as more independent of British control than they really were. Impressment offers a good example. The Royal Navy had the right to impress men when needed, yet even in the midst of the French and Indian War, American colonists viewed impressment as an unwarranted infringement on their rights as British subjects. Many colonists had also begun to see smuggling, domestic manufacturing, and local self-governance as rights rather than privileges. Thus when British officials decided to assert greater control, many colonists protested.

To King George III and to Parliament, asserting control over the colonies was both right and necessary. In 1763 King George appointed George Grenville to lead the British government. As prime minister and chancellor of the Exchequer, Grenville faced an economic depression in England, rebellious farmers opposed to a new tax on domestic cider, and growing numbers of unemployed soldiers returning from the war. He believed that regaining political and economic control in the colonies abroad could help resolve these crises at home.

Eighteenth-century wars, especially the French and Indian War, cost a fortune. British subjects in England paid taxes to help offset the nation's debts, even though few of them benefited as directly from the British victory as did their counterparts in the American colonies. The colonies would cost the British treasury more if the crown could not control colonists' movement into Indian territories, limit smuggling and domestic manufacturing, and house British troops in the colonies cheaply. With more British troops and officials stationed in or visiting the colonies during the French and Indian War, they had greater opportunities to observe colonial life. Many of these observers voiced concern about the extent of criminality in the colonies and the rebellious spirit that existed among many servants, seamen, frontiersmen, tenants, and even women and slaves. Others feared that the religious enthusiasm of the Great Awakening had nurtured disdain for established authority among the colonists. Clearly it was time to impose a true imperial order.

To establish order, Parliament launched a three-prong program. First, it sought stricter enforcement of existing laws and established a Board of Trade to centralize policies and ensure their implementation. The **Navigation Acts**, which prohibited smuggling, established guidelines for legal commerce, and set duties on trade items, were the most important laws to be enforced. Second, Parliament extended wartime policies into peacetime. For example, the Quartering Act of 1765 ensured that British troops would remain in the colonies to enforce imperial policy. Colonial governments were expected to support them by allowing them to use vacant buildings and providing them with food and supplies.

The third part of Grenville's colonial program was the most important. It called for the passage of new laws to raise funds and reestablish the sovereignty of British rule. The first revenue act passed by Parliament was the American Duties Act of 1764, known as the **Sugar Act**. It imposed an **import duty**, or tax, on sugar, coffee, wines, and other luxury items. The act also reduced the import tax on foreign molasses but insisted that the duty be collected, a shock to the many colonial merchants and rum distillers who relied on cheap molasses smuggled in from the French and Spanish Caribbean. The crackdown on smuggling increased the power of customs officers and established the first vice-admiralty courts in North America to ensure that the Sugar Act raised money for the crown. That same year, Parliament passed the Currency Act, which prohibited colonial assemblies from printing paper money or bills of credit. Taken together, these provisions meant that colonists would pay more money into the British treasury even as the supply of money (and illegal goods) diminished in the colonies.

SAMUEL A. OTIS

Has juft imported, and is determined to fell at the loweft Advance, at Store No. 5. South Side of the Town-Dock, by Wholefale and Retail,

CHoice Jamaica Sugars by the Hogfhead, Barrel, or fingle C.wt.
Weft-India and New-England-Rum.
Cotton Wool
Pepper
Pipes   Wool Cards
Spices of all Kinds
Ruffia and Ravens Duck
Codlines
Junk
Frying Pans
Iron Pots and Kettles.
White Beans

3-4, ⅞ and yard wide Linnens
Irifh Linnens
Cotton Checks
Pins of all Numbers
Gun Powder
Ticklinburgs & Oznabrigs
Kilmarnock Caps
Belladine Sewing Silk
London Scythes
Seeming Twine——&c.
Cotton Cards
Roll Brimftone
Copperas
Allum

Beft Sperma Ceti Candles,

Warranted Pure,

MADE AND SOLD by JOHN LANGDON in Fleet-Street, above HANCOCK's Wharf, near the Old North Meeting Houfe. He alfo fells the beft Refin'd Sperma Ceti Oil by the Barrel. Beft Tallow Candles mould and dipp'd, and Bayberry Wax Candles. ALL as low as they can be had at any Place in Town.

To be Sold this Fall or next Spring.

A collection of an Hundred of the beft Sorts of young Grafted and Inoculated Englifh Fruit Trees—of Apples—Pears-Plumbs-- Cherries—Peaches—Apricots—Nectons—Quinces—Lime-Trees—Englifh Elms—and Mulberry Trees for Silk Worms—Grape Vines of all Sorts—Red and White Dutch Currant Bufhes—Englifh Goofeberry Bufhes of all Sorts—Afparagus Plants of the large Early Sort—and Box for Edgings of Walks—Alfo, Garlick—Shalots—and Horfe Radifh 5f. Old Tenor a Pound.—All forts of Dried Sweet Herbs.
N. B. Garden Seeds faved here moft fuitable for the Weft-Indies than any Imported, and warranted Good, &c. all at the very loweft Price for Cafh, &c.—By William Davidfon, Gardiner, in Seven-Star Lane, Bofton.

TO BE SOLD,

By Jofeph Dennie,

In Union-Street, opposite Mr. James Jackfon's,
BOHEA TEA by the Cheft or Hundred, Nutmegs, Pepper by the Bag or Hundred.

Boston Advertisements

Advertisements from the *Boston Gazette and Country Journal* show the array of consumer goods brought in to Boston Harbor. Among the items listed were rum, tea, and English cloth, all of which were subject to import duties and trade restrictions. As boycotts developed in the colonies, Bostonians would have to choose which of these items to continue buying. Courtesy of the Massachusetts Historical Society

---

Some colonial leaders protested the Sugar Act through speeches, pamphlets, and petitions, and Massachusetts established a **committee of correspondence** to circulate concerns to leaders in other colonies. However, dissent remained disorganized and ineffective. Nonetheless, the passage of the Sugar and Currency Acts caused anxiety among many colonists, which was heightened by passage of the Quartering Act the next year. Colonial responses to these developments marked the first steps in an escalating conflict between British officials and their colonial subjects.

REVIEW & RELATE

How did Britain's postwar policies lead to the emergence of unified colonial protests?

Why did British policymakers believe they were justified in seeking to gain greater control over Britain's North American colonies?

✔ *LEARNINGCurve* bedfordstmartins.com/hewittlawson/LC

Resistance to Britain Intensifies

Over the next decade, between 1764 and 1774, the British Parliament sought to extend its political and economic control over the American colonies, and the colonists periodically resisted. With each instance of resistance, Parliament demanded further submission to royal authority. With each demand for submission, colonists responded with greater assertions of their rights and autonomy. Yet no one—neither colonists nor British officials—could have imagined in 1764, or even in 1774, that a revolution was in the making.

The Stamp Act Inspires Coordinated Resistance

Grenville decided that his next step would be to impose a stamp tax on the colonies similar to that long used in England. The stamp tax required that a revenue stamp be affixed to all transactions involving paper items, from newspapers and contracts to playing cards and diplomas. Grenville announced his plans in 1764, a full year before Parliament enacted the **Stamp Act** in the spring of 1765. The tax was to be collected by colonists appointed for the purpose, and the money was to be spent within the colonies at the direction of Parliament for "defending, protecting and securing the colonies." To Grenville and a majority in Parliament, the Stamp Act seemed completely fair. After all,

Englishmen paid on average 26 shillings in tax annually, while Bostonians averaged just 1 shilling. Moreover, the act was purposely written to benefit the American colonies.

The colonists viewed it in a more threatening light. The Stamp Act differed from earlier parliamentary laws in three important ways. First, by the time of its passage, the colonies were experiencing rising unemployment, falling wages, and a downturn in trade. All of these developments were exacerbated by the Sugar, Currency, and Quartering Acts passed by Parliament the previous year. Indeed, in cities like Boston, British soldiers often competed with colonists for scarce jobs in order to supplement their low wages. Second, critics viewed the Stamp Act as an attempt to control the *internal* affairs of the colonies. It was not an indirect tax on trade, paid by importers and exporters, but a direct tax on daily business: getting a marriage certificate, selling land, and publishing or buying a newspaper or an almanac. Third, such a direct intervention in the economic affairs of the colonies unleashed the concerns of leading colonial officials, merchants, lawyers, shopkeepers, and ministers that Parliament was taxing colonists who had no representation in its debates and decisions. Their arguments resonated with ordinary women and men, who were affected far more by the stamp tax than by an import duty on sugar, molasses, or wine.

By announcing the Stamp Act a year before its passage, Grenville assured that colonists had plenty of time to organize their opposition. In New York City, Boston, and other cities, merchants, traders, and artisans formed groups dedicated to the repeal of the Stamp Act. Soon Sons of Liberty, Daughters of Liberty, Sons of Neptune, Vox Populi, and similar organizations emerged to challenge the imposition of the Stamp Act. Even before the act was implemented, angry mobs throughout the colonies attacked stamp distributors. Some were beaten, others tarred and feathered, and all were forced to take an oath never to sell stamps again.

Colonists lodged more formal protests with the British government as well. The Virginia House of Burgesses, led by Patrick Henry, acted first. It passed five resolutions, which it sent to Parliament, denouncing taxation without representation. The Virginia Resolves were reprinted in many colonial newspapers and repeated by orators to eager audiences in Massachusetts and elsewhere. At the same time, the Massachusetts House adopted a circular letter—a written protest circulated to the other colonial assemblies—calling for a congress to be held in New York City in October 1765 to consider the threat posed by the Stamp Act.

In the meantime, popular protests multiplied. The protests turned violent in Boston, where **Sons of Liberty** leaders like Samuel Adams organized mass demonstrations. Adams modeled his oratory on that of itinerant preachers,

but with a political twist. Sons of Liberty also spread anti-British sentiment through newspapers and handbills that they posted on trees and buildings throughout the city and in surrounding towns. At dawn on August 14, 1765, the Boston Sons of Liberty hung an effigy of stamp distributor Andrew Oliver on a tree and called for his resignation. A mock funeral procession, joined by farmers, artisans, apprentices, and the poor, marched to Boston Common. The crowd, led by twenty-seven-year-old Ebenezer Mackintosh—a shoemaker, a veteran of the French and Indian War, and a popular working-class leader—carried the fake corpse to the Boston stamp office and destroyed the building. Demonstrators saved pieces of lumber, "stamped" them, and set them on fire outside Oliver's house. Oliver, wisely, had already left town.

Oliver's brother-in-law, Lieutenant Governor Thomas Hutchinson, arrived at the scene and tried to quiet the crowd, but he only angered them further. They soon destroyed Oliver's stable house, coach, and carriage, which the crowd saw as signs of aristocratic opulence. Twelve days later, demonstrators attacked the homes of Judge William Story, customs officer Benjamin Hallowell, and Lieutenant Governor Hutchinson.

The battle against the Stamp Act unfolded across the colonies with riots, beatings, and resignations reported from Newport, Rhode Island, to New Brunswick, New Jersey, to Charles Town (later Charleston), South Carolina. In Charleston, slave trader and stamp agent Henry Laurens was attacked by white artisans who hanged him in effigy and then by white workers and finally by slaves who harassed him with chants of "Liberty! Liberty!!" On November 1, 1765, when the Stamp Act officially took effect, not a single stamp agent remained in his post in the colonies.

Protesters carefully chose their targets: stamp agents, sheriffs, judges, and colonial officials. Even when violence erupted, it remained focused, with most crowds destroying stamps and stamp offices first and then turning to the private property of Stamp Act supporters. These protests made a mockery of notions of deference toward British rule. But they also revealed growing autonomy on the part of middling- and working-class colonists who attacked men of wealth and power, sometimes choosing artisans rather than wealthier men as their leaders. However, this was not primarily a class conflict because many wealthier colonists made common cause with artisans, small farmers, and the poor. Indeed, colonial elites considered themselves the leaders, inspiring popular uprisings through the power of their political arguments and oratorical skills, although they refused to support actions they considered too radical. For example, when Levellers in the Hudson valley proclaimed themselves Sons of Liberty and sought assistance from

Stamp Act rebels in New York City, the merchants, judges, and large landowners who led the protests there refused to help them.

It was these more affluent protesters who dominated the Stamp Act Congress in New York City in October 1765, which brought together twenty-seven delegates from nine colonies. The delegates petitioned Parliament to repeal the Stamp Act, arguing that taxation without representation was tyranny and that such laws "have a manifest Tendency to subvert the Rights and Liberties of the Colonists." Delegates then urged colonists to boycott British goods and refuse to pay the stamp tax. Yet they still proclaimed their loyalty to king and country.

The question of representation became a mainstay of colonial protests. Whereas the British accepted the notion of "virtual representation," by which members of Parliament gave voice to the views of particular classes and interests, the North American colonies had developed a system of representation based on locality. According to colonial leaders, only members of Parliament elected by colonists could represent their interests.

Even as delegates at the Stamp Act Congress declared themselves disaffected but loyal British subjects, they participated in the process of developing a common identity in the American colonies. Christopher Gadsden of South Carolina expressed the feeling most directly. "We should stand upon the broad common ground of natural rights," he argued. "There should be no New England man, no New-Yorker, known on the continent, but all of us Americans."

Eventually the British Parliament was forced to respond to colonial protests and even more to rising complaints from English merchants and traders whose business had been damaged by the colonists' boycott. Parliament repealed the Stamp Act in March 1766, and King George III granted his approval a month later. When news reached the colonies in May, crowds celebrated in the streets, church bells rang, and fireworks and muskets saluted the victory. Colonists now looked forward to a new and better relationship between themselves and the British government.

From the colonists' perspective, the crisis triggered by the passage of the Stamp Act demonstrated the limits of parliamentary control. Colonists had organized effectively and forced Parliament to repeal the hated legislation. Protests had raged across the colonies and attracted support from a wide range of colonists, including young and old, men and women, merchants, lawyers, artisans, and farmers. Individual leaders, like Patrick Henry of Virginia and Samuel Adams of Massachusetts, became more widely known through their fiery oratory and their success in appealing to the masses. The Stamp Act agitation also

demonstrated the growing influence of ordinary citizens who led parades and demonstrations and joined in attacks on stamp agents and the homes of British officials. And the protests revealed the growing power of the written word and printed images in disseminating ideas among colonists. Broadsides, political cartoons, handbills, newspapers, and pamphlets circulated widely, reinforcing discussions and proclamations at taverns, rallies, demonstrations, and more formal political assemblies.

Explore

See Documents 5.2 and 5.3 for two different types of dissent.

For all the success of the Stamp Act protests, American colonists still could not imagine in 1765 that protest would ever lead to open revolt against British sovereignty. More well-to-do colonists were concerned that a revolution against British authority might fuel a dual revolution in which small farmers, tenants, servants, slaves, and laborers would rise up against their political and economic superiors in the colonies. Even most middling- and working-class protesters believed that the best solution to the colonies' problems was to gain greater economic and political rights within the British empire, not to break from it. After all, Great Britain was the most powerful nation in the world, and the colonies could only benefit from their place in its far-reaching empire.

The Townshend Act and the Boston Massacre

The repeal of the Stamp Act in March 1766 led directly to Parliament's passage of the Declaratory Act. That act declared that Parliament had the authority to pass any law "to bind the colonies and peoples of North America" closer to Britain. No new tax or policy was established; Parliament simply wanted to proclaim Great Britain's political supremacy in the aftermath of the successful stamp tax protests.

Following this direct assertion of British sovereignty, relative harmony prevailed in the colonies for more than a year. Having rid themselves of the burden of parliamentary taxation, colonists were content to abide by less offensive restrictions on smuggling, domestic manufacturing, and similar matters. Then in June 1767, a new chancellor of the Exchequer, Charles Townshend, rose to power in England. He persuaded Parliament to return to the model offered by the earlier Sugar Act. The **Townshend Act**, like the Sugar Act, instituted an import tax on a range of items sent to the colonies, including glass, lead, paint, paper, and tea.

Now, however, even an indirect tax led to immediate protests and calls for a boycott of the items subject to the tax. In February 1768, Samuel Adams wrote a circular letter reminding colonists of the importance of the boycott, and the

DOCUMENTS 5.2 AND 5.3

Protesting the Stamp Act: Two Views

The announcement of the Stamp Act in 1764 ignited widespread protests throughout the colonies. Colonial governments petitioned Parliament for its repeal, crowds attacked stamp agents and distributors, broadsides and newspapers denounced "taxation without representation," and boycotts and mass demonstrations were organized in major cities, some of which turned violent. Protests were not limited to the colonists, however, as shown in the petition to Parliament from London merchants, who argued that they were losing revenue because of colonial boycotts of British goods. The second document celebrates the repeal of the Stamp Act by depicting a funeral for the act led by its supporters. Dr. William Scott, who published letters supporting the Stamp Act in a London newspaper, leads the procession.

Explore

5.2 London Merchants Petition to Repeal the Stamp Act, 1766

And that, in consequence of the trade between the colonies and the mother country, as established and permitted for many years, and of the experience which the petitioners have had of the readiness of the Americans to make their just remittances to the utmost of their real ability, they have been induced to make and venture such large exportations of British manufactures, as to leave the colonies indebted to the merchants of Great Britain in the sum of several millions sterling; at that at this time the colonists, when pressed for payment, appeal to past experience, in proof of their willingness; but declare it is not in their power, at present, to make good their engagements, alleging, that the taxes and restrictions laid upon them, and the extension of the jurisdiction of vice admiralty courts established by some late acts of parliament, particularly . . . by an act passed in the fifth year of his present Majesty, for granting and applying certain stamp duties, and other duties, in the British colonies and plantations in America, with several regulations and restraints, which, if founded in acts of parliament for defined purposes, are represented to have been extended in such a manner as to disturb legal commerce and harass the fair trader, have so far interrupted the usual and former most fruitful branches of their commerce, restrained the sale of their produce, thrown the state of the several provinces into confusion, and brought on so great a number of actual bankruptcies, that the former opportunities and means of remittances and payments are utterly lost and taken from them; and that the petitioners are, by these unhappy events, reduced to the necessity of applying to the House, in order to secure themselves and their families from impending ruin; to prevent a multitude of manufacturers from becoming a burthen to the community, or else seeking their bread in other countries, to the irretrievable loss of this kingdom; and to preserve the strength of this nation entire.

Source: Guy Steven Callender, *Selections from the Economic History of the United States, 1765–1860* (Boston: Ginn, 1909), 146–47.

5.3 The Repeal, 1766

Library of Congress

Interpret the Evidence

- How do both the petition and the cartoon emphasize the economic arguments against the Stamp Act? What role, if any, do arguments about political representation play in these documents?

- Who do you think was the intended audience for each of these documents? What evidence can you find in each document to support your answer?

Put It in Context

What do these documents suggest about the more general relations among the colonies, British merchants, and Parliament in 1766?

Massachusetts Assembly disseminated it to other colonial assemblies. In response, Parliament posted two more British army regiments in Boston and New York City to enforce the law, including the Townshend Act. Angry colonists did not retreat when confronted by this show of military force. Instead, a group of outspoken colonial leaders demanded that colonists refuse to import goods of any kind from Britain.

Explore

See Document 5.4 for one colonist's objection to the Townshend Act.

This boycott depended especially on the support of women, who were often in charge of the day-to-day purchase of household items that appeared on the boycott list. Women were expected to boycott a wide array of British goods—gloves, hats, shoes, cloth, sugar, and tea among them. Single women and widows who supported themselves as shopkeepers were expected to join male merchants and store owners in refusing to sell British goods. To make up for the boycotted goods, wives, mothers, and daughters produced homespun shirts and dresses and brewed herbal teas to replace British products.

Despite the hardships, many colonial women embraced the boycott. Twenty-two-year-old Charity Clarke voiced the feelings of many colonists when she wrote to a friend in England, "If you English folks won't give us the liberty we ask . . . I will try to gather a number of ladies armed with spinning wheels [along with men] who shall learn to weave & keep sheep, and will retire beyond the reach of arbitrary power." Women organized spinning bees in which dozens of participants produced yards and yards of homespun cloth. By 1770 wearing homespun came to symbolize women's commitment to the colonial cause.

Refusing to drink tea offered another way for women to show their support of protests against parliamentary taxation. In February 1770, more than "300 Mistresses of Families, in which number the Ladies of the Highest Rank and Influence," signed a petition in Boston and pledged to abstain from drinking tea, and dozens of women from less prosperous families signed their own boycott agreement.

Boston women's refusal to drink tea and their participation in spinning bees were part of a highly publicized effort to make their city the center of opposition to the Townshend Act. Printed propaganda, demonstrations, rallies, and broadsides announced to the world that Bostonians rejected Parliament's right to impose its will, or at least its taxes, on the American colonies. Throughout the winter of 1769–1770, boys and young men confronted British soldiers stationed in Boston. Although they were angry over Parliament's taxation policies, Boston men also considered the soldiers, who moonlighted for extra pay, as economic competitors. The taunts and tension soon escalated into violence.

By March 1770, 1,700 British troops were stationed in Boston, a city of 18,000 people. On the evening of March 5, boys began throwing snowballs and insults at the lone soldier guarding the Boston Customs House. An angry crowd began milling about, now joined by a group of sailors led by Crispus Attucks, an ex-slave of mixed African and Indian ancestry. The nervous guard called for help, and Captain Thomas Preston arrived at the scene with seven British soldiers. He appealed to the "gentlemen" present to disperse the crowd. Instead, the harangues of the crowd continued, and snowballs, stones, and other projectiles flew in greater numbers. Then a gun fired, and soon more shooting erupted. Eleven men in the crowd were hit, and four were "killed on the Spot," including Crispus Attucks.

Despite confusion about who, if anyone, gave the order to fire, colonists expressed outrage at the shooting of ordinary men on the streets of Boston. Samuel Adams and other Sons of Liberty, though horrified by the turn of events, recognized the incredible potential for anti-British propaganda. Adams organized a mass funeral for those killed, and thousands watched the caskets being paraded through the city. Newspaper editors and broadsides printed by the Sons of Liberty labeled the shooting a "massacre." When the accused soldiers were tried in Boston for the so-called **Boston Massacre** and the jury acquitted six of the eight of any crime, colonial leaders became more convinced that British rule had become tyrannical and that such tyranny must be opposed. **See Document Project 5: The Boston Massacre, page 153**.

To ensure that colonists throughout North America learned about the Boston Massacre, committees of correspondence formed once again to spread the news. These committees became important pipelines for sending information about plans and protests across the colonies, connecting seaport cities with one another and with like-minded colonists in the countryside. They also circulated an engraving by Bostonian Paul Revere that suggested the soldiers purposely shot at a peaceful crowd.

In the aftermath of the shootings, public pressure increased on Parliament to repeal the Townshend duties. Merchants in England and North America pleaded with Parliament to reconsider policies that had resulted in economic losses on both sides of the Atlantic. In response, Parliament repealed all of the Townshend duties except the import tax on tea. Parliament retained the tea tax to prove its political authority to do so.

Continuing Conflicts at Home

As colonists in Boston and other seaport cities rallied to protest British taxation, other residents of the thirteen colonies continued to challenge authorities closer to home. In the same years as the Stamp Act and Townshend Act

DOCUMENT 5.4

John Dickinson | Letter from a Farmer, 1768

In 1767 the British Parliament passed a series of taxes on the American colonies to raise revenue and gain greater control of colonial government and trade. The Townshend duties, as they were called, outraged many colonists. John Dickinson, a prominent Pennsylvania attorney who had been a representative at the Stamp Act Congress, wrote the most famous attacks on the Townshend Act. Published under the pseudonym "A Farmer," Dickinson's letters criticized British taxation policies and called for peaceful resistance to them.

Explore

I hope to demonstrate before these letters are concluded, yet even in such a supposed case, these colonies ought to regard the act with abhorrence. For who are a free people? Not those over whom government is reasonably and equitably exercised but those who live under a government, so *constitutionally checked* and *controuled*, that proper provision is made against its being otherwise exercised. The late act is founded on the destruction of this constitutional security.

If the parliament have a right to lay a duty of four shillings and eight pence on a hundred weight of glass, or a ream of paper, they have a right to lay a duty of any other sum on either. They may raise the duty, as the author before quoted says has been done in some countries, till it "exceeds seventeen or eighteen times the value of the commodity." In short, if they have a right to levy a tax of *one penny* upon us, they have a right to levy a *million* upon us: For where does their right stop? At any given number of pence, shillings, or pounds? To attempt to limit their right, after granting it to exist at all, is

as contrary to reason, as granting it to exist at all is contrary to justice. If they have any right to tax us, then, whether our own money shall continue in our own pockets, or not, depends no longer on *us*, but on *them*. "There is nothing which we can call our own," or to use the words of Mr. Locke, "What property have we in that, which another may, by right, take, when he pleases, to himself?"

These duties, which will inevitably be levied upon us, and which are now levying upon us, are expressly laid for the sole purpose of taking money. This is the true definition of taxes. They are therefore taxes. This money is to be taken from us. We are therefore taxed. Those who are taxed without their own consent, given by themselves, or their representatives, are slaves. We are taxed without our own consent given by ourselves, or our representatives. We are therefore—I speak it with grief—I speak it with indignation—we are slaves.

Source: John Dickinson, *Letters from a Farmer in Pennsylvania to the Inhabitants of the British Colonies* (New York: The Outlook Company, 1903), 75–78.

Interpret the Evidence

- Is Dickinson's main criticism of the Townshend duties that they are an economic burden, or is it broader than that?
- What is Dickinson's definition of a just government?

Put It in Context

What does Dickinson's complaint about colonists being treated as slaves suggest about the limits of his political vision?

protests, tenants in New Jersey and the Hudson valley continued their campaign for economic justice. So, too, did Herman Husband and the Sandy Creek Association. Governor Tryon of North Carolina had been among those who claimed that Parliament had abused its power in taxing the colonies, but he did not recognize such abuses in his own colony. Instead, he viewed the Regulators, formed during the

campaign against the Townshend Act, as traitors. The Regulators, however, insisted that they were simply trying to protect farmers and laborers from deceitful speculators, corrupt politicians, and greedy employers. A year after the Boston Massacre, Governor Tryon sent troops to quell what he viewed as open rebellion on the Carolina frontier. The Regulators amassed two thousand farmers to defend

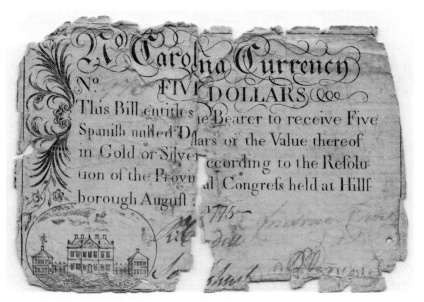

The Regulators and Governor William Tryon

When the Regulators rebelled against the Townshend duties in 1771 along the North Carolina frontier, Governor Tryon, who also questioned British tax policies, nevertheless dispatched colonial troops and crushed the rebellion. Tryon's lavish palace in New Bern appears in the lower left corner of this $5 bill, issued in 1775 on the eve of the American Revolution.   North Carolina Collection, University of North Carolina at Chapel Hill

themselves, although Husband, a pacifist, was not among them. But when twenty Regulators were killed and more than a hundred wounded at the Battle of Alamance Creek in May 1771, he surely knew many of the fallen. Six Regulators were hanged a month later in front of Governor Tryon, local officials, and hundreds of neighboring farm families. Although North Carolina Regulators did not proclaim this the Alamance Massacre, many local residents harbored deep resentments against colonial officials for what they viewed as the slaughter of honest, hardworking men. Herman Husband fled the Carolina frontier and headed north.

Resentments against colonial leaders were not confined to North Carolina. An independent Regulator movement emerged in South Carolina in 1767. Far more effective than their North Carolina counterparts, South Carolina Regulators seized control of the western regions of the colony, took up arms, and established their own system of frontier justice. By 1769 the South Carolina Assembly negotiated a settlement with the Regulators, establishing new parishes in the colony's interior that ensured greater representation for frontier areas and extending colonial political institutions, such as courts and sheriffs, to the region.

Tea and Widening Resistance

For a brief period after the Boston Massacre, conflicts within the colonies generally overshadowed protests against British policies. During this period, the tea tax was collected, the increased funds ensured that British officials in the colonies were less dependent on local assemblies to carry out their duties, and general prosperity seemed to lessen the antagonism between colonists and royal authorities. In May 1773, however, all that changed. That month Parliament passed a new act that granted the East India Company a monopoly on shipping and selling tea in the colonies. Although this did not add any new tax or raise the price of tea, it did fuel a new round of protests.

Founded in the early seventeenth century, the East India Company had been one of the major trading companies in the British empire and a symbol of British commercial supremacy for more than 150 years. By the 1770s, however, it was on the verge of economic collapse and asked for a monopoly on the tea trade and the right to sell tea through its own agents rather than through independent shopkeepers and merchants in the colonies. Many members of Parliament had invested in the East India Company, so their decision to grant it a monopoly on tea involved financial as well as political considerations. Still, the decision was not seen as especially controversial since East India Company tea sold by company agents cost less, even with the tax, than smuggled Dutch or French tea.

Samuel Adams, Patrick Henry, Christopher Gadsden, and other radicals had continued to view the tea tax as an illegal imposition on colonists and refused to pay it as a matter of principle. They had established committees of correspondence to keep up the pressure for a colony-wide boycott, and Adams published and circulated "Rights of the Colonies," a pamphlet that listed a range of grievances against British policies. Their concerns became the basis for a new round of protests when Parliament granted the East India Company its monopoly. By eliminating colonial merchants from the profits to be made on tea and implementing a monopoly for a single favored company, Parliament pushed merchants into joining with radicals to demand redress.

Committees of correspondence quickly organized another colony-wide boycott. In some cities, like Charleston, South Carolina, tea was unloaded from East India Company ships but never sold. In others, like New York, the ships were turned back at the port. Only in Boston, however, did violence erupt as ships loaded with tea, and protected by British troops, sat anchored in the harbor. On the night of December 16, 1773, the Sons of Liberty organized a "tea party." After a massive rally against British policy, a group of about fifty men disguised as Indians boarded the British ships and dumped forty-five tons of tea into the sea.

Although hundreds of spectators knew who had boarded the ship, witnesses refused to provide names or other information to British officials investigating the incident. The Boston Tea Party was a direct challenge to British authority and resulted in massive destruction of valuable property.

Parliament responded immediately with a show of force. The **Coercive Acts**, passed in 1774, closed the port of Boston until residents paid for the tea, moved Massachusetts court cases against royal officials back to England, and revoked the colony's charter in order to strengthen the authority of royal officials and weaken that of the colonial assembly. The British government also approved a new Quartering Act, which forced Boston residents to accommodate more soldiers in their own homes or build more barracks.

The royal government passed the Coercive Acts to punish Massachusetts and to discourage similar protests in other colonies. Instead, the legislation, which colonists called the **Intolerable Acts**, spurred a militant reaction. Committees of correspondence spread news of the fate of Boston and the entire colony of Massachusetts. Colonial leaders, who increasingly identified themselves as patriots, soon formed committees of safety—armed groups of colonists who gathered weapons and munitions and vowed to protect themselves against British encroachments on their rights and institutions. Other colonies sent support, both political and material, to Massachusetts and instituted a boycott of British goods. All ranks of people—merchants, laborers, farmers, housewives—throughout the colonies joined the boycott.

Explore

See Document 5.5 for a British reaction to colonial women's efforts to boycott tea.

At the same time, a group of patriots meeting in Williamsburg, Virginia, in the spring of 1774 called for colonies to send representatives to a **Continental Congress** to meet in Philadelphia the following September to discuss relations between the North American colonies and Great Britain.

By passing the Coercive Acts, Parliament had hoped to dampen the long-smoldering conflict with the colonies. Instead, it flared even brighter, with radical leaders committing themselves to the use of violence, moderate merchants and shopkeepers making common cause with radicals, and ordinary women and men embracing a boycott of all British goods.

The Continental Congress and Colonial Unity

When the Continental Congress convened in Philadelphia's Carpenter Hall in September 1774, fifty-six delegates

First Continental Congress

This 1783 French engraving depicts the meeting of the first Continental Congress, held in Philadelphia in September 1774. Fifty-six delegates attended from every colony but Georgia. After spending most of the first day debating whether to start the meeting off with a prayer, the congress got down to the business of petitioning King George III to remedy the colonists' grievances.   The Granger Collection, New York

represented every colony but Georgia. Many of these men—and they were all men—had met before. Some had worked together in the Stamp Act Congress in 1765; others had joined forces in the intervening years on committees of correspondence or in petitions to Parliament. Still, the representatives disagreed on many fronts. Some were radicals like Samuel Adams, Patrick Henry, and Christopher Gadsden. Others held moderate views, including George Washington of Virginia and John Dickinson of Pennsylvania. And a few, like John Jay of New York, voiced more conservative positions.

Despite their differences, all the delegates agreed that the colonies must resist further parliamentary encroachments on their liberties. They did not talk of independence, but rather of reestablishing the freedoms that colonists had enjoyed in an earlier period: freedom from British taxes and from the presence of British troops and the right to control local economic and political affairs. Washington voiced the sentiments of many. Although opposed to the idea of independence, he echoed John Locke by refusing to submit "to the loss of those valuable rights and privileges, which are essential to the happiness of every free State, and without which life, liberty, and property are rendered totally insecure."

DOCUMENT 5.5

The Edenton Proclamation, 1774

When colonial leaders called for a boycott of tea following the 1773 Tea Act, women throughout the colonies joined in the campaign. In Edenton, North Carolina, a group of women published a proclamation stating their allegiance to the cause of liberty by refusing to serve or drink British tea. Their public statement received much attention in both the American and the British press. The following political cartoon, which satirizes the Edenton women who signed the public declaration, appeared in several London newspapers.

Explore

What is the significance of the female slave holding the inkstand?

How are the women portrayed in this cartoon?

What is the presence of the infant and dog on the floor meant to suggest about the character of female petitioners?

A SOCIETY of PATRIOTIC LADIES,
AT
EDENTON in NORTH CAROLINA.

Plate V.

Library of Congress

Put It in Context

How does the cartoon use contemporary understandings of women's role in society to undermine their actions?

To demonstrate their unified resistance to the Coercive Acts, delegates called on colonists to continue the boycott of British goods and to end all colonial exports to Great Britain. Committees were established in all of the colonies to coordinate and enforce these actions. Delegates also insisted that Americans were "entitled to a free and exclusive power of legislation in their several provincial legislatures." By 1774 a growing number of colonists supported these measures and the ideas on which they were based.

The delegates at the Continental Congress could not address all the colonists' grievances, and most had no interest in challenging race and class relations within the colonies themselves. Nonetheless, it was a significant event because the congress drew power away from individual colonies—most notably Massachusetts—and local organizations like the Sons of Liberty and placed the emphasis instead on colony-wide plans and actions. To some extent, the delegates shifted leadership of colonial protests away from more radical artisans, like Ebenezer Mackintosh, and put planning back in the hands of men of wealth and standing. Moreover, even as they denounced Parliament, many representatives felt a special loyalty to the king and sought his intervention to rectify relations between the mother country and the colonies.

REVIEW & RELATE

How and why did colonial resistance to British policies escalate in the decade following the conclusion of the French and Indian War?

How did internal social and economic divisions shape the colonial response to British policies?

☑ *LEARNINGCurve* bedfordstmartins.com/hewittlawson/LC

Conclusion: Liberty within Empire

From the Sugar Act in 1764 to the Continental Congress in 1774, colonists reacted strongly to parliamentary efforts to impose greater control over the colonies. Their protests grew increasingly effective as colonists developed organizations, systems of communication, and arguments to buttress their position. Residents of seacoast cities like Boston and New York City developed especially visible and effective challenges, in large part because they generally had the most to lose if Britain implemented new economic, military, and legislative policies.

In frontier areas, such as the southern backcountry, the Hudson valley, and northern New England, complaints against British tyranny vied with those against colonial land

speculators and officials throughout the 1760s and 1770s. Still, few of these agitators questioned the right of white colonists to claim Indian lands or enslave African labor. In this sense, at least, most frontier settlers made common cause with more elite colonists who challenged British authority, including the many planters and large landowners who attended the Continental Congress.

One other tie bound the colonists together in 1774. No matter how radical the rhetoric, the aim continued to be resistance to particular policies, not independence from the British empire. Colonists sought greater liberty within the empire, focusing on parliamentary policies concerning taxation, troops, and local political control. Only on rare occasions did a colonist question the fundamental framework of imperial governance, and even then, the questions did not lead to a radical reformulation of economic or political relations. And despite some colonists' opposition to certain parliamentary acts, many others supported British policies. While royal officials and many of their well-to-do neighbors were horrified by the new spirit of lawlessness that had erupted in the colonies, the majority of colonists did not participate in the Sons or Daughters of Liberty, the colonial congresses, or the petition campaigns. Small farmers and backcountry settlers were often far removed from centers of protest activity, while poor families in seaport cities who purchased few items to begin with had little interest in boycotts of British goods. Finally, some colonists still hesitated to consider open revolt against British rule for fear of a revolution from below. The activities of land rioters, Regulators, evangelical preachers, female petitioners, and African American converts to Christianity reminded more well-established settlers that the colonies harbored their own tensions and conflicts.

The fates of George Washington and Herman Husband suggest the uncertainties that still plagued the colonies and individual colonists in 1774. As Washington returned to his Virginia estate from the Continental Congress, he began to devote more time to military affairs. He took command of the volunteer militia companies in the colonies and chaired the committee on safety in his home county. Although still opposed to rebellion, he was nonetheless preparing for it. Herman Husband, on the other hand, had already watched his rebellion against oppressive government fail at the Battle of Alamance Creek. When the Continental Congress met in Philadelphia, he was living on the Pennsylvania frontier, trying to reestablish his farm and family there. Whether ruled by Great Britain or eastern colonial elites, he was most concerned with the rights of poor and working people. Yet he and Washington would have agreed with the great British parliamentarian Edmund Burke, who, on hearing of events in the American colonies in 1774, lamented, "Clouds, indeed, and darkness, rest upon the future."

Chapter Review

Online Study Guide ▶ bedfordstmartins.com/hewittlawson

KEY TERMS

Albany Congress (p. 131)
Peace of Paris (p. 133)
Proclamation Line of 1763 (p. 135)
Regulators (p. 137)
benign neglect (p. 140)
Navigation Acts (p. 140)
Sugar Act (p. 140)
import duty (p. 140)
committee of correspondence (p. 141)
Stamp Act (p. 141)
Sons of Liberty (p. 142)
Townshend Act (p. 143)
Boston Massacre (p. 146)
Coercive Acts (Intolerable Acts) (p. 149)
Continental Congress (p. 149)

REVIEW & RELATE

1. How did the French and Indian War and the subsequent peace treaty affect relations between Britain and its North American subjects?

2. How did the French and Indian War and the increasing power of large landowners contribute to conflict between average colonists and colonial elites?

3. How did Britain's postwar policies lead to the emergence of unified colonial protests?

4. Why did British policymakers believe they were justified in seeking to gain greater control over Britain's North American colonies?

5. How and why did colonial resistance to British policies escalate in the decade following the conclusion of the French and Indian War?

6. How did internal social and economic divisions shape the colonial response to British policies?

TIMELINE OF EVENTS

1754–1763	French and Indian War
1754	George Washington launches surprise attack on Fort Duquesne
	Albany Congress convenes
1757	William Pitt takes charge of British war effort
May 1763	Pontiac launches pan-Indian revolt to drive out British
June 1763	Peace of Paris
October 1763	British establish Proclamation Line of 1763
December 1763	Paxton Boys attack Conestoga Indians
1764	Green Mountain Boys resist New York authorities
	Sugar Act passed
1765	Stamp Act passed
	Stamp Act Congress convenes
1766	Sandy Creek Association formed
	Stamp Act repealed and Declaratory Act passed
1767	Townshend Act passed
1770	Boston Massacre
1771	Battle of Alamance Creek, North Carolina
1773	Boston Tea Party
1774	Coercive Acts passed
	Continental Congress convenes in Philadelphia

DOCUMENT PROJECT **5**

The Boston Massacre

The Boston Massacre was a critical episode in the American independence movement. The origins of this skirmish between Bostonians and British troops lie in the passage of the Townshend Act in 1767, three years before the so-called massacre.

There was widespread resistance to the Townshend duties, including public demonstrations, petitions to King George and Parliament, and boycotts against British goods. Boston was the scene of numerous disturbances, and the situation in Boston was so tense that four thousand British troops were brought in to enforce the Townshend Act. Then in late February 1770, a British sympathizer, Ebenezer Richardson, tore down an anti-British poster. When an angry mob threw stones at Richardson's house and hit his wife, Ebenezer fired into the crowd and killed an eleven-year-old boy. A mass funeral for the boy set the stage for the events of March 5, 1770.

On that chilly evening, an exchange between a local tradesman and a British officer outside the Customs House escalated when companions on both sides joined in the dispute. Church bells were rung, bringing more colonists to the scene (Document 5.6). Captain Thomas Preston, the officer in charge that day, tried to gain control of the situation by calling in reinforcements (Document 5.9). In the ensuing melee, Bostonians overwhelmed the British regulars, who sought to protect themselves. Someone fired his gun, and a number of British soldiers then followed suit, killing three men immediately and fatally injuring two others (Documents 5.6 and 5.9).

Within the month, Preston and eight British soldiers were indicted for murder and tried in fall 1770. Unable to find attorneys willing to defend himself and his troops, Preston appealed directly to patriot John Adams, who agreed to take the case to ensure a fair trial. Preston was tried separately and was acquitted. Six other soldiers were also acquitted, but two were found guilty of murder, a charge later reduced to manslaughter. Parliament repealed all of the Townshend duties except for the tax on tea.

The following documents reveal the chaos of that night from the differing perspectives of Bostonians and British soldiers. They also illustrate the ways that colonial leaders used the event to promote the patriot cause (Documents 5.7, 5.8, and 5.10).

DOCUMENT 5.6

Deposition of William Wyatt, March 7, 1770

Just two days after the Boston Massacre, city officials began deposing dozens of witnesses to the event. They later published these descriptions as part of a pamphlet that criticized the event as a "Horrid Massacre." The following selection is from the testimony of William Wyatt and describes his version of the scene just as British soldiers were loading their weapons.

That last Monday evening, being the fifth day of March current, I was in Boston, down on Treat's wharf, where my vessel was lying, and hearing the bells ring, supposed there was a fire in the town, whereupon I hastened up to the Town-house, on the south side of it, where I saw an officer of the army lead out of the guard-house there seven or eight soldiers of the army, and lead them down in seeming haste, to the Custom-house on the north side of King street, where I followed them, and when the officer had got there with the men, he bid them face about. I stood just below them on the left wing, and the said officer ordered his men to load, which they did accordingly, with the utmost dispatch, then they remained about six minutes, with their firelocks rested and bayonets fixed, but not standing in exact order. I observed a considerable number of young lads, and here and there a man amongst them, about the middle of the street, facing the soldiers, but not within ten or twelve feet distance from them; I observed some of them, viz., the lads, etc., had sticks in their hands, laughing, shouting, huzzaing, and crying fire; but could not observe that any of them threw anything at the soldiers, or threatened any of them. Then the said officer retired from before the soldiers and stepping behind them, towards the right wing, bid the soldiers fire; they not firing, he presently again bid 'em fire, they not yet firing, he stamped and said, "Damn your bloods, fire, be the consequence what it will"; then the second man on the left wing fired off his gun, then, after a very short pause, they fired one after another as quick as possible, beginning on the right wing; the last man's gun on the left wing flashed in the pan, then he primed again, and the people being withdrawn from before the soldiers, most of them further down the street, he turned his gun toward them and fired upon them. Immediately after the principal firing, I saw three of the people fall down in the street; presently after the last gun was fired off, the said officer, who had commanded the soldiers (as above) to fire, sprung before them, waving his sword or stick, said, "Damn ye, rascals, what did ye fire for?" and struck up the gun of one of the soldiers who was loading again, whereupon they seemed confounded and fired no more.

Source: *A Short Narrative of the Horrid Massacre in Boston Perpetrated in the Evening of the Fifth Day of March, 1770, by the Soldiers of the 29th Regiment* (Boston, 1770), republished with additional material by John Doggett Jr. (New York, 1849), 72.

DOCUMENT 5.7

Account of Boston Massacre Funeral Procession, March 12, 1770

One week after the Boston Massacre, a massive public funeral was held for the four victims who had already died: Samuel Gray, Samuel Maverick, James Caldwell, and Crispus Attucks. In the scene described here, shops were closed and church bells marked the event in Boston and also in nearby Charlestown and Roxbury. Note that the article mentions that Bostonians from all ranks attended the funeral.

Last Thursday, agreeable to a general request of the inhabitants, and by the consent of parents and friends, were carried to their grave in succession, the bodies of Samuel Gray, Samuel Maverick, James Caldwell, and Crispus Attucks, the unhappy victims who fell in the bloody massacre of the Monday evening preceding!

On this occasion most of the shops in town were shut, all the bells were ordered to toll a solemn peal, as were also those in the neighboring towns of Charlestown, Roxbury, etc. The procession began to move between the hours of 4 and 5 in the afternoon; two of the unfortunate sufferers, Messrs. James Caldwell and Crispus Attucks, who were strangers [not residents of Boston], borne from Faneuil Hall, attended by a numerous train of persons of all ranks; and the other two, Mr. Samuel Gray, from the house of Mr. Benjamin Gray (his brother), on the north side of the Exchange, and Mr. Maverick, from the house of his distressed mother, Mrs. Mary Maverick, in Union Street, each followed by their respective relations and friends: The several hearses forming a junction in King Street, the theatre of the inhuman tragedy! proceeded from thence through the Main Street, lengthened by an immense concourse of people, so numerous as to be obliged to follow in ranks of six, and brought up by a long train of carriages belonging to the principal gentry of the town. The bodies were deposited in one vault in the middle burying ground. The aggravated circumstances of their death, the distress and sorrow visible in every countenance, together with the peculiar solemnity with which the whole funeral was conducted, surpass description.

Source: *Boston Gazette and Country Journal*, March 12, 1770.

DOCUMENT 5.8

Paul Revere | Etching of the Boston Massacre, 1770

Published three weeks after the Boston Massacre, Paul Revere's famous etching of the event stirred anti-British sentiment among the colonists. Revere was not at the Customs House on March 5 and largely copied this image from the engraving of another artist, Henry Pelham. Revere's etching depicts an organized line of British soldiers firing into a crowd of unarmed colonists. At the time of the Boston Massacre, Revere was a prominent silversmith and a member of the Sons of Liberty.

Library of Congress

DOCUMENT 5.9

Account of Captain Thomas Preston, June 25, 1770

Seven months after the Boston Massacre, British troops involved in the event went on trial. Captain Thomas Preston was the officer in charge the night of March 5, and he was tried separately from the other soldiers. His trial centered on whether or not he had ordered his men to fire on the crowd. Assuming that defendants in criminal trials would perjure themselves to gain an acquittal, English legal custom prohibited them from testifying. But Preston had presented his version of events to British authorities just a week after the event. While imprisoned in Boston, he released this account of events, which was published in the *Boston Gazette* on March 12, 1770. In April, it appeared in London papers and was republished in the *Boston Evening-Post* on June 25, 1770. Thus it is likely that jurors in his trial knew that he strenuously denied the charges against him.

ON MONDAY NIGHT about Eight o' Clock two Soldiers were attacked and beat. But the Party of the Towns-People, in order to carry Matters to the utmost Length, broke into two Meeting-Houses, and rang the Alarm Bells, which I supposed was for Fire as usual, but was soon undeceived. About Nine some of the Guard came to and informed me, the Town-Inhabitants were assembling to attack the Troops, and that the Bells were ringing as the Signal for that Purpose, and not for Fire, and the Beacon intended to be fired to bring in the distant People of the Country. This, as I was Captain of the Day, occasioned my repairing immediately to the Main-Guard. In my Way there I saw the People in great Commotion, and heard them use the most cruel and horrid Threats against the Troops. In a few Minutes after I reached the Guard, about an hundred People passed it, and went towards the Custom-House, where the King's Money is lodged. They immediately surrounded the Sentinel posted there, and with Clubs and other Weapons threatened to execute their Vengeance on him. I was soon informed by a Townsman, their Intention was to carry off the Soldier from his Post, and probably murder him. On which I desired him to return for further Intelligence; and he soon came back and assured me he heard the Mob declare they would murder him. This I feared might be a Prelude to their plundering the King's Chest. I immediately sent a non-commissioned Officer and twelve Men to protect both the Sentinel and the King's-Money, and very soon followed myself, to prevent (if possible) all Disorder; fearing lest the Officer and Soldiery by the Insults and Provocations of the Rioters, should be thrown off their Guard and commit some rash Act. They soon rushed through the People, and, by charging their Bayonets in half Circle, kept them at a little Distance. Nay, so far was I from intending the Death of any Person, that I suffered the Troops to go to the Spot where the unhappy Affair took Place, without any Loading in their Pieces, nor did I ever give Orders for loading them. This remiss Conduct in me perhaps merits Censure; yet it is Evidence, resulting from the Nature of Things, which is the best and surest that can be offered, that my Intention was not to act

(continued on page 158)

offensively, but the contrary Part, and that not without Compulsion. The mob still increased, and were more outrageous, striking their clubs or bludgeons one against another, and calling out, "Come on you rascals, you bloody backs, you lobster scoundrels, fire if you dare, G–d damn you, fire and be damned; we know you dare not"; and much more such language was used. At this time I was between the soldiers and the mob, parleying with and endeavouring all in my power to persuade them to retire peaceably; but to no purpose. They advanced to the points of the bayonets, struck some of them, and even the muzzles of the pieces, and seemed to be endeavouring to close with the soldiers. On which some well-behaved persons asked me if the guns were charged. I replied, yes. They then asked me if I intended to order the men to fire. I answered no, by no means; observing to them that I was advanced before the muzzles of the men's pieces, and must fall a sacrifice if they fired; that the soldiers were upon the half-cock and charged bayonets, and my giving the word fire under those circumstances would prove me no officer. While I was thus speaking, one of the soldiers, having received a severe blow with a stick, stepped a little on one side and instantly fired, on which turning to and asking him why he fired without orders, I was struck with a club on my arm, which for some time deprived me of the use of it, which blow, had it been placed on my head, most probably would have destroyed me. On this a general attack was made on the men by a great number of heavy clubs, and snowballs being thrown at them, by which all our lives were in imminent danger; some persons at the same time from behind calling out, "Damn your bloods, why don't you fire?" Instantly three or four of the soldiers fired, one after another, and directly after three more in the same confusion and hurry.

The mob then ran away, except three unhappy men who instantly expired, in which number was Mr. Gray, at whose rope-walk the prior quarrel took place; one more is since dead, three others are dangerously, and four slightly wounded. The whole of this melancholy affair was transacted in almost 20 minutes. On my asking the soldiers why they fired without orders, they said they heard the word "Fire" and supposed it came from me. This might be the case, as many of the mob called out "Fire, fire," but I assured the men that I gave no such order, that my words were, "Don't fire, stop your firing."

Source: *Supplement to the Boston Evening-Post*, June 25, 1770.

DOCUMENT 5.10

John Hancock | Oration on the Boston Massacre, 1774

In the years following the Boston Massacre, the city of Boston held an annual Massacre Day commemoration on March 5. On the fourth anniversary of the event, John Hancock delivered an emotional speech to the crowd. His tribute tied the Boston Massacre to the growing independence movement and demonstrated that the event remained a source of inspiration for years afterward. The last Massacre Day memorial was celebrated with the end of the American Revolutionary War in 1783.

Some boast of being friends to government; I am a friend to righteous government, to a government founded upon the principles of reason and justice; but I glory in publicly avowing my eternal enmity to tyranny. Is the present system, which the British administration have adopted for the government of the colonies, a righteous government—or is it tyranny? Here suffer me to ask (and would to heaven there could be an answer), what tenderness, what regard, respect or consideration has Great Britain shown, in their late transactions, for the security of the persons or properties of the inhabitants of the colonies? Or rather what have they omitted doing to destroy that security?

They have declared that they have ever had, and of right ought ever to have, full power to make laws of sufficient validity to bind the colonies in all cases whatever. They have exercised this pretended right by imposing a tax upon us without our consent; and lest we should show some reluctance at parting with our property, her fleets and armies are sent to enforce their mad pretensions. . . .

But I forbear, and come reluctantly to the transactions of that dismal night when in such quick succession we felt the extremes of grief, astonishment, and rage; when heaven in anger, for a dreadful moment, suffered hell to take the reins; when Satan with his chosen band opened the sluices of New England's blood, and sacrilegiously polluted our land with the dead bodies of her guiltless sons!

Let this sad tale of death never be told without a tear; let not the heaving bosom cease to burn with a manly indignation at the barbarous story through the long tracts of future time: let every parent tell the shameful story to his listening children until tears of pity glisten in their eyes and boiling passions shake their tender frames; and whilst the anniversary of that ill-fated night is kept a jubilee in the grim court of pandemonium, let all America join in one common prayer to heaven that the inhuman, unprovoked murders of the 5th of March, 1770, planned by Hillsborough and a knot of treacherous knaves in Boston, and executed by the cruel hand of Preston and his sanguinary coadjutors, may ever stand on history without a parallel. . . .

We have all one common cause; let it, therefore, be our only contest who shall most contribute to the security of the liberties of America. And may the same kind Providence which has watched over this country from her infant state still enable us to defeat our enemies.

Source: Mayo Williamson Hazeltine, ed., *Orations from Homer to McKinley* (New York: P. F. Collier and Sons, 1903), 7:2628–29, 2631, 2637.

Interpret the Evidence

1. How accurate is Paul Revere's etching of the Boston Massacre (Document 5.8)? Why would he have chosen to depict the scene as he did?

2. Compare Revere's portrayal of the event with the testimonies of William Wyatt (Document 5.6) and Captain Preston (Document 5.9).

3. Why did the funeral procession (described in Document 5.7) further incite popular sentiment against the British?

4. In what ways does William Wyatt's deposition (Document 5.6) support the colonists' view of the event? In what ways might it support the British view? Where does it overlap with Captain Preston's account (Document 5.9)?

5. How does John Hancock (Document 5.10) connect the Boston Massacre with the ongoing struggle for American independence?

Put It in Context

- What events had occurred between March 1770 and March 1774 that made the Boston Massacre a touchstone of resistance?

- How might the deaths of the five colonists and the outcome of the trial have changed the way patriots and ordinary colonists viewed the British authorities?

akg-images

Library of Congress

The Battle of Bunker Hill, June 17, 1775.

Slaves destroy a statue of King George III in New York City on July 9, 1776.

6

Revolutions

1775–1783

Everett Collection

African American slave James Armistead worked as a spy for the Americans during the Revolutionary War.

AMERICAN HISTORIES

On November 30, 1774, Thomas Paine arrived in Philadelphia aboard a ship from London. At age thirty-seven, Paine had failed at several occupations and two marriages. But he was an impassioned writer. A pamphlet he wrote caught the eye of Benjamin Franklin, who helped him secure a job on *The Pennsylvania Magazine* just as tensions between the colonies and Great Britain neared open conflict.

Born in 1737, Paine was raised in an English market town by parents who owned a small grocery store and made whalebone corsets. The Paines managed to send him to school for a few years before his father introduced him to the trade of corset-making. Over the next dozen years, Paine also worked as a seaman, a preacher, a teacher, and an excise (or tax) collector. He drank heavily and beat both his wives. Yet despite his personal vices, Paine tried to improve himself and the lot of other British workers. He taught working-class children how to read and write and attended lectures on science and politics in London. As an excise collector in 1762, he wrote a pamphlet that argued for better pay and working conditions for tax collectors. He was fired from his job, but Franklin convinced Paine to try his luck in Philadelphia.

Paine quickly gained in-depth political knowledge of the conflicts between the colonies and Great Britain and gained patrons among Philadelphia's economic and political elite. When armed conflict with British troops erupted in April 1775, colonial debates over whether to declare independence intensified. Pamphlets were a popular means of influencing these debates, and Paine hoped to write one that would tip the balance in favor of independence.

In January 1776, his pamphlet *Common Sense* did just that.

An instant success, *Common Sense* provided a rationale for independence and an emotional plea for creating a new democratic republic. Paine urged colonists not only to separate from England but also to establish a political structure that would ensure liberty and equality for all Americans: "A government of our own is our natural right," he concluded. " 'Tis time to part."

When *Common Sense* was published in 1776, sixteen-year-old Deborah Sampson was working as a servant to Jeremiah and Susanna Thomas in Marlborough, Massachusetts. Indentured at the age of ten, she looked after the Thomases' five sons and worked hard in both the house and the fields. Jeremiah Thomas thought education was above the lot of servant girls, but Sampson insisted on reading whatever books she could find. However, her commitment to American independence likely developed less from reading and more from the fighting that raged in Massachusetts and drew male servants and the Thomas sons into the Continental Army in the 1770s.

When Deborah Sampson's term of service ended in 1778, she sought work as a weaver and then a teacher. In March 1782, she disguised herself as a man and enlisted in the Continental Army, which was then desperate for recruits. Her height and muscular frame allowed her to fool local recruiters, and she accepted the bounty paid to those who enlisted. But Deborah never reported for duty, and when her charade was discovered, she was forced to return the money.

In May 1782, Sampson enlisted a second time under the name Robert Shurtliff. To explain the absence of facial hair, she told the recruiter that she was only seventeen years old. For the next year, Sampson, disguised as Shurtliff, marched, fought, and lived with her Massachusetts regiment. Her ability to carry off the deception was helped by lax standards of hygiene: Soldiers rarely undressed fully to bathe, and most slept in their uniforms.

Even after the formal end of the war in March 1783, Sampson/Shurtliff continued to serve in the Continental Army. In the fall of 1783, she was sent to Philadelphia to help quash a mutiny by Continental soldiers angered over the army's failure to provide back pay. While there, Sampson/Shurtliff fell ill with a raging fever, and a doctor at a local army hospital discovered that "he" was a woman. He reported the news to General John Paterson, and Sampson was honorably discharged, having served the army faithfully for more than a year. ●

AS THE AMERICAN HISTORIES of Thomas Paine and Deborah Sampson demonstrate, the American Revolution transformed individual lives as well as the political life of the nation. Paine had failed financially and personally in England but gained fame in the colonies through his skills as a patriot pamphleteer. Sampson, who was forced into an early independence by her troubled family, excelled as a soldier. Still, while the American Revolution offered opportunities for some colonists, it promised hardship for others. Most Americans had to choose sides long before it was clear whether the colonists could defeat Great Britain, and the long years of conflict (1775–1783) took a toll on families and communities across the thirteen colonies. Over the course of a long and difficult war, could the patriots attract enough Tom Paines and Deborah Sampsons to secure independence and establish a new nation?

The Question of Independence

The Continental Congress that met to protest the Coercive Acts (see chapter 5) adjourned in October 1774, but delegates reconvened in May 1775. During the intervening months, patriot leaders honed their arguments for resisting British tyranny, and committees of correspondence circulated the latest news and debates. While leading patriots began to advocate resistance in the strongest possible terms, the eruption of armed clashes between British soldiers and local farmers fueled the argument for independence. It also led the Continental Congress to establish a Continental Army in June 1775. A year later, in July 1776, as the fighting continued, the congress finally declared independence.

Armed Conflict Erupts

As debates over independence intensified, the Sons of Liberty and other patriot groups not only spread propaganda against the British but also gathered and stored weapons and organized and trained local militia companies. Female patriots continued the boycott of British goods but began to manufacture bandages and bullets as well. Some northern colonists freed enslaved African Americans who agreed to enlist in the militia. Others kept close watch on the movements of British troops.

On April 18, 1775, Boston patriots observed British soldiers boarding boats in the harbor. The British were headed to Lexington, intending to confiscate guns and ammunition hidden there and in neighboring Concord and perhaps arrest patriot leaders. Hoping to warn his fellow patriots of the approaching soldiers, Paul Revere beat them to Lexington but was stopped on the road to Concord by the British. By that time, however, a network of riders was spreading the alarm. One of them alerted Concord residents of the impending danger.

Early in the morning of April 19, the first shots rang out on the village green of Lexington. After a brief exchange between British soldiers and local militiamen—known as minutemen for the speed with which they assembled—eight colonists lay dead. The British troops then moved on to Concord, where they uncovered and burned colonial

The Battle of Lexington
On April 19, 1775, British soldiers fought local militias, killing eight Lexington minutemen before marching off to Concord. Two visitors from Connecticut witnessed the battle on the village green in Lexington: Amos Doolittle, a silversmith, and Ralph Earl, a portraitist. From Earle's sketches, Doolittle engraved the militiamen scrambling for safety, while the main redcoat column advances from the north.
Superstock/Everett Collection

supplies. However, patriots in nearby towns had now been alerted. Borrowing guerrilla tactics from American Indians, colonists hid behind trees, walls, and barns and battered the British soldiers as they marched back to Boston, killing 73 and wounding 200.

Word of the conflict traveled quickly. Outraged Bostonians attacked British troops and forced them to retreat to ships in the harbor. The victory was short-lived, however, and the British soon regained control of Boston. But colonial forces entrenched themselves on hills just north of the city. Then in May, Ethan Allen and his Green Mountain Boys from Vermont joined militias from Connecticut and Massachusetts to capture the British garrison at Fort Ticonderoga, New York. The battle for North America had begun.

When the **Second Continental Congress** convened in Philadelphia on May 10, 1775, the most critical question for delegates like Pennsylvania patriot John Dickinson was how to ensure time for discussion and negotiation. Armed conflict had erupted, but did that mean that independence should, or must, follow? Other delegates insisted that independence was the only appropriate response to armed attacks on colonial residents. Patrick Henry of Virginia declared, "Gentlemen may cry 'peace, peace' but there is no peace. The war is actually begun!"

Less than a month later, on June 16, British forces under General Sir William Howe attacked patriot fortifications on Breed's Hill and Bunker Hill, north of the city. The British won the day when patriots ran out of ammunition. But the redcoats—so called because of their bright red uniforms—suffered more than 1,000 casualties, while only half that number of patriots were killed or wounded. This costly victory allowed the British to maintain control of Boston for nine more months, but the heavy losses emboldened patriot militiamen.

Building a Continental Army

The Battle of Bunker Hill convinced the congress to establish an army for the defense of the colonies and appoint forty-three-year-old Brigadier General George Washington as commander in chief. More comfortable leading troops than debating politics, Washington gave up his seat at the Continental Congress and on June 23 headed to Cambridge, Massachusetts, to take command of ten companies of frontier marksmen along with militia companies already engaged in battle.

Since the Continental Congress had not yet proclaimed itself a national government, Washington depended largely on the willingness of local militia companies to accept his command and of individual colonies to supply soldiers, arms, and ammunition. Throughout the summer of 1775,

Washington wrote dozens of letters to patriot political leaders, including delegates at the Continental Congress, detailing the army's urgent need for men, supplies, and discipline. He sought to remove incompetent officers and improve order among the troops, who spent too much time drinking, gambling, visiting prostitutes, and fighting with militiamen from other locales.

As he sought to forge a disciplined army, Washington and his officers developed a twofold military strategy.

1. Americanischer Scharffschütz oder Jäger (Rifleman)
2. reguläre Infanterie von Pensylvanien.

Militiamen

This 1784 German illustration shows a uniform worn by a sharpshooter (left) and a Pennsylvania regular infantryman (right). Patriot soldiers often dressed in the uniforms of their local militia, which gave the Continental Army a very diverse appearance. Many Germans (Hessians) who fought as mercenaries for the British would have seen these uniforms.   Anne S. K. Brown Military Collection, Brown University Library

Concerned about British forces and their Indian allies in Canada and New York, they sought to drive the British out of Boston and to secure the colonies from attack by enemy forces farther north. In November 1775, American troops under General Richard Montgomery captured Montreal. However, the difficult trek in cold weather decimated the patriot reinforcements led by General Benedict Arnold, and American troops failed to dislodge the British from Quebec. Smallpox ravaged many of the survivors.

Despite the disastrous outcome of the invasion of Canada, the Continental Army secured important victories in the winter of 1775–1776. To improve Washington's position in eastern Massachusetts, General Henry Knox retrieved weapons captured at Fort Ticonderoga. In March, Washington positioned the forty-three cannons on Dorchester Heights and surprised the British with a bombardment that drove them from Boston. General Howe was forced to retreat with his troops to Nova Scotia.

Reasons for Caution and for Action

As the British retreated from Boston, the war had already spread into Virginia. In the spring of 1775, local militias had forced Lord Dunmore, Virginia's royal governor, to take refuge on British ships in Norfolk harbor. Dunmore encouraged white servants and black slaves to join him there, and thousands did so. When Dunmore led his army back into Virginia in November 1775, hundreds of black men fought with British troops at the Battle of Great Bridge. Once he reclaimed the governor's mansion in Williamsburg, Dunmore issued an official proclamation that declared "all indent[ur]ed Servants, Negroes or others (appertaining to Rebels)" to be free if they were "able and willing to bear Arms" for the British.

Dunmore's Proclamation, which offered freedom to slaves willing to fight for the crown, heightened concerns among patriot leaders about the consequences of declaring independence. Although they wanted liberty for themselves, most did not want to disrupt the plantation economy or the existing social hierarchy. Could the colonies throw off the shackles of British tyranny without loosening other bonds at the same time? Given these concerns, many delegates at the Continental Congress, which included large planters, successful merchants, and professional men, hesitated to act.

Moreover, some still hoped for a negotiated settlement. But the king and Parliament refused to compromise in any way with colonies that they considered to be in rebellion. Instead, in December 1775, the king prohibited any negotiation or trade with the colonies, adding further weight to the claims of radicals that independence was a necessity. The January 1776 publication of Tom Paine's **Common Sense**,

which sold more than 120,000 copies in three months, helped turn the tide toward independence as well.

Paine rooted his arguments both in biblical stories familiar to American readers and in newer scientific analogies, such as Isaac Newton's theory of gravity. It was Paine's ability to wield both religious and scientific ideas—appealing to the spirit and the intellect—that made *Common Sense* attractive to diverse groups of colonists. Within weeks of its publication, George Washington wrote to a friend that "the sound Doctrine and unanswerable reasoning contain [in] Common Sense" would convince colonists of the "Propriety of a Separation." Farmers and artisans also applauded *Common Sense*, debating its claims at taverns and coffeehouses, which had become increasingly popular venues for political discussion in the 1760s and 1770s.

Explore

Read Paine's words and a rebuttal in Documents 6.1 and 6.2.

By the spring of 1776, a growing number of patriots believed that independence was necessary. Colonies began to take control of their legislatures and instruct their delegates to the Continental Congress to support independence. The congress also sent an agent to France to request economic and military assistance for the patriot cause. And in May, the congress advised colonies that had not yet done so to establish independent governments.

Declaring Independence

Taken together, the spread of armed conflict and the rationale offered in *Common Sense* convinced patriots that the time to declare independence was at hand. In early June 1776, Richard Henry Lee of Virginia introduced a motion to the Continental Congress, resolving that "these United Colonies are, and of right ought to be, Free and Independent States." A heated debate followed in which Lee and John Adams argued passionately for independence. Eventually, even more cautious delegates, like Robert Livingston of New York, were convinced. Livingston concluded that "they should yield to the torrent if they hoped to direct it." He then joined Adams, Thomas Jefferson, Benjamin Franklin, and Roger Sherman on a committee to draft a formal statement justifying independence.

The thirty-three-year-old Jefferson took the lead in preparing the declaration. Building on ideas expressed by Paine, Adams, Lee, and George Mason, he drew on language used in the dozens of local "declarations" written earlier by town meetings, county officials, and colonial assemblies. The Virginia Declaration of Rights drafted by Mason in May 1776, for example, claimed that "all men are

Debating Independence: Two Views

Thomas Paine's *Common Sense* was the most widely read pamphlet supporting American independence. Paine's plain style and use of biblical allusions appealed to ordinary people and ignited the Revolutionary movement. But not all colonists were convinced. Charles Inglis, rector of Trinity Church in New York City, published loyalist pamphlets, though often anonymously and from the safety of the British-occupied city. His 1776 pamphlet *The True Interest of America Impartially Stated* provided one of the most influential loyalist arguments.

Explore

6.1 Thomas Paine | *Common Sense*, January 1776

In England a King hath little more to do than to make war and give away places; which, in plain terms, is to impoverish the nation, and set it together by the ears. A pretty business, indeed, for a man to be allowed eight hundred thousand sterling a year for, and worshipped into the bargain! Of more worth is one honest man to society, and in the sight of God, than all the crowned ruffians that ever lived. . . .

But where, say some, is the King of America? I will tell you, friend, he reigns above, and does not make havock of mankind like the royal brute of Great Britain. Yet that we may not appear to be defective even in earthly honors, let a day be solemnly set apart for proclaiming the charter; let it be brought forth, placed on the divine law, the word of God: let a crown be placed thereon, by which the world may know that so far we approve of monarchy, that in America, THE LAW IS KING. For as in absolute governments the King is law, so in free countries the Law *ought* to be King; and there ought to be no other. But lest any ill use should afterwards arise, let the crown, at the conclusion of the ceremony, be demolished, and scattered among the people whose right it is.

A government of our own is our natural right; and when a man seriously reflects on the precariousness of his human affairs, he will become convinced, that it is infinitely wiser and safer, to form a constitution of our own in a cool deliberate manner, while we have it in our power, than to trust such an interesting event to time and chance.

Source: Thomas Paine, *Common Sense; Addressed to the Inhabitants of America* (London: H. D. Symonds, 1792), 11, 20.

born equally free and independent, and have certain inherent natural Rights." Central to many of these documents was the contract theory of government proposed by the seventeenth-century British philosopher John Locke. He argued that sovereignty resided in the people, who submitted voluntarily to laws and authorities in exchange for protection of their life, liberty, and property. The people could therefore reconstitute or overthrow a government that abused its powers. Jefferson summarized this argument and then listed the abuses and crimes perpetrated by King George III against the colonies, which justified patriots' decision to break their contract with British authorities.

Once prepared, the **Declaration of Independence** was then debated and revised. In the final version, all references to slavery were removed. But delegates agreed to list among the abuses suffered by the colonies the fact that the king "excited domestic insurrections amongst us," referring to the threat posed by Dunmore to the institution of slavery. On July 2, 1776, delegates from twelve colonies approved the Declaration, with only New York abstaining. Independence was publicly proclaimed on July 4 when the Declaration was published as a broadside to be circulated throughout the colonies, although such an act was tantamount to treason.

REVIEW & RELATE

- What challenges did Washington face when he was given command of the Continental Army?

- How and why did proponents of independence prevail in the debates that preceded the publication of the Declaration of Independence?

Explore

6.2 Charles Inglis | The True Interest of America Impartially Stated, March 1776

Suppose we were to revolt from Great Britain, declare ourselves independent, and set up a republic of our own—what would be the consequence? I stand aghast at the prospect; my blood runs chill when I think of the calamities, the complicated evils that must ensue, and may be clearly foreseen—it is impossible for any man to foresee them all. . . .

The Americans are properly Britons. They have the same manners, habits, and ideas of Britons; and have been accustomed to a similar form of government. But Britons never could bear the extremes, either of monarchy or republicanism. Some of their kings have aimed at despotism, but always failed. Repeated efforts have been made toward democracy, and they equally failed. Once, indeed, republicanism triumphed over the constitution; the despotism of one person ensued; both were finally expelled. . . . Limited monarchy is the form of government which is most favorable to liberty, which is best adapted to the genius and temper of Britons; although here and there among us a crackbrained zealot for democracy or absolute monarchy may be sometimes found.

Source: The Reverend Charles Inglis, *The True Interest of America Impartially Stated* (Philadelphia, 1776).

Interpret the Evidence

- How do Paine and Inglis differ in what they consider the proper form of government for the Americas?
- Why might Inglis have chosen to attack Paine's argument in *Common Sense* so vehemently?

Put It in Context

Why did the pamphlet emerge as a popular form of political discourse during the Revolutionary era?

Choosing Sides

Probably no more than half of American colonists actively supported the patriots. Perhaps a fifth actively supported the British, including many merchants and most officials appointed by the king and Parliament. The rest tried to stay neutral or were largely indifferent unless the war came to their doorstep. Both patriots and loyalists included men and women from all classes and races and from both rural and urban areas.

Recruiting Supporters

Men who took up arms against the British before independence was declared and the women who supported them clearly demonstrated their commitment to the patriot cause. In some colonies, patriots had organized local committees, courts, and assemblies to assume governance should British officials lose their authority. White servants and enslaved blacks in Virginia who fled to British ships or marched with Lord Dunmore made their loyalties known as well. Some Indians, too, declared their allegiance early in the conflict. In May 1775, Guy Johnson, the British superintendent for Indian affairs for the northern colonies, left Albany, New York, and sought refuge in Canada. He was accompanied by 120 British loyalists and 90 Mohawk warriors. The latter were led by the mission-educated chief of the Mohawks, Joseph Brant (Thayendanegea), who had translated the Anglican prayer book into Mohawk and who had fought with the British in the French and Indian War.

The Continental Congress, like Johnson, recognized the importance of Indians to the outcome of any colonial war. It appointed commissioners from the "United Colonies" to meet with representatives of the six nations of the Iroquois Confederacy in August 1775. While Brant's group of Mohawk warriors had already committed to supporting the British, some Oneida Indians, influenced by missionary and patriot sympathizer Samuel Kirkland, wanted to support the colonies. Others, however, urged neutrality, at least for the moment.

> **Explore**
>
> See Document 6.3 for one Oneida leader's reasons for remaining neutral.

Once independence was declared, there was far more pressure on all groups to choose sides. The stance of political and military leaders and soldiers was clear. But to win against Great Britain required the support of a large portion of the civilian population as well. As battle lines shifted back and forth across New England, the Middle Atlantic region, and the South, many civilians caught up in the fighting were faced with difficult choices.

DOCUMENT 6.3

Oneida Address to Connecticut Governor Jonathan Trumbull, June 1775

American Indians faced a potentially perilous choice once the Revolutionary War began. Like the undecided colonists, Indians had to determine whether to align with the patriots or with the loyalists. The members of the Oneida tribe in Connecticut sought a middle course, hoping to stake out neutral ground between the opposing sides. The following statement from the chief warriors of the Oneida to the governor of Connecticut outlines the tribe's reasoning. The Oneidas eventually did take a side; unlike most tribes, they fought alongside the colonists.

Explore

BROTHERS: We have heard of the unhappy differences and great contention between you and Old England. We wonder greatly, and are troubled in our minds.

BROTHERS: Possess your minds in peace respecting us Indians. We cannot intermeddle in this dispute between two brothers. The quarrel seems to be unnatural. You are *two brothers of one blood*. We are unwilling to join on either side in such a contest, for we bear an equal affection to both you Old and New England. Should the great king of England apply to us for aid, we shall deny him; if the Colonies apply, we shall refuse. The present situation of you two brothers is new and strange to us. We Indians cannot find, nor recollect in the traditions of our ancestors, the like case, or a similar instance.

BROTHERS: For these reasons possess your minds in peace, and take no umbrage that we Indians refuse joining in the contest. We are for peace.

BROTHERS: Was it an alien, a foreign nation, who had struck you, we should look into the matter. We hope, through the wise government and good pleasure of God, your distresses may soon be removed and the dark clouds be dispersed.

BROTHERS: As we have declared for peace, we desire you will not apply to our Indian brethren in New England for their assistance. Let us Indians be all of one mind, and live with one another; and you white people settle your own disputes between yourselves.

Source: William Leete Stone, *Life of Joseph Brant—Thayendanegea* (New York: Anderson V. Blake, 1838), 1:62–63.

Interpret the Evidence

• Why does the Oneida chief address his audience as "brothers"?

• How does the chief justify the Oneidas' neutral stance?

Put It in Context

Why was it difficult, if not impossible, for Indians and colonists to remain neutral once the fighting started?

Many colonists who remained loyal to the king found safe haven in cities like New York, Newport, and Charleston, which remained under British control throughout much of the war. **Loyalist** men were welcomed as reinforcements to the British army. Still, those who made their loyalist sympathies clear risked a good deal. When British troops were forced out of cities or towns they had temporarily occupied, many loyalists faced harsh reprisals. Patriots had no qualms about invading the homes of loyalists, punishing women and children, and destroying or confiscating property. Grace Galloway was denounced by former friends and evicted from her Philadelphia home after her loyalist husband, Joseph, fled to New York City in 1777.

Many loyalists were members of the economic and political elite, but others came from ordinary backgrounds. Tenants, small farmers, and slaves joined the loyalist cause in defiance of their landlords, their owners, and wealthy planters. The Hudson valley was home to many poorer loyalists, whose sympathy for the British was heightened by the patriot commitments of their wealthy landlords. When the fighting moved south, many former Regulators (see chapter 5) also supported the British as a result of their hostility to patriot leaders among North Carolina's eastern elite.

Perhaps most importantly, the majority of Indian nations ultimately sided with the British. The Mohawk, Seneca, and Cayuga nations in the North and the Cherokee and Creek nations in the South were among Great Britain's leading allies. Although British efforts to limit colonial migration, such as the Proclamation Line of 1763, had failed, most Indian nations still believed that a British victory offered the only hope of ending further encroachments on their territory.

Choosing Neutrality

Early in the war, many Indian nations proclaimed their neutrality. The Delaware and Shawnee nations, caught between British and American forces in the Ohio River valley, were especially eager to stay out of the fighting. The Shawnee chief Cornstalk worked tirelessly to maintain his nation's neutrality, but American soldiers killed him under a flag of truce in 1777. Eventually the Shawnees, like the Delawares, chose to ally with the British side after patriot forces refused to accept their claims of neutrality.

Colonists who sought to remain neutral during the war also faced hostility and danger. Some 80,000 Quakers, Mennonites, Amish, Shakers, and Moravians considered war immoral and embraced neutrality. These men refused to bear arms, hire substitutes, or pay taxes to new state

governments. The largest number of religious pacifists lived in Pennsylvania. Despite Quakerism's deep roots there, pacifists were treated as suspect by both patriots and loyalists.

In June 1778, Pennsylvania authorities jailed nine Mennonite farmers who refused to take an oath of allegiance to the revolutionary government. Their worldly goods were sold by the state, leaving their wives and children destitute. Quakers were routinely fined and imprisoned for refusing to support the patriot cause and harassed by British authorities in the areas they controlled. At the same time, Quaker meetings regularly disciplined members who offered aid to either side, disowning more than 1,700 members during the Revolution. Betsy Ross was among those disciplined when her husband joined the patriot forces and she sewed flags for the Continental Army.

Committing to Independence

After July 4, 1776, the decision to support independence took on new meaning. If the United States failed to win the war, all those who actively supported the cause could be considered traitors. The families of Continental soldiers faced especially difficult decisions as the conflict spread across the colonies and soldiers moved farther and farther from home. Men too old or too young to fight proved their patriotism by gathering arms and ammunition and patrolling local communities.

Meanwhile some female patriots accompanied their husbands or fiancés as camp followers, providing food, laundry, sewing, and other material resources to needy soldiers. Most patriot women remained at home, however, and demonstrated their commitment to independence by raising funds, gathering information, and sending clothes, bedding, and other goods to soldiers at the front. The Continental Army was desperately short of supplies from the beginning of the war. Northern women were urged to increase cloth production, while farm women in the South were asked to plant crops to feed the soldiers. The response was overwhelming. Women in Hartford, Connecticut, produced 1,000 coats and vests and 1,600 shirts in 1776 alone. Mary Fraier of Chester County, Pennsylvania, was one of many women who collected clothing door-to-door and then washed and mended it before delivering it to troops stationed nearby. Other women opened their homes to soldiers wounded in battle or ill with fevers, dysentery, and other diseases.

Some African American women also became ardent patriots. Phillis Wheatley of Boston, whose owners taught her to read and write, published a collection of poems in

1776 and sent a copy to General Washington. She urged readers to recognize Africans as children of God:

> Remember Christians, Negroes, black as Cain,
> May be refin'd, and join th' angelic train

Rewarded with freedom by her master, Wheatley was among a small number of blacks who actively supported the patriot cause. Of course, the majority of black Americans labored as slaves in the South. While some joined the British in hopes of gaining their freedom, most were not free to choose sides.

REVIEW & RELATE

How did colonists choose sides during the Revolutionary War? What factors influenced their decisions?

Why did so many Indian tribes try to stay neutral during the conflict? Why was it so difficult for Indians to remain neutral?

✔ *LEARNINGCurve* bedfordstmartins.com/hewittlawson/LC

Fighting for Independence

After July 4, 1776, battles between British and colonial troops intensified, and the patriots suffered a series of military defeats that must have made some wonder about the wisdom of undertaking a revolution. It was more than five months after independence was declared before patriots celebrated a military victory against the British. In 1777, however, the tide turned for the Continental Army, although British forces remained formidable. A year later, it was clear that victory would not be easily won and that each side needed support from women on the home front as well as men on the battlefront.

British Troops Gain Early Victories

In the summer of 1776, when General Washington tried to lead his army out of Boston to confront British troops en route to New York City, many soldiers deserted and returned home. They believed that New York men should defend New York. Among the soldiers who remained with Washington, many were landless laborers whose wives and sisters followed the troops as their only means of support. Although Washington deemed these "camp followers" undesirable, the few hundred women provided critical services to ordinary soldiers. Ultimately, Washington arrived in New York with 19,000 men, many of whom were poorly armed and poorly trained and some of whom were coerced into service by local committees of safety.

The ragtag Continental force faced a formidable foe with a powerful navy and a far larger and better-trained army. Throughout the summer, British ships sailed into New York harbor or anchored off the coast of Long Island. General Howe, hoping to overwhelm the colonists, ordered 10,000 troops to march into the city in the weeks immediately after the Declaration of Independence was signed. But the Continental Congress rejected Howe's offer of peace and a royal pardon.

So Howe prepared to take control of New York City by force and then march up the Hudson valley, isolating New York and New England from the rest of the rebellious colonies. He was aided by some 8,000 Hessian mercenaries (German soldiers being paid to fight for the British) and naval reinforcements under the command of Admiral Richard Howe. On August 27, 1776, British forces clashed with a far smaller contingent of Continentals on Long Island. More than 1,500 patriots were killed or wounded in the fierce fighting, diminishing the army's strength even further.

By November, the British had captured Fort Lee in New Jersey and attacked the Continental Army at Fort Washington, north of New York City. The large community of loyalists in the New York/New Jersey region served as ready hosts for General Howe and his officers, and ordinary redcoats survived by looting the stores, farms, and homes of patriots. Meanwhile Washington led his weary troops and camp followers into Pennsylvania, while the Continental Congress, fearing a British attack on Philadelphia, fled to Baltimore.

Although General Howe might have ended the patriot threat right then by a more aggressive campaign, he was interested primarily in wearing down the Continental Army so that the colonies would plead for peace. Neither he nor Washington engaged in full-scale frontal assaults. Washington did not have the troops or arms to do so, but he also hoped that the British would accept American independence once they saw the enormous effort it would take to defeat the colonies.

Patriots Prevail in New Jersey

The Continental Army had not gained a single military victory between July 1776, when the colonies declared independence, and December. Fortunately for Washington, Howe followed the European tradition of waiting out the winter months and returning to combat after the spring thaw. This tactic gave the patriots the opportunity to regroup, repair weapons and wagons, and recruit soldiers. Yet Washington was not eager to face the cold and discomfort of the winter with troops discouraged by repeated defeats and retreats.

Camped in eastern Pennsylvania, Washington discovered that General Howe had sent Hessian troops to occupy

The British Burn New York City, 1776

This print by François Xavier Haberman shows several buildings along a New York City street set ablaze by the British troops of General William Howe on September 19, 1776. It also depicts citizens being beaten by redcoats while African slaves engage in looting. The British promised slaves their freedom if they opposed the patriots.   Library of Congress

the city of Trenton, New Jersey, just across the Delaware River. On Christmas Eve, Washington crossed the river with some 2,500 soldiers and attacked Trenton. The Continentals quickly routed the surprised Hessians. Then they marched on Princeton, where they battled three regiments of regular British troops, defeating them on January 3, 1777. The British army retreated from New Jersey, settling back into New York City, and the Continental Congress returned to Philadelphia. By January 1777, it seemed clear to both sides that the conflict would indeed be harder, more costly, and more deadly than anyone had imagined in the spring of 1775.

A Critical Year of Warfare

The British and Continental armies emerged from their winter camps in the spring of 1777. The British forces, including regular army units, American loyalists, Indian allies, Hessians, and naval men-of-war, were concentrated largely in New York City and Canada. The Continental forces, numbering fewer than 5,000 men, were entrenched near Morristown, New Jersey, far from the patriot centers of New England and from the coastal areas controlled by the British army and navy. Although the Continental Congress had returned to Philadelphia, it feared that the British would seek to capture the city and split the United States in two.

General Howe also believed that the key to victory was capturing Philadelphia, and he hoped that success there might lead the patriots to surrender. Washington's force was too small to defeat Howe's army, but it delayed his advance on the capital city by attacks along the way. En route, Howe learned that he was still expected to reinforce General John Burgoyne's soldiers, who were advancing south from Canada. Too late to redirect his efforts, Howe continued to Philadelphia and captured it in September 1777. Meanwhile Burgoyne and his 7,200 troops had regained control of Fort Ticonderoga on July 7. He continued south along the Hudson valley, but by late July his forces stalled as they waited for supplies from Canada and reinforcements from Howe and General Barry St. Leger.

In July, St. Leger had marched east through New York State while Joseph Brant and his sister Molly Brant, a powerful Indian leader in her own right, gathered a force of Mohawk, Seneca, and Cayuga warriors to support the British forces. But on August 6, they suffered a stunning defeat. At Oriskany, New York, a band of German American farmers led by General Nicholas Herkimer held off the British advance, allowing General Arnold to reach nearby Fort Stanwix with reinforcements. On August 23, the British and Indian troops were forced to retreat to Canada (Map 6.1).

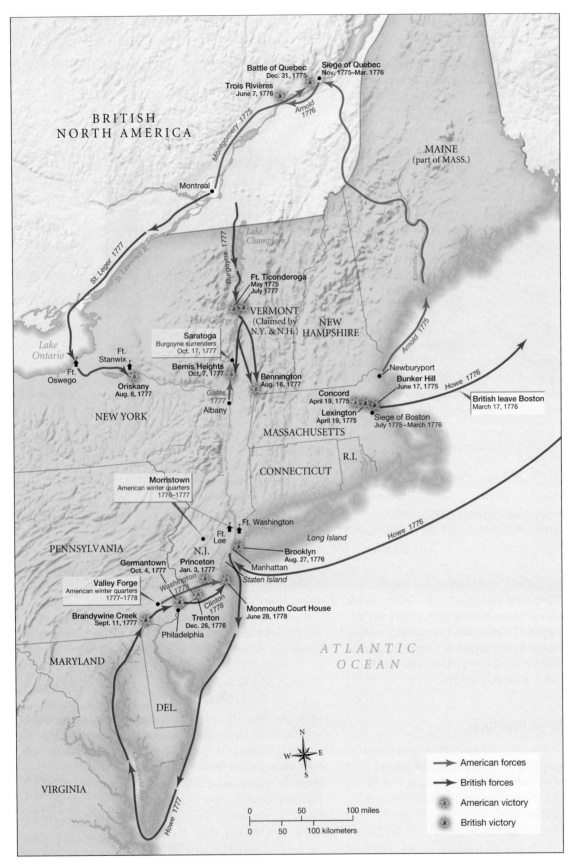

MAP 6.1 The War in the North, 1775–1778

After early battles in Massachusetts, patriots invaded Canada but failed to capture Quebec. The British army captured New York City in 1776 and Philadelphia in 1777, but New Jersey remained a battle zone through 1778. Meanwhile General Burgoyne secured Canada for Britain and then headed south, but his forces were defeated by patriots at the crucial Battle of Saratoga.

General Howe's reinforcements never materialized, and Burgoyne now faced a brutal onslaught from patriot militiamen. Vermont's Green Mountain Boys, Continental soldiers under the command of Generals Horatio Gates and Benedict Arnold, and their Oneida allies also poured into the region. In September, patriots defeated the British at Freeman's Farm, with the British suffering twice the casualties of the Continentals. Fighting intensified in early October, when Burgoyne lost a second battle at Freeman's Farm. Ten days later, he surrendered his remaining army of 5,800 men to General Gates at nearby Saratoga, New York.

The Continental Army's victory in the **Battle of Saratoga** stunned the British and strengthened the patriots. It undercut the significance of Howe's victory at Philadelphia and indicated the general's misunderstanding of the character of the patriot cause and the nature of the war he was fighting. The patriot victory gave hope to General Washington as his troops dug in at Valley Forge for another long winter and to members of the Continental Congress who had temporarily retreated to York, Pennsylvania. It also gave Benjamin Franklin greater leverage to convince French officials to support the American cause.

Patriots Gain Critical Assistance

Despite significant victories in the fall of 1777, the following winter proved especially difficult for Continental forces. The quarters at **Valley Forge** were again marked by bitter cold, poor food, inadequate clothing, and scarce supplies. Discipline deteriorated, and many recent recruits were poorly trained. Critical assistance arrived through the voluntary efforts of Baron Friedrich von Steuben, a Prussian officer recruited by Benjamin Franklin, who took charge of drilling soldiers. Other officers experienced in European warfare also joined the patriot cause during the winter of 1777–1778: the Marquis de Lafayette of France, Johann Baron de Kalb of Bavaria, and Thaddeus Kosciusko and Casimir Count Pulaski, both of Poland. The Continental Army continued to be plagued by problems of recruitment, discipline, wages, and supplies. But the contributions of Steuben, Lafayette, and other foreign volunteers, along with the leadership of Washington and his officers, sustained the military effort.

Patriots on the home front were also plagued by problems in 1777–1778. Families living in battlefield areas were especially vulnerable to the shifting fortunes of war. When British troops captured Philadelphia in the fall of 1777, a British officer commandeered the house of Elizabeth Drinker, a well-to-do Quaker matron. An angry Drinker reported that the officer moved in with "3 Horses 2 Cows 2 Sheep and 3 Turkeys" along with "3 Servants 2 White Men and one Negro Boy." Meanwhile women who lived far from the conflict were forced to fend for themselves as soldiers moved wherever the Continental Army took them. The wives of political leaders also faced long years alone while their husbands remained at their posts. To hasten the end, many women formed voluntary associations, like the Ladies Association of Philadelphia, to provide critical resources for the army and thus aid the patriot cause. **See Document Project 6: Women in the Revolution, page 185.**

While most women worked tirelessly on the home front, some cast their fate with the army. Camp followers continued to provide critical services to the military, including cooking, washing, sewing, and nursing. They suffered along with the troops in the face of scarce supplies and harsh weather and depended like the soldiers on food, clothing, and bedding supplied by female volunteers in Philadelphia, Boston, Baltimore, and other cities.

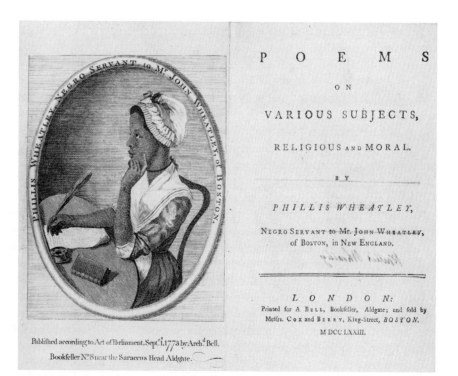

Phillis Wheatley

This portrait of Phillis Wheatley appears on the title page of her book of poems, printed in London in 1773. Like Deborah Sampson, Phillis Wheatley sided with the patriots, but as a writer, not a soldier. She won her personal freedom as a result of her efforts. The Pierpont Morgan Library/Art Resource, NY

Women with sufficient courage and resources served as spies and couriers for British and Continental forces. Lydia Darragh, a wealthy Philadelphian, eavesdropped on conversations among the British officers who occupied her house and then carried detailed notes to Washington hidden in the folds of her dress. Some women, like Nancy Hart Morgan of Georgia, took more direct action. Morgan protected her backcountry home from half a dozen British soldiers by lulling them into a sense of security at dinner, hiding their guns, and shooting two before neighbors came to hang the rest.

Some patriot women took up arms on the battlefield. A few, such as Margaret Corbin, accompanied their husbands to the front lines and were thrust into battle. When her husband was killed in battle at Fort Washington in November 1776, Corbin took his place loading and firing cannons until the fort fell to the British. In addition, a small number of women, like Deborah Sampson, disguised themselves as men and enlisted as soldiers.

Surviving on the Home Front

Whether black or white, enslaved or free, women and children faced hardship, uncertainty, loneliness, and fear as a result of the war. Even those who did not directly engage enemy troops took on enormous burdens during the conflict. Farm wives had to take on the tasks of plowing or planting in addition to their normal domestic duties. In cities, women worked ceaselessly to find sufficient food, wood, candles, and cloth to maintain themselves and their children. One desperate wife, Mary Donnelly, wrote, "[I was] afraid to open my Eyes on the Daylight [lest] I should hear my infant cry for Bread and not have it in my power to relieve him."

As the war spread, women watched as Continental and British forces slaughtered cattle and hogs for food, stole corn and other crops or burned them to keep the enemy from obtaining supplies, looted houses and shops, and kidnapped or liberated slaves and servants. Some home invasions turned savage. Both patriot and loyalist papers in New York, Philadelphia, and Charleston reported cases of rape.

Despite the desperate circumstances, most women knew they had to act on their own behalf to survive. Faced with merchants who hoarded goods in hopes of making greater profits when prices rose, housewives raided stores and warehouses and took coffee, sugar, and other items they needed. Others learned as much as they could about family finances so that they could submit reports to local officials if their houses, farms, or businesses were damaged or looted. Growing numbers of women banded together to assist one another, to help more impoverished families, and to supply troops badly in need of clothes, food, bandages, and bullets.

REVIEW & RELATE

How did the patriot forces fare in 1776? How and why did the tide of war turn in 1777?

What role did colonial women and foreign men play in the conflict in the early years of the war?

LEARNINGCurve bedfordstmartins.com/hewittlawson/LC

Governing in Revolutionary Times

Amid the constant upheavals of war, patriot leaders established governments to replace those abolished by declaring independence. At the national level, responsibilities ranged from coordinating and funding military operations to developing diplomatic relations with foreign countries and Indian nations. At the state level, constitutions had to be drafted and approved, laws enforced, and military needs assessed and met. Whether state or national, new governments had to assure their followers that they were not simply replacing old forms of oppression with new ones. Yet few states moved to eliminate the most oppressive institution in the nation, slavery.

Colonies Become States

For most of the war, the Continental Congress acted in lieu of a national government while the delegates worked to devise a more permanent structure. But the congress had little authority of its own and depended mainly on states for funds and manpower. Delegates did draft the **Articles of Confederation** in 1777 and submitted them to the states for approval. Eight of the thirteen states ratified the plan for a national government by mid-1778. But nearly three more years passed before the last state, Maryland, approved the Articles. The lack of a central government meant that state governments played a critical role throughout the war.

Even before the Continental Congress declared American independence, some colonies had forced royal officials to flee and established new state governments. Some states abided by the regulations in their colonial charters or by English common law. Others, including Delaware, South Carolina, Virginia, New Jersey, and Pennsylvania, created new governments based on a written constitution. Because the earliest constitutions were written in the midst of war, they were often completed in haste, sometimes by legislative bodies without any specific authorization and without popular approval of the final document.

These constitutions reflected the fear of centralized power that emerged from the struggle against British tyranny. In Pennsylvania, radical patriots influenced by Tom Paine developed one of the most democratic constitutions, enhancing the power of voters and legislators and limiting the power of the executive branch. The constitution established only one legislative house, elected by popular vote, and the governor was replaced by an executive council. Those elected to the legislature could not serve for more than four in any seven years to discourage the formation of a political aristocracy in the state. Although Pennsylvania's constitution was among the most radical, all states limited centralized power in some way.

Finally, most states, building on the model offered by Virginia, included in their constitutions a bill of rights that ensured citizens freedom of the press, freedom of elections, speedy trials by one's peers, humane punishments, and the right to form militias. Some state constitutions expanded these rights to include freedom of speech and assembly, the right to petition and to bear arms, and equal protection of the laws. The New Jersey constitution, written in 1776, enfranchised all free inhabitants who met the property qualifications, thereby allowing some single or widowed women and free blacks to vote in local and state elections. This surprising decision was apparently made with little debate or dissent.

Patriots Divide over Slavery

Although state constitutions were revolutionary in many respects, few of them addressed the issue of slavery. Only Vermont abolished slavery in its 1777 constitution. Legislators in Pennsylvania approved a gradual abolition law by which slaves born after 1780 could claim their freedom at age twenty-eight. In Massachusetts, two slaves sued for their freedom in county courts in 1780–1781. Quock Walker, who had been promised his freedom by a former master, sued his current master to gain manumission (release from slavery). About the same time, an enslaved woman, Mumbet, who was the widow of a Revolutionary soldier, initiated a similar case. Mumbet won her case and changed her name to Elizabeth Freeman. When Walker's owner appealed the local court's decision to free his slave, the Massachusetts Supreme Court cited the Mumbet case and ruled that slavery conflicted with the state constitution, which declared "all men . . . free and equal." Walker, too, was freed.

In southern states, however, slaves had little recourse to the law. No state south of Pennsylvania abolished the institution of slavery. And southerners held about 400,000 of the nation's 450,000 slaves. In states such as Virginia, the Carolinas, and Georgia, life for enslaved women and men

Elizabeth "Mumbet" Freeman

This watercolor portrait of Elizabeth "Mumbet" Freeman was painted on ivory by Susan Anne Ridley Sedgwick in 1811 when Freeman was sixty-nine. The first slave to be freed in Massachusetts as a result of a court case, she later worked as a domestic servant for her attorney, Theodore Sedgwick, Susan Ridley Sedgwick's father-in-law. © Massachusetts Historical Society, Boston/The Bridgeman Art Library

grew increasingly harsh during the war. Because British forces promised freedom to blacks who fought with them, slave owners and patriot armies in the South did everything possible to ensure that African Americans did not make it behind British lines. The thousands who did manage to flee to British-controlled areas were often left to defend themselves when the redcoats retreated. There were exceptions. Lord Dunmore took a few thousand blacks with him when he fled Virginia in 1776, and British forces under General Sir Henry Clinton carried some 20,000 African Americans aboard ships retreating from Charleston and Savannah in 1781.

Despite the uncertain prospects for African Americans, the American Revolution dealt a blow to the institution of slavery. For many blacks, Revolutionary ideals required the end of slavery. Northern free black communities grew rapidly during and after the war, especially in seaport cities like New York, Philadelphia, and Boston where labor was in high demand. In the South, too, thousands of slaves gained freedom during the war, either by joining the British or by fleeing in the midst of battlefield chaos. As many as one-quarter of South Carolina's slaves had emancipated themselves by the end of the Revolution. Yet as the Continental Congress worked toward developing a framework for a national government, few delegates considered slavery or its abolition a significant issue.

France Allies with the Patriots

The Continental Congress considered an alliance with France far more critical to patriot success than the issue of slavery. French financial and military support could aid the patriots immensely, and France's traditional rivalry with Great Britain made an alliance plausible.

For France, defeat of the British would mean increased trade with North America and redressing the balance of power in Europe, where Great Britain had gained the upper hand since France's defeat in the French and Indian War. Indeed, in 1775 the French government had secretly provided funds to smuggle military supplies to the colonies. In December 1776, the Continental Congress sent Benjamin Franklin to Paris to serve as an unofficial liaison for the newly independent United States. Franklin was enormously successful, securing supplies and becoming a favorite among the French aristocracy and ordinary citizens alike.

But the French were initially unwilling to forge a formal compact with the upstart patriots. Only when the

Continental Army defeated General Burgoyne at Saratoga in October 1777 did King Louis XVI agree to an official alliance. By February 1778, Franklin had secured an agreement that approved trading rights between the United States and all French possessions. France then recognized the United States as an independent nation, relinquished French territorial claims on mainland North America, and sent troops to reinforce the Continental Army. In return, the United States promised to defend French holdings in the Caribbean. A year later, Spain allied itself with France to protect its own North American holdings.

British leaders, infuriated by the alliance, declared war on France. Yet doing so ensured that military conflicts would spread well beyond North America as French forces attacked British outposts in Gibraltar, the Bay of Bengal, Senegal in West Africa, and Grenada in the West Indies. British military expenditures skyrocketed from £4 million in 1775 to £20 million in 1782. Meanwhile, in addition to their attacks on British outposts, the French supplied the United States with military officers, weapons, funds, and critical naval resources. Spain contributed by capturing British forts in West Florida and using New Orleans as a base for privateering expeditions against British ships.

Explore

To read one French volunteer soldier's experience, see Document 6.4.

Washington's French Allies

This late-eighteenth-century painting by James Peale the Elder shows Washington and his generals at Yorktown, site of the final major battle of the Revolutionary War. Among Washington's generals were the Frenchmen the Marquis de Lafayette and the Comte de Rochambeau. Peale was not at Yorktown, but he fought in the Continental Army for three years.   Private Collection/Photo © Christie's Images/The Bridgeman Art Library

Faced with this new alliance, Britain's prime minister, Lord North (1771–1782), decided to concentrate British forces in New York City. This tactic forced the British army to abandon Philadelphia and return the city to patriot control in the summer of 1778. For the remainder of the war, New York City provided the sole British stronghold in the North, serving as a supply center and prisoner-of-war camp. At the same time, the American cause gained the support of the French navy, a critical addition given the limited state of American naval forces.

DOCUMENT 6.4

Chevalier de Pontgibaud | A French Volunteer at Valley Forge, 1828

After a string of defeats in the fall of 1777, the Continental Army needed an encampment to wait out the winter and prepare for the fighting to resume in the spring. General George Washington chose to station his men in Valley Forge, Pennsylvania. The conditions proved formidable; more than 2,000 men died from disease, exacerbated by poor housing and scant supplies. In the following selection, from a memoir written in 1828, Chevalier de Pontgibaud, a French volunteer in the Continental Army, describes his arrival at Valley Forge in December 1777.

Explore

What problems seem particularly troublesome to Pontgibaud?

What is the significance of the woolen coats worn by Continental officers?

Why does Pontgibaud believe the colonial cause was eventually successful?

Soon I came in sight of the camp. My imagination had pictured an army with uniforms, the glitter of arms, standards, etc., in short, military pomp of all sorts. Instead of the imposing spectacle I expected, I saw, grouped together or standing alone, a few militia men, poorly clad, and for the most part without shoes; many of them badly armed, but all well supplied with provisions, and I noticed that tea and sugar formed part of their rations. I did not then know that this was not unusual, and I laughed, for it made me think of the recruiting sergeants on the Quai de la Ferraille at Paris, who say to the yokels, "You will want for nothing when you are in the regiment, but if bread should run short you must not mind eating cakes." Here the soldiers had tea and sugar. In passing through the camp I also noticed soldiers wearing cotton night-caps under their hats, and some having for cloaks or great-coats, coarse woollen blankets, exactly like those provided for the patients in our French hospitals. I learned afterwards that these were the officers and generals.

Such, in strict truth, was—at the time I came amongst them—the appearance of this armed mob, the leader of whom was the man who has rendered the name of Washington famous; such were the colonists—unskilled warriors who learned in a few years how to conquer the finest troops that England could send against them. Such also—at the beginning of the War of Independence—was the state of want in the insurgent army, and such was the scarcity of money, and the poverty of that government, now so rich, powerful, and prosperous, that its notes, called Continental Paper Money, were nearly valueless.

Source: Chevalier de Pontgibaud, *A French Volunteer of the War for Independence*, ed. and trans. Robert Douglas (New York: J. W. Bouton, 1897), 40–41.

Put It in Context

How did the Continental Army differ from the military forces of European nations?

Raising Armies and Funds

The French alliance did create one unintended problem for the Continental Army. When Americans heard that France was sending troops, fewer men volunteered for military service, even when bounties were offered. Others took the bounty and then failed to report for duty. Local officials had the authority to draft men into the army or to accept substitutes for draftees. By the late 1770s, some draftees forced enslaved men to take their place; others hired landless laborers, the handicapped, or the mentally unfit as substitutes.

As the war spread south and west in 1778–1779, Continental forces were stretched thin, and enlistments faltered further. Soldiers faced injuries, disease, and shortages of food and ammunition. Soldiers also risked capture by the British, one of the worst fates to befall a Continental. Most patriot prisoners were held in jails in New York City or on ships in the harbor under abusive, unsanitary conditions. Colonel Ethan Allen, a captive for two and a half years, described the filthy accommodations, inadequate water, and horrid stench of the British prisons and noted the "hellish delight and triumph of the tories . . . exulting over the dead bodies of their murdered country-men." A few brave women like Elizabeth Burgin carried food and other supplies to patriot prisoners of war. Alto-gether, between 8,000 and 11,500 patriots died in British prisons in New York—more than died in battle.

The Continental Congress could do little to aid prisoners or their families, given the financial problems it faced. With no authority to impose taxes on American citizens, the congress had to find other ways to meet its financial responsibilities. It borrowed money from wealthy patriots, accepted loans from France and the Netherlands, and printed money of its own—some $200 million by 1780. However, money printed by the states was still used far more widely than were Continental dollars. "Continentals" depreciated so quickly that by late 1780 it took one hundred continentals to buy one silver dollar's worth of goods.

The situation in Philadelphia, the seat of national government, demonstrated the difficulties caused by inflation. In January 1779, housewives, sailors, and artisans gathered on the cold streets to protest high prices and low wages. Although officials tried to regulate prices, riots erupted and flour merchants were especially targeted by mobs of women and young people. By October, Philadel-phia militiamen joined the protests, marching on the house of James Wilson, a Philadelphia lawyer who sided with merchants accused of hoarding goods. Hours of rioting followed, and eventually fifteen militiamen were arrested and fined. But in the following days, city officials distrib-uted much-needed food to the poor. The Fort Wilson riot echoed events in towns and cities across the young nation.

The congress finally improved its financial standing slightly by using a $6 million loan from France to back certificates issued to wealthy patriots. Meanwhile states raised money through taxes to provide funds for govern-ment operations, backing for its paper money, and other expenses. Most residents found such taxes incredibly burdensome given wartime inflation, and even the most patriotic began to protest further efforts to squeeze money out of them. Thus the financial status of the new nation remained precarious.

Indian Affairs and Land Claims

The congress also sought to settle land claims in the western regions of the nation and build alliances with additional Indian nations. The two issues were intertwined, and both were difficult to resolve. Most Indian nations had long-standing complaints against colonists who intruded on their lands, and many patriot leaders made it clear that indepen-dence would mean further expansion into western lands.

In the late 1770s, British forces and their Indian allies fought bitter battles against patriot militias and Continental forces all along the frontier. Each side destroyed property, ruined crops, and killed civilians. In the summer and fall of 1778, Indian and American civilians suffered through a series of brutal attacks in Wyoming, Pennsylvania; Ono-quaga, New York (Brant's home community); and Cherry Valley, New York. Patriots and Indians also battled along the Virginia frontier after pioneer and militia leader Daniel Boone established a fort there in 1775.

In the South, 6,000 patriot troops laid waste to Cherokee villages in the Appalachian Mountains in retaliation for the killing of white intruders along the Watauga River by a renegade Cherokee warrior, Dragging Canoe. Yet a cousin of Dragging Canoe, Nancy Ward (Nanye-hi), who had married a white trader, remained sympathetic to the patriot cause. During the Revolution, she warned patriots of pending attacks by pro-British Cherokee warriors in 1776 and 1780, allowing the patriots to launch their own attacks. Ward apparently believed that white settlement was inevitable and that winning the friendship of patriots was the best way to ensure the survival of the Cherokee nation. Hers, however, was a minority voice among frontier Indians.

Much western land had already been claimed by individual states like Virginia, Massachusetts, Connecticut, New York, and Georgia. States with western claims hoped to use the lands to reward soldiers and expand their settlements. Maryland spoke for states without such claims, arguing that if such lands were "wrested from the common enemy by the blood and treasure of the thirteen States," they should be considered "common property, subject to be parcelled out by Congress into free and independent governments." In 1780 New York State finally ceded its western claims to the Continental Congress, and Connecti-cut and Massachusetts followed suit.

With land disputes settled, Maryland ratified the Articles of Confederation in March 1781, and a new national government was finally formed. But the congress's guarantee that western lands would be "disposed of for the common benefit of the United States" ensured continued conflicts with Indians.

REVIEW & RELATE

What values and concerns shaped state governments during the Revolutionary War?

What issues and challenges did the Continental Congress face even after the French joined the patriot side?

LEARNINGCurve bedfordstmartins.com/hewittlawson/LC

Winning the War and the Peace

From 1778 to 1781, the battlefront in the Revolution moved south and west. As conflicts with Britain and its Indian allies intensified along the western frontier, British troops reinforced by African American fugitives fought patriots in the Carolinas and Georgia. In the final years of the war, the patriots' ability to achieve victory rested on a combination of superb strategy, alliances with France and Spain, and the continued material support of affluent men and women. However, even after Britain's surrender in October 1781, the war dragged on while peace terms were negotiated. The celebrations of victory following the signing of a peace treaty were tempered by protests among Continental soldiers demanding back pay and by the realization of the new nation's looming problems.

Fighting in the West

While the congress debated the fate of western land claims, battles continued in the Ohio and Mississippi River valleys. British commanders at Fort Michilimackinac on Lake Huron recruited Sioux, Chippewa, and Sauk warriors to attack Spanish forces along the Mississippi, while soldiers at Fort Detroit armed Ottawa, Fox, and Miami warriors to assault American settlers flooding into the Ohio River valley. British forces from Fort Detroit also moved deeper into this region, establishing a post at Vincennes on the Wabash River.

The response to these British forays was effective, if not well coordinated. In 1778 a young patriot surveyor, George Rogers Clark of Virginia, organized a patriot expedition to counter Indian raids in the west and to reinforce Spanish and French allies in the upper Mississippi valley. He fought successfully against British and Indian forces at Kaskaskia

and Cahokia on the Mississippi River. Then Clark marched his troops through the bitter February cold and launched a surprise attack on British forces at Vincennes. Although Detroit remained in British hands, Spanish troops defeated British-allied Indian forces that attacked St. Louis, giving the patriots greater control in the Ohio valley (Map 6.2).

In the summer of 1779, General John Sullivan led 4,000 patriot troops on a campaign to wipe out Mohawk, Seneca, Cayuga, and Onondaga villages in central and western New York. He succeeded in ending most attacks by Britain's Iroquois allies and disrupting the supplies being sent by British forces at Fort Niagara. Patriot attacks in Ohio also continued. In one of the worst atrocities fomented by patriots, Pennsylvania militiamen massacred more than one hundred Delaware men, women, and children near present-day Canton, Ohio, even though the Delawares had converted to Christianity and declared their neutrality.

Battles between Indian nations and American settlers did not end with the American Revolution. For the moment, however, patriot militia units and Continental forces supported by French and Spanish allies had defeated British and Indian efforts to control the Mississippi and Ohio River valleys.

War Rages in the South

Meanwhile British troops sought to regain control of southern states from Georgia to Virginia. British troops captured Savannah, Georgia, in 1778 and soon extended their control over the entire state. When General Clinton was called north in late 1778 to lead British troops against Washington's Continentals in New Jersey, he left the southern campaign in the hands of Lord Charles Cornwallis.

In May 1780, General Cornwallis reclaimed Charleston, South Carolina, and accepted the surrender of 5,000 Continental soldiers, the largest surrender of patriot troops during the war. He then evicted patriots from the city, purged them from the state government, gained military control of the state, and imposed loyalty oaths on all Carolinians able to fight. To aid his efforts, local loyalists organized militias to battle patriots in the interior. Banastre Tarleton led one especially vicious company of loyalists who slaughtered civilians and murdered many who surrendered. In retaliation, planter and merchant Thomas Sumter organized 800 men who showed a similar disregard for regular army procedures, raiding largely defenseless loyalist settlements near Hanging Rock, South Carolina, in August 1780.

Conflicts between patriots and loyalists raged across the South until the war's end (see Map 6.2). As retaliatory violence erupted in the interior of South Carolina, General Gates marched his Continental troops south to join 2,000 militiamen from Virginia and North Carolina. But his

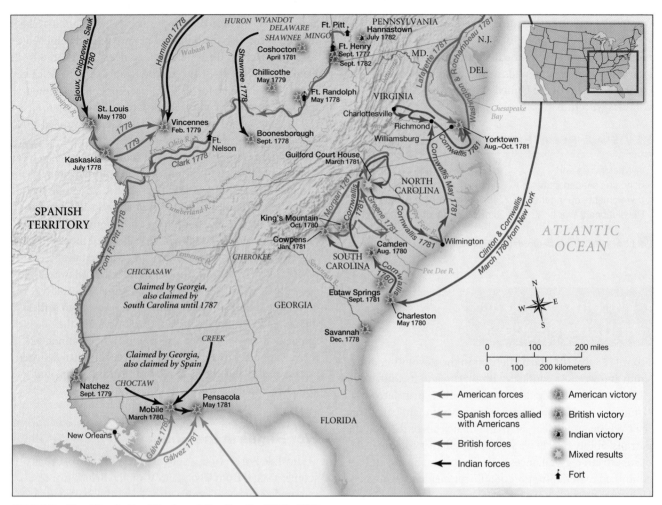

MAP 6.2   The War in the West and the South, 1777–1782

Between 1780 and 1781, major battles between Continental and British troops took place in Virginia and the Carolinas, and the British general Cornwallis finally surrendered at Yorktown, Virginia, in October 1781. But patriot forces also battled British troops and their Indian allies from 1777 to 1782 in the Ohio River valley, the lower Mississippi River, and the Gulf coast.

troops were exhausted and short of food, and on August 16 Cornwallis won a smashing victory against the combined patriot forces at Camden, South Carolina. Soon after news of Gates's defeat reached General Washington, he heard that Benedict Arnold, commander at West Point, had defected to the British. Indeed, he had been passing information to the British for some time.

Suddenly, British chances for victory seemed more hopeful. Clinton had moved the bulk of northern troops into New York City and could send units south from there to bolster Cornwallis. Cornwallis was in control of Georgia and South Carolina, and local loyalists were eager to gain control of the southern countryside. Meanwhile Continental soldiers in the North mutinied in early 1780 over terms of enlistment and pay. Patriot morale was low, funds were scarce, and civilians were growing weary of the war.

Yet somehow the patriots prevailed. A combination of luck, strong leadership, and French support turned the tide.

In October 1780, when Continental hopes looked especially bleak, a group of 800 frontier sharpshooters routed Major Patrick Ferguson's loyalist troops at King's Mountain in South Carolina. The victory kept Cornwallis from advancing into North Carolina and gave the Continentals a chance to regroup.

Shortly after the battle at King's Mountain, Washington sent General Nathanael Greene of Rhode Island to replace Gates as head of southern operations. Taking advice from local militia leaders like Daniel Morgan and Francis Marion, Greene divided his limited force into even smaller units. Marion and Morgan each led 300 Continental soldiers into the South Carolina backcountry, picking up hundreds of local militiamen along the way. At the village of Cowpens, Morgan drew Tarleton's much larger force into a circle of sharpshooters backed by Continentals and an armed cavalry. While Tarleton escaped, 100 of his men died and 800 were captured.

Cornwallis, enraged at the patriot victory, pursued Continental forces as they retreated. But Cornwallis's troops had outrun their cannons, and Greene circled back and attacked them at Guilford Court House. Although Cornwallis eventually forced the Continentals to withdraw from the battlefield, his troops suffered enormous losses. In August 1781, frustrated at the ease with which patriot forces still found local support in the South, he hunkered down in Yorktown on the Virginia coast and waited for Clinton to send reinforcements from New York.

Washington now coordinated strategy with his French allies. Comte de Rochambeau marched his 5,000 troops south from Rhode Island to Virginia as General Lafayette led his troops south along Virginia's eastern shore. At the same time, French naval ships headed north from the West Indies. One unit cut off a British fleet trying to resupply Cornwallis by sea. Another joined up with American privateers to bombard Cornwallis's forces. By mid-October, British supplies had run out, and it was clear that Clinton was not going to send reinforcements. On October 19, 1781, the British army admitted defeat.

Francis Marion

Francis Marion, known as "the Swamp Fox," and his militia waged guerrilla warfare against the British in South Carolina. Marion wreaked havoc by avoiding frontal assaults, instead conducting quick surprise attacks. This print from an 1836 painting by John Blake White shows Marion in striking headgear inviting a British officer to share a meal, while Marion's slave Oscar kneels by the table.   Anne S. K. Brown Military Collection, Brown University Library

An Uncertain Peace

The Continental Army had managed the impossible. It had defeated the British army and won the colonies' independence. Yet even with the surrender at **Yorktown**, the war continued in fits and starts. Peace negotiations in Paris dragged on as French, Spanish, British, and American representatives sought to settle a host of issues. Meanwhile British forces challenged Continental troops in and around New York City even as American recruiters found it nearly impossible to find new enlistments.

Some Continental soldiers continued to fight, but others focused on the long-festering issue of overdue wages. When the congress decided in June 1783 to discharge the remaining troops without providing back pay, a near mutiny erupted in Pennsylvania. Nearly 300 soldiers marched on the congress in Philadelphia. Washington sent troops, including Deborah Sampson/Robert Shurtliff, to put down the mutiny, and bloodshed was avoided when the Pennsylvania soldiers agreed to accept half pay and certificates for the remainder. Despite this compromise, the issue of back pay would continue to plague the nation over the next decade.

Meanwhile patriot representatives in Paris—Benjamin Franklin, John Adams, and John Jay—continued to negotiate peace terms. Rising antiwar sentiment on the British home front, especially after the surrender at Yorktown, forced the government's hand. But the Comte de Vergennes, the French foreign minister, opposed the Americans' republican principles and refused to consider the American delegates as his political equals. Given the importance of the French to the American victory, the congress had instructed its delegates to defer to French wishes. This blocked the American representatives from signing a separate peace with the British.

Eventually, however, U.S. delegates finalized a treaty that secured substantial benefits for the young nation. The United States gained control of all lands south of Canada and north of Louisiana and Florida stretching to the Mississippi River. In addition, the treaty recognized the United States to be "free Sovereign and independent states." Spain signed a separate treaty with Great Britain in which it regained control of Florida. Despite their role in the war, none of the Indian nations that occupied the lands under negotiation were consulted.

When the **Treaty of Paris** was finally signed on September 2, 1783, thousands of British troops and their supporters left the colonies for Canada, the West Indies, or England. British soldiers on the western frontier were supposed to be withdrawn at the same time, but they remained for many years and continued to foment hostilities between Indians in the region and U.S. settlers along the frontier.

The evacuation of the British also entailed the exodus of thousands of African Americans who had fought against the patriots. At the end of the war, British officials granted certificates of manumission to more than 1,300 men, 900 women, and 700 children. The largest number of these freed blacks settled in Nova Scotia, where they received small allotments of land from the British. Most, however, lacked the money, tools, or livestock to make such homesteads profitable. Despite these obstacles, some created a small Afro-Canadian community in Nova Scotia, while others migrated to areas considered more hospitable to black residents, such as Sierra Leone. Although thousands gained their freedom by taking up arms for the British, few were well rewarded for their efforts.

Explore

See Document 6.5 for a black loyalist's petition to the British cabinet.

A Surprising Victory

Americans had managed to defeat one of the most powerful military forces in the world. That victory resulted from the convergence of many circumstances. Certainly Americans benefited from fighting on their own soil. Their knowledge of the land and its resources as well as earlier experiences fighting against Indians and the French helped prepare them for battles against the British.

Just as important, British troops and officers were far removed from centers of decision making and supplies. Even supplies housed in Canada could not be easily transported the relatively short distance into New York. British commanders were often hesitant to make decisions independently, but awaiting instructions from England proved costly on several occasions, especially since strategists in London often had little sense of conditions on the ground in America.

Both sides depended on outsiders for assistance, but here, too, Americans gained the advantage. While the British army certainly outnumbered its Continental adversary, it relied heavily on German mercenaries, Indian allies, and freed blacks to bolster its regular troops. In victory, such "foreign" forces were relatively reliable, but in defeat, many of them chose to look out for their own interests. The patriots meanwhile marched with French and Spanish armies well prepared to challenge British troops and motivated to gain advantages for France and Spain if Britain was defeated.

Perhaps most importantly, a British victory was nearly impossible without conquering the American colonies one by one. Because a large percentage of colonists supported the patriot cause, British troops had to contend not only with Continental soldiers but also with an aroused citizenry fighting for its independence.

REVIEW & RELATE

How and why did the Americans win the Revolutionary War?

What uncertainties and challenges did the new nation face in the immediate aftermath of victory?

LEARNINGCurve bedfordstmartins.com/hewittlawson/LC

Conclusion: Legacies of the Revolution

After the approval of the Declaration of Independence, Thomas Hutchinson, the British official who had gained fame during the Stamp Act upheavals in Boston, charged that patriot leaders had "sought independence from the beginning." But the gradual and almost reluctant move from resistance to revolution in the American colonies suggests otherwise. When faced with threats from British troops, a sufficient number of colonists took up arms to create the reality of war, and this surge of hostilities finally gave the advantage to those political leaders urging independence.

The victory over Great Britain won that independence but left the United States confronting difficult problems. Most soldiers simply wanted to return home and reestablish their former lives. But the government's inability to pay back wages and the huge debt the nation owed to private citizens and state and foreign governments hinted at difficult economic times ahead.

Like many soldiers, Deborah Sampson embraced a conventional life after the war. But times were hard. A decade after she was discharged, Massachusetts finally granted her a small pension for her wartime service. In 1804 Paul Revere successfully appealed to the U.S. Congress to grant her a federal pension. When Sampson died in 1827, a special congressional act awarded her children additional money. Many men also waited years to receive compensation for their wartime service while they struggled to reestablish farms and businesses and pay off the debts that accrued while they were fighting for independence.

Political leaders tried to address the concerns of former soldiers and ordinary citizens while they developed a governmental structure to manage an expansive and diverse nation. Within a few years of achieving independence, financial distress among small farmers and tensions with Indians on the western frontier intensified concerns about the ability of the

DOCUMENT 6.5

Thomas Peters | Petition to the British Cabinet, 1790

During the war, thousands of African Americans fled from slavery to join the British. Former slave Thomas Peters escaped from his owner in North Carolina and became a sergeant in a British regiment called the Black Pioneers. Like other loyalists, he settled in Nova Scotia after the war. He soon realized that even in Canada blacks were treated unequally. In 1790 he went to London to present the following petition to the British cabinet on behalf of other black loyalists. Faced with persistent inequality, Peters and many other ex-slaves eventually migrated to Sierra Leone.

Explore

The humble Memorial and Petition of Thomas Peters a free Negro and late a Serjt. [sergeant] in the Regiment of Guides and Pioneers serving in North America under the command of Genl. Sir Henry Clinton on Behalf of himself and others the Black Pioneers and loyal Black Refugees hereinafter described

Sheweth

That your Memorialist and the said other Black Pioneers having served in North America as aforesaid for the Space of seven years and upwards, during the War, afterwards went to Nova Scotia under the Promise of obtaining the usual Grant of Lands and Provision.

That notwithstanding they have made repeated Applications to all Persons in that Country who they conceived likely to put them in Possession of the due Allotments, the said Pioneers with their Wives and Children amounting together in the whole to the Number of 102 People now remain at Annapolis Royal have not yet obtained their Allotments of Land except one single Acre of land each for a Town Lot and tho' a further Proportion of 20 Acres each Private man (viz) about a 5th part of the Allowance of Land that is due to them was actually laid out and located for them agreeable to the Governor's Order it was afterwards taken from them on Pretense that it had been included in some former Grant and they have never yet obtained other Lands in Lieu thereof and remain destitute and helpless.

Source: Great Britain, Public Record Office, Colonial Office file CO217/63fol. 63, reprinted in David Northrup, *Crosscurrents in the Black Atlantic* (Boston: Bedford/St. Martin's, 2008), 39–40.

Interpret the Evidence

- On what grounds do Peters and his supporters base their claims to land in Nova Scotia?
- How were they rewarded for their service in the British military?

Put It in Context

What was required to make freedom meaningful for ex-slaves living in the United States or abroad?

confederation government to secure order and prosperity. In response, some patriots demanded a new political compact to strengthen the national government. But others feared that such a change would simply replicate British tyranny.

Leading revolutionaries engaged in heated debates over the best means to unify and stabilize the United States in the decade following the Revolution. However, some key leaders lived abroad in this period. Although Thomas Paine was awarded land and money by Pennsylvania and the U.S. Congress, in 1791 he moved to France, where he wrote pamphlets advocating revolution there. His increasingly radical political views and attacks on organized religion led many Americans to malign the former hero. He returned to

the United States in 1802, but his death in New York City in 1809 was mentioned only briefly in most newspapers. Other patriot leaders remained celebrated figures, but Thomas Jefferson, Benjamin Franklin, and John Adams all spent significant amounts of time in England and France as ambassadors for the young nation. There they played key roles in building ties to European powers, thus ensuring U.S. security.

The legacies of the Revolution seemed far from clear in the decade following the American victory. As problems escalated, Americans were challenged to reimagine their political future while holding on to the republican impulses that drove them to revolution.

LEARNING*Curve*
Check what you know.
bedfordstmartins.com/hewittlawson/LC

Chapter Review

Online Study Guide ▶ bedfordstmartins.com/hewittlawson

KEY TERMS

Second Continental Congress (p. 164)
Dunmore's Proclamation (p. 165)
Common Sense (p. 165)
Declaration of Independence (p. 166)
loyalist (p. 169)
Battle of Saratoga (p. 173)
Valley Forge (p. 173)
Articles of Confederation (p. 174)
Yorktown (p. 181)
Treaty of Paris (p. 182)

REVIEW & RELATE

1. What challenges did Washington face when he was given command of the Continental Army?

2. How and why did proponents of independence prevail in the debates that preceded the publication of the Declaration of Independence?

3. How did colonists choose sides during the Revolutionary War? What factors influenced their decisions?

4. Why did so many Indian tribes try to stay neutral during the conflict? Why was it so difficult for Indians to remain neutral?

5. How did the patriot forces fare in 1776? How and why did the tide of war turn in 1777?

6. What role did colonial women and foreign men play in the conflict in the early years of the war?

7. What values and concerns shaped state governments during the Revolutionary War?

8. What issues and challenges did the Continental Congress face even after the French joined the patriot side?

9. How and why did the Americans win the Revolutionary War?

10. What uncertainties and challenges did the new nation face in the immediate aftermath of victory?

TIMELINE OF EVENTS

April 19, 1775	Battles of Lexington and Concord
June 1775	Continental Congress establishes Continental Army
June 16, 1775	Battle of Bunker Hill
August 1775	Representatives of the Continental Congress meet with representatives of the six nations of the Iroquois Confederacy
November 1775	Dunmore issues his proclamation
1776	New Jersey constitution enfranchises all free inhabitants, including women and free blacks, who meet property qualifications
January 1776	Thomas Paine publishes *Common Sense*
July 4, 1776	Continental Congress publicly declares independence
July 1776– mid-December 1776	British forces defeat Continental Army and force retreat
December 1776– January 1777	Patriot victories at Trenton and Princeton, New Jersey
October 1777	Patriot victory at Saratoga
Winter 1777–1778	Continental Army encamps at Valley Forge, Pennsylvania
1778	Articles of Confederation ratified by eight states
February 1778	France enters into formal alliance with the United States
Summer 1779	Patriot forces wipe out Iroquois Confederacy villages on New York frontier
1780–1781	Quock Walker and Elizabeth "Mumbet" Freeman successfully sue for their freedom in Massachusetts
March 1781	Articles of Confederation ratified
October 19, 1781	British surrender at Yorktown, Virginia
May 1782	Deborah Sampson enlists in Continental Army under the name Robert Shurtliff
September 2, 1783	Treaty of Paris signed

Women in the Revolution

The Revolutionary War had a tremendous impact on the lives of women, just as women helped shape the course of that conflict. As in all wars, women faced the fear and hardships brought on by absent men, inadequate supplies, roaming enemy soldiers, and nearby battles. But at a time when women were supposed to limit their activities to domestic concerns, the war also opened up new opportunities. On the home front, they ran family farms and shops, raised money, and produced homespun goods for the Continental Army, and they defended themselves and their homes. Women also spied on enemy encampments, provided medical care for soldiers, and even fought alongside men on the battlefield. Women gained new skills, felt pride in their independence and abilities, and, like their male counterparts, gained satisfaction and sometimes fame in supporting the cause in which they believed. They cast their everyday responsibilities in a political light, even as the war generally failed to expand women's legal or political rights.

The women represented in the following documents demonstrate a variety of experiences during the war. Some women, like Christian Barnes (Document 6.6), remained loyal to Great Britain and suffered attacks by patriot neighbors and soldiers. As a Seneca, Mary Jemison (Document 6.10) sought to remain neutral during the war, but she also faced hardships brought on by pillaging colonial soldiers. The other documents offer a window into the lives of patriot women who worked to defend their new country and their families during the war. Even here, there were differences between the activities of wealthy women (Documents 6.7 and 6.9) and those of ordinary women (Document 6.8). In reading these documents, think about the extent to which being a woman shaped how they experienced the war. Almost all women faced new challenges, but some were also offered new opportunities. Still, even the innovative roles women played were often justified in domestic or familial terms.

DOCUMENT 6.6

Christian Barnes | Letter to Elizabeth Inman, April 29, 1775

As the conflict intensified between Great Britain and America, colonists were forced to choose sides. Whether patriots or loyalists, women were often terrorized by enemy soldiers. One such woman was Christian Barnes, the wife of a well-known loyalist who fled to Marlborough, Massachusetts, to avoid capture by the colonial government. The following selection is from a letter written by Barnes in the spring of 1775, in which she describes a frightening visit by a colonial soldier.

IT IS NOW A WEEK since I had a line from my dear Mrs. Inman, in which time I have had some severe trials, but the greatest terror I was ever thrown into was on Sunday last. A man came up to the gate and loaded his musket, and before I could determine which way to run he entered the house and demanded a dinner. I sent him the best I had upon the table. He was not contented, but insisted upon bringing in his gun and dining with me; this terrified the young folks, and they ran out of the house. I went in and endeavored to pacify him by every method in my power, but I found it was to no purpose. He still continued to abuse me, and said that when he had eat his dinner he should want a horse and if I did not let him have one he would blow my brains out. He pretended to have an order from the General for one of my horses, but did not produce it. His language was so dreadful and his looks so frightful that I could not remain in the house, but fled to the store and locked myself in. He followed me and declared he would break the door open. Some people very luckily passing to meeting prevented his doing any mischief and staid by me until he was out of sight, but I did not recover from my fright for several days. The sound of drum or the sight of a gun put me into such a tremor that I could not command myself. I have met with but little molestation since this affair, which I attribute to the protection sent me by Col. Putnam and Col. Whitcomb. I returned them a card of thanks for their goodness tho' I knew it was thro' your interest I obtained this favor. . . . The people here are weary at his [Mr. Barnes's] absence, but at the same time give it as their opinion that he could not pass the guards. . . . I do not doubt but upon a proper remonstrance I might procure a pass for him through the Camp from our two good Colonels. . . . I know he must be very unhappy in Boston. It was never his intention to quit the family.

Source: Nina M. Tiffany, ed., *Letters of James Murray, Loyalist* (Boston, 1901), 187–88.

DOCUMENT 6.7

Deborah Champion | Letter to Patience, October 2, 1775

Deborah Champion was the daughter of Henry Champion, a high-ranking officer in the Continental Army. In the fall of 1775, she traveled from Connecticut to Boston to deliver secret messages from her father to George Washington. Accompanied by a family slave named Aristarchus, she was stopped by British troops several times during her journey. Several days after her return home, she described the adventure in a letter to a friend, excerpted here.

FATHER LAID HIS HAND on my shoulder, (a most unusual caress with him) and said almost solemnly, "Deborah I have need of thee. Hast thee the courage to go out and ride, it may be even in the dark and as fast as may be, till thou comest to Boston town?" He continued, "I do not believe Deborah, that there will be actual danger to threaten thee, else I would not ask it of thee, but the way is long, and in part lonely. I shall send Aristarchus with thee and shall explain to him the urgency of the business. Though he is a slave, he understands the mighty matters at stake, and I shall instruct him yet further. There are reasons why it is better for you a woman to take the despatches I would send than for me to entrust them to a man; else I should send your brother Henry. Dare you go? . . ."

Everywhere we heard the same thing, love for the Mother Country, but stronger than that, that she must *must* give us our rights, that we were fighting not for independence, though that might come and would be the war-cry if the oppression of unjust taxation was not removed. Nowhere was a cup of imported tea offered us. It was a glass of milk, or a cup of "hyperion" the name they gave to a tea made of raspberry leaves. We heard that it would be almost impossible to avoid the British, unless by going so far out of the way that too much time would be lost, so plucked up what courage I could as darkness began to come on at the close of the second day. I secreted the papers in a small pocket in a saddle bag under some eatables that mother had put up. We decided to ride all night. Providentially the moon just past full, rose about 8 o'clock and it was not unpleasant, for the roads were better. I confess that I began to be weary. It was late at night or rather very early in the morning, that I heard a sentry call and knew that if at all the danger point was reached. I pulled my calash [a large hood] as far over my face as I could, thanking my wise mother's forethought, and went on with what boldness I could muster. I really believed I heard Aristarchus' teeth chatter as he rode to my side and whispered "De British missus for sure." Suddenly I was ordered to *halt*. As I could not help myself I did so. A soldier in a red coat appeared and suggested that I go to headquarters for examination. I told him "It was early to wake his Captain and to please let me pass for I had been sent in urgent haste to see a friend in need," which was true, if a little ambiguous. To my joy he let me go saying "Well, you are only an old woman any way." Evidently as glad to be rid of me as I of him.

Source: Deborah Champion to Patience, 2 October 1775, in *Women's Letters: America from the Revolutionary War to the Present*, ed. Lisa Grunwald and Stephen J. Adler (New York: Dial Press, 2005), 25–28.

DOCUMENT 6.8

Abigail Adams | Letter to John Adams, July 13, 1777

Food shortages among colonial militias during the Revolutionary War are well documented, but civilian populations also struggled with high prices and scarce resources. Because women were responsible for their family budgets, they dealt with these problems on a daily basis during the war, just as they had during the prewar boycotts. In July 1777, some women in Boston found an unusual solution, which Abigail Adams describes in a letter to her husband, John.

I have nothing new to entertain you with, unless it is an account of a new set of mobility [popular uprising], which has lately taken the lead in Boston. You must know that there is a great scarcity of sugar and coffee, articles which the female part of the state is very loth to give up, especially whilst they consider the scarcity occasioned by the merchants having secreted a large quantity. There had been much rout and noise in the town for several weeks. Some stores had been opened by a number of people, and the coffee and sugar carried into the market, and dealt out by pounds. It was rumored that an eminent, wealthy, stingy merchant (who is a bachelor) had a hogshead of coffee in his store, which he refused to sell to the committee under six shillings per pound. A number of females, some say a hundred, some say more, assembled with a cart and trucks, marched down to the warehouse, and demanded the keys, which he refused to deliver. Upon which, one of them seized him by his neck, and tossed him into the cart. Upon his finding no quarter, he delivered the keys, when they tipped up the cart and discharged him; then opened the warehouse, hoisted out the coffee themselves, put it into the truck, and drove off.

It was reported, that he has personal chastisement [physical beating] among them; but this, I believe was not true. A large concourse of men stood amazed, silent spectators of the whole transaction.

Source: Charles F. Adams, ed., *Letters of Mrs. Adams, the Wife of John Adams*, 4th ed. (Boston: Wilkins, Carter, 1848), 84–85.

DOCUMENT 6.9

Esther De Berdt Reed | The Sentiments of an American Woman, 1780

Esther De Berdt Reed was born and raised in England, moving to Philadelphia only after her marriage to merchant Joseph Reed in 1770. Joseph was a leading patriot and was elected president (governor) of Pennsylvania during the war. In June 1780, Esther Reed, the mother of five young children and recently recovered from smallpox, called on women in Philadelphia to aid the Continental Army. Her broadside "The Sentiments of an American Woman" was the foundation of the Ladies Association of Philadelphia, which raised large sums by going door-to-door and soliciting contributions from women. Reed's goal was to give money directly to the soldiers, but at George Washington's request the money was instead used to make clothing for the troops.

WHO KNOWS IF PERSONS DISPOSED TO censure, and sometimes too severely with regard to us, may not disapprove our appearing acquainted even with the actions of which our sex boasts? We are at least certain, that he cannot be a good citizen who will not applaud our efforts for the relief of the armies which defend our lives, our possessions, our liberty? . . .

We know that at a distance from the theatre of war, if we enjoy any tranquility, it is the fruit of your watchings, your labours, your dangers. If I live happy in the midst of my family; if my husband cultivates his field, and reaps his harvest in peace; if, surrounded with my children, I myself nourish the youngest, and press it to my bosom, without being affraid of seeing myself separated from it, by a ferocious enemy; if the house in which we dwell; if our barns, our orchards are safe at the present time from the hands of those incendiaries, it is to you that we owe it. And shall we hesitate to evidence to you our gratitude? Shall we hesitate to wear a cloathing more simple; hair dressed less elegant, while at the price of this small privation, we shall deserve your benedictions. Who, amongst us, will not renounce with the highest pleasure, those vain ornaments, when she shall consider that the valiant defenders of America will be able to draw some advantage from the money which she may have laid out in these; that they will be better defended from the rigours of the seasons, that after their painful toils, they will receive some extraordinary and unexpected relief; that these presents will perhaps be valued by them at a greater price, when they will have it in their power to say: *This is the offering of the Ladies.* The time is arrived to display the same sentiments which animated us at the beginning of the Revolution, when we renounced the use of teas, however agreeable to our taste, rather than receive them from our persecutors; when we made it appear to them that we placed former necessaries in the rank of superfluities, when our liberty was interested; when our republican and laborious hands spun the flax, prepared the linen intended for the use of our soldiers; when exiles and fugitives we supported with courage all the evils which are the concomitants of war. Let us not lose a moment; let us be engaged to offer the homage of our gratitude at the altar of military valour, and you, our brave deliverers, while mercenary slaves combat to cause you to share with them, the irons with which they are loaded, receive with a free hand our offering, the purest which can be presented to your virtue,

BY AN AMERICAN WOMAN

Source: Esther De Berdt Reed, "The Sentiments of an American Woman" (Philadelphia: John Dunlop, 1780).

DOCUMENT 6.10

Mary Jemison | The War's Impact on Native Americans, 1823

Many Indian communities chose to aid either the British or the colonists, but even those who sought to remain neutral were often affected by the war. In the following passage, Mary Jemison describes the impact of the war on her Seneca community. Jemison, an Irish immigrant to the Americas, had been captured in 1758 at the age of fifteen by Shawnee Indians. Though most of her family was killed in the attack, she was spared and eventually given to the Seneca tribe. She married a Seneca man and had six children. In 1823 she recounted her capture and life among the Senecas in *Life of Mrs. Mary Jemison*, which became one of the best-selling books of the 1820s.

In one or two days after the skirmish at Conesus Lake, Sullivan and his army arrived at Genesee River, where they destroyed every article of the food kind that they could lay their hands on. A part of our corn they burnt, and threw the remainder into the river. They burnt our houses, killed what few cattle and horses they could find, destroyed our fruit-trees, and left nothing but the bare soil and timber. But the Indians had eloped, and were not to be found.

Having crossed and recrossed the river, and finished the work of destruction, the army marched off to the east. Our Indians saw them move off, but, suspecting it was Sullivan's intention to watch our return, and then to take us by surprise, resolved that the main body of our tribe should hunt where *we* then were, till Sullivan had gone so far that there would be no danger of his returning to molest us.

This being agreed to, we hunted continually till the Indians concluded that there could be no risk in our once more taking possession of our lands. Accordingly, we all returned; but what were our feelings when we found that there was not a mouthful of any kind of sustenance left—not even enough to keep a child one day from perishing with hunger.

The weather by this time had become cold and stormy; and as we were destitute of houses, and food, too, I immediately resolved to take my children, and look out for myself, without delay. With this intention, I took two of my little ones on my back, bade the other three follow, and traveled up the river to Gardeau Flats, where I arrived that night.

At that time, two negroes, who had run away from their masters some time before, were the only inhabitants of those flats. They lived in a small cabin, and had planted and raised a large field of corn, which they had not yet harvested. As they were in want of help to secure their crop, I hired them to husk corn till the whole harvest arrived. . . .

The next summer after Sullivan's campaign, our Indians, highly incensed at the whites for the treatment they had received, and the sufferings which they had consequently endured, determined to obtain some redress, by destroying their frontier settlements.

Source: James E. Seaver, ed., *Life of Mrs. Mary Jemison*, 4th ed. (New York: Miller, Orton, and Mulligan, 1856), 123–24; 126.

Interpret the Evidence

1. What types of activities did female patriots undertake in the service of the colonies? What evidence is offered about how men responded to these activities?

2. In addition to carrying secret messages to General Washington, how else does Deborah Champion reveal her support for the colonial cause (Document 6.7)?

3. What unique dangers did women face during the war, whether loyalist, neutral, or patriot? In what ways did being female offer new opportunities during a time of war?

4. Although many women had participated actively in pre-Revolutionary boycotts and protests, they were still confined largely to the domestic sphere. How did these women justify their public and political actions (Documents 6.7, 6.8, and 6.9)?

5. How did the different social and economic backgrounds of the women represented here affect their experiences during the war?

6. What groups of women are not represented in the documents? How might historians study the lives of these women?

Put It in Context

- What were women's main contributions to the war effort? How did their efforts shape the outcome of the war and the lives of their families?

background photos: page 188, Pennsylvania State Archives; page 190, akg-images

© Chicago History Museum, USA/The Bridgeman Art Library

The Granger Collection, New York

● The Treaty of Greenville, 1785.

● Portrait of Catherine Brass Yates, 1794.

7

Political Cultures

1783–1800

The Granger Collection, New York

Farmer plowing near Moravian settlement of Salem, North Carolina, 1787.

Like many young farmers in Massachusetts, Daniel Shays enlisted in a local militia company in the early 1770s. Born to Irish parents in Hopkinton, Massachusetts, in 1747 and one of six children, Daniel received little formal education. In 1772 he married, had a child, and settled into farming. But in April 1775, he, his father, and his brother grabbed muskets and raced toward Concord to meet the British forces. By June, he was among the patriots defending Breed's Hill and Bunker Hill.

After distinguished service in the Continental Army, Shays resigned from service in 1780 and purchased a farm in Pelham, Massachusetts. He hoped to return to a normal life, but in the years following the Revolution, the nation entered a period of economic turmoil. Farmers in western Massachusetts, many deeply in debt, were especially hard hit. Debtors, including former soldiers and their families, lost their land, tools, livestock, clothes, and furniture, and many were also imprisoned. Although Shays managed to keep his farm, many of his neighbors faced eviction. Shays was chosen to represent his town at county conventions that petitioned the state government for economic relief. However, the Massachusetts legislature, sitting in Boston, largely ignored their concerns.

Angered by the legislature's failure to act, armed groups of farmers attacked courthouses throughout western Massachusetts in 1786. Although Shays was reluctant to lead the movement, he soon headed the largest contingent of farmer-soldiers, a band that eventually numbered more than a thousand men. After a series of small skirmishes against local militias, Massachusetts governor James Bowdoin

193

Daniel Shays and Alexander Hamilton

moved to quash the rebellion. In January 1787, Shays and his men headed to the federal arsenal at Springfield, Massachusetts, to seize guns and ammunition. The farmers were routed by state militia and pursued by the governor's army. Many rebel leaders were captured; others, including Shays, escaped to Vermont and later New York State. Four were convicted and two were hanged before Bowdoin granted amnesty to the rest of the rebels, in hopes of avoiding further conflict.

This uprising, known as Shays's Rebellion, fueled grave concern on the part of many state and national leaders. They feared that the U.S. government was too weak to put down such insurgencies and advocated amending or replacing the Articles of Confederation to create a new political structure that would strengthen federal power. Among those outraged by the rebels was Alexander Hamilton, a young New York politician with an admirable record of military service. Hamilton was born illegitimate and impoverished in the British West Indies. Orphaned at eleven, he was apprenticed to a firm of merchants, where his gift for commerce and finance quickly became clear. The firm sent him for schooling to the American colonies, where he was drawn into the activities of radical patriots. Hamilton joined the Continental Army in 1776 and gained a reputation as courageous, even reckless, in the pursuit of military glory.

During the war, Hamilton fell in love with Elizabeth Schuyler, who came from a wealthy New York family, and they married in December 1780. After the American victory, Hamilton used military and marital contacts to establish himself as a lawyer and financier in New York City. In 1786 he focused his efforts on improving the state of the nation's finances. He was elected to the New York State legislature that spring and by fall was serving as a delegate to a convention on interstate commerce held in Annapolis, Maryland. Hamilton was among a small group of delegates who sought to strengthen the central government. They pushed through a resolution calling for a second convention "to render the constitution of the Federal Government adequate to the exigencies of the Union."

Although the initial response to the call was lukewarm, the eruption of Shays's Rebellion and the federal government's financial problems soon convinced many in the congress and the states that change was required. Although Hamilton played only a small role in the 1787 convention in Philadelphia, he worked tirelessly for ratification of the Constitution drafted there. Once the new federal government was established, in the fall of 1789 Hamilton accepted appointment to the job he most deeply desired, secretary of the treasury. ●

photos: The Granger Collection, New York; Library of Congress

---

AS ALEXANDER HAMILTON took charge of the nation's economic policy, Daniel Shays retreated to a modest living on the frontiers of New York State. Despite the suppression of Shays's Rebellion, the grievances that fueled the uprising persisted, and other problems confronted the new nation as well. Moreover, Hamilton's efforts to stabilize and strengthen the national economy, although deemed successful by many political and economic elites, sparked controversy and conflicts in the years ahead. As the American histories of Daniel Shays and Alexander Hamilton demonstrate, Americans may have come together to win the Revolutionary War, but not

all Americans shared a common vision of the independent nation that military victory made possible.

Postwar Problems

The United States faced serious financial instability in its formative years. Other issues also threatened the emerging nation. Indians, with support from British allies, continued to launch raids against frontier settlements. Western migrants fueled these conflicts and forced the confederation government to take a more active role in governing its frontier territories. Meanwhile Spain closed the port of New Orleans to U.S. trade as states struggled to regulate commerce within the nation and abroad. Another threat to American trade arose off the coast of North Africa, where Barbary pirates attacked U.S. merchant ships. Issues of trade and piracy required diplomacy with European powers, but diplomatic relations were plagued with uncertainty given America's outstanding war debts and the relative weakness of the confederation government.

Officers Threaten Mutiny

As the American Revolution ground to an end, issues of military pay and government finances sparked conflict. Uprisings by ordinary soldiers were common but successfully put down. Threats by Continental officers, however, posed a greater problem. In March 1783, some five hundred officers were still encamped at Newburgh, New York. Many officers came from wealthy families and had served without pay during the war. In 1780 they had extracted a promise from the Continental Congress for half pay for life but had received no compensation since.

Some confederation leaders were sympathetic to the officers' plight and hoped to use pressure from this formidable group to enhance the powers of the congress. Hamilton was among the leaders pressing state governments to grant the confederation congress a new duty of 5 percent on imported goods. The federal government would thereby gain an independent source of revenue by which it could begin paying off its debts and ensure the loyalty of wealthy Americans who had helped finance the war. Perhaps the actions of the officers at Newburgh could convince states like New York to agree to the collection of this import duty.

Quietly encouraged by these supporters, dissident officers circulated petitions that included veiled threats of a military takeover. When the officers met on March 15, however, they were confronted by General George Washington, who urged the officers to respect civilian control of the government and to allow the fragile U.S. government time to prove itself. Most of the Newburgh officers quickly retreated from the "infamous propositions" circulated earlier. At the same time, congressional leaders, fearing a mutiny, promised the officers full pay for five years. Within weeks, news arrived that a peace treaty was near completion in Paris, and over the next three months the officers headed home.

Indians, Land, and the Northwest Ordinance

One anonymous petitioner at Newburgh suggested that the officers move as a group to "some unsettled country" and let the confederation fend for itself. In reality, no such unsettled country existed beyond the thirteen states. Numerous Indian nations and American settlers claimed control of these western lands, and more American settlers were arriving all the time. In 1784 some two hundred Indian leaders from the Iroquois, Shawnee, Creek,

George Washington's Headquarters
Hasbrouck House, the Revolutionary War headquarters of George Washington, was located near Newburgh, New York, sixty miles north of New York City. In operation from April 1782 to August 1783, this base housed a group of affluent officers who considered a military takeover of the government. Washington convinced them to abandon the idea.   Ivy Close Images/Landov

Cherokee, and other nations gathered in St. Louis, where they complained to the Spanish governor that the Americans were "extending themselves like a plague of locusts."

Despite the continued presence of British and Spanish troops in the Ohio River valley, the United States hoped to convince Indian nations—both friendly and hostile—that it controlled the territory. The confederation congress sought to strengthen these claims by signing treaties with the vanquished nations. In the fall of 1784, U.S. commissioners met with Iroquois delegates at Fort Stanwix, New York, and demanded land cessions that covered all of western New York and Pennsylvania as well as areas farther west. They backed up their demands with the threat of force. Although

the six Indian nations in the council later refused to ratify the treaty, the U.S. government acted as though the treaty was valid. With a similar mix of negotiation and coercion, U.S. commissioners signed treaties at Fort McIntosh, Pennsylvania (1785), and Fort Finney, Ohio (1786), and claimed lands held by the Wyandots, Delawares, Shawnees, and others.

As more and more eastern Indians were pushed into the Ohio River valley, they crowded onto lands already claimed by other nations. Initially, these migrations increased conflict among Indians, but eventually some leaders used this forced intimacy to launch pan-Indian movements against further American encroachment on their land.

DOCUMENTS 7.1 AND 7.2

Conflicts over Western Lands: Two Views

Following the Revolutionary War, one of the most pressing issues that the confederation government faced was the disposition of western lands. To resolve these issues, the U.S. government negotiated with a number of Indian tribes to gain clear title to western lands, but it backed these negotiations with the threat of force. The following documents offer very different views of these negotiations. The first selection is from the journal of General Richard Butler, who had fought against Indians in the region. In 1786, he was appointed to negotiate with the Shawnee tribe, a British ally during the Revolutionary War. In his exchange with an Indian representative, Butler mentions a "string," which refers to a wampum belt. A black belt was a sign of war, and a white belt represented peace. The second selection comes from a speech given at a pan-Indian council meeting. The speech was addressed to the U.S. Congress and expressed the Indians' united stance and their hopes for fair and open dealings with the United States.

Explore

7.1 General Richard Butler | Fort Finney Treaty Negotiations, 1786

It rests now with you, the destruction of your women and children, or their future happiness, depends on your present choice. Peace or war is in your power; make your choice like men, and judge for yourselves. We shall only add this: had you judged as it is your interest to do, you would have considered us as your friends, and followed our counsel; but if you choose to follow the opinion which you have expressed, you are guided either by evil counsel or rashness, and are blinded. We plainly tell you that this country belongs to the United States—their blood hath defended it, and will forever protect it. Their proposals are liberal and just; and you instead of acting as you have done,

and instead of persisting in your folly, should be thankful for the forgiveness and offers of kindness of the United States, instead of the sentiments which this string imparts, and the manner in which you have delivered it. . . .

. . . Kekewepellethe [the Indian representative] then arose and spoke as follows:

. . . Brethren, our people are sensible of the truths you have told them. You have every thing in your power—you are great, and we see you own all the country; we therefore hope, as you have every thing in your power, that you will take pity on our women and children.

Source: Neville B. Craig, ed., *The Olden Time* (Pittsburgh, 1848), 2:524.

Explore

See Documents 7.1 and 7.2 for two perspectives on U.S.-Indian interactions.

Indians and U.S. political leaders did share one concern over western lands: the vast numbers of squatters, mainly white men and women, who moved onto land to which they had no legal claim. In the fall of 1784, George Washington traveled with family members and slaves to survey nearly thirty thousand acres of western territory he had been granted as a reward for military service. He found much of the land occupied by squatters who refused to purchase their homesteads or pay rent to Washington. Unable to impose his will on the squatters, he became more deeply concerned about the weaknesses of the confederation government.

Washington feared that the federal government was not strong enough to protect his and others' property rights. Indeed, the confederation congress struggled just to convince the remaining states with western land claims to cede that territory to federal control. Slowly, however, between 1783 and 1785, the congress convinced the two remaining states with the largest western land claims, Virginia and Massachusetts, to relinquish all territory north of the Ohio River (Map 7.1).

Explore

7.2 United Indian Nations Council | Message to Congress, 1786

To the Congress of the United States of America:

Brethren of the United States of America: It is now more than three years since peace was made between the King of Great Britain and you, but we, the Indians, were disappointed, finding ourselves not included in that peace, according to our expectations: for we thought that its conclusion would have promoted a friendship between the United States and Indians, and that we might enjoy that happiness that formerly subsisted between us and our elder brethren. . . . In the course of our councils, we imagined we hit upon an expedient that would promote a lasting peace between us.

Brothers: We are still of the same opinion as to the means which may tend to reconcile us to each other; and we are sorry to find, although we had the best thoughts in our minds, during the beforementioned period, mischief has, nevertheless, happened between you and us. We are still anxious of putting our plan of accommodation into execution, and we shall briefly inform you of the means that seem most probable to us of effecting a firm and lasting peace and reconciliation: the first step towards which should, in our opinion, be, that all treaties carried on with the United States, on our parts, should be with the general voice of the whole confederacy, and carried on in the most open manner, without any restraint on either side; and especially as landed matters are often the subject of our councils with you, a matter of the greatest importance and of general concern to us, in this case we hold it indispensably necessary that any cession of our lands should be made in the most public manner, and by the united voice of the confederacy; holding all partial treaties as void and of no effect.

Source: *American State Papers, Class II: Indian Affairs* (Washington, 1832), 1:8.

Interpret the Evidence

- What does Butler's journal reveal about his view of U.S.-Indian relations? How does he see the power dynamic between the two groups?
- Does the United Indian Nations Council frame U.S.-Indian relations as between dominant and dependent peoples or as between two separate and equal nations? How do the Indians' views compare with those of Butler?
- Why do you think the Indians emphasize the importance of the entire confederacy's participation in treaty negotiations?

Put It in Context

How did the United States use divisions among Indians to its advantage?

MAP 7.1   Cessions of Western Land, 1782–1802

Beginning with the congress established under the Articles of Confederation, political leaders sought to resolve competing state claims to western territory based on colonial charters. The confederation congress and, after ratification of the Constitution, the U.S. Congress gradually persuaded all states to cede their claims and create a "national domain," part of which was then organized as the Northwest Territory.

To regulate this vast territory, Thomas Jefferson drafted the **Northwest Land Ordinance** in 1785. It provided that the territory be surveyed and divided into adjoining townships of thirty-six sections, each 1 square mile (640 acres) in area. He hoped to carve fourteen small states out of the region to enhance the representation of western farmers and to ensure the continued dominance of agrarian views in the national government. The congress revised his proposal, however, stipulating that only three to five states be created from the vast territory.

The population of the territory grew rapidly, with speculators buying up huge tracts of land and selling smaller parcels to eager settlers. In response, congressional leaders modified the original Northwest Ordinance in 1787 and clarified the process by which territories could become states. The congress appointed territorial officials and guaranteed residents the basic rights of U.S. citizens. After a territory's population reached 5,000, residents could choose an assembly, but the territorial governor retained the power to veto all legislation. When a prospective state reached a population of 60,000, it could apply for admission to the United States on an equal basis with the existing states. Thus the congress established an orderly system by which territories became states in the Union.

The 1787 ordinance also addressed concerns about race and political power in the region, though with mixed results. It encouraged fair treatment of Indian nations, although it did not include any means of enforcing such treatment and failed to resolve Indian land claims. It abolished slavery throughout the territory, but the law included a clause that mandated the return of fugitive slaves to their owners to forestall a flood of fugitives into the Northwest Territory. By restricting the number of states established in the territory, the ordinance also sought to limit the future clout of western settlers in the federal government.

Meanwhile, ownership of the region south of the Ohio River and west of the original thirteen states remained in dispute. By 1785 thirty thousand Americans had settled in Kentucky, and thousands more streamed into Tennessee. Spanish officials claimed rights to this land and signed treaties with Creek, Choctaw, and Chickasaw tribes in the area. Supplied with weapons by Spanish traders, these Indians along with Cherokees harassed Anglo-American settlers in the lower Mississippi valley. The region would remain an arena of conflict for decades to come.

Depression and Debt

Disputes over western lands were deeply intertwined with the economic difficulties that plagued the new nation. Victory in the Revolution was followed by years of economic depression and mushrooming debt. The war had fueled the demand for domestic goods and ensured high employment. However, after the peace settlement, both the demand and the jobs declined. In addition, international trade was slow to recover from a decade of disruption. Meanwhile, the nation was saddled with a huge war debt. Individuals, the states, and the federal government each viewed western lands as a solution to their problems. Farm families could move west and start over on "unclaimed" land; states could distribute land in lieu of cash payments to veterans or creditors; and the congress could sell land to fund its debts. Yet there was never enough land to meet these conflicting needs, nor did the United States hold secure title to the territory.

Some national leaders, including Hamilton, focused on other ways of repaying the war debt. Fearing that wealthy creditors would lose faith in the new nation if it could not repay its debts, they wanted to grant the federal government the right to collect a percentage of import duties as a way to increase its revenue. Meanwhile, legislators in a number of states, including Massachusetts, passed hard-money laws that required debts to be repaid in gold or silver rather than in paper currency. Creditors—mainly well-to-do merchants and professionals—favored hard-money measures to ensure repayment in full. Artisans and small farmers, including many veterans who had borrowed paper money during the war, were now asked to repay loans in hard currency as the money supply shrank. Taxes, too, were rising as states sought to cover the interest on wartime bonds held by affluent investors.

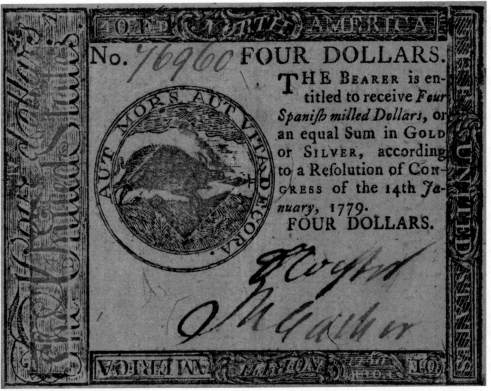

Revolutionary War Currency

In 1779 the Continental Congress authorized the issuance of paper currency, including this $4 bill. The congress backed up these notes with either gold or silver to encourage their acceptance. The insignia on the front shows a wild boar charging into a spear with the motto *Aut mors aut vita decora* (Either death or an honorable life).   Reproduced from the original held by the Department of Special Collections of the University Libraries of Notre Dame

Failures of American diplomacy weakened the nation's economy further. In 1783 the British Parliament denied the United States the right to trade with the British West Indies, and New England merchants lost lucrative markets for fish, grain, and lumber. The following year, Spain, unhappy with Americans' insistence on pushing into disputed western territories, prohibited U.S. ships from accessing the port of New Orleans. This embargo closed off a primary trade route for western settlers. Spain and Great Britain also threatened U.S. sovereignty by conspiring with American citizens on the frontier and promising them protection from Indians. At the same time, British troops that had refused to abandon forts in the western United States urged Indians to harass frontier settlers.

The United States fared better in its relations with France and Holland. Both nations granted American ships the right to trade with their West Indies colonies. Yet the continuation of America's wartime alliance with France also ensured continued conflicts with Great Britain.

REVIEW & RELATE

What challenges did the new nation face in the immediate aftermath of the Revolutionary War?

How and why did the conflict between America and Great Britain continue after the war ended?

LEARNINGCurve bedfordstmartins.com/hewittlawson/LC

On the Political Margins

In the aftermath of the Revolution, the United States was forced to the political margins in international affairs. At the same time, as the new Republic moved from war to peace to nationhood, some groups within the nation were marginalized as well. Small farmers were among those who suffered in the postwar period, but they were not alone. Church leaders who had enjoyed government support in the colonial period now had to compete for members and funds. African Americans, whose hopes for freedom had been raised by the Revolution, continued to fight for full-fledged citizenship and an end to slavery. Women, too, faced challenges as they sought to claim a greater voice in the nation.

Separating Church and State

Government support of churches largely ended with the establishment of the United States. Anglican churches had long benefited from British support and collected taxes to support their ministry during the Revolution. Then in 1786

the Virginia Assembly approved the Statute of Religious Freedom, which was drafted earlier by Thomas Jefferson and made church attendance and support voluntary and eliminated many Anglican privileges. Other states soon followed suit, affecting all churches that had previously counted on government support.

Most states did require that officeholders be Christians, or even Protestants. But by the 1780s, that designation included a wide array of denominations. Especially in frontier areas, Baptists and Methodists, the latter of which broke off from the Anglican Church in 1784, gained thousands of converts. The Society of Friends, or Quakers, and the Presbyterians also gained new adherents in this period, while Catholics and Jews experienced greater tolerance than in the colonial era. In fact, in 1790 the Vatican appointed John Carroll the first Roman Catholic bishop of the United States. As a result of this diversity, no single religious voice or perspective dominated in the new nation. Instead, all denominations competed for members, money, and political influence.

Many Protestant churches were also challenged from within by free blacks who sought a greater role in church governance. In 1794 Richard Allen, a preacher who had been born a slave, led a small group of Philadelphia blacks who founded the first African American church in the United States. The Bethel African-American Methodist Church initially remained within the larger Methodist fold. By the early 1800s, however, Allen's church would serve as the basis for the first independent black denomination, the African Methodist Episcopal Church.

African Americans Struggle for Rights

Black churches provided one arena in which African Americans could demonstrate their independence. It was no accident that the Bethel African-American Methodist Church was founded in Philadelphia, which attracted large numbers of free blacks after passage of the state's gradual emancipation law in 1780. Although the northern states with the largest enslaved populations—New York and New Jersey—did not pass such laws until 1799 and 1804, the size of the free black population increased throughout the region.

Many of these free blacks were migrants from the South, where tens of thousands of enslaved women and men gained their freedom during or immediately following the Revolution (see chapter 6). A few slave owners took Revolutionary ideals to heart and emancipated their slaves following the war. Many others emancipated slaves in their wills. In addition, several states prohibited the importation of slaves from Africa during or immediately following the Revolution, including Delaware, Pennsylvania, Virginia, and Maryland. Despite these emancipations and prohibitions, the number of individuals enslaved in the United States in 1800 was far greater than in 1776, and the enslaved population continued to grow rapidly thereafter. Now, however, slavery was increasingly confined to the South. As northern states passed gradual abolition laws, southern states moved in the opposite direction, making it more difficult for owners to free their slaves and for free blacks to remain in the South.

The limits on emancipation in the South nurtured the growth of free black communities in the North, especially in seaport cities like Philadelphia, New York, Boston, and New Bedford, Massachusetts. In these areas, most African Americans focused on establishing families, finding jobs, and securing the freedom of relatives still enslaved. Others, like Richard Allen, sought to build black communities by establishing churches, schools, and voluntary societies and demanding a political voice. Some northern states, such as New Jersey, granted property-owning blacks the right to vote. Others, such as Pennsylvania, did not specifically exclude them. Records suggest that few black men participated in elections in the early Republic, yet many petitioned state and local governments—in the North and the South—to provide African American communities with schooling, burial grounds, and other forms of assistance.

Explore

To read a petition from free blacks, see Document 7.3.

Although blacks gained little support from most white Americans, they did have some allies. The Society of Friends, the only religious denomination to oppose slavery in the colonial period, became more adamant in its stance in the post-Revolutionary period. Many affluent Quakers finally freed their slaves and withdrew from the slave trade. Anthony Benezet, a Quaker writer and educator, advocated tirelessly for the abolition of slavery within the Society of Friends and directed the Negro School in Philadelphia, which he had founded in 1770.

Women Seek Wider Roles

Quaker women as well as men testified against slavery in the 1780s, writing statements on the topic in separate women's meetings. Although few other women experienced such spiritual autonomy, many gained a new sense of economic and political independence during the Revolution. Once peace was achieved, should they demand rights based on their wartime service or create new roles for themselves in the new Republic? Differences of age, wealth, region, race, and religion shaped women's responses to these questions.

The most famous Revolutionary claim for women's rights was penned by Abigail Adams in 1776 when she warned her husband, John, that "if particular care and attention is not paid to the Ladies we are determined to foment a Rebellion [*sic*], and will not hold ourselves bound by any Laws in which we have no voice, or Representation." Adams and other elite women sought a more public voice following the Revolution as well. Only in New Jersey could women—widowed or single, property-owning women—vote, and many cast ballots in state and local elections by the early nineteenth century.

The vast majority of women, however, could shape political decisions only by influencing their husbands, sons, and brothers. Fortunately, many leaders of the early Republic viewed virtuous wives and mothers as necessary to the development of a strong nation. In 1787 Benjamin Rush, a signer of the Declaration of Independence, published his *Essay on Female Education*. He believed that women could best shape political ideas and relations by "instructing their sons in principles of liberty and government" and rewarding husbands engaged in public service with "approbation and applause." To prepare young women for this enhanced domestic role, Rush suggested educating them in literature, music, composition, geography, history, and bookkeeping.

A more radical approach to women's education was presented by Judith Sargent Murray. Murray argued that "girls should be enabled to procure for themselves the necessaries of life; independence should be placed within their grasp." In addition to such practical instruction, Murray also advocated an education for girls that included science, mathematics, Latin, and Greek. She argued that at age two, boys and girls were intellectually equal. But from then on, "the one is taught to aspire, and the other is early confined and limited." A few American women in the late eighteenth century did receive broad educations, and some ran successful businesses; wrote plays, poems, and histories; and established urban salons where women and men discussed the issues of the day. In 1789 Massachusetts became the first state to institute free elementary education for all children, and female academies also multiplied in this period. Still, most girls' education was focused on preparing them for domesticity, and most women wielded what influence they had as an extension of their domestic responsibilities.

While women's influence was praised in the post-Revolutionary era, state laws rarely expanded women's rights. All states limited women's economic autonomy, although a few allowed married women to enter into business. Divorce was also legalized in many states but was still available only to the wealthy and well connected. Meanwhile women were excluded from juries and legal training and with rare exceptions from voting rights.

African American and Indian women lived under even more severe restraints than white women did. By the 1790s, the number of enslaved women began to increase rapidly once again. Even black women who gained their freedom

Petition from Free Blacks of Charleston, 1791

Although most African Americans in the early Republic were slaves, small free black communities existed in both the North and the South. However, their civil and political rights were often significantly curtailed. In South Carolina, free blacks lived under the harsh rules of the Negro Act of 1740, passed in the wake of the Stono rebellion, which restricted their freedom of movement and assembly, among other constraints. In 1791 free blacks in Charleston petitioned the state legislature for increased judicial rights.

Explore

How do free blacks in Charleston view their citizenship status?

What are these petitioners asking for?

On what grounds do the petitioners base their claims?

That in the enumeration of free citizens by the Constitution of the United States for the purpose of representation of the Southern states in Congress your memorialists [petitioners] have been considered under that description as part of the citizens of this state.

Although by the fourteenth and twenty-ninth clauses in an Act of Assembly made in the year 1740 . . . commonly called the Negro Act, now in force, your memorialists are deprived of the rights and privileges of citizens by not having it in their power to give testimony on oath in prosecutions on behalf of the state; from which cause many culprits have escaped the punishment due to their atrocious crimes, nor can they give their testimony in recovering debts due to them, or in establishing agreements made by them within the meaning of the Statutes of Frauds and Perjuries in force in this state except in cases where persons of color are concerned, whereby they are subject to great losses and repeated injuries without any means of redress.

That by the said clauses in the said Act, they are debarred of the rights of free citizens by being subject to a trial without the benefit of a jury and subject to prosecution by testimony of slaves without oath by which they are placed on the same footing.

Your memorialists show that they have at all times since the independence of the United States contributed and do now contribute to the support of the government by cheerfully paying their taxes proportionable to their property with others who have been during such period, and now are, in full enjoyment of the rights and immunities of citizens, inhabitants of a free independent state.

Source: Petition of Thomas Cole, Peter Bassnett Matthewes, and Matthew Webb to the South Carolina Senate, January 1, 1791, Records of the General Assembly, no. 181.

Put It in Context

What does this petition reveal about life for free blacks in the early Republic?

could find jobs only as domestic servants or agricultural workers. Indian women also faced a difficult future. Years of warfare had enhanced men's role as warriors and diplomats while restricting women's political influence. Furthermore, American officials and missionaries encouraged Indians to embrace gender roles that mirrored those of Anglo-American culture by giving men hoes and women spinning wheels. When forced to move farther west, Indian women also lost political and economic authority that was linked to their traditional control over land, crops, and households.

Indebted Farmers Fuel Political Crises

Although many Americans struggled economically in the 1780s, ordinary men did gain a greater voice in politics. Under constitutions written during the Revolution, most state governments broadened the electorate, allowing men with less property (or in some cases no property) to vote and hold office. They also increased representation from western areas. Although most elected officials still came from the wealthier classes, many felt some responsibility to address the claims of the less fortunate.

Still, the economic interests of poor farmers and of wealthy merchants and landowners diverged sharply. As conflicts between rich and poor, debtors and creditors, escalated between 1783 and 1787, state governments came down firmly on the side of those with money. When petitions and elections failed, impoverished workers and farmers mounted protests. In New Hampshire, debt-ridden farmers marched on the original state capital at Exeter to demand reform. They were confronted by cavalry units, who quickly seized and imprisoned their leaders.

In addition to rebellions by farmers and debtors, many political and economic leaders were worried about the continued efforts of Great Britain and Spain to undercut U.S. sovereignty, ongoing struggles with Indian nations, and attacks on private property by squatters. When James Madison and Alexander Hamilton attended the 1785 convention in Annapolis to address problems related to interstate commerce, they discovered that their concerns about the weakness of the confederation were shared by many large landowners, planters, and merchants. Despite these concerns, state legislatures were reluctant to give up the powers conferred on them under the Articles.

Shays's Rebellion, the 1786 armed uprising by disgruntled, indebted farmers in western Massachusetts, turned the tide by crystallizing fears among prominent patriots about the limits of the confederation model. On December 26, 1786, Washington wrote Henry Knox to express his concerns about the rebellion and other upheavals along the frontier: "If the powers [of the central government] are inadequate, amend or alter them; but do not let us sink into the lowest states of humiliation and contempt." Hamilton, too, believed that Shays's Rebellion marked "almost the last stage of national humiliation." Speaking of the confederation government, he claimed that this "frail and toddering edifice seems ready to fall upon our heads and crush us beneath its ruins."

Daniel Shays

This sketch is the only eighteenth-century illustration in existence of Daniel Shays (on the left in this detail). In it he stands with Jacob Shattuck, another anti-government leader. The picture appeared in a pro-Constitution Boston almanac, which ridiculed the two rebels by showing them in fancy uniforms and holding swords, in contrast to what would have been their usual homespun appearance. National Portrait Gallery, Smithsonian Institution/Art Resource, NY

REVIEW & RELATE

How did America's experience of the Revolutionary War change the lives of African Americans and women?

What do uprisings by farmers and debtors tell us about social and economic divisions in the early Republic?

LEARNINGCurve bedfordstmartins.com/hewittlawson/LC

Reframing the American Government

The delegates who met in Philadelphia in 1787 did not agree on the best way to reform the government. Some delegates, like James Monroe of Virginia, hoped to strengthen the existing government by amending the Articles of Confederation. Others joined with Madison and Hamilton, who argued for nothing less than a new structure for governing the United States. Once representatives agreed to draft a new constitution, they still disagreed over questions of representation, the relations between state and national governments, and the limits of popular democracy.

Even after the ratification of the Constitution and the election of George Washington as president, there was much to do. The Senate, House of Representatives, and Supreme Court had to be organized. The president had to select administrators to help him implement policies and programs. A system for levying, collecting, and distributing funds had to be put in place, and a host of economic problems had to be addressed. Foreign powers and Indian nations needed to be assured that treaties would be honored and diplomatic relations reestablished. A bill of rights, demanded in so many ratifying conventions, had to be drafted and approved. Finally, both proponents and opponents of the Constitution had to be convinced that the U.S. government could respond to the varied needs of its citizens.

The Philadelphia Convention of 1787

The fifty-five delegates who attended the Philadelphia convention were composed of white, educated men of property, mainly lawyers, merchants, and planters. Although many delegates had played important roles in the Revolution, only eight had signed the Declaration of Independence two decades earlier. The elite status of the delegates and the paucity of leading patriots raised concern among those who saw the convention as a threat to the rights of states and of citizens. Whatever changes they imagined, all the delegates realized that discussions about restructuring the U.S. government could alarm many

Americans, and thus they agreed to meet in secret until they had concluded their business.

On May 25, the convention opened, and delegates quickly turned to the key question: Was the convention going to revise the Articles of Confederation or draft an entirely new framework of governance? The majority of men came to Philadelphia with the intention of amending the Articles. However, a core group of federalists, who sought a more powerful central government, met in the weeks before the convention and drafted a plan to replace the Articles. This **Virginia Plan** proposed a strong centralized state, including a bicameral (two-house) legislature in which representation was to be based on population. Members of the two houses would select the national executive and the national judiciary. The new Congress would retain all the powers held by the confederation, and it would gain the power to settle disputes between states and veto legislation passed by an individual state. According to the Virginia Plan, Congress would not have the power to tax citizens or to regulate interstate or international commerce. Although most delegates opposed the Virginia Plan, it launched discussions in which strengthening the central government was assumed to be the goal.

Discussions of the Virginia Plan raised another issue that nearly paralyzed the convention: the question of representation. Heated debates pitted large states against small states even though political interests were not necessarily determined by size. Yet delegates held on to size as the critical issue in determining representation. In mid-June, William Patterson of New Jersey introduced a "small-state" plan in which Congress would consist of only one house, with each state having equal representation. Although Patterson's congressional plan was doomed to failure, he also articulated ideas of constitutional supremacy and judicial review that became key elements in the American legal system.

With few signs of compromise, the convention finally appointed a special committee of one delegate from each state to hammer out the problem of representation. Their report broke the logjam. Members of the House of Representatives were to be elected by voters in each state; members of the Senate would be appointed by state legislatures. Representation in the House would be determined by population—counted every ten years in a national census—and each state, regardless of size, would have equal representation in the Senate. The Senate could approve treaties and presidential appointments, try cases of impeachment, and initiate certain kinds of legislation. The House, however, had the singular authority to introduce all funding bills.

Included within this compromise was one of the few considerations of slavery at the Philadelphia convention. With little apparent debate, the committee decided that

James Madison

James Madison of Virginia was one of the framers of the Constitution and one of the authors of *The Federalist Papers*, which supported its ratification. This striking portrait of Madison was painted around 1792 by the artist Charles Willson Peale, who had served during the Revolutionary War in the Pennsylvania militia and attained the rank of captain.   Independence National Historical Park

representation in the House of Representatives was to be based on an enumeration of the entire free population and three-fifths of "all other persons," that is, slaves. If delegates had moral scruples about this **three-fifths compromise**, most found them outweighed by the urgency of settling the troublesome question of representation.

Still, slavery was on the minds of delegates. In the same week that the Philadelphia convention tacitly accepted the institution of slavery, the confederation congress meeting in New York City outlawed slavery in the Northwest Territory. It was perhaps news of that decision that inspired representatives from Georgia and South Carolina to insist that the Constitution protect the slave trade. Delegates in Philadelphia agreed that "the migration or importation of such persons as any of the states now existing shall think proper to admit" would not be interfered with for twenty years. At the same time, northern delegates insisted that the three-fifths

formula be used in assessing taxation as well as representation, ensuring that the South paid for the increased size of its congressional delegation with increased taxes.

Two other issues provoked considerable debate in the following weeks: the balance of power between states and the central government, and the degree of popular participation in selecting national leaders. The delegates supported federalism, a system in which states and the central government share power. But the new Constitution increased the powers of the central government significantly over those granted by the Articles of Confederation. The new Congress was granted the right to raise revenue by levying and collecting taxes and tariffs and coining money; to raise armies; to regulate interstate commerce; to settle disputes between the states; to establish uniform rules for the naturalization of immigrants; and to make treaties with foreign nations and Indians. But Congress could veto state laws only when those laws challenged "the supreme law of the land," and states retained all rights that were not specifically granted to the federal government.

One of the important powers retained by the states was the right to determine who was eligible to vote, but delegates in Philadelphia decided how much influence eligible voters would have in national elections. Members of the House of Representatives were to be elected directly by popular vote for two-year terms. Senators—two from each state—were to be selected by state legislatures for a term of six years. Voters were also involved only indirectly in the selection of the president. The president would be selected for a four-year term by an electoral college, members of which were appointed by state legislatures and equal to the whole number of senators and representatives to which the state was entitled. Finally, the federal judicial system was to be wholly removed from popular influence. Justices on the Supreme Court were to be appointed by the president and approved by the Senate. Once approved, they served for life to protect their judgments from the pressure of popular opinion.

With the final debates concluded, delegates agreed that approval by nine states, rather than all thirteen, would make the Constitution the law of the land. Some delegates sought formal reassurance that the powers granted the federal government would not be abused and urged inclusion of a bill of rights, modeled on the Virginia Declaration of Rights. But weary men eager to finish their business voted down the proposal. On September 17, 1787, the Constitution was approved and sent to the states for ratification.

Americans Battle over Ratification

Although the confederation congress neither approved nor rejected the Constitution, it did circulate the document to state legislatures and asked them to call conventions to consider ratification. At the same time, printers published thousands of copies of the Constitution in newspapers and as broadsides. Soon Americans were proclaiming their opinions from pulpits, papers, and other public platforms. In homes, churches, and taverns, ordinary citizens debated the wisdom of abolishing the confederation and establishing a stronger central government.

There were many opinions on the Constitution, but the states were not allowed to modify the document, only to accept or reject it in whole. Fairly quickly then, two sides emerged. The **Federalists**, who supported ratification, came mainly from urban and commercial backgrounds and lived in towns and cities along the Atlantic coast. They viewed a stronger central government as essential to the economic and political stability of the nation. Their opponents, who were generally more rural, less wealthy, and more likely to live in interior or frontier regions, opposed increasing the powers of the central government. Known more for what they stood against than what they stood for, opponents were labeled **Antifederalists**.

The pro-Constitution position was most fully expressed in a series of eighty-five editorials that appeared in New York newspapers in 1787–1788 and were published collectively as *The Federalist Papers*. Written by James Madison, John Jay, and Alexander Hamilton, these brilliant essays articulated broad principles embraced by most supporters of the Constitution. Most notably, in *Federalist* No. 10, Madison countered the common wisdom that small units of government were most effective in representing the interests of their citizens and avoiding factionalism. Recognizing that factions were inevitable, he argued that in a large political body, groups with competing interests had to collaborate and compromise in order to rule. This check on the "tyranny of the majority" protected the rights and freedoms of all. Although these editorials did not have a profound impact on delegates during the ratification process, they had a major influence in shaping the government that emerged after ratification.

Antifederalists continued to view a large and powerful central government as leading to tyranny, invoking the actions of the British king and Parliament to illustrate their point. Small farmers worried that a strong central government filled with merchants, lawyers, and planters might place the interests of creditors above those of ordinary (and indebted) Americans. Some wealthy patriots, like Mercy Otis Warren of Boston, feared that the Constitution would hand over power to a few individuals who remained isolated from the "true interests of the people." Finally, many Americans were concerned about the absence of a bill of rights.

Explore

See Document 7.4 for one farmer's concerns about a strong central government.

Federalists worked in each state to soften their critics by persuasive arguments, flattering hospitality, and timely compromises regarding a bill of rights. They also gained strength from a few states that ratified the Constitution quickly. By January 1788, Delaware, Pennsylvania, New Jersey, Georgia, and Connecticut had all approved the Constitution. Federalists also gained the support of the most influential newspapers, which were based in eastern cities and tied to commercial interests.

Despite the Federalists' successes, the contest in many states became heated. In Massachusetts, Antifederalists, including some leaders of Shays's Rebellion, gained the majority among convention delegates. Many were deeply opposed to the centralization of power established by the Constitution. Federalists worked hard to overcome the objections of their opponents, drafting a bill of rights to be proposed for adoption following the Constitution's ratification. Finally, on February 6, the Massachusetts delegates voted 187 to 168 in favor of ratification. Maryland and South Carolina followed in April and May. A month later, New Hampshire Federalists won a close vote, making it the ninth state to ratify the Constitution.

Two of the most populous and powerful states, New York and Virginia, had not yet ratified. Passionate debates erupted in both states. Finally, after promising that a bill of rights would be added quickly, Virginia Federalists won the day by a few votes. A month later, New York also approved the Constitution by a narrow margin. The divided nature of the votes, and the fact that two states (North Carolina and Rhode Island) had still not ratified, meant that the new government would have to prove itself quickly (Table 7.1).

TABLE 7.1 Votes of State-Ratifying Conventions

State	Date	For	Against
Delaware	December 1787	30	0
Pennsylvania	December 1787	46	23
New Jersey	December 1787	38	0
Georgia	January 1788	26	0
Connecticut	January 1788	128	40
Massachusetts	February 1788	187	168
Maryland	April 1788	63	11
South Carolina	May 1788	149	73
New Hampshire	June 1788	57	47
Virginia	June 1788	89	79
New York	July 1788	30	27
North Carolina	November 1788	194	77
Rhode Island	May 1790	34	32

DOCUMENT 7.4

Amos Singletary | Speech to the Massachusetts Ratifying Convention, 1788

By the time of the Massachusetts ratifying convention in January 1788, five of the nine required states had already ratified the federal Constitution. But the debates in Massachusetts were fierce, with the memory of Shays's Rebellion still fresh in the delegates' minds. Amos Singletary, a farmer and a convention delegate, claimed to represent the "little folk" when he addressed the convention. He sided with the Antifederalists and framed the debate about the Constitution in class terms and in the context of the pre-Revolutionary struggle between Britain and the colonists.

Explore

We contended with Great Britain—some said for a threepenny duty on tea; but it was not that—it was because they claimed a right to tax us and bind us in all cases whatever. And does not this constitution do the same? Does it not take away all we have—all our property? Does it not lay all taxes, duties, imposts, and excises? And what more have we to give? . . . These lawyers, and men of learning, and monied men, that talk so finely and gloss over matters so smoothly, to make us poor illiterate people swallow down the pill, expect to get into Congress themselves; they expect to be the managers of this constitution, and get all the power and all the money into their own hands, and then they will swallow up all us little folks, like the great Leviathan, Mr. President; yes, just as the whale swallowed up Jonah.

Source: Albert Bushell Hart, ed., *American Patriots and Statesmen from Washington to Lincoln,* vol. 2, 1775–1789 (New York: P. F. Collier and Sons, 1916), 335–36.

Interpret the Evidence

- What can we infer from this speech about Singletary's understanding of the causes of the Revolution?
- What connections does Singletary seem to make among education, money, and power? What motives does he ascribe to supporters of the Constitution?

Put It in Context

What light does this speech shed on Singletary's view of social and economic relations in the early Republic?

Organizing the Federal Government

Most political leaders hoped that the partisanship of the Federalist/Antifederalist struggle would fade away with the ratification of the Constitution. The electoral college's unanimous decision to name George Washington the first president helped calm some of this political turmoil. John Adams was selected as vice president. On April 30, 1789, Washington and Adams were sworn in at the nation's capital in New York City.

Washington quickly established four departments—State, War, Treasury, and Justice—to bring order to his administration. Thomas Jefferson was named secretary of state; Henry Knox, secretary of war; Alexander Hamilton, secretary of the treasury; and Edmund Randolph, attorney general, head of the Department of Justice. These men had been major figures in the Revolution and helped draft the Constitution.

Congress was also busy in the spring of 1789. The Constitution called for a Supreme Court, but it offered little guidance on its practical organization. The Judiciary Act of 1789 established a Supreme Court composed of six justices along with thirteen district courts and three circuit courts to hear cases appealed from the states. Congress also worked quickly to establish a bill of rights. Representative James Madison gathered more than two hundred resolutions passed by state ratifying conventions and honed them down to twelve amendments, which Congress approved and submitted to the states for ratification. In 1791 ten of the amendments were ratified by the necessary three-fourths of the states, and these became the **Bill of Rights**. It guaranteed the rights of individuals and states in the face of a more powerful central government, including freedom of speech, the press, religion, and the right to petition.

Federal Hall

This drawing shows Federal Hall, located on Wall Street in New York City. Originally built in 1700 as City Hall, the building housed the Stamp Act Congress in 1765 and the confederation congress from 1785 to 1788. In 1789 it became the seat of Congress under the new Constitution and the site of President Washington's first inauguration.   New York Public Library/Art Resource, NY

Hamilton Forges an Economic Agenda

Even as the new government was being organized, its leaders recognized that without a stable economy, the best political structure could falter. Thus Washington's appointment of Alexander Hamilton as secretary of the treasury was especially significant. In formulating the nation's economic policy, Hamilton's main goal was to establish the nation's credit. This would strengthen the United States in the eyes of the world and tie wealthy Americans more firmly to the federal government.

Hamilton formulated a policy that involved funding the national debt at face value and assuming the remaining state debts as part of the national debt. To pay for this policy, he planned to raise revenue through government bonds, an excise tax on goods traded within the United States, and tariffs on imported goods. Hamilton also called for the establishment of a central bank to carry out the financial operations of the United States. His ideas were bold and controversial, but he had the support of

Washington and key Federalists in Congress. Hamilton also had the charm and intellectual ability to persuade skeptics of the utility of his proposals and the wisdom to compromise when necessary. In three major reports to Congress—on public credit and a national bank in 1790 and on manufactures in 1791—he laid out a system of state-assisted economic development.

Hamilton's proposal to repay at face value the millions of dollars in securities issued by the confederation to foreign and domestic creditors was particularly controversial. Thousands of soldiers, farmers, artisans, and shop owners had been paid with these securities during the war, but most had long ago sold them for a fraction of their value to speculators. Thus speculators would make enormous profits if the securities were paid off at face value. Madison argued that the original owners of the securities should be rewarded in some way. Others, such as Patrick Henry, claimed that Hamilton's policy was intended "to erect, and concentrate, and perpetuate a large monied interest" that would prove "fatal to the existence of American liberty." Despite the passion of his opponents, Hamilton won the day.

The federal government's assumption of the remaining state war debts also faced fierce opposition, especially from southern states like Virginia that had already paid off their debt. Hamilton again won his case, though this time by agreeing to "redeem" (that is, reimburse) the money spent by states that had repaid their debts. In addition, Hamilton and his supporters had to agree to move the nation's capital from Philadelphia to a more central location along the Potomac River.

Funding the national debt, assuming the remaining state debts, and reimbursing states for debts already paid would cost $75.6 million (about $1.5 billion today). Rather than paying off the entire debt, Hamilton proposed the establishment of a Bank of the United States, funded by $10 million in stock to be sold to private stockholders and the national government. The bank would serve as a repository for income generated by taxes and tariffs and would grant loans and sell bills of credit to merchants and investors, thereby creating a permanent national debt. This, he argued, would bind investors to the United States, turning the national debt into a "national blessing."

Not everyone agreed with Hamilton's plans. Jefferson and Madison argued vehemently against the Bank of the United States, noting that there was no constitutional sanction for a federal bank. The secretary of the treasury fought back, arguing that Congress had the right to make "all Laws which shall be necessary and proper" for carrying out the provisions of the Constitution. Once again, Hamilton prevailed. Congress chartered the bank for a period of twenty years, and Washington signed the legislation into law.

The final piece of Hamilton's plan focused on raising revenue. Congress quickly passed tariffs on a range of imported goods. Tariffs generated some $4 million to $5 million annually for the federal government. Excise taxes placed on the consumption of wine, tea, coffee, and distilled spirits and on the sale of whiskey generated another $1 million each year. Some congressmen viewed these tariffs as a way to protect new industries in the United States, such as the furniture, tobacco, upholstery, hatmaking, and shoemaking industries. Hamilton was most concerned with generating income for the Treasury, but he also supported industrial development.

Hamilton's financial policies proved enormously successful in stabilizing the American economy, repaying outstanding debts, and tying men of wealth to the new government. The federal bank functioned effectively to collect and distribute the nation's resources. Commerce flourished, revenues rose, and confidence revived among foreign and domestic investors. Hamilton's support for "infant industries," expressed in his 1791 *Report on Manufactures*, also proved prescient even as farmers remained the backbone of the economy for decades to come.

REVIEW & RELATE

What issues attracted the most intense debate during the drafting and ratification of the Constitution? Why?

What role did Hamilton imagine the federal government playing in the American economy? Why were his proposals controversial?

✔ *LEARNINGCurve* bedfordstmartins.com/hewittlawson/LC

Years of Crisis, 1792–1796

By 1792 Hamilton had succeeded in implementing his plan for U.S. economic development. Yet as Washington began his second term in the spring of 1793, signs of strain appeared throughout the nation. The French Revolution, which had begun to dissolve into chaos and terror, posed challenges to foreign trade and diplomacy. Reduced prices for western land fueled migration to the frontier, intensified conflicts between Indians and white settlers, and increased hostilities between the United States and Great Britain. Finally, the excise tax on whiskey inspired discontent among frontier farmers. This cluster of crises reinforced disagreements among Federalists, splitting them into warring factions during Washington's second term.

Foreign Trade and Foreign Wars

Jefferson and Madison led the faction opposed to Hamilton's policies. Their supporters were mainly southern Federalists who envisioned the country's future rooted in agriculture, not the commerce and industry supported by Hamilton and his allies. Jefferson agreed with the Scottish economist Adam Smith that an international division of labor could best provide for the world's people. Americans could supply Europe with food and raw materials in exchange for clothes and other items manufactured in Europe. When wars in Europe, including a revolution in France, disrupted European agriculture in the 1790s, Jefferson's views were reinforced.

The French Revolution (1789–1799) had broader implications for U.S. politics than simply increasing the profits from American wheat. The efforts of French revolutionaries to overthrow the monarchy, end feudal practices, and institute a republic gained enthusiastic support from many Americans, especially the followers of Jefferson and Madison. They formed Republican societies, modeled on the

A Connecticut Merchant

This 1789 portrait of Elijah Boardman by Ralph Earl depicts a successful merchant in his Connecticut dry goods store. Boardman served in the Continental Army and became a political supporter of Thomas Jefferson. The Neutrality Act of 1793 increased commercial opportunities abroad, especially in the West Indies, allowing affluent merchants to expand their businesses, hire skilled craftsmen, and build elegant homes. Image copyright © The Metropolitan Museum of Art. Image source: Art Resource, NY

of the royal family in the Reign of Terror, wealthy Federalists grew more anxious. The beheading of King Louis XVI horrified them, as did the revolution's condemnation of Christianity. When France declared war against Prussia, Austria, and finally Great Britain, merchants worried about the impact on trade, and Hamilton feared a loss of valuable revenue from tariffs. In response, Congress passed the **Neutrality Act** in 1793, prohibiting ships of belligerent nations—including France or Great Britain—from using American ports. This act overrode a 1778 treaty, signed in the midst of the American Revolution, in which the United States had agreed to defend France in any war with Britain.

The immediate effect of the Neutrality Act was positive for American merchants. They eagerly increased trade with colonies in the British and French West Indies, and U.S. ships captured much of the lucrative sugar trade. Employment rose, and a building boom transformed seacoast cities as affluent residents hired carpenters, masons, and other craftsmen to construct fashionable homes in the "Federal" style. At the same time, farmers in the Chesapeake and Middle Atlantic regions benefited from European demand for grain, and the price of American wheat soared.

Yet these benefits did not bring about a political reconciliation. Instead, tensions escalated in the spring of 1793 when the French diplomat Edmond Genêt visited the United States. Republican clubs poured out to hear Citizen Genêt speak, and their members donated generously to support the French Revolution. Thousands of young Americans enlisted as volunteers on privateering vessels that harassed British and Spanish shipping in the Caribbean. At the same time, the British navy began stopping U.S. ships carrying French sugar and seized more than 250 vessels. American merchants were outraged and demanded that the government intervene to protect the "free trade" guaranteed by the Neutrality Act.

President Washington sent John Jay to England to negotiate a settlement with the British. In the meantime, Genêt's popularity began to fade as he sought to pull the United States into the war. Pro-British Federalists were more adamant than Republicans in their disapproval, arguing that Genêt was seeking to provoke conflict. Finally, in August 1793, just as yellow fever erupted in the nation's capital, Washington demanded Genêt's recall to France. Jay returned from England in 1794 with a treaty negotiated

Sons of Liberty, to keep tabs on Federalist encroachments on American rights. Many members adopted the French term *citizen* when addressing each other. Moreover, the strong presence of workers and farmers among France's revolutionary forces sparked further critiques of the "monied power" that drove Federalist policies.

In late 1792, as French revolutionary leaders began executing thousands of priests, aristocrats, and members

with the British, although many congressmen thought he had given away too much and were hesitant to ratify it. The treaty, for instance, did not include an agreement by the British to stop impressing American seamen.

The Whiskey Rebellion

Despite these foreign crises, it was the effect of Federalist policies on the American frontier that crystallized Republican opposition and led to the development of a **Democratic-Republican Party**. In the early 1790s, Republican societies from Maine to Georgia had demanded the removal of British and Spanish troops from frontier areas, while frontier farmers lashed out at Federalist enforcement of the so-called whiskey tax. Many farmers on the frontier grew corn and turned it into whiskey to make it easier to transport and more profitable to sell. The whiskey tax hurt these farmers, who considered themselves "industrious citizens" and "friends of liberty." Hundreds of them in Pennsylvania, North Carolina, and Kentucky petitioned the federal government for relief.

Much like their counterparts in Massachusetts in the 1780s, western Pennsylvania farmers rallied in 1792 and 1793 to protest the tax and those who enforced it. Former North Carolina Regulator Herman Husband was one of the most outspoken critics of the excise tax (see chapter 5). They burned sheriffs in effigy, marched on courthouses, assaulted tax collectors, and petitioned the federal government. Washington and his advisers failed to respond, paralyzed by a yellow fever epidemic in Philadelphia that ground government operations to a halt. By 1794 an all-out rebellion erupted, with protesters adopting slogans from Stamp Act protests, Shays's Rebellion, and even the French Revolution.

President Washington and his advisers worried that the rebellion could spread and feared that uprisings by white settlers might encourage Indians to rise up as well. Furthermore, Spanish and British soldiers were eager to foment trouble along the frontier, and the **Whiskey Rebellion** might spark intervention by either Spain or Great Britain. Federalists suspected that pro-French immigrants from Scotland and Ireland were behind the insurgency.

When Shays's Rebellion had erupted in 1787, the confederation government had had no power to intervene. Now, however, the United States could raise an army to quash such insurgencies. In August 1794, Washington federalized militias from four states, calling up nearly thirteen thousand soldiers. The president asked Hamilton, author of the whiskey tax, to accompany the troops into battle. The army that marched into western Pennsylvania in September vastly outnumbered the "whiskey rebels"

and easily suppressed the uprising. Having gained victory, only two of the leaders were tried and convicted, and they were later pardoned by Washington. **See Document Project 7: The Whiskey Rebellion, page 218**.

Washington proved that the Constitution provided the necessary powers to put down internal threats. Yet in doing so, the administration horrified many Americans who viewed the force used against the farmers as excessive. Jefferson, who had resigned as secretary of state in 1793, joined Madison in his outrage at the government's action. Despite a strong aversion to partisan politics among leaders of the Revolutionary generation, the divisions inspired by Hamilton's policies convinced Jefferson and Madison to launch an opposition party known as the Democratic-Republican Party.

Further Conflicts on the Frontier

In one area, Federalists and Democratic-Republicans voiced common concerns: the continued threats to U.S. sovereignty by Indian, British, and Spanish forces. In 1790 Congress had passed the Indian Trade and Intercourse Act to regulate Indian-white relations on the frontier and to ensure fair and equitable dealings. However, the act was widely ignored. Traders regularly cheated Indians, settlers launched private expeditions to claim Indian lands illegally, and government agents approved sham treaties. Federal troops sent to the Northwest Territory to enforce the law ended up fighting against the Indians.

The government's failure to stem the flood of settlers into the Ohio and Mississippi River valleys proved costly. In 1790 Little Turtle, a war chief of the Miami nation, gathered a large force of Shawnee, Delaware, Ottawa, Chippewa, Sauk, Fox, and other Indians. This pan-Indian alliance successfully attacked federal troops in the Ohio valley that fall. A year later, the allied Indian warriors defeated a large force under General Arthur St. Clair, governor of the Northwest Territory (Map 7.2). The stunning defeat shocked Americans, who continued to blame British forces encamped in forts on U.S. soil for encouraging Little Turtle and his warriors. In the meantime, Spanish authorities negotiated with Creeks and Cherokees to attack U.S. settlements on the southern frontier.

Washington decided to deal with problems in the Northwest Territory first, sending 2,000 men under the command of General Anthony Wayne into the Ohio frontier. In the spring of 1794, Wayne's troops built Fort Defiance in the heart of Ohio territory. Augmented by several hundred mounted Kentucky riflemen, Wayne's forces then attacked some 1,500 to 2,000 Indians gathered at a nearby British fort. In the Battle of Fallen Timbers, the

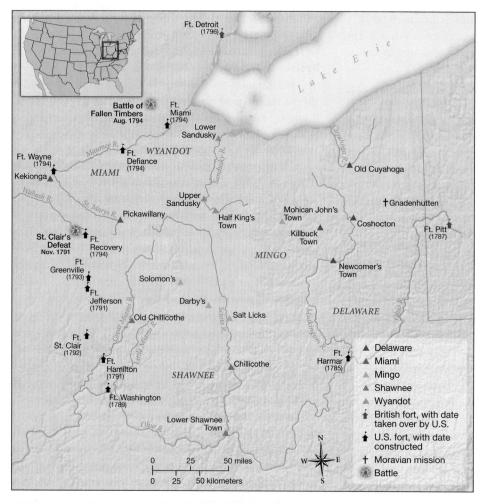

MAP 7.2   American Indians in the Ohio River Valley, c. 1785–1795

In the early to mid-eighteenth century, despite periodic conflicts, Indian tribes in the Ohio River valley forged trade and diplomatic relations with various colonial powers. But once the United States established the Northwest Territory in 1785, conflicts between Indians and U.S. settlers and soldiers escalated dramatically. As tribes forged pan-Indian alliances, the United States constructed numerous forts in the region.

pan-Indian forces, led by Little Turtle, suffered a bitter defeat. A year later, the warring Indians in the Northwest Territory signed the Treaty of Greenville, granting the United States vast tracts of land.

Amid this turmoil, in November 1794 the Senate finally approved the **Jay Treaty** with Great Britain, which required the withdrawal of British forces from U.S. soil by 1796. But it also required Americans to make "full and complete compensation" to British firms for debts outstanding at the time of the American Revolution and limited U.S. trade with the British West Indies. Before Jay's controversial treaty took effect, Spain agreed to negotiate an end to hostilities on the southern frontier of the United States. Envoy Thomas Pinckney, a South Carolina planter,

negotiated the treaty, which recognized the thirty-first parallel as the boundary between U.S. and Spanish territory in the South and opened the Mississippi River and the port of New Orleans to U.S. shipping. The **Pinckney Treaty**, ratified in 1796, advanced the interests of the South, while the Jay Treaty promoted those of the North.

REVIEW & RELATE

How did events overseas shape domestic American politics in the 1790s?

What common concerns underlay the Whiskey Rebellion and Shays's Rebellion? How did the U.S. government deal differently with each?

LEARNINGCurve bedfordstmartins.com/hewittlawson/LC

The First Party System

In 1796 executive power was placed in the hands of politicians who represented opposing factions in the national government: John Adams (a Federalist) became president and Thomas Jefferson (a Democratic-Republican) vice president. The two disagreed fundamentally on a wide range of issues, and events soon heightened these divisions. Foreign crises once again fueled political antagonisms as fear of war with Britain or France intensified. In response to the increasingly passionate debates over foreign policy, Federalists in Congress passed two acts in 1798 relating to aliens (immigrants) and to sedition (activities that promote civil disorder). Instead of resolving tensions, however, these laws exacerbated opposition to Federalist rule. By 1800, as the nation's fourth presidential election approached, partisan debates had crystallized into opposing factions, and the Democratic-Republicans threatened to oust the Federalists from power.

The Adams Presidency

The election of 1796 was the first to be contested by candidates identified with opposing factions. After private consultations among party leaders, Federalists supported John Adams for president and Thomas Pinckney for vice president. Though less well organized, Democratic-Republicans chose Thomas Jefferson and Aaron Burr of New York to represent their interests. When the electoral college was established, political parties did not exist and, in fact, were seen as promoting conflict. Thus electors were asked to choose the best individuals to serve, regardless of their views. In 1796 they picked Adams for president and Jefferson for vice president, perhaps hoping to lessen partisan divisions by forcing men of different views to work together. Instead, the effects of an administration divided against itself were nearly disastrous, and opposing interests became even more thoroughly entrenched.

Adams and Jefferson had disagreed on almost every major policy issue during Washington's administration. Not surprisingly, the new president rarely took advice from his vice president, who continued to lead the opposition. At the same time, Adams retained most of Washington's appointees, who repeatedly sought advice from Hamilton, which further undercut Adams's authority. Worse still, the new president had poor political instincts and faced numerous challenges.

At first, foreign disputes enhanced the authority of the Adams administration. The Federalists remained pro-British, and French seizures of U.S. ships threatened to provoke war.

In 1798 Adams tried to negotiate compensation for the losses suffered by merchants. When an American delegation arrived in Paris, however, three French agents demanded a bribe to initiate talks.

The Democratic-Republicans in Congress believed that Adams was exaggerating the issue to undermine U.S.-French relations. Adams then made public secret correspondence from the French agents, whose names were listed only as X, Y, and Z. Americans, including Democratic-Republicans, expressed outrage at this French insult to U.S. integrity, which became known as the **XYZ affair**. Congress quickly approved an embargo act that prohibited trade with France and permitted privateering against French ships. In May 1798, Congress allocated funds to build up the navy and defend the American coastline against attack. For the next two years, the United States fought an undeclared war with France.

Despite widespread support for his handling of the XYZ affair, Adams feared dissent from opponents at home and abroad. Consequently, the Federalist majority in Congress passed a series of security acts in 1798. The Alien Act allowed the president to order the imprisonment or deportation of noncitizens and was directed primarily at Irish and Scottish dissenters who criticized the government's pro-British policies. Congress also approved the Naturalization Act, which raised the residency requirement for citizenship from five to fourteen years. Finally, Federalists pushed through the Sedition Act, which outlawed "false, scandalous, or malicious statements against President or Congress" and penalized those who incited hatred of the government.

The First Amendment stated that Congress "shall make no law . . . abridging the freedom of speech, or of the press." However, as a Federalist newspaper explained, in the current situation, "All who are against us are at war." No opposition to Federalist policies would be tolerated. Over the next several months, nearly two dozen Democratic-Republican editors and legislators were arrested for sedition, and some were fined and imprisoned.

Democratic-Republicans were, understandably, infuriated by the **Alien and Sedition Acts**. They considered the attack on immigrants an attempt to limit the votes of farmers, artisans, and frontiersmen, who formed the core of their supporters. The Sedition Act also challenged the party since it was Republican critics who faced arrest. Jefferson and Madison encouraged states to pass resolutions that would counter this violation of the Bill of Rights. Accepting resolutions drafted by Jefferson and Madison, legislators in Virginia and Kentucky declared the Alien and Sedition Acts "void and of no force." Virginia went even further, claiming that states had a right to nullify any powers exercised by the federal government that were not explicitly granted to it.

He in a trice struck Lyon thrice
Upon his head, enrag'd, fir,

Who seiz'd the tongs to ease his wrongs,
And Grifwold thus engag'd, fir.

Congress Hall,
in Philad.ª Feb. 15. 1798.
S. K. Cor. 6.ᵗʰ & Chesnut St.

Matthew Lyon and Roger Griswold

This political cartoon depicts a fight on the floor of the House of Representatives in February 1798 between Representatives Matthew Lyon of Vermont, a Democratic-Republican brandishing tongs, and Roger Griswold of Connecticut, a Federalist waving a cane. A newspaper editor and a critic of the Alien and Sedition Acts, Lyon was later convicted of sedition but won reelection while in jail.   Library of Congress

Although the Alien and Sedition Acts curbed dissent in the short run, they reinforced popular concerns about the power wielded by the Federalists. Combined with the ongoing war with France, continuing disputes over taxes, and relentless partisan attacks and denunciations in the press, these acts set the stage for the presidential election of 1800.

The Election of 1800

By 1800 Adams had negotiated a peaceful settlement of U.S. conflicts with France, considering it one of the greatest achievements of his administration. However, other Federalists, including Hamilton, disagreed, continuing to seek open warfare and an all-out victory. Thus the Federalists faced the election of 1800 deeply divided. Democratic-Republicans meanwhile, although more loosely organized than the Federalists, united behind Jefferson. They portrayed the Federalists as the "new British," tyrants who abused their power and violated the rights guaranteed ordinary citizens.

For the first time, congressional caucuses selected candidates for each party. The Federalists agreed on Adams and Charles Cotesworth Pinckney of South Carolina. The Democratic-Republicans again chose Jefferson and Burr as their candidates. The campaign quickly escalated into a series of bitter accusations, with advocates for each side denouncing the other.

In the first highly contested presidential election, the different methods states used to record voters' preferences gained more attention. Only five states determined members of the electoral college by popular vote. In the rest of the states, legislatures appointed electors. In some states, voters orally declared their preference for president; in other states, voters submitted paper ballots. In addition, because the idea of party tickets was new, the members of the electoral college were not prepared for the situation

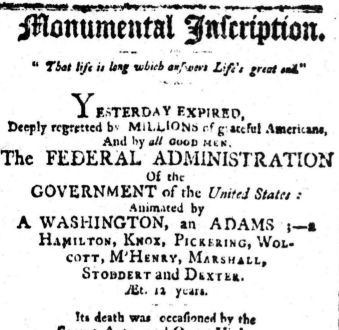

Monumental Inscription.

" *That life is long which answers Life's great end.*"

YESTERDAY EXPIRED,
Deeply regretted by MILLIONS of grateful Americans,
And by *all* GOOD MEN,
The FEDERAL ADMINISTRATION
Of the
GOVERNMENT of the *United States :*
Animated by
A WASHINGTON, an ADAMS ;— a
HAMILTON, KNOX, PICKERING, WOL-
COTT, M'HENRY, MARSHALL,
STODDERT and DEXTER.
Æt. 12 years.

Its death was occasioned by the
Secret Arts, and Open Violence;
Of Foreign and Domestic Demagogues :
Notwithstanding its whole Life
Was devoted to the Performance of every Duty
to promote
The UNION, CREDIT, PEACE, PROSPER-
ITY, HONOR, and
FELICITY OF ITS COUNTRY.

At its birth it found
The Union of the States dissolving like a Rope of snow ;
It hath left it
Stronger than the Threefold cord.

It found the United States
Bankrupts in Estate and Reputation ;
It hath left them
Unbounded in Credit ; and respected throughout
the World.

The Election of 1800

The election of 1800 marked the first transfer of political power in the United States from one party to another. The Democratic-Republican candidate for president, Thomas Jefferson, defeated the Federalist Party incumbent, John Adams. On March 4, 1801, the *Columbian Centinel*, a Federalist newspaper in Boston, viewed Jefferson's inauguration as the end of the peace, prosperity, and honor achieved under the Federalists. The Granger Collection, New York

---

they faced in January 1801, when Jefferson and Burr received exactly the same number of votes. After considerable political maneuvering, Jefferson, the intended presidential candidate, emerged victorious.

Jefferson labeled his election a revolution achieved not "by the sword" but by "the suffrage of the people." The election of 1800 was hardly a popular revolution, given the restrictions on suffrage (of some 5.3 million Americans, only about 550,000 could vote) and the limited participation of voters in selecting the electoral college. Still, partisan factions had been transformed into opposing parties, and the United States had managed a peaceful

transition from one party in power to another, which was a development few other nations could claim in 1800.

REVIEW & RELATE

What were the main issues dividing the Federalists and the Democratic-Republicans?

What do the Alien and Sedition Acts tell us about attitudes toward political partisanship in late-eighteenth-century America?

Conclusion: A Young Nation Comes of Age

In the 1780s and 1790s, the United States faced numerous obstacles to securing its place as a nation. Financial hardship, massive debts, hostile Indians, and shifting European alliances and conflicts had to be addressed by a federal government that, under the Articles of Confederation, was relatively weak. Yet despite these challenges, the confederation congress did initiate diplomatic relations with European and Indian nations and successfully organized the vast Northwest Territory. Nonetheless, by 1787 concerns about national security, fueled by rebellious farmers and frontier conflicts, led to the drafting of a new constitution. After a fierce battle in many states, the Constitution was ratified, and the federal government's power to raise money, raise armies, and regulate interstate commerce was enhanced.

George Washington served as the first American president, and his administration implemented policies that enhanced U.S. power at home and abroad. Most important, Secretary of the Treasury Alexander Hamilton implemented a series of measures to stabilize the American economy, pay off Revolutionary War debts, and promote trade and industry. Yet these policies also aroused opposition among political leaders like Jefferson and Madison, who viewed agriculture as the foundation of the American nation. And specific acts like the whiskey tax also fueled antagonism among ordinary farmers and frontiersmen. Although the Federalists continued to support Hamilton's economic policies and pro-British diplomacy, they faced growing opposition from agrarian and pro-French Democratic-Republicans.

In 1798 the Federalist-controlled Congress passed the Alien and Sedition Acts, further unifying Democratic-Republicans. By 1800 the Democratic-Republicans had created an opposition party that was less solid in its structure than the Federalists but sufficiently powerful to win control of Congress and the presidency. This peaceful transition in power boded well for the young United States.

Despite political setbacks, the Federalist legacy remained powerful. Many of Hamilton's policies would continue to shape national economic growth, and the Federalists retained their political power in the Northeast for years to come. Hamilton himself retreated from public service following Jefferson's election. Marginalized by the defeat of the Federalists and tainted after admitting to an adulterous affair, he focused on his law practice. Yet he could not stay entirely clear of politics. In 1804 Aaron Burr was passed over as the vice presidential candidate by the Democratic-Republicans and decided to seek the governorship of New York instead. Hamilton worked tirelessly to defeat Burr, and when the vice president lost, he challenged his nemesis to a duel. On July 11, 1804, Burr fatally shot Hamilton. Even in death, though, Hamilton retained his stature as the architect of the nation's first economic policy.

Meanwhile Democratic-Republicans, many of whom were small farmers and frontiersmen, often fared worse than their Federalist counterparts, at least economically, even after Jefferson's election. We do not know whether Daniel Shays voted in 1800, but he likely supported Jefferson. The rebellion Shays led in 1787 had helped convince many political leaders of the need for a new constitution, yet his role in creating the new nation was largely forgotten. Indeed, Shays, like many ordinary Continental soldiers, spent the rest of his life in relative obscurity. Having moved with his family to eastern New York in 1788, he finally received a federal military pension in 1818, just seven years before he died.

Shays's pension was granted by a U.S. Congress still controlled by Democratic-Republicans. The Democratic-Republican Party would not be seriously challenged for national power until 1824, giving it nearly a quarter century to implement its vision of the United States. Yet developing a vision in opposition to that of the Federalists proved far easier than implementing that vision once the Democratic-Republicans—a heterogeneous group—held the power of the central government in their own hands.

LEARNINGCurve
Check what you know.
bedfordstmartins.com/hewittlawson/LC

Chapter Review

Online Study Guide ▶ bedfordstmartins.com/hewittlawson

KEY TERMS

Northwest Land Ordinance (1785 and 1787) (p. 198)
Shays's Rebellion (p. 203)
Virginia Plan (p. 204)
three-fifths compromise (p. 205)
Federalists (p. 206)
Antifederalists (p. 206)
Bill of Rights (p. 207)
Neutrality Act (p. 210)
Democratic-Republican Party (p. 211)
Whiskey Rebellion (p. 211)
Jay Treaty (p. 212)
Pinckney Treaty (p. 212)
XYZ affair (p. 213)
Alien and Sedition Acts (p. 213)

REVIEW & RELATE

1. What challenges did the new nation face in the immediate aftermath of the Revolutionary War?

2. How and why did the conflict between America and Great Britain continue after the war ended?

3. How did America's experience of the Revolutionary War change the lives of African Americans and women?

4. What do uprisings by farmers and debtors tell us about social and economic divisions in the early Republic?

5. What issues attracted the most intense debate during the drafting and ratification of the Constitution? Why?

6. What role did Hamilton imagine the federal government playing in the American economy? Why were his proposals controversial?

7. How did events overseas shape domestic American politics in the 1790s?

8. What common concerns underlay the Whiskey Rebellion and Shays's Rebellion? How did the U.S. government deal differently with each?

9. What were the main issues dividing the Federalists and the Democratic-Republicans?

10. What do the Alien and Sedition Acts tell us about attitudes toward political partisanship in late-eighteenth-century America?

TIMELINE OF EVENTS

1780–1804	Northern states pass gradual emancipation laws
March 1783	Officers encamped at Newburgh, New York, threaten to mutiny
1784	U.S. commissioners meet with Iroquois delegates at Fort Stanwix, New York
1785	Northwest Land Ordinance passed
	Annapolis Convention
1786–1787	Shays's Rebellion
1787	Constitutional Convention in Philadelphia
	Northwest Land Ordinance revised
June 1788	U.S. Constitution ratified
1789	Alexander Hamilton named secretary of the treasury
	Judiciary Act of 1789 passed
1789–1799	French Revolution
1790–1794	Little Turtle leads pan-Indian alliance against American settlements in the Ohio valley
1791	Bill of Rights ratified
1793	Neutrality Act passed
July–October 1793	Yellow fever epidemic paralyzes Philadelphia
1794	Whiskey Rebellion
	Bethel African-American Methodist Church in Philadelphia founded
1796	Jay Treaty and Pinckney Treaty ratified
	Democratic-Republicans and Federalists contest presidential election
1798	Alien and Sedition Acts passed

The Whiskey Rebellion

In 1791 Alexander Hamilton, the first secretary of the treasury, sought a way to reduce the national debt, and he convinced Congress to pass the first internal revenue tax in the form of an excise tax on distilled spirits. This direct tax angered many Americans, especially farmers who turned their excess grain into whiskey, a lucrative and easily transported product. Their resentment increased because of provisions that taxed smaller producers at almost twice the rate as large producers and required that all stills be federally registered.

Farmers in western Pennsylvania were particularly resistant to the new tax. Many refused to pay the tax, and towns sent petitions to state and federal officials asking that the tax be repealed (see Document 7.5). When this did not work, angry farmers resorted to violence. By the summer of 1794, the Whiskey Rebellion, as it became known, reached a crisis state. Tax collectors were tarred and feathered, groups of farmers burned the homes of tax officials in western counties, and armed rebels attacked neighbors who supported the whiskey tax. Sympathetic residents in towns like Pittsburgh offered their support as farmers prepared for an armed confrontation (Document 7.6).

Washington and his cabinet feared that the revolt would become another Shays's Rebellion, and Hamilton described the rebels accordingly (Documents 7.8 and 7.9). When the "whiskey rebels" refused to negotiate with government representatives, Washington placed the militias of four states under federal control (Document 7.7). When this force of 13,000 men arrived in Pennsylvania, however, most of the rebels had dispersed. The leaders were arrested and tried for treason, but only two leaders were convicted. Washington eventually pardoned all those involved in the revolt.

The Whiskey Rebellion was Washington's most serious domestic crisis and a test of the federal government's powers under the Constitution (Document 7.9). Washington successfully defeated the rebels, but many Americans were outraged that force had been used against their fellow citizens. In response, Thomas Jefferson and James Madison, dissatisfied with this and other Federalist policies, formed the Democratic-Republican political party (Document 7.10).

DOCUMENT 7.5

Resolution to the Pennsylvania Legislature, 1791

Throughout the summer of 1791, farmers in Pennsylvania met to discuss and protest the excise tax on whiskey. In September, representatives from several western counties, including the former North Carolina Regulator Herman Husband, met in Pittsburgh (see chapter 5). There they drafted a resolution to be printed in the *Pittsburgh Gazette* and sent to the U.S. Congress and the Pennsylvania legislature. The following selection highlights the farmers' objections to the whiskey tax.

Resolved, That the said law is deservedly obnoxious to the feelings and interests of the people in general, as being attended with infringements on liberty, partial in its operations, attended with great expense in the collection, and liable to much abuse. It operates on a domestic manufacture, a manufacture not equal through the States. It is insulting to the feelings of the people to have their vessels marked, houses painted and ransacked, to be subject to informers, gaining by the occasional delinquency of others. It is a bad precedent tending to introduce the excise laws of Great Britain and of countries where the liberty, property, and even the morals of the people are sported with, to gratify particular men in their ambitious and interested measures.

Resolved, That in the opinion of this committee, the duties imposed by the said act on spirits distilled from the produce of the soil of the United States, will eventually discourage agriculture, and a manufacture highly beneficial in the present state of the country, that those duties which fall heavy, especially upon the western parts of the United States, which are, for the most part, newly settled, and where the aggregate of the citizens is of the laborious and poorer class, who have not the means of procuring the wines, spirituous liquors, etc., imported from foreign countries.

Source: Pennsylvania Archives, 2nd Series, 4:21.

DOCUMENT 7.6

The Pittsburgh Resolution, 1794

As the Whiskey Rebellion reached a climax in the summer of 1794, its leaders called on armed volunteers to meet at Braddock's Field near Pittsburgh. At the same time, towns across western Pennsylvania held meetings to consider how best to support the rebels. Pittsburgh residents met on July 31 and drafted their own resolution to support the protesters, a portion of which follows.

In consequence of certain letters sent by the last mail, certain persons were discovered as advocates of the excise law, and enemies to the interests of the country, and that a certain Edward Day, James Brison, and Abraham Kirkpatrick, were particularly obnoxious, and that it was expected by the country that they should be dismissed without delay; whereupon, it was resolved it should be so done, and a committee of twenty-one were appointed to see this resolution carried into effect.

Also, that, whereas it is a part of the message from the gentlemen of Washington, that a great body of the people of the country will meet to-morrow at Braddock's Field, in order to carry into effect measures that may seem to them advisable with respect to the excise law, and the advocates of it.

Resolved, That the above committee shall, at an early hour, wait upon the people on the ground, and assure the people that the above resolution, with respect to the proscribed persons, has been carried into effect.

Resolved, also, That the inhabitants of the town shall march out and join the people on Braddock's Field, as brethren, to carry into effect with them any measure that may seem to them advisable for the common cause.

Resolved, also, That we shall be watchful among ourselves of all characters that, by word or act, may be unfriendly to the common cause; and, when discovered, will not suffer them to live amongst us, but they shall instantly depart the town.

Resolved, That the town committee shall exist as a committee of information and correspondence, as an organ of our sentiments until our next town meeting. And that *whereas,* a general meeting of delegates from the townships of the country, on the west of the mountains, will be held at Parkinson's Ferry, on the Monongahela, on the 14th of August next.

Resolved, That delegates shall be appointed to that meeting, and that the 9th August next be appointed for a town meeting to elect such delegates.

Source: Pennsylvania Archives, 2nd Series, 4:21, 80–81.

DOCUMENT 7.7

George Washington | Proclamation against the Rebels, 1794

In August 1794, President Washington met with his cabinet and the governor of Pennsylvania in order to formulate a response to the rebels' growing threat. Washington then issued a proclamation that called on the rebels and anyone "aiding, abetting, or comforting" them to end their revolt and return home. In the proclamation, Washington also utilized the Militia Act of 1792 to call up troops from Maryland, New Jersey, Pennsylvania, and Virginia to put down the rebellion.

And whereas, By a law of the United States, intitled "An Act to provide for calling forth the Militia to execute the laws of the Union; suppress insurrections and repel invasions," it is enacted that whenever the laws of the United States shall be opposed, or the execution thereof obstructed in any State by combinations too powerful to be suppressed by the ordinary course of judicial proceedings, or by the powers vested in the Marshal by that act, the same being notified by an associate Justice or a district Judge, it shall be lawful for the President of the United States to call forth the Militia of such State to suppress such combinations, and to cause the laws to be duly executed. And if the Militia of a State where such combinations may happen, shall refuse or be insufficient to suppress the same, it shall be lawful for the President, if the Legislature shall not be in session, to call forth and employ such numbers of the Militia of any other State or States most convenient thereto, as may be necessary; and the use of the militia so to be called forth may be continued, if necessary, until the expiration of thirty days after the commencement of the ensuing session: *Provided, always*, That whenever it may be necessary, in the judgment of the President, to use the Militia force hereby directed to be called forth, the President shall forthwith, and previous thereto, by Proclamation, command such insurgents to disperse and retire peaceably to their respective abodes within the limited time: . . .

And whereas, it is, in my judgment, necessary under the circumstances of the case to take measures for calling forth the militia in order to suppress the combinations aforesaid, and to cause the laws to be duly executed, and I have accordingly determined so to do, feeling the deepest regret for the occasion, but withal the most solemn conviction that the essential interest of the Union demand it, that the very existence of the government and the fundamental principles of social order are materially involved in the issue, and that the patriotism and firmness of all good citizens are seriously called upon as occasion may require, to aid in the suppression of so fatal a spirit;

Wherefore, and in pursuance of the proviso above recited, I, George Washington, President of the United States, do hereby command all persons, being insurgents, as aforesaid, and all others whom it may concern, on or before the first day of September next to disperse and retire peaceably to their respective abodes. And I do moreover warn all persons whomsoever against aiding, abetting, or comforting the perpetrators of the aforesaid treasonable acts; and do require all officers and other citizens, according to their respective duties and the laws of the land, to exert their utmost endeavors to prevent and suppress such dangerous proceedings.

Source: Pennsylvania Archives, 2nd Series, 4:21, 125–27.

DOCUMENT 7.8

Alexander Hamilton | Letter to George Washington, August 5, 1794

Washington's military preparations resulted in large part from the increasing violence occurring in western Pennsylvania. Tax collectors in particular faced the wrath of angry farmers and other citizens sympathetic to their plight. In the following letter, Alexander Hamilton relays to Washington reports of the violence that had occurred since the rebellion began. He also offers his own explanation of the types of people responsible for attacking not only government officials but also anyone who offered any support for the whiskey tax.

Sometime in October 1791, an unhappy man of the name of Wilson, a stranger in the county and manifestly disordered in his intellects, imagining himself to be a collector of the revenue, or invested with some trust in relation to it, was so unlucky as to make inquiries concerning distillers who had entered their stills, giving out that he was to travel through the United States to ascertain and report to Congress the number of stills, etc. This man was pursued by a party in disguise, taken out of his bed, carried about five miles back to a smith's shop, stripped of his clothes, which were afterwards burnt, and having been himself inhumanly burnt in several places with a heated iron, was tarred and feathered and about day-light dismissed naked, wounded and otherwise in a very suffering condition. These particulars are communicated in a letter from the inspector of the revenue of the 17th of November, who declares that he had then himself seen the unfortunate maniac, the abuse of whom, as he expresses it, exceeded description and was sufficient to make human nature shudder. The affair is the more extraordinary as persons of weight and consideration in that county are understood to have been actors in it, and as the symptoms of insanity were, during the whole time of inflicting the punishment, apparent; the unhappy sufferer displaying the heroic fortitude of a man who conceived himself to be a martyr to the discharge of some important duty.

Not long after a person of the name of Roseberry underwent the humiliating punishment of tarring and feathering with some aggravations for having in conversation hazarded the very natural and just but unpalatable remark that the inhabitants of that county could not reasonably expect protection from a government whose laws they so strenuously opposed.

The audacity of the perpetrators of these excesses was so great that an armed banditti ventured to seize and carry off two persons who were witnesses against the rioters in the case of Wilson in order to prevent their giving testimony of the riot to a court then sitting or about to sit.

Designs of personal violence against the inspector of the revenue himself, to force him to a resignation, were repeatedly attempted to be put in execution by armed parties, but, by different circumstances, were frustrated.

Source: Pennsylvania Archives, 2nd Series, 4:21, 88–89.

DOCUMENT 7.9

Alexander Hamilton | Tully's Pamphlet, 1794

Many Americans criticized Washington's decision to organize troops against the whiskey rebels. Fearful that public sentiment would make it impossible to find enough militia recruits, Alexander Hamilton (using the pen name Tully) wrote a series of pamphlets in support of the government. These pamphlets, one of which is excerpted here, were so compelling that militias had to turn away volunteers.

Fellow citizens: You are told that it will be intemperate to urge the execution of the laws which are resisted. What? Will it be indeed intemperate in your Chief Magistrate, sworn to maintain the Constitution, charged faithfully to execute the laws, and authorized to employ for that purpose force, when the ordinary means fail—will it be intemperate in him to exert that force, when the Constitution and the laws are opposed by force? Can he answer it to his conscience, to you, not to exert it?

Yes, it is said; because the execution of it will produce civil war—the consummation of human evil.

Fellow citizens: Civil war is, undoubtedly, a great evil. It is one that every good man would wish to avoid, and will deplore if inevitable. But it is incomparably a less evil than the destruction of government. The first brings with it serious but temporary and partial ills: the last undermines the foundations of our security and happiness; and where should we be if it were once to grow into a maxim that force is not to be used against the seditious combinations of parts of the community to resist the laws? This would be to give a carte blanche to ambition, to licentiousness, to foreign intrigue, to make you the prey of the gold of other nations—the sport of the passions and vices of individuals among yourselves. The hydra Anarchy would rear its head in every quarter. The goodly fabric you have established would be rent asunder and precipitated into the dust. You knew how to encounter civil war rather than surrender your liberty to foreign domination; you will not hesitate now to brave it rather than to surrender your sovereignty to the tyranny of a faction; you will be as deaf to the apostles of anarchy now as you were to the emissaries of despotism then. Your love of liberty will guide you now as it did then; you know that the power of the majority and liberty are inseparable. Destroy that, and this perishes. But, in truth, that which properly can be called civil war is not to be apprehended—unless from the act of those who endeavor to fan the flame, by rendering the Government odious. A civil war is a contest between two great parts of the same empire. The exertion of the strength of the nation to suppress resistance to its laws, by a sixtieth part of itself, is not of that description.

Source: John C. Hamilton, ed., *The Works of Alexander Hamilton* (New York: Charles F. Francis, 1851), 7:166–67.

You will learn from the newspapers and official communications the unfortunate scene in the Western parts of Pennsylvania which unfolded itself during the recess. The history of its remote and immediate causes, the measures produced by it, and the manner in which it has been closed, does not fall within the compass of a letter. It is probable, also, that many explanatory circumstances are yet but imperfectly known. I can only refer to the printed accounts, which you will receive from the Department of State, and the comments which your memory will assist you in making on them. The event was, in several respects, a critical one for the cause of liberty, and the real authors of it, if not in the service, were, in the most effectual manner, doing the business of Despotism. You well know the general tendency of insurrections to increase the momentum of power. You will recollect the particular effect of what happened some years ago in Massachusetts. Precisely the same calamity was to be dreaded on a larger scale in this case. There were enough, as you may well suppose, ready to give the same turn to the crisis, and to propagate the same impressions from it. It happened most auspiciously, however, that, with a spirit truly Republican, the people every where, and of every description, condemned the resistance to the will of the majority, and obeyed with alacrity the call to vindicate the authority of the laws. You will see, in the answer of the House of Representatives to the President's speech, that the most was made of this circumstance, as an antidote to the poisonous influence to which Republicanism was exposed. If the insurrection had not been crushed in the manner it was, I have no doubt that a formidable attempt would have been made to establish the principle that a standing army was necessary for *enforcing the laws*. When I first came to this City, about the middle of October, this was the fashionable language. Nor am I sure that the attempt would not have been made, if the President could have been embarked in it, and particularly if the temper of New England had not been dreaded on this point. I hope we are over that danger for the present. You will readily understand the business detailed in the newspapers relating to the denunciation of the "self-created Societies." The introduction of it by the President was, perhaps,

DOCUMENT 7.10
James Madison | Letter to James Monroe, December 4, 1794

James Madison and Thomas Jefferson were the leading critics of the Federalist policies of George Washington and Alexander Hamilton. Washington's decision to raise an army to put down the western Pennsylvania rebels confirmed Madison's fears that the national government had become too strong. In his letter to James Monroe, then serving as U.S. minister to France, Madison expresses his concern about Washington's use of military force and the dangers of a standing army. He also criticizes Federalist efforts to link rebellious farmers with the Republican societies (also sometimes called Democratic societies) established in support of the French Revolution and the emerging political opposition in the United States.

the greatest error of his political life. For his sake, as well as for a variety of obvious reasons, I wished it might be passed over in silence by the House of Representatives. The answer was penned with that view, and so reported. This moderate course would not satisfy those who hoped to draw a party advantage out of the President's popularity. The game was to connect the Democratic Societies with the odium of the insurrection; to connect the Republicans in Congress with those Societies; to put the President ostensibly at the head of the other party, in opposition to both, and by these means prolong the illusions in the North, and try a new experiment on the South. To favor the project, the answer of the Senate was accelerated, and so framed as to draw the President into the most pointed reply on the subject of the Societies. At the same time, the answer of the House of Representatives was procrastinated, till the example of the Senate and the commitment of the President could have their full operation. You will see how nicely the House was divided, and how the matter went off. As yet, the discussion has not been revived by the newspaper combatants. If it should, and equal talents be opposed, the result cannot fail to wound the President's popularity more than anything that has yet happened. It must be seen that no two principles can be either more indefensible in reason, or more dangerous in practice, than that—1. Arbitrary denunciations may punish what the law permits, and what the Legislature has no right by law to prohibit; and that, 2. The Government may stifle all censure whatever on its misdoings; for if it be itself the Judge, it will never allow any censures to be just; and if it can suppress censures flowing from one lawful source, it may those flowing from any other—from the press and from individuals, as well as from Societies, &c.

The elections for the House of Representatives are over in New England and Pennsylvania. In Massachusetts, they have been contested so generally as to rouse the people compleatly from their lethargy, though not sufficiently to eradicate the errors which have prevailed there. The principal members have been all severely pushed; several changes have taken place, rather for the better, and *not one* for the worse.

Interpret the Evidence

1. What are the chief complaints of the whiskey rebels and their supporters (Documents 7.5 and 7.6)? Are they opposed only to the economic burden of a tax? Which of their arguments do you find the most convincing?

2. What arguments do Washington and Hamilton make in favor of government action against the rebels (Documents 7.7 and 7.9)? Which do you find most convincing?

3. According to Hamilton's letter (Document 7.8), who was responsible for carrying out the violence of the Whiskey Rebellion? How does Hamilton characterize the attackers and the victims? How can we evaluate his claims?

4. Why do you think Hamilton's pamphlets elicited such overwhelming support for the government and militia (Document 7.9)? Why did he write them under a pen name?

5. On what basis does James Madison criticize President Washington's actions in response to the rebellion? Why does he believe that the Federalists' response to the rebellion is of greater concern than the rebellion itself (Document 7.10)?

6. Washington justified his use of force to put down the revolt by pointing to the violence employed by the rebels. What other strategies did the rebels use to protest the tax? How else might the federal government have responded to armed rebellion among its citizens?

Put It in Context

- What role did the Whiskey Rebellion play in the formation of a new political party?

- What Democratic-Republican ideas are represented in the documents written by the whiskey rebels and their supporters, including James Madison?

Private Collection/Peter Newark American Pictures/The Bridgeman Art Library

Private Collection/The Bridgeman Art Library

Eli Whitney's cotton gin operated by black slaves, 1793.

Portrait of Meriwether Lewis, 1815.

8
New Frontiers
1790–1820

The Granger Collection, New York

Birthplace of Abigail Adams, Weymouth, Massachusetts.

When Parker Cleaveland graduated from Harvard University in 1799, his well-to-do family might have expected him to pursue a career in medicine, law, or the ministry. Instead, he turned to teaching. In 1805 Cleaveland secured a position in Brunswick, Maine, a territory that was then part of the state of Massachusetts, as the first professor of mathematics and natural philosophy at Bowdoin College.

In 1806 he married Martha Bush, who joined him on the Maine frontier. The Cleavelands emerged as leading citizens of Brunswick, a community of some three thousand residents. Most local families supported themselves in the lumbering or shipbuilding trades, but the recently opened college attracted middle-class professionals, whose intellectual interests and consumption habits transformed Brunswick into a more cosmopolitan town.

Over the next twenty years, the Cleavelands raised eight children, boarded and fed dozens of students, entertained faculty and visiting scholars, and corresponded with professors at other institutions. The busy couple served as a model of new ideals of companionate marriage, in which husbands and wives shared interests, friendship, and affection. They also instilled republican virtue and scientific principles in their charges. While Parker taught the students math and science, Martha trained them in manners and morals.

Professor Cleaveland believed in using scientific research to benefit society. Thus when local workers asked him to identify colored rocks found in the river, Parker began studying geology and chemistry. In 1816 he published his *Elementary Treatise on Mineralogy and*

227

Geology, which served as a text for college students and a handbook for travelers interested in the topic. He also lectured throughout New England, displaying mineral samples and performing chemical experiments.

The Cleavelands viewed Bowdoin College and the surrounding community as a laboratory in which distinctly American values and ideas could be taught and sustained. So, too, did the residents of other college towns. Although less than 1 percent of men in the United States and no women attended universities at the time, frontier colleges were considered important vehicles for bringing republican virtue—especially the desire to act for the public good rather than for personal gain—to the far reaches of the young nation. Yet these colleges were also enmeshed in the country's racial history. Several were constructed with the aid of slave labor, and all were built on land purchased or confiscated from Indians. In Maine, the Penobscot nation lost considerable territory to whites following the American Revolution, much of it under the direction of Massachusetts governor John Bowdoin II, the college's namesake. Moreover, the Indians' displacement continued as the success of colleges like Bowdoin attracted more white families to frontier regions.

The purchase of the Louisiana Territory by President Thomas Jefferson in 1803 marked out a new American frontier and ensured further encroachments on native lands. This vast territory covered 828,000 square miles and stretched from the Mississippi River to the Rocky Mountains and from New Orleans to present-day Montana. The area was home to tens of thousands of Indian inhabitants.

In the late 1780s, a baby girl, later named Sacagawea, was born to a family of Shoshone Indians who lived in an area later included in the Louisiana Purchase. In 1800 she was on a berry-picking expedition when her group was attacked by a Hidatsa raiding party that killed several Shoshones and took a number of women and children captive. Sacagawea and her fellow captives were marched some five hundred miles to a Hidatsa-Mandan village near present-day Bismarck, North Dakota. Eventually Sacagawea was sold to a French fur trader, Toussaint Charbonneau, along with another young Shoshone woman, and both became his wives.

In November 1804, an expedition led by Meriwether Lewis and William Clark set up winter camp near the village where Sacagawea lived. Lewis and Clark had been hired by the U.S. government to lead an exploring party through the newly acquired Louisiana Territory. Both Charbonneau, who spoke French and Hidatsa, and Sacagawea joined the expedition as interpreters in April 1805.

The only woman in the party, Sacagawea traveled with her infant son strapped to her back. Her presence was crucial, as Clark noted in his journal: "The Wife of Chabono our interpreter we find reconsiles all the Indians, as to our friendly intentions. A woman with a party of men is a token of peace." •

BOTH CLEAVELAND AND SACAGAWEA forged new identities on the frontiers of the United States. Yet while Cleaveland gained fame as "the father of American mineralogy," Sacagawea was rarely mentioned in accounts of the journey over the following decades. The American histories of both Sacagawea and Cleaveland were shaped by the efforts of political leaders and ordinary citizens to extend the boundaries of the emerging nation. Their different fates make clear that the young United States was marked by stark racial, class, and gender divisions—divisions that were more often deepened than bridged by the nation's expansion westward.

Creating an American Identity

In his inaugural address in March 1801, President Thomas Jefferson noted that the United States was "kindly separated by nature and a wide ocean from the exterminating havoc of one quarter of the globe," that is, Europe. He believed that the distance allowed Americans to develop their own unique culture and institutions. Jefferson also viewed the nation's extensive frontiers as a boon to its development, providing room for "our descendants to the thousandth and thousandth generation."

For many Americans, education offered one means of ensuring a distinctive national identity. Public schools could train American children in republican values, while the wealthiest among them could attend private academies and colleges. Written works such as newspapers, sermons, books, and magazines helped forge a common identity among the nation's far-flung citizens. Even the presence of Indians and Africans contributed to art and literature that were uniquely American. In addition, the construction of a new capital city to house the federal government offered a potent symbol of nationhood.

Yet these developments also illuminated underlying conflicts that defined the young nation. The decision to move the U.S. capital south from Philadelphia was prompted by concerns among southern politicians about the power of northern economic and political elites. The very construction of the capital, in which enslaved and free workers labored side by side, highlighted racial and class differences in the nation. Educational opportunities differed by race and class as well as by sex. The question thus remained: Could a singular notion of American identity be forged in a country where differences of race, class, and sex loomed so large?

Education for a New Nation

The desire to create a specifically American culture began as soon as the Revolution ended. In 1783 Noah Webster, a schoolmaster, declared that "America must be as independent in *literature* as in *Politics*, as famous for *arts* as for *arms*." To this end, the twenty-five-year-old Webster published the *American Spelling Book*, which by 1810 had become the second best-selling book in the United States (the Bible was the first). In 1828 Webster produced his *American Dictionary of the English Language*.

Webster's books were widely used in the nation's expanding network of schools and academies and led to more standardized spelling and pronunciation of commonly used words. Before the Revolution, public education for children, which focused on basic reading and writing skills, was widely available in New England and the Middle Atlantic region. In the South, only those who could afford private schooling—perhaps a quarter of the boys and 10 percent of the girls—received any formal instruction. Few young people enrolled in high school in any part of the colonies, and far fewer attended college.

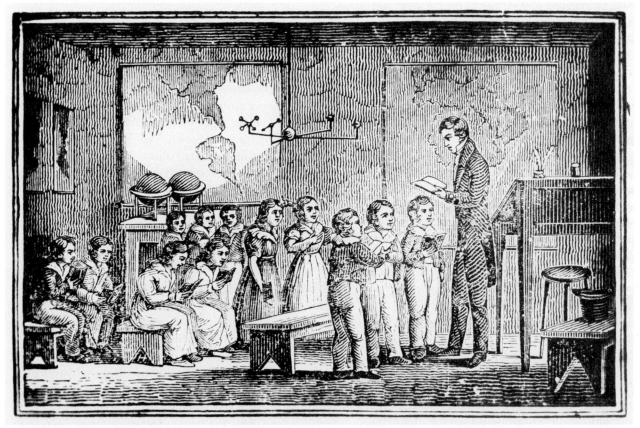

New England Grammar School

In this New England grammar school in the 1790s, boys and girls gather for instruction by their schoolmaster. They likely used one of Noah Webster's spellers or readers. The schoolmaster surely taught lessons in geography, as can be seen by the wall map and the two globes at the rear of the room.   The Granger Collection, New York

Following the Revolution, state and national leaders proposed ambitious plans for public education. In 1789 Massachusetts became the first state to institute free public elementary education for all children, and private academies and boarding schools proliferated throughout the nation.

Before 1790, the American colonies boasted nine colleges that provided further education for young men, including Harvard, Yale, King's College (Columbia), Queen's College (Rutgers), and the College of William and Mary. After independence, many Americans worried that these institutions were tainted by British and aristocratic influences. Situated in urban centers or crowded college towns, they were also criticized as centers of vice where youth might be corrupted by "scenes of dissipation and amusement." New colleges based on republican ideals needed to be founded.

Frontier towns offered opportunities for colleges to enrich the community and benefit the nation. Located in isolated villages, these colleges assured parents that students would focus on education. The young nation benefited as well, albeit at the expense of Indians and their lands. The founders of Franklin College in Athens, Georgia, encouraged white settlement in the state's interior, an area still largely populated by Creeks and Cherokees. And frontier colleges provided opportunities for ethnic and religious groups outside the Anglo-American mainstream—like Scots-Irish Presbyterians—to cement their place in American society.

Frontier colleges were organized as community institutions in which extended families—composed of administrators and faculty, their wives and children, servants and slaves, and students—played the central role. The familial character of these colleges—and their lower tuition fees—was also attractive to parents. Women were viewed as exemplars of virtue in the new nation, and the wives of professors were thus especially important in maintaining a refined atmosphere. They held salons where students could learn proper deportment and social skills. They also served as maternal figures for young adults living away from home. In some towns, students in local female academies joined college men on field trips and picnics to cultivate proper relations between the sexes.

Literary and Cultural Developments

While frontier colleges expanded educational and cultural opportunities, older universities also contributed to the development of a national identity. A group known as the Hartford Wits, most of them graduates of Yale, gave birth to a new literary tradition. This circle of poets, playwrights, and essayists expressed distinctly American (though largely Federalist) perspectives. Members of the Hartford Wits published paeans to democracy, satires about Shays's Rebellion, and plays about specifically American dilemmas, such as the proper role of the central government in a republican nation.

The young nation also produced a number of novelists. Advances in printing and the production of paper increased the circulation of novels, a literary genre developed in Britain and continental Europe at the turn of the eighteenth century. At the same time, improvements in girls' education produced a growing audience among women, who were thought to be the genre's most avid readers. Novelists like Susanna Rowson and Charles Brockden Brown sought to educate readers about virtuous action by placing ordinary women and men in moments of high drama that tested their moral character. They also emphasized new marital ideals, by which husbands and wives became partners and companions in building a home and family.

Explore

See Document 8.1 for a dramatic warning to young women from novelist Susanna Rowson.

Among the most important American literary figures to emerge in the early nineteenth century was Washington Irving. While living in Europe in the 1810s, he wrote a series of short stories and essays, including "The Legend of Sleepy Hollow" and "Rip Van Winkle," that were published in his *Sketchbook* in 1820. These popular folktales drew on the Dutch culture of the Hudson valley region in New York and often poked fun at more celebratory tales of early American history. But Irving also wrote serious essays. One challenged colonial accounts of Indian-English conflicts, which he argued ignored courageous actions by Indians while applauding atrocities committed by whites.

While Irving achieved fame by making fun of romanticized versions of American history, books that glorified the nation's past were also enormously popular. Among the most influential were a three-volume *History of the Revolution* (1805) written by Mercy Otis Warren and the *Life of Washington* (1806), a celebratory if somewhat fanciful biography by an Anglican clergyman, Mason "Parson" Weems. The influence of American authors increased as residents in both urban and rural areas purchased growing numbers of books. By 1820–1821, for instance, an astonishing 80 percent of households of middling wealth in Chester County, Pennsylvania, owned books.

DOCUMENT 8.1

Susanna Rowson | *Charlotte Temple*, 1791

The English-born novelist Susanna Rowson lived much of her life in Massachusetts, where she was educated mainly by private tutors. She based her plots on historical events and in 1791 published *Charlotte Temple*, which enjoyed enormous popularity in the United States. This sentimental (and, for its time, racy) story focused on the seduction and betrayal of a young woman by a British naval officer.

Explore

In affairs of love, a young heart is never in more danger than when attempted by a handsome young soldier. A man of an indifferent appearance will, when arrayed in a military habit, show to advantage, but when beauty of person, elegance of manner, and an easy method of paying compliments are united to the scarlet coat, smart cockade, and military sash, ah! well-a-day for the poor girl who gazes on him: she is in imminent danger; but if she listens to him with pleasure, 'tis all over with her, and from that moment she has neither eyes nor ears for any other object.

. . . I mean no more by what I have here advanced than to ridicule those romantic girls who foolishly imagine a red coat and silver epaulet constitute the fine gentleman; and should that fine gentleman make half a dozen fine speeches to them they will imagine themselves so much in love as to fancy it a meritorious action to jump out of a two-pair of stairs window, abandon their friends, and trust entirely to the honor of a man who, perhaps, hardly knows the meaning of the word, and if he does, will be too much the modern man of refinement to practise it in their favor. . . .

Oh, my dear girls—for to such only am I writing—listen not to the voice of love, unless sanctioned by paternal approbation: be assured, it is now past the days of romance: no woman can be run away with contrary to her own inclination: then kneel down each morning and request kind Heaven to keep you free from temptation, or should it please to suffer you to be tried, pray for fortitude to resist the impulse of inclination when it runs counter to the precepts of religion and virtue.

Source: Susanna Haswell Rowson, *Charlotte Temple: A Tale of Truth* (New York: Funk and Wagnalls, 1905), 51–54.

Interpret the Evidence

- How would you describe Rowson's literary style?
- What was Rowson's advice to her readers? How did she use this story to help elevate the moral character of women?

Put It in Context

Why do you think *Charlotte Temple* became so popular in the early 1790s? Who might have viewed the book as controversial?

Artists, too, devoted considerable attention to historical themes. Charles Willson Peale painted Revolutionary generals while serving in the Continental Army and became best known for his portraits of George Washington. Samuel Jennings offered a more radical perspective on the nation's character when he presented *Liberty Displaying the Arts and Sciences* (1792) to the Philadelphia Library Company. Many of the library's directors opposed slavery, and Jennings portrayed Lady Liberty offering a book to a group of attentive African Americans. Engravings, which were less expensive than paintings, circulated widely, and many also highlighted national symbols like flags, eagles, and Lady Liberty.

Engravings of nature were especially popular. Books like Cleaveland's *Elementary Treatise on Mineralogy and Geology* included plates that illustrated rocks and geological formations. William Bartram's *Travels* (1791), based on his journey through the southeastern United States and Florida, illustrated plants and animals, such as the alligator, previously unknown to Anglo-American scientists.

Illustration by William Bartram, Naturalist

William Bartram was a naturalist from Pennsylvania who traveled through the South during the 1770s. He visited Indian villages and sketched plant and animal life, including alligators and other animals that most Americans had never seen. This drawing of a great yellow bream was among many illustrations that he published in his *Travels* (1791), a popular compendium of his work.   HarperCollins Publishers/ The Art Archive at Art Resource, NY

In the 1780s, Benjamin Franklin helped found the American Philosophical Society in Philadelphia to promote American literature and science. Like-minded gentlemen in Boston and Salem established the American Academy of Arts and Sciences. Colleges like Bowdoin, Franklin, and Dickinson advanced scientific research in frontier regions, while the University of Pennsylvania in Philadelphia established the nation's first medical school. As in the arts, American scientists built on developments in continental Europe and Great Britain, but the young nation prided itself on contributing its own expertise.

The Racial Limits of American Culture

One subject that received significant attention from writers and scientists in the United States was the American Indian. White Americans in the late eighteenth century often wielded native names and symbols as they worked to create a distinct national identity. In long-settled regions along the Atlantic seaboard, where Indian nations no longer posed a significant threat, some Americans followed in the tradition of the Boston Tea Party, dressing as Indians to protest economic and political tyranny. Antirent rioters in the Hudson valley, participants in the Whiskey Rebellion, and squatters in the backcountry of Maine disguised themselves as Indians before attacking landlords, tax collectors, and land speculators. More well-to-do whites also embraced Indian names, costumes, and symbols. Tammany societies, for example, which were named after a mythical Delaware chief called Tammend, promoted patriotism and republicanism in the late eighteenth century and attracted large numbers of skilled artisans, lawyers, and merchants.

Poets, too, focused on American Indians. In his 1787 poem "Indian Burying Ground," Philip Freneau offered a sentimental portrait that highlighted the lost heritage of a nearly extinct native culture in New England. The theme of lost cultures and heroic (if still savage) Indians became even more pronounced in American poetry in the following decades.

Such sentimental portraits of American Indians were less popular along the nation's frontier, where Indians still posed a threat. Even a woman like Sacagawea, who aided the efforts of Lewis and Clark, did not become the object of literary or artistic efforts for several generations. Sympathetic depictions of Africans and African Americans by white artists and authors appeared with even less frequency. Most were produced in the North and were intended, like Jennings's *Liberty*, for the rare patrons who opposed slavery. Typical images of blacks and Indians were far more demeaning. Especially when describing Indians in frontier regions, authors, artists, politicians, and soldiers tended to focus on their savagery, their duplicity, or both. Most images of Africans and African Americans highlighted their innate inferiority and exaggerated their perceived physical and intellectual differences from white Americans.

Whether their depiction was realistic, sentimental, or derogatory, Africans, African Americans, and American Indians were almost always presented to the American public through the eyes of whites. Few blacks or Indians had access to English-language schools, books, or newspapers, and few whites were willing to publish or purchase works by those who did. Educated African Americans like the Reverend Richard Allen of Philadelphia or the Reverend Thomas Paul of Boston generally wrote for black audiences or corresponded privately with sympathetic whites. Similarly, cultural leaders among American Indians worked mainly within their own nation either to maintain traditional languages and customs or to introduce their people to Anglo-American ideas and beliefs.

White Americans who demanded improved education generally ignored or excluded blacks and Indians. Most southern planters had little desire to teach their slaves to read and write. Even in the North, states did not generally incorporate black children into their plans for public education. It was African Americans in cities with large free black populations who established the most long-lived schools for their race. The Reverend Allen opened a Sunday school for children in 1795 at his African Methodist Church, and other free blacks formed literary and debating societies for young people and adults. Still, only a small percentage of African Americans received an education equivalent to that available to whites in the new Republic.

U.S. political leaders were more interested in the education of American Indians, but government officials never proposed any systematic method of providing them with schools. Instead, various religious groups sent missionaries to the Seneca, Cherokee, and other tribes. A few of the most successful students were then sent to American colleges to be trained as ministers or teachers for their own people. However, just as with African Americans, only a small percentage of American Indians were taught to read or write in English, and whites made almost no efforts to teach Indians the languages and histories of their own nations.

The divergent approaches that whites took to Indian and African American education demonstrated broader assumptions about the two groups rooted in geographical expansion and slave labor. Most white Americans believed that Indians were untamed and uncivilized, but not innately different from Europeans. Africans and African Americans, on the other hand, were assumed to be inferior, and most whites believed that no amount of education could make blacks their intellectual or moral equals. As U.S. frontiers expanded, white Americans considered ways to "civilize" Indians and incorporate them into the nation. But the requirements of slavery made it much more difficult for whites to imagine African Americans as anything more than lowly laborers, despite free blacks who clearly demonstrated otherwise. **See Document Project 8: Race Relations in the Early Republic, page 250.**

Emigration and Colonization

Some African Americans did question the benefits of remaining in the United States. In the late 1780s, the Newport African Union Society in Rhode Island developed a plan to establish a community for American blacks in Africa.

Many whites, too, viewed the settlement of blacks in Africa as the only way to solve the nation's racial dilemma. William Thornton, a Quaker physician who had inherited his father's sugar plantation in the West Indies, joined a group in London who tried to establish a free black commonwealth on the west coast of Africa. He traveled to the United States to promote what he called colonization. But when Thornton presented his plans to the Free African Society in Philadelphia in 1787, local leaders opposed the effort.

Over the next three decades, the idea of emigration (as blacks viewed it) or colonization (as whites saw it) received widespread attention. Those who opposed slavery hoped to persuade slave owners to free or sell their human property on the condition that they be shipped to Africa. Others assumed that free blacks could find opportunities for economic, religious, and political leadership in Africa that did not exist in the United States. Still others simply wanted to rid the nation of its race problem by ridding it of blacks. In 1817 a group of southern slave owners and northern merchants formed the **American Colonization Society (ACS)** to carry "civilization" and Christianity to the African continent and establish colonies of freed slaves and free-born American blacks there. Although some African Americans supported this scheme, northern free blacks generally opposed it, viewing colonization as an effort originating "more immediately from prejudice than philanthropy."

Ultimately the plans of the ACS proved impractical. Particularly as cotton production expanded from the 1790s on, few slave owners were willing to emancipate their workers. Indeed, even in the supposedly enlightened communities where higher education flourished, slavery was widely accepted. In southern colleges, in particular, slaves cleared land, constructed buildings, cleaned rooms, did laundry, and prepared meals.

Building a National Capital

The construction of Washington City, the nation's new capital, depended on the labor of slaves as well. The capital was situated along the Potomac River in an area surrounded by farms and plantations. More than 300,000 slaves lived in Virginia and Maryland, the states that provided the land for the federal district, and the commissioners appointed to oversee the city's construction held almost 100 slaves themselves. Between 1792 and 1809, dozens of enslaved men were hired out by their owners, who were paid $50 to $70 annually for their slaves' labor on the city. Most enslaved men cleared land, built roads, and constructed the White House and the Capitol. Some performed skilled labor as carpenters and sawyers (who cut trees and lumber) or as assistants to stonemasons and

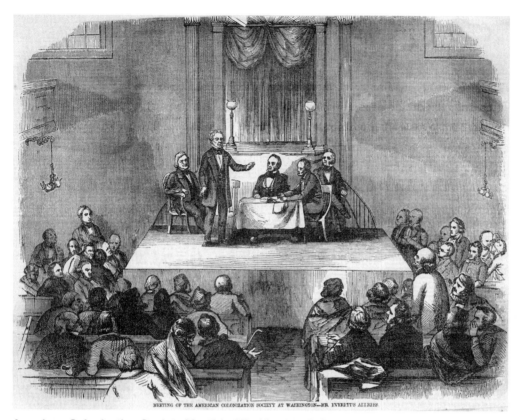

MEETING OF THE AMERICAN COLONIZATION SOCIETY AT WASHINGTON—MR. EVERETT'S ADDRESS.

American Colonization Society Meeting, Washington, D.C.

Formed in 1817, the American Colonization Society consisted of northern merchants and southern plant-ers who sought to resolve the race problem in the United States by shipping free and enslaved blacks to Africa. Although the society helped found Liberia, most African Americans opposed the venture, and as slave labor became increasingly profitable, few slaveholders allowed their enslaved workers to emigrate.
© Bettman/CORBIS

surveyors. A few enslaved women were hired as cooks, nurses, and washerwomen.

Free blacks also participated in the development of Washington, working in many of the same positions as slaves did. One of the most noteworthy African Americans involved in the project was Benjamin Banneker, a self-taught clock maker, astronomer, and surveyor. He was hired as an assistant to the surveyor, Major Andrew Ellicott, in 1791, helping to plot the 100-square-mile area on which the capital was to be built.

African Americans worked alongside whites, including many Irish immigrants, whose wages were kept in check by the availability of slave labor. Most workers, regardless of race, faced poor housing, sparse meals, and limited medical care as well as malarial fevers. Despite these obstacles, in less than a decade, a system of roads was laid out and cleared, the Executive Mansion was built, and the north wing of the Capitol was completed.

Although Washington City was considered a symbol of the nation, it was experts from abroad who created the U.S.

capital. The streets were laid out according to plans developed by the French engineer Pierre L'Enfant, the Executive Man-sion was designed by the Irish-born James Hoban, and the Capitol building was envisioned by the West Indian physician turned architect (and colonizationist) William Thornton. The Capitol's construction was directed by the English architect Benjamin Latrobe, and African Americans and immigrants made up the majority of the labor force. What was perhaps most "American" about the nation's capital were the diverse races and nationalities that designed and built it.

Washington's founders envisioned the city as a beacon to the world, proclaiming the advantages of republican principles. But its location on a slow-moving river and its clay soil left the area hot, humid, and dusty in the summer and muddy and damp in the winter and spring. When John Adams and his administration moved to Washington in June 1800, they considered themselves on the frontiers of civilization. The mile-long road from the Capitol to the Executive Mansion was filled with tree stumps and was nearly impossible to navigate in a carriage. On rainy days, when roads proved impassable, officials walked or rode horses to work. That November, when Abigail Adams moved into the Executive Mansion, she complained that the roof leaked, the huge house was hard to heat, and firewood was difficult to obtain. Abigail Adams was not alone in criticizing the capital city. Although the founders considered it "an experiment in republican simplicity," most residents painted Washington in harsh tones. New Hampshire representative Ebenezer Matroon wrote a friend, "If I wished to punish a culprit, I would send him to do penance in this place . . . this swamp—this lonesome dreary swamp, secluded from every delightful or pleasing thing." Others described the city as a "fever-stricken morass."

Despite the drawbacks, the new capital played an important role in the social and political world of American elites, drawing wealthy and influential Americans to this center of federal power. From January through March, the height of the social season, the wives of congressmen, judges, and other officials created a lively schedule of teas, parties, and balls in the new capital city. When Thomas Jefferson became president, he opened the White House to visitors on a regular basis, a style that seemed appropriate for the man who had drafted the Declaration of Independence. This, too, helped reshape the Washington social scene. Yet for all his republican principles, Jefferson moved into the Executive Mansion with a retinue of slaves.

In decades to come, Washington City would become Washington, D.C., a city with broad boulevards decorated with beautiful monuments to the American political experiment. And the Executive Mansion would become the White House, a proud symbol of republican government.

The United States Capitol

This watercolor by William Russell Birch presents a view of the Capitol in Washington, D.C., before it was burned down by the British during the War of 1812. Birch had emigrated from England in 1794 and lived in Philadelphia. As this painting suggests, neither the Capitol nor the city was as yet a vibrant center of republican achievements.   Library of Congress

Still, Washington was characterized by wide disparities in wealth, status, and power, which were especially visible when Jefferson occupied the Executive Mansion and slaves labored in its kitchen, laundry, and yard. Moreover, President Jefferson's efforts to incorporate new territories into the United States only exacerbated these divisions by providing more economic opportunities for planters, investors, and white farmers while ensuring the expansion of slavery and the decimation of American Indians.

REVIEW & RELATE

How did developments in education, literature, and the arts contribute to the emergence of a distinctly American identity?

What place did blacks and American Indians inhabit in the predominant white view of American society and culture?

✔ *LEARNINGCurve* bedfordstmartins.com/hewittlawson/LC

Extending U.S. Borders

Thomas Jefferson, like other leading Democratic-Republicans, favored limited government, imagining a nation made up of small, independent farmers who had little need and less desire for an expansive federal government (see chapter 7). Initially, the president was successful in imposing his vision on the young government. By the middle of his first term, however, developments in international affairs converged with Supreme Court rulings to expand federal power. Jefferson contributed directly to this expansion by purchasing the Louisiana Territory from France. In turn, the development of this vast territory raised new questions about the place of Indians and African Americans in a republican society.

A New Administration Faces Challenges

In 1801 Democratic-Republicans worked quickly to implement their vision of limited federal power. Holding the majority in Congress, they repealed the hated whiskey tax and let the Alien and Sedition Acts expire. The Senate also approved Jefferson's appointment of Albert Gallatin, who served as a lawyer for the whiskey rebels, as secretary of the treasury. The president significantly reduced government expenditures, and he and Gallatin immediately set about slashing the national debt, cutting it nearly in half by the end of Jefferson's second term. Democratic-Republicans also worked to curb the powers granted to the Bank of the United States and the federal court system.

Soon, however, international upheavals forced Jefferson to make fuller use of his presidential powers. The U.S. government had paid tribute to the Barbary States of North Africa during the 1790s to gain protection for American merchant ships. The new president opposed this practice and in 1801 refused to continue the payments. The Barbary pirates quickly resumed attacks on American ships, and Jefferson was forced to send the U.S. navy and Marine Corps to retaliate. Although the combined American and Arab mercenary force did not achieve their objective of capturing Tripoli, the Ottoman viceroy agreed to negotiate a new agreement with the United States. Seeking to avoid all-out war, Congress accepted a treaty with the Barbary States that reduced the tribute payment.

Jefferson had also followed the developing crisis in the West Indies during the 1790s. In 1791 slaves on the sugar-rich island of Saint Domingue launched a revolt against French rule. The **Haitian Revolution** escalated into a complicated conflict in which free people of color, white slave owners, and slaves formed competing alliances with British and Spanish forces as well as with leaders of the French Revolution. Finally, in December 1799, Toussaint L'Ouverture, a former slave and military leader, claimed the presidency of the new Republic of Haiti. But Napoleon Bonaparte seized power in France that same year and sent thousands of troops to reclaim the island. Although Toussaint was shipped off to France, where he died in prison, other Haitian rebels continued the fight. As the struggle intensified, thousands of Haitian refugees, black and white, fled to the United States. However, by November 1803, prolonged fighting, yellow fever, and the loss of sixty thousand soldiers forced Napoleon to admit defeat. Haiti became the first independent black-led nation in the Americas.

Explore

See Document 8.2 for a vivid description of the uprising in Haiti.

Incorporating the Louisiana Territory

Thomas Jefferson had enthusiastically supported the American and French revolutions, but he was not sympathetic to an independent black nation. Nonetheless, in France's defeat he saw an opportunity to gain navigation rights on the Mississippi River, which the French controlled. This was a matter of crucial concern to Americans living west of the Appalachian Mountains. Jefferson sent fellow Virginian James Monroe to France to offer Napoleon $2 million to ensure Americans the right of navigation and deposit (that is, offloading cargo from ships) on the Mississippi. To Jefferson's surprise, Napoleon offered instead to sell the entire **Louisiana Territory** for $15 million.

DOCUMENT 8.2

Mary Hassal | *Secret History*, 1808

The Haitian Revolution elicited a range of emotions from Americans who read or heard about the island's violent slave uprising. Unlike most people in the United States, however, Mary Hassal of Philadelphia was in Haiti during the historic event. She relayed her firsthand interpretation of the revolution in a series of letters to her uncle, Vice President Aaron Burr. The following excerpt describes the grim fate of three black rebels.

Explore

Cape Francois

What did these slaves do to receive such severe punishment?

How does Hassal describe the men's reactions to their deaths?

What effect did the executions have on the people of Cape Francois, white and black?

Ah, my dear friend, where shall I find expressions to convey to you an idea of the horror that fills my soul; how describe scenes at which I tremble even now with terror?

Three negroes were caught setting fire to a plantation near the town. They were sentenced to be burnt alive; and the sentence was actually executed. When they were tied to the stake and the fire kindled, one of them, I understand, held his head over the smoke and was suffocated immediately. The second made horrible contortions, and howled dreadfully. The third, looking at him contemptuously said, Peace! Do you not know how to die? and preserved an unalterable firmness till the devouring flames consumed him. This cruel act has been blamed by everybody as giving a bad example to the negroes, who will not fail to retaliate on the first prisoners they take. But it has been succeeded by a deed which has absolutely chilled the hearts of the people. Everyone trembles for his own safety, and silent horror reigns throughout the place.

Source: Mary Hassal, *Secret History; or, The Horrors of Santo Domingo* (Philadelphia: Bradford and Inskeep, 1808), 99–100.

Put It in Context

How might reports like this one have contributed to American slaveholders' fear of slave revolts?

The president agonized over the constitutionality of such a purchase. Since the Constitution contained no provisions for buying land from foreign nations, a strict interpretation would not allow the purchase. In the end, though, the opportunity proved too tempting, and in late 1803 the president finally agreed to buy the Louisiana Territory based on a loose interpretation of the Constitution. Because the acquisition of the vast territory proved enormously popular among both politicians and ordinary Americans, few cared that it expanded presidential and congressional powers.

Congress soon appropriated funds for an exploratory expedition known as the **Corps of Discovery** to map the terrain. This effort, which Sacagawea and her husband joined, was led by Captain Meriwether Lewis, who had served as Jefferson's personal secretary, and William Clark, an army officer. Beginning on May 14, 1804, Lewis, Clark, and three dozen men traveled thousands of miles up the Missouri River, through the northern plains, over the Rocky Mountains, and beyond the Louisiana Territory to the Pacific coast. Members of the expedition meticulously recorded observations about local plants and animals as well as Indian residents, providing valuable evidence for young scientists like Parker Cleaveland and fascinating information for ordinary Americans.

Sacagawea was the only Indian to travel as a permanent member of the expedition, but other native women and men assisted the Corps when it journeyed near their villages. They provided food and lodging for the travelers, hauled baggage up steep mountain trails, and offered food, horses, and other trade items. The one African American on the expedition, a slave named York, also helped negotiate trade with local Indians. York recognized his value as a trader, hunter, and scout and asked Clark for his freedom when the expedition ended in 1806. York did eventually become a free man, but it is not clear whether it was by Clark's choice or because York escaped.

Other expeditions followed Lewis and Clark's successful venture. In 1806 Lieutenant Zebulon Pike led a group to explore the southern portion of the Louisiana Territory (Map 8.1). After traveling from St. Louis to the Rocky Mountains, the expedition traveled into Mexican territory. In early 1807, Pike and his men were captured by Mexican forces. They were returned to the United States at the Louisiana border that July. Pike had learned a great deal about lands that would eventually become part of the United States and about Mexican desires to overthrow Spanish rule, information that proved valuable over the next two decades.

Early in this series of expeditions, in November 1804, Jefferson stood for reelection, winning an easy victory. His popularity among farmers, already high, increased when Congress passed an act that reduced the minimum allotment for federal land sales from 320 to 160 acres. This act allowed more farmers to purchase land on their own rather than via speculators. Yet by the time of his second inauguration in March 1805, the president's vision of limiting the powers of the federal government had been shattered by his own actions and those of the Supreme Court.

The Supreme Court Extends Its Reach

The Supreme Court, the last bastion of Federalist power, extended its reach during Jefferson's presidency. In 1801, just before the Federalist-dominated Congress turned over

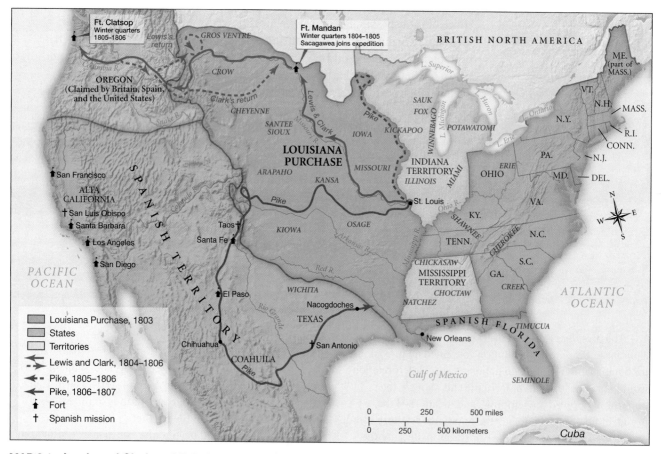

MAP 8.1   Lewis and Clark and Zebulon Pike Expeditions, 1804–1807

The expeditions led by Meriwether Lewis, William Clark, and Zebulon Pike illustrate the vast regions explored in just four years after the purchase of the Louisiana Territory by the United States. Lewis and Clark as well as Pike journeyed through and beyond the borders of that territory, gathering important information about Indian nations, plants, animals, and the natural terrain throughout the West.

power to the Democratic-Republicans, it passed a new **Judiciary Act**. The act created six additional circuit courts and sixteen new judgeships, which President Adams filled with Federalist "midnight appointments" before he left office. Jefferson accused the Federalists of having "retired into the judiciary" and worried that "from that battery all the works of Republicanism are to be beaten down and destroyed." Meanwhile John Marshall, who sat as the chief justice of the Supreme Court (1801–1835), insisted that the powers of the Court must be equal to and balance those of the executive and legislative branches.

One of the first cases to test the Court's authority involved a dispute over President Adams's midnight appointments. Jefferson's newly appointed secretary of state, James Madison, refused to deliver the appointment papers to several of these appointees, including William Marbury. Marbury and three others sued Madison to receive their commissions. In *Marbury v. Madison* (1803), the Supreme Court ruled that it was not empowered to force the executive branch to give Marbury his commission. But in his decision, Chief Justice Marshall declared that the Supreme Court did have the duty "to say what the law is." He thus asserted a fundamental constitutional point: that the Supreme Court had the authority to decide what federal laws were constitutional. The following year, the Court also claimed the right to rule on the constitutionality of state laws. In doing so, the Court rejected the view of Democratic-Republicans who claimed that state legislatures had the power to repudiate federal law.

Over the next dozen years, the Supreme Court continued to assert Federalist principles. In 1810, to strengthen its claims for judicial review, the nation's highest court insisted that it was the proper and sole arena for determining matters of constitutional interpretation. In another case, *McCulloch v. Maryland* (1819), the Federalist-dominated Court reinforced its loose interpretation of the Constitution's implied powers clause. This clause gave the federal government the right to "make all laws which shall be necessary and proper" for carrying out the explicit powers granted to it by the Constitution. Federalists had used this clause to establish the first national bank. Despite Democratic-Republicans' early opposition to a national bank, Congress chartered the Second Bank of the United States in 1816. Its branch banks issued notes that circulated widely in local business communities. Legislators in Maryland, believing that these banks had gained excessive power, approved a tax on their operations. Marshall's Court ruled that the establishment of the bank was "necessary and proper" for the functioning of the national government and rejected Maryland's right to tax the branch bank, claiming that "the power to tax involves the power to destroy."

By 1820 the Supreme Court, under the forceful direction of John Marshall, had established the power of judicial review—the authority of the nation's highest court to rule on cases involving states as well as the nation. From the Court's perspective, the judiciary was as important an institution in framing and preserving a national agenda as Congress or the president.

Democratic-Republicans Expand Federal Powers

Although Democratic-Republicans generally opposed Marshall's rulings, they, too, continued to expand federal power. Once again, international developments drove the Jefferson administration's political agenda. By 1805 the security of the United States was threatened by continued conflicts between France and Great Britain. Both sought alliances with the young nation, and both ignored U.S. claims of neutrality. Indeed, each nation sought to punish Americans for trading with the other. Britain began stopping American ships carrying sugar and molasses from the French West Indies on the pretense of searching them for British deserters. Between 1802 and 1811, the Royal Navy impressed (forced into service) more than eight thousand sailors taken from such ships, including many American citizens. Remembering similar abuses during the colonial period, Americans demanded action. Yet the United States was in no position to launch a war against Great Britain. France claimed a similar right to stop American ships if they continued to trade with Great Britain.

Unable to convince foreign powers to recognize U.S. neutrality, Jefferson and Madison pushed for congressional passage of an embargo that they hoped would, like colonial boycotts, force Great Britain's hand. In 1807 Congress passed the **Embargo Act**, which prohibited U.S. ships from leaving their home ports until Britain and France repealed their restrictions on American trade. Although the act kept the United States out of war, it had a devastating impact on national commerce.

New England merchants immediately voiced their outrage. Some merchants began sending items to Europe via Canada. In response, Congress passed the Force Act, granting extraordinary powers to customs officials to end such smuggling. The economic pain spread well beyond the merchant class. Young professionals like Parker Cleaveland were affected by the embargo-fueled recession; he was forced to sell his home to the Bowdoin trustees and become their tenant in 1807. Farmers and planters also suffered the embargo's effects, as did urban workers, especially in port cities where sailors and dockworkers faced escalating unemployment. The recession raised deep concerns about the expansion of federal power.

Opposition to the Embargo Act

Although Congress repealed the Embargo Act in 1809, lawmakers still barred the United States from trading with Great Britain and France, both of which attacked American shipping in violation of American neutrality. This political cartoon by Alexander Anderson criticizes the embargo, which proved costly to merchants, sailors, and dockworkers. Here a merchant carrying a barrel of goods curses the snapping turtle "Ograbme," which is *embargo* spelled backward.   The Granger Collection, New York

Congress and the president had not simply regulated international trade; they had brought it to a halt.

In Jefferson's first inaugural address, he acknowledged that "it will rarely fall to the lot of imperfect man to retire from this station [the presidency] with the reputation and the favor which bring him into it." Not only had Jefferson failed to contain the powers of the federal government, but the Embargo Act also threatened the livelihood of those who had once seen him as their champion. At the end of his second term, a Philadelphia seaman wrote to him, claiming that because of the Embargo Act he had lost what little he owned and threatening to "throttle his honored neck."

Despite such sentiments, many Americans still viewed Jefferson favorably. He had devoted his adult life to the creation of the American Republic, and he had purchased the Louisiana Territory, opening up vast lands to American exploration and development. This geographical boon had encouraged inventors and artisans to pursue ideas that would help the young nation take full advantage of its resources and recover from its current economic plight.

REVIEW & RELATE

How did Jefferson and the Democratic-Republicans contribute to the expansion of the role of the federal government in American life?

How did the conflict between France and Great Britain in the late eighteenth and early nineteenth centuries lead to domestic problems in the United States?

Remaking the U.S. Economy

As the United States expanded geographically, technological ingenuity became a highly valued commodity. The spread of U.S. settlements into new territories necessitated improved forms of transportation and increased the need for muskets and other weapons to protect the nation's frontier. The growing population also fueled improvements in agriculture and manufacturing to meet demands for clothing, food, and farm equipment. Continued conflicts with Great Britain and France also highlighted the need to develop the nation's natural resources and technological capabilities. Still, the daily lives of most Americans changed only slowly. And some workers, especially enslaved women and men, found that technological advances just added to their burdens.

The U.S. Population Grows and Migrates

Although Democratic-Republicans initially hoped to limit the powers of the national government, the rapid growth of the United States pulled in the opposite direction. An increased population, combined with the exhaustion of farmland along the eastern seaboard, fueled migration to the west as well as the growth of cities. By 1820 one-quarter of non-Indian Americans lived west of the Appalachian Mountains. These developments heightened conflicts with Indians and over slavery, but they also encouraged advances in transportation and communication and improvements in agriculture and manufacturing.

Sacagawea must have realized that the expedition she accompanied was a harbinger of white expansion, but many Indians only gradually came to realize that the few dozen men who joined Lewis and Clark heralded the arrival of hundreds and then thousands of migrants from the East. As white Americans encroached farther and farther on lands long settled by native peoples, Indian tribes in the eastern United States and the midsection of the nation were forced westward. As early as 1800, groups like the Shoshones, who originally inhabited the Great Plains, had been forced into the Rocky Mountains by Indians moving into the plains from the Mississippi and Ohio valleys (Map 8.2).

At the same time, although the vast majority of Americans continued to live in rural areas, a growing number moved to cities (defined as places with 8,000 or more inhabitants). New York City and Philadelphia both counted more than 100,000 residents by 1810. In New York, immigrants, most of them Irish, made up about 10 percent of the population in 1820 and twice that percentage five years later. During this time, the number of African Americans in New York City increased to more than 10,000. New cities began to emerge along the nation's frontier as well. After the United States acquired the Louisiana Territory, New Orleans grew rapidly, and western migration fueled the development of Cincinnati. Even smaller frontier towns served important functions for migrants traveling west. Trading posts appeared across the Mississippi valley, which eased the migration of thousands headed farther west. They served as sites of exchange between Indians and white Americans and created the foundations for later cities (Table 8.1).

Most Americans who headed west hoped to benefit from the increasingly liberal terms offered by the federal government for purchasing land. Yeomen farmers sought sufficient acreage to support their families and grow some additional crops for sale. They were eager to settle in western sections of the

original thirteen states, in the Ohio River valley, or in newly opened territories along the Missouri and Kansas Rivers. In the South, small farmers had to compete with slave-owning planters who headed west in the early nineteenth century. Migrants to the Mississippi valley also had to contend with a sizable population of long-settled Spanish residents and French planters who had taken refuge from Saint Domingue with their slaves, as well as Chickasaw and Creek Indians in the South and Shawnee, Chippewa, Sauk, and Fox Indians farther north.

The development of roads and turnpikes hastened the movement of people and the transportation of goods. Frontier farmers required methods to get their produce to eastern markets quickly and cheaply. Before completion of the Lancaster Turnpike in Pennsylvania, it cost as much to carry wheat and other items overland the sixty-two miles to Philadelphia as it did to ship them by sea from Philadelphia to London. Those who lived farther west faced

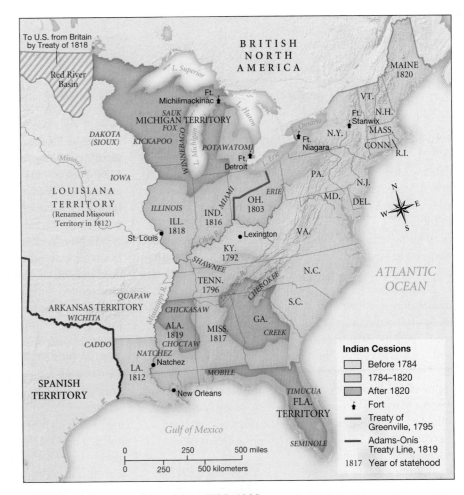

MAP 8.2　Indian Land Cessions, 1790–1820

With the ratification of the Constitution, the federal government gained greater control over Indian relations, including land cessions. At the same time, large numbers of white settlers poured into regions west of the Appalachian Mountains. The U.S. government gained most Indian land by purchase or treaty, but these agreements were often the consequence of military victories by the U.S. army.

TABLE 8.1 Prices at George Davenport's Trading Post, Rock Island, Illinois, c. 1820

Item	Price	Item	Price
Ax	$6.00	Large copper kettle	$30.00
Beaver trap	$8.00	Lead	$0.20 per pound
Black silk handkerchief	$2.00	Lead shot for guns	$1.00 per 5 pounds
Breechcloth	$3.00	Medium copper kettle	$10.00
Bridles	$2.00–$10.00	Muskrat spear	$2.00
Chain for staking down traps	$0.75 per 6 feet	Muskrat trap	$5.00
Combs	$1.00 per pair	Muslin or calico shirt	$3.00
File (for sharpening axes)	$2.00	Ordinary butcher knife	$0.50
Flannel	$1.00 per yard	Sheet iron kettle	$10.00
Flannel mantle	$3.00	Small copper kettle	$3.00
Gunflints	$1.00 per 15	Spurs	$6.00 per pair
Hand-size mirrors	$0.25	Tin kettle	$14.00
Heavy wool cloth	$10.00 per yard	Tomahawk	$1.50
Hoe	$2.00	Trade gun	$20.00–$25.00
Horn of gunpowder	$1.50	Wool blanket	$4.00
Horses	$35.00–$50.00	Wool mantle (short cloak or shawl)	$4.00

Source: Will Leinicke, Marion Lardner, and Ferrel Anderson, *Two Nations, One Land* (Rock Island, IL: Citizens to Preserve Black Hawk Park, 1981).

even greater challenges. With the admission of Kentucky (1792), Tennessee (1796), and Ohio (1803) to the Union, demands for congressional assistance in building transportation routes grew louder. By 1819 five more states were admitted along the Mississippi River, from Louisiana to Illinois.

During Jefferson's administration, Albert Gallatin urged Congress to fund internal improvements—that is, roads and canals—to enhance the economic development of the nation. Legislatures chartered and sometimes helped fund improved transportation in their own states, but Gallatin focused on transportation across regions. He advocated a "great turnpike road" along the Atlantic seaboard from Maine to Georgia as well as roads to connect the four main rivers that flowed from the Appalachians to the Atlantic Ocean. In 1815 Congress approved funds for one such project, the **National Road** from western Maryland through southwestern Pennsylvania to Wheeling, West Virginia. This so-called Cumberland Road was completed in 1818, and in the following decades it was extended into Ohio and Illinois.

Carrying people and goods by water was even faster and cheaper than transporting them over land, but rivers ran mainly north and south. In addition, although loads could be delivered quickly downstream, the return voyage was long and slow. While politicians advocated the construction of canals along east-west routes to link river systems, inventors and mechanics focused on building boats powered by steam to overcome the problems of sending goods upriver.

Oliver Evans, a machinist in Philadelphia, developed a steam-powered gristmill—to produce flour from grain—in 1788. Then in 1804 he invented a high-pressure steam engine attached to a dredge that cleaned the silt around the docks in Philadelphia harbor. He had insufficient funds, however, to pursue work on a steam-powered boat.

In New York State, Robert Fulton sought to improve on Evans's efforts, using the low-pressure steam engine developed in England. Fulton had moved to Paris in the early nineteenth century to train as a painter. While there, he met the wealthy ambassador Robert Livingston, who helped negotiate the Louisiana Purchase. Livingston convinced Fulton to focus on engineering and provided funds for him to do so. In 1807 Fulton launched the first successful steamboat, the *Clermont*, which traveled up the Hudson River from New York City to Albany in only thirty-two hours. The powerful Mississippi River proved a greater challenge, but by combining Evans's high-pressure steam engine with a flat-bottom hull that avoided the river's sandbars, mechanics who worked along the frontier improved Fulton's original design and launched the steamboat era in the West.

Technology Reshapes Agriculture and Industry

Advances in agricultural and industrial technology paralleled the development of roads and steamboats. Here, too, a single invention spurred others, inducing a **multiplier effect** that inspired additional dramatic changes during the decades following the Revolution. Two inventions—the cotton gin and the spinning machine—were especially notable in transforming southern agriculture and northern industry, transformations that were deeply intertwined.

American developments were also closely tied to the earlier rise of industry in Great Britain. By the 1770s, British manufacturers had built spinning mills in which steam-powered machines spun raw cotton into yarn. Importing cotton from Britain's colonies, British manufacturers thrived. Eager to maintain their monopoly on industrial technology, the British made it illegal for engineers to emigrate. They could not, however, keep everyone who worked in a cotton mill from leaving the country. At age fourteen, Samuel Slater was hired as an apprentice in an English mill that used a yarn-spinning machine designed by Richard Arkwright. Slater was promoted to supervisor of the factory, but at age twenty-one he sought greater opportunities in America. While working in New York City, he learned that Moses Brown, a wealthy Rhode Island merchant, was seeking help in developing a machine like Arkwright's. Funded by Rhode Island investors and assisted by local craftsmen, Slater designed and built a spinning mill in Pawtucket.

The mill opened in December 1790 and began producing yarn, which was then woven into cloth in private shops and homes. By 1815 a series of cotton mills, most built to look like New England meetinghouses in order to limit hostility from local farmers, dotted the Pawtucket River. These factories promised a steady income for workers in the mills, most of whom were the wives and children of farmers, and ensured employment for weavers in the countryside. They also increased the demand for cotton in New England just as British manufacturers sought new sources of the crop as well.

Ensuring a steady supply of cotton, however, required another technological innovation, this one created by Eli Whitney. After graduating from Yale at age twenty-seven, Whitney agreed to serve as a private tutor for a planter family in South Carolina. On the ship carrying him to his new position, Whitney met Catherine Greene, widow of the Revolutionary War general Nathanael Greene. He ended up staying on her Mulberry Plantation near Savannah, Georgia, where local planters complained to him about the difficulty of making a profit on cotton in the area. Long-staple cotton, grown in the Sea Islands, yielded enormous profits, but the soil in most of the South could sustain only the short-staple variety, which required hours of intensive labor to separate its sticky green seeds from the cotton fiber.

The Cotton Gin

Invented by Eli Whitney in 1793, the cotton gin, which separated cotton fibers from seed, transformed American industry and agriculture. As presented in this engraving, which was likely part of the patent application, Whitney's invention was a relatively simple device that had an enormous impact on the South and the nation at large.　Culver Pictures/The Art Archive at Art Resource, NY

In 1793, in as little as ten days, Eli Whitney built a machine that could ease the labor of deseeding short-staple cotton. His **cotton gin** consisted of a wooden box with a mesh screen, rollers, brushes, and wire hooks. The cotton boll was drawn through the mesh, where wire hooks caught the seeds and the rotating brushes then swept the cotton lint into a tray. Whitney's gin could clean as much cotton fiber in one hour as several workers could clean in a day. Recognizing the gin's value, Whitney received a U.S. patent, but because the machine was easy to duplicate, he never profited from his invention.

Fortunately, Whitney had other ideas that proved more profitable. In June 1798, amid U.S. fears of a war with France, the U.S. government granted him an extraordinary contract to produce 4,000 rifles in eighteen months. Rifles were then produced individually by highly trained artisans, but the inventor claimed he could devise a machine to manufacture guns in large quantities. By January 1801, having produced only 500 rifles, Whitney met with national political leaders to reassure them that success was near. Adapting the plan of Honoré Blanc, a French mechanic who devised a musket with interchangeable parts, Whitney demonstrated the potential for using machines to produce various parts of a musket, which could then be assembled in mass quantities. With Jefferson's enthusiastic support, the federal government extended Whitney's contract, and by 1809 his New Haven factory was turning out 7,500 guns annually.

Whitney's factory became a model for the **American system of manufacturing**, in which water-powered machinery and the division of production into many small tasks allowed less skilled workers to produce mass quantities of a particular item, like guns or shoes. Whitney viewed this system as a boon to men and women who were unable or unwilling to obtain apprenticeships in skilled crafts. In factories, they could be trained quickly to do a particular task and thereby support themselves or supplement family earnings from farming.

The factories developed by Whitney and Slater became training grounds for younger mechanics and inventors who devised improvements in machinery or set out to solve new technological puzzles. Their efforts also transformed the lives of generations of workers—enslaved and free—who planted and picked the cotton, spun the yarn, wove the cloth, and sewed the clothes that cotton gins and spinning mills made possible.

Transforming Household Production

Slater and Whitney were among the most influential American inventors, but both required the assistance and collaboration of other inventors, machinists, and artisans to implement their ideas. The achievement of these enterprising individuals was seen by many Americans as part of a larger spirit of inventiveness and technological ingenuity that marked the United States as a young

---

DOCUMENTS 8.3 AND 8.4

Industrial Beginnings in Massachusetts: Two Views

American industry began in earnest in New England, and Massachusetts mills garnered great attention from interested observers at home and abroad, many of whom assessed the success and potential of American industry. In the first document, Henry Wansey, a retired clothier from England who visited New England's mills in 1794 to determine whether they would provide competition for his home country, describes his visit. In the second document, Timothy Dwight, the president of Yale College, surveys the mills in Worcester, Massachusetts.

Explore

8.3 Henry Wansey | An Excursion to the United States, 1794

Near Boston are the following manufactories established, according to the accounts given me by a considerable merchant there: A cotton and carpet manufactory at Worcester, carried on by Peter Stowell and Co. with a good capital; and one of woollen, by Thomas Stowell; at Newbury Port, Joseph Brown, a clothier, makes a variety of woollen goods of the coarse kinds. . . . But all these I judge rather the seeds of manufactories, than any large or permanent establishments. That energy which is created in our country by necessity and difficulty of living cannot take place there for many years; nor need England fear a rivalship there, or in any other country. France, when disburdened of her present military government, will be many years in recovering her manufactories.

When we consider that the United States, with scarcely four million inhabitants, import annually of our manufactures more than twelve million dollars in value, it follows that when her inhabitants are increased to eight million, she will want manufactures to the annual amount of twenty-four million dollars. From hence I conclude that her population and prosperity are an advantage to Great Britain. I am convinced that the ability of the United States to manufacture cannot keep pace by any means with her increasing population; at least for a century. It therefore follows, that she must increase her demand for foreign manufactures; and the Americans generally acknowledge that no country can supply them so well as Great Britain.

Source: Henry Wansey, *An Excursion to the United States of North America, in the Summer of 1794* (London: Salisbury, 1798), 29–30.

nation. That spirit led to a cascade of inventions between 1790 and 1820.

Cotton gins and steam engines, steamboats and interchangeable parts, gristmills and spinning mills—each of these items and processes was improved upon over time and led to myriad other inventions. For instance, in 1811 Francis Cabot invented a power loom for weaving, a necessary step once spinning mills began producing more yarn than hand weavers could use. Similarly, Jethro Wood perfected the cast-iron plow in 1819, ensuring that western farmers could provide adequate food for the small but rising population of city dwellers and factory workers.

Despite these rapid technological advances, the changes that occurred in the early nineteenth century were more evolutionary than revolutionary. Most political leaders and social commentators viewed gradual improvement as a blessing. For many Americans, the ideal situation consisted of either small mills scattered through the countryside or household enterprises that could supply neighbors with finer cloth, wool cards, or other items that improved home production.

Explore

For two distinct views on the progress of manufacturing in early New England, see Documents 8.3 and 8.4.

The importance of domestic manufacturing increased after passage of the Embargo Act as imports of cloth and other items fell dramatically. Small factories, like those along the Pawtucket River, increased their output, and so did ordinary housewives. Blacksmiths, carpenters, and

Explore

8.4 Timothy Dwight | Travels in New England, 1821

Few towns in New-England exhibit so uniform an appearance of neatness and taste or contain so great a proportion of good buildings, and so small a proportion of those which are indifferent, as Worcester. There is probably more wealth in it also than in any other, which does not exceed it in dimensions and number of inhabitants. Its trade, considering its inland situation, is believed to be extensive and profitable. . . .

There are in Worcester four grist-mills, four saw-mills, two fulling-mills, and a large paper-mill. The proprietors of the fulling-mills carry on the Clothiers' business to a great extent; and with skill supposed not to be excelled in the State. Scarlet and blue have for some time been dyed here in a superiour manner.

On the subject of *mills* I wish you to observe, once for all, that I shall rarely mention them. There is scarcely a township in New-England which has not a complete set of grist-mills and saw-mills. . . . There is, probably, no country in the world where mill-streams are so numerously and universally dispersed, or grist-mills and saw-mills so universally erected as in New-England. Conveniences of this kind may be said, almost if not quite literally, to be furnished in abundance to every Parish in the Country. To reiterate this fact would be to take very effectual means for wearing out your patience.

Source: Timothy Dwight, *Travels; in New-England and New-York* (New Haven: Timothy Dwight, 1821), 366–67.

Interpret the Evidence

- According to Wansey, would the mills in Worcester and other Massachusetts towns be able to compete with their British counterparts? Why or why not?
- How does Dwight characterize Worcester? Do you think he would agree with Wansey's assessment of America's industrial prospects?

Put It in Context

What do these reports reveal about the industrial innovations occurring in the United States in the late eighteenth and early nineteenth centuries?

wheelwrights busily repaired and improved the spindles, looms, and other equipment that allowed family members to produce more and better cloth from wool, flax, and cotton. New ideas about companionate marriage, which emphasized affection and mutual obligations between spouses, may have encouraged husbands and wives to work more closely in these domestic enterprises. While husbands generally carried out the heavier or more skilled parts of home manufacturing, like weaving, wives spun yarn and sewed together sections of cloth into finished goods.

At the same time, daughters, neighbors, and servants remained critical to the production of household items. In Hallowell, Maine, in the early nineteenth century, the midwife Martha Ballard worked alongside her daughters and a niece, producing the goods necessary to survive on the northern frontier, even as she supplemented her husband's income as a surveyor. In more populated areas, older forms of mutuality continued alongside newer patterns of companionate marriage. Neighbors shared tools and equipment while those with specialized skills assisted neighbors—threading a loom, for instance—in exchange for items they needed. Yet young couples who joined in these activities no doubt imagined themselves embarking on more egalitarian marriages than those of their parents. If they ended up living on the southern frontier, however, they might well discover that traditional patterns of hierarchical marriage prevailed there, shaping both household production and social life.

In wealthy households, whatever the contours of marriage, servants and slaves took on a greater share of domestic labor by the late eighteenth and early nineteenth centuries. Most female servants in the North were young and unmarried. Some arrived with children in tow or became pregnant while on the job, a mark of the rising rate of out-of-wedlock births following the Revolution. Planters' wives in the South had fewer worries in this regard because if household slaves became pregnant, their children added to the slave owner's labor supply. And on larger plantations, owners increasingly assigned a few enslaved women to spin, cook, wash clothes, make candles, and wait on table. Plantation mistresses also hired the wives of small farmers and landless laborers to turn cotton into yarn, weave yarn into cloth, and sew clothing for slaves and children. While mistresses in both regions continued to engage in household production, they also expanded their roles as domestic managers.

Still, at the turn of the nineteenth century, most people continued to live on family farms; to produce or trade locally for food, clothing, and other basic needs; and to use techniques handed down for generations to produce candles and soap, prepare meals, and deliver

babies. Yet by 1820, their lives, like those of wealthier Americans, were transformed by the expanding market economy. More and more families sewed clothes with machine-spun thread made from cotton ginned in the American South, worked their fields with cast-iron plows, and varied their diet by adding items shipped from other regions by steamboats.

Technology, Cotton, and Slaves

Some of the most dramatic technological changes occurred in agriculture, and none was more significant than the cotton gin, which led to the vast expansion of agricultural production in the South. This in turn fueled regional specialization, ensuring that residents in one area of the nation—the North, South, or West—depended on those in other areas. Southern planters relied on a growing demand for cotton from northern merchants and manufacturers. At the same time, planters, merchants, manufacturers, and factory workers became more dependent on western farmers to produce the grain and livestock needed to feed the nation.

As cotton gins spread across the South, any thoughts of abolishing slavery in the region disappeared. Instead, cotton and slavery expanded into the interior of many southern states as well as into the lower Mississippi valley. Cotton was not the only crop produced in the South—in Louisiana, planters made their fortunes on sugar and in South Carolina on rice—but it quickly became the most important. In 1790 southern farms and plantations produced about 3,000 bales of cotton, each weighing about 300 pounds. By 1820, with the aid of the cotton gin, the South produced more than 330,000 bales annually (Table 8.2). For southern blacks, increased production meant increased burdens. Because seeds could be separated from raw cotton with much greater efficiency, farmers could plant vastly larger quantities of the crop. On small farms, the work was still performed primarily by family members, neighbors, or hired hands. But planters could purchase additional slaves, particularly as cotton prices rose in the early nineteenth century.

The dramatic increase in the amount of cotton planted and harvested each year was paralleled by a jump in the size of the slave population. Thus even as northern states began to abolish the institution and the international slave trade ended (in 1808), southern planters significantly increased the number of slaves they held. Some smuggled in women and men from Africa and the Caribbean. Most planters, however, depended on enslaved women to bear more children, increasing the size of their labor force through natural reproduction. In addition, planters in the Deep South—from Georgia and the Carolinas west to

TABLE 8.2 Growth of Cotton Production in the United States, 1790–1830

Year	Production in Bales
1790	3,135
1795	16,719
1800	73,145
1805	146,290
1810	177,638
1815	208,986
1820	334,378
1825	532,915
1830	731,452

Source: Lewis Cecil Gray, *History of Agriculture in the Southern United States to 1860*, vol. 2 (Gloucester, MA: Peter Smith, 1958).

Louisiana—began buying slaves from farmers in Maryland and Virginia, where cotton and slavery were less profitable.

In 1790 there were fewer than 700,000 slaves in the United States. By 1820 there were nearly 1.5 million. Still, because of the increased competition for field hands to plant, maintain, and harvest the cotton crop, the price of slaves increased, roughly doubling between 1795 and 1805. The dramatic growth of slave markets in Charleston and New Orleans was one measure of the continued importance of the slave trade as cotton lands moved west.

In the early nineteenth century, most white southerners believed that there was enough land to go around. And the rising price of cotton allowed small farmers to imagine they would someday be planters. Some southern Indians also placed their hopes in cotton. Cherokee and Creek Indians cultivated the crop, even purchasing black slaves to increase production. Some Indian villages now welcomed ministers to their communities, hoping that embracing Protestantism and "American" culture might allow them to retain their current lands. Yet other native residents foresaw the increased pressure for land that cotton cultivation produced and organized to defend themselves from whites invading their territory. Regardless of the policies adopted by Indians, cotton and slavery expanded rapidly into Cherokee- and Creek-controlled lands in the interior of Georgia and South Carolina. And the admission of the states of Louisiana, Mississippi, and Alabama between 1812 and 1819 marked the rapid spread of southern agriculture farther westward.

Enslaved men and women played critical roles in the South's geographical expansion. Without their labor, neither cotton nor sugar could have become mainstays of the South's economy. Because clearing new cotton fields and planting and harvesting sugarcane involved heavy labor, most planters selected young slave men and women to move west, breaking apart families in the process. Some slaves resisted their removal to new plantations. If forced to go, they could still use their role in the labor process to limit owners' control. Slaves worked slowly, broke tools, and feigned illness or injury. Enslaved women and men hid out temporarily as a respite from brutal work regimes or harsh punishments. Others ran to areas controlled by Indians, hoping for better treatment, or to regions where slavery was no longer legal.

Still, given the power and resources wielded by whites, most slaves had to find ways to improve their lives within the system of bondage. The end of the international slave trade helped blacks in this regard since planters then had to depend more on natural reproduction to increase their labor supply. To ensure that slaves lived longer and healthier lives, planters were forced to provide sturdier housing, better clothing, and increased food allotments. Some slaves gained leverage to fish, hunt, or maintain small gardens in order to improve their diet. With the birth of more children, southern blacks also developed more extensive kinship networks, ensuring that family members could care for children if their parents were compelled to move west. Enslavement was still brutal, but slaves made small gains that improved their chances of survival.

Southern slaves also established their own religious ceremonies, often held in the woods or swamps at night. African Americans were swept up as well in the religious revivals that burned across the southern frontier beginning in the 1790s. Itinerant preachers, or circuit riders, held camp meetings that tapped into deep emotional wells of spirituality. Baptist and Methodist clergy drew free and enslaved blacks as well as white frontier families to their gatherings. They encouraged physical displays of spiritual rebirth, from trembling and quaking to calling out and dancing, offering release from the oppressive burdens of daily life for poor whites and blacks alike.

Evangelical religion, combined with revolutionary ideals promoted in the United States and Haiti, proved a potent mix, and planters rarely lost sight of the potential dangers this posed to the system of bondage. Outright rebellions occurred only rarely, yet the successful revolt of blacks in Haiti reminded slaves and owners alike that uprisings were possible. In 1800 Gabriel, an enslaved blacksmith in Richmond, Virginia, plotted such a rebellion. His supporters rallied around the demand for "Death or Liberty." Gabriel's plan to kill all whites except those who opposed slavery failed when informants betrayed him to local authorities. Nonetheless, news of the plot traveled across the South and terrified white residents, reminding them that the promise of new frontiers could not be separated from the dangers embedded in the nation's oppressive racial history.

REVIEW & RELATE

How did new inventions and infrastructure improvements contribute to the development of the American economy?

Why did slavery expand rapidly and become more deeply entrenched in southern society in the early nineteenth century?

LEARNINGCurve bedfordstmartins.com/hewittlawson/LC

Conclusion: New Frontiers and New Challenges

The geographical and economic expansion that marked the period from 1790 to 1820 inspired scientific and technological advances as well as literary and artistic paeans to a distinctly American identity. For young, ambitious men like Parker Cleaveland, Eli Whitney, Washington Irving, and Meriwether Lewis, the frontiers that opened in education, science, literature, and exploration offered opportunities for fame and financial success. Though his name is unfamiliar today, Cleaveland was offered prestigious professorships as well as the presidency of Bowdoin College during the early decades of the nineteenth century. He chose, however, to live out his life as a professor of mathematics, chemistry, and mineralogy in Brunswick, Maine, where he died in 1858.

Of course, not all white men had the luxury of a college education or the resources to invest in commercial enterprises or technological improvements. Many sought opportunities on the frontier, hoping to find fertile land, abundant wildlife, or opportunities for trade. In some cases, they and their families faced Indians angered by the constant encroachment of white Americans on their lands. In other cases, land speculators and planters bought up western lands, raising prices and pushing the frontier farther west.

The same developments that provided opportunities for enterprising white men also transformed the lives of white women. Those of elite or middling status benefited from improved educational opportunities and new ideals that highlighted mothers' role in raising children and

marriage based on companionship and mutual responsibilities. Yet these changes occurred gradually and unevenly, and many men expected their wives to fulfill all their traditional household obligations while also providing their husband with greater affection and attention. At the same time, domesticity itself changed as the market economy allowed some women to purchase goods they had once produced at home. Such changes increased expectations regarding the quality of domestic life, even though many women still had to supply most of their needs through intensive household labor.

Transformations in white society introduced even more difficult challenges for African Americans. While blacks in the North had greater hopes of gaining their freedom, most remained enslaved until the 1820s or later. Southern slaves faced far worse prospects. As cotton cultivation expanded into new territories, many slaves were forced to move west and to labor on bigger farms and plantations. There they honed means of survival and resistance that became even more crucial in the decades ahead.

At the same time, all along the expanding U.S. frontier, American Indians faced continued pressure to embrace white culture, leave their lands, or both. In 1810 Sacagawea, Charbonneau, and their son Baptiste apparently traveled to St. Louis at the invitation of William Clark, who offered to pay for Baptiste's education. The next spring, Charbonneau and his wife returned to their village, leaving Baptiste in Clark's care. It is not clear whether Sacagawea ever saw her son again, but William Clark penned the phrase "Se car ja we au Dead" on the cover of his cash book for 1825–1828, suggesting that she died during those years. By then, the Shoshone and Hidatsa nations where she was raised had begun to face the onslaught of white settlement. They, along with Indians living in older areas like Georgia, the Carolinas, and Tennessee, resisted the claims of the United States on their ancestral lands and struggled to control the embattled frontier.

Thus even as the young nation conquered new frontiers in education, technology, and the arts, it was forced to defend itself against attacks both internal and external. In the 1810s and 1820s, new conflicts erupted over slavery and against Indians. But the United States also faced its first major economic crisis, while Great Britain and France challenged American sovereignty. New frontiers created new opportunities but also intensified older challenges and conflicts.

LEARNINGCurve
Check what you know.
bedfordstmartins.com/hewittlawson/LC

Chapter Review

Online Study Guide ▶ bedfordstmartins.com/hewittlawson

KEY TERMS

American Colonization Society (ACS) (p. 233)
Haitian Revolution (p. 236)
Louisiana Territory (p. 236)
Corps of Discovery (p. 237)
Judiciary Act of 1801 (p. 239)
Marbury v. Madison (p. 239)
McCulloch v. Maryland (p. 239)
Embargo Act (p. 239)
National Road (p. 242)
multiplier effect (p. 242)
cotton gin (p. 243)
American system of manufacturing (p. 244)

REVIEW & RELATE

1. How did developments in education, literature, and the arts contribute to the emergence of a distinctly American identity?

2. What place did blacks and American Indians inhabit in the predominant white view of American society and culture?

3. How did Jefferson and the Democratic-Republicans contribute to the expansion of the role of the federal government in American life?

4. How did the conflict between France and Great Britain in the late eighteenth and early nineteenth centuries lead to domestic problems in the United States?

5. How did new inventions and infrastructure improvements contribute to the development of the American economy?

6. Why did slavery expand rapidly and become more deeply entrenched in southern society in the early nineteenth century?

TIMELINE OF EVENTS

1789	Massachusetts institutes free public elementary education for all children
1790	Spinning mill designed and built by Samuel Slater opens
1790–1820	Cotton production in the South increases from 3,000 to 330,000 bales annually
	U.S. slave population more than doubles from 700,000 to 1.5 million
1791–1803	Free and enslaved blacks revolt against French rule in Saint Domingue
1792–1809	New capital of Washington City constructed
1793	Eli Whitney invents cotton gin
1801	Federalists pass new Judiciary Act
	Jefferson sends U.S. force to challenge Barbary pirates
1803	United States purchases Louisiana Territory from France
	Haiti established as the first independent black-led nation in the Americas
	Marbury v. Madison
1804–1806	Corps of Discovery explores Louisiana Territory
April 1805	Sacagawea joins Corps of Discovery
1807	Robert Fulton launches first successful steamboat
	Embargo Act passed
1810	Population of both New York and Philadelphia exceeds 100,000
1816	Parker Cleaveland publishes *Elementary Treatise on Mineralogy and Geology*
1817	American Colonization Society founded
1819	*McCulloch v. Maryland*
1820	One-quarter of non-Indian Americans live west of the Appalachian Mountains
	Washington Irving publishes *Sketchbook*
1828	Noah Webster publishes *American Dictionary of the English Language*

Race Relations in the Early Republic

In the late eighteenth century, the United States was far from extending the promises of equality and democracy championed in the Revolutionary War to all Americans. African Americans and Indians in particular were denied most civil and political rights. Indeed, Thomas Jefferson (Document 8.5) and many others were uncertain about whether the two groups could be fully incorporated into white society. When Jefferson bought the Louisiana Territory in 1803, he acquired lands inhabited by numerous Indian communities. In Document 8.6, Meriwether Lewis describes his encounter with Indians in the region. Despite promises of aid, Indian nations in the West fared no better than those in the eastern United States as white settlers, backed by government force, gradually took over Indian lands.

The majority of African Americans in the early Republic era were enslaved, and eight of the first ten presidents were slaveholders. As cotton production expanded in the South, slavery did as well, and the slave population increased dramatically after 1790. With the end of the international slave trade in 1808, owners grew even more reluctant to free their slaves. As Andrew Jackson's 1804 ad for a runaway slave demonstrates (Document 8.8), slavery was a brutal system. The English Quaker Robert Sutcliff noted this physical brutality in his travels to Virginia and Pennsylvania (Document 8.9). While slave revolts were rare, those that occurred involved extensive planning, as suggested by the confession of a slave involved in one plot (Document 8.7).

Even free blacks lacked political and civil rights and suffered severe discrimination. However, some free blacks managed to create vibrant communities, as in Philadelphia. There African Americans agitated publicly against racism despite being denied the formal rights of citizenship (Document 8.10). The following documents reveal popular white perceptions of African Americans and Indians. They also suggest how blacks and Indians sought to carve out a place for themselves in the early Republic.

DOCUMENT 8.5

Thomas Jefferson | Letter to the Marquis de Chastellux, 1785

Thomas Jefferson sent copies of the first edition of his *Notes on the State of Virginia* to several friends in Europe, including the Marquis de Chastellux. In this book, he defended America against the claims of those who thought that human beings, plants, and animals degenerated in the New World. In a letter to the marquis, which is excerpted here, Jefferson repeats some of his arguments in the book, including his opinions about American Indians in relation to whites. He also hazards a tentative view about African Americans in relation to Indians.

AND I AM SAFE in affirming, that the proofs of genius given by the Indians of North America place them on a level with whites in the same uncultivated state. The North of Europe furnishes subjects enough for comparison with them, and for a proof of their equality. I have seen some thousands myself, and conversed much with them, and have found in them a masculine, sound understanding. I have had much information from men who had lived among them, and whose veracity and good sense were so far known to me, as to establish a reliance on their information. They have all agreed in bearing witness in favor of the genius of this people. As to their bodily strength, their manners rendering it disgraceful to labor, those muscles employed in labor will be weaker with them, than with the European laborer; but those which are exerted in the chase, and those faculties which are employed in the tracing an enemy or a wild beast, in contriving ambuscades [ambushes] for him, and in carrying them through their execution, are much stronger than with us, because they are more exercised. I believe the Indian, then, to be, in body and mind, equal to the white man. I have supposed the black man, in his present state, might not be so; but it would be hazardous to affirm, that, equally cultivated for a few generations, he would not become so.

Source: Willson Whitman, ed., *Jefferson's Letters* (Eau Claire, WI: Hale, 1900), 23.

DOCUMENT 8.6

Meriwether Lewis | Journal Entry, 1805

Throughout the Lewis and Clark expedition, both men kept journals and extensive notes on the plants, animals, terrain, and people they encountered. The following journal entry, in which Meriwether Lewis describes his encounter with Sacagawea's tribe, the Shoshone, was written fifteen months into the journey in what is today Idaho.

I can discover that these people are by no means friendly to the Spaniards. Their complaint is, that the Spaniards will not let them have fire arms and amunition, that they put them off by telling them that if they suffer them to have guns they will kill each other, thus leaving them defenceless and an easy prey to their bloodthirsty neighbours to the East of them, who being in possession of fire arms hunt them up and murder them without rispect to sex or age and plunder them of their horses on all occasions. They told me that to avoid their enemies who were eternally harrassing them that they were obliged to remain in the interior of these mountains at least two thirds of the year where the[y] suffered as we then saw great heardships for the want of food sometimes living for weeks without meat and only a little fish roots and berries. But this added Câmeahwait [a Shoshone leader], with his ferce eyes and lank jaws grown meager for the want of food, would not be the case if we had guns, we could then live in the country of buffaloe and eat as our enimies do and not be compelled to hide ourselves in these mountains and live on roots and berries as the bear do. We do not fear our enimies when placed on an equal footing with them. I told them that the Minnetares Mandans & Recares [other native tribes] of the Missouri had promised us to desist from making war on them & that we would indevour to find the means of making the Minnetares of fort d Prarie or as they call them Pahkees desist from waging war against them also. That after our finally returning to our homes towards the rising sun whitemen would come to them with an abundance of guns and every other article necessary to their defence and comfort, and that they would be enabled to supply themselves with these articles on reasonable terms in exchange for the skins of the beaver Otter and Ermin [long-tailed weasel] so abundant in their country. They expressed great pleasure at this information and said they had been long anxious to see the whitemen that traded guns; and that we might rest assured of their friendship and that they would do whatever we wished them.

Source: Reuben Gold Thwaites, ed., *Original Journals of the Lewis and Clark Expedition, 1804–1808* (New York: Dodd, Mead, 1904), 383–84.

DOCUMENT 8.7

Confession of Solomon, September 1800

Gabriel's Conspiracy was a plan for a massive slave rebellion in Virginia during the summer of 1800. The revolt's leader, Gabriel, was a slave and blacksmith on a tobacco plantation near Richmond who was often hired out to businesses in Richmond, where he recruited others to his plan. Gabriel was strongly influenced by the ideals of liberty advocated by participants in the American and Haitian revolutions. When some of the slaves involved confessed the plan to their masters before the revolt began, Governor James Monroe ordered the state militia to round up the leaders of the conspiracy. Gabriel's brother Solomon was caught in the initial patrols and gave his confession, excerpted here, while several leaders were still at large. Gabriel was caught several weeks later, and Gabriel, Solomon, and twenty-five other slaves were executed for the conspiracy.

My brother Gabriel was the person who influenced me to join him and others in order that (as he said) we might conquer the white people and possess ourselves of their property. I enquired how we were to effect it. He said by falling upon them (the whites) in the dead of night, at which time they would be unguarded and unsuspicious. I then enquired who was at the head of the plan. He said Jack, alias Jack Bowler. I asked him if Jack Bowler knew anything about carrying on war. He replied he did not. I then enquired who he was going to employ. He said a man from Caroline who was at the siege of Yorktown, and who was to meet him (Gabriel) at the Brook and proceed on to Richmond, take, and then fortify it. This man from Caroline was to be commander and manager the first day, and then, after exercising the soldiers, the command was to be resigned to Gabriel. If Richmond was taken without the loss of many men they were to continue there some time, but if they sustained any considerable loss they were to bend their course for Hanover Town or York, they were not decided to which, and continue at that place as long as they found they were able to defend it, but in the event of a defeat or loss at those places they were to endeavor to form a junction with some negroes which, they had understood from Mr. Gregory's overseer, were in rebellion in some quarter of the country. This information which they had gotten from the overseer, made Gabriel anxious, upon which he applied to me to make scythe-swords, which I did to the number of twelve. Every Sunday he came to Richmond to provide ammunition and to find where the military stores were deposited. Gabriel informed me, in case of success, that they intended to subdue the whole of the country where slavery was permitted, but no further.

The first places Gabriel intended to attack in Richmond were, the Capitol, the Magazine, the Penitentiary, the Governor's house and his person. The inhabitants were to be massacred, save those who begged for quarter and agreed to serve as soldiers with them. The reason why the insurrection was to be made at this particular time was, the discharge of the number of soldiers, one or two months ago, which induced Gabriel to believe the plan would be more easily executed.

Source: H. W. Flournoy, ed., *Calendar of Virginia State Papers and Other Manuscripts from January 1, 1799, to December 31, 1807* (Richmond, 1890), 9:147.

DOCUMENT 8.8

Andrew Jackson | Runaway Slave Advertisement, 1804

STOP THE RUNAWAY.
FIFTY DOLLARS REWARD.

Eloped from the subscriber, living near Nashville, on the 25th of June last, a Mulatto Man Slave, about thirty years old, six feet and an inch high, stout made and active, talks sensible, stoops in his walk, and has a remarkably large foot, broad across the root of the toes—will pass for a free man, as I am informed he has obtained by some means, certificates as such—took with him a drab great-coat, dark mixed body coat, a ruffled shirt, cotton home spun shirts, and overalls. He will make for Detroit, through the states of Kentucky and Ohio, or the upper part of Louisiana. The above reward will be given any person that will take him and deliver him to me or secure him in jail so that I can get him. If taken out of the state, the above reward, and all reasonable expenses paid— and ten dollars extra for every hundred lashes any person will give him to the amount of three hundred.

Andrew Jackson, near Nashville, State of Tennessee

Source: *Tennessee Gazette*, November 7, 1804.

Future president Andrew Jackson bought his first slaves in 1794 and by 1804 owned 9 slave men and women. In that same year, he bought the Hermitage, a Tennessee cotton plantation, and slowly increased the size of his property and its slave population. By the time he was president, he owned 100 slaves and would own more than 160 before his death in 1845. Although Jackson was known to provide adequate food and housing for his slaves, he was not above employing corporal punishment, as is evidenced by the following advertisement he placed for a runaway slave in 1804.

DOCUMENT 8.9

Robert Sutcliff, *Travels in Some Parts of North America*, 1812

Robert Sutcliff, an English Quaker, arrived in the United States on a business trip in 1804. Over the next three years, he recorded his travels in the country and published his experiences as a book in 1812. In the following excerpts, Sutcliff describes his encounters with the institution of slavery in the area around Richmond, Virginia, which include a reference to Gabriel's Conspiracy, and then in the last segment, near Philadelphia, Pennsylvania.

9th Month, 25th [1804].

I pursued my way to Richmond in the mail stage, through a beautiful country, but clouded and debased by Negro slavery. At the house where I breakfasted, which is called the Bowling-green, I was told that the owner had in his possession 200 slaves. In one field near the house, planted with tobacco, I counted nearly 20 women and children, employed in picking grubs from the plant. In the afternoon I passed by a field in which several poor slaves had lately been executed, on the charge of having an intention to rise against their masters. A lawyer who was present at their trials at Richmond, informed me that on one of them being asked what he had to say to the court on his defence, he replied in a manly tone of voice: "I have nothing more to offer than what General Washington would have had to offer, had he been taken by the British and put to trial by them. I have adventured my life in endeavouring to obtain the liberty of my countrymen, and am a willing sacrifice in their cause: and I beg, as a favour, that I may be immediately led to execution. I know that you have pre-determined to shed my blood, why then all this mockery of a trial?" . . .

8th Month, 15th [1805].

I spent this day at Richmond. In the evening I walked to Manchester, over the bridge at James's River, which at this place is nearly half a mile wide. From my own observations, and the information I received from an inhabitant, Richmond appears to be a place of great dissipation; chiefly arising from the loose and debauched conduct of the white people with their black female slaves. It sometimes happens here, as in other places, that the white inhabitants, in selling the offspring of these poor debased females, sell their own sons and daughters with as much indifference as they would sell their cattle. By such means, every tender sentiment of the human breast is laid waste, and men become so degraded that their feelings rank but little above those of the beasts in the field. In their treatment of their offspring, how far do some of the brute creation surpass them! . . .

1st Month, 25th [1806].

In crossing the Schuylkill [River, at Philadelphia] on the floating bridge at the upper ferry, I passed a Negro boy apparently about 12 years of age. Round his neck an iron collar was locked, and from each side of it an iron bow passed over his head. His dress was a light linsey jacket and trowsers, without hat, shoes, or stockings. Soon after passing the boy, whom I supposed to be a runaway slave, I met a person of whom I inquired the reason of the boy's having so much iron about him. The man replied that the boy was his, and was so often running away that he had used that method to prevent him.

Source: Robert Sutcliff, *Travels in Some Parts of North America, in the Years 1804, 1805, and 1806* (Philadelphia: B&T Kite, 1812), 50, 94, 181.

Resolved unanimously, That the following address, signed on behalf of the meeting by the Chairman and Secretary, be published and circulated.

To the humane and benevolent Inhabitants of the city and county of Philadelphia.

The free people of color, assembled together, under circumstances of deep interest to their happiness and welfare, humbly and respectfully lay before you this expression of their feelings and apprehensions.

Relieved from the miseries of slavery, many of us by your aid, possessing the benefits which industry and integrity in this prosperous country assure to all its inhabitants, enjoying the rich blessings of religion, by opportunities of worshipping the only true God, under the light of Christianity, each of us according to his understanding; and having afforded to us and to our children the means of education and improvement; we have no wish to separate from our present homes for any purpose whatever. Contented with our present situation and condition, we are not desirous of increasing their prosperity but by honest efforts, and by the use of those opportunities for their improvement, which the constitution and laws allow to all. It is therefore with painful solicitude and sorrowing regret we have seen a plan for colonizing the free people of color of the United States on the coast of Africa brought forward under the auspices and sanction of gentlemen whose names give value to all they recommend, and who certainly are among the wisest, the best, and the most benevolent of men in this great nation.

If the plan of colonizing is intended for our benefit and those who now promote it will never seek our injury; we humbly and respectfully urge that it is not asked for by us nor will it be required by any circumstances, in our present or future condition; as long as we shall be permitted to share the protection of the excellent laws and just government which we now enjoy, in common with every individual of the community.

DOCUMENT 8.10

Free Blacks in Philadelphia Oppose Colonization, 1817

Many African Americans fiercely resisted the idea of colonization—that free blacks and slaves should be returned to their ancestral homeland of Africa. The following document lists the resolutions of a group of prominent free blacks who met in Philadelphia in 1817 to express opposition to the American Colonization Society. The chair of the committee, sailmaker James Forten, was one of the wealthiest African Americans in the country.

We, therefore, a portion of those who are the objects of this plan, and among those whose happiness, with that of others of our color, it is intended to promote; with humble and grateful acknowledgements to those who have devised it, renounce and disclaim every connexion with it; and respectfully but firmly declare our determination not to participate in any part of it.

If this plan of colonization now proposed, is intended to provide a refuge and a dwelling for a portion of our brethren, who are now held in slavery in the south, we have other and stronger objections to it, and we entreat your consideration of them.

The ultimate and final abolition of slavery in the United States, by the operation of various causes, is, under the guidance and protection of a just God, progressing. Every year witnesses the release of numbers of the victims of oppression, and affords new and safe assurances that the freedom of all will be in the end accomplished. As they are thus by degrees relieved from bondage, our brothers have opportunities for instruction and improvement; and thus they become in some measure fitted for their liberty. Every year, many of us have restored to us by the gradual, but certain march of the cause of abolition—parents, from whom we have long been separated—wives and children whom we had left in servitude—and brothers, in blood as well as in early sufferings, from whom we had been long parted.

But if the emancipation of our kindred shall, when the plan of colonization shall go into effect, be attended with transportation to a distant land, and shall be granted on no other condition; the consolation for our past sufferings and of those of our color who are in slavery, which have hitherto been, and under the present situation of things would continue to be, afforded to us and to them, will cease for ever. The cords, which now connect them with us, will be stretched by the distance to which their ends will be carried, until they break; and all the sources of happiness, which affection and connexion and blood bestow, will be ours and theirs no more.

Source: William Lloyd Garrison, *Thoughts on African Colonization; or, An Impartial Exhibition of the Doctrines, Principles, and Purposes of the American Colonization Society, together with the Resolutions, Addresses, and Remonstrances of the Free People of Color* (Boston: Garrison and Knapp, 1832), part 2, 10–11.

Interpret the Evidence

1. What do Thomas Jefferson's letter (Document 8.5) and Meriwether Lewis's journal entry (Document 8.6) tell us about how American Indians were perceived in the early Republic? How would you compare their opinions of Indians?

2. What encouraged slaves to revolt (Documents 8.7 and 8.9)? What do these documents reveal about slavery in Richmond and in Virginia more generally?

3. What does the runaway slave advertisement in Document 8.8 tell us about Andrew Jackson as a slave owner? Does the fact that it was written by a future president shape how you view it? Why or why not?

4. What does Robert Sutcliff's report (Document 8.9) reveal about the treatment that slaves in the North and in the South endured? Judging from his writing, how does Sutcliff's English and Quaker background affect his views of slavery?

5. Given the horrors of slavery in the North and the South and the near impossibility of overthrowing the institution, why did free blacks in Philadelphia oppose colonization (Document 8.10)? What language did they use to address their audience?

Put It in Context

- According to these documents, how did race relations in the United States change between 1785 and 1817 as slavery expanded along with white Americans' movement into new western territories?

The Granger Collection, New York

The Granger Collection, New York

• View of Broadway in New York City, c. 1830s.

• Portrait presumed to be Tecumseh by an unknown artist.

9

Defending and Redefining the Nation

1809–1832

© Collection of the New-York Historical Society, USA/The Bridgeman Art Library

Junction of Erie and Northern Canals, c. 1830–1832.

AMERICAN HISTORIES

Dolley Payne, a future First Lady, was raised on a Virginia plantation. But her Quaker parents, moved by the Society of Friends' growing antislavery sentiment, decided to free their slaves. In 1783, when Dolley was fifteen, the Paynes moved to Philadelphia. There, Dolley's father suffered heavy economic losses, and Dolley lost her first husband and her younger son to yellow fever. In 1794 the young widow met and married Virginia congressman James Madison. The two made a perfect political couple. James was brilliant but reserved, while Dolley, witty and charming, loved entertaining. When the newly elected president Thomas Jefferson appointed James secretary of state in 1801, the couple moved to Washington.

Since Jefferson and his vice president, Aaron Burr, were widowers, Dolley Madison served as hostess for White House affairs. When James Madison succeeded Jefferson as president in 1809, he, too, depended on his wife's social skills and networks. Dolley held lively informal receptions to which she invited Federalists, Democratic-Republicans, diplomats, cabinet officers, and their wives. These social events helped bridge the ideological differences that continued to divide Congress and proved crucial in creating a unified front when Congress declared war on Great Britain in 1812.

During the War of 1812, British forces attacked Washington City and burned the Executive Mansion. With the president away, his wife was left to secure important state papers, emerging as a symbol of national courage at a critical moment in the war. When peace came the following year, Dolley Madison quickly reestablished a busy social calendar to help mend conflicts that had erupted during the war.

In 1817, at the end of the president's second term, the Madisons left Washington for Virginia just as a young Scots-Cherokee trader named John Ross entered the political arena. Born in 1790 in the Cherokee nation, John (also known as Guwisguwi) was the son of a Scottish trader and his wife, who was both Cherokee and Scottish. John Ross was raised in an Anglo-Indian world in eastern Tennessee where he played with Cherokee children and attended tribal ceremonies and festivals but was educated by private tutors and in Protestant missionary schools. At age twenty, Ross was appointed as a U.S. Indian agent among the Cherokees and during the War of 1812 served as an adjutant (or administrative assistant) in a Cherokee regiment.

After the war, Ross focused on business ventures in Tennessee, including the establishment of a plantation. He also became increasingly involved in Cherokee political affairs, using his bilingual skills and Protestant training to represent Indian interests to government officials. In 1819 Ross was elected president of the Cherokee legislature. In the 1820s, he moved to Georgia, near the Cherokee capital of New Echota, where he served as president of the Cherokee constitutional convention in 1827. Having overseen the first written constitution produced by an Indian nation, Ross was then elected principal chief in 1828. Over the next decade, he battled to retain the Cherokee homeland in Georgia, North Carolina, and Tennessee against the pressures of white planters and politicians. •

AMERICAN POLITICS IN the early nineteenth century was a white man's world, but, as the American histories of Dolley Madison and John Ross demonstrate, it was possible for some of those on the political margins to influence national developments. Both Madison and Ross sought to defend and expand the democratic ideals that defined the young nation. The First Lady helped forge social networks and nurture a nascent political culture in Washington that included women as well as men. At the same time, she struggled with the issue of slavery on her husband's Montpelier plantation. Ross encouraged the Cherokee people to embrace Anglo-American religion, language, and political ideals in the hopes of providing them with a path to inclusion in the United States. Yet ultimately, given the nation's economic growth, he could not overcome the power of white planters and politicians to wrest territory from even the most Americanized Indians. Although Ross most directly confronted the limits of American democracy, Dolley Madison also grappled with the dilemmas posed to the nation's democratic ideals by the expansion of slavery and the limits of citizenship.

Conflicts at Home and Abroad

When Thomas Jefferson completed his second term as president in March 1809, he was succeeded by his friend and ally James Madison. Madison was the principal author of the Constitution; coauthor of *The Federalist Papers*, which ensured its ratification; and secretary of state in Jefferson's administration. Like Jefferson, he sought to end foreign interference in American affairs and to resolve conflicts between Indians and white residents on the nation's frontier. Congress itself was divided over how best to address these problems. By 1815 the United States had weathered a series of domestic and foreign crises, including another war with Britain, but American sovereignty remained fragile. At the same time, even though Madison (like Jefferson) believed in a national government with limited powers, he found himself expanding federal authority.

Tensions at Sea and on the Frontier

When President Madison took office, Great Britain and France remained embroiled in the Napoleonic Wars in Europe and refused to modify their policies toward American shipping or to recognize U.S. neutrality. American ships were subject to seizure by both nations, and British authorities continued to impress "deserters" into the Royal Navy. In response, the new president convinced Congress to pass the **Non-Intercourse Act** in 1809, which allowed Americans to trade with every nation except France and Britain. When that act failed to satisfy the warring nations or improve the economy, Congress approved a bill that opened trade with both Great Britain and France but allowed the president to reimpose an embargo on one nation if the other lifted its restrictions. When Napoleon promised to lift all restrictions on U.S. shipping, Madison stalled, giving British officials time to match France's policy. Britain refused.

In the midst of these crises, Madison also faced difficulties in the Northwest Territory. In 1794 General "Mad Anthony" Wayne had won a decisive victory against a multitribe coalition led by the Shawnees at the Battle of Fallen Timbers. But this victory inspired two forceful native leaders to create a pan-Indian alliance in the Ohio River valley. The Shawnee prophet Tenskwatawa and his half-brother Tecumseh, a warrior, encouraged native peoples to resist white encroachments on their territory and to give up all aspects of white society and culture, including clothing, liquor, and other popular trade goods. They imagined an Indian nation that stretched from the Canadian border to the Gulf of Mexico.

Although powerful Creek and Choctaw nations in the lower Mississippi valley refused to join the alliance, bands of Indians in the upper Midwest, frustrated with continuing white encroachments, rallied around the brothers. In 1808 Tenskwatawa and Tecumseh established Prophet Town along the Tippecanoe River in Indiana Territory. The next year, William Henry Harrison, the territorial governor, plied several Indian leaders with liquor and persuaded them to sign a treaty selling three million acres of land to the United States for only $7,600. Tecumseh was enraged by Harrison's methods and dismissed the treaty, claiming the land belonged to all the Indians together.

Explore

Read part of Tecumseh's response to Harrison in Document 9.1.

In November 1811, fearing the growing power of the Shawnee leaders, President Madison ordered Harrison to attack Prophet Town. With more troops and superior weapons, the U.S. army defeated the Shawnees, and soldiers then burned Prophet Town to the ground. The rout damaged Tenskwatawa's stature as a prophet, and he and his supporters fled to Canada. Skirmishes continued between Indians and U.S. troops along the Canadian border, but federal officials now returned their attention to conflicts with Great Britain.

War Erupts with Britain

Convinced that British officials in Canada fueled Indian resistance, supporters of war with Great Britain demanded an end to British intervention on the western frontier. They were even more concerned about British interference with transatlantic trade. Yet merchants in the Northeast, who depended on trade with Great Britain and the British West Indies, feared the commercial disruptions that war entailed. Once staunch supporters of expanding the power of the national government, New England Federalists now adamantly opposed a declaration of war.

For months, Madison avoided taking a clear stand for or against war. On June 1, 1812, however, having exhausted diplomatic efforts and seeing no end to these conflicts as long as the Napoleonic Wars raged across Europe, Madison sent a secret message to Congress outlining American grievances against Great Britain. Within weeks, Congress declared war by a sharply divided vote of 79 to 49 in the House of Representatives and 19 to 13 in the Senate.

Supporters claimed that a victory over Great Britain would end threats to U.S. sovereignty and raise Americans' stature in Europe, but the nation was ill prepared to launch a major offensive against such an imposing foe. Cuts in federal spending and falling tax revenues over the previous decade had diminished military resources. Democratic-Republicans had also failed to renew the charter of the Bank of the United States when it expired in 1811, so the nation lacked a vital source of credit. Nonetheless, many in Congress believed that Britain would be too distracted and overcommitted by the ongoing conflict with France to attack North America.

Meanwhile U.S. commanders devised plans to attack Canada. The most enthusiastic advocates of war imagined that the United States could defeat Britain and gain control of all of North America. Initially, however, the U.S. army and navy proved no match for Great Britain and its Indian allies. Tecumseh, who was appointed a brigadier general in the British army, helped capture Detroit. Joint British and Indian forces also launched successful attacks on Fort Dearborn, Fort Mackinac, and other points along the U.S.-Canadian border.

Even as U.S. forces faced defeat after defeat in the summer and fall of 1812, American voters reelected James

DOCUMENT 9.1

Tecumseh | Speech to William Henry Harrison, 1810

In 1809 William Henry Harrison, governor of the Indiana Territory, negotiated a treaty with a coalition of native peoples to cede three million acres to the United States. Unhappy with this treaty, two Shawnee brothers, Tecumseh and Tenskwatawa, united with other Indian nations to resist American settlement of the region. In August 1810, Tecumseh confronted Harrison and delivered a speech, excerpted here, urging him to return the land. Harrison refused, and in the fall of 1811 U.S. troops attacked and defeated the Shawnees at Prophet Town.

Explore

Brother. Since the peace was made you have kill'd some of the Shawanese, Winebagoes, Delawares, and Miamies and you have taken our lands from us, and I do not see how we can remain at peace with you if you continue to do so. You have given goods to the Kickapoos for the sale of their lands . . . which has been the cause of many deaths among them. You have promised us assistance but I do not see that you have given us any.

You try to force the red people to do some injury. It is you that is pushing them on to do mischief. You endeavor to make distinctions, you wish to prevent the Indians to do as we wish them: to unite and let them consider their land as the common property of the whole.

You take tribes aside and advise them not to come into this measure [coalition] and untill our design is accomplished we do not wish to accept of your invitation to go and visit the President.

The reason I tell you this is you want by your distinctions of Indian tribes in allotting to each a particular track of land to make them to war with each other. You never see an Indian come and endeavour to make the white people do so. You are continually driving the red people when at last you will drive them into the great Lake where they can't eather stand or work.

Source: Logan Esarey, ed., *Messages and Letters of William Henry Harrison* (Indianapolis: Indiana Historical Commission, 1922), 1:465.

Interpret the Evidence

- How does Tecumseh's view of Indian land differ from that negotiated in the treaty?
- What blame does he place on other Indians? Why does Tecumseh consider white Americans untrustworthy?

Put It in Context

What does this document reveal about the relationship between American Indians and the U.S. government by the 1810s?

Madison as president. His narrow victory demonstrated the geographical divisions caused by the war. Madison won most of the western and southern states, where the war was most popular, and was defeated in New England and New York, where Federalist opponents held sway.

After a year of fighting, U.S. forces—with the aid of crucial naval victories on the Great Lakes—finally drove the British back into Canada (Map 9.1). Tecumseh was killed in Canada at the Battle of the Thames, and U.S. forces burned York (present-day Toronto). Yet just as U.S. prospects in the war improved, New England Federalists demanded retreat. In the fall of 1813, state legislatures in New England

withdrew their support for any invasions of "foreign British soil," and Federalists in Congress sought to block appropriations for the war and challenge the deployment of local militia units into the U.S. army.

New England Federalists did not have sufficient power to change national policy, but they called a meeting at Hartford, Connecticut, in 1814 to consider their options. Some participants at the **Hartford Convention** called for New England's secession from the United States. Most, however, supported amendments to the U.S. Constitution that would limit presidents to a single term and ensure that presidents were elected from diverse states (so that Virginia planters could not dominate the executive branch). Other amendments would limit embargoes to sixty days and require a two-thirds majority in Congress to declare war, prohibit trade, or admit new states.

The ideas debated at Hartford gained increased attention as British forces once again launched attacks into the United States and British warships blockaded U.S. ports. In August 1814, the British sailed up the Chesapeake. As American troops retreated, Dolley Madison and a family slave, Peter Jennings, gathered up government papers and valuable belongings before fleeing the city. The redcoats then burned and sacked Washington City. The invasion of the U.S. capital was humiliating, but American troops quickly rallied to defeat the British in Maryland and expel them from Washington and New York.

Meanwhile news arrived from the South that in March 1814 militiamen from Tennessee led by Andrew Jackson had defeated a force of Creek Indians, important allies of the British. Cherokee warriors (and adjutant John Ross), longtime foes of the Creeks, joined the fight as well. At the Battle of Horseshoe Bend, in present-day Alabama, the combined U.S.-Cherokee forces slaughtered some eight hundred Creek warriors. Jackson then demanded punitive terms, and in the resulting treaty the Creek nation lost two-thirds of its tribal domain.

Despite sporadic U.S. victories, America was no closer to winning the war. In June 1814, the British finally defeated Napoleon, ending the war in Europe. And in December of that year, the British fleet landed thousands of seasoned troops at New Orleans, threatening U.S. control of that crucial port city. But exhausted from twenty years of European warfare, the British were losing steam as well. As a result, representatives of the two countries met in Ghent, Belgium, to negotiate a peace settlement. On Christmas Eve 1814, the Treaty of Ghent was signed, returning to each nation the lands it controlled before the war.

Although the war had officially ended, it took time for the news to reach the United States. In January 1815, American troops under General Andrew Jackson attacked and routed the British army at New Orleans. The victory

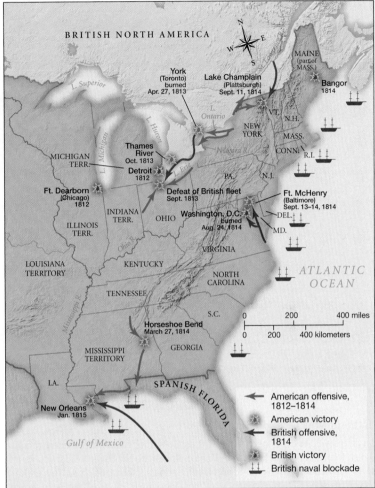

MAP 9.1   The War of 1812

Most conflicts in this war occurred in the Great Lakes region or around Washington, D.C. Yet two of the most significant victories were achieved by General Andrew Jackson in the South. At Horseshoe Bend, his troops defeated Creek allies of the British, and at New Orleans they beat British forces two weeks after a peace agreement was signed in Europe.

cheered Americans, who did not know that peace had already been achieved, and Jackson became a national hero.

Although the War of 1812 achieved no official territorial gains, Jackson's late victory in the Battle of New Orleans made it appear that American forces had vanquished Great Britain. The war did represent an important defense of U.S. sovereignty and garnered international prestige for the young nation. In addition, Indians on the western frontier lost a powerful ally when British representatives at Ghent failed to act as advocates for their allies. Thus, in practical terms, the U.S. government gained greater control over vast expanses of land in the Ohio and Mississippi River valleys held by these Indian nations.

A CORRECT VIEW of the BATTLE Near the City of NEW ORLEANS, on the Eighth of January 1815, Under the Command of Genl. Andw. Jackson, Over 10,000 British Troops, in which 3 of their most distinguished Generals were killed & several wounded and upwards of 3,000 of their choisest Soldiers were killed & wounded. and made Prisoners, &c

Battle of New Orleans

On January 8, 1815, General Andrew Jackson's troops launched grapeshot and canister bombs against British forces in New Orleans in this final battle of the War of 1812. Jackson's troops included Indian allies, backcountry immigrants, and French-speaking black soldiers. This engraving by Francisco Scacki shows the slain British commander, Major General Sir Edward Pakenham, in the center foreground.

The Granger Collection, New York

REVIEW & RELATE

How were conflicts with Indians in the West connected to ongoing tensions between the United States and Great Britain on land and at sea?

What were the long-term consequences of the War of 1812?

✓ *LEARNINGCurve* bedfordstmartins.com/hewittlawson/LC

Expanding the Economy and the Nation

By further expanding federal powers, the War of 1812 reinforced political changes that had been under way for more than a decade. At the Hartford Convention, Federalists who had once advocated broad national powers called for restrictions on federal authority. By contrast, the Democratic-Republicans, who gained support in 1800 by demanding restraints on federal power, now applauded its expansion. Indeed, Democratic-Republicans in Congress sought to use federal authority to settle boundary disputes in the West, make investments in transportation, and reestablish a national bank. Increasingly, many ordinary Americans viewed such federal assistance as critical to the continued development of industry and agriculture.

Governments Fuel Economic Growth

At the nation's founding, Alexander Hamilton led a coalition that advocated the use of federal power to fuel commercial development. Over the following decade, this coalition's efforts to expand federal authority in the interest of commerce and industry inspired opposition within Federalist ranks. In 1800 Thomas Jefferson captured the presidency by advocating a reduction in federal powers and a renewed emphasis on the needs of small farmers and working men. Once in power, however, Jefferson and his Democratic-Republican supporters faced a series of economic and political developments that led many of them to embrace Hamilton's loose interpretation of the U.S. Constitution and support federal efforts to aid economic growth (see chapter 8). In the 1810s, for example, Democratic-Republican representative Henry Clay of Kentucky sketched out a plan called the **American System**, which combined federally funded internal improvements to aid farmers with federal tariffs to protect U.S. manufacturing and a national bank to oversee economic development.

Western expansion helped fuel the demand for federally funded internal improvements. The non-Indian population west of the Appalachian Mountains more than doubled between 1810 and 1820, from 1,080,000 to 2,234,000. The new residents included veterans of the War of 1812, many of whom received 160-acre parcels of land between the Illinois and Mississippi Rivers. They and their families established farms, shops, and communities throughout the territory. Four frontier states were admitted to the Union in just four years: Indiana (1816), Mississippi (1817), Illinois (1818), and Alabama (1819).

Population growth and commercial expansion moved hand in hand. In 1811 the first steamboat traveled down the Mississippi from the Ohio River to New Orleans; over the next decade, steamboat traffic expanded, and freight charges dropped precipitously. This development helped western and southern residents but hurt trade on overland routes between northeastern seaports and the Ohio River valley. The Cumberland Road, a federally funded highway linking Maryland and Ohio, reestablished this connection, and Congress passed bills to fund more ambitious federal transportation projects. But President Madison vetoed much of this legislation, believing that it overstepped even a loose interpretation of the Constitution.

Congress also developed new trade routes by negotiating treaties with Indian nations. For instance, an ancient trail from Missouri to Santa Fe, a town in northern Mexico, cut across territory claimed by the Osage Indians. White traders began using the trail in 1821, and four years later Congress approved a treaty with the Osage nation to guarantee right of way for U.S. merchants. In the following decade, the Santa Fe Trail became a critical route for commerce between the United States and Mexico.

East of the Appalachian Mountains, most internal improvement projects were funded by individual states. The most significant of these was New York's **Erie Canal**, a 363-mile waterway stretching from the Mohawk River to Buffalo that was completed in 1825. Tolls on the Erie Canal quickly repaid the tremendous cost of its construction. Freight charges and shipping times plunged. In 1820 transporting a ton of grain by land from Buffalo to New York City cost $100 and took 20 days; in 1825 shipping a ton of grain by canal between those two cities cost only $9 and took 6 days. And by linking western farmers to the Hudson River, the Erie Canal ensured that New York City became the nation's premier seaport (Map 9.2).

The Erie Canal's success inspired hundreds of similar projects in other states. Canals carried manufactured goods from New England and the Middle Atlantic states to rural households in the Ohio River valley. Western farmers, in turn, shipped hogs, hemp, flour, whiskey, and other farm products back east. Just as important, canals linked smaller cities within Pennsylvania and Ohio, facilitating the rise of commercial and manufacturing centers like Harrisburg, Pittsburgh,

ENTERPRISE ON HER FAST TRIP TO LOUISVILLE, 1815.

Steamboat *Enterprise*

In 1814 the steamboat *Enterprise* made its maiden voyage, traveling six hundred miles from Louisville to Pittsburgh. The voyage showed that steamboats could overcome the strong currents of the Ohio River. Later that year, the *Enterprise* departed from Pittsburgh carrying arms to supply General Jackson's troops at New Orleans, proving it could also navigate the waters of the mighty Mississippi River. Beinecke Rare Book and Manuscript Library, Yale University

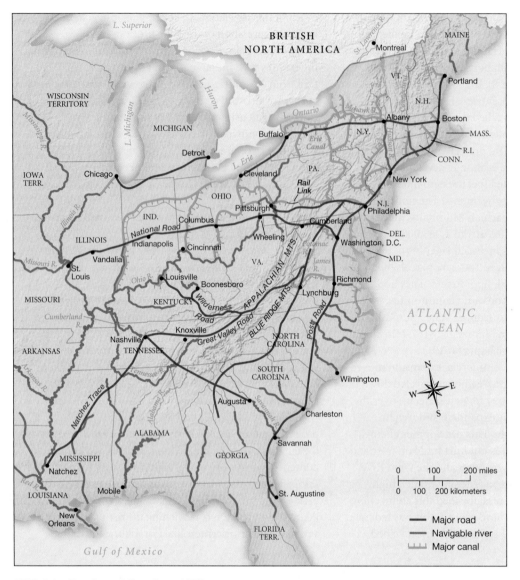

MAP 9.2   Roads and Canals to 1837

During the 1820s and 1830s, state and local governments as well as private companies built roads and canals to foster migration and commercial development. The Erie Canal, completed in 1825, was the most significant of these projects. But many other states, particularly in the Northeast and the old Northwest, sought to duplicate that canal's success over the following decade.

Cincinnati, and Toledo. Canals also allowed vast quantities of coal to be transported out of the Allegheny Mountains, fueling industrial development throughout the Northeast.

Americans Expand the Nation's Borders

In 1816, in the midst of the nation's economic resurgence, James Monroe, a Democratic-Republican from Virginia, won an easy victory in the presidential election over Rufus King, a New York Federalist. Monroe, who had served as secretary of state under Madison, hoped to use improved relations with Great Britain to resolve Indian problems on the frontier. Believing that hostile Indians would "lose their terror" once

the British no longer encouraged them, he sent John Quincy Adams to London to negotiate treaties that limited U.S. and British naval forces on the Great Lakes, set the U.S.-Canadian border at the forty-ninth parallel, and provided for joint British-U.S. occupation of the Oregon Territory. In 1817 and 1818, the Senate approved these treaties, which further limited Indian rights and power in the North.

President Monroe harbored grave concerns about the nation's southern boundary as well. He sought to limit Spain's power in North America and stop Seminole Indians in western Florida and Alabama from claiming lands ceded to the United States by the defeated Creeks. Shifting from diplomacy to military force, in 1817 the president sent

General Andrew Jackson and his Tennessee militia to force the Seminoles back into Florida. Nonetheless, he ordered Jackson to avoid direct conflict with Spanish forces for fear of igniting another war. But in the spring of 1818, having chased the Seminoles deep into Florida, Jackson attacked two Spanish forts, hanged two Seminole chiefs, and executed two British citizens allied with local Indians.

Jackson's attacks spurred outrage among Spanish and British officials and many members of Congress. Indeed, the threat of conflict with Britain, Spain, and hostile Indians prompted President Monroe to establish the nation's first peacetime army in 1818. In the end, however, the British chose to ignore the execution of citizens engaged in "unauthorized" activities, while Spain decided to sell the Florida Territory to the United States rather than fight to retain it. In the Adams-Onís Treaty (1819), negotiated by John Quincy Adams, Spain ceded all its lands east of the Mississippi to the United States along with ancient claims to the Oregon Territory.

Success in acquiring Florida encouraged the administration to look for other opportunities to limit European influence in the Western Hemisphere. By 1822 Argentina, Chile, Peru, Colombia, and Mexico had all overthrown Spanish rule. In March of that year, President Monroe recognized the independence of these southern neighbors, and Congress quickly established diplomatic relations with the new nations. Yet Monroe also secretly attempted to survey Mexican lands in hopes of gaining more territory for the United States. The following year, President Monroe added a codicil to a treaty with Russia that claimed that the Western Hemisphere was part of the U.S. sphere of influence. Although the United States did not have sufficient power to enforce what later became known as the **Monroe Doctrine**, it had quietly declared its intention to challenge Europeans for authority in the Atlantic world.

By the late 1820s, U.S. residents were moving to and trading with newly independent Mexican territories. Southern whites began occupying Mexican lands in east Texas, while midwestern traders traveled the Santa Fe Trail. Meanwhile New England manufacturers and merchants had begun shipping their wares via clipper ships to another Mexican territory, Alta California, whose residents eagerly purchased U.S.-made shoes, cloth, and tools.

Some Americans looked even farther afield. U.S. merchants had begun trading with China in the late eighteenth century, and by the early nineteenth century, ships from eastern ports carried otter pelts and other merchandise across the Pacific, returning with Chinese porcelains and silks. In the 1810s and 1820s, the Alta California and China trades converged, expanding the reach of U.S. merchants and the demand for U.S. manufactured goods. The desire to expand trade also led some Americans to look to the Pacific, especially Hawaii and Samoa, for additional markets and land.

Extended trade routes along with wartime disruptions of European imports fueled the expansion of U.S. manufacturing. By 1813 the area around Providence, Rhode Island, boasted seventy-six spinning mills with more than 51,000 spindles. Two years later, Philadelphia claimed pride of place as the nation's top industrial city, turning out glass, chemicals, metalwork, leather goods, and dozens of other products. Workers in factories, artisans' shops, and homes as well as in prisons and poorhouses contributed to an economic boom that seemed boundless.

Regional Economic Development

Clay's American System was intended to bind the various regions of the United States together. Yet even as roads, rivers, canals, and steamboats helped unify a growing nation, they also reinforced the development of regional economies. Although regional ties remained fluid, between 1815 and 1830 increasingly distinct economies developed that promoted the rise of particular labor systems and political priorities.

In the South, for instance, the defeat of the Creek nation, vast Indian land cessions, and the acquisition of Florida ensured the growth of cotton cultivation, which had been initiated by the invention of the cotton gin (see chapter 8). Although the foreign slave trade had ended in 1808, planters extended slavery into new lands to produce cash crops like cotton, sugar, and rice. They used profits from these goods to buy food from the West and shoes and cloth from the North. Small farmers, too, sought to benefit from rising cotton prices, planting as much of their land in cotton as they could. Because continuous cultivation drained nutrients from the soil, planters and small farmers constantly sought more fertile fields, leading to further pressure on those Indians who still controlled large areas of rich southern soil.

When James and Dolley Madison returned to Montpelier in 1817, they experienced the new possibilities and problems of southern agriculture. Plantation homes in long-settled areas like the Virginia piedmont became more fashionable as they incorporated luxury goods imported from China and Europe. The Madisons entertained hundreds of guests, hosted dinners and dances, and provided beds and meals for three dozen people at a time. But soil exhaustion in the region limited the profits from tobacco and made a shift to cotton impossible. While some Virginia planters made money by selling slaves to other planters farther south, James Madison refused to break up slave families who had worked the plantation for decades. With no desire to leave for lands farther west, he and Dolley were forced to reduce their standard of living.

Other white Americans, however, benefited from the expansion of southern agriculture. Of course, many cotton farmers made substantial profits in the 1810s. So did western farmers, who shipped vast quantities of food and other farm products to the South. Towns like Cincinnati, located across the Ohio River from Kentucky, sprang up as regional centers of commerce. In 1811 Cincinnati settlers still confronted Indians along the nearby White Water River. Eight years later, the booming town was incorporated as a city with nearly ten thousand residents.

Americans living in the Northeast increased their commercial connections with the South as well. Northern merchants became more deeply engaged in the southern cotton trade, opening warehouses in port cities like Savannah and Charleston and sending cotton factors, or agents, into the countryside to broker deals with planters. Meanwhile the southern cotton boom fueled industrial expansion. Indeed, factory owners in New England shipped growing amounts of yarn, thread, and cloth along with shoes, tools, and leather goods to the South. As merchants in New England and New York focused on the cotton trade, those in Philadelphia and Pittsburgh built ties to western farmers, exchanging manufactured goods for agricultural products across the Appalachian Mountains.

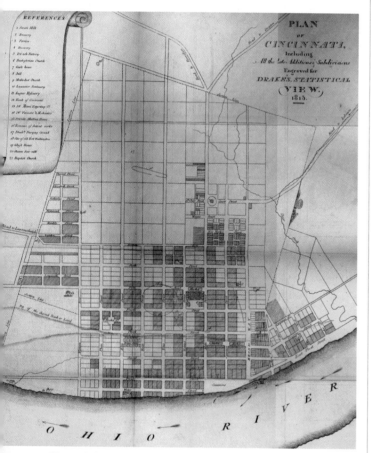

Plan of Cincinnati, 1815

This map, drawn four years before Cincinnati was incorporated as a city, illustrates the importance of the Ohio River to the city's development. Nestled along the riverbank, the village of Cincinnati was laid out in a grid pattern. The map lists a steam mill; two breweries; ferries; a potash factory, sugar refinery, and sawmill; churches; banks; and other important locations. Courtesy Archives & Rare Books Library, University of Cincinnati

REVIEW & RELATE

What role did government play in early-nineteenth-century economic development?

How and why did economic development contribute to regional differences and shape regional ties?

LEARNINGCurve bedfordstmartins.com/hewittlawson/LC

Economic and Political Crises

As America's regions developed distinct economies in the 1810s, they became more, not less, dependent on each other. Western farmers needed manufactured goods from the North; northern manufacturers needed raw cotton from the South; southern planters needed food crops from the West. The growth in trade required the expansion of commercial institutions such as banks, which forged economic links across the United States. This economic integration stimulated the economy, but interdependence also made the nation more vulnerable when financial crises hit. The panic of 1819, the nation's first severe recession, brought economic growth to an abrupt halt. At the same time, when Missouri applied for statehood in 1819, it set off the first serious national debate over slavery.

The Panic of 1819

The **panic of 1819** resulted primarily from irresponsible banking practices in the United States and was deepened by the declining overseas demand for American goods, especially cotton. Beginning in 1816, American banks, including the Second Bank of the United States (BUS), loaned out huge sums to settlers seeking land on the frontier and to merchants and manufacturers expanding their businesses. Many of these loans were not backed by sufficient collateral. Banks, meanwhile, issued notes without adequate hard currency as European governments, fearful of growing turmoil in South America, hoarded gold and silver. State and local banks and their clients were betting on continued economic growth to ensure repayment. Western banks were especially reckless in offering discounted loans. Then, as agricultural production in Europe revived with the end of the Napoleonic Wars, the demand for American foodstuffs dropped sharply. Farm income plummeted by roughly one-third in the late 1810s.

In 1818 the directors of the Second Bank, fearing a continued expansion of the money supply, tightened the credit it provided to branch banks. This sudden effort to curtail credit led to economic panic. Some branch banks failed immediately. Others survived by calling in loans to companies and individuals, who in turn demanded repayment from those to whom they had extended credit. The chain of indebtedness pushed more people to the brink of economic ruin just as factory owners cut their workforce and merchants limited orders for new goods. Both individuals and enterprises faced bankruptcy and foreclosures on mortgages. In New York State, property values fell from a total of $315 million in 1818 to $256 million in 1820. In Richmond, Virginia, property values fell by half during the panic.

Bankruptcies, foreclosures, unemployment, and poverty spread like a plague across the country. Cotton farmers were especially hard hit by declining exports and falling prices. Planters who had gone into debt to purchase land in Alabama and Mississippi were unable to pay their mortgages. Many western residents, who had invested all they had in new farms, lost their land or simply stopped paying their mortgages. This put further strains on state banks, some of which simply collapsed, leaving the Second Bank holding mortgages on vast amounts of western territory. At the same time, public land sales plummeted from $13.6 million in 1818 to $1.3 million in 1821.

Many Americans viewed banks as the cause of the panic. Some states defied the Constitution and the Supreme Court by trying to tax BUS branches or printing state banknotes with no specie (gold or silver) to back them. Some Americans called for government relief, but there was no system to provide the kinds of assistance needed. Meanwhile Congress debated how to reignite the nation's economic engines. Northern manufacturers called for even higher tariffs to protect U.S. products from foreign competition, but southern planters argued that high tariffs raised the price of manufactured goods even as agricultural profits declined. And working men, small farmers, and frontier settlers feared that their economic needs were being ignored by politicians with ties to bankers, planters, manufacturers, and merchants.

By 1823 the panic had largely dissipated, but the prolonged economic crisis had shaken national confidence, and citizens became more skeptical of federal authority and more suspicious of banks. From 1819 until the Civil War, one of the greatest limitations on national expansion remained the cycle of economic expansion and contraction, which was tied ever more closely to unregulated national and international markets. **See Document Project 9: The Panic of 1819, page 284**.

Slavery in Missouri

The spread of slavery fueled a second national crisis. In February 1819, the Missouri Territory applied for statehood. New York congressman James Tallmadge Jr. proposed that it be admitted only if it banned further importation of slaves and passed a gradual emancipation law modeled on those in many northern states. With the support of southern

congressmen, however, whites in the territory defeated Tallmadge's proposals. The northern majority in the House of Representatives then rejected Missouri's admission.

Southern politicians were outraged, claiming that since the Missouri Territory allowed slavery, so should the state of Missouri. Although the region bordered the Northwest Territory, where slavery was outlawed in 1787, it also bordered the slave states of Kentucky and Tennessee. With cotton production moving ever westward, southern congressmen wanted to ensure the availability of new lands. They also wanted to ensure the South's power in Congress. Because the northern population had grown more rapidly than that in the South, by 1819 northern politicians controlled the House of Representatives. The Senate, however, was evenly divided, with two senators representing each state: eleven slave and eleven free. If northerners could block the admission of slave states like Missouri while allowing the admission of free states, the balance of power in the Senate would tip in the North's favor. Thus southern senators blocked the admission of Maine, which sought to separate itself from Massachusetts and become a free state.

For southern planters, the decision on Missouri defined the future of slavery. With foreign trade in slaves outlawed, planters relied on natural increase and trading slaves from older to newer areas of cultivation to meet the demand for labor. Moreover, with free blacks packing the congressional galleries in Washington to listen to congressmen debate Missouri statehood, supporters of slavery worried that divisions among whites could fuel resistance to slavery and even open revolt. Two rebellions had occurred in recent memory. In 1811 some four hundred slaves in Louisiana had killed two whites and burned several plantations. Their advance on New Orleans was stopped only when U.S. troops killed more than sixty rebels. Even more immediately, several hundred fugitive slaves had joined forces with Seminole Indians in 1817, raiding Georgia plantations and establishing autonomous communities in central Florida. Andrew Jackson's 1818 attack halted their activities, but most of the fugitive blacks escaped deep into Florida.

In 1820 Representative Henry Clay of Kentucky forged a compromise that resolved the immediate issues and promised a long-term solution. Maine was to be admitted as a free state and Missouri as a slave state, thereby maintaining the balance between North and South in the U.S. Senate (Map 9.3). At the same time, Congress agreed that the southern border of Missouri—latitude 36°30′—was to serve as the boundary between slave and free states throughout the Louisiana Territory.

Explore

Compare two critiques of the Missouri Compromise in Documents 9.2 and 9.3.

DOCUMENTS 9.2 AND 9.3

Protesting the Missouri Compromise: Two Views

Missouri's statehood application sparked a crisis over the future of slavery in America, and the resulting Missouri Compromise did little to ease the fears of Americans who wanted to contain its spread. Timothy Claimright and Thomas Jefferson both opposed the Missouri Compromise, but they offered different reasons for doing so. Claimright of Brunswick, Maine, argues in a poem published as a broadside that his home state should not join the Union if it means inviting the admission of Missouri as a slave state. Thomas Jefferson predicts in a letter that the temporary solution of the compromise will only lead to a future tragedy.

Explore

9.2 Timothy Claimright | Maine Not to Be Coupled with the Missouri Question, 1820

If the South will not yield, to the West be it known,
That Maine will declare for a *King* of her own;
And *three hundred thousand* of freemen demand
The justice bestow'd on each State in the land.
Free whites of the East are not blacks of the West,
And Republican souls on this principle rest,
That if no respect to their rights can be shown,
They know how to vindicate what are their own. . . .

They are founded on freedom, humanity's right,
Ordained by God against slavery to fight.
And Heaven born liberty sooner than yield,
The whites of Missouri shall dress their own field.
We are hardy and healthy, can till our own soil,
In labour delight; make a pleasure of toil. . . .
They too lazy to work, drive slaves, whom they fear;
We school our own children, and brew our own beer.
We do a day's work and go fearless to bed;
Tho' lock'd up, they dream of slaves, whom they dread. . . .
They may boast of their blacks; we boast of our plenty,
And swear to be free, eighteen hundred and twenty.
South and West, now be honest, to MAINE give her due,
If you call her a child, she's an Hercules too.
A Sister in Union admit her, as free;
To be coupled with slaves, she will never agree.

Source: Timothy Claimright, *Maine Not to Be Coupled with the Missouri Question* (Brunswick, ME, 1820), Library of Congress Ephemera Collection.

9.3 Thomas Jefferson | Letter to John Holmes, 1820

Monticello, April 22, 1820

I thank you, dear Sir, for the copy you have been so kind as to send me of the letter to your constituents on the Missouri question. It is a perfect justification to them. I had for a long time ceased to read newspapers, or pay any attention to public affairs, confident they were in good hands, and content to be a passenger in our bark [ship] to the shore from which I am not distant. But this momentous question, like a fire-bell in the night, awakened and filled me with terror. I considered it at once as the knell of the Union. It is hushed, indeed, for the moment. But this is a reprieve only, not a final sentence. A geographical line, coinciding with a marked principle, moral and political, once conceived and held up to the angry passions of men, will never be obliterated; and every new irritation will mark it deeper and deeper. I can say, with conscious truth, that there is not a man on earth who would sacrifice more than I would to relieve us from this heavy reproach, in any *practicable* way. The cession of that kind of property [slavery], for so it is misnamed, is a bagatelle [an insignificant thing] which would not cost me a second thought, if, in that way, a general emancipation and *expatriation* could be effected; and, gradually, and with due sacrifices, I think it might be. But as it is, we have the wolf by the ears, and we can neither hold him, nor safely let him go. Justice is in one scale, and self-preservation in the other. Of one thing I am certain, that as the passage of slaves from one State to another, would not make a slave of a single human being who would not be so without it, so their diffusion over a greater surface would make them individually happier, and proportionally facilitate the accomplishment of their emancipation, by dividing the burthen on a greater number of coadjutors.

Source: Thomas Jefferson Randolph, ed., *Memoirs, Correspondence, and Private Papers of Thomas Jefferson* (London: Henry Colburn and Richard Bentley, 1829), 4:332.

Interpret the Evidence

- Why does Claimright oppose the Missouri Compromise? How does he differentiate Maine and other northern states from the slave societies of the South?
- Why does Jefferson believe that the Missouri Compromise would exacerbate the conflict over slavery? Does he offer a solution to the slavery issue in the United States?

Put It in Context

How might supporters of the Missouri Compromise have responded to the arguments of Claimright and Jefferson?

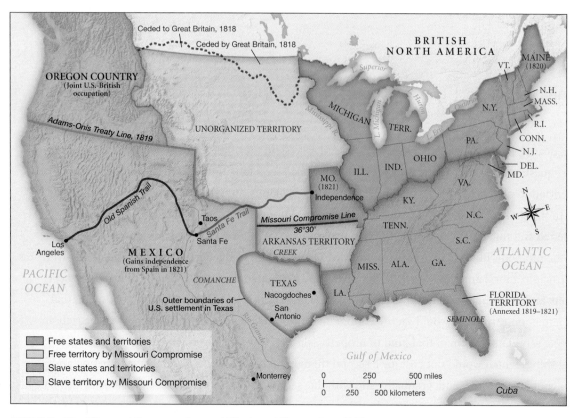

MAP 9.3   The Missouri Compromise and Westward Expansion, 1820s

The debate over the Missouri Compromise occurred just as the United States began expanding farther westward. Within a few years of its adoption, the growth of U.S. settlements in eastern Texas and increased trade with a newly independent Mexico suggested the importance of drawing a clear boundary between slave and free states.

The **Missouri Compromise** gained the support of a majority of representatives and senators and ended the crisis for the moment. Still, the debates made clear how quickly a disagreement over slavery could escalate into clashes that threatened the survival of the nation.

REVIEW & RELATE

What were the political consequences of the panic of 1819?

What regional divisions did the conflict over slavery in Missouri reveal?

✔ *LEARNINGCurve* bedfordstmartins.com/hewittlawson/LC

Redefining American Democracy

With the frontier moving ever westward and the panic of 1819 shaking many Americans' faith in traditional political and economic leaders, the nation was ripe for

change. Working men, small farmers, and frontier settlers, who had long been locked out of the electoral system by property qualifications and eastern elites, demanded the right to vote. They also looked for a different kind of candidate to champion their cause. Frontier heroes like Andrew Jackson, with few ties to banks, business, and eastern power brokers, appealed to this new constituency. The resulting political movement widened voting rights in the United States and brought more diverse groups of men into the electorate. Yet the new democratic movement advanced the interests only of white men. During the 1820s, African Americans lost political and civil rights in most northern and western states. Indians, too, fared poorly under the new political regime. While some white women gained greater access to political activities as a result of the expanded voting rights of fathers and husbands, they did not achieve independent political rights. Finally, during the 1820s and 1830s, ongoing conflicts over slavery, tariffs, and the rights of Indian nations transformed party alignments as a wave of new voters entered the political fray.

Expanding Voting Rights

Between 1788 and 1820, the U.S. presidency was dominated by Virginia elites and after 1800 by Democratic-Republicans. With little serious political opposition at the national level, few people bothered to vote in presidential elections. Far more people engaged in partisan and popular political activities at the state and local level. Many towns held public celebrations on the Fourth of July and election days, and politicians of every stripe invited women to participate. Female participants often sewed symbols of their partisan loyalties on their clothes and joined in parades and feasts organized by men.

This popular political activity stimulated interest in presidential elections following the panic of 1819, when, as Scottish traveler James Flint noted, "the faith of the people was shaken." Laboring men, who were especially vulnerable to economic downturns, demanded the right to vote as a means of forcing politicians to respond to their concerns.

In New York State, Martin Van Buren, a rising star in the Democratic-Republican Party, led the fight to eliminate property qualifications for voting. At the state constitutional convention of 1821, the committee on suffrage reflected his views, arguing that the only qualification for voting should be "the virtue and morality of the people." By the word *people*, Van Buren and the committee meant white men, but even this limited demand aroused heated opposition. A year earlier, attorney Daniel Webster had been elected to the Massachusetts constitutional convention, where he argued vociferously that "political power naturally and necessarily goes into the hands which hold the property."

Although many wealthy conservatives supported Webster's views, he lost the debate, and both Massachusetts and New York instituted universal white male suffrage. By 1825 most states along the Atlantic seaboard had lowered or eliminated property qualifications on

Election Day in Philadelphia, 1815
John Lewis Krimmel, a recent German immigrant, painted this image of an election day celebration in Philadelphia in 1815. The image highlights the widespread popular participation of men, women, and children in political events even before the expansion of voting rights for white men in the 1820s.　Courtesy, Winterthur Museum

white male voters. Meanwhile states along the frontier that had joined the Union in the 1810s established universal white male suffrage from the beginning. And by 1824 three-quarters of the states (18 of 24) allowed voters, rather than state legislatures, to elect members of the electoral college.

Yet as white men gained political rights in the 1820s, democracy did not spread to other groups. Indian nations were considered sovereign entities, so Indians voted in their own nations, not in U.S. elections. Women were excluded from voting because of their perceived dependence on men. New Jersey had granted single or widowed property-owning women the right to vote during the Revolution, but in 1807 the state legislature rescinded that right—along with suffrage for African American men—when small numbers of female and black voters proved they could make a difference in contested elections.

African American men faced challenges to their rights well beyond New Jersey. No southern legislature had ever granted blacks the right to vote, and in the 1820s northern states began to disfranchise African Americans. In many cases, expanded voting rights for white men went hand in hand with new restrictions on black men. In New York State, for example, the constitution of 1821, which eliminated property qualifications for white men, raised property qualifications for African American voters, disfranchising most African Americans in the state in the process.

When African American men protested their disfranchisement in northern states, some whites spoke out on their behalf. They claimed that denying rights to men who had in no way abused the privilege of voting set "an ominous and dangerous precedent." In response, opponents of black suffrage offered explicitly racist justifications. Some worried that blacks might eventually secure seats in state legislatures, on juries, and in Congress. Some argued that black voting would lead to interracial socializing, even marriage. However, the growing population of free blacks in northern cities posed the greatest threat. Once again, white politicians feared that black voters might hold the balance of power in close elections, forcing white civic leaders to accede to their demands. Gradually, racist arguments won the day, and by 1840, 93 percent of free blacks in the North were excluded from voting.

Racial Restrictions and Antiblack Violence

Restrictions on voting followed other constraints on African American men and women. As early as 1790, Congress limited naturalization (the process of becoming a citizen) to white aliens, or immigrants. It also excluded blacks from enrolling in federal militias. In 1820 Congress authorized city officials in Washington, D.C., to adopt a separate legal code governing free blacks and slaves. This federal legislation encouraged states to add their own restrictions, including segregation of public schools, public transportation, and public accommodations like churches and theaters. Such laws were passed in the North as well as in the South. Some northern legislatures even denied African Americans the right to settle in their state.

In addition, blacks faced mob and state-sanctioned violence across the country. In 1822 officials in Charleston, South Carolina, accused Denmark Vesey of following the revolutionary leader Toussaint L'Ouverture's lead and plotting a conspiracy to free the city's slaves. One of 1,500 free blacks residing in the city, Vesey had helped to organize churches, mutual aid societies, and other black institutions. Whites viewed these efforts as a threat to the future of slavery because such accomplishments challenged assumptions about black inferiority. Vesey may have organized a plan to free slaves in the city, but it is also possible that white officials concocted the plot in order to terrorize free blacks and slaves in the area and to shore up the power of ruling white elites. Despite scant evidence, Vesey and 34 of his alleged co-conspirators were found guilty and hanged. Another 18 were exiled outside the United States. The African Methodist Episcopal church where they supposedly planned the insurrection was torn down.

Northern blacks also suffered from violent attacks by whites. Assaults on individual African Americans often went unrecorded, but race riots received greater attention. For example, in 1829 white residents of Cincinnati attacked black neighborhoods, and more than half of the city's black residents fled. Many of them resettled in Ontario, Canada. They were soon joined by Philadelphia blacks who had been attacked by groups of white residents in 1832. Such attacks continued in northern cities throughout the 1830s.

Political Realignments

Restrictions on black political and civil rights converged with the decline of the Federalists in the North. Federalist majorities in New York State had approved the gradual abolition law of 1799. In 1821 New York Federalists advocated equal rights for black and white voters as long as property qualifications limited suffrage to respectable citizens. But Federalists were losing power by this time, and the concerns of African Americans were low on the Democratic-Republican agenda.

Struggles among Democratic-Republicans in the 1820s turned to a large extent on the same issue that had earlier divided them from Federalists: the limits of federal power. After nearly a quarter century in power, many Democratic-Republicans embraced a more expansive view of federal authority and a looser interpretation of the U.S.

Constitution. Yet others in the party argued forcefully for a return to Jeffersonian principles of limited federal power and a strict construction of the Constitution. At the same time, rising young politicians—like Martin Van Buren and Andrew Jackson—and newly enfranchised voters sought to seize control of the party from its longtime leaders.

The election of 1824 brought these conflicts to a head, splitting the Democratic-Republicans into rival factions that by 1828 had coalesced into two distinct entities: the **Democrats** and the **National Republicans**. Unable to agree on a single presidential candidate in 1824, the Democratic-Republican congressional caucus fractured into four camps backing separate candidates: John Quincy Adams, Andrew Jackson, Henry Clay, and Secretary of the Treasury William Crawford. John C. Calhoun, Monroe's secretary of war, eventually threw his support behind Jackson and sought the vice presidency.

As the race developed, Adams and Jackson emerged as the two strongest candidates. John Quincy Adams's stature rested on his diplomatic achievements and the reputation of his father, former president John Adams. Like Clay, he favored internal improvements and protective tariffs that would bolster northern industry and commerce. Jackson, on the other hand, relied largely on his fame as a war hero and Indian fighter to inspire popular support. Like Crawford, he advocated limited federal power.

As a candidate who appealed to ordinary voters, Jackson held a decided edge. Jackson, outgoing and boisterous, claimed to support "good old Jeffersonian Democratic republican principles" and organized a campaign that took his case to the people. Emphasizing his humble origins, he appealed to small farmers and northern workers who hoped to emulate his success as a self-made man. Just as important, Jackson gained the support of Van Buren, who also wanted to expand the political clout of the "common [white] man" and limit the reach of a central government that was becoming too powerful.

The four presidential candidates created a truly competitive race. With more white men eligible to vote and more states allowing voters to choose members of the electoral college, turnout at the polls increased to more than a quarter of eligible voters. Jackson won the popular vote by carrying Pennsylvania, New Jersey, the Carolinas, and much of the West and led in the electoral college with 99 electors. But with no candidate gaining an absolute majority in the electoral college, the Constitution called for the House of Representatives to choose the president from the three leading contenders—Jackson, Adams, and Crawford. Clay, who came in fourth, asked his supporters to back Adams, ensuring his election. Once in office, President Adams appointed Clay his secretary of state. Jackson claimed that the two had engineered a "corrupt

bargain" that denied the will of the people. Yet the decisions of Clay and Adams involved a logical alliance between two candidates who agreed on the need to increase federal investment in internal improvements, raise tariffs, and expand the powers of the BUS.

But when President Adams sought to implement his agenda, he ran into vigorous opposition in Congress led by Van Buren. Calhoun, who had been elected vice president, also opposed his policies. Van Buren argued against federal funding for internal improvements since New York State had financed the Erie Canal with its own monies. Calhoun, meanwhile, joined other southern politicians in opposing any expansion of federal power for fear it would then be used to restrict the spread of slavery.

The most serious battle in Congress, however, involved tariffs. The tariff of 1816 had excluded most cheap English cotton cloth from the United States, thereby allowing New England textile manufacturers to gain control of the domestic market. In 1824 the tariff was extended to more expensive cotton and woolen cloth and to iron goods. During the presidential campaign, Adams and Clay appealed to northern voters by advocating even higher duties on these items. When Adams introduced tariff legislation that extended duties to raw materials like wool, hemp, and molasses, he gained support from both Jackson and Van Buren, who considered these tariffs beneficial to farmers on the frontier. Despite the opposition of Vice President Calhoun and congressmen from older southern states, the tariff of 1828 was approved, raising duties on imports to an average of 62 percent.

The tariff of 1828, however, was Adams's only notable legislative victory. His foreign policy was also stymied by a hostile Congress. Moreover, Jackson's supporters gained a majority in the midterm elections of 1826, intensifying conflicts among Democratic-Republicans. Adams thus entered the 1828 election campaign with little to show in the way of domestic or foreign achievements, and Jackson and his supporters took full advantage of the president's political vulnerability.

The Presidential Election of 1828

The election of 1828 tested the power of the two major factions in the Democratic-Republican Party. President Adams followed the traditional approach of "standing" for office. He told supporters, "If my country wants my services, she must ask for them." Jackson and his supporters, who deeply distrusted established political leaders, chose instead to "run" for office. They took their case directly to the voters, introducing innovative techniques to create enthusiasm among the electorate.

Van Buren managed the first truly national political campaign in U.S. history, seeking to re-create the original Democratic-Republican coalition among farmers, northern artisans, and southern planters while adding a sizable constituency of frontier voters. He was aided in the effort by Calhoun, who again ran for vice president and supported the Tennessee war hero despite their disagreement over tariffs. Jackson's supporters organized state party conventions to nominate him for president rather than relying on the congressional caucus. They established local Jackson committees in critical states such as Virginia and New York. They organized newspaper campaigns and developed a logo, the hickory leaf, based on the candidate's nickname "Old Hickory."

Jackson traveled the country to build loyalty to himself as well as to his party. His Tennessee background, rise to great wealth, and reputation as an Indian fighter ensured his popularity among southern and western voters. He also reassured southerners that he advocated "judicious" duties on imports, suggesting that he might try to lower the rates imposed in 1828. At the same time, his support of the tariff of 1828 and his military credentials created enthusiasm among northern working men and frontier farmers.

President Adams's supporters demeaned the "dissolute" and "rowdy" men who poured out for Jackson rallies, and they also launched personal attacks on the candidate.

Dragging politicians' private lives into public view was nothing new, but opposition papers focused their venom this time on the candidate's wife, Rachel. They questioned the timing of her divorce from her first husband and remarriage to Jackson, suggesting she was an adulterer and a bigamist. Rachel Jackson felt humiliated, but her husband refused to be intimidated by scandal.

Adams distanced himself from his own campaign. He sought to demonstrate his statesmanlike gentility by letting others speak for him. This strategy worked well when only men of wealth and property could vote. But with an enlarged electorate and an astonishing turnout of more than 50 percent of eligible voters, Adams's approach failed and Jackson became president. Jackson won handily in the South and the West and carried most of the Middle Atlantic states as well as New York. Adams dominated only in New England (Figure 9.1).

The election of 1828 formalized a new party alignment. During the campaign, Jackson and his supporters referred to themselves as "the Democracy" and forged a new national Democratic Party. In response, Adams's supporters called themselves National Republicans. The competition between Democrats and National Republicans heightened interest in national politics among ordinary voters and ensured that the innovative techniques introduced by Jackson would be widely adopted in future campaigns.

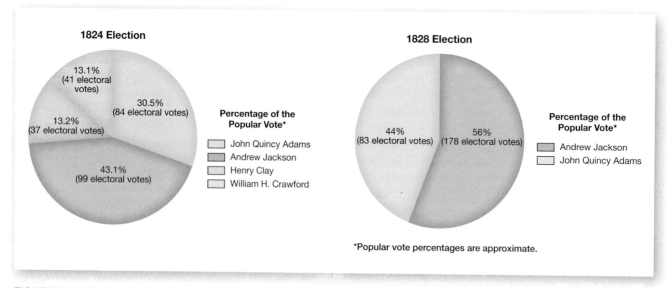

FIGURE 9.1   The Elections of 1824 and 1828

Andrew Jackson lost the 1824 election to John Quincy Adams when the decision was thrown into the House of Representatives. In 1828 Jackson launched the first popular campaign for president, mobilizing working-class white men who were newly enfranchised. Three times as many men—more than one million voters—cast ballots in 1828 than in 1824, ensuring Jackson's election as president.

REVIEW & RELATE

How and why did the composition of the electorate change in the 1820s?

How did Jackson's 1828 campaign represent a significant departure from earlier patterns in American politics?

✔ *LEARNINGCurve* bedfordstmartins.com/hewittlawson/LC

Jacksonian Democracy in Action

Many ordinary Americans held high expectations for Jackson's presidency, and Jackson hoped to make government more responsive to the "common man." But the president's notion of democracy, while inclusive of white men regardless of wealth or property, did not extend to Indians or African Americans. During his presidency, Indian nations would actively resist his efforts to take more of their land, and blacks would continue to resist their enslavement. Of more immediate importance, since President Jackson had to take clear positions on tariffs and other controversial issues, he could not please all of his constituents. He also confronted experienced adversaries like Clay, Webster, and John Quincy Adams, who was elected to the House of Representatives from Massachusetts in 1830. The president thus faced considerable difficulty in translating popular support into public policy.

A Democratic Spirit?

On March 4, 1829, crowds of ordinary citizens came to see their hero's inauguration. Jackson's wife Rachel had died less than three months earlier, leaving her husband devastated. Now Jackson, dressed in a plain black suit, walked alone to the Capitol as vast throngs of supporters waved and cheered. Wealthy planters were jammed shoulder to shoulder with frontier farmers and working men and

President Andrew Jackson's First Inauguration, 1829

This illustration by the British artist Robert Cruikshank, entitled *President's Levee, or All Creation Going to the White House*, depicts crowds in front of the White House during Andrew Jackson's first inaugural reception in 1829. The crowds of ordinary people were so enthusiastic and unrestrained that President Jackson had to flee out the back of the White House to escape injury.   The Granger Collection, New York

women. Local African Americans also turned out for the spectacle. A somber Jackson read a brief inaugural address, took the oath of office, and then rode his horse through the crowds to the White House.

The size and enthusiasm of the crowds soon shattered the decorum of the inauguration. Author Margaret Bayard Smith reported mobs "scrambling, fighting, [and] romping" through the White House reception. Jackson was nearly crushed to death by "rabble" eager to shake his hand. Tubs of punch laced with rum, brandy, and champagne were finally placed on the lawn to draw the crowds outdoors.

Nonetheless, Jackson and his supporters viewed the event as a symbol of a new democratic spirit. Others were less optimistic. Bayard Smith warned against putting too much faith in "the people," who "have been found in all ages and countries where they get power in their hands, that of all tyrants, they are the most ferocious, cruel, and despotic." She and other conservative political leaders also saw echoes of the French Revolution in the unruly behavior of the masses. Supreme Court justice Joseph Story, too, feared "the reign of King 'Mob.'"

Tensions between the president and the capital's traditional leaders intensified in the first months of his administration. Jackson's appointment of Tennessee senator John Eaton as secretary of war added to the rancor. Eaton had had an affair with a woman thought to be of questionable character and later married her. When Jackson announced his plans to appoint Eaton to his cabinet, congressional leaders urged him to reconsider. When the president appointed Eaton anyway, the wives of Washington's leading politicians snubbed Mrs. Eaton and refused to accept her social calls. This time Jackson was outmaneuvered in what became known as the **Petticoat Affair**, and Eaton was eventually forced from office.

From the days of Dolley Madison, political wives had wielded considerable influence in Washington. In 1831 they pressured Eaton to resign. But the Petticoat Affair also led Jackson's entire cabinet to resign, after which his legislative agenda stalled in Congress and National Republicans regained the momentum lost after Adams's defeat. The Eaton appointment had reinforced concerns that the president used his authority to reward his friends. So, too, did his reliance on an informal group of advisers, known as the Kitchen Cabinet, rather than his official cabinet. While his administration opened up government posts to a wider range of individuals, ensuring more democratic access, he often selected appointees based on personal ties. The resulting **spoils system**—introduced by Jackson and continued by future administrations—assigned federal posts as gifts for partisan loyalty rather than as jobs that required experience or expertise.

Confrontations over Tariffs and the Bank

The Democratic Party that emerged in the late 1820s was built on an unstable foundation. The coalition that formed around Jackson included northern workers who benefited from high tariffs as well as southern farmers and planters who did not. It brought together western voters who sought federal support for internal improvements and strict constructionists who believed that such expenditures were unconstitutional. Weakened by conflicts over appointments, Jackson had to decide which factions to reward. In 1830 Congress passed four internal improvement bills with strong support from National Republicans. Jackson vetoed each one, claiming that the "voice of the people" demanded careful spending. These vetoes worried his frontier supporters but pleased his southern constituency.

Southern congressmen, however, were more interested in his stand on tariffs. The tariff of 1828 still enraged many southern planters and politicians, but most believed that once Jackson reached the White House, he would reverse course and reduce this "Tariff of Abominations." Instead, he avoided the issue, and southern agriculture continued to suffer. Agricultural productivity in Virginia, South Carolina, and other states of the Old South was declining from soil exhaustion, while prices for staples like cotton and rice had not fully recovered after the panic of 1819. At the same time, higher duties on manufactured items meant that southerners had to pay more for the goods they bought.

Even as Calhoun campaigned with Jackson in 1828, the South Carolinian developed a philosophical argument to negate the effects of high tariffs on his state. Like opponents of the War of 1812, Calhoun drew on states' rights doctrines outlined in the Kentucky and Virginia Resolutions of 1798 (see chapter 7). In *The South Carolina Exposition and Protest*, published anonymously in 1828, Calhoun argued that states should have the ultimate power to determine the constitutionality of laws passed by Congress. When Jackson, after taking office, realized that his vice president advocated **nullification**—the right of individual states to declare individual laws void within their borders—it further damaged their relationship, which was already frayed by the Eaton affair.

When Congress debated the tariff issue in 1830, South Carolina senator Robert Hayne defended nullification. He claimed that the North intended to crush the South economically and that only the right of states to nullify federal legislation could protect southern society. In response, Daniel Webster denounced nullification and the states' rights doctrine on which it was built. At a banquet held after the Hayne-Webster debate, Jackson further antagonized southern political leaders by supporting Webster's position.

Matters worsened in 1832 when northern and western congressmen ignored their southern counterparts and confirmed the high duties set four years earlier. Jackson signed the 1832 tariff into law. In response, South Carolina held a special convention that approved an Ordinance of Nullification. It stated that duties on imports would not be collected in the state after February 1, 1833, and threatened secession if federal authorities tried to collect them. Many of the state's residents believed armed conflict was at hand, and some planters raised regiments to secure their property and defend what they viewed as the state's rights.

The tariff crisis thus escalated in the fall of 1832 just as Jackson faced reelection. The tariff debates had angered many southerners, and Calhoun refused to run again as his vice president. Fortunately for Jackson, however, opponents in Congress had provided him with another issue that could unite his supporters and highlight his commitment to the common man: the renewal of the BUS charter.

Clay and Webster persuaded Nicholas Biddle, head of the BUS, to request an early recharter of the bank. Jackson's opponents in Congress knew they had the votes to pass a new charter in the summer of 1832, and they hoped Jackson would veto the bill and thereby split the Democratic Party just before the fall elections. The Second Bank was a political quagmire. Although a private institution, it was chartered, or granted the right to operate, by the federal government, which owned 20 percent of its stock. The bank had stabilized the economy during the 1820s by regularly demanding specie (gold or silver) payments from state-chartered banks. This kept those banks from issuing too much paper money and thereby prevented inflation and higher prices. The Second Bank's tight-money policies also kept banks from expanding too rapidly in the western states. Bankers, merchants, and entrepreneurs in eastern cities as well as most planters applauded the bank's efforts, but its tight-money policies aroused hostility among the wider public. When state-chartered banks closed because of lack of specie, ordinary Americans were often stuck with worthless paper money. Tight-money policies also made it more difficult for individuals to get credit to purchase land, homes, or farm equipment.

As the president's opponents had hoped, Congress approved the new charter, and Jackson vetoed it. Yet rather than dividing the Democrats, Jackson's veto gained enormous support from voters across the country. In justifying his action, the president cast the Second Bank as a "monster" that was "dangerous to the liberties of the people"—particularly farmers, mechanics, and laborers—and promoted "the advancement of the few." Finally, Jackson noted that wealthy Britons owned substantial shares of the bank's stock and that national pride demanded ending the Second Bank's reign over the U.S. economy. Jackson rode the enthusiasm for his bank veto to

reelection over National Republican candidate Henry Clay. Within a year, the Second Bank was dead, deprived of government deposits by Jackson.

Explore

For a satirical view of Jackson's attack on the BUS, see Document 9.4.

Soon after his reelection, however, the president faced a grave political crisis related to the tariff issue. Jackson now supported lower tariffs, but he was adamant in his opposition to nullification. In early 1833, he persuaded Congress to pass a Force Bill, which gave him authority to use the military to enforce national laws in South Carolina. At the same time, Jackson made clear that he would work with Congress to reduce tariffs, allowing South Carolina to rescind its nullification ordinance without losing face. Open conflict was averted, but the question of nullification was not resolved.

Contesting Indian Removal

On another long-standing issue—the acquisition of Indian land—Jackson gained the support of white southerners and most frontier settlers. Yet not all Americans agreed with his effort to remove or exterminate Indians. In the 1820s, nations like the Cherokee that sought to maintain their homelands gained the support of Protestant missionaries who hoped to "civilize" Indians by converting them to Christianity and "American" ways. In 1819 Congress had granted these groups federal funds to establish schools and churches to help acculturate and convert Indian men and women. Presidents James Monroe and John Quincy Adams supported the rights of Indians to maintain their sovereignty if they embraced missionary goals. Jackson was much less supportive of efforts to incorporate Indians into the United States and sided with political leaders who sought to force eastern Indians to accept homelands west of the Mississippi River.

In 1825, three years before Jackson was elected president, Creek Indians in Georgia and Alabama were forcibly removed to Unorganized Territory (previously part of Arkansas Territory and later called Indian Territory) based on a fraudulent treaty. Jackson supported this policy. When he became president, politicians and settlers in Georgia, Florida, the Carolinas, and Illinois demanded federal assistance to force Indian communities out of their states.

The largest Indian nations vehemently protested their removal. The Cherokees, who had fought against the Creeks alongside Jackson at Horseshoe Bend, adopted a republican form of government in 1827 based on the U.S. Constitution. John Ross served as the president of the Cherokee constitutional convention, and a year later he was

General Jackson Slaying the Many Headed Monster, 1836

Few issues exposed the differences between the Democrats and the National Republicans more clearly than the battle over the national bank. This political cartoon depicts President Andrew Jackson, holding a cane marked "Veto," with his ally Vice President Martin Van Buren and a character named Major Jack Downing. The three attempt to slay "the many headed monster." The American humorist Seba Smith created the fictional Downing to represent a provincial Maine "down-easterner" who used a very broad dialect. He was presented as a close chum of Andrew Jackson to satirize the goings-on in Washington. The hydra features the faces of Nicholas Biddle, the president of the Bank of the United States, and other men who represent the banks of the various states. Biddle wears a hat that says "Penn" and "$35,000,000," which refers to the state of Pennsylvania's effort to recharter the BUS in defiance of Jackson's efforts to destroy it.

Explore

How does the artist characterize Jackson, Van Buren, and Downing?

How does Jackson intend to eliminate the bank?

Why do you think the artist portrayed the banks as a hydra?

GENERAL JACKSON SLAYING THE MANY HEADED MONSTER.

Private Collection/Peter Newark American Pictures/The Bridgeman Art Library

Put It in Context

What do you think the artist believes about the feasibility of the Jackson administration's efforts to destroy the bank?

Cherokee Phoenix

As U.S. officials pressured the Cherokee nation to relocate west of the Mississippi River, Cherokee leaders sought to convince them that the tribe had become Americanized. Elias Boudinot, whose Cherokee name was Galagina Uwatie, attended Christian mission schools and married a white woman. In 1828 he published the bilingual *Phoenix* to build internal unity and gather support against Cherokee removal.   Library of Congress

chosen principal chief in the first constitutional election. He and the other chiefs then declared themselves a sovereign nation within the borders of the United States. The Georgia legislature rejected the Cherokee claims of independence and argued that Indians were simply guests of the state. When Ross appealed to Jackson to recognize Cherokee sovereignty, the president refused. Instead, Jackson proclaimed that Georgia, like other states, was "sovereign over the people within its borders." At his urging, Congress passed the **Indian Removal Act** in 1830, by which the Cherokee and other Indian nations would be forced to exchange ancient claims on lands in the Southeast for a "clear title forever" on territory west of the Mississippi River. Still, the majority of Cherokees refused to accept these terms and worked assiduously to maintain control of their existing territory.

As the dispute between the Cherokee nation and Georgia unfolded, Jackson made clear his intention to implement the Indian Removal Act. In 1832 he sent federal troops into western Illinois to force Sauk and Fox peoples to move farther west. Instead, whole villages, led by Chief

Black Hawk, fled to the Wisconsin Territory. Black Hawk and a thousand warriors confronted U.S. troops at Bad Axe, but the Sauk and Fox warriors were decimated in a brutal daylong battle. The survivors were forced to move west. Meanwhile the Seminole Indians, who had fought against Jackson when he invaded Florida in 1818, prepared for another pitched battle to protect their territory, while John Ross pursued legal means to resist removal through state and federal courts. The contest for Indian lands would continue well past Jackson's presidency, but the president's desire to force indigenous nations westward would ultimately prevail.

REVIEW & RELATE

What did President Jackson's response to the Eaton affair and Indian removal reveal about his vision of democracy?

To what extent did Jackson's policies favor the South? Which policies benefited or antagonized which groups of Southerners?

✓ LEARNING Curve bedfordstmartins.com/hewittlawson/LC

Conclusion: The Nation Faces New Challenges

From the 1810s through the early 1830s, the United States was buffeted by a series of crises. The War of 1812 threatened the stability of the nation, not only due to attacks on its recently constructed capital city but also because New Englanders so deeply opposed the conflict that some considered seceding from the Union. The panic of 1819 then threw the nation into economic turmoil and led to demands for expanded voting rights for white men. It also heightened disputes over banks and tariffs as residents of various regions and classes sought to ensure their own financial security. The admission of Missouri similarly intensified debates over slavery as white southerners saw themselves losing out in population growth and political representation to the North. At the same time, the western expansion that allowed territories like Missouri to claim statehood also escalated struggles over Indian rights. By the 1820s, those struggles involved a diverse array of Indian nations as well as deep differences among white Americans over the future of native peoples who had embraced Christianity and other forms of "civilization."

In navigating these difficult issues, some Americans sought to find a middle ground. Dolley Madison worked to overcome partisan divisions through social networking. After the death of her husband, James, in 1836, she returned to Washington where her house on Lafayette Street became a center of social activity for politicians, ambassadors, and their wives. Although her son's mismanagement of Montpelier forced her to sell the beloved estate, Dolley secured her old age when Congress purchased President James Madison's papers from her. Similarly, John Ross wielded his biracial heritage to seek rights for Indians within a white-dominated world. He served as both a lobbyist for Cherokee interests in Washington and an advocate of acculturation to Anglo-American ways among the Cherokee. Still, congressional passage of the Indian Removal Act in 1830 challenged Ross's efforts to maintain his tribe's sovereignty and homeland. When Henry Clay was reelected to the U.S. Senate in November 1831, he spoke out against Cherokee removal. But Clay was more widely known for helping to forge key compromises on the admission of Missouri and on tariffs. In each case, he hoped to bring a deeply divided Congress together and provide time for the nation's political leaders to develop more permanent solutions.

Yet despite the efforts of Madison, Ross, Clay and others, differences often led to division in the 1820s and 1830s. Indeed, Henry Clay provided the final push that ensured John Quincy Adams's selection as president in 1824. In the aftermath of that election, two distinct political parties emerged out of the once-united Democratic-Republicans: the Democrats and the National Republicans. In the context of the political, military, and economic upheaval that marked the early Republic, it is not surprising that a charismatic but divisive figure like Andrew Jackson emerged to lead the new Democratic Party. Transforming the process of political campaigning, he gave voice to the "common man," but he also introduced the spoils system to government, smashed the Second Bank of the United States, and forced thousands of Indians off their lands. The extermination and removal of Indians then fostered the geographical expansion of American settlements southward and westward, ensuring the growth of slavery.

Dolley Madison, who lived into the late 1840s, and John Ross, who survived the Civil War, observed the continuing conflicts created by geographical expansion and partisan agendas. Madison remained a beloved figure in Washington, escorted through the Executive Mansion by President James K. Polk in February 1849, just months before her death. Ross, however, faced much more difficult circumstances as the Cherokee nation divided over whether to accept removal. Ross fought to delay removal as long as possible but eventually oversaw the forced march west of thousands of Cherokees. In their new homes, Cherokees continued to fight each other and the U.S. government. Indeed, Ross died in 1866 in Washington, D.C., while trying to negotiate a new treaty with the federal government.

Despite the dramatically different backgrounds and careers of Madison and Ross, both worked to bridge differences in the young nation, and both defended it against attack. Both harbored democratic ideals of a nation that could incorporate women as well as men, Indians as well as whites. Ultimately, however, neither had the power to overcome the partisan rivalries and economic crises that shaped the young nation or to halt the rising tensions over Indian lands and slave labor that would continue to plague Americans in the decades to come.

LEARNING*Curve*
Check what you know.
bedfordstmartins.com/hewittlawson/LC

Chapter Review

Online Study Guide ▶ bedfordstmartins.com/hewittlawson

KEY TERMS

Non-Intercourse Act (p. 261)
Hartford Convention (p. 262)
American System (p. 265)
Erie Canal (p. 265)
Monroe Doctrine (p. 267)
panic of 1819 (p. 268)
Missouri Compromise (p. 272)
Democrats and National Republicans (p. 275)
Petticoat Affair (p. 278)
spoils system (p. 278)
nullification (p. 278)
Indian Removal Act (p. 281)

REVIEW & RELATE

1. How were conflicts with Indians in the West connected to ongoing tensions between the United States and Great Britain on land and at sea?

2. What were the long-term consequences of the War of 1812?

3. What role did government play in early-nineteenth-century economic development?

4. How and why did economic development contribute to regional differences and shape regional ties?

5. What were the political consequences of the panic of 1819?

6. What regional divisions did the conflict over slavery in Missouri reveal?

7. How and why did the composition of the electorate change in the 1820s?

8. How did Jackson's 1828 campaign represent a significant departure from earlier patterns in American politics?

9. What did President Jackson's response to the Eaton affair and Indian removal reveal about his vision of democracy?

10. To what extent did Jackson's policies favor the South? Which policies benefited or antagonized which groups of Southerners?

TIMELINE OF EVENTS

1809	Non-Intercourse Act passed
1811	First steamboat travels down the Mississippi to New Orleans
	William Henry Harrison defeats Shawnees at Prophet Town
June 1812	War of 1812 begins
1814	Hartford Convention
March 1814	Battle of Horseshoe Bend
August 1814	British burn Washington City
December 1814	Treaty of Ghent
1815	Battle of New Orleans
1817–1818	Andrew Jackson fights Spanish and Seminole forces in Florida
1818	Great Britain and U.S. agree to joint occupation of Oregon Territory
1819	Spain cedes Florida to U.S.; establishes boundary between U.S. and Spanish territory through the Adams-Onís Treaty
	Panic of 1819 sparks severe recession that lasts until 1823
1820	Missouri Compromise
1821	White traders begin using Santa Fe Trail
1822	Denmark Vesey accused of organizing a slave uprising
1823	Monroe Doctrine articulated
1825	Erie Canal completed
1828	Tariff of 1828 passed
	John Ross elected principal chief of the Cherokee nation
1829	Petticoat Affair
1830	Indian Removal Act passed
1832	South Carolina passes Ordinance of Nullification
1833	Force Bill passed

The Panic of 1819

The panic of 1819 lasted more than four years and was the first serious economic recession faced by the United States. It resulted primarily from irresponsible banking practices and the declining demand for cotton, foodstuffs, and other American goods in Europe. This combination prompted farm foreclosures, factory layoffs, bank failures, and widespread personal and business bankruptcies. In every region of the country, people were left jobless, homeless, and destitute, and thousands auctioned off their household goods or were thrown into debtors' prisons (Documents 9.5 and 9.6). Private charities were overwhelmed, and most could not meet the demand for clothes, housing, and food.

In the midst of this tremendous suffering, the public focused its blame on bankers and government officials. There was much disagreement, however, about the proper remedy for the economic recession. Some sought permanent restriction of bank credit, whereas others believed that cheaper credit would enable the economy to grow. Proposals were put forward to give direct government relief to debtors, abolish debtors' prisons, and start public works projects. Debates over whether to increase protective tariffs revealed the sectional differences emerging in the United States. In 1816 Congress had passed a tariff raising duties on foreign imports, and during the panic northern manufacturers wanted this tariff increased to further protect the U.S. market from foreign competition. Southern planters, on the other hand, blamed tariffs for raising the costs of manufactured goods and felt they benefited the North at the expense of the South (Document 9.7). The panic also led to calls for political reforms, especially by those who felt the government was not responsive to the needs of the laboring classes. Many states considered lowering or even abolishing property qualifications for eligible voters. Documents 9.8 and 9.9 demonstrate both sides of this debate as it was taken up at the New York constitutional convention in 1821. By 1823 the panic had ended, but the economic and political changes it engendered reshaped American society and politics and would influence future responses to economic crises.

DOCUMENT 9.5

Auction in Chatham Square, 1820

Cities throughout the United States were hit hard by the panic, and in the first year of the crisis the number of paupers in New York City increased from 8,000 to 13,000. Widespread unemployment resulted in evictions and homelessness for thousands of families. The following image of Chatham Square in lower Manhattan, painted in 1843, reveals a common scene in urban areas—the public auction of goods from an evicted family. Artist E. Didier depicted Chatham Square as it was in 1820, the last year auctions were held there as the area became increasingly residential.

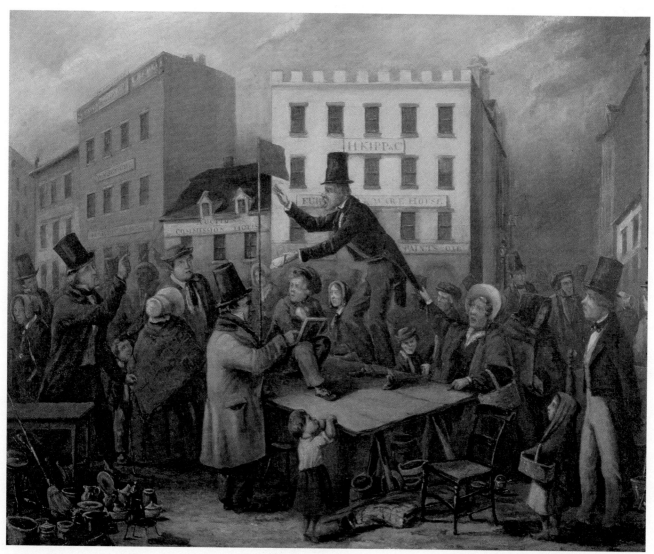

DOCUMENT 9.6

James Flint | Account of the Panic, 1820

The Scottish traveler James Flint was touring America when the panic hit. In his letters home, he described the impact of the economic recession on banks, factories, and merchants. The following passage is from a letter he wrote from Jeffersonville, Indiana, describing the impossible conditions that many American workers faced.

Merchants in Cincinnati, as elsewhere, have got into debt, by buying property, or by building houses, but are now secure in the possession. Such people, notwithstanding complain of the badness of the times, finding that the trade of buying without paying cannot be continued. Those who have not already secured an independence for life, may soon be willing to have trade and fair dealing as formerly. Property laws deprive creditors of the debts now due to them; but they cannot force them to give credit as they were wont to do.

Agriculture languishes—farmers cannot find profit in hiring labourers. The increase of produce in the United States is greater than any increase of consumpt that may be pointed out elsewhere. To increase the quantity of provisions, then, without enlarging the numbers of those who eat them, will be only diminishing the price farther. Land in these circumstances can be of no value to the capitalist who would employ his funds in farming. The spare capital of farmers is here chiefly laid out in the purchase of lands.

Labourers and mechanics are in want of employment. I think I have seen upwards of 1500 men in quest of work within eleven months past, and many of these declared, that they had no money. Newspapers and private letters agree in stating, that wages are so low as eighteen and three-fourth cents (about ten-pence) per day, with board, at Philadelphia, and some other places. Great numbers of strangers lately camped in the open field near Baltimore, depending on the contributions of the charitable for subsistence. You have no doubt heard of emigrants returning to Europe without finding the prospect of a livelihood in America. Some who have come out to this part of the country do not succeed well. Labourers' wages are at present a dollar and an eighth part per day. Board costs them two three-fourths or three dollars per week, and washing three-fourths of a dollar for a dozen of pieces. On these terms, it is plain that they cannot live two days by the labour of one, with the other deductions which are to be taken from their wages. Clothing, for example, will cost about three times its price in Britain: and the poor labourer is almost certain of being paid in depreciated money; perhaps from thirty to fifty per cent. under par. I have seen several men turned out of boarding houses, where their money would not be taken. They had no other resource left but to lodge in the woods, without any covering except their clothes. They set fire to a decayed log, spread some boards alongside of it for a bed, laid a block of timber across for a pillow, and pursued their labour by day as usual. . . .

Employers are also in the habit of deceiving their workmen, by telling them that it is not convenient to pay wages in money, and that they run accounts with the storekeeper, the tailor, and the shoemaker, and that from them they may have all the necessities they want very cheap. The workman who consents to this mode of payment procures orders from the employer, on one or more of these citizens, and is charged a higher price for the goods than the employer actually pays for them. This is called *paying in trade.* . . .

In the district of Jeffersonville, there has been an apparent interruption of the prosperity of the settlers. Upwards of two hundred quarter sections of land are by law forfeited to the government, for non-payment of part of the purchase money due more than a year ago. A year's indulgence was granted by Congress, but unless farther accommodation is immediately allowed, the lands will soon be offered a second time for sale. Settlers seeing the danger of losing their possessions are now offering to transfer their rights for less sums than have already been paid; it being still in the power of purchasers to retain the lands on paying up the arrears due in the land office. This marks the difficulty that individuals at present have in procuring small sums of money in this particular district.

Source: Reuben Gold Thwaites, ed., *Early Western Travels, 1748–1846* (Cleveland: Arthur H. Clark, 1904), 9:226–28; 236.

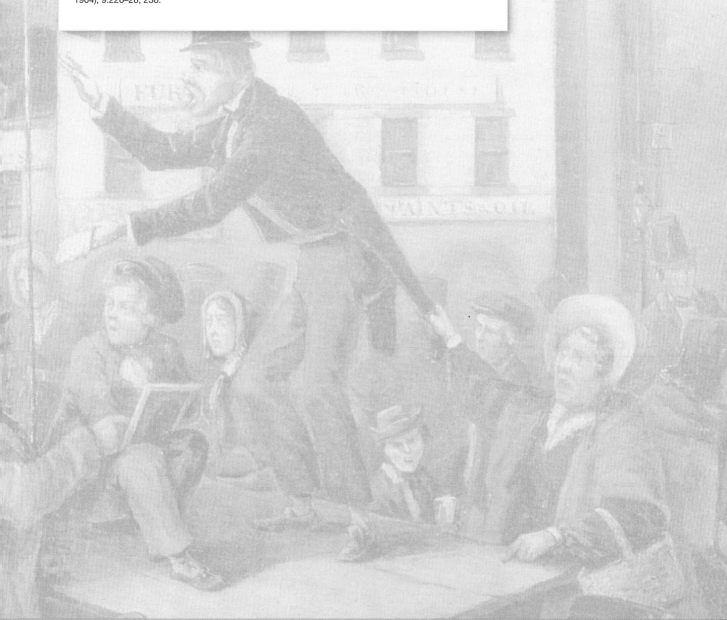

DOCUMENT 9.7

Virginia Agricultural Society | Antitariff Petition, 1820

As political debates raged on whether to raise the protective tariff on imported goods, many groups around the country wrote Congress to support or protest the tariff. Most southern planters and farmers spoke out against the tariff, including the Virginia Agricultural Society of Fredericksburg. In January 1820, the organization sent a petition to Congress, from which the following selection is taken. In the aftermath of the panic, Congress passed the tariff of 1824, which raised duties on foreign imports.

THAT HOSTILITY, resulting from true republican principles, to partial taxation, exclusive privileges, and monopolies created by law, was the primary cause of our glorious and ever-memorable revolution.

That, although most of us are only the descendants of those patriots who achieved that revolution, by the lavish expenditure of their treasure and their blood, yet that we inherit enough of their spirit to feel equal aversion to similar oppressions; at the same time, we confidently trust that neither we, nor our sons after us, will ever be found backward or reluctant in offering up at the shrine of national good and national happiness any sacrifices, however great, which *their* promotion and preservation may obviously and necessarily require. But we have been taught to believe that a parental Government—a Government founded upon the immutable and sacred principles of truth, justice, and liberty—if she required sacrifices at all from those whom she is so solemnly bound to protect, would make them such as should operate equally upon every member of the community.

That we view with great concern, both nationally and individually, certain late attempts, on the part of various descriptions of domestic manufacturers, to induce your honorable body to increase the duties upon imports, already so high as to amount, upon many articles, nearly to a prohibition. This increased cost upon some of these may truly be designated a tax upon knowledge, if not a bounty to ignorance; such, for example, as the duty upon books in foreign languages, and upon philosophical, mathematical, surgical, and chemical instruments.

That, although these attempts are sustained under the plausible pretext of "promoting national industry," they are calculated (we will not say in *design*, but certainly in *effect*) to produce a tax highly impolitic in its nature, partial in its operation, and oppressive in its effects: a tax, in fact, to be levied principally on the great body of agriculturists, who constitute a large majority of the whole American people, and who are the chief consumers of all foreign imports.

That such a tax would be a flagrant violation of the soundest and most important principles of political economy, amongst which we deem the following to be incontrovertibly true: that, as the interests of dealers and consumers necessarily conflict with each other, the first always aiming to *narrow*, whilst the latter, who form the majority of every nation, as constantly endeavor to *enlarge* competition; by which enlargement alone extravagant prices and exorbitant profits are prevented, it is the duty of every wise and just government to secure the consumers against both exorbitant profits and extravagant prices by leaving competition as free and open as possible.

Source: "Remonstrance against Increase of Duties on Imports," House of Representatives, January 17, 1820, no. 570, 16th Cong., 1st sess., *American State Papers: Finance*, 3:447–48.

DOCUMENT 9.8

James Kent | Arguments against Expanding Male Voting Rights, 1821

The economic crisis spawned debates throughout the country about the political system and its responsiveness to all classes of American citizens. The New York constitutional convention of 1821 included a committee that reviewed the state's voting laws and considered implementing "universal suffrage," that is, granting voting rights to all white men regardless of wealth or property. The committee heard testimony from supporters and opponents of property qualifications for voting. Chief Justice and Chancellor James Kent of New York argued in favor of property qualifications.

I have reflected upon the report of the select committee with attention and with anxiety. We appear to be disregarding the principles of the constitution, under which we have so long and so happily lived, and to be changing some of its essential institutions. . . .

The tendency of universal suffrage is to jeopardize the rights of property and the principles of liberty. . . .

The notion that every man that works a day on the road, or serves an idle hour in the militia, is entitled as of right to an equal participation in the whole power of the government is most unreasonable and has no foundation in justice. We had better at once discard from the report such a nominal test of merit. If such persons have an equal share in one branch of the legislature, it is surely as much as they can in justice or policy demand. Society is an association for the protection of property as well as of life, and the individual who contributes only one cent to the common stock ought not to have the same power and influence in directing the property concerns of the partnership as he who contributes his thousands. He will not have the same inducements to care, and diligence, and fidelity. His inducements and his temptation would be to divide the whole capital upon the principles of agrarian law [to ensure a more equal distribution of land to all classes].

Liberty, rightly understood, is an inestimable blessing, but liberty without wisdom, and without justice, is no better than wild and savage licentiousness. The danger which we have hereafter to apprehend, is not the want, but the abuse, of liberty. We have to apprehend the oppression of minorities, and a disposition to encroach on private right—to disturb chartered privileges—and to weaken, degrade, and overawe the administration of justice; we have to apprehend the establishment of unequal, and consequently, unjust systems of taxation, and all the mischiefs of a crude and mutable legislation. A stable senate, exempted from the influence of universal suffrage, will powerfully check these dangerous propensities.

Source: *Report of the Proceedings and Debates of the Convention of 1821* (Albany, 1821), 219, 221–22.

DOCUMENT 9.9

Nathan Sanford | Arguments for Expanding Male Voting Rights, 1821

Nathan Sanford, a former U.S. senator and a delegate to the New York constitutional convention, argued in favor of removing property qualifications. Sanford and his supporters won the debate, and property qualifications were removed for white male voters. However, property qualifications were increased for black male voters, thus denying most African Americans the right to vote in the state.

The question before us is the right of suffrage—who shall, or who shall not, have the right to vote. The committee have presented the scheme they thought best; to abolish all existing distinctions and make the right of voting uniform. Is this not right? Where did these distinctions arise? They arose from British precedents. In England, they have their three estates, which must always have their separate interests represented. Here there is but one estate—the people. To me, the only qualifications seem to be the virtue and morality of the people; and if they may be safely entrusted to vote for one class of our rulers, why not for all? In my opinion, these distinctions are fallacious. We have the experience of almost all the other states against them. The principle of the scheme now proposed is that those who bear the burthens of the state should choose those that rule it. There is no privilege given to property, as such; but those who contribute to the public support, we consider as entitled to share in the election of rulers. . . .

. . . But how is the extension of the right of suffrage unfavourable to property? Will not our laws continue the same? Will not the administration of justice continue the same? And if so, how is private property to suffer? Unless these are changed, and upon them rest the rights and security of property, I am unable to perceive how property is to suffer by the extension of the right of suffrage. But we have abundant experience on this point in other states. Now, sir, in many states the right of suffrage has no restriction; every male inhabitant votes. Yet what harm has been done in those states? What evil has resulted to them from this cause? The course of things in this country is for the extension and not the restriction of popular rights. I do not know that in Ohio or Pennsylvania, where the right of suffrage is universal, there is not the same security for private rights and private happiness as elsewhere.

Source: *Report of the Proceedings and Debates of the Convention of 1821* (Albany, 1821), 178–79.

Interpret the Evidence

1. How might images such as the one of the public auction (Document 9.5) have shaped public opinion about the panic?

2. How does James Flint (Document 9.6) describe the panic, and what comparisons does he make between American society and conditions in Europe?

3. On what grounds does the Virginia Agricultural Society of Fredericksburg protest the tariff (Document 9.7)? How does it place its struggles within the context of American history?

4. Compare the arguments of James Kent (Document 9.8) and Nathan Sanford (Document 9.9) in the debate over voting rights in New York. How do they conceptualize the principles of justice, rights, and equality? Which arguments do you find the most convincing, and why?

5. Do you think the members of the Virginia Agricultural Society would agree more with Nathan Sanford or with James Kent? What about James Flint or the creator of the public auction image?

Put It in Context

- How did the devastating impact of the panic of 1819 shape state and national-level debates over economic policies and political rights?

- How did the policies implemented during and immediately after the panic of 1819—particularly voting rights and tariff laws—change the U.S. political and economic landscape over the following decade?

The Granger Collection, New York

Private Collection/Peter Newark Western Americana/The Bridgeman Art Library

● The storming of the Alamo, 1836.

● Painting of a Sioux village, by George Catlin.

10
Slavery Expands South and West

1830–1850

The Granger Collection, New York

A planter's home near New Orleans, Louisiana.

AMERICAN HISTORIES

Although James Henry Hammond became one of the richest plantation owners in South Carolina, he began life more modestly. Born in 1807 near Newberry, South Carolina, he was the only one of six siblings to earn a college degree. Certain that a legal career would lead to wealth and power, James opened a law practice in Columbia, the state capital, in 1828. Two years later, bored by his profession, he established a newspaper, the *Southern Times*. Writing bold editorials that supported nullification of the "Tariff of Abominations," Hammond quickly gained attention and acclaim.

While launching his journalistic career, James courted Catherine Fitzsimmons, the daughter of a wealthy, politically connected family. When they married in June 1831, James became master of Silver Bluff, a 7,500-acre plantation worked by 147 slaves. Giving up his editorial career to focus on managing the estate, he quickly gained prominence as an agricultural reformer and was elected to the U.S. House of Representatives in 1834.

Hammond's political career was erratic. In 1836 he led a campaign that resulted in congressional passage of the so-called gag rule, ensuring that antislavery petitions would be tabled rather than read on the floor of the House. Soon afterward, he took ill and resigned from Congress, but he returned to politics in 1842 as governor of South Carolina. His ambitions were stymied once more, however, when Catherine discovered that James had made sexual advances on his four nieces, aged thirteen to sixteen. Fearing public exposure, Hammond withdrew from politics, but he soon joined southern

intellectuals in arguing that slavery was a positive good rather than a necessary evil.

This proslavery argument intensified in the late 1840s as northern reformers sought to halt the spread of slavery into newly acquired lands in the West. In the early nineteenth century, a thriving trade in enslaved workers had developed between the Upper South and more fertile areas in the Lower South. It bolstered the economy in both regions but also highlighted the brutalities of bondage. With westward expansion, this internal trade in slaves burgeoned.

Solomon Northrup was among tens of thousands of African Americans who endured the ravages of the internal slave trade. Unlike the vast majority, however, Northrup was born free in Minerva, New York, in 1808. His father, Mintus, had been born into slavery but was freed by his owner's will. Once free, Mintus acquired sufficient property to qualify to vote, an impressive achievement for a former slave.

After his marriage to Anne Hampton at the age of twenty-one, Solomon found employment transporting goods along the region's waterways. He was also hired as a fiddle player for local dances, while Anne worked as a cook in neighborhood taverns. In 1834 the couple moved to Saratoga Springs, a tourist haven that provided more job opportunities. There they raised their three children until tragedy struck.

In March 1841, Solomon met two white circus performers who hired him to play fiddle for them on tour. They paid his wages up front and told him to obtain documents proving his free status. After reaching Washington, D.C., however, Northrup was drugged, chained, and sold to James Birch, a notorious slave trader. Northrup was resold in New Orleans to William Ford, whom he later described as a "kind, noble, candid Christian man" who was nonetheless blind "to the inherent wrong at the bottom of the system of Slavery." Ford gave Northrup a new name, Platt, and put him to work as a raftsman while Northrup tried unsuccessfully to get word to his wife.

In 1842 Ford sold "Platt" to a neighbor, John Tibeats, who whipped and abused his workers. When Tibeats attacked his newly acquired slave with an ax, Northrup fought back and fled to Ford's house. His former owner shielded him from Tibeats's wrath and arranged his sale to Edwin Epps, who owned a large cotton plantation. For the next ten years, Northrup worked the fields and played the fiddle at local dances.

Finally, in 1852 Samuel Bass, a Canadian carpenter who openly acknowledged his antislavery views, came to work on Epps's house. Northrup persuaded Bass to send a letter to his wife in Saratoga Springs. Anne Northrup, astonished to hear from her husband after more than a decade, took the letter to lawyer Henry Northrup, the son of Mintus's former owner. After months of legal efforts, Henry traveled to Louisiana and, with the help of a local judge, freed Solomon Northrup in January 1853. •

THE AMERICAN HISTORIES of Solomon Northrup and James Henry Hammond were both intertwined in the struggle over slavery. By 1850 slave labor had become central to the South's and the nation's economic success, even as slave ownership became concentrated in the hands of a smaller proportion of wealthy white families. The concentration of more slaves on each plantation created a stronger sense of community and a truly African American culture, although it did not negate the brutality of the institution. At the same time, the volatility of the cotton market fueled economic instability, which planters claimed could be resolved only by cultivating more cotton. In response, sympathetic administrations in Washington forcibly removed Indians from the Southeast, supported independence for Texas, and proclaimed war on Mexico. But these policies led to growing conflicts with western Indian nations and heightened political conflicts over slavery and the nation's future.

Planters Expand the Slave System

The cotton gin, developed in the 1790s, ensured the growth of southern agriculture into the 1840s (see chapter 8). As the cotton kingdom spread west, planters forged a distinctive culture around the institution of slavery. But slavery limited the development of cities, technology, and educational institutions, leaving the South increasingly dependent on the North and West for food, industrial goods, commercial resources, books and magazines, and even higher education. In addition, westward expansion extended the trade in slaves within the South, shattering black families. Still, southern planters viewed themselves as national leaders, both the repository of traditional American values and the engine of economic progress.

A Plantation Society Develops in the South

Plantation slavery existed throughout the Americas in the early nineteenth century. British, French, Dutch, Portuguese, and Spanish colonies in the West Indies and South America all housed large numbers of slaves and extensive plantations. In the U.S. South, however, the volatile cotton market and a scarcity of fertile land kept most plantations relatively small before 1830. But from the early 1840s on, territorial expansion and profits from cotton, as well as from rice and sugar, fueled a period of conspicuous consumption. Successful southern planters now built grand houses and purchased a variety of luxury goods.

South Carolina Plantation

This wood engraving from the mid-nineteenth century depicts a planter's residence on the Cumbee River, South Carolina. When cotton prices began to rise after 1843, leading planters invested more of their profits in fancy houses and luxurious furnishings. They bought expensive clothing and jewelry for their wives and daughters and traveled abroad with their families.   The Granger Collection, New York

As plantations grew, especially in states like South Carolina and Mississippi where slaves outnumbered whites, a wealthy aristocracy sought to ensure productivity by employing harsh methods of discipline. Masters whipped slaves for a variety of offenses, from not picking enough cotton to breaking tools or running away. Although James Henry Hammond imagined himself a progressive master, he used the whip liberally, hoping thereby to ensure that his estate generated sufficient profits to purchase fancy furnishings, trips to Europe, fashionable clothing, and fine jewelry.

Increased attention to comfort and luxury helped make the heavy workload of plantation mistresses tolerable. Although mistresses were idealized for their beauty, piety, and grace, they took on considerable managerial responsibilities. They directed the domestic slaves as well as the feeding, clothing, and medical care of the entire labor force. They were expected to organize and preside over lavish social events, host relatives and friends for extended stays, and direct the plantation in their husband's absence. When James was traveling, Catherine Hammond struggled to manage the estate while caring for their seven children.

Of course, plantation mistresses were relieved of the most arduous labor by enslaved women, who cooked, cleaned, and washed for the family, cared for the children, and even nursed the babies. Wealthy white women benefited from the best education, the greatest access to music and literature, and the finest clothes and furnishings to be had in the region. Yet the pedestal on which plantation mistresses stood was shaky, built on a patriarchal system in which husbands and fathers held substantial power. For example, most wives were forced to ignore the sexual relations that husbands initiated with female slaves. As Mary Boykin Chesnut explained in her diary, "Every lady tells you who is the father of all the Mulatto children in everybody's household, but those in her own, she seems to think drop from the clouds or pretends to think so." In 1850, when Catherine Hammond discovered James's sexual relations with an enslaved mother and daughter, she moved to Charleston with her two youngest daughters. Most wives, however, stayed put, and some took out their anger and frustration on slave women already victimized by their husbands. Moreover, some mistresses owned slaves themselves, traded them on the slave market, and gave them as gifts or bequests to family members and friends.

Not all slaveholders were wealthy planters like the Hammonds, with fifty or more slaves and extensive landholdings. Far more planters in the 1830s and 1840s owned between twenty and fifty slaves, and an even larger number of farmers owned just three to six slaves. These small planters and farmers could not afford to emulate the lives of the largest slave owners. Still, as Hammond wrote a friend in 1847, "The planters here are essentially what the nobility are in other countries. They stand at the head of society & politics."

Urban Life in the Slave South

The insistence on the supremacy of slave owners had broad repercussions. The richest men in the South invested in slaves, land, and household goods, with little left to develop industry, technology, or urban institutions. The largest factory in the South, the Tredegar Iron Works in Richmond, Virginia, was constructed in 1833, and by 1850 it employed several hundred free and enslaved African Americans. Most southern industrialists, however, like South Carolina textile manufacturer William Gregg, employed poor white women and children. But neither Tredegar nor a scattering of textile mills fundamentally reshaped the region's economy.

The South also fell behind in urban development. The main exception was port cities, which boasted fine shops, a growing professional class, and ready access to national and international news. Yet even in Baltimore, Charleston, and Savannah, commerce was often directed by northern agents, especially cotton brokers. In addition, nearly one-third of southern whites had no access to cash and instead bartered goods and services, further restricting the urban economy. In the South, only Baltimore and New Orleans reached a population of 100,000 by 1850.

Despite their relative scarcity, southern cities attracted many free blacks, providing them with the best hope of finding employment and distancing themselves from hostile planters. The growing demand for cheap domestic labor in urban areas and planters' greater willingness to emancipate less valuable single female slaves meant that free black women generally outnumbered men in southern cities. These women worked mainly as washerwomen, cooks, and general domestics, while free black men labored as skilled artisans, dockworkers, or sailors in southern seaports. In these jobs, free blacks competed with slaves and with growing numbers of Irish, German, and Jewish immigrants who flocked to southern cities in the 1840s and 1850s. The presence of immigrants and free blacks and the reputation of ports as escape hatches for runaway slaves ensured that cities remained suspect in the South.

The scarcity of cities and industry also curtailed the development of transportation. State governments and private citizens invested little in roads, canals, and railroads. Most small farmers traded goods locally, and planters used the South's extensive river system to ship goods to commercial hubs. Where rivers did not meet this need, rail lines were sometimes built. However, only Virginia and Maryland, with their proximity to the nation's capital, developed extensive rail networks.

New Orleans, 1841
New Orleans was one of the few major urban areas in the South and, like Baltimore and Charleston, prospered through its seaport. Not only did the port of New Orleans attract sailing ships engaged in foreign commerce, but it was also the destination for steamships carrying goods along the Mississippi River.   Eileen Tweedy/The Art Archive at Art Resource, NY

The Consequences of Slavery's Expansion

Outside the South, industry and agriculture increasingly benefited from technological innovation. Indeed, the booming textile industry in New England fueled the demand for cotton and drove up prices during the 1840s and 1850s. Planters, however, continued to rely on intensive manual labor. Even reform-minded planters focused on fertilizer and crop rotation rather than machines to enhance productivity. The limited use of new technologies—such as iron plows or seed drills—resulted from a lack of investment capital and planters' attitudes toward African American laborers. Believing them to be inherently lazy, ignorant, and untrustworthy, planters refused to purchase expensive equipment that might be broken or purposely sabotaged. Instead, they relied on continually expanding the acreage under cultivation.

One result of these practices was that a declining percentage of white Southerners came to control vast estates with large numbers of enslaved laborers. Between 1830 and 1850, the absolute number of both slaves and owners grew. But slave owners became a smaller proportion of all white Southerners because the white population grew faster than the number of slave owners. At the same time, distinctions among wealthy planters, small slaveholders, and whites who owned no slaves also increased.

The concern with productivity and profits and the concentration of more slaves on large plantations did have some benefits for black women and men. The end of the international slave trade in 1808 forced planters to rely more heavily on natural reproduction to increase their labor force. Thus many planters thought more carefully about how they treated their slaves, who were increasingly viewed as "valuable property." It was no longer good business to work slaves to death, cripple them with severe whippings, or cut off fingers, ears, or other body parts.

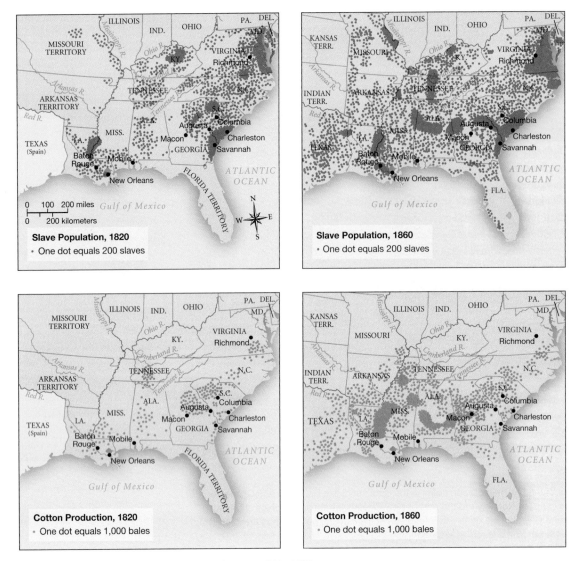

MAP 10.1 The Spread of Slavery and Cotton, 1820–1860

While tobacco, rice, and sugar remained important crops in a few states, cotton became the South's and the nation's major export. The need to find more fertile fields led planters to migrate to Alabama, Mississippi, and Louisiana. As a result of cotton's success, the number of enslaved people increased dramatically, the internal slave trade expanded, and labor demands intensified.

Nonetheless, owners continued to whip slaves with regularity and made paltry investments in diet and health care for enslaved workers. Most slaves lived in small houses with dirt floors and minimal furniture and were given three or four suits of clothes a year despite laboring six days a week. They ate a diet high in calories, especially fats and carbohydrates, but with little meat, fish, fresh vegetables, or fruits. The high mortality rate among slave infants and children—more than twice that of white children to age five—reflected the limits of planters' care.

The spread of slavery into Mississippi, Louisiana, Alabama, Missouri, and Texas affected both white and black families, though again not equally. The younger sons of wealthy planters were often forced to move to the frontier, and their families generally lived in rough quarters on isolated plantations. Such moves were far more difficult for slaves, however. Between 1830 and 1850, more than 440,000 slaves were forced to move from the Upper South to the Lower South (Map 10.1). On the southern frontier, they endured especially harsh conditions as they carved out new cotton fields and rice paddies or planted and harvested sugarcane. Many of these frontier slaves had been torn away from their families and communities.

Explore

See Document 10.1 for one visitor's description of a slave pen in Washington, D.C.

By the 1830s, slave markets blossomed in Richmond, Charleston, Savannah, Natchez, New Orleans, and Washington, D.C. Solomon Northrup described one in Washington, D.C., in 1841 where a woman named Eliza watched as her son Randall was "won" by a planter from Baton Rouge. She promised "to be the most faithful slave that ever lived" if he would also buy her and her daughter. The slave trader threatened the desperate mother with a hundred lashes, but neither his threats nor her tears could change the outcome. As slavery spread westward, such scenes were repeated thousands of times.

DOCUMENT 10.1

Edward Strutt Abdy | Description of Washington, D.C., Slave Pen, 1833

Slavery and the slave trade had always been legal in Washington, D.C., and enslaved laborers cleared land and constructed buildings. As the debate over slavery increased in the nineteenth century, abolitionists often highlighted the incongruence of slavery in the capital city of American democracy. Visitors wrote with disgust about slave auctions held within sight of the Capitol steps. In the 1830s, the English writer Edward Strutt Abdy toured the United States and described the scene at a slave pen.

Explore

How does Abdy describe the construction of the slave pen and its relation to the U.S. Capitol?

How are whites and blacks described?

How might northern and southern audiences have reacted to this description of a slave pen? How might readers in Great Britain, where slavery had just been abolished, have responded?

One day I went to see the "slaves' pen"—a wretched hovel, "right against" the Capitol, from which it is distant about half a mile, with no house intervening. The outside alone is accessible to the eye of a visitor; what passes within being reserved for the exclusive observation of its owner (a man of the name of Robey) and his unfortunate victims. It is surrounded by a wooden paling fourteen or fifteen feet in height, with the posts outside to prevent escape, and separated from the building by a space too narrow to admit of a free circulation of air. At a small window above, which was unglazed and exposed alike to the heat of summer and the cold of winter, so trying to the constitution, two or three sable faces appeared, looking out wistfully to while away the time and catch a refreshing breeze; the weather being extremely hot. In this wretched hovel, all colors, except white—the only guilty one—both sexes, and all ages, are confined, exposed indiscriminately to all the contamination which may be expected in such society and under such seclusion. The inmates of the gaol, of this class I mean, are even worse treated; some of them, if my informants are to be believed, having been actually frozen to death, during the inclement winters which often prevail in the country. While I was in the city, Robey had got possession of a woman, whose term of slavery was limited to six years. It was expected that she would be sold before the expiration of that period, and sent away to a distance, where the assertion of her claim would subject her to ill-usage. Cases of this kind are very common.

Source: Edward Strutt Abdy, *Journal of a Residence and Tour in the United States of North America, from April, 1833, to October, 1834* (London: John Murray, 1835), 2:96–97.

Put It in Context

How did the gradual elimination of slavery in the northern United States and in other parts of the world affect views of slavery in the American South?

REVIEW & RELATE

- What role did the planter elite play in southern society and politics?
- What were the consequences of the dominant position of slave-based plantation agriculture in the southern economy?

LEARNINGCurve bedfordstmartins.com/hewittlawson/LC

Slave Society and Culture

Because slave labor formed the backbone of the southern economy, enslaved workers gained some leverage against owners and overseers. But these women and men did not simply define themselves in relation to whites. They also developed relationships and identities within the slave quarters. By maintaining aspects of African culture, creating strong kinship networks, and embracing religion, southern blacks found ways to lighten their bondage. Many also found small ways to resist their enslavement on an everyday basis. Others resisted more openly, and a small number organized rebellions against their masters.

Slaves Fuel the Southern Economy

The labor of enslaved blacks drove the nation's economy as well as the South's. In 1820 the South produced some 500,000 bales of cotton, much of it exported to England. By 1850 the region produced nearly 3 million bales, feeding textile mills in New England and abroad. A decade later, cotton accounted for nearly two-thirds of the U.S. export trade and added nearly $200 million a year to the American economy.

Carpenters, blacksmiths, and other skilled slaves were sometimes hired out and allowed to keep a small amount of the money they earned. They traveled to nearby households, compared their circumstances to those on other plantations, and sometimes made contact with free blacks. Some skilled slaves also learned to read and write and had access to tools and knowledge denied to field hands. And they were less likely to be sold to slave traders. Still, they were constantly hounded by whites who demanded travel passes and deference, were more acutely aware of alternatives to slavery, and were often suspected of involvement in rebellions.

Household slaves sometimes received old clothes and bedding or leftover food from their owners. Yet they were under the constant surveillance of whites, and women especially were vulnerable to sexual abuse. Moreover, the work they performed was physically demanding. Enslaved women chopped wood, hauled water, baked food, and washed clothes. Fugitive slave James Curry recalled that his mother, a cook in North Carolina, rose early each morning to milk fourteen cows, bake bread, and churn butter. She was responsible for meals for her owners and the slaves. In summer, she cooked her last meal around eight o'clock, after which she milked the cows again. Then she returned to her

Plantation Slaves at Work

Slaves performed a wide variety of labor, such as planting and harvesting crops, domestic work, and carpentry and blacksmithing. These two panels painted by William Henry Brown in about 1842 illustrate slaves hauling a week's worth of picking. Although most tasks were physically demanding, workers who carried goods to market at least had the chance to briefly leave the plantation. The Historic New Orleans Collection, accession no. 1975.93.1 and 1975.93.2

quarters, put her children to bed, and often fell asleep while mending clothes.

Field hands often left their youngest children in the care of cooks and washerwomen. But once slaves reached the age of eleven or twelve, they were put to work full-time. Although field labor was defined by its relentless pace and drudgery, it also brought together large numbers of slaves for the entire day and thus helped forge bonds among laborers on the same plantation. Songs provided a rhythm for their work and offered slaves the chance to communicate their frustrations or their hopes.

Field labor was generally organized by task or by gang. Under the task system, typical on rice plantations, a slave could return to his or her quarters once the day's task was completed. This left time for some slaves to cultivate gardens, fish for supper, make quilts, or repair furniture. In the gang system, widely used on cotton plantations, men and women worked in groups under the supervision of a driver and swept across fields hoeing, planting, or picking.

Developing an African American Culture

Amid hard work and harsh treatment, slaves created social bonds and a rich culture of their own. Thus blacks in America continued to employ African names, like Cuffee and Binah, generations after their enslavement. Even if masters gave them English names, they might use African names in the slave quarters to sustain family and community networks and memories. Some also retained elements of West African languages. Along the South Carolina and Georgia coast, enslaved workers spoke Gullah, a dialect that combined African words and speech patterns with English. Agricultural techniques, medical practices, forms of dress, folktales, songs and musical instruments, dances, and courtship rituals—all demonstrated the continued importance of West African and Caribbean culture to African Americans. This **syncretic culture**, which combined elements from Africa and the Caribbean with those from the United States, was disseminated as slaves hauled cotton to market, forged families across plantation boundaries, or were sold farther south. It was also handed down across generations through storytelling, music, rituals, and religious services.

Religious practices offer an important example of syncretic cultural forms. Africans from Muslim communities often continued to pray to Allah even if they were also required to attend Protestant churches. Black preachers who embraced Christianity developed rituals that combined African and American elements. In the early nineteenth century, slaves eagerly embraced the evangelical teachings offered by Baptist and Methodist preachers, which echoed some of the expressive spiritual forms in West Africa. By midcentury, African Americans made up one-third of Baptist and perhaps one-quarter of Methodist church membership. On Sunday mornings, slaves might listen to white ministers proclaim that slavery was God's will; that evening, they might gather in the woods to hear their own preachers tell of God's love and the possibilities of black liberation, at least in the hereafter. Slaves often incorporated drums, conch shells, dancing, or other West African elements into these worship services.

Although most black preachers were men, a few women gained a spiritual following in slave communities. Many female slaves embraced religion enthusiastically, hoping that Christian baptism might substitute for West African rituals that protected newborn babies. Enslaved women also called on church authorities to intervene when white owners or overseers or even enslaved men abused them. They also considered the church one means of sanctifying slave marriages that were not recognized legally.

Slaves also generally provided health care for their community. Most slave births were attended by black midwives, and African American healers often turned to herbal medicines, having discovered southern equivalents to cures used in West Africa. Forced to labor in the fields, gather branches and roots in the forest, and supplement their meager rations with local plants, slaves were far more attuned to the natural world than were their owners.

Resistance and Rebellion

Many owners worried that black preachers and West African folktales inspired blacks to resist enslavement. Fearing defiance, planters went to incredible lengths to control seemingly powerless slaves. Although they were largely successful in quelling open revolts, they were unable to eliminate more subtle forms of opposition, like slowing the pace of work, feigning illness, and damaging white-owned equipment, food, and clothing. Even slaves' ability to sustain a distinct African American culture was viewed by some planters as undermining the institution of bondage. More overt forms of resistance—such as truancy and running away, which disrupted work and lowered profits—also proved impossible to stamp out.

The forms of everyday resistance slaves employed varied in part on their location and resources. Skilled artisans, mostly men, could do more substantial damage because they used more expensive tools, but they were less able to protect themselves through pleas of ignorance. Field laborers could damage only hoes and a few cotton

Nat Turner's Rebellion

This woodcut depicts the rebellion in the top panel and the capture of rebels below. It was published in 1831 by Samuel Warner, a New York publisher who based his lurid account on eyewitness testimony and the supposed confessions of participants. He linked the Turner rebellion to the Haitian Revolution and to suspected (though unproven) conspiracies elsewhere in the South. Library of Congress

plants, but they could do so on a regular basis without exciting suspicion. House slaves could burn dinners, scorch shirts, break china and glassware, and even poison owners or burn down houses. Often considered the most loyal slaves, they were also among the most feared because of their intimate contact with white families. Single male slaves were the most likely to run away, planning their escape carefully to get as far as possible before their owners noticed they were missing. Women who fled plantations were more likely to hide out for short periods in the local area and return at night to get food and visit family. Eventually, isolation, hunger, or concern for children led most of these truants to return if slave patrols did not find them first.

Despite their rarity, efforts to organize slave uprisings, such as that planned by Gabriel (see chapter 8) and the one supposedly hatched by Denmark Vesey (see chapter 9) in the early nineteenth century, continued to haunt southern whites. Rebellions in the West Indies, especially the one in Saint Domingue, also echoed through the early nineteenth century. Then in 1831 a seemingly obedient slave named Nat Turner organized a revolt in rural Virginia that stunned whites across the South. Turner was a self-styled preacher and religious visionary who believed that God had given him a mission. On the night of August 21, he and his followers killed their owners, the Travis family, and then headed to nearby plantations in Southampton County. The bloody insurrection led to the deaths of 57 white men, women, and children and liberated more than 50 slaves. But on August 22, outraged white militiamen burst on the scene and eventually captured the black rebels. Turner managed to hide out for two months but was eventually caught. Tried and convicted on November 5, he was hanged six days later. Virginia executed 55 other African Americans suspected of assisting Turner. White mobs also beat, tortured, or killed some 200 more blacks with no connection to the rebellion.

Nat Turner's rebellion instilled panic among white Southerners, who now worried they might be killed in their sleep by a seemingly submissive slave. News of the uprising traveled through slave communities as well, inspiring both pride and anxiety. The execution of Turner and his followers reminded African Americans how far whites would go to protect the institution of slavery.

REVIEW & RELATE

How did enslaved African Americans create ties of family, community, and culture?

How did enslaved African Americans resist efforts to control and exploit their labor?

LEARNINGCurve bedfordstmartins.com/hewittlawson/LC

Planters Tighten Control

Fears of rebellion led to stricter regulations of black life, and actual uprisings temporarily reinforced white solidarity. Yet yeomen farmers, poor whites, and middle-class professionals all voiced some doubts about the ways in which human bondage affected southern society. To unite these disparate groups, planters wielded their economic and political authority, highlighted bonds of kinship and religious fellowship, and promoted an ideology of white supremacy. Their efforts intensified as northern states and other nations began eradicating slavery.

Harsher Treatment for Southern Blacks

Slave revolts led many southern states to impose harsher controls; however, Nat Turner's rebellion led some white Virginians to question slavery itself. In December 1831, the state Assembly established a special committee to consider the crisis. Representatives from western counties, where slavery was never profitable, argued for the gradual abolition of slavery and the colonization of the state's black population in Africa. Hundreds of women in the region sent petitions to the Virginia legislature supporting these positions. But slaveholders from eastern districts claimed that even discussing emancipation might encourage blacks who observed the Assembly's debates to rebel.

Advocates of colonization gained significant support, but the state's leading intellectuals spoke out adamantly for the benefits of slavery. Professor Thomas Dew, president of the College of William and Mary, emphasized the advantages for planters and slaves alike. Dew claimed that slaveholders performed godly work in raising Africans from the status of brute beast to civilized Christian. Dew's proslavery argument turned the tide, and in the fall of 1832 the Virginia legislature rejected gradual emancipation and imposed new restrictions on slaves and free blacks.

Explore

See Documents 10.2 and 10.3 for opposing views on abolition in Virginia.

From the 1820s to the 1840s, more stringent codes were passed across the South. Most southern legislatures prohibited owners from manumitting their slaves, made it illegal for whites to teach slaves to read or write, limited the size and number of independent black churches, abolished slaves' already-limited access to courts, outlawed slave marriage, banned antislavery literature as obscene, defined rape as a crime only against white women, and outlawed assemblies of more than three blacks without a white person present.

States also regulated the lives of free blacks. Some prohibited free blacks from residing within their borders, others required large bonds to ensure good behavior, and most forbade free blacks who left the state from returning. The homes of free blacks could be raided at any time on suspicion of possessing stolen goods or harboring runaways, and the children of free black women were subject to stringent apprenticeship laws that kept many in virtual slavery.

Planters, aided by state legislatures and local authorities, proved largely successful in controlling slaves, but there was a price to pay. Laws to regulate black life tended to restrict education, mobility, and urban development for southern whites as well. Such laws also characterized the region's primary labor force as savage, heathen, and lazy,

hardly a basis for sustained economic development. And the regulations increased tensions between poorer whites, who were often responsible for enforcement, and wealthy whites, who benefited most clearly from their imposition.

White Southerners without Slaves

Yeomen farmers, independent landowners who did not own any slaves, had a complex relationship with the South's plantation economy. Many were related to slave owners, and they often depended on planters to ship their crops to market. Some hoped to rise into the ranks of slaveholders one day, and others made extra money by hiring themselves out to planters. Yet yeomen farmers also recognized that their economic interests often diverged from those of planters. As growing numbers gained the right to vote in the 1820s and 1830s, they voiced their concerns in county and state legislatures.

Most yeomen farmers believed in slavery, but they sometimes challenged planters' authority and assumptions. In the Virginia slavery debates, small farmers from western districts advocated gradual abolition. In other states, they advocated more liberal policies toward debtors and the protection of fishing rights. Yeomen farmers also questioned certain ideals embraced by elites. Although plantation mistresses considered manual labor beneath them, the wives and daughters of many small farmers had to work in the fields, haul water, chop wood, and perform other arduous tasks. Still, yeomen farmers' ability to diminish planter control was limited by the continued importance of cotton to the southern economy.

In their daily life, however, many small farmers depended more on friends and neighbors than on the planter class. Barn raisings, corn shuckings, quilting bees, and other collective endeavors offered them the chance to combine labor with sociability. Church services and church socials also brought communities together. Farmers lost such ties when they sought better land on the frontier. There, families struggled to establish new crops and new lives in relative isolation but hoped that fertile fields might offer the best chance to rise within the South's rigid class hierarchy.

One step below the yeomen farmers were the even larger numbers of white Southerners who owned no property at all. These poor whites depended on hunting and fishing in frontier areas, performing day labor on farms and plantations, or working on docks or as servants in southern cities. Poor whites competed with free blacks and slaves for employment and often harbored resentments as a result. Yet they also built alliances based on their shared economic plight. Poor immigrants from Ireland, Wales, and Scotland were especially hostile to American planters, who reminded them of English landlords.

DOCUMENTS 10.2 AND 10.3

Debating Slavery: Two Views

Nat Turner's rebellion in Southampton, Virginia, sparked discussions about slavery nationwide. In Virginia, the General Assembly debated whether to gradually abolish slavery in the state. Arguments for and against abolition flooded the legislature. Although they never mentioned Nat Turner by name, women in Augusta County indicated the ways in which his revolt had intensified their fears, and they concluded that eliminating slavery was the only way to ensure their safety. Slavery proponents had no more forceful advocate than Thomas Dew, president of the College of William and Mary, who argued that slavery was beneficial for slaves and their owners. The Virginia legislature took no action on the issue of emancipation and instead passed laws that further restricted free and enslaved blacks in Virginia.

Explore

10.2 Memorial of the Ladies of Augusta to the Virginia General Assembly, January 19, 1832

We pretend not to conceal from [you], our fathers & brothers, our protectors . . . , the fears which agitate our bosoms, and the dangers which await us, as revealed to us by recent tragical deeds; our fears, we admit, [are] great, but we do not concede that they are the effects of blind & unreflecting cowardice: we do not concede that they spring from the superstitious timidity of our sex. Alas! . . . we appeal to your manly reason, to your more matured wisdom, to attest the justice & propriety of our fears, when we call to your remembrance the late slaughter of our sisters & their little ones in certain parts of our land, & the strong probability, that that slaughter was but a partial execution of a widely projected scheme of carnage. We know not, we cannot know the right, nor the unguarded moments, by day or by night, which is pregnant with our destruction & that of our husbands & brothers, & sisters & children; but we do know that we are at every moment, exposed to the means of our own excision & of all that is dear to us in life. The bloody monster which threatens us is warmed & cherished on our own hearths. O hear our prayer & remove it, ye protectors of our persons, ye guardians of our peace!

   Our fears teach us to reflect & reason: and our reflections & reasonings have taught us that the peace of our homes, the welfare of society, the prosperity of future generations call aloud & imperatively for some decisive & efficient measure—and that measure cannot, we believe, be decisively efficient, or of much benefit if it have not, for its ultimate object, the extinction of slavery from amongst us.

Source: Virginia General Assembly, Legislative Petitions: Petition of the Females of Augusta County, 19 January 1832, Accession 36121, State Records Collection, The Library of Virginia, Richmond, Virginia.

Some poor whites remained in the same community for decades, establishing themselves on the margins of society. They attended church regularly, performed day labor for affluent families, and taught their children to defer to their betters. In Savannah and other southern cities, wealthy families organized benevolent associations and more affluent immigrants established mutual aid societies to help poorer members of their community in hard times. It was the most respectable among this downtrodden class who had the best chance of securing assistance.

Other poor whites moved frequently and survived by combining legal and illegal ventures. Some rejected laws and customs established by elites and joined forces with blacks or other poor whites. These men and women often had few ties to local communities, little religious training or education, and settled scores with violence. Although poor whites unnerved southern elites by flouting the law and sometimes befriending poor blacks, they could not mount any significant challenge to planter control.

Explore

10.3 Thomas Dew | The Proslavery Argument, 1832

Every one acquainted with southern slaves knows that the slave rejoices in the elevation and prosperity of his master; and the heart of no one is more gladdened at the successful debut of young master or miss on the great theatre of the world than that of either the young slave who has grown up with them and shared in all their sports, and even partaken of all their delicacies—or the aged one who has looked on and watched them from birth to manhood, with the kindest and most affectionate solicitude, and has ever met from them all the kind treatment and generous sympathies of feeling, tender hearts. Judge Smith, in his able speech on Foote's Resolutions in the Senate, said, in an emergency, he would rely upon his own slaves for his defence—he would put arms into their hands, and he had no doubt they would defend him faithfully. In the late Southampton insurrection, we know that many actually convened their slaves and armed them for defence, although slaves were here the cause of the evil which was to be repelled.

Source: William Harper, James Henry Hammond, William Gilmore Simms, and Thomas Roderick Dew, *The Pro-Slavery Argument* (Philadelphia: Lippincott, Grambo, 1853), 457–58.

Interpret the Evidence

- On what grounds do the women of Augusta County argue for an end to slavery, and how does their petition reflect their status as women?
- Why does Dew argue that slavery is beneficial for slaves? How do you think the Augusta women would respond to Dew's arguments?

Put It in Context

What do these statements convey about the divide over slavery in Virginia following Nat Turner's rebellion?

Unlike poor whites, the South's small but growing middle class sought stability and respectability. These middle-class Southerners, who worked as doctors, lawyers, journalists, teachers, and shopkeepers, often looked to the North for models to emulate. Many were educated in northern schools and developed ties with their commercial or professional counterparts in northern cities. They were avid readers of newspapers, religious tracts, and literary periodicals published in the North. And like middle-class Northerners,

southern businessmen often depended on their wives' social and financial skills to succeed.

Nonetheless, middle-class southern men shared many of the social attitudes and political priorities of slave owners. They participated alongside planters in benevolent associations, literary and temperance (antialcohol) societies, and agricultural reform organizations. Most middle-class Southerners also adamantly supported slavery and benefited from planters' demands for goods and services. In

SC [c.1850]

Gentlemen's Fashions

The owner of Welch's clothing store was among Charleston's well-known entrepreneurs. With this ad he appealed to middle-class men visiting the city on business as well as local residents, who he assumed shared a common sense of proper dress. The ad declares that Danskin's Pattern shirts received the "commendation of gentlemen in all parts of the United States." Courtesy, David M. Rubenstein Rare Book & Manuscript Library, Duke University, Durham, North Carolina

fact, some suggested that bound labor might be as useful to industry as it was to agriculture, and they sought to expand the institution further. Despite the emergence of a small middle class, however, the gap between rich and poor continued to expand in the South.

Planters Seek to Unify Southern Whites

Planters faced another challenge as nations in Europe and South America began to abolish slavery. Antislavery views, first expressed by a few Enlightenment thinkers and Quakers, gained growing support among evangelical

Protestants in Great Britain and the United States and among political radicals in Europe. Slave rebellions in Saint Domingue (Haiti) and the British West Indies in the early nineteenth century intensified these efforts. In 1807 the British Parliament forbade the sale of slaves within its empire and in 1834 emancipated all those who remained enslaved. France followed suit in 1848. As Spanish colonies such as Mexico and Nicaragua gained their independence in the 1820s and 1830s, they, too, eradicated the institution. Meanwhile gradual abolition laws in the northern United States slowly eliminated slavery there. Although slavery continued in Brazil and in Spanish colonies such as Cuba and serfdom remained in Russia, international attitudes toward human bondage were shifting.

In response, planters wielded their political and economic power to forge tighter bonds among white Southerners. According to the three-fifths compromise in the U.S. Constitution, areas with large slave populations gained more representatives in Congress than those without. The pattern held for state elections, too. In addition, well-educated planters and their allies were the likeliest candidates for office and the most successful. Planters also used their resources to provide credit for those in need, offer seasonal employment for poorer whites, transport crops to market for yeomen farmers, and contribute food, clothing, and other goods in times of crisis. Few poorer whites could afford to antagonize these affluent benefactors.

Wealthy planters also emphasized ties of family and faith. James Hammond, for example, assisted his siblings and other family members financially throughout their lives. Many slave owners also worshipped alongside their less well-to-do neighbors, and both the pastor and the congregation benefited from maintaining good relations with the wealthiest congregants. Many church members, like many relatives and neighbors, genuinely admired and respected planter elites who looked out for them.

Still, planters did not take white solidarity for granted. From the 1830s on, they relied on the ideology of white supremacy to cement the belief that all whites, regardless of class or education, were superior to all blacks. Following on Thomas Dew, southern elites argued with growing vehemence that the moral and intellectual failings of blacks meant that slavery was not just a necessary evil but actually a positive good. At the same time, they insisted that blacks harbored deep animosity toward whites, which could be controlled only by regulating every aspect of their lives. Combining racial fear and racial pride, planters forged bonds with poor and middling whites to guarantee their continued dominance. They also sought support from officials in the nation's capital.

REVIEW & RELATE

What groups made up white southern society? How did their interests overlap? How did they diverge?

How and why did the planter elite seek to reinforce white solidarity?

✓ *LEARNINGCurve* bedfordstmartins.com/hewittlawson/LC

Democrats Face Political and Economic Crises

Southern planters depended on federal power to expand and sustain the system of slavery. Although President Andrew Jackson disappointed slave owners on issues such as the tariff and states' rights, he stood with them on the policies of Indian removal and independence for Texas. Jackson's successor in the White House, Martin Van Buren, continued his predecessor's Indian policies and his support for the Republic of Texas. But Van Buren faced a more well-organized opposition in the **Whig Party**, which formed in the 1830s, while Texas rebels faced powerful resistance from Mexican and Comanche forces. Then in 1837 a prolonged and severe economic panic gripped the nation, creating an opportunity for the Whigs to end Democratic control of the federal government.

Continued Conflicts over Indian Lands

In 1830 Congress had passed the Indian Removal Act in hopes of settling the powerful Cherokee and Seminole tribes on land west of the Mississippi River. Not all Indian peoples went peacefully. As federal authorities forcibly removed the majority of Seminoles to Indian Territory between 1832 and 1835, a minority fought back. Jackson and his military commanders expected that this **Second Seminole War** would be short-lived. However, they misjudged the Seminoles' strength; the power of their charismatic leader, Osceola; and the resistance of African American fugitives living among the Seminoles. Hundreds of southern slaves had fled to Florida in the early nineteenth century seeking freedom. Some married Seminole women, while others were reenslaved by Seminole Indians. But the Seminoles treated slaves with more leniency than did southern whites, allowing them to live on small farms with their own families and enjoy many of the rights of full members of the tribe. Thus free and enslaved blacks fought fiercely against Seminole removal.

The war continued long after Jackson left the presidency. During the seven-year guerrilla war, 1,600 U.S. troops died and the government spent more than $30 million. U.S. military forces defeated the Seminoles in 1842 only by luring Osceola into an army camp with false promises of a peace settlement. Instead, officers took him captive, finally breaking the back of the resistance. Still, to end the conflict, the U.S. government had to allow fugitive slaves living among the Seminoles to accompany the tribe to Indian Territory.

Members of the Cherokee nation also resisted removal, but they fought their battles in the arena of public opinion and in the courts. Throughout the early nineteenth century, growing numbers of Cherokees had embraced "Americanization" programs offered by white missionaries, educators, and government agents. John Ross and other Indian leaders urged Cherokee people to accommodate to white ways, believing it was the best means to ensure the continued control of their own communities. When Georgia officials sought to impose new regulations on the Cherokees living within the state's borders, tribal leaders took them to court and sought to use evidence of their Christianity, domesticity, and republican government to maintain their rights.

In 1831 *Cherokee Nation v. Georgia* reached the Supreme Court, where Indian leaders demanded recognition as a separate nation as stipulated in the U.S. Constitution. Chief Justice John Marshall spoke for the majority when he ruled that all Indians in the United States were "domestic dependent nations" rather than fully sovereign governments. The Court thus denied a central part of the Cherokees' claim. Yet the following year, in *Worcester v. Georgia*, Marshall and the Court declared that the state of Georgia could not impose *state* laws on the Cherokees, for they had "territorial boundaries, within which their authority is exclusive," and that both their land and their rights were protected by the federal government.

President Jackson held a distinctly different view. He argued that only the removal of the Cherokees west of the Mississippi River could ensure their "physical comfort," "political advancement," and "moral improvement." Most southern whites agreed because they sought to expand cotton production into fertile Cherokee fields. But Protestant women and men in the North launched a massive petition campaign in 1830 supporting the Cherokees' right to their land. The Cherokees themselves forestalled action through Jackson's second term, but many federal and state officials continued to press for the tribe's removal.

Explore

Read a petition from Cherokee women resisting their removal in Document 10.4.

Petition of the Women's Councils to the Cherokee National Council, 1831

Throughout the early nineteenth century, Cherokee women fought against land cessions and removal and argued for communal land use rather than individual allotments. Traditionally, land and political authority passed through the mother's line, but as the Cherokee people adopted Anglo-American ways, patrilineal descent and men's authority replaced this matrilineal system. Despite this change, Cherokee women continued to petition the Cherokee National Council, urging the council to resist land cessions and removal. The following excerpt comes from an 1831 petition.

Explore

To the Committee and Council,

We the females, residing in Salequoree and Pine Log, believing that the present difficulties and embarrassments under which this nation is placed demands a full expression of the mind of every individual, on the subject of emigrating to Arkansas, would take upon ourselves to address you. Although it is not common for our sex to take part in public measures, we nevertheless feel justified in expressing our sentiments on any subject where our interest is as much at stake as any other part of the community.

We believe the present plan of the General Government to effect our removal West of the Mississippi, and thus obtain our lands for the use of the State of Georgia, to be highly oppressive, cruel, and unjust. And we sincerely hope there is no consideration which can induce our citizens to forsake the land of our fathers of which they have been in possession from time immemorial, and thus compel us, against our will, to undergo the toils and difficulties of removing with our helpless families hundreds of miles to unhealthy and unproductive country. We hope therefore the Committee and Council will take into deep consideration our deplorable situation, and do everything in their power to avert such a state of things. And we trust by a prudent course their transactions with the General Government will enlist in our behalf the sympathies of the good people of the United States.

Source: *Cherokee Phoenix*, November 12, 1831, in *The Cherokee Removal: A Brief History with Documents*, 2nd ed., ed. Theda Purdue and Michael Green (Boston: Bedford/St. Martin's, 2005), 134.

Interpret the Evidence

- On what grounds did the women protest Cherokee removal?
- How did the women use references to their gender to inspire sympathy and support from council members?

Put It in Context

What light does the petition shed on the women's understanding of the politics and government of the United States?

In December 1835, U.S. officials convinced a small group of Cherokee men—without tribal sanction—to sign the **Treaty of New Echota**. It proposed the exchange of 100 million acres of Cherokee land in the Southeast for $68 million and 32 million acres in Indian Territory. Cherokee leaders, including John Ross, lobbied Congress to reject the treaty, but to no avail. In May 1836, Congress approved the treaty by a single vote and set the date for final removal two years later. Although most of the

17,000 Cherokees resisted this plan, they had few means left to defy the U.S. government (Map 10.2).

In May 1838, the U.S. army began to forcibly remove any Cherokee who had not yet resettled in Indian Territory. General Winfield Scott, assisted by 7,000 U.S. soldiers, forced some 15,000 Cherokees into forts and military camps that June. The Cherokees spent the next several months without sufficient food, water, sanitation, or medicine. The situation went from bad to worse. In

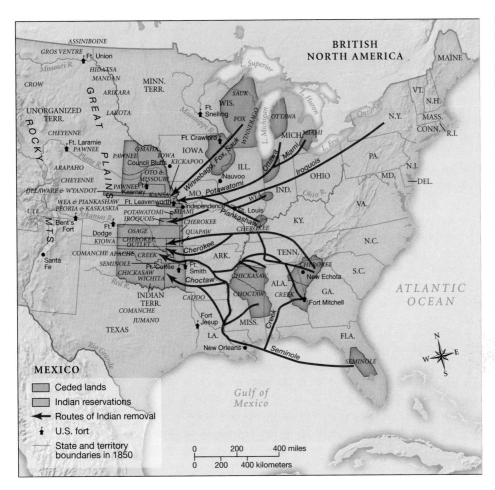

MAP 10.2　Indian Removals and Relocations, 1820s–1850s

In the 1820s and 1830s, the federal government used a variety of tactics, including military force, to expel Indian nations residing east of the Mississippi River. As these tribes resettled in the West, white migration along the Oregon and other trails began to increase. The result, by 1850, was the forced relocation of many western Indian nations as well.

October, when the Cherokees began the march west, torrential rains were followed by snow. Although the U.S. army planned for a trip of less than three months, the journey actually took five months. As supplies ran short, many Indians, weakened by disease and hunger, died, including Ross's wife. The remaining Cherokees completed this **Trail of Tears**, as it became known, in March 1839. But thousands remained near starvation a year later.

The Battle for Texas

While whites in Georgia sought Cherokee land, those on the frontier looked toward Texas. Some Southerners had moved into Texas in the early nineteenth century, but the Adams-Onís Treaty of 1819 guaranteed Spanish control of the territory. Then in 1821 Mexicans overthrew Spanish rule and claimed Texas as part of the new Republic of Mexico. But Mexicans, like the Spaniards before them, faced serious competition from Comanche Indians, who controlled vast areas to the north and west and launched raids into Texas for horses and other livestock.

Eager to increase settlement in the area and to create a buffer against the Comanches, the Mexican government granted U.S. migrants some of the best land in eastern Texas. It hoped these settlers—many of whom brought slaves to cultivate cotton—would eventually spread into the interior, where Comanche raids had devastated Mexican communities. To entice more Southerners, the Mexican government negotiated a special exemption for U.S. planters when it outlawed slavery in 1829. But rather than spreading into the interior, U.S. farmers and planters stayed east of the Colorado River, out of reach of Comanche raiders and close to U.S. markets in Louisiana.

While the Mexican residents of Texas developed a vibrant Tejano culture that combined Catholicism, Spanish language and culture, and indigenous customs, U.S. settlers resisted acculturation. Instead, they continued to worship as Protestants, speak English, send their children to separate schools, and trade mainly with the United States. By 1835 the 27,000 white Southerners and their 3,000 slaves far outnumbered the 3,000 Mexicans living in eastern Texas.

Comanche Lodge
George Catlin's painting of a buffalo-skin lodge in the mid-1830s shows Little Spaniard, of mixed Spanish and Indian heritage, arriving in camp. The introduction of horses on the Great Plains allowed nomadic hunters like the Comanches, who had relied on dogs to transport the poles and covers of their tepees, to live in much bigger and heavier shelters. Smithsonian American Art Museum, Washington, DC/Art Resource, NY

Forming a majority of the east Texas population and eager to expand their plantations and trade networks, growing numbers of U.S. settlers demanded independence. **See Document Project 10: Claiming Texas, page 319.** Then in 1836 Mexicans elected a strong nationalist leader, General Antonio López de Santa Anna, as president. He sought to rein in **Tejanos** angered over their vulnerability to Comanche attacks and to curb American settlers seeking further concessions. When Santa Anna appointed a military commander to rule Texas, independence-minded U.S. migrants organized a rebellion. On March 2, they declared eastern Texas an independent republic and adopted a constitution that legalized slavery. Some elite Tejanos, long neglected by authorities in Mexico City, sided with the rebels. The rebellion appeared to be short-lived, however. On March 6, 1836, General Santa Anna crushed settlers defending the **Alamo** in San Antonio. His troops killed all 250 men at the fort but freed the women and children. Soon thereafter, Santa Anna captured the U.S. settlement at Goliad.

Although Santa Anna's troops suffered more than 1,500 casualties, several times those of the rebel forces, the general was convinced that the uprising was over. But the U.S. government, despite its claims of neutrality, aided the rebels with funds and army officers. Newspapers in New Orleans and New York picked up the story of the Alamo and published dramatic accounts of the battle, describing the Mexican fighters as brutal butchers bent on saving Texas for the pope. These stories, though more fable than fact, increased popular support for the war at a time when many Americans were growing increasingly hostile to Catholic immigrants in the United States.

As hundreds of armed volunteers headed to Texas, General Sam Houston led rebel forces in a critical victory at San Jacinto in April 1836. While the Mexican government refused to recognize rebel claims, it did not try to regain the lost ground in east Texas. Few of the U.S. volunteers arrived in time to participate in the fighting, but some settled in the newly liberated region. Still, the failure of Santa Anna to recognize Texan independence kept the

U.S. government from granting the territory statehood for fear it would lead to war with Mexico. Fortunately for the rebels, the Comanche nation did recognize the Republic of Texas and developed trade relations with residents to gain access to the vast U.S. market.

Meanwhile President Jackson worried that admitting a new slave state might split the national Democratic Party just before the fall elections. To limit debate on the issue, Congress passed a **gag rule** in March 1836 that tabled all antislavery petitions without being read. Nevertheless, thousands of women and men from Ohio to Massachusetts still flooded the House of Representatives with petitions opposing the annexation of Texas.

Van Buren and the Panic of 1837

With Jackson suffering from tuberculosis, the Democratic convention chose Vice President Martin Van Buren to run for president in 1836. The Whigs hoped to defeat Van Buren by bringing together diverse supporters: financiers and commercial farmers who advocated internal improvements and protective tariffs; merchants and manufacturers who favored a national bank; evangelical Protestants who objected to Jackson's Indian policy; and Southerners who were antagonized by the president's heavy-handed use of federal authority. But these disparate interests led the Whigs to nominate three different men for president, and this lack of unity allowed Democrats to fend off an increasingly powerful opposition. Although Van Buren won the popular vote by only a small margin (50.9 percent), he secured an easy majority in the electoral college.

Inaugurated on March 4, 1837, President Van Buren soon faced another crisis that threatened the Democrats' hold on power. The **panic of 1837** started in the South and was rooted in the changing fortunes of American cotton in Great Britain. During the 1830s, the British invested heavily in cotton plantations and brokerage firms, and southern planters used the funds to expand cotton production and improve shipping facilities. British banks also lent large sums to states such as New York to fund internal improvements. This infusion of British money into the U.S. economy fueled inflation, and in February 1837 rising prices prompted protests by farmers and workers. But worse problems lay ahead.

In late 1836, the Bank of England, faced with bad harvests and declining demand for textiles, had tightened credit to limit the flow of money out of the country. This forced British investors to call in their loans and drove up interest rates in the United States just as cotton prices started to fall. Some of the largest American cotton merchants were forced to declare bankruptcy. The banks

where they held accounts then failed—ninety-eight of them in March and April 1837 alone.

The economic crisis hit the South hard. Cotton prices fell by nearly half in less than a year. Land values declined dramatically, many southern whites lost farms and homes, port cities came to a standstill, and cotton communities on the southern frontier collapsed. The damage soon radiated throughout the United States. Northern brokers, shippers, and merchants were devastated by losses in the cotton trade, and northern banks were hit by unpaid debts incurred for canals and other internal improvements. Entrepreneurs who borrowed money to expand their businesses defaulted in large numbers. Shopkeepers, artisans, and farmers in the North and Midwest suffered unemployment and foreclosures.

Many Americans, especially in the North and West, blamed Jackson's war against the Bank of the United States for precipitating the panic. They were also outraged at Van Buren's refusal to intervene in the crisis. Probably no federal policy could have resolved the problems created by the "credit bubble," which had been brought on by the ready availability of British money. Still, the president's apparent disinterest in the plight of the people inspired harsh criticisms from ordinary citizens as well as political opponents. Worse, despite brief signs of recovery in 1838, the depression deepened in 1839 and continued for four more years.

The Whigs Win the White House

Van Buren was clearly vulnerable as he faced reelection in 1840. Eager to exploit the Democrats' weakness, the Whig Party organized its first national convention that fall and united behind military hero William Henry Harrison (see chapter 9). Harrison was born to a wealthy planter family in Virginia, but the sixty-eight-year-old soldier was portrayed as a self-made man who lived in a simple log cabin in Indiana. His running mate, John Tyler, another Virginia gentleman and a onetime Democrat, joined the Whigs because of his opposition to Jackson's stand on nullification. Whig leaders hoped he would attract southern voters. Taking their cue from the Democrats, the Whigs organized rallies, barbecues, parades, and mass meetings. They turned the tables on their foe by portraying Van Buren as an aristocrat who enjoyed fine wines and expensive clothes and Harrison as the hero of the common man. Reminding voters that Harrison had defeated Tenskwatawa at the Battle of Tippecanoe, the Whigs adopted the slogan "Tippecanoe and Tyler Too."

Explore

See Document 10.5 for a poster from Harrison's "log cabin" campaign.

DOCUMENT 10.5

William Henry Harrison Campaign Poster, 1840

The 1840 presidential campaign pitted the incumbent Martin Van Buren against William Henry Harrison. Harrison, the Whig Party candidate, was portrayed as a man from humble origins even though he was the son of a wealthy Virginia planter. His campaign slogan "Tippecanoe and Tyler Too" highlighted his military background and leadership in the defeat of Tenskwatawa at the Battle of Tippecanoe. The campaign was a rousing success, and Harrison and his running mate, John Tyler, handily defeated Van Buren with 53 percent of the popular vote.

Library of Congress

Interpret the Evidence

- What impression of Harrison and his background was the poster meant to convey?
- What characteristics does the poster associate with the "common man" and, by extension, Harrison?

Put It in Context

How does this poster illustrate the democratization of American politics in the first half of the nineteenth century?

The Whigs also welcomed women into the campaign. By 1840 thousands of women had circulated petitions against Cherokee removal, organized temperance societies, promoted religious revivals, and joined charitable associations. They embodied the kind of moral force that the Whig Party claimed to represent. In October 1840, Whig senator Daniel Webster spoke to a gathering of 1,200 women. He praised women's moral virtues and asked audience members to encourage their brothers and husbands to vote for Harrison.

The Whig strategy paid off handsomely on election day when some 80 percent of eligible voters cast ballots. Harrison won easily, and the Whigs gained a majority in Congress. Yet the election's promise was shattered when "old Tippecanoe" died of pneumonia a month after his inauguration. Whigs in Congress now had to deal with John Tyler, whose sentiments were largely southern and Democratic. Frustrating Whig plans for reform with vetoes, Tyler allowed the Democratic Party to regroup and set the stage for close elections in 1844 and 1848.

REVIEW & RELATE

How and why did Indian nations in the Southeast resist removal to the West while some Indians in the West forged ties with U.S. markets?

What events and developments led to a Whig victory in the election of 1840?

LEARNINGCurve bedfordstmartins.com/hewittlawson/LC

The National Government Looks to the West

Despite the Whig victory in 1840, planters wielded considerable clout in Washington, D.C., because of the importance of cotton to the U.S. economy. In turn, Southerners needed federal support to expand into more fertile areas. The presidential election of 1844 turned on this issue, with Democratic candidate James K. Polk demanding continued expansion into Oregon and Mexico. Once Polk was in office, his claims were contested not only by Britain and Mexico but also by the Comanches, who controlled the southern plains. After the United States won vast Mexican territories in 1848, conflicts with Indians and debates over slavery only intensified.

Expanding to Oregon and Texas

Southerners eager to expand the plantation economy looked not only to the West for additional lands but also to Cuba and Nicaragua in the 1830s and 1840s. Although efforts to capture these areas failed, planters continued to press for expansion. Yet expansion was not merely a southern strategy. Northerners demanded that the United States renounce its joint occupation of the Oregon Country with Great Britain. And some northern politicians and businessmen believed that acquisition of lands in Hawaii and Samoa could benefit U.S. trade. In 1844 the Democratic Party built on these expansionist dreams to recapture the White House.

Initially, Democrats could not agree on a candidate, but they ultimately nominated a Tennessee congressman and governor, James K. Polk. The Whigs, unwilling to nominate Tyler for president, chose the well-known Kentucky senator Henry Clay. Polk ran on a platform that proclaimed the "Reoccupation of Oregon and the Annexation of Texas." Clay, meanwhile, remained uncommitted on the issue of Texas. This proved his undoing when the small but growing Liberty Party, adamantly opposed to slavery, denounced annexation. Liberty Party candidate James G. Birney captured just enough votes in New York State to throw the state and the election to Polk.

In February 1845, a month before Polk took office, Congress passed a joint resolution annexing the Republic of Texas. The day before Polk's inauguration, Florida was also admitted to statehood. That summer, John L. O'Sullivan, editor of the *Democratic Review*, captured the American mood by declaring that nothing must interfere with "the fulfillment of our manifest destiny to overspread the continent allotted by Providence for the free development of our yearly multiplying millions." This vision of **manifest destiny**—of the nation's God-given right to expand its borders—defined Polk's presidency.

With the Florida and Texas questions seemingly resolved, President Polk turned his attention to Oregon, which stretched from the forty-second parallel to latitude 54°40′ and was jointly occupied by Great Britain and the United States. Residents of either nation could settle anywhere in the region, but most of the British lived north of the Columbia River, while most Americans settled to the south.

In 1842, three years before Polk took office, settlers' glowing reports of the mild climate and fertile soil around Puget Sound had inspired thousands of farmers and traders to migrate to Oregon. Americans flooded into the Willamette valley, and merchants involved in the China trade imagined a thriving U.S. trading post on the Oregon coast. Alarmed by this "Oregon fever," the British tried to confine Americans to areas south of the Columbia River. But American settlers demanded access to the entire territory, proclaiming "Fifty-four forty or fight!" As president, Polk encouraged migration into Oregon, but he was unwilling to risk war with

Astoria, Oregon, 1848

In 1845 the British army sent Lieutenant Henry Warre to the Oregon Country to gather intelligence on American settlements in case of war with the United States. Warre sketched Astoria, which lies at the mouth of the Columbia River. The first permanent settlement in the Oregon Country, it was established by John Jacob Astor's Pacific Fur Company in 1811.   The Granger Collection, New York

Great Britain. Instead, diplomats negotiated a treaty in 1846 that extended the border with British Canada (the forty-ninth parallel) to the Pacific Ocean. Over the next two years, Congress admitted Iowa and Wisconsin to statehood, reassuring northern residents that expansion benefited all regions of the nation.

Many of the lands newly claimed by the U.S. government were home to vast numbers of Indians. Indeed, the West had become more crowded as the U.S. government forced eastern tribes to move west of the Mississippi (see Map 10.2). When the Cherokee and other southeastern tribes were removed to Indian Territory, for example, they confronted local tribes such as the Osage. Pushed into the Southwest, the Osages came into conflict with the Comanches, who had earlier fought the Apaches for control of the southern plains. Other Indian nations were pushed onto the northern plains from the Old Northwest. There the Sioux became the dominant tribe by the 1830s after seizing hunting grounds from the Omahas, Iowas, and Cheyennes, who resettled farther south and west.

The flood of U.S. migrants into Texas and the southern plains transformed relations among Indian nations as well as with Mexico. In the face of Spanish and then Mexican claims on their lands, for example, the Comanches forged alliances with former foes like the Wichitas and the Osages. The Comanches also developed commercial ties with tribes in Indian Territory and with Mexican and Anglo-American traders on the frontiers of their respective nations. In these ways, they hoped to benefit from the imperial ambitions of the United States and Mexico while strengthening bonds among Indians in the region.

Comanche expansion was especially problematic for Mexico once it achieved independence in 1821. The young nation did not have sufficient resources to sustain the level of gift giving that Spanish authorities used to maintain peace. As a result, Comanche warriors launched continual raids against Tejano settlements in Texas. But the Comanches also developed commercial relations with residents of New Mexico, who flaunted trade regulations promulgated in Mexico City in order to maintain peace with neighboring

Indians. By 1846 Comanche trade and diplomatic relations with New Mexican settlements had seriously weakened the hold of Mexican authorities on their northern provinces.

Pursuing War with Mexico

At the same time, with Texas now a state, Mexico faced growing tensions with the United States. Conflicts centered on Texas's western border. Mexico insisted on the Nueces River as the boundary line, while Americans claimed all the land to the Rio Grande. In January 1846, Polk secretly sent emissary John Slidell to negotiate with Mexico, offering

President José Herrera $30 million for New Mexico and California after securing the Rio Grande boundary. But Polk also sent U.S. troops under General Zachary Taylor across the Nueces River. Mexican officials refused to see Slidell and instead sent their own troops across the Rio Grande. Meanwhile U.S. naval commanders prepared to seize San Francisco Bay if war was declared. The Mexican government responded to these hostile overtures by sending more troops into the disputed Texas territory.

When fighting erupted near the Rio Grande in May 1846 (Map 10.3), Polk claimed that "American blood had been shed on American soil" and declared a state of war.

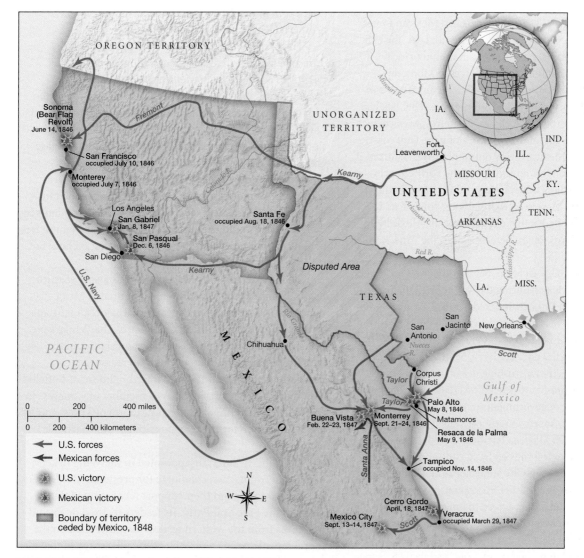

MAP 10.3   The Mexican-American War, 1846–1848

Although a dispute over territory between the Nueces River and the Rio Grande initiated the Mexican-American War, most of the fighting occurred between the Rio Grande and Mexico City. In addition, U.S. forces in California launched battles to claim independence for that region even before gold was discovered there.

Many Whigs in Congress protested, arguing that the president had provoked the conflict. Congressman Abraham Lincoln of Illinois demanded that Polk "show me the spot" where U.S. blood was shed. However, antiwar Whigs failed to convince the Democratic majority, and Congress voted to finance the war.

The South was solidly behind the war. As the Charleston, South Carolina, *Courier* declared: "Every battle fought in Mexico and every dollar spent there, but insures the acquisition of territory which must widen the field of Southern enterprise and power in the future." Most Northerners also supported the war. Although ardent opponents of slavery protested, most Americans considered westward expansion a boon (see Map 10.3).

Once the war began, battles erupted in a variety of locations. In May 1846, U.S. troops defeated Mexican forces in Palo Alto and Resaca de la Palma. A month later, the U.S. army captured Sonoma, California, with the aid of local settlers. John Frémont then led U.S. forces to Monterey, California, where the navy launched a successful attack and declared the territory part of the United States. That fall, U.S. troops gained important victories at Monterrey, Mexico, just west of the Rio Grande, and Tampico, along the Gulf coast.

Although the Mexican army outnumbered U.S. forces, it failed to capitalize on this advantage. In the northern provinces, Mexican soldiers were ill equipped for major battles, and in the heart of Mexico divisions among political and military leaders limited battlefield success. Still, Mexican soldiers and residents fought fiercely against the American invaders.

Despite major U.S. victories, Santa Anna, who reclaimed the presidency of Mexico during the war, refused to give up. In February 1847, his troops attacked General Taylor's forces at Buena Vista and nearly secured a victory. Polk then agreed to send General Winfield Scott to Veracruz with 14,000 soldiers. Capturing the port in March, Scott's army marched on to Mexico City. After a crushing defeat of Santa Anna at Cerro Gordo, the president-general was removed from power, and the new Mexican government sought peace.

With victory ensured, U.S. officials faced a difficult decision: How much Mexican territory should they claim? The U.S. army in central Mexico faced continued guerrilla attacks. Meanwhile Whigs and some northern Democrats denounced the war as a southern conspiracy to expand slavery. In this context, Polk agreed to limit U.S. claims to the northern regions of Mexico. Eager to unite the Democratic Party before the fall election, the president signed the **Treaty of Guadalupe Hidalgo** in February 1848, and the U.S. Senate ratified it in March. The treaty committed the United States to pay Mexico $15 million in return for control over Texas north and east of the Rio Grande plus California and the New Mexico territory.

Debates over Slavery Intensify

News of the U.S. victory traveled quickly across the United States. In the South, planters imagined slavery spreading into the lands acquired from Mexico. Northerners, too, applauded the expansion of U.S. territory but focused on California as a center for agriculture and commerce. Yet the acquisition of new territory only heightened sectional conflicts. Debates over slavery had erupted during the war, with a few northern Democrats joining Whigs in denouncing "the power of SLAVERY" to "govern the country, its Constitutions and laws." In August 1846, Democratic congressman David Wilmot of Pennsylvania proposed outlawing slavery in all territory acquired from Mexico so that the South could not profit from the war. The **Wilmot Proviso** passed in the House, but in the Senate, Southerners and proslavery northern Democrats killed it.

The presidential election of 1848 opened with the unresolved question of whether to allow slavery in the territories acquired from Mexico. Polk, exhausted by the war effort and divisions among Democrats, refused to run for a second term. In his place, Democrats nominated Lewis Cass, a senator from Michigan and an ardent expansionist. He had suggested that the United States purchase Cuba from Spain in 1848 and advocated seizing all of Oregon and more of Mexico. Hoping to keep northern antislavery Democrats in the party, Cass campaigned for what he called "squatter sovereignty," by which residents in each territory would decide whether to make the region free or slave. This strategy put the slavery question on hold but satisfied almost no one.

The Whigs, too, hoped to avoid the slavery issue for fear of losing southern votes. They nominated Mexican-American War hero General Zachary Taylor, a Louisiana slaveholder with no political experience. The Whigs were pleased that he had not taken a stand on slavery in the western territories. But they sought to reassure their northern wing by nominating Millard Fillmore of Buffalo, New York, for vice president. As a member of Congress in the 1830s, he had opposed the annexation of Texas, and he had a reputation for fiscal responsibility and charitable endeavors.

The Liberty Party, disappointed in the Whig ticket, decided to run its own candidate for president. But leaders who hoped to expand their support reconstituted themselves as the Free-Soil Party. Its leaders focused on excluding slaves from the western territories rather than on the moral injustice of slavery. Still, Free-Soilers argued that slavery empowered "aristocratic men" and threatened the rights of "the great mass of the people." The party nominated former president Martin Van Buren and appealed to small farmers and urban workers who hoped to benefit from western expansion.

Once again, the presence of a third party affected the outcome of the election. While Whigs and Democrats tried to avoid the slavery issue, Free-Soilers demanded attention to it. By focusing on the exclusion of slavery in western territories rather than its abolition, the Free-Soil Party won more adherents in northern states. Indeed, Van Buren won enough northern Democrats so that Cass lost New York State and the 1848 election. Zachary Taylor and the Whigs won, but only by placing a southern slaveholder in the White House.

REVIEW & RELATE

- How did western expansion both benefit Americans and exacerbate conflicts among them?

- How did the Mexican-American War reshape national politics and intensify debates over slavery?

✔️ *LEARNINGCurve* bedfordstmartins.com/hewittlawson/LC

Conclusion: Geographical Expansion and Political Division

By the mid-nineteenth century, the United States stood at a crossroads. Most Americans considered expansion advantageous and critical to revitalizing the economy.

Planters believed it was vital to slavery's success. While most white Northerners were willing to leave slavery alone where it already existed, many hoped to keep it out of newly acquired territories. The vast lands gained from Mexico in 1848 intensified these debates. Between 1830 and 1850, small but growing numbers of Northerners joined slaves, American Indians, and Mexicans in protesting U.S. expansion. Even some yeomen farmers and middle-class professionals in the South questioned whether extending slavery benefited the region economically and politically. But these challenges remained limited until 1848, when the fight over slavery in the territories fractured the Democratic Party, created a crisis for the Whigs, and inspired the growth of the Free-Soil Party.

Political realignments continued over the next decade, fueled by growing antislavery sentiment in the North and proslavery ideology in the South. In 1853 Solomon Northrup horrified thousands of antislavery readers with his book *Twelve Years a Slave*, which vividly described his life in bondage. Such writings alarmed planters like James Henry Hammond, who continued to believe that slavery was "the greatest of all the great blessings which Providence has bestowed upon our glorious region." Yet in insisting on the benefits of slave labor, the planter elite inspired further conflict with Northerners, whose lives were increasingly shaped by commercial and industrial developments and the expansion of free labor.

LEARNINGCurve
Check what you know.
bedfordstmartins.com/hewittlawson/LC

Chapter Review

Online Study Guide ▶ bedfordstmartins.com/hewittlawson

KEY TERMS

syncretic culture (p. 301)
Nat Turner's rebellion (p. 302)
yeomen farmers (p. 303)
Whig Party (p. 307)
Second Seminole War (p. 307)
Treaty of New Echota (p. 308)
Trail of Tears (p. 309)
Tejanos (p. 310)
Alamo (p. 310)
gag rule (p. 311)
panic of 1837 (p. 311)
manifest destiny (p. 313)
Treaty of Guadalupe Hidalgo (p. 316)
Wilmot Proviso (p. 316)

REVIEW & RELATE

1. What role did the planter elite play in southern society and politics?

2. What were the consequences of the dominant position of slave-based plantation agriculture in the southern economy?

3. How did enslaved African Americans create ties of family, community, and culture?

4. How did enslaved African Americans resist efforts to control and exploit their labor?

5. What groups made up white southern society? How did their interests overlap? How did they diverge?

6. How and why did the planter elite seek to reinforce white solidarity?

7. How and why did Indian nations in the Southeast resist removal to the West while some Indians in the West forged ties with U.S. markets?

8. What events and developments led to a Whig victory in the election of 1840?

9. How did western expansion both benefit Americans and exacerbate conflicts among them?

10. How did the Mexican-American War reshape national politics and intensify debates over slavery?

TIMELINE OF EVENTS

1820–1850	Southern cotton production increases from about 500,000 bales to 3 million bales
1821	Mexico overthrows Spanish rule and encourages U.S. settlement in Texas
1830–1850	440,000 slaves from the Upper South sold to owners in the Lower South
1831	*Cherokee Nation v. Georgia*
August 1831	Nat Turner leads slave uprising in Virginia
December 1831	Virginia's Assembly establishes special committee on slavery
1832	*Worcester v. Georgia*
1833	Tredegar Iron Works established
1834	Britain abolishes slavery
1835–1842	Second Seminole War
1836	Treaty of New Echota
March 2, 1836	U.S. settlers declare eastern Texas an independent republic
March 6, 1836	General Santa Anna crushes U.S. rebels at the Alamo
March 1836	James Hammond leads campaign that results in congressional gag rule
1837	Panic of 1837 triggers recession
October 1838–March 1839	Trail of Tears
1840	Whigs win the presidency and gain control of Congress
1841	Solomon Northrup kidnapped and sold into slavery
1845	U.S. annexes Texas
1846	U.S. settles dispute with Great Britain over Oregon
May 1846–February 1848	Mexican-American War
August 1846	David Wilmot proposes Wilmot Proviso
March 1848	Treaty of Guadalupe Hidalgo
1853	Solomon Northrup publishes *Twelve Years a Slave*

DOCUMENT PROJECT **10**

Claiming Texas

When Mexico overthrew Spanish control in 1821, the newly formed Mexican government encouraged more U.S. residents to move into Texas, hoping to expand settlement on its northern frontier. Some families, like the one led by Moses Austin, acquired huge tracts of land and then resold land titles to other American families. These settlers were mostly interested in the rich farmland they found, and they brought their slaves with them to cultivate cotton and other plantation-style crops (Document 10.6). Throughout the 1830s, conflicts erupted between these recent settlers and the Mexican government over control of the region. By 1836 open rebellion broke out in east Texas, and in March of that year U.S.-born Texans declared their region an independent republic (Document 10.7). But after declaring independence, rebels at the Alamo in San Antonio were overrun by Mexican forces, who killed all 250 men stationed there. Stories of the heroic efforts of Americans at the Alamo reached the eastern United States, including letters such as the one from Colonel William Travis (Document 10.8), who pleaded for reinforcements in a desperate attempt to hold the fort. Although reinforcements arrived too late to save the Alamo, hundreds of volunteers flocked to Texas from the United States. They helped General Sam Houston win a decisive victory against Mexican forces just a month later at the Battle of San Jacinto. Still the Mexican government refused to recognize Texas as an independent republic, and the U.S. government refused to annex Texas, fearing it would lead to war with Mexico.

As an independent republic, Texas had to resolve both the issue of slavery and relations with Indians. Leaders drafted a constitution in 1836 that legalized slavery, and many new settlers supported the provision. In response, abolitionists in the United States opposed statehood for Texas. Documents 10.9 and 10.10 demonstrate opposing sides of this debate, one that continued even after Texas was admitted as a state in 1845. At the same time, Texas sought to ensure its stability by sometimes seeking peace with and at other times making war on the numerous Indian tribes on its borders. Likewise, Comanche, Caddo, Shawnee, and other Indian nations alternately traded with and raided the Texas settlements. After years of broken treaties, hostage taking, and warfare, Texas officials and Indian chiefs finalized a treaty in October 1844 to ensure peace and improve trade in the region (Document 10.11).

DOCUMENT 10.6

Mary Austin Holley | Letter to Charles Austin, 1831

In 1831 Mary Holley visited her cousin Stephen Austin at his home in Texas. It was her first visit to the region, and her letters home were filled with vivid, if idealized, descriptions of the people and land she encountered there. Her letters were published in 1833, and she later wrote the first English-language history of Texas. Although she never permanently settled in Texas, Holley's writings attracted many others to the region.

Bolivar, Texas, December, 1831

One's feelings in Texas are unique and original, and very like a dream or youthful vision realized. Here, as in Eden, man feels alone with the God of nature, and seems, in a peculiar manner, to enjoy the rich bounties of heaven, in common with all created things, The animals, which do not fly from him; the profound stillness; the genial sun and soft air—all are impressive, and are calculated both to delight the imagination and to fill the heart with religious emotions.

With regard to the state of society here, as is natural to expect, there are many incongruities. It will take some time for people gathered from the north and from the south, from the east, and from the west to assimilate and adapt themselves to new situations. The people are universally kind and hospitable, which are redeeming qualities. Everybody's house is open and table spread to accommodate the traveller. There are no poor people here, and none rich; that is, none who have much money. The poor and the rich, to use the correlatives, where distinction, there is none, get the same quantity of land on arrival, and if they do not continue equal, it is for want of good management on the one part, or superior industry and sagacity on the other. All are happy because busy; and none meddle with the affairs of their neighbours because they have enough to do to take care of their own. They are bound together by a common interest, by sameness of purpose and hopes. As far as I could learn, they have no envyings, no jealousies, no bickerings, through politics or fanaticism. . . .

. . . I should say, industrious farmers will certainly do well, and cannot fail of success; that is to say, if abundant crops and a ready market with high prices will satisfy them. Substantial planters with capital and hands may enlarge their operations here to any extent and with enormous profits. One gentleman, for instance, whom I visited, has ninety-three acres under cultivation by seven hands. His crop this year consists of eighty bales of cotton, two thousand bushels of corn, five hundred bushels of sweet potatoes, besides other articles of minor importance.

Source: Mary Austin Holley, *Texas: Observations, Historical, Geographical, and Descriptive, in a Series of Letters, Written during a Visit to Austin's Colony, with a View of a Permanent Settlement in That Country, in the Autumn of 1831* (Baltimore: Armstrong & Plaskitt, 1833), 127–29.

DOCUMENT 10.7

Colonel Gregorio Gomez | Call to Arms against the Texans, 1835

In the early 1830s, more and more settlers from the United States moved to Texas. They viewed Mexican/Tejano culture and Catholicism with suspicion, while Mexicans considered these "Texian colonists" as outsiders with little claim to the land. By 1835 these tensions erupted in armed conflict. In the following selection, Colonel Gregorio Gomez calls on Mexicans to defend their nation against U.S. invaders. The next month, Gomez waged a successful battle at Tampico under the leadership of Mexican exile José Antonio Mexia.

October 17, 1835

Gregorio Gomez, colonel of the battalion Tres Villas, and commandant of this town, to his brothers in arms and to the inhabitants.

Friends: It is now proved that the fears of all good Mexicans have been too well founded. The hypocritical and false promises of the Texian colonists have not deceived the enlightened part of the nation: These ungrateful traitors, these unnatural guests, in return for the liberality and the favors shown them by our country, are attempting now to plunge a murderous poignard [knife] in her bosom. The crisis in which the republic is now involved has favored their plans. They have openly declared their rebellion; and attempt no less than dismembering that rich part of our territory, where they have been received with such liberal hospitality. By the last official accounts we have learned that they have already begun to act. The weak garrison stationed at Bahia del Espiritu Santo has been captured by the rebels, who have taken military possession of the place. What will be the consequence of such wanton proceedings, if not the complete annihilation of those usurpers? Is there a Mexican who would not be fired with indignation at beholding the national honor and integrity of territory violated by a gang of lawless foreigners? Foreigners they are certainly by birth and principles; and by their treacherous conduct they have forfeited all the privileges and immunities granted to them by our too generous country.

It is now [not?] an internal question, when the members of the same family may be involved in domestic quarrels; but it is a question where adventurous foreigners are preying upon us, to rob us of one of our most precious gems, whilst we are deliberating on the ways and means to regulate properly the whole of our public concerns. Thousand curses on the Mexican who should be dastardly enough to join the murderous and anti-national plot! His name should be branded with infamy; and his crime never forgotten by his brethren. Let us then appeal to arms, let us rally round the government, and, with the native bravery of Mexicans, let us rush on these gangs of perfidious foreigners. Let us dispel them as the wind doth a flying cloud; and let us avenge her [the country's] honor, sullied in so atrocious a manner. Such are the sentiments of your brother in arms, and of your comrade who is ever ready to sacrifice his life in defence of such a noble cause.

Source: *Niles' Weekly Register*, November 21, 1835, 188.

DOCUMENT 10.8

Colonel William Travis | Appeal for Reinforcements, March 3, 1836

In February 1836, a small group of Texian colonists gathered at the Alamo in San Antonio to defend their settlements against Mexican forces. The rebels held out for thirteen days, during which time one of the co-commanders, twenty-six-year-old William Travis, wrote several letters appealing to supporters in the United States for reinforcements, including his last appeal, which was sent on March 3.

I hope your honorable body will hasten on reinforcements, ammunition, and provisions to our aid, as soon as possible. We have provisions for twenty days for the men we have: our supply of ammunition is limited. At least five hundred pounds of cannon powder, and two hundred rounds of six, nine, twelve, and eighteen pound balls—ten kegs of rifle powder, and a supply of lead, should be sent to this place without delay, under a sufficient guard.

If these things are promptly sent and large reinforcements are hastened to this frontier, this neighborhood will be the great and decisive battle ground. The power of Santa Ana is to be met here, or in the colonies; we had better meet them here, than to suffer a war of desolation to rage in our settlements. A blood-red banner waves from the church of Bejar, and in the camp above us, in token that the war is one of vengeance against rebels; they have declared us such, and demanded that we should surrender at discretion, or that this garrison should be put to the sword. Their threats have had no influence on me, or my men, but to make all fight with desperation, and that high souled courage which characterizes the patriot, who is willing to die in defence of his country's liberty and his own honor.

The citizens of this municipality are all our enemies except those who have joined us heretofore; we have but three Mexicans now in the fort: those who have not joined us in this extremity, should be declared public enemies, and their property should aid in paying the expenses of the war.

The bearer of this will give your honorable body a statement more in detail should he escape through the enemies lines.

God and Texas—Victory or Death!!

Your obedient ser't
W. Barrett Travis, Lieut. Col. Comm.

P.S. The enemies troops are still arriving and the reinforcement will probably amount to two or three thousand.

Source: *Telegraph and Texas Register*, March 12, 1836, 3.

DOCUMENT 10.9

Benjamin Lundy | The War in Texas, 1836

As battles raged in Texas, many Americans outside the territory debated whether or not the United States should annex it. Slavery was at the heart of this debate, with abolitionists fearing that the added Texas territory would strengthen the power of slaveholders. Benjamin Lundy, a Quaker and an ardent abolitionist who published several antislavery newspapers, was well known for his 1836 publication *The War in Texas*, in which he argued against the annexation of Texas.

It is generally admitted that the war in Texas has assumed a character which must seriously affect both the interests and honor of this nation. It implicates the conduct of a large number of our citizens, and even the policy and measures of the government are deeply involved in it. The subject, as now presented to our view, is indeed one of vital importance to the people of the United States; and it particularly invites the attention—the most solemn and deliberate consideration—of all who profess to be guided by the true principles of justice and philanthropy. It is not only to be viewed as a matter of interest, at the present day. The great fundamental principles of universal liberty—the perpetuity of our free republican institutions—the prosperity, the welfare, and the happiness of future generations—are measurably connected with the prospective issue of this fierce and bloody conflict.

But the prime cause and the real objects of this war are not distinctly understood by a large portion of the honest, disinterested, and well-meaning citizens of the United States. Their means of obtaining correct information upon the subject have been necessarily limited; and many of them have been deceived and misled by the misrepresentations of those concerned in it, and especially by hireling writers for the newspaper press. They have been induced to believe that the inhabitants of Texas were engaged in a legitimate contest for the maintenance of the sacred principles of Liberty, and the natural, inalienable Rights of Man: whereas, the motives of its instigators, and their chief incentives to action, have been, from the commencement, of a directly opposite character and tendency. It is susceptible of the clearest demonstration, that the immediate cause and the leading object of this contest originated in a settled design, among the slaveholders of this country (with land speculators and slave-traders), to wrest the large and valuable territory of Texas from the Mexican Republic, in order to re-establish the SYSTEM OF SLAVERY; to open a vast and profitable SLAVE-MARKET therein; and, ultimately, to annex it to the United States. And further, it is evident—nay, it is very generally acknowledged—that the insurrectionists are principally citizens of the United States, who have proceeded thither for the purpose of revolutionizing the country; and that they are dependent upon this nation, for both the physical and pecuniary means, to carry the design into effect. We have a still more important view of the subject. The Slaveholding Interest is now paramount in the Executive branch of our national government; and its influence operates, indirectly, yet powerfully, through that medium, in favor of this Grand Scheme of Oppression and Tyrannical Usurpation. Whether the national Legislature will join hands with the Executive, and lend its aid to this most unwarrantable, aggressive attempt, will depend on the VOICE OF THE PEOPLE, expressed in their primary assemblies, by their petitions, and through the ballot-boxes.

Source: Benjamin Lundy, *The War in Texas* (Philadelphia: Merrihew and Gunn, 1837), 3.

DOCUMENT 10.10

Southerners Support Texas Settlers, 1837

Throughout the South, slaveholders and politicians urged support for American settlers in Texas and sought annexation of the territory. The southern press defended Texas slavery and bitterly denounced northern and abolitionist resistance to annexation. The following selection from the *Charleston Mercury* outlined the prevailing southern opinion on Texas and the "slavery question."

That Texas will be the cause of a severe sectional struggle is almost certain. Either the establishment of her independence as a separate state, or her admission into the Union, would tend greatly to strengthen the South, and ensure the stability and security of Southern institutions, placing the question of slavery beyond the reach of Northern agitation; and it is a grave question for the South and one of difficult decision, whether we should prefer that Texas should be a powerful and independent slave holding state upon our borders, untrammelled by Northern connections, or that she should become a member of the Union. That either her admission, or the acknowledgment of her Independence, will be opposed by a powerful Northern party, there is no doubt. But we fear not for the result. When the question arises, we can say to the North, now make good your oft repeated pledges—make the South forever safe on the subject of Slavery. Set our minds at rest by perpetuating Slavery. The North may be blind enough to wish to refuse, but the West is becoming every day more aware of the value of its connection with this section, and our just demand will be complied with. The North may then choose between the Union with Texian Independence—with the establishment of Slavery above the reach of fanaticism—and no Union; and when they are compelled to choose, we have no fear of their abhorrence of Slavery driving them to disunion. Until then the South and South West will rally upon Texas, which is already de facto an independent state, and will never want the means to maintain her Independence, while there are rifles in our back woods.

Source: *Charleston Mercury*, as reprinted in *Telegraph and Texas Register*, January 11, 1837, 3.

DOCUMENT 10.11

Treaty of Tehuacana Creek, October 9, 1844

For eight years following the achievement of independence, Texas residents and Comanches and other local Indian nations engaged in sporadic warfare and almost constant raids on each other's settlements. Men, women, and children were killed and taken hostage on both sides, and barns, fields, and villages were devastated. In 1840, following a smallpox epidemic, Comanche chiefs sought peace and sent a large group to San Antonio to negotiate terms. Instead, white officials and San Antonio residents murdered thirty-five of them. A year later, Sam Houston, a leader of the Texas rebellion but an advocate of fair treatment for Indians, was elected president of the Republic of Texas. After numerous discussions, Texas officials and the Comanches, along with nine other Indian tribes, signed the Treaty of Tehuacana Creek.

The commissioners of the Republic of Texas, and the Chiefs and head men of the before mentioned tribes of Indians, being met in council at Tehuacana Creek on the ninth day of October, in the Year 1844, have concluded, accepted, and agreed to and signed the following articles of treaty:

Article I. Both parties agree and declare, that they will forever live in peace, and always meet as friends and brothers. The tomahawk shall be buried, and no more blood appear in the path between them now made white. The Great Spirit will look with delight upon their friendship, and will frown in anger upon their enmity.

Article II. They further agree and declare, that the Government of Texas shall permit no bad men to cross the line into the hunting grounds of the Indians; and that if the Indians should find any such among them, they will bring him or them to some one of the agents, but not do any harm to his or their person or property. . . .

Article V. They further agree and declare, that the Indians shall no more steal horses or other property from the whites; and if any property should be stolen, or other mischief done by the bad men among the tribes, that they will punish those who do so and restore the property taken to some one of the agents. . . .

Article VII. They further agree and declare, that the Government of Texas shall establish trading houses for the convenience and benefit of the Indians, and such articles shall be kept for the Indian trade as they may need for their support and comfort.

Article VIII. They further agree and declare, that when peace is fully established between the white and the red people, and no more war or trouble exists, the Indians shall be supplied with powder, lead, guns, spears, and other arms to enable them to kill game and live in plenty. . . .

Article XV. They further agree and declare, that the President may send among the Indians such black-smiths and other mechanics, as he may think best, for their benefit: and also that he may send schoolmasters and families for the purpose of instructing them in a Knowledge of the English language and Christian Religion, as well as other persons to teach them how to cultivate the soil and raise corn. . . .

Article XIX. They further agree and declare, that they will mutually surrender and deliver up all the prisoners which they have of the other party for their own prisoners; and that they will not be friendly with any people or nation, or enter into treaty with them, who will take prisoners from Texas, or do its citizens any injury. . . .

Source: Dorman H. Winfrey and James M. Day, eds., *The Indian Papers of Texas and the Southwest, 1825–1916* (Austin, TX: Pembroke Publishers, 1966), 2:114–19.

Interpret the Evidence

1. How does Mary Austin Holley (Document 10.6) describe Texas as a unique place for settlers? What accounts for its distinctiveness?

2. How does Gregorio Gomez's description of Americans in Texas (Document 10.7) compare to Holley's? How do you explain the differences? On what grounds does Gomez attempt to gain support for the fight against "Texian colonists" from the United States?

3. According to William Travis (Document 10.8), why was defending the Alamo important? Why do you think the defeat of Americans there gained so much attention in the United States?

4. Compare the discussions of Texas found in Benjamin Lundy's *The War in Texas* (Document 10.9) and the article from the *Charleston Mercury* (Document 10.10). How is slavery described, and how do the attitudes expressed in the documents affect each author's view about the fighting in Texas? What do the two documents reveal about the differences between the North and the South in the 1830s?

5. What does the Treaty of Tehuacana Creek (Document 10.11) suggest about what Indians hoped to gain from negotiating peace with the Republic of Texas? What do the specific articles in the treaty suggest about the issues that mattered most to white Texans?

Put It in Context

- What do the various documents presented here suggest about the ongoing debates over statehood for Texas in the United States?

- How would the United States benefit from adding Texas to the Union, and what problems might admitting Texas create?

The Granger Collection, New York

Library of Congress

View of New York from Brooklyn Heights, 1849.

Portrait of Jarena Lee, the first female preacher of the African Methodist Episcopal Church, 1844.

11
Social and Cultural Ferment in the North

1820–1850

From *Memoir of Samuel Slater, the Father of American Manufactures*, 1836

Engraving of a textile mill from the memoir of the English-American industrialist Samuel Slater, 1836.

AMERICAN HISTORIES

Charles Grandison Finney, one of the greatest preachers of the nineteenth century, was born in 1792 and raised in rural New York State. As a young man, Finney studied the law. But in 1821, like many others of his generation, he experienced a powerful religious conversion. No longer interested in a legal career, he turned to the ministry instead.

After being ordained in the Presbyterian Church, Finney joined "New School" ministers who rejected the more conservative traditions of the Presbyterian Church and embraced a vigorous evangelicalism. In the early 1830s, while his wife, Lydia, remained at home with their growing family, the Reverend Finney traveled throughout New York State preaching about Christ's place in a changing America. He held massive revivals in cities along the Erie Canal, most notably in Rochester, and then moved on to New York City. He achieved his greatest success in places experiencing rapid economic development and an influx of migrants and immigrants, where the clash of cultures and classes fueled fears of moral decay. Spiritual renewal could rescue the young nation from sin and depravity.

Finney urged Christians to actively seek salvation. Once individuals reformed themselves, he said, they should work to abolish poverty, intemperance, prostitution, and slavery. He expected women to participate in revivals and good works but advised them to balance these efforts with their domestic responsibilities, an ideal modeled by his own wife.

In many ways, Amy Kirby Post fit Finney's ideal. She raised five children while devoting herself to spiritual and social reform. However, Amy Kirby was born into a large, close-knit Quaker family in the farming community of Jericho, New York. While most Quakers believed in quiet piety rather than evangelical revivals, their faith also provided solace in times of sorrow. In 1823, at age twenty-one, Amy became engaged to a fellow Quaker in central New York, where her sister Hannah lived with her husband, Isaac Post. But her fiancé died in June 1825 just before their wedding. Hannah took sick a year later, and Amy nursed her until her death in April 1827. She stayed on to care for Hannah's two young children and two years later married Isaac Post.

Amy experienced these personal upheavals in the midst of heated religious controversies among Quakers. In the 1820s, Elias Hicks claimed that the Society of Friends had abandoned its spiritual roots and become too much like a traditional church. His followers, called Hicksites, insisted that Friends should reduce their dependence on disciplinary rules, elders, and preachers and rely instead on the "Inner Light"— the spirit of God dwelling within each individual. When the Society of Friends divided into Hicksite and Orthodox branches in 1827, Amy Kirby and Isaac Post joined the Hicksites.

In 1836 Amy Post moved with her husband and four children to Rochester, New York. In a city marked by the spirit of Finney's revivals, Quakers emphasized quiet contemplation rather than fiery sermons and emotional conversions. But the Society of Friends allowed women to preach when moved by the spirit. Quaker women also held separate meetings to discipline female congregants, evaluate marriage proposals, and write testimonies on important religious issues.

Amy Post's spiritual journey was increasingly shaped by the rising tide of abolition. Committed to ending slavery, she joined non-Quakers in signing an 1837 antislavery petition. Five years later, she helped found the Western New York Anti-Slavery Society, which included Quakers and evangelicals, women and men, and blacks and whites. Post's growing commitment to abolition caused tensions in the Hicksite Meeting since some members opposed working in "worldly" organizations alongside non-Quakers. By 1848 Post and other radical Friends had withdrawn from the Hicksite Meeting and invited like-minded people to join them in the newly established Congregational Friends. Their meetings attracted abolitionists, advocates of Indian rights and women's rights, and peace activists, all causes Post embraced. ●

THE AMERICAN HISTORIES of Charles Finney and Amy Post were shaped by the dynamic religious, social, and economic developments in the early-nineteenth-century United States. Finney changed the face of American religion, aided by masses of evangelical Protestants. The rise of cities and the expansion of industry in the northern United States made problems like poverty, unemployment, alcohol abuse, crime, and prostitution more visible, drawing people to Finney's message. Other Americans brought their own religious traditions to bear on the problems of the day. Some, like Post, were so outraged by the moral stain of slavery that they burst traditional religious bonds and reconsidered what it meant to do God's work. For both Finney and Post, Rochester—the fastest-growing city in the nation between 1825 and 1835—exemplified the problems and the possibilities created by urban expansion and social change.

The Growth of Cities

Commercial and industrial development, immigration from Europe, and migration from rural areas led to the rapid growth of U.S. cities from 1820 on. Urbanization stimulated economic expansion but also created social upheaval. Cultural divisions intensified in urban areas where Catholics and Protestants, workers and the well-to-do, immigrants, African Americans, and native-born whites lived side by side. The emergence of a middle class of shopkeepers, professionals, and clerks might have bridged these divides, but most middle-class Americans highlighted their distinctiveness from both the wealthy few at the top and the mass of workers and the poor at the bottom.

The Lure of Urban Life

Across the North, urban populations boomed. As centers of national and international commerce, seaports like New York and Philadelphia gained the greatest population in the early to mid-nineteenth century. But boomtowns also emerged along inland waterways. Rochester, New York, first settled in 1812, was flooded by goods and people once the Erie Canal was completed in 1825. Between 1820 and 1850, the number of cities with 100,000 inhabitants grew from two to six. In the Northeast, some farm communities doubled or tripled in size and were incorporated into neighboring cities such as Philadelphia. By 1850, among the nation's ten most populous urban centers, only two—Baltimore and New Orleans—were located in the South.

Cities increased not only in size but also in the diversity of their residents. During the 1820s, some 150,000 European immigrants entered the United States; during the 1830s, nearly 600,000; and during the 1840s, more than 1,700,000. This surge of immigrants included more Irish and German settlers than ever before as well as large numbers of Scandinavians. Many settled along the eastern seaboard, but others added to the growth of frontier cities such as Cincinnati, St. Louis, and Chicago.

Irish families had settled in North America early on, most of them Scots-Irish Presbyterians. Then in the 1830s and 1840s, the Irish countryside was plagued by bad weather, a potato blight, and harsh economic policies imposed by the English government. In 1845–1846 a full-blown famine forced thousands of Irish farm families—most of them Catholic—to emigrate. Young Irish women emigrated in especially large numbers, working as seamstresses and domestics to help fund passage to the United States for other family members. Poor harvests, droughts, failed revolutions, and repressive landlords convinced large

numbers of Germans and Scandinavians to flee their homelands as well. By 1850 the Irish made up about 40 percent of immigrants to the United States, and Germans nearly a quarter (Figure 11.1).

Commerce and industry attracted immigrants to northern cities. These newcomers provided an expanding pool of cheap labor that further fueled economic growth. Banks, mercantile houses, and dry goods stores multiplied. Industrial enterprises in cities such as New York and Philadelphia included mechanized factories as well as traditional workshops in which master craftsmen oversaw the labor of apprentices. Credit and insurance agencies were created to aid entrepreneurs in their ventures. The increase in business also drove the demand for ships, newspapers catering to merchants and businessmen, warehouses, and other trade necessities, which created a surge in jobs and attracted even more people.

Businesses that focused on leisure also flourished. In the 1830s, theater became affordable to working-class families, who attended comedies, musical revues, and morality plays. They also joined middle- and upper-class

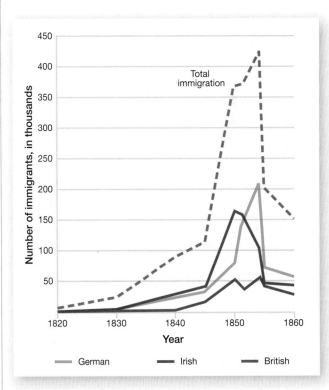

FIGURE 11.1 Immigration to the United States, 1820–1860

Famine, economic upheaval, and political persecution led masses of people from Ireland, Germany, and Britain to migrate to the United States from the 1820s through the 1850s. The vast majority settled in cities and factory towns in the North or on farms in the Midwest. An economic recession in the late 1850s finally slowed immigration, though only temporarily.

Leisure Pursuits

City residents who lived a more sedentary life used their leisure time to keep fit. This 1850 lithograph advertising Dr. Rich's Institute for Physical Education shows newly developed exercises and gymnastic equipment that have become standard today. Dr. Rich's Institute was one of many urban gymnasiums that promoted health through systematic physical training. © Museum of the City of New York, USA/The Bridgeman Art Library

audiences at productions of Shakespeare and nationalistic dramas in which strong and clever Americans triumphed over English aristocrats. Minstrel shows mocked self-important capitalists but also portrayed African Americans in crude caricatures. One of the most popular characters was Jim Crow, who appeared originally in an African American song. In the 1820s, he was incorporated into a song-and-dance routine by Thomas Rice, a white performer who blacked his face with burnt cork.

Museums, too, became a favorite destination for city dwellers. Many were modeled on P. T. Barnum's American Museum on lower Broadway in New York City. These museums were not staid venues for observing the fine arts or historical artifacts. Instead, they offered an abundance of exhibits and entertainment, including wax figures, archaeological antiquities, medical instruments, and insect collections, as well as fortune-tellers, bearded ladies, and snake charmers.

The lures of urban life were especially attractive to the young. Single men and women and newly married couples flocked to cities. By 1850 half the residents of New York City, Philadelphia, and other seaport cities were under sixteen years old. Young men sought work in construction, in the maritime trades, or in banks and commercial houses, while young women competed for jobs as seamstresses and domestic servants.

The Roots of Urban Disorder

In addition to stimulating economic growth by providing the labor that made industrial development possible, immigrants also transformed the urban landscape in the nineteenth century. They filled factories and workshops, crowded into houses and apartments, and built ethnic institutions, including synagogues and convents—visible indicators of the growing diversity of the American city.

Such marks of difference aroused growing concern among native-born Protestants. Crude stereotypes of immigrant groups appeared more frequently, and anti-Catholicism and anti-Semitism flourished in the 1830s and 1840s. Jews, who were long denied admission to skilled crafts and professions in Europe, had little choice but to pursue commercial ventures. Yet they were portrayed not as well-educated businessmen but as manipulative money-lenders. Similarly, many Irishmen enjoyed a beer with friends after laboring at difficult and low-paid jobs. But rather than being viewed as hardworking comrades, they were often pictured as habitual drunkards.

Rural Americans, seeking better jobs and new social experiences, added to urban diversity. Native-born white men often set out on their own, but most white women settled in cities under the supervision of a husband, a landlady, or an employer. African Americans, too, sought greater opportunities in urban areas. In the 1830s, more blacks joined Philadelphia's vibrant African American community, attracted by its churches, schools, and mutual aid and literary societies. New Bedford, Massachusetts, a thriving whaling center, provided employment for black men, including growing numbers of fugitive slaves, as well as for American Indians from the region. Although relative racial tolerance prevailed in New Bedford, in most urban areas racial minorities faced hostility and discrimination that limited their opportunities.

Even as cities promised better lives for many immigrants and migrants, they also posed dangers. Battles erupted between immigrant and native-born residents, Protestant and Catholic gangs, and white and black workers. Robberies, gambling, prostitution, and other criminal activities flourished. Diseases spread quickly through densely populated neighborhoods. When innovations in transportation made it possible for more affluent residents to distance themselves from crowded inner cities, they leaped at the chance. The first horse-drawn streetcar line was built in New York City in 1832, and as lines multiplied there and elsewhere, wealthy families moved to less crowded neighborhoods away from the urban center.

Violence increased as economic competition intensified in the 1840s. Native-born white workers and employers pushed Irish immigrants to the bottom of the economic ladder, where they competed with African Americans. Yet Irish workers insisted that their whiteness gave them a higher status than skilled blacks. When black temperance reformers organized a parade in Philadelphia in August 1842, white onlookers—mostly Irish laborers—attacked the marchers. Blacks fought back, and the conflict escalated into a riot.

Americans who lived in small towns and rural areas regularly read news of urban riots, murders, robberies, and vice. Improvements in printing created vastly more and cheaper newspapers. Tabloids wooed readers by publishing sensational stories of crime, sex, and scandal. Even more respectable newspapers carried stories about urban mayhem, and religious periodicals warned their parishioners against the city's moral temptations. After Congress funded construction of the first telegraph line in 1844 between Baltimore and Washington, D.C., news could travel even more quickly. In response to both a real increase in crime and a heightened perception of urban dangers, cities—beginning with Boston in 1845—replaced voluntary night watchmen with police forces. Fire companies, too, became established parts of city government, and city and county jails expanded with the population.

The New Middle Class

Members of the emerging middle class were among the most avid readers of the burgeoning numbers of newspapers and magazines. They included ambitious businessmen, successful shopkeepers, doctors, and lawyers as well as teachers, journalists, ministers, and other salaried employees. In Britain, the middle class emerged at the turn of the nineteenth century. In the United States, it was still a class in the making, rather than a stable entity, in the first half of the nineteenth century. At the top rungs, wealthy entrepreneurs and professionals adopted luxurious lifestyles. At the lower rungs, a growing cohort of salaried clerks and managers hoped that their hard work, honesty, and thrift would be rewarded with upward mobility.

Education, religious affiliation, and sobriety were important indicators of middle-class status. A well-read man who attended a well-established church and drank in strict moderation was marked as belonging to this new rank. A middle-class man was also expected to own a comfortable home, marry a pious woman, and raise well-behaved children. Entrance to the middle class required the efforts of wives as well as husbands, and so couples adopted new ideas about marriage and family. They believed that marital relationships should be based on affection and companionship rather than the husband's supreme authority. As partners for life, the husband focused on achieving financial security while the wife managed the household. The French traveler Alexis de Tocqueville captured this development in *Democracy in America* (1835). "In no country," he wrote, "has such constant care been taken . . . to trace two clearly distinct lines of action for the two sexes." The millions of women who toiled on farms and plantations or as mill workers and domestic servants certainly challenged this notion of **separate spheres** for men and women, but it captured the middle-class ideal.

The rise of the middle class inspired a flood of advice books, ladies' magazines, religious periodicals, and novels that advocated new ideals of womanhood, ideals that emphasized the centrality of child rearing and homemaking to women's identities. This cult of domesticity seemed to restrict wives to home and hearth, where they provided their husbands with respite from the cares and corruptions of the world. But wives were also expected to cement social and economic bonds by visiting the wives of business

Middle-Class Shoppers

Although middle-class women did most of the daily shopping for the family, this 1847 lithograph shows that men were involved as well. This store on Main Street in Worcester, Massachusetts, sold goods from the West Indies, no doubt including rum, which attracted a male clientele. The store hired young boys to help load the purchased items.   The Granger Collection, New York

associates, serving in local charitable societies, and attending prayer circles. In carrying out these duties, the ideal woman bolstered her family's status by performing public as well as private roles.

Middle-class families also played a crucial role in the growing market economy. Although wives and daughters were not expected to work for wages, they were responsible for much of the family's consumption. They purchased factory-produced shoes and cloth, handcrafted clocks and cast-iron stoves, fine European crystal, and porcelain figures imported from China. Some middling housewives also bought basic goods once made at home, such as butter and candles. And middle-class children required books, pianos, and dancing lessons.

Although increasingly recognized for their ability to consume wisely, middle-class women still performed significant domestic labor. Only upper-middle-class women could afford servants. Most middle-class women, aided by daughters or temporary "help," cut and sewed garments, cultivated gardens, canned fruits and vegetables, plucked chickens, cooked meals, and washed and ironed clothes. As houses expanded in size and clothes became fancier, these chores continued to be laborious and time-consuming. But they were also increasingly invisible, focused inwardly on the family rather than outwardly as part of the market economy.

Middle-class men contributed to the consumer economy as well. Most directly, they created and invested in industrial and commercial ventures. But in carrying out their business and professional obligations, they supported new leisure pursuits. Many joined colleagues at restaurants, the theater, or sporting events. They also attended plays and lectures with their wives, visited museums, and took their children to the circus.

REVIEW & RELATE

Why did American cities become larger and more diverse in the first half of the nineteenth century?

What values and beliefs did the emerging American middle class embrace?

LEARNINGCurve bedfordstmartins.com/hewittlawson/LC

The Rise of Industry

Although the percentage of Americans employed in manufacturing never rose above 10 percent of the laboring population in the mid-nineteenth century, industrial enterprises in the Northeast transformed the nation's economy. In the 1830s and 1840s, factories grew considerably in size, and some investors, especially in textiles, constructed factory towns. Textile mills now relied heavily on the labor of girls and young women recruited from rural areas, while urban workshops hired varied groups of workers, including children, young women and men, and older adults. As industry expanded, however, working men's access to highly skilled jobs declined. The panic of 1837 exacerbated this trend and also increased tensions within the working class, especially among workers from different ethnic and racial backgrounds.

Factory Towns and Women Workers

In the late 1820s, investors and manufacturers joined forces to create factory towns in the New England countryside, the most famous of which was constructed in Lowell, Massachusetts, along the Merrimack River. Funded by the Boston Associates, a group of investors from eastern Massachusetts, the Lowell mills were based on an earlier experiment in nearby Waltham. In the Waltham system, every step of the production process was mechanized. The factories were far larger than earlier ones and were built as part of a planned community that included boardinghouses, government offices, and churches. Agents for the Waltham system traveled throughout New England to recruit the daughters of farm families as workers. They assured parents that their daughters would be watched over by managers and foremen as well as by landladies. The young women were required to attend church and observe curfews, and their labor was regulated by clocks and bells to ensure discipline and productivity.

Textile towns allowed young women to contribute to family finances while living in a well-ordered environment. Farm families needed more cash because of the growing market economy, and daughters could save money for the clothes and linens required for married life. Factory jobs also provided an alternative to marriage as young New England men moved west and left a surplus of women behind. The boardinghouses provided a relatively safe, all-female environment for the young workers, and sisters and neighbors often lived together. Despite constant regulation and supervision, many rural women viewed factory work as an adventure. They could send money home and still set aside a bit for themselves, and they could attend lectures and concerts, meet new people, and acquire a wider view of the world.

Initially, factory towns offered many benefits to young women and their families, but by the 1830s working conditions began to deteriorate. Factory owners cut wages, lengthened hours, and sped up machines, forcing women to produce more cloth in less time for lower pay. Many boardinghouses became overcrowded, and company officials regulated both rents and expenses, so higher prices

for lodging did not necessarily mean better food or furnishings. Factory workers launched numerous strikes in the 1830s against longer hours, wage cuts, and speedups in factory production. The solidarity required to sustain these strikes was forged in boardinghouses and at church socials as well as on the factory floor.

> **Explore**
>
> See Documents 11.1 and 11.2 for firsthand accounts of life in the mills.

Despite the mill workers' solidarity, it was not easy to overcome the economic power wielded by manufacturers. Working women's efforts at collective action were generally short-lived, lasting only as long as the strike itself. Then employees returned to their jobs until the next crisis hit. And as competition increasingly cut into profits, owners resisted mill workers' demands more vehemently. When the panic of 1837 intensified fears of job loss, women's organizing activities were doomed until the economy recovered.

Deskilling and the Response of Working Men

While the construction of factory towns expanded economic opportunities for young women, the gradual decline of time-honored crafts narrowed the prospects for working men. As craft workshops increased in size, they hired fewer skilled workers and more men who learned only a single aspect of production—cutting barrel staves or attaching soles to shoes. Like mill operatives, these workers performed distinct tasks, many of which were mechanized over the course of the nineteenth century. The final product was less distinctive than an item crafted by a skilled artisan, but it was also less expensive and available in mass quantities.

The shift from craft work to factory work threatened to undermine working men's skills, pay, and labor conditions. Soon masters hired foremen to regulate the workforce and installed bells and clocks to regulate the workday. Artisans were offended by the new regime, which treated them as wage-earning dependents rather than as independent craftsmen. As the process of **deskilling** transformed shoemaking, printing, bookbinding, tailoring, and other trades, laboring men fought to maintain their status.

Some workers formed mutual aid societies to provide assistance in times of illness, injury, or unemployment. Others participated in religious revivals or joined fraternal orders, such as the Masons and the Red Men, to find the camaraderie they once enjoyed at work. The expansion of voting rights in the 1820s offered another avenue for action. The first workingmen's political party was founded in Philadelphia in 1827, and soon white farmers, mechanics,

DOCUMENTS 11.1 AND 11.2

Life in the Mills: Two Views

In the 1820s, the textile mills of Lowell, Massachusetts, provided the daughters of local farmers a way to contribute to their family incomes and experience some adventure. Soon, however, a slowing economy led to reduced wages, longer hours, and demands for increased productivity. The Lowell workers organized to protest these changes and went on strike several times during the late 1820s and the 1830s. The first selection below is from an 1844 edition of *The Lowell Offering*, a magazine to which mill workers contributed stories and poems. Factory owners controlled the content of the magazine to ensure an idealized vision of life in the mills. Still, the letter from "Susan" below does highlight the physical toll of industrial labor. Susan was a pseudonym for Harriet Farley, a weaver and the editor of *The Lowell Offering*. The selection at right is by Harriet Robinson, who entered the mills at age ten in 1834. She published a memoir in 1898 in which she recalls the growing dissatisfaction of the women workers and her critical role in a strike in 1836.

Explore

11.1 Letter from a Lowell Factory Worker, 1844

It makes my feet ache and swell to stand so much, but I suppose I shall get accustomed to that too. The girls generally wear old shoes about their work, and you know nothing is easier; but they almost all say that when they have worked here a year or two they have to procure shoes a size or two larger than before they came. The right hand, which is the one used in stopping and starting the loom, becomes larger than the left; but in other respects the factory is not detrimental to a young girl's appearance. Here they look delicate, but not sickly; they laugh at those who are much exposed, and get pretty brown; but I, for one, had rather be brown than pure white. I never saw so many pretty looking girls as there are

here. Though the number of men is small in proportion there are many marriages here, and a great deal of courting. I will tell you of this last sometime. . . .

You ask if the work is not disagreeable. Not when one is accustomed to it. It tried my patience sadly at first, and does now when it does not run well; but, in general, I like it very much. It is easy to do, and does not require very violent exertion, as much of our farm work does.

You also ask how I get along with the girls here. Very well indeed.

Source: Harriet Farley, "Letters from Susan, Second Letter," *The Lowell Offering*, June 1844, 170–71.

and workingmen started joining forces throughout the North to advocate for principles of liberty and equality. Self-educated artisans like Thomas Skidmore of New York City argued for the redistribution of property and the abolition of inheritance to equalize wealth in the nation. However, most workingmen's parties focused on more practical proposals: government distribution of free land in the West, the abolition of compulsory militia service and imprisonment for debt, public funding for education, and the regulation of banks and corporations. Although the

success of these parties at the polls was modest, by the 1830s Democrats and Whigs adopted many of their proposals.

Workingmen, like workingwomen, also formed unions to demand better wages and working conditions. In the 1820s and 1830s, skilled journeymen held mass meetings to protest employers' efforts to extend the workday from ten to eleven hours, merge smaller workshops into larger factories, and cut wages. In New York City in 1834, labor activists formed a citywide federation, the General Trades Union, which provided support for striking workers. The National

11.2 Harriet Robinson |
Reflections on the 1836 Lowell
Mills Strike, 1898

My own recollection of this first strike (or "turn out" as it was called) is very vivid. I worked in a lower room, where I had heard the proposed strike fully, if not vehemently, discussed; I had been an ardent listener to what was said against this attempt at "oppression" on the part of the corporation, and naturally I took sides with the strikers. When the day came on which the girls were to turn out, those in the upper rooms started first, and so many of them left that our mill was at once shut down. Then, when the girls in my room stood irresolute, uncertain what to do, asking each other, "Would you?" or "Shall we turn out?" and not one of them having the courage to lead off, *I*, who began to think they would not go out, after all their talk, became impatient, and started on ahead, saying, with childish bravado, "I don't care what you do, I am going to turn out, whether any one else does or not"; and I marched out, and was followed by the others.

As I looked back at the long line that followed me, I was more proud than I have ever been since at any success I may have achieved, and more proud than I shall ever be again until my own beloved State gives to its women citizens the right of suffrage.

The agent of the corporation where I then worked took some small revenges on the supposed ringleaders; on the principle of sending the weaker to the wall, my mother [a landlady] was turned away from her boarding-house, that functionary saying, "Mrs. Hanson, you could not prevent the older girls from turning out, but your daughter is a child, and *her* you could control."

It is hardly necessary to say that so far as results were concerned this strike did no good. The dissatisfaction of the operatives subsided, or burned itself out, and though the authorities did not accede to their demands, the majority returned to their work, and the corporation went on cutting down the wages.

Source: Harriet H. Robinson, *Loom and Spindle; or, Life among the Early Mill Girls* (New York: Thomas Y. Crowell, 1898), 84–86.

Interpret the Evidence

- How did life on the farm differ from life in the factory? How does "Susan" describe her own adjustment to industrial work?
- What connections does Robinson make between the strike and the larger social and political context of 1830s Massachusetts? How does she see herself and her actions?

Put It in Context

Were "Susan" and Robinson typical factory workers in this period? Why or why not?

Trades Union was established later that year, with delegates representing more than twenty-five thousand workers across the North. These organizations aided skilled workers but refused admission to women and unskilled men.

Broad labor organizations proved difficult to sustain because of differences in skill and ethnicity as well as in age and marital status among members. Even workingmen's parties, which recruited men across occupations and ages, refused to recruit laborers who could not vote—women, new immigrants, and most blacks. With the onset of the

panic of 1837, the common plight of workers became clearer. But the economic crisis made unified action nearly impossible as individuals sought to hold on to what little they had by any means available.

The Panic of 1837 in the North

The panic of 1837 began in the South, but it hit northern cotton merchants hard (see chapter 10). Textile factories drastically cut production, metal foundries that supplied

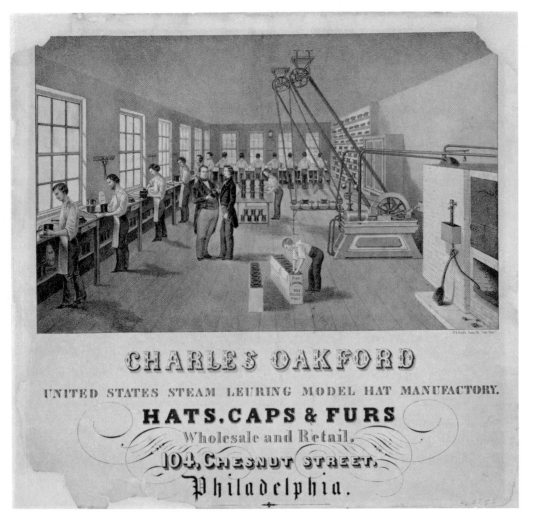

Hat Manufacturing, 1850

This 1850 lithograph advertises Charles Oakford's hat factory in Philadelphia. Like many industries, hat making became increasingly mechanized in the 1840s. Here Oakford talks with a client in the center of the room, across from his steam-powered lathe, while workers stand at stations shaping and stacking hats. A boy packs the merchandise into a box ready for shipping.   © Philadelphia History Museum at the Atwater Kent/The Bridgeman Art Library

their machinery were wiped out, workers lost their jobs, and merchants and investors went broke. Those who kept their jobs saw their wages cut in half. As with the panic of 1819, hunger plagued urban residents while crops rotted in the Midwest because farmers could not afford to harvest them. In Rochester, the Posts were among hundreds who lost their homes to foreclosure. Petty crime, prostitution, and violence also rose as men and women struggled to make ends meet.

In Lowell and other textile towns, hours increased and wages fell. Just as important, the process of deskilling intensified. Factory owners considered mechanization one way to improve their economic situation. In the 1830s and 1840s, the sewing machine was invented and

improved. When it came into widespread use in the 1850s, factories began to mass-produce inexpensive clothing, employing women who worked for low wages. Mechanical reapers, steam boilers, and the steam press transformed other occupations as manufacturers invested more of their resources in machines. At the same time, the rising tide of immigrants provided a ready supply of relatively cheap labor. Artisans tried to maintain their traditional skills and status, but in many trades they were fighting a losing battle.

By the early 1840s, when the panic subsided, new technologies did spur new jobs. Factories demanded more workers to handle new machines that ran at a faster pace. The ease of harvesting wheat inspired changes in flour milling that required engineers to design machines and mechanics to build and repair them. The steam press allowed publication of more newspapers and magazines, creating positions for editors, publishers, printers, engravers, reporters, and sales agents. Advertising became an occupation unto itself.

Following the panic, new labor organizations also emerged to address workers' changing circumstances. Many of these unions were made up of a particular trade or ethnic group, and almost all continued to address primarily the needs of skilled male workers. Textile operatives remained the one important group of organized female workers. In the 1840s, workingwomen joined with workingmen in New England to fight for a ten-hour day. Slowly, however, farmers' daughters abandoned the fight and left the mills as Irish immigrants flooded the labor market and agreed to accept lower pay and longer hours.

For most women in need, charitable organizations offered more support than unions did. Organizations like Philadelphia's Female Association for the Relief of Women and Children in Reduced Circumstances provided a critical safety net for many poor families since public monies for such purposes were limited. Although nearly every town and city provided some form of public assistance in this period, municipalities never had sufficient resources to meet the needs of growing populations, much less the extraordinary demands posed by hard times. Despite financial constraints, towns and cities continued to expand almshouses and workhouses, offer some financial assistance, and provide land and supplemental funds for private benevolent ventures like orphan asylums.

Rising Class and Cultural Tensions

By the 1840s, leaders of both public and private charitable endeavors linked relief to the moral character of those in need and generally measured that character by the standards of affluent Protestants. Upper-class Americans had long debated whether the poor would learn habits of industry and thrift if they were simply given aid without working for it. Concern over the "idle poor"—those who were physically able to work but did not—intensified as more and more immigrants joined the ranks of the needy. The debate was deeply gendered. Women and children were considered the worthiest recipients of aid, and middle- and upper-class women the appropriate dispensers of charity. Successful men, meanwhile, often linked poverty to weakness and considered giving pennies to a beggar an unmanly act that indulged the worst traits of the poor. They focused on building workhouses or expanding almshouses, though preferably at little expense to city residents.

The panic of 1837 convinced some benevolent leaders that public workhouses and almshouses offered the best hope for helping the poor. Alternatively, charitable societies sought to improve the environment in an effort to change the conditions that produced poverty. In the 1840s and 1850s, they built orphan asylums, schools, hospitals, and homes for working women to provide vulnerable residents with housing, education, domestic skills, and advice.

The "undeserving" poor faced grimmer choices. They received public assistance only through the workhouse or the local jail. Rowdy men who gambled away what little they earned, prostitutes who tempted respectable men into vice, and immigrants who preferred idle poverty to virtuous labor figured in newspaper articles, investigative reports, and novels. In fictional portrayals, naive girls were often the victims of immoral men or unfortunate circumstance. One of the first mass-produced books in the United States, Nathaniel Hawthorne's *The Scarlet Letter* (1850) was set in Puritan New England but addressed contemporary concerns about the seduction of innocents. It illustrated the social ostracism and poverty suffered by a woman who bore a child out of wedlock.

Other fictional tales placed the blame for fallen women on foreigners, especially Catholics. Such works drew vivid portraits of young nuns ravished by priests and then thrown out pregnant and penniless. These stories attracted tens of thousands of readers in the United States and heightened anti-Catholic sentiment, which periodically boiled over into attacks on Catholic homes, schools, churches, and convents.

Economic competition further intensified conflicts between immigrants and native-born Americans. By the 1840s, Americans who opposed immigration took the name **nativists** and launched public campaigns against foreigners, especially Irish Catholics. In May 1844, nativists clashed with Irishmen in Philadelphia after shots were fired from a firehouse. A dozen nativists and one Irishmen were killed the first day. The next night, nativists looted and burned Irish businesses and Catholic churches.

Explore

See Document 11.3 for an example of nativist sentiment from a well-known inventor.

Most native-born workers distanced themselves from immigrants, but others believed that class solidarity was crucial to overcoming the power wielded by employers. Nevertheless, only highly skilled immigrants were likely to gain entrance to labor organizations. Although immigrants with sufficient resources to open businesses or establish themselves in professions might

DOCUMENT 11.3

Samuel F. B. Morse | The Dangers of Foreign Immigration, 1835

Samuel Morse is best remembered as a painter and the inventor of the telegraph, but he was also a leader in the nativist movement of the mid-nineteenth century, and he wrote and spoke out against immigration throughout his life. He viewed Catholicism in particular as a grave threat to American democracy and advocated strict restriction of immigration from countries with large Catholic populations. The following passage is from an anti-immigration book Morse wrote in 1835.

Explore

Let us examine this point a little more minutely. These materials are the *varieties of Foreigners* of the same Creed, the Roman Catholic, over all of whom the Bishops or Vicars General hold, as a matter of course, ecclesiastical rule; and we well know what is the nature of Roman Catholic ecclesiastical rule—it is the double refined spirit of despotism, which, after arrogating to itself the prerogatives of Deity, and so claiming to bind or loose the *soul* eternally, makes it, in the comparison, but a mere trifle to exercise absolute sway in all that relates to the body. The notorious ignorance in which the great mass of these emigrants have been all their lives sunk, until their minds are dead, makes them but senseless machines; they obey orders mechanically, for it is the habit of their education, in the despotic countries of their birth. And can it be for a moment supposed by any one that by the act of coming to this country, and being naturalized, their darkened intellects can suddenly be illuminated to discern the nice boundary where their *ecclesiastical obedience* to their priests *ends*, and their *civil independence* of them *begins*? The very supposition is absurd. They obey their priests as demigods, from the habit of their whole lives; they have been taught from infancy that their priests are infallible in the greatest matters, and can they, by mere importation to this country, be suddenly imbued with the knowledge that in civil matters their priests may err, and that they are not in these also their infallible guides? Who will teach them this? Will their priests? Let common sense answer this question. Must not the priests, as a matter almost of *certainty*, control the opinions of their ignorant flock in civil as well as religious matters? and do they not do it?

Source: Samuel F. B. Morse, *Imminent Dangers to the United States through Foreign Immigration* (New York: E. B. Clayton, 1835), 13.

Interpret the Evidence

- Why does Morse single out Catholicism as a threat to the United States?
- Why does Morse believe most immigrants are incapable of becoming good citizens?

Put It in Context

What is the relationship among Morse's hostility to Catholic immigrants, the growth and increasing diversity of cities, and rising class tensions in this period?

gain middle-class status, only pious immigrants from Protestant backgrounds were likely to be truly accepted into middle-class society.

REVIEW & RELATE

How and why did American manufacturing change over the course of the first half of the nineteenth century?

How did Northerners respond to the hard times that followed the panic of 1837? How did responses to the crisis vary by class, ethnicity, and religion?

✓ *LEARNINGCurve* bedfordstmartins.com/hewittlawson/LC

Saving the Nation from Sin

Americans had established Bible societies, prayer circles, and urban missions as early as the 1810s. These efforts were infused with new energy as evangelical fires—lit by southern camp meetings in the early nineteenth century—swept across the North. Men and women of all classes and races embraced this **Second Great Awakening** to express deeply held beliefs and reclaim a sense of the nation's godly mission. Yet evangelical Protestantism was not the only religious tradition to thrive in the 1830s and 1840s. The Quaker and Unitarian faiths also grew in this period. Catholic churches and Jewish synagogues expanded along with immigration, and new religious groups—including Mormons and Millerites—attracted thousands of followers. At the same time, transcendentalists sought deeper engagements with nature as another path to spiritual renewal.

The Second Great Awakening

Although diverse religious traditions flourished in the United States, evangelical Protestantism proved the most powerful in the 1820s and 1830s. Evangelical churches hosted revivals, encouraged conversions, and organized prayer and missionary societies. This second wave of religious revivals began in Cane Ridge, Kentucky, in 1801, took root across the South, and then spread northward. Although revivals had diminished by the late 1830s, they erupted periodically through the 1850s and again during the Civil War. But it was the revivals of the 1830s that transformed Protestant churches and the social fabric of northern life.

Northern ministers like Charles Grandison Finney adopted techniques first wielded by southern Methodists and Baptists: plain speaking, powerful images, and mass meetings. But Finney molded these techniques for a more

affluent audience and held his "camp meetings" in established churches. Northern evangelicals also insisted that religious fervor demanded social responsibility and that good works were a sign of salvation.

In the late 1820s, boomtown growth along the Erie Canal aroused deep concerns about the rising tide of sin. In September 1830, the Reverend Finney arrived in Rochester and began preaching in the city's Presbyterian churches. Arguing that "nothing is more calculated to beget a spirit of prayer, than to unite in social prayer with one who has the spirit himself," Finney led prayer meetings that lasted late into the night. Individual supplicants walked to special benches designated for anxious sinners, who were prayed over in public. Female parishioners played crucial roles, encouraging their husbands, sons, friends, and neighbors to submit to God.

Thousands of Rochester residents joined in the evangelical experience as Finney's powerful message spilled over into other denominations (Map 11.1). But the significance of the Rochester revivals went far beyond a mere increase in church membership. Finney had converted "the great mass of the most influential people" in the city: merchants, lawyers, doctors, master craftsmen, and

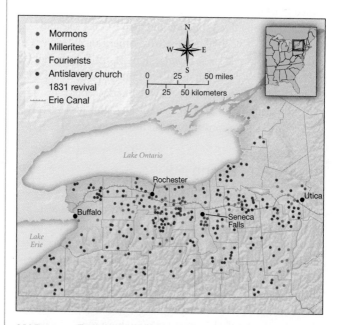

MAP 11.1 Religious Movements in the Burned-Over District, 1831–1848

Western and central New York State were burned over by the fires of religious revivalism in the 1830s and 1840s. But numerous other religious groups also formed or flourished in the region at the same time, including radical Quakers, Mormons, and Millerites. In the 1840s, Fourierist phalanxes, the Oneida community, and other utopian experiments also flourished here.   Source: Whitney R. Cross, *The Burned-Over District: The Social and Intellectual History of Enthusiastic Religion in Western New York, 1800–1850* (1950).

shopkeepers. Equally important, he proclaimed that if Christians were "united all over the world the Millennium [Christ's Second Coming] might be brought about in three months." Local preachers in Rochester and the surrounding towns took up his call, and converts committed themselves to preparing the world for Christ's arrival.

Lyman Beecher, a powerful Presbyterian minister in Boston, declared that the spiritual renewal of the early 1830s was the greatest revival of religion the world had ever seen. Middle-class and wealthy Americans were swept into Presbyterian, Congregational, and Episcopalian churches, while Baptists and Methodists ministered mainly to laboring women and men. Black Baptists and Methodists evangelized in their own communities, where independent black churches combined powerful preaching with haunting spirituals. In Philadelphia, African Americans built fifteen churches between 1799 and 1830. Over the next two decades, a few black women, such as Jarena Lee, joined men in evangelizing among African American Methodists and Baptists.

Tens of thousands of Christian converts both black and white embraced evangelicals' message of moral outreach. They formed Bible, missionary, and charitable societies; Sunday schools; and reform organizations. No movement gained greater impetus from the revivals than did **temperance**, which sought to moderate and then ban the sale and consumption of alcohol. In the 1820s, Americans fifteen years and older consumed six to seven gallons of distilled alcohol per person per year (about double the amount consumed today). Middle-class evangelicals, who once accepted moderate drinking as healthful and proper, now insisted on eliminating alcohol consumption in the United States.

New Spirits Rising

Although enthusiasm for temperance and other reforms waned during the panic of 1837 and many churches lost members, the Second Great Awakening revived following the panic. Increasingly, however, evangelical ministers competed for souls with a variety of other religious groups. In the 1840s, diverse religious groups flourished, many of which supported good works and social reform. The Society of Friends, or Quakers, the first religious group to refuse fellowship to slaveholders, grew throughout the early and mid-nineteenth century. Having divided in 1827 and then again in 1848, the Society of Friends continued to grow. So, too, did its influence in reform movements as activists like Amy Post carried Quaker testimonies against alcohol, war, and slavery into the wider society. Unitarians also combined religious worship with social reform. Their primary difference from other Christians was their belief in a single unified higher spirit rather than the Trinity of the Father,

the Son, and the Holy Spirit. First established in Boston in 1787, Unitarian societies spread across New England in the 1820s, emerging mainly out of Congregational churches. Opposed to evangelical revivalism, Unitarians nonetheless spread west and south in the 1830s and 1840s, attracting well-to-do merchants and manufacturers as well as small farmers, shopkeepers, and laborers. Dedicated to a rational approach to understanding the divine, Unitarian church members included prominent literary figures such as Ralph Waldo Emerson and Harvard luminaries such as William Ellery Channing.

Other churches grew as a result of immigration. Dozens of Catholic churches were established to meet the needs of many Irish and some German immigrants. With the rapid increase in the number of Catholic churches, more Irish priests were ordained in the United States, and women's religious orders also became increasingly Irish in the 1840s and 1850s. By 1860 the Irish numbered 1.6 million of the 2.2 million Catholics in the United States. Meanwhile synagogues, Hebrew schools, and Hebrew aid societies signaled the growing presence of Jews in the United States. They came chiefly from Germany, though Jews were far fewer in number than Catholics.

Entirely new religious groups also flourished in the 1840s. One of the most important was the Church of Jesus Christ of Latter-Day Saints, or Mormons, founded by Joseph Smith. Smith claimed that he began to receive visions from God at age fifteen and was directed to dig up gold plates inscribed with instructions for redeeming the Lost Tribes of Israel. *The Book of Mormon* (1830), supposedly based on these inscriptions, granted spiritual authority to the unlearned and mercy to the needy while it castigated the pride and wealth of those who oppressed the humble and the poor. At the same time, Smith founded the Church of Jesus Christ of Latter-Day Saints, which he led as the Prophet. Although seeking converts, the church did not admit African Americans to worship.

Smith founded not only a church but a theocracy (a community governed by religious leaders). In the mid-1830s, Mormons established a settlement at Nauvoo, Illinois, built homes and churches, and recruited followers from the eastern United States and from England. But after Smith received revelations sanctioning polygamy, local authorities arrested him and his brother, and a mob lynched them. Brigham Young, a successful missionary, took over as Prophet and in 1846 led 12,000 followers west, 5,000 of whom built a thriving theocracy near the Great Salt Lake, in what would become the Utah Territory in 1850.

New religious groups also formed by separating from established denominations, just as Unitarians had split from Congregationalists. William Miller, a prosperous farmer and Baptist preacher, led one such movement.

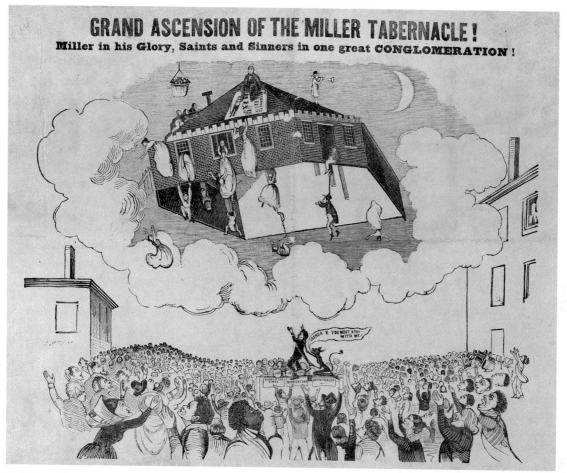

GRAND ASCENSION OF THE MILLER TABERNACLE!
Miller in his Glory, Saints and Sinners in one great CONGLOMERATION!

Religious Fervor

This broadside depicts the rapture that Baptist minister William Miller predicted would occur when Jesus Christ returned between March 21, 1843, and March 21, 1844. Although the failure of this and later predictions caused many Americans to satirize Miller and his followers, some Millerites continued to believe the Second Coming was imminent and formed the Seventh-Day Adventists.   The New-York Historical Society

He claimed that the Bible proved that the Second Coming of Jesus Christ would occur in 1843. Thousands of Americans read Millerite pamphlets and newsletters and attended sermons by Millerite preachers. When various dates for Christ's Second Coming passed without incident, however, Millerites developed competing interpretations for the failure and divided into distinct groups. The most influential group formed the Seventh-Day Adventist Church in the 1840s.

Transcendentalism

Another important movement for spiritual renewal was rooted in the transcendent power of nature. The founder of this transcendentalist school of thought was Ralph Waldo Emerson, a Unitarian pastor who gave up his post to travel and read. In 1836 he published an essay entitled "Nature"

that expressed his newfound belief in a Universal Being. This Being existed as an ideal reality beyond the material world and was accessible through nature. The natural world Emerson described was distinctly American and offered hope that moral perfection could be achieved in the United States despite the corruptions of civil society and man-made governments. Emerson expressed his ideas in widely read essays and books and in popular lectures to packed houses.

From the 1830s on, Emerson's town of Concord, Massachusetts, served as a haven for writers, poets, intellectuals, and reformers who embraced his views. Many Unitarians and other liberal Protestants in the Boston area were drawn to **transcendentalism** as well. In 1840 Margaret Fuller, a close friend of Emerson, became the first editor of *The Dial*, a journal dedicated to transcendental thought. In 1844 she moved to New York City, where the editor Horace Greeley hired her as a critic at the *New York Tribune*. While in New York, she published her ideas about the conflict between women's assigned roles and their innate abilities in *Woman in the Nineteenth Century* (1845), which combined transcendental ideas with arguments for women's rights.

Henry David Thoreau also followed the transcendentalist path. He grew up in Concord and read "Nature" while a student at Harvard. In July 1845, Thoreau moved to a cabin near Walden Pond and launched an experiment in simple living. A year later, he was imprisoned overnight for refusing to pay his taxes as a protest against slavery and the Mexican-American War. In the anonymous *Civil Disobedience* (1846), he argued that individuals of conscience had the right to resist government policies they believed to be immoral. Five years later, Thoreau published *Walden*, which offered a classic statement of the interplay among a simple lifestyle, natural harmony, and social justice.

Emerson also urged Americans to break their cultural dependence on Europe, and American artists agreed. Led by Thomas Cole, members of the Hudson River School painted romanticized landscapes from New York's Catskill and Adirondack Mountains. The sweeping vistas tied the nation's power to its natural beauty. Western vistas inspired artistic efforts as well. George Catlin portrayed the dramatic scenery of western mountains, gorges, and waterfalls and offered moving portraits of Plains Indians, who, he feared, faced extinction. Other artists captured birds, plants, and animals distinctive to the West. Although relatively few Americans had yet visited the region, many hung copies of frontier paintings on their walls or marveled at them in books and magazines. Clearly the hand of God must be at work in such glorious landscapes.

REVIEW & RELATE

What impact did the Second Great Awakening have in the North?	What new religious organizations and viewpoints emerged in the first half of the nineteenth century, *outside* of Protestant evangelical denominations?

✔ *LEARNINGCurve* bedfordstmartins.com/hewittlawson/LC

Organizing for Change

Both religious commitments and secular problems spurred social activism in the 1830s and 1840s. In cities, small towns, and rural communities, Northerners founded organizations, launched campaigns, and established institutions to better the world around them. Yet even those

Americans who agreed that society needed to be reformed did not share a common sense of priorities or solutions. Moreover, while some activists worked to persuade Americans to follow their lead, others insisted that change would occur only if imposed by law.

Varieties of Reform

Middle-class Protestant women and men formed the core of many reform movements in the early to mid-nineteenth century. They had more time and money to devote to social reform than did their working-class counterparts and were less tied to traditional ways than were their wealthy neighbors. Nonetheless, workers and farmers, African Americans and immigrants, Catholics and Jews also participated in efforts to improve society. The array of causes reformers pursued was astonishing: charity to the poor and sick; establishing religious missions; prison reform, health reform, dress reform, and educational reform; eradicating prostitution; aid to orphans, the deaf, the blind, the mentally ill, and immigrants; the exclusion of immigrants; the rights of workers, of women, and of Indians; ending alcohol and tobacco abuse; abolishing capital punishment; racial justice; and the abolition of slavery.

Explore

See Document 11.4 for an illustration of the dangers of alcohol.

Reformers used different techniques to pursue their goals. Since women could not vote, for example, they were excluded from direct political participation. Instead, they established charitable associations, distributed food and medicine, constructed asylums, circulated petitions, organized boycotts, arranged meetings and lectures, and published newspapers and pamphlets. Other groups with limited political rights—African Americans and immigrants, for instance—embraced similar modes of action. White men wielded these forms of activism but also organized political campaigns and lobbied legislators. The techniques employed were also affected by the goals of a particular movement. Moral suasion worked best with families, churches, and local communities, while legislation was more likely to succeed if the goal involved transforming people's behavior across a whole state or region.

Reformers often used a variety of tactics to support a single cause, and many changed their approach over time. For instance, reformers who sought to eradicate prostitution began by praying in front of urban brothels and attempting to rescue "fallen" women. They soon

DOCUMENT 11.4

Drunkard's Home, 1850

Temperance societies undertook a variety of activities to publicize the dangers of alcohol. Public lectures, ceremonies, and parades were popular venues, as were newspapers and books. This engraved illustration is from *The National Temperance Offering*, an 1850 publication of the Sons of Temperance of North America. Founded in New York City in 1842, the Sons of Temperance was one of the oldest temperance organizations in the United States. It was also a mutual aid society that offered members life insurance, funeral benefits, and assistance if they were injured or ill.

Explore

How does the father's drinking seem to affect the family's economic situation?

In this illustration, what is the source of the father's violence?

How does alcohol affect each member of this family?

The National Temperance Offering, and Sons and Daughters of Temperance Gift (PS1265.N3 1850), University of Virginia Library

Put It in Context

What moral arguments did members of the temperance movement use to support their cause?

launched *The Advocate of Moral Reform*, a newspaper that published morality tales, advice to mothers, and the names of men who visited brothels. Moral reform societies in small towns and rural areas worked to alert young women and men to the dangers of city life. Those in cities opened Homes for Virtuous and Friendless Females in the 1840s to provide safe havens for vulnerable women. But moral reformers also started to petition state legislators to make punishments for men who hired prostitutes as harsh as those for prostitutes themselves.

The Temperance Movement

Many moral reformers also advocated temperance. Organized temperance work began in 1826 with the founding of the American Temperance Society, an all-male organization led by clergy and businessmen who focused on alcohol abuse among working-class men. Religious revivals then inspired the establishment of some 5,000 local chapters with more than 100,000 members. Over time, the temperance movement changed the goal from moderation to total abstinence, targeted middle-class and elite as well as working-class men, and welcomed women's support. Wives and mothers were expected to persuade family members to stop drinking, sign a temperance pledge, and commit their newly sober souls to God. To promote this work, women founded dozens of female temperance societies in the 1830s. African Americans, too, created their own temperance organizations.

Some white working men viewed temperance as a way to gain dignity and respect. For Protestants, in particular, embracing temperance distinguished them from Irish Catholic workers, who were caricatured as happy drunkards. Some working-class temperance advocates also criticized liquor dealers, whom they considered to be greedy capitalists overseeing "the vilest, meanest, most earth-cursing and hell-filling business ever followed."

Despite the rapid growth of temperance organizations, moral suasion failed to reduce alcohol consumption significantly. As a result, many temperance advocates turned to legal reform in the 1840s, hoping to legislate where they could not persuade. In 1851 Maine passed legislation that prohibited the sale of all alcoholic beverages. By 1855 twelve states had joined Maine in restricting the manufacture or sale of alcohol. Yet these stringent measures inspired a backlash. Hostile to the imposition of middle-class Protestant standards on the population at large, Irish workers in Maine organized the Portland Rum Riot in 1855. It led to the law's repeal the next year.

Legal strategies generally complemented rather than replaced moral arguments. Temperance advocates continued to publish short stories, magazine articles, sermons, and novels alerting Americans to the dangers of "demon rum." Working-class families were often the subjects of didactic tales written by and for the middle class. But laboring men and women had their own ideas about how to deal with alcohol abuse. Small groups of men who abused alcohol gathered together in the 1840s and formed Washingtonian societies—named in honor of the nation's founder—to help each other stop drinking. Martha Washington societies appeared shortly thereafter, composed not of female alcoholics but of the wives, mothers, and sisters of male alcoholics.

Temperance advocates thus used various strategies to limit alcohol abuse and its consequences. Over the course of the nineteenth century, these efforts gradually reduced the consumption of beer, wine, and spirits, although they did not eliminate the problem.

Utopian Communities

While most reformers reached out to the wider society to implement change, some activists withdrew into self-contained communities that they hoped would serve as models for other groups. The architects of these **utopian societies** turned to European intellectuals and reformers for inspiration as well as to American religious and republican ideals.

In the 1820s, Scottish and Welsh labor radicals such as Frances Wright, Robert Owen, and his son Robert Dale Owen established utopian communities in the United States. They believed that a young nation founded on republican principles would be particularly open to experiments in communal labor, gender equality, and (in Wright's case) racial justice. Their efforts ultimately failed, but they did arouse impassioned debate. After founding the community of New Harmony, Indiana, in 1828 with his father, Robert Dale Owen returned briefly to Europe. He then joined Wright in New York City, where they established a reform newspaper, reading room, and medical dispensary. Resettling in New Harmony in 1833, Owen continued to advocate for workers' rights, birth control, and the abolition of slavery. But he also embraced Jacksonian democracy and won election to the Indiana House of Representatives and then the U.S. Congress. Owen thus pursued both utopian communalism and political activism in the larger society.

Former Unitarian minister George Ripley also sought to bridge a critical divide—between physical and intellectual labor. He established a transcendentalist community at Brook Farm in Massachusetts in 1841. In 1845 the farm was reconfigured according to the principles of the French socialist Charles Fourier, who believed that cooperation across classes was necessary to temper the conflicts inherent in capitalist society. He developed a plan for communities, called phalanxes, where residents chose jobs based on their individual interests and were paid according to the contribution of each job to the community's well-being. Fourier also advocated equality for women. More than forty Fourierist phalanxes were founded in the northern United States during the 1840s.

Explore

See Document 11.5, in which Ripley invites Ralph Waldo Emerson to join Brook Farm.

A more uniquely American experiment, the Oneida community, was established in central New York by John Humphrey Noyes in 1848. He and his followers believed that Christ's Second Coming had already occurred and embraced the communalism of the early Christian church. But Noyes also advocated sexual freedom and developed a plan for "complex marriage" in which women were liberated from male domination and constant childbearing. Divorce and remarriage were permitted, children were raised communally, and a form of birth control was instituted. Despite the public outrage provoked by Oneida's sexual practices, the community recruited several hundred residents and thrived for more than three decades.

DOCUMENT 11.5

George Ripley | Letter to Ralph Waldo Emerson, November 9, 1840

George Ripley was a Unitarian minister and an avid reformer. In 1840 he wrote to Ralph Waldo Emerson, the well-known transcendentalist, inviting him to join his planned utopian community, Brook Farm. Although Emerson rejected the invitation, Brook Farm began operations in 1841 in West Roxbury, Massachusetts. The Brook Farmers lived and dined communally and divided their time between farm work and artistic and scholarly pursuits. The community could not sustain itself financially, however, and a year after a devastating fire in 1846, the experiment ended. In the following excerpt, Ripley explains his ideas about the importance of combining physical and mental labor.

Explore

Our objects, as you know, are to insure a more natural union between intellectual and manual labor than now exists; to combine the thinker and the worker, as far as possible, in the same individual; to guarantee the highest mental freedom, by providing all with labor, adapted to their tastes and talents, and securing to them the fruits of their industry; to do away [with] the necessity of menial services, by opening the benefits of education and the profits of labor to all; and thus to prepare a society of liberal, intelligent, and cultivated persons, whose relations with each other would permit a more simple and wholesome life, than can be led amidst the pressure of our competitive institutions.

To accomplish these objects, we propose to take a small tract of land, which, under skillful husbandry, uniting the garden and the farm, will be adequate to the subsistence of the families; and to connect with this a school or college, in which the most complete instruction shall be given, from the first rudiments to the highest culture. Our farm would be a place for improving the race of men that lived on it; thought would preside over the operations of labor, and labor would contribute to the expansion of thought; we should have industry without drudgery, and true equality without its vulgarity.

Source: Octavius Brooks Frothingham, *George Ripley* (Boston: Houghton Mifflin, 1882), 307–8.

Interpret the Evidence

- How does Ripley describe the benefits of combining physical and mental labor at Brook Farm?
- Why might George Ripley be interested in persuading Ralph Waldo Emerson to join the Brook Farm community?

Put It in Context

How does Ripley's plan for his utopian community fit with the visions of social reformers more generally in this period?

How did the temperance movement reflect the range of tactics and participants involved in reform during the 1830s and 1840s?

What connections can you identify between utopian communities and mainstream reform movements in the first half of the nineteenth century?

LEARNINGCurve bedfordstmartins.com/hewittlawson/LC

Abolitionism Expands and Divides

For a small percentage of Northerners, slavery was the ultimate injustice. While most Northerners applauded themselves for ridding their region of the institution, antislavery advocates urged them to recognize the North's continued complicity in human bondage. After all, slaves labored under brutal conditions to provide cotton for New England factories, sugar and molasses for northern tables, and profits for urban traders. Free blacks were among the most vocal advocates of abolition. Yet their leadership became a source of conflict as more whites joined the movement in the 1830s. The place of the church, of women, and of politics in antislavery efforts also caused controversy. In addition, abolitionists disagreed over whether to focus on abolishing slavery in the South or simply preventing its extension into western territories. Although these debates often weakened individual organizations, they expanded the number and range of antislavery associations and campaigns.

The Beginnings of the Antislavery Movement

In the 1820s, African Americans and a few white Quaker allies led the fight to abolish slavery. They published pamphlets, lectured to small audiences, and helped runaway slaves escape. In 1829 David Walker wrote the most militant statement of black abolitionist sentiment, *Appeal . . . to the Colored Citizens*. The free son of an enslaved father, Walker left his North Carolina home for Boston in the 1820s. There he became an agent and a writer for *Freedom's Journal*, the country's first newspaper published by African Americans. In his *Appeal*, Walker criticized the false promises of African colonization and warned that slaves would claim their freedom by force if whites did not agree to emancipate them. Quaker abolitionists, such as Benjamin Lundy, the editor of the *Genius of Universal Emancipation*, admired Walker's courage but rejected his call for violence.

William Lloyd Garrison, a white Bostonian who worked on Lundy's Baltimore newspaper, was inspired by Walker's radical stance. In 1831 he returned to Boston and launched his own abolitionist newspaper, the *Liberator*, urging white antislavery activists to embrace the black perspective. White reformers, he claimed, worried more about the moral and practical problems that slavery posed for whites than about the wrongs it imposed on blacks. From blacks' perspective, Garrison claimed, the goal must be immediate, uncompensated emancipation.

The *Liberator* demanded that whites take an absolute stand against slavery where it existed and halt its spread. With the aid of like-minded reformers in Boston, Philadelphia, and New York City, Garrison organized the **American Anti-Slavery Society (AASS)** in 1833. By the end of the decade, the AASS boasted branches in dozens of towns and cities, from Boston to Salem, Ohio. Members supported lecturers and petition drives, criticized churches that refused to denounce slavery, and proclaimed that the U.S. Constitution was a proslavery document. Some Garrisonians also participated in the work of the **underground railroad**, a secret network of activists who assisted fugitives fleeing enslavement.

In 1835 Sarah and Angelina Grimké joined the AASS and soon began lecturing for the organization. Daughters of a prominent South Carolina planter, they had moved to Philadelphia and converted to Quakerism. As Southerners, their denunciations of slavery carried particular weight. Yet as women, their public presence aroused fierce opposition. In 1837 Congregationalist ministers in Massachusetts decried their presence in front of "promiscuous" audiences of men and women.

The Grimkés were not the first women to speak out against slavery. Maria Stewart, a free black widow, lectured in Boston in 1831–1832. She demanded that northern blacks take more responsibility for ending slavery in the South and for fighting racial discrimination everywhere. In 1833 free black and white Quaker women formed an interracial organization, the Philadelphia Female Anti-Slavery Society. The organization built on the earlier efforts of white Quakers and free blacks in Philadelphia to boycott slave-produced goods such as cotton and sugar.

The abolitionist movement and the AASS quickly expanded to the frontier, and by 1836 Ohio claimed more antislavery groups than any other state. That year, Ohio women initiated a petition to abolish slavery in the District of Columbia, which was circulated from Rhode Island to Illinois. The petition campaign inspired the first national meeting of women abolitionists, held in New York City in 1837. But in Ohio and the rest of the Midwest, female and male abolitionists worked side by side, claiming it was their Christian duty "to *unite* our efforts for the accomplishment of the holy object of our association."

Death of Capt. Ferrer, the Captain of the Amistad, July, 1839.

The *Amistad* Revolt, 1839

This illustration depicts the mutiny of forty-nine African slaves led by Cinqué on board the Spanish ship *Amistad* off the coast of Cuba. After the rebels killed Captain Ramón Ferrer, they sailed to Long Island, New York. In subsequent judicial proceedings, the federal courts ruled that the slaves were entitled to their freedom, and they were returned to Africa.   Beinecke Rare Book and Manuscript Library, Yale University

Abolition Gains Ground and Enemies

The abolitionist movement shocked many Northerners, and in the late 1830s violence often erupted in response to antislavery agitation. Mobs threatened participants at the 1838 Antislavery Convention of American Women at Pennsylvania Hall in Philadelphia. After black and white women left the meeting arm in arm, the hall was burned to the ground. From 1834 to 1838, mobs routinely attacked antislavery meetings, lecturers, and presses as AASS agents crisscrossed the North recruiting followers and organizing local societies.

The massive petition campaigns in 1836 and 1837 generated both support and opposition. Thousands of women and men, including Amy Post and her husband Isaac, signed their names to petitions to ban slavery in the District of Columbia, end the internal slave trade, and oppose the annexation of Texas. While some evangelical women considered such efforts part of their Christian duty, evangelical ministers (including the Reverend Finney) condemned antislavery work as outside women's sphere. Many female evangelicals retreated in the face of clerical disapproval, but others continued their efforts alongside their nonevangelical sisters. **See Document Project 11: The Second Great Awakening and Women's Activism, page 352**. Many politicians were also opposed to mass petitioning, whether by women or men, so in 1836 Congress passed the gag rule (see chapter 10).

But gag rules did not silence abolitionists. In the 1840s, fugitive slaves helped alert Northerners to the horrors of slavery. The most important of the fugitive abolitionists was Frederick Douglass, a Maryland-born slave who fled to New Bedford, Massachusetts, in 1838. He met Garrison in 1841, joined the AASS, and four years later published his life story, *Narrative of the Life of Frederick Douglass, as Told by Himself*. Having revealed his identity as a fugitive slave, Douglass sailed for England, where he launched a successful two-year lecture tour. He then returned to the United States; moved to Rochester, New York; and began publishing his own antislavery newspaper, the *North Star*. Amy Post befriended Douglass, and the Western New York Anti-Slavery Society raised funds and subscribers to support his work.

While eager to have fugitive slaves tell their dramatic stories, many abolitionist leaders did not match Post's vigorous support of African American activists asserting an independent voice. Although these abolitionists opposed slavery, they still believed that blacks were inferior to whites. Thus several affiliates of the AASS refused to accept black members. Those that did often faced resignations from members who opposed the innovation. Ultimately, the independent efforts of black activists such as Douglass helped to expand the antislavery movement even as they made clear the limits of white abolitionist ideals.

Conflicts also arose over the responsibility of churches to challenge slavery. The major Protestant denominations included southern as well as northern churches. If mainstream churches such as Presbyterians, Baptists, or Methodists refused communion to slave owners, their southern branches would certainly secede. Still, from the 1830s on, abolitionists pressured their churches to take Christian obligations seriously and denounce human bondage.

Antislavery Meeting

This daguerreotype (an early form of photograph) shows the abolitionist Frederick Douglass seated at a table beside a Quaker woman, with two other former slaves from Washington, D.C., Mary and Emily Edmondson, standing behind him. The open-air meeting in Cazenovia, New York, was held on August 22, 1850, to protest the impending passage of the Fugitive Slave Act, which penalized individuals who aided escaped slaves. The Granger Collection, New York

Abolitionism and Women's Rights

Women were increasingly active in the AASS and the "come outer" movement, but their growing participation aroused opposition even among abolitionists. By 1836–1837, female societies formed the backbone of antislavery petition campaigns. More women also joined the lecture circuit, including Abby Kelley, a fiery Quaker orator who demanded that women be granted an equal role in the movement. But when Garrison and his supporters appointed Kelley to the AASS business committee in the spring of 1839, they triggered a crisis. At the AASS annual convention that May, debates erupted over the propriety of women participating "in closed meetings with men." Of the 1,000 abolitionists in attendance, some 300 walked out in protest. The opposition came mainly from the evangelical wing of the movement and included Lewis Tappan, one of the chief financiers of the AASS. The dissidents soon formed a new organization, the American and Foreign Anti-Slavery Society, which excluded women from public lecturing and officeholding but encouraged them to support men's efforts.

The Garrisonians responded by expanding the roles of women in the AASS. In 1840 local chapters appointed a handful of female delegates, including Lucretia Mott, to the World Anti-Slavery Convention in London. The majority of men at the meeting, however, rejected the female delegates' credentials. Women were then forced to watch the proceedings from a separate section of the hall, confirming for some that women could be effective in campaigns against slavery only if they gained more rights for themselves.

Finally, in July 1848, a small circle of women, including Lucretia Mott and a young American she met in London, Elizabeth Cady Stanton, organized the first convention focused explicitly on women's rights. Held in Stanton's hometown of Seneca Falls, New York, the convention attracted three hundred women and men, including Garrisonian abolitionists, radical Quakers, and members of the antislavery Liberty Party. James Mott presided over part of the convention and Frederick Douglass spoke, but women dominated the proceedings. One hundred participants signed a **Declaration of Sentiments** that called for women's equality in everything from education and employment to legal rights and voting. Two weeks later,

Individual churches responded, but aside from the Society of Friends, larger denominations failed to follow suit.

In response, abolitionists urged individual Christians to break with churches that continued to accept slaveholders. Antislavery preachers and parishioners pushed the issue, and some worshippers "came out" from mainstream churches to form antislavery congregations. Union churches, composed of evangelical "come outers" from various denominations, were founded in New York State and New England. White Wesleyan Methodists and Free Will Baptists joined African American Methodists and Baptists in insisting that congregants oppose slavery in order to gain membership. Although these churches remained small, they served as constant reminders to mainstream denominations of their continued ties to slavery.

a second convention in Rochester, New York, took the radical action of electing a woman, Abigail Bush, to preside. Here, too, Douglass and other black abolitionists as well as local working women participated.

Although abolitionism provided much of the impetus for the women's rights movement, it was not the only influence. Strikes by seamstresses and mill workers in the 1830s and 1840s highlighted women's economic needs. Utopian communities experimented with gender equality, and temperance reformers focused attention on domestic violence against women and called for changes in divorce laws. A diverse coalition advocated for married women's property rights. Women's rights were also debated among the Seneca Indians in western New York. Like the Cherokees, Seneca women had lost traditional rights over land and tribal policy as their nation adopted more Anglo-American ways. In the summer of 1848, the creation of a written constitution threatened to enshrine these losses in writing. The Seneca constitution did strip women of their role in selecting chiefs but protected their right to vote on any decision to sell tribal lands. Earlier in 1848, revolutions had erupted against repressive regimes in France and elsewhere in Europe. Antislavery papers like the *North Star* covered developments in detail, including European women's demands for political and civil recognition. French rebels such as Jeanne Deroin and German revolutionaries such as Mathilde Anneke were especially noted for their advocacy of women's rights. The meetings in Seneca Falls and Rochester drew on these ideas and influences even as they attended primarily to the rights of white American women.

The Rise of Antislavery Parties

As women's rights conventions began calling for female suffrage, debates over the role of partisan politics in the antislavery campaign intensified. Keeping slavery out of western territories depended on the actions of Congress, as did abolishing slavery in the nation's capital and ending the internal slave trade. Moral suasion had seemingly done little to change minds in Congress or in the South. To force abolition onto the national political agenda, the **Liberty Party** was formed in 1840. Many Garrisonians were appalled at the idea of participating in what they considered a proslavery government, but the Liberty Party gained significant support among abolitionists in New York, the Middle Atlantic states, and the Midwest.

The Whigs and Democrats sought to avoid the antislavery issue in order to keep their southern and northern wings intact, but that strategy became much more difficult once the Liberty Party entered campaigns. In 1840 the party won less than 1 percent of the popular vote but

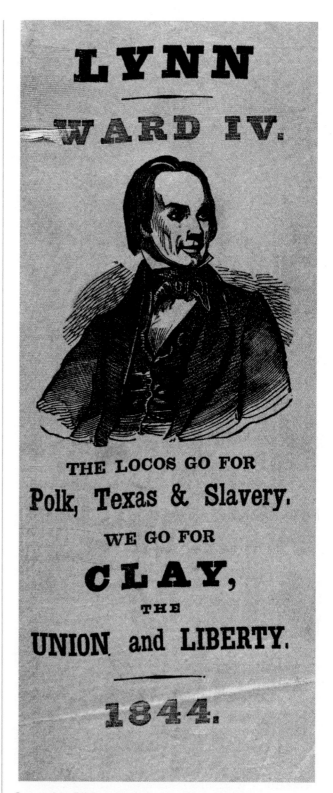

Campaign Ribbon from the Election of 1844

The Liberty Party, though fiercely opposed to the proslavery presidential candidate James K. Polk, helped turn the 1844 election in Polk's favor by taking votes away from the Whig contender, Henry Clay, who compromised on slavery. This Whig campaign ribbon from the fourth ward in Lynn, Massachusetts, proclaims "Clay, the Union and Liberty." © David J. and Jane L. Frent Collection/CORBIS

organized large rallies that attracted men, women, and children. In sparsely settled regions like Illinois, Garrisonians even joined Liberty Party supporters to get out the antislavery message. In 1844 the party won a little more than 2 percent of the vote, but this time its presence in the race was enough to ensure a victory for James K. Polk over the Whig candidate, Henry Clay (see chapter 10).

When President Polk led the United States into war with Mexico, interest in an antislavery political party surged. In 1848 the Liberty Party gained the support of antislavery Whigs, also called Conscience Whigs; northern Democrats who opposed the extension of slavery into the territories; and African American leaders like Frederick Douglass, who broke with Garrison on the issue of electoral politics. Seeing a political opportunity, more practically minded political abolitionists founded the Free-Soil Party, which quickly subsumed the Liberty Party. Free-Soilers focused less on the moral wrongs of slavery than on the benefits of keeping western territories free for northern whites. The Free-Soil Party nominated Martin Van Buren, a former Democrat, for president in 1848 and won 10 percent of the popular vote. Once again, the result was to send a slaveholder to the White House—Zachary Taylor, who had led U.S. troops in the war with Mexico. Nonetheless, the Free-Soil Party had expanded beyond the Liberty Party, raising fears in the South and in the two major parties that the battle over slavery could no longer be contained.

REVIEW & RELATE

How did the American Anti-Slavery Society differ from earlier abolitionist organizations?

How did conflicts over gender and race shape the development of the abolitionist movement in the 1830s and 1840s?

✓ *LEARNINGCurve* bedfordstmartins.com/hewittlawson/LC

Conclusion: From the North to the Nation

Charles Grandison Finney followed these developments from Oberlin College, where he served as president in the 1840s. Resistant to women's growing demands for rights and skeptical that politics could transform society, he continued to view individual conversions as the wellspring of change. As the nation expanded westward, he trained ministers to travel the frontier converting American Indians to Christianity and reminding Christian pioneers of their religious obligations. After the discovery of gold in California in 1848, religious leaders of every faith feared that the desire for material gain would once again lead Americans to neglect spiritual responsibilities.

Amy Post watched close friends leave for California with husbands struck by gold fever. Other friends and coworkers moved to Ohio, Michigan, and Kansas. Those who remained in Rochester became even more immersed in abolitionist campaigns but continued to clash over the best strategies for achieving their goals. Amy Post, like most Quakers, rejected participation in a government that accepted slavery and fomented war, causing a rift with Frederick Douglass. The disagreement caused her deep personal anguish, but the debates revitalized the movement, creating new opportunities for action.

Finney and Post were among tens of thousands of Northerners inspired by religious and reform movements between 1820 and 1850. Driven by urban and industrial development, immigration, and moral concerns, activists focused on a wide range of causes. But abolitionism carried the most powerful national implications. The addition of vast new territories at the end of the Mexican-American War in 1848 ensured that those concerns would become even more pressing in the decade ahead.

LEARNINGCurve
Check what you know.
bedfordstmartins.com/hewittlawson/LC

Chapter Review ⌐ Online Study Guide ▶ bedfordstmartins.com/hewittlawson

KEY TERMS

separate spheres (p. 331)
deskilling (p. 333)
nativists (p. 337)
Second Great Awakening (p. 339)
temperance (p. 340)
transcendentalism (p. 341)
utopian societies (p. 344)
Appeal . . . to the Colored Citizens (p. 346)
Liberator (p. 346)
American Anti-Slavery Society (AASS) (p. 346)
underground railroad (p. 346)
Declaration of Sentiments (p. 348)
Liberty Party (p. 349)

REVIEW & RELATE

1. Why did American cities become larger and more diverse in the first half of the nineteenth century?

2. What values and beliefs did the emerging American middle class embrace?

3. How and why did American manufacturing change over the course of the first half of the nineteenth century?

4. How did Northerners respond to the hard times that followed the panic of 1837? How did responses to the crisis vary by class, ethnicity, and religion?

5. What impact did the Second Great Awakening have in the North?

6. What new religious organizations and viewpoints emerged in the first half of the nineteenth century, *outside* of Protestant evangelical denominations?

7. How did the temperance movement reflect the range of tactics and participants involved in reform during the 1830s and 1840s?

8. What connections can you identify between utopian communities and mainstream reform movements in the first half of the nineteenth century?

9. How did the American Anti-Slavery Society differ from earlier abolitionist organizations?

10. How did conflicts over gender and race shape the development of the abolitionist movement in the 1830s and 1840s?

TIMELINE OF EVENTS

1820–1850	Size, number, and diversity of northern cities grow; immigration surges
1823	Textile factory town built in Lowell, Massachusetts
1826	American Temperance Society founded
1827	First workingmen's political party founded
1829	David Walker publishes *Appeal . . . to the Colored Citizens*
1830	Joseph Smith publishes *The Book of Mormon*
September 1830	Charles Grandison Finney brings Second Great Awakening to Rochester, New York
1833	William Lloyd Garrison founds American Anti-Slavery Society (AASS)
1837–1842	Panic of 1837
1839	American Anti-Slavery Society splits over the role of women in the society
1840	Liberty Party formed
	World Anti-Slavery Convention, London
1842	Amy Post helps found the Western New York Anti-Slavery Society
1843	William Miller predicts Second Coming of Christ
1844	Congress funds construction of the first telegraph line
May 1844	Anti-immigrant violence rocks Philadelphia
1845	Frederick Douglass publishes *Narrative of the Life of Frederick Douglass*
	Margaret Fuller publishes *Woman in the Nineteenth Century*
1845–1846	Irish potato famine
1846	Henry David Thoreau publishes *Civil Disobedience*
1848	Free-Soil Party formed
	Frederick Douglass publishes the *North Star*
July 1848	Seneca Falls Woman's Rights Convention
1851	Maine prohibits the sale of alcoholic beverages

The Second Great Awakening and Women's Activism

From the 1790s through the 1830s, a religious movement known as the Second Great Awakening swept through communities across the United States. Revivals and camp meetings transformed many denominations, and evangelical Protestant churches were especially affected by this religious fervor, which not only altered the nature of church services but also led to a surge in church membership. In Documents 11.6 and 11.7, evangelist Charles Grandison Finney and the English traveler Frances Trollope describe the character of revivals in quite different terms.

The Second Great Awakening's social impact extended beyond church membership, and many of the newly converted sought to put their religious beliefs into action through good works. Especially in the North, this meant joining movements designed to rid American society of what they believed were the consequences of sin. Temperance societies, charitable organizations, antiprostitution campaigns, and the abolitionist movement all benefited from this commitment to social reform.

Women formed the backbone of the Second Great Awakening, bringing their husbands, sons, and brothers to mass meetings. It was natural, then, that they also sought to extend their beliefs into reform activities. As women slowly took on a more public role in reform efforts, their actions generated passionate and heated debates over the proper place for women in American society. Several of the documents that follow explore these debates through the lens of the abolitionist movement. Document 11.9, the pastoral letter from Congregationalist ministers, is an example of the criticism directed at women when they engaged in public antislavery work. The female abolitionists in Documents 11.8 and 11.10 defend themselves by appealing to religious doctrines and also the principles of American democracy. Women's reform impulse eventually led some to argue for an expansion of women's rights. While small numbers of abolitionist, temperance, and moral reform activists initiated the women's rights movement of the mid-nineteenth century, many of them came from Quaker and Unitarian rather than evangelical backgrounds.

DOCUMENT 11.6

Charles Grandison Finney | What Revival Is, 1835

In 1835 Charles Finney moved from New York City to Ohio, where he became a professor at Oberlin College and Theological Seminary. In Ohio, Finney continued to preach and also trained new generations of ministers to carry on his theological message. He reached out to an even wider audience through the publication of *Lectures on Revivals of Religion*. Originally a series of sermons printed in the *New York Evangelist*, Finney's book was enormously popular and sold twelve thousand copies in three months. The following selection is from the first lecture, "What Revival Is."

A REVIVAL ALWAYS INCLUDES conviction of sin on the part of the church. Backslidden professors cannot wake up and begin right away in the service of God, without deep searchings of heart. The fountains of sin need to be broken up. In a true revival, Christians are always brought under such convictions; they see their sins in such a light, that often they find it impossible to maintain a hope of their acceptance with God. It does not always go to that extent; but there are always, in a genuine revival, deep convictions of sin, and often cases of abandoning all hope.

Backslidden Christians will be brought to repentance. A revival is nothing else than a new beginning of obedience to God. Just as in the case of a converted sinner, the first step is a deep repentance, a breaking down of heart, a getting down into the dust before God, with deep humility, and forsaking of sin.

Christians will have their faith renewed. While they are in their backslidden state they are blind to the state of sinners. Their hearts are as hard as marble. The truths of the Bible only appear like a dream. They admit it to be all true; their conscience and their judgment assent to it; but their faith does not see it standing out in bold relief, in all the burning realities of eternity. But when they enter into a revival, they no longer see men as trees walking, but they see things in that strong light which will renew the love of God in their hearts. This will lead them to labor zealously to bring others to him. They will feel grieved that others do not love God, when they love him so much. And they will set themselves feelingly to persuade their neighbors to give him their hearts. So their love to men will be renewed. They will be filled with a tender and burning love for souls. They will have a longing desire for the salvation of the whole world. They will be in an agony for individuals whom they want to have saved; their friends, relations, enemies. They will not only be urging them to give their hearts to God, but they will carry them to God in the arms of faith, and with strong crying and tears beseech God to have mercy on them, and save their souls from endless burnings.

A revival breaks the power of the world and of sin over Christians. It brings them to such vantage ground that they get a fresh impulse towards heaven. They have a new foretaste of heaven, and new desires after union with God; and the charm of the world is broken, and the power of sin overcome.

When the churches are thus awakened and reformed, the reformation and salvation of sinners will follow, going through the same stages of conviction, repentance, and reformation. Their hearts will be broken down and changed. Very often the most abandoned profligates are among the subjects. Harlots, and drunkards, and infidels, and all sorts of abandoned characters, are awakened and converted. The worst part of human society are softened and reclaimed, and made to appear as lovely specimens of the beauty of holiness.

Source: Charles G. Finney, *Lectures on Revivals of Religion* (New York: Leavitt, Lord, 1835), 14–15.

DOCUMENT 11.7

Frances Trollope |
Description of a Revival Meeting, 1832

Frances Trollope was an English author who toured the United States and lived briefly in Cincinnati in the early 1830s. In 1832 she published *Domestic Manners of the Americans*, a critical and often biting account of American society. The book was a best seller in the United States and Europe, and Trollope was both widely praised and criticized for the work. She discussed a variety of topics and aimed much of her criticism at the influence of the Second Great Awakening and evangelicalism on Americans. In the following selection, she describes a revival meeting in Indiana.

Four high frames, constructed in the form of altars, were placed at the four corners of the inclosure; on these were supported layers of earth and sod, on which burned immense fires of blazing pinewood. On one side a rude platform was erected to accommodate the preachers, fifteen of whom attended this meeting, and with very short intervals for necessary refreshment and private devotion, preached in rotation, day and night, from Tuesday to Saturday.

When we arrived, the preachers were silent; but we heard issuing from nearly every tent mingled sounds of praying, preaching, singing, and lamentation. The curtains in front of each tent were dropped, and the faint light that gleamed through the white drapery, backed as it was by the dark forest, had a beautiful and mysterious effect, that set the imagination at work; and had the sounds which vibrated around us been less discordant, harsh, and unnatural, I should have enjoyed it; but listening at the corner of a tent, which poured forth more than its proportion of clamour, in a few moments chased every feeling derived from imagination, and furnished realities that could neither be mistaken nor forgotten. . . .

At midnight, a horn sounded through the camp, which, we were told, was to call the people from private to public worship; and we presently saw them flocking from all sides to the front of the preachers' stand. Mrs. B. and I contrived to place ourselves with our backs supported against the lower part of this structure, and we were thus enabled to witness the scene which followed without personal danger. There were about two thousand persons assembled.

One of the preachers began in a low nasal tone, and, like all other Methodist preachers, assured us of the enormous depravity of man as he comes from the hands of his Maker, and of his perfect sanctification after he had wrestled sufficiently with the Lord to get hold of him, *et cætera*. The admiration of the crowd was evinced by almost constant cries of "Amen! Amen!" "Jesus! Jesus!" "Glory! Glory!" and the like. . . .

. . . Above a hundred persons, nearly all females, came forward, uttering howlings and groans so terrible that I shall never cease to shudder when I recall them. They appeared to drag each other forward, and on the word being given, "let us pray," they all fell on their knees; but this posture was soon changed for others that permitted greater scope for the convulsive movements of their limbs; and they were soon all lying on the ground in an indescribable confusion of heads and legs. They threw about their limbs with such incessant and violent motion, that I was every instant expecting some serious accident to occur.

But how am I to describe the sounds that proceeded from this strange mass of human beings? I know no words which can convey an idea of it. Hysterical sobbings, convulsive groans, shrieks and screams the most appalling, burst forth on all sides. I felt sick with horror. As if their hoarse and overstrained voices failed to make noise enough, they soon began to clap their hands violently. . . .

Many of these wretched creatures were beautiful young females. The preachers moved about among them, at once exciting and soothing their agonies. I heard the muttered "Sister! dear sister!" I saw the insidious lips approach the cheeks of the unhappy girls; I heard the murmured confessions of the poor victims, and I watched their tormentors, breathing into their ears consolations that tinged the pale cheek with red. Had I been a man, I am sure I would have been guilty of some rash act of interference. . . .

One woman near us continued to "call on the Lord," as it is termed, in the loudest possible tone, and without a moment's interval, for the two hours that we kept our dreadful station. She became frightfully hoarse, and her face so red as to make me expect she would burst a blood-vessel. Among the rest of her rant, she said, "I will hold fast to Jesus, I never will let him go; if they take me to hell, I will still hold him fast, fast, fast!"

The stunning noise was sometimes varied by the preachers' beginning to sing; but the convulsive movements of the poor maniacs only became more violent. At length the atrocious wickedness of this horrible scene increased to a degree of grossness and drove us from our station; we returned to the carriage at about three o'clock in the morning, and passed the remainder of the night listening to the ever-increasing tumult at the pen. To sleep was impossible.

Source: Frances Trollope, *Domestic Manners of the Americans* (London: Whittaker, Treacher, 1832), 140, 142–45.

DOCUMENT 11.8

Elizabeth Emery and Mary P. Abbott | Letter to the *Liberator*, 1836

Many women's experiences in the religious revivals of the Second Great Awakening moved them to engage in social activism. Abolitionism attracted female activists who believed they were called to rid America of a grave sin. Like many women across the country, women in Andover, Massachusetts, organized a Female Antislavery Society. Elizabeth Emery and Mary Abbott, two leaders in the society, wrote a letter to the antislavery newspaper the *Liberator*, expressing their belief that women had a moral responsibility to work to end slavery.

Mr. Editor:

In these days of women's doings, it may not be amiss to report the proceedings of some ladies in Andover. The story is now and then told of a new thing done here, as the opening of a railroad, or the building of a factory, but we have news better than all—it is the formation of a "Female Antislavery Society."

The call of our female friends across the waters—the energetic appeal of those untiring sisters in the work of emancipation in Boston—above all, the sighs, the groans, the deathlike struggles of scourged sisters in the South—these have moved our hearts, our hands. We feel that woman has a place in this Godlike work, for woman's woes, and woman's wrongs, are borne to us on every breeze that flows from the South; woman has a place, for she forms a part in God's created intelligent instrumentality to reform the world. God never made her to be inactive nor in all cases to follow in the wake of man. When man proves recreant to his duty and faithless to his Maker, woman, with her feeling heart, should rouse him—should start his sympathies—should cry in his ear, and raise such a storm of generous sentiment, as shall never let him sleep again. We believe God gave woman a heart to feel—an eye to weep—a hand to work—a tongue to speak. Now let her use that tongue to speak on slavery. Is it not a curse—a heaven-daring abomination? Let her employ that hand, to labor for the slave. Does not her sister in bonds, labor night and day without reward? Let her heart grieve, and her eye fill with tears, in view of a female's body dishonored—a female's mind debased—a female's soul forever ruined! Woman nothing to do with slavery! Abhorred the thought!! We will pray to abhor it more and more. Is not woman abused—woman trampled upon—woman spoiled of her virtue, her probity, her influence, her joy! And this, not in India—not in China—not in Turkey—not in Africa but in America—in the United States of America, in the birthplace of Washington, the father of freedom, the protector of woman, the friend of equality and human rights!

Woman out of her place, in feeling, praying, and acting for the slave! Impious idea! Her oppressed sister cries aloud for help. She tries to lift her manacled hand—to turn her bruised face—to raise her tearful eye, and by all these, to plead a remembrance in our prayers—an interest in our labors. . . . As Christian women, we will do a Christian woman's duty. . . .

Our preamble gives our creed:

"We believe American Slavery is a sin against God—at war with the dictates of humanity, and subversive of the principles of freedom, because it regards rational beings as goods and chattel; robs them of compensation for their toil—denies to them the protection of law—disregards the relation of husband and wife, brother and sister, parent and child; shuts out from the intellect the light of knowledge; overwhelms hope in despair and ruins the soul—thus sinking to the level of brutes, more than one million of American females, who are created in God's image, a little lower than the angels', and consigns them over to degradation, physical, social, intellectual, and moral: consequently, every slaveholder is bound instantly to cease from all participation in such a system. We believe that we should have no fellowship with these works of darkness, but rather reprove them—and that the truth spoken in love, is mighty to the removal of slavery, as of all other sins." . . .

May fearful foreboding lead the slave holder to timely repentance.

Source: Elizabeth Emery and Mary P. Abbott, "Letter to *The Liberator*," *The Liberator*, August 27, 1836, 138.

DOCUMENT 11.9
Pastoral Letter to the *Liberator*, 1837

As women's involvement in abolitionism became more public, it generated controversy from inside and outside of the movement. In August 1837, ministers from the Congregational Church wrote a letter to the *Liberator* denouncing women's public abolitionist efforts. Their immediate concern was the work of Angelina and Sarah Grimké, sisters and speakers on the abolitionist lecture circuit. The lectures the Grimkés presented to mixed-sex audiences infuriated these Congregationalist ministers, whose letter broadly condemned all women's public activism.

We invite your attention to the dangers which at present seem to threaten the female character with wide-spread and permanent injury. The appropriate duties and influence of woman are clearly stated in the New Testament. Those duties and that influence are unobtrusive and private, but the source of mighty power. When the mild, dependent, softening influence of woman upon the sternness of man's opinions is fully exercised, society feels the effects of it in a thousand ways. The power of woman is in her dependence, flowing from the consciousness of that weakness which God has given her for her protection, and which keeps her in those departments of life that form the character of individuals and of the nation. There are social influences which females use in promoting piety and the great objects of Christian benevolence which we cannot too highly commend. We appreciate the unostentatious prayers and efforts of woman in advancing the cause of religion at home and abroad; in Sabbath-schools; in leading religious inquirers to the pastors for instruction; and in all such associated effort as becomes the modesty of her sex; and earnestly hope that she may abound more and more in these labors of piety and love.

But when she assumes the place and tone of man as a public reformer, our care and protection of her seem unnecessary; we put ourselves in self-defence against her; she yields the power which God has given her for protection, and her character becomes unnatural. If the vine, whose strength and beauty is to lean upon the trellis-work and half conceal its clusters, thinks to assume the independence and the over-shadowing nature of the elm, it will not only cease to bear fruit, but fall in shame and dishonor into the dust. We cannot, therefore, but regret the mistaken conduct of those who encourage females to bear an obtrusive and ostentatious part in measures of reform, and countenance any of that sex who so far forget themselves as to incinerate in the character of public lecturers and teachers. . . . We especially deplore the intimate acquaintance and promiscuous conversation of females with regard to things "which ought not to be named"; by which that modesty and delicacy which is the charm of domestic life, and which constitutes the true influence of woman in society, is consumed, and the way opened, as we apprehend, for degeneracy and ruin. We say these things, not to discourage proper influences against sin, but to secure such reformation as we believe is Scriptural, and will be permanent.

Source: "Pastoral Letter of the General Association of Massachusetts to the Congregational Churches under Their Care," *The Liberator*, August 11, 1837.

DOCUMENT 11.10

Sarah Grimké | Response to the Pastoral Letter, 1837

In response to the ministers' criticism, Sarah Grimké wrote her own letter to the *Liberator*, which defended her work and that of her sister, Angelina. Daughters of a slave owner in South Carolina, the Grimké sisters had moved to Philadelphia in the 1820s. Their conversion to Quakerism strengthened their belief in the evils of slavery, and by 1837 they were nationally known abolitionist activists. Their work included public lectures on behalf of the American Anti-Slavery Society. Criticisms of this work led the sisters to develop arguments in support of women's rights.

Dear Friend,

When I last addressed thee, I had not seen the Pastoral Letter of the General Association. It has since fallen into my hands, and I must digress from my intention of exhibiting the condition of women in different parts of the world, in order to make some remarks on this extraordinary document. I am persuaded that when the minds of men and women become emancipated from the thraldom [bondage] of superstition and "traditions of men," the sentiments contained in the Pastoral Letter will be recurred to with as much astonishment as the opinions of Cotton Mather and other distinguished men of his day, on the subject of witchcraft; nor will it be deemed less wonderful, that a body of divines should gravely assemble and endeavor to prove that woman has no right to "open her mouth for the dumb," than it now is that judges should have sat on the trials of witches, and solemnly condemned nineteen persons and one dog to death for witchcraft.

But to the letter. It says, "We invite your attention to the dangers which at present seem to threaten the female character with wide-spread and permanent injury." I rejoice that they have called the attention of my sex to this subject, because I believe if woman investigates it, she will soon discover that danger is impending, though from a totally different source from that which the Association apprehends—danger from those who, having long held the reins of *usurped* authority, are unwilling to permit us to fill that sphere which God created us to move in, and who have entered into league to crush the immortal mind of woman. I rejoice, because I am persuaded that the rights of woman, like the rights of slaves, need only be examined to be understood and asserted, even by some of those who are now endeavoring to smother the irrepressible desire for mental and spiritual freedom which glows in the breast of many who hardly dare to speak their sentiments.

"The appropriate duties and influence of women are clearly stated in the New Testament. Those duties are unobtrusive and private, but the sources of *mighty power*. When the mild, *dependent*, softening influence of woman upon the sternness of man's opinions is fully exercised, society feels the effects of it in a thousand ways." No one can desire more earnestly than I do, that woman may move exactly in the sphere which her Creator has assigned her; and I believe her having been displaced from that sphere has introduced confusion into the world. It is, therefore, of vast importance to herself and to all the rational creation, that she should ascertain what are her duties and her privileges as a responsible and immortal being. . . .

But the influence of woman, says the Association, is to be private and unobtrusive; her light is not to shine before man like that of her brethren; but she is passively to let the lords of the creation, as they call themselves, put the bushel over it, lest peradventure [perhaps] it might appear that the world has been benefitted by the rays of *her* candle. So that her quenched light, according to their judgment, will be of more use than if it were set on the candlestick. "Her influence is the source of mighty power." This has ever been the flattering language of man since he laid aside the whip as a means to keep woman in subjection. He spares her body; but the war he has waged against her mind, her heart, and her soul, has been no less destructive to her as a moral being. How monstrous, how anti-christian, is the doctrine that woman is to be dependent on man! Where, in all the sacred Scriptures, is this taught? Alas! she has too well learned the lesson, which MAN has labored to teach her. She has surrendered her dearest RIGHTS, and been satisfied with the privileges which man has assumed to grant her; she has been amused with the show of power, whilst man has absorbed all the reality into himself. He has adorned the creature whom God gave him as a companion, with baubles and gew-gaws [showy things], turned her attention to personal attractions, offered incense to her vanity, and made her the instrument of his selfish gratification, a plaything to please his eye and amuse his hours of leisure. . . .

. . . We are told, "the power of woman is in her dependence, flowing from a consciousness of that weakness which God has given her for her protection." If physical weakness is alluded to, I cheerfully concede the supe-riority; if brute force is what my brethren are claiming, I am willing to let them have all the honor they desire; but if they mean to intimate, that mental or moral weakness belongs to woman, more than to man, I utterly disclaim the charge. Our powers of mind have been crushed, as far as man could do it, our sense of morality has been impaired by his interpretation of our duties; but no where does God say that he made any distinc-tion between us, as moral and intelligent beings.

. . . As to the pretty simile, introduced into the Pastoral Letter, "If the vine whose strength and beauty is to lean upon the trellis work, and half conceal its clusters, thinks to assume the independence and the overshad-owing nature of the elm," etc. I shall only remark that it might well suit the poet's fancy, who sings of spar-kling eyes and coral lips, and knights in armor clad; but it seems to me utterly inconsistent with the dignity of a Christian body, to endeavor to draw such an anti-scriptural distinction between men and women. Ah! how many of my sex feel in the dominion, thus unrighteously exercised over them, under the gentle appellation of *protection*, that what they have leaned upon has proved a broken reed at best, and oft a spear.

Source: Sarah Grimké, *Letters on the Equality of the Sexes and the Condition of Woman* (Boston: Isaac Knapp, 1838), 14–18, 21.

Interpret the Evidence

1. What ideas in Charles Finney's *Lectures on Revivals of Religion* (Document 11.6) might have strengthened the connection between the Second Great Awakening and the social reform movements of the nineteenth century?

2. What seem to be Frances Trollope's main criticisms of the camp meeting in Indiana (Document 11.7)? How might Finney and other ministers have responded to those criticisms?

3. Since Trollope's *Domestic Manners of the Americans* was so popular within the United States, how might her views of women and revivalism have shaped public opinion?

4. How do the criticisms of female activism in the pastoral letter of 1837 (Document 11.9) compare with Trollope's criticism of women at revivals?

5. How do both Elizabeth Emery and Mary Abbott (Document 11.8) and Sarah Grimké (Document 11.10) use religious principles to support women's public role in the abolitionist movement?

Put It in Context

- How do the arguments of Emery, Abbott, and Grimké affirm mid-nineteenth-century beliefs about the differences between men and women? In what ways do they challenge those beliefs?

Library of Congress

Peter Newark American Pictures/The Bridgeman Art Library

Emigrant party headed to California, 1850.

Slaves fleeing Maryland coast to Delaware, 1850.

12

Imperial Ambitions and Sectional Crises

1848–1861

© Collection of the New-York Historical Society, USA/The Bridgeman Art Library

California town, 1855.

AMERICAN HISTORIES

John C. Frémont, a noted explorer and military leader and the first presidential nominee of the Republican Party, rose from humble beginnings. He was the illegitimate child of Anne Beverley Whiting Pryor of Savannah, Georgia, who abandoned her wealthy husband and ran off with a French immigrant, Jean Charles Fremon. As a young man, John changed his last name to Frémont, either reclaiming the original spelling or seeking to create a more aristocratic one. He attended the College of Charleston, where he excelled at mathematics, but was eventually expelled for neglecting his studies. Frémont was hired to teach aboard a navy ship in 1833 through the help of an influential South Carolina politician. He then obtained a surveying position to map new railroad lines and Cherokee lands in Georgia and was finally appointed a second lieutenant in the Corps of Topographical Engineers.

In 1840 Lieutenant Frémont traveled to Washington, D.C., to assist in publishing maps and reports from an expedition along the upper Mississippi River. The following year, the twenty-eight-year-old explorer eloped with Jessie Benton, the seventeen-year-old daughter of Missouri senator Thomas Hart Benton. Despite the scandal, Senator Benton supported his son-in-law's selection for a federally funded expedition to the West. In 1842 Frémont and his guide, Kit Carson, led twenty-three men along the emerging Oregon Trail. Two years later, John returned to Washington, where he and his wife Jessie wrote a vivid report on the Oregon Territory and California. Congress published the report, which inspired a wave of hopeful migrants to head west.

John Frémont shared many Americans' imperial ambitions, but his success was tainted by a quest for personal glory. On a federal mapping expedition in 1845, he left his post and headed to California. Arriving in the Sacramento valley in the winter of 1846, he stirred support among U.S. settlers for war with Mexico. His brash behavior nearly provoked a battle that would have wiped out his small company. Frémont then fled to the Oregon Territory, where he and Kit Carson became involved in conflicts with Modoc Indians. Then, as the nation moved closer to war with Mexico, Frémont returned to California, where he supported Anglo-American settlers' efforts to declare the region an independent republic. Although Frémont was denied the republic's governorship, he worked tirelessly for California's admission to the Union and served as one of the state's first senators. With his wife's encouragement, he also embraced abolition and in 1856 was nominated for president by the new Republican Party.

Dred Scott also traveled the frontier in the 1830s and 1840s, but not of his own free will. Born a slave in Southampton, Virginia, around 1800, he and his master, Peter Blow, moved west to Alabama in 1818 and then relocated to St. Louis, Missouri, in 1830. Three years later, short of funds, Blow sold Scott to Dr. John Emerson, an assistant surgeon in the U.S. army. In 1836 Emerson took Scott to Fort Snelling in the Wisconsin Territory, a free territory that offered glimpses of a different life. There Scott met Harriet Robinson, a young African American woman who was enslaved to the local Indian agent. Her master was also a justice of the peace and agreed to marry the couple in 1837 and transfer ownership of Harriet to Dr. Emerson. When Emerson was transferred back to St. Louis, the Scotts returned with him. After his death in 1843, the couple was hired out to local residents in St. Louis by Emerson's widow.

In April 1846, the Scotts initiated lawsuits in the Missouri courts seeking their freedom. The Missouri Supreme Court had ruled in earlier cases that slaves who resided for any time in free territory must be freed, and the Scotts had lived and married in Wisconsin. Dred Scott's former owners, the Blows, supported his suit, and in 1850 the Missouri Circuit Court ruled in the Scotts' favor. However, the Emerson family appealed the decision to the state Supreme Court, with Harriet's case to follow the outcome of her husband's. Two years later, that court ruled against all precedent and overturned the lower court's decision. Dred Scott then appealed to the U.S. Supreme Court, but it, too, ultimately ruled against the Scotts, leaving them enslaved. •

both photos: Library of Congress

THE AMERICAN HISTORIES of John Frémont and Dred Scott were shaped by the explosive combination of westward expansion and the growing regional division over the issue of slavery. Whereas Frémont joined expeditions to map and conquer the West, Scott followed the migrations of slave owners and soldiers. Both Frémont and Scott found strength through marriage. Jessie Frémont served as her husband's confidante and coauthor, providing both practical and emotional support through nearly fifty years of marriage. Harriet Scott joined her husband in the prolonged litigation to win their freedom. Frémont also opposed slavery, but he focused on legislative means to end it. From their different positions, these two men reflected the dramatic changes that occurred as westward expansion pushed the issues of empire and slavery to the center of national debate.

Wagon Train, 1860

This early photograph, taken in 1860, shows a train of covered wagons, oxen, and men on horseback setting out from Manhattan, Kansas.   Kansas State Historical Society

Claiming the West

During the 1830s and 1840s, national debates over slavery intensified. The most important battles now centered on western territories gained through victory in the war with Mexico. Before 1848, government-sponsored expeditions had opened up vast new lands for American pioneers seeking opportunity. Eastern migrants, along with immigrants from Germany and Scandinavia, moved west in growing numbers. Then, following the Mexican-American War and the discovery of gold in California, tens of thousands of men rushed to the Pacific coast seeking riches. But the West was already home to a diverse population that included Indians, Mexicans, Mormons, and missionaries. Eager pioneers converged, and often clashed, with these groups.

Traveling the Overland Trail

In the 1830s, a few white families had ventured to the western frontier. Some traveled around the southern tip of South America by ship or across the Isthmus of Panama by boat and mule train. But a growing number followed overland trails to the far West. In 1836 Narcissa Whitman and Eliza Spaulding joined a group traveling to the Oregon Territory, the first white women to make the trip. They accompanied their husbands, both Presbyterian ministers, who hoped to convert the region's Indians. Their letters to friends and associates back east described the rich lands and needy souls in the Walla Walla valley and encouraged further migration.

The panic of 1837 also prompted Americans to head west as thousands of U.S. migrants and European immigrants sought new opportunities in the 1840s. They were drawn to Oregon, the Rocky Mountain region, and the eastern plains. The Utah Territory, not yet officially part of the United States, attracted large numbers of Mormons. Some pioneers opened trading posts in the West where Indians exchanged goods with Anglo-American settlers or with merchants back east. Small settlements developed around these posts and near the expanding system of forts that dotted the region.

For many pioneers, the journey on the **Oregon Trail** began at St. Louis. From there, they traveled by wagon train across the Great Plains and the Rocky Mountains to the Pacific coast. By 1860 some 350,000 Americans had made the journey, claimed land from the Mississippi to the Pacific, and transformed the United States into an expanding empire.

Because the trip to the West required funds for wagons and supplies, most pioneers were of middling status. The three- to six-month journey was also physically demanding, and most pioneers traveled with family members to help share the labor and provide support, though men outnumbered women and children, comprising some 60 percent of western migrants.

Explore

See Document 12.1 for one account of the journey west.

DOCUMENT 12.1

Elizabeth Smith Geer | Oregon Trail Diary, 1847

Like thousands of families, Elizabeth and Cornelius Smith and their seven children set out for the Oregon Territory in the spring of 1847. They fared well through the summer, but in the fall heavy rains made things difficult, as Elizabeth describes in the following diary entry, and by November Cornelius had become sick. The Smiths continued on to Oregon, arriving in Portland by Thanksgiving, where Cornelius died two months later. In 1849 Elizabeth married Joseph Geer, the father of ten children whose wife died after making the rough journey on the Oregon Trail.

Explore

November 18.

It rains and snows. We start around the falls this morning with our wagons. We have five miles to go. I carry my babe and lead, or rather carry another, through snow, mud, and water almost to my knees. It is the worst road a team could possibly travel. I went ahead with my children and I was afraid to look behind me for fear of seeing the wagons overturn into the mud and water with everything in them. My children gave out with cold and fatigue and could not travel, and the boys had to unhitch the oxen and bring them and carry the children on to camp. I was so cold and numb that I could not tell by the feeling that I had any feet. We started this morning at sunrise and did not camp until after dark, and there was not one dry thread on one of us—not even on the babe. I had carried my babe and I was so fatigued that I could scarcely speak or step. When I got here I found my husband lying in Welch's wagon very sick. He had brought Mrs. Polk down the day before and was taken sick. We had to stay up all night for our wagons were left halfway back. I have not told half we suffered. I am not adequate to the task.

Source: Theodore Thurston Geer, *Fifty Years in Oregon* (New York: Neale, 1912), 146.

Interpret the Evidence

- This diary entry reflects common experiences of women, and especially mothers, on the Oregon Trail. Why do you think so many women were willing to make the journey?
- What does this diary reveal about how women experienced the trip differently from how men did?

Put It in Context

Despite widespread fear of Indian attacks on the trail, what were the most serious dangers that pioneers faced on the journey west?

Early in the journey, women and men generally followed their customary roles: Men hunted, fished, and drove the wagons, while women cooked, washed, and watched the children. But traditional roles often broke down on the trail, and even conventional domestic tasks posed novel problems. Women had to cook unfamiliar food over open fires in all kinds of weather and with only a handful of pots and utensils. They washed laundry in rivers or streams, and on the plains they had to haul water for cooking or cleaning from great distances. Wood, too, was scarce on the plains, and women and children gathered buffalo dung (called "chips") for fuel. Men frequently had to gather food rather than hunt and fish, or they had to learn to catch strange (and sometimes dangerous) animals, such as jack rabbits and rattlesnakes. Few men were prepared for the arduous work of pulling wagons out of ditches or floating them across rivers with powerful currents. Nor were many of them expert in shoeing horses or fixing wagon wheels, tasks that were performed by skilled artisans at home.

Expectations changed dramatically when men took ill or died on the journey. Then wives drove the wagon, gathered or hunted for food, and learned to repair axles and other wagon parts. When large numbers of men were injured or ill, women might serve as scouts and guides or pick up guns to defend wagons under attack by Indians or wild animals. Yet despite the growing burdens on pioneer women, they gained little power over decision making. Moreover, the addition of men's jobs to women's responsibilities was rarely reciprocated. Few men cooked, did laundry, or cared for children on the trail. Single men generally paid women on the trail to perform such chores for them, and a husband who lost his wife on the journey generally relied on "neighbor" women as he would at home.

In one area, however, relative equality reigned. Men and women were equally susceptible to disease, injury, and death on the trail. Accidents, gunshot wounds, drowning, broken bones, and infections affected individuals on every wagon train. Some groups were struck as well by influenza, cholera, measles, mumps, or scarlet fever—all deadly in the early nineteenth century. In addition, about 20 percent of women on the overland trail became pregnant, which posed even greater dangers than at home given rough roads, a lack of water, the abundance of dirt, and the frequent absence of midwives and doctors. Some 20 percent of women lost children or spouses on the trip west, though most had little time to mourn. Wagon trains usually stopped only briefly to bury the dead, leaving a cross or a pile of stones to mark the grave, and then moved on. Overall, about one in ten to fifteen migrants died on the western journey, leaving some 65,000 graves along the trails west.

The Gold Rush

Despite the hazards, more and more Americans traveled the Oregon Trail, the Santa Fe Trail, and other paths to the Pacific coast. Initially only a few thousand Americans settled in California. Some were agents sent by New England merchants to purchase fine leather made from the hides of Spanish cattle raised in the area. Several of these agents married into families of elite Mexican ranchers, known as Californios, and adopted their culture, even converting to Catholicism.

However, the Anglo-American presence in California changed dramatically after 1848 when gold was discovered at Sutter's Mill in northeastern California. News of the discovery brought tens of thousands of new settlers from the eastern United States, South America, Europe, and Asia. In the **gold rush**, "forty-niners" raced to claim riches in the California mountains, and men vastly outnumbered women. Single men came with brothers, neighbors, or friends. Married men left wives and children behind, promising to send for them once they struck gold. Some 80,000 arrived in 1849 alone.

The rapid influx of gold seekers heightened tensions between newly arrived whites, local Indians, and Californios. Forty-niners confiscated land owned by Californios, shattered the fragile ecosystem in the California mountains, and

Gold Rush Miner, 1849

This prospector was one of some 80,000 who arrived in northeast California in 1849 after gold was discovered at Sutter's Mill. Photographed fully equipped with the tools of his trade—pickax, hoe, and pan—he, like other miners, was capable of digging out only surface gold. Armed with two pistols, the prospector in this photograph also suggests the dangers miners faced.   Private Collection/ Peter Newark American Pictures/The Bridgeman Art Library

forced Mexican and Indian men to labor for low wages or a promised share in uncertain profits. New conflicts erupted when foreign-born migrants joined the search for wealth. Forty-niners from the United States regularly stole from and assaulted foreign-born competitors—whether Asian, European, or South American. With the limited number of sheriffs and judges in the region, most criminals knew they were unlikely to be arrested, much less tried and convicted.

The gold rush also led to conflicts over gender roles as thousands of male migrants demanded food, shelter, laundry, and medical care. Some women in the region earned a good living by renting rooms, cooking meals, washing clothes, or working as prostitutes. But many faced heightened forms of exploitation. Indian and Mexican women were especially vulnerable to sexual harassment and rape, while Chinese women were imported specifically to provide sexual services for male miners.

Chinese men were also victims of abuse by whites, as evidenced by Chinese workers who were hired by a

British mining company and then run off their claim by Anglo-American gold seekers. Yet some Chinese men used the skills traditionally assigned them in their homeland—cooking and washing clothes—to earn a far steadier income than prospecting for gold could provide. Other men also took advantage of the demand for goods and services. Levi Strauss, a twenty-four-year-old German Jewish immigrant, moved from New York to San Francisco to open a dry goods store in 1853. He was soon producing canvas and then denim pants that could withstand harsh weather and long wear. These blue jeans made Strauss far richer than any forty-niner seeking gold.

A Crowded Land

While U.S. promoters of migration continued to depict the West as an open territory waiting to be tamed and cultivated, it was in fact the site of competing imperial ambitions in the late 1840s. Despite granting statehood to Texas in 1845 and winning the war against Mexico in 1848, the United States had to compete with Comanche, Sioux, and other powerful Indian nations for control of the Great Plains (see chapter 10). As the U.S. government sought to secure land for railroads and forts and as American migrants and European immigrants carved out farms and villages, they had to contend with a range of Indian nations that refused to relinquish control (Map 12.1).

Although attacks on wagon trains were rare, Indians did threaten frontier settlements throughout the 1840s and 1850s. Settlers often retaliated, and U.S. army troops joined them in efforts to push Indians back from areas newly claimed by whites. Yet in many parts of the West, Indians were as powerful as whites, and they did not cede territory without a fight. For example, the Reverend Marcus Whitman and his wife Narcissa became victims of their success in promoting western settlement. In 1843 Marcus returned east and led one thousand Christian emigrants on a "Great Migration" to the Oregon Territory. The settlers were enthusiastic about their new homes, but the arrival of more whites proved disastrous for local Indians. The pioneers brought a deadly measles epidemic to the region, killing thousands of Cayuse and Nez Percé Indians. In 1847, convinced that whites brought disease but no useful medicine, a group of Cayuse Indians killed the Whitmans and ten other white settlers.

Yet violence against whites could not stop the flood of migrants into the Oregon Territory. Indeed, attacks by one Indian tribe were often used to justify assaults on any Indian tribe. For example, John Frémont and Kit Carson, whose party had been attacked by a group of Modoc Indians in Oregon in 1846, took their revenge by destroying a Klamath Indian village and killing men, women,

and children there. The defeat of Mexico and the discovery of gold in California in 1848 only intensified these conflicts.

Although Indians and white Americans were the main players in many battles, Indian nations also competed with each other. In the southern plains, drought and disease exacerbated those conflicts in the late 1840s and dramatically changed the balance of power in the region. In 1845 the southern plains were struck by a dry spell, which lasted on and off until the mid-1860s. Three years later, smallpox ravaged Comanche villages, and then forty-niners heading to California introduced a virulent strain of cholera that killed prominent Comanche leaders as well as hundreds of their followers. In the late 1840s, the Comanches were the largest Indian nation, with about twenty thousand members; by the mid-1850s, less than half that number remained.

Yet the collapse of the Comanche empire was not simply the result of outside forces. As the Comanches expanded their trade networks and incorporated smaller Indian nations into their orbit, they overextended their reach. Most important, they allowed too many bison to be killed in order to meet the needs of their Indian allies and the demand for bison robes by Anglo-American and European traders. The Comanches also herded growing numbers of horses, which required expansive grazing lands and winter havens in the river valleys and pushed the bison onto more marginal lands. Opening up the Santa Fe Trail to commerce multiplied the problems by destroying vegetation, polluting springs, and thus damaging some of the last refuges for bison. The prolonged drought then completed the depopulation of the bison on the southern plains. Without bison, the Comanches lost one of their most critical trade items; by the late 1850s, they were left without the goods or leverage to sustain their commercial and political networks. As the Comanche empire collapsed, former Indian allies sought to advance their own interests. These two developments reignited Indian wars on the southern plains as tens of thousands of Anglo-Americans and European immigrants poured through the region.

African Americans also participated in these western struggles. Many were held as slaves by southeastern tribes forced into Indian Territory, while others were freed and married Seminole or Cherokee spouses. The Creeks proved harsh masters, prompting some slaves to escape north to free states or south to Mexican or Comanche territory. Yet as southern officers in the U.S. army moved to frontier outposts to secure American dominance, they carried more slaves into the region. Many, including Dr. Emerson, changed posts frequently, taking slaves like Dred Scott into western territories that

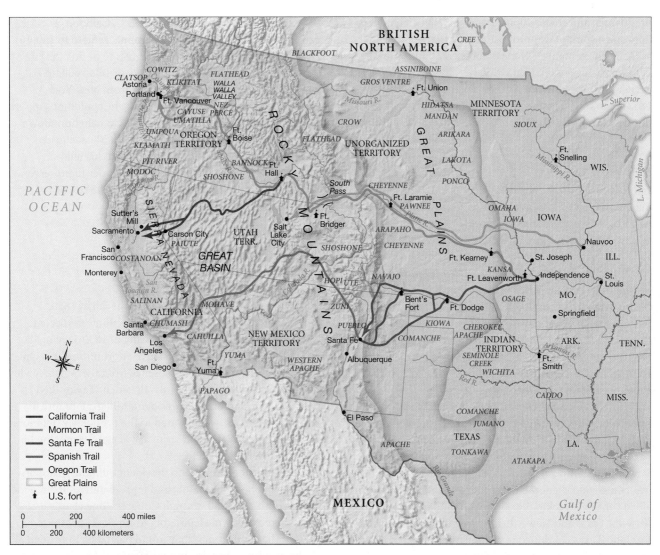

MAP 12.1   Western Trails and Indian Nations, c. 1850

As wagon trains and traders journeyed west in rapidly growing numbers during the 1830s and 1840s, the United States established forts along the most well-traveled routes. At the same time, Indians claimed or were forced into new areas through the pressure of Indian removals, white settlement, and the demands of hunting, trade, and agriculture.

were alternately slave and free. Still, it was white planters who brought the greatest numbers of African Americans into Texas, Missouri, and Kansas, pushing the frontier of slavery ever westward. At the same time, some free blacks joined the migration voluntarily in hopes of finding better economic opportunities and less overt racism on the frontier.

REVIEW & RELATE

Why did Americans go west in the 1830s and 1840s, and what was the journey like?

What groups competed for land and resources in the West? How did competition lead to violence?

Expansion and the Politics of Slavery

The place of African Americans and of slavery in the West aroused intense political debates as territories in the region began to seek statehood. Debates over the eradication of slavery and limits on its expansion had shaped the highly contested presidential election of 1848 (see chapters 10 and 11). After the Mexican-American War, the battle between proponents and opponents of slavery intensified and focused more specifically on its westward expansion. Each time a territory achieved the requirements for statehood, a new crisis erupted. To resolve these crises required strong presidential and congressional leadership, judicial moderation, and a spirit of compromise among the people as well as their representatives. None of these conditions prevailed. Instead, passage of the Fugitive Slave Act in 1850 aroused deeper hostilities, and President Franklin Pierce (1853–1857) encouraged further expansion but failed to address the crises that ensued.

California and the Compromise of 1850

In the winter of 1849, just before Zachary Taylor's March inauguration, California applied for admission to the Union as a free state. Some California political leaders opposed slavery on principle. Others wanted to "save" the state for whites by outlawing slavery, discouraging free blacks from migrating to the state, and restricting the rights of American Indian, Mexican, and Chinese residents. Yet the internal debates among Californians were not uppermost in the minds of those in Congress. Southerners were concerned about the impact of California's free-state status on the sectional balance in Congress, while northern Whigs were shocked when President Taylor suggested that slavery should be allowed anywhere in the West.

Other debates percolated in Congress at the same time. Many Northerners were horrified by the spectacle of slavery and slave trading in the nation's capital and argued that it damaged America's international reputation. Southerners, meanwhile, complained that the Fugitive Slave Act of 1793 was being widely ignored in the North, as abolitionists aided runaways seeking freedom. A boundary dispute between Texas and New Mexico irritated western legislators, and Texas continued to claim that debts it accrued while an independent republic and during the Mexican-American War should be assumed by the federal government.

Senator Henry Clay of Kentucky, the Whig leader who had hammered out the Missouri Compromise in 1819–1820, again tried to resolve the many conflicts that stalled congressional action. He offered a compromise by which California would be admitted as a free state; the remaining land acquired from Mexico would be divided into two territories—New Mexico and Utah—and slavery there would be decided by popular sovereignty; the border dispute between New Mexico and Texas would be decided in favor of New Mexico, but the federal government would assume Texas's war debts; the slave trade (but not slavery) would be abolished in the District of Columbia; and a new and more effective fugitive slave law would be approved. Although Clay's compromise offered something to everyone, his colleagues did not immediately embrace it.

By March 1850, after months of debate, the sides remained sharply divided, with senators on both sides of the issue opposing the measure. John C. Calhoun, a proslavery senator from South Carolina, refused to support any compromise that allowed Congress to decide the fate of slavery in the western territories. Meanwhile William H. Seward, an antislavery Whig senator from New York, proclaimed that in all good conscience he could not support a compromise that forced Northerners to help hunt down fugitives from slavery. Daniel Webster, a Massachusetts Whig and an elder statesman, appealed to his fellow senators to support the compromise in order to preserve the Union, but Congress adjourned with the fate of California undecided.

Explore

See Document 12.2 for Calhoun's final attempt to reject a compromise.

Before the Senate reconvened in the fall of 1850, however, the political landscape changed in unexpected ways. Henry Clay retired in the spring of 1850, leaving the Capitol with his last great legislative effort unfinished. On March 31, Calhoun died; his absence from the Senate made compromise more likely. In July, President Taylor died unexpectedly, and his vice president, Millard Fillmore of Buffalo, New York, was elevated to the presidency. Fillmore then appointed Webster as secretary of state, removing him from the Senate as well.

In September 1850, with President Fillmore's support, a younger cohort of senators and representatives steered the **Compromise of 1850** through Congress, one clause at a time, thereby allowing legislators to support only those parts of the compromise they found palatable. In the end, all the provisions passed, and Fillmore quickly signed the bills into law. California entered the Union as a free state, and John C. Frémont entered Congress as one of that state's first two senators. The Compromise of 1850, like the Missouri Compromise thirty years earlier, fended off a sectional crisis, but it also signaled future problems. Would popular sovereignty prevail when later territories sought admission to the Union, and would Northerners abide by a fugitive slave law that called on them to aid directly in the capture of runaway slaves?

The Fugitive Slave Act Inspires Northern Protest

The fugitive slave laws of 1793 and 1824 mandated that all states aid in apprehending and returning runaway slaves to their owners. The **Fugitive Slave Act of 1850** was different in two important respects. First, it eliminated jury trials for alleged fugitives. Second, the law required individual citizens, not just state officials, to help return runaways or

John C. Calhoun | On the Compromise of 1850, 1850

California's application for statehood in 1849 prompted another crisis over slavery. Southerners feared that admitting California as a free state would tip the balance in Congress against them. Senator Henry Clay tried to broker a compromise that would admit California as a free state but toughen the fugitive slave law. Amid vigorous congressional debate, South Carolina senator John C. Calhoun insisted that slavery be preserved. A colleague read Calhoun's address for the aging and ill senator. Calhoun's death a few weeks later helped pave the way for final passage of the Compromise of 1850.

Explore

How can the Union be saved? To this I answer, there is but one way by which it can be, and that is, by adopting such measures as will satisfy the States belonging to the Southern section that they can remain in the Union consistently with their honor and their safety. . . .

. . . The South asks for justice, simple justice, and less she ought not to take. She has no compromise to offer but the Constitution, and no concession or surrender to make. She has already surrendered so much that she has little left to surrender. Such a settlement would go to the root of the evil, and remove all cause of discontent, by satisfying the South that she could remain honorably and safely in the Union, and thereby restore the harmony and fraternal feelings between the sections which existed anterior to the Missouri agitation. . . .

But can this be done? Yes, easily; not by the weaker party, for it can of itself do nothing—not even protect itself—but by the stronger. The North has only to will it to accomplish it—to do justice by conceding to the South an equal right in the acquired territory, and to do her duty by causing the stipulations relative to fugitive slaves to be faithfully fulfilled—to cease the agitation of the slave question, and to provide for the insertion of a provision in the Constitution, by an amendment, which will restore to the South in substance the power she possessed of protecting herself, before the equilibrium between the sections was destroyed by the action of this Government. There will be no difficulty in devising such a provision—one that will protect the South, and which at the same time will improve and strengthen the Government, instead of impairing and weakening it.

Source: *The Congressional Globe*, 31st Cong., 2nd Sess. (1850), 453, 455.

Interpret the Evidence

- Calhoun objects to the Compromise of 1850 because it does not sufficiently protect southern rights. Which rights does he think need protection, and why does he think those rights are in jeopardy?
- Calhoun wants to regain the "harmony and fraternal feelings" between the sections that existed before "the Missouri agitation." Why does he pinpoint the Missouri Compromise as the moment when sectional divisions took hold?

Put It in Context

What developments in the 1840s led Calhoun and other southern leaders to fear that the South was becoming weaker, at least politically, compared to the North? Would northern senators have agreed?

else risk being fined or imprisoned. The act angered many Northerners who believed that the federal government had gone too far in protecting the rights of slaveholders and thereby aroused sympathy for the abolitionist cause.

Before 1850, the most well-known individuals aiding fugitives were free blacks such as David Ruggles in New York City; Jermaine Loguen in Syracuse, New York; and, after his own successful escape, Frederick Douglass in Rochester, New York. Their main allies in this work were white Quakers such as Amy and Isaac Post in Rochester; Thomas Garrett in Chester County, Pennsylvania; and Levi and Catherine Coffin in Newport, Indiana. The work was dangerous. Charles Turner Torrey, a white Congregationalist minister, may have aided as many as four hundred fugitives, but he was eventually caught and imprisoned. He died of tuberculosis in a Baltimore jail in 1846.

Following passage of the Fugitive Slave Act, the number of slave owners and hired slave catchers pursuing fugitives increased dramatically. But so, too, did the number of northern abolitionists helping blacks escape. Enslaved women and men followed various paths northward from rural plantations and southern cities. Once they crossed into free territory, most fugitives contacted free blacks or individuals known to be sympathetic to their cause. They then began the often slow progress along the underground railroad, from house to house or barn to barn, until they found safe haven. A small number of fortunate slaves were led north by fugitives like Harriet Tubman, who returned south repeatedly to free dozens of family members and other enslaved men and women. Fugitives followed disparate paths through the Midwest, Pennsylvania, New York, and New England, and there was little coordination among the "conductors" from one region or state to another. But the underground railroad was nonetheless an important resource for fugitives, some of whom sought refuge in Canada while others hoped to blend into free black communities in the United States.

Free blacks were endangered by the claim that slaves hid themselves in their midst. In Chester County, Pennsylvania, on the Maryland border, newspapers reported on at least a dozen free blacks who were kidnapped or arrested as runaways in the first three months of 1851. One provision of the Fugitive Slave Act encouraged such arrests: Commissioners were paid $10 for each slave sent back but only $5 if a slave was not returned. Without the right to a trial, a free black could easily be sent south as a fugitive. It was this fear that prompted hundreds of African Americans, both free and enslaved, to flee to Canada.

At the same time, a growing number of Northerners challenged the federal government's right to enforce the law. Blacks and whites organized protest meetings throughout the free states. At a meeting in Boston in 1851, abolitionist William Lloyd Garrison denounced the law: "We execrate it, we spit upon it, we trample it under our feet." Abolitionists also joined forces to rescue fugitives who had been arrested. In Syracuse, New York, in October 1851, Jermaine Loguen, Samuel Ward, and the Reverend Samuel J. May led a well-organized crowd as it broke into a Syracuse courthouse to rescue a fugitive slave known as Jerry. They successfully hid him from authorities and then spirited him to Canada. As such incidents increased across the North, Daniel Webster bemoaned the lack of respect for federal law, and President Fillmore lamented the rise of "mob rule." But northern abolitionists gained growing sympathy from their neighbors and became bolder in denouncing both the Fugitive Slave Act and "the bloodhound kidnappers" who sought to enforce it.

Meanwhile members of Congress continued to debate the law's effects. Senator Frémont was among the legislators who helped defeat a bill that would have imposed harsher

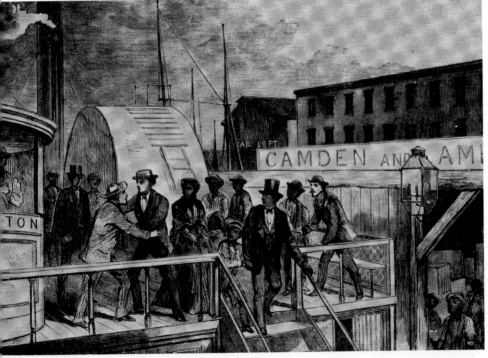

Rescue of Fugitive Slaves

This 1872 illustration portrays the dramatic rescue of the North Carolina slave Jane Johnson and her two children aboard a Philadelphia ferry in 1855 as they accompanied their owner on a trip through the free state of Pennsylvania. They were liberated by members of the Pennsylvania Anti-Slavery Society, led by the black abolitionist William Still, who boarded the boat and removed them to safety. Photo Researchers, Inc.

penalties on those who assisted runaways. And Congress felt growing pressure to calm the situation, including from foreign officials who were horrified by the violence required to sustain slavery in the United States. Abolitionist speakers like Frederick Douglass, who spent six months denouncing the Fugitive Slave Act across Canada, Ireland, and England, intensified foreign concern over the law. Great Britain and France had already abolished slavery in their West Indian colonies and found it hard to support what they saw as extreme policies to keep the institution alive in the United States. Yet neither southern slaveholders nor northern abolitionists were willing to compromise any further.

Pierce Encourages U.S. Expansion

In the presidential election of 1852, the Whigs and the Democrats tried once again to appeal to voters across the North-South divide by running candidates who either skirted the critical issues of the day or held ambiguous views. The Democrats, who had great difficulty choosing a candidate, finally nominated Franklin Pierce. A successful New Hampshire lawyer who opposed abolition, Pierce had served in Congress from 1833 to 1842 and in the U.S. army during the Mexican-American War. The Whigs rejected Vice President Millard Fillmore, who had angered many in the party by supporting popular sovereignty and vigorous enforcement of the Fugitive Slave Act. The Whig Party turned instead to another military leader, General Winfield Scott of Virginia, to head the ticket. General Scott had served with distinction in the war against Mexico, but he had not expressed any proslavery views. The Whigs thus hoped to gain southern support while maintaining their northern base. The Free-Soil Party, too, hoped to expand its appeal, given northern hostility to the Fugitive Slave Act. But Free-Soilers were unable to take advantage of the moment, nominating John P. Hale, a relatively unknown former Democratic senator from New Hampshire.

Franklin Pierce's eventual victory left the Whigs and the Free-Soilers in disarray. A third of southern Whigs threw their support to the Democrats, seeking a truly proslavery party. Many Democrats who had supported Free-Soilers in 1848, like Martin Van Buren, were driven to vote for Pierce by their enthusiasm over the admission of California as a free state. But despite the Democratic triumph, that party also remained fragile. The nation now faced some of its gravest challenges under a president with limited political experience and no firm base of support. His cabinet included men of widely differing views, part of an effort to appease the various factions of the Democratic Party. But when confronted with difficult decisions, Pierce often received contradictory advice and generally pursued his own expansionist vision.

Early in his administration, Pierce focused on expanding U.S. trade and extending the "civilizing" power of U.S. institutions to other parts of the world. Inspired by the promise of new markets, Pierce and his supporters sought to shift Americans' attention outward. Trade with China had declined in the 1840s, but the United States had begun commercial negotiations with Japan in 1846. These came to fruition in 1854, when U.S. emissary Commodore Matthew C. Perry obtained the first formal treaty with Japan that allowed for mutual trading. Within four years, Pierce and his agent, international trader Townsend Harris, succeeded in expanding commercial ties and enhancing diplomatic relations with Japan, in large part by ensuring U.S. support for the island nation against its traditional enemies in China, Russia, and Europe.

Although the president rejected Commodore Perry's offer to take military possession of Formosa and other territories near Japan, Pierce was willing to consider conquests in the Caribbean and Central America. For decades, U.S. politicians, particularly Southerners, had looked to gain control of Cuba, Mexico, and Nicaragua. A "Young America" movement within the Democratic Party imagined manifest destiny reaching southward as well as westward. In hopes of stirring up rebellious Cubans against Spanish rule, some Democrats joined with private adventurers to send three expeditions, known as *filibusters*, to invade Cuba under the leadership of Cuban exile General Narciso Lopez. In 1854 the capture of one of the filibustering ships led to an international incident. Spanish officials confiscated the ship, while Democrats eager to add Cuba to the United States urged Pierce to seek an apology and redress from Spain. But many northern Democrats rejected any effort to obtain another slave state, and Pierce was forced to withdraw even tacit federal approval for the filibusters.

Other politicians still pressured Spain to sell Cuba to the United States. These included Pierce's secretary of state, William Marcy, and the U.S. ambassador to Great Britain, James Buchanan, as well as the ministers to France and Spain. In October 1854, these ministers met in Ostend, Belgium, and sent a letter to Pierce: "If we possess the power, [the United States is justified] by every law, human and Divine" in taking Cuba by force. When this Ostend Manifesto was leaked to the press, Northerners were outraged. They viewed the whole episode as "a dirty plot" to gain more slave territory and forced Pierce to give up any plans to obtain Cuba. In 1855 a private adventurer named William Walker, who had organized four filibusters to Nicaragua, invaded that country and set himself up as ruler. He then invited southern planters to take up vast lands he had confiscated from local farmers and to reintroduce slavery in Nicaragua. Pierce and many Democrats endorsed his plan, but neighboring Hondurans forced Walker from power in 1857 and executed him by firing squad three years later. Although Pierce's expansionist dreams failed, his efforts heightened sectional tensions.

REVIEW & RELATE

What steps did legislators take in the 1840s and early 1850s to resolve the issue of the expansion of slavery?

How were slavery and American imperialist ambitions intertwined in the 1840s and 1850s?

✔ *LEARNINGCurve* bedfordstmartins.com/hewittlawson/LC

Sectional Crises Intensify

The political crises that divided Americans in the 1850s infused cultural as well as political life, leading to a lively trade in antislavery literature. This cultural turmoil, combined with the weakness and fragmentation of the existing political parties, helped give rise to the Republican Party in 1854. Although it spoke almost solely for North-erners who opposed the continued expansion of slavery, the Republican Party soon absorbed enough Free-Soilers, Whigs, and northern Democrats to become a major political force. The events that drove these cultural and political developments included continued challenges to the Fugitive Slave Act, a battle over the admission of Kansas to the Union, and a Supreme Court ruling in the *Dred Scott* case.

Popularizing Antislavery Sentiment

The Fugitive Slave Act had forced Northerners to recon-sider their role in sustaining the institution of slavery. In 1852, just months before Franklin Pierce was elected president, their concerns were heightened by the publica-tion of the novel ***Uncle Tom's Cabin*** by Harriet Beecher Stowe. Stowe's father, Lyman Beecher, and brother Henry were among the nation's leading evangelical clergy, and her sister Catharine had opposed Cherokee removal and promoted women's education. Stowe was inspired to write *Uncle Tom's Cabin* by passage of the Fugitive Slave Act in 1850, and the story originally ran as a forty-installment serial in an abolitionist periodical, the *National Era*. Once published in book form, the novel sold more than 350,000 copies in a matter of months.

Uncle Tom's Cabin built on accounts by former slaves as well as tales gathered by abolitionist lecturers and writers. During the 1850s, tales of life in bondage received growing attention in the North in both abolitionist circles and the mainstream press. The autobiographies of

Frederick Douglass (1845), Josiah Henson (1849), and Henry Bibb (1849) set the stage for Stowe's novel. So, too, did the expansion of the antislavery press, which by the 1850s included dozens of newspapers across the North, the Midwest, and eastern Canada. Antislavery poems and songs also circulated widely and were performed at abolitionist conventions and fund-raising fairs.

Still, nothing captured the public's attention as did *Uncle Tom's Cabin*. Read by millions in the United States and England and translated into French and German, the book reached a mass audience, far exceeding the reach of other abolitionist literature. Its sentimental portrait of saintly slaves and its vivid depiction of cruel masters and overseers offered white Northerners a way to identify with enslaved blacks. Although some African Americans were frustrated by its demeaning portraits of northern free blacks, they recognized that it helped to fuel anger at the Fugitive Slave Act and at efforts to expand slavery into new territories. Its success and its limitations also convinced other fugitives, including Harriet Jacobs, to publish their real-life stories.

Explore

See Documents 12.3 and 12.4 for two contrasting literary depictions of slavery.

In some cases, the real-life stories of fugitive slaves surpassed their fictional counterparts for emotional impact. In May 1854, abolitionists sought to free fugitive slave Anthony Burns from a Boston courthouse, where his master was attempting to reclaim him. They failed to secure his release, and Burns was soon marched to the docks to be shipped south. Twenty-two companies of state militia held back tens of thousands of Bostonians who lined the streets, hissing and shouting "Kidnappers!" at the soldiers and police. A year later, supporters purchased Burns's freedom from his master, but the incident raised anguished ques-tions among local residents. In a city that was home to intellectual, religious, and antislavery leaders such as Ralph Waldo Emerson, the Reverend Theodore Parker, and William Lloyd Garrison, Bostonians wondered how they had come so far in aiding and abetting slavery.

The Kansas-Nebraska Act Stirs Dissent

Kansas provided the first test of the effects of *Uncle Tom's Cabin* on northern sentiments toward slavery's expansion. As white Americans slowly displaced Indian nations from their homelands, large and diverse groups of Indians settled in the northern half of the Louisiana Territory. This unorganized region had once been considered beyond the reach of white settlement, but Senator Stephen Douglas of

Illinois was eager to have a transcontinental railroad run through his home state. He needed the federal government to gain control of land along the route he proposed, and therefore he argued for the establishment of a vast Nebraska Territory. But to support his plan, Douglas also needed to convince southern congressmen, who sought a route through their own region. Much of the unorganized territory lay too far north to support plantation slavery, but a small portion lay directly west of Missouri, the northernmost slave state. According to the Missouri Compromise, states lying above the southern border of Missouri were automatically free. To gain southern support, Douglas sought to reopen the question of slavery in the territories. Pointing to the Compromise of 1850, by which territories acquired from Mexico would decide the fate of slavery by popular sovereignty, he argued that the same standard should apply to all new territories.

In January 1854, Douglas introduced the **Kansas-Nebraska Act** to Congress. The act extinguished Indians' long-held treaty rights in the region and repealed the Missouri Compromise. Two new territories—Kansas and Nebraska— would be carved out of the unorganized lands, and each would determine whether to enter the nation as a slave or a free state by a referendum of eligible voters (Map 12.2). The act spurred intense opposition from most Whigs and some northern Democrats who wanted to retain the Missouri Compromise line. Months of fierce debate followed. Finally, on May 25, Douglas's proposed act passed by a comfortable majority when most Democrats followed the party line to vote yes. President Pierce quickly signed the bill into law.

Passage of the Kansas-Nebraska Act enraged many Northerners, who considered the dismantling of the Missouri Compromise a sign of the rising power of the South. They were infuriated that the South—or what some now called the Slave Power Conspiracy—had once again benefited from northern politicians' willingness to compromise. Although few of these opponents considered the impact of the law on Indians, the act also shattered treaty provisions that had protected the Arapaho, Cheyenne, Ponco, Pawnee, and Sioux nations. These Plains Indians lost half the land they had held by treaty as thousands of settlers swarmed into the newly organized territories. In the fall of 1855, conflicts between white settlers and Indians erupted across the southern and central plains. The U.S. army then sent six hundred troops to retaliate against a Sioux village, killing eighty-five residents of Blue Water in the Nebraska Territory and triggering continued violence throughout the region.

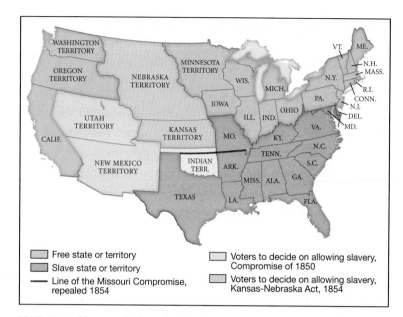

MAP 12.2 Kansas-Nebraska Territory

From 1820 on, Congress attempted to limit sectional conflict. But the Missouri Compromise (1820) and the Compromise of 1850 failed to resolve disagreements over slavery's expansion. The creation of the Kansas and Nebraska territories in 1854 also heightened sectional conflict and ensured increased hostilities with Indians in the region.

As tensions escalated across the nation, Americans faced the 1854 congressional elections. The Democrats, increasingly viewed as supporting the priorities of slave-holders, lost badly in the North. But the Whig Party also proved weak, having failed to stop the Slave Power from extending its leverage over federal policies. A third party, the American Party, was founded in the early 1850s and attracted native-born workers and Protestant farmers who were drawn to its anti-immigrant and anti-Catholic message (see chapter 11). Responding to these political realignments, another new party—the Republicans—was founded in the spring of 1854. Led by antislavery Whigs, the **Republican Party** slowly attracted former Free-Soilers to its ranks. Among its early members was a Whig politician from Illinois, Abraham Lincoln.

Born in Kentucky in 1809, Lincoln moved north to Illinois with his family and worked as a farmhand and surveyor. He also taught himself the rudiments of the law and was elected to the state legislature in 1834. In 1842 he married Mary Todd, the daughter of a wealthy banker, and established a lucrative law practice. Four years later, Lincoln was elected as a Whig to the House of Representatives. Serving his two-year term during the crisis over war with Mexico, he challenged Polk's claim that the first blood had been shed on U.S. soil (see chapter 11). After resuming his Springfield law practice, Lincoln joined the new Republican Party in 1856.

DOCUMENTS 12.3 AND 12.4

Slavery in Literature: Two Views

The 1852 publication of *Uncle Tom's Cabin* by Harriet Beecher Stowe helped mobilize northern antislavery sentiment but provoked a hostile reaction among Southerners, who said she misrepresented their way of life. Written in response to Stowe's work, Caroline Hentz's novel *The Planter's Northern Bride* argued that slaves' lives were better than those of working-class and poor Northerners. Hentz defended southern values and traditions, including slavery. The following excerpt from *Uncle Tom's Cabin* depicts a scene in which the overseer Simon Legree punishes Tom for helping another slave. In the second selection, from *The Planter's Northern Bride*, Hentz's main character, Eulalia Moreland, describes meeting the slaves on her husband's plantation.

Explore

12.3 Harriet Beecher Stowe | *Uncle Tom's Cabin*, 1852

"Well, here's a pious dog, at last, let down among us sinners!—a saint, a gentleman, and no less, to talk to us sinners about our sins! Powerful holy critter, he must be! Here, you rascal, you make believe to be so pious—didn't you never hear, out of yer Bible, 'Servants, obey yer masters'? An't I yer master? Didn't I pay down twelve hundred dollars, cash, for all there is inside yer old cussed black shell? An't yer mine, now, body and soul?" he said, giving Tom a violent kick with his heavy boot; "tell me!"

In the very depth of physical suffering, bowed by brutal oppression, this question shot a gleam of joy and triumph through Tom's soul. He suddenly stretched himself up, and, looking earnestly to heaven, while the tears and blood that flowed down his face mingled, he exclaimed,

"No! no! no! my soul an't yours, Mas'r! You haven't bought it—ye can't buy it! It's been bought and paid for, by one that is able to keep it—no matter, no matter, you can't harm me!"

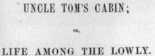

Original Cover of *Uncle Tom's Cabin*
Newberry Library, Chicago, Illinois, USA/ The Bridgeman Art Library

"I can't!" said Legree, with a sneer; "we'll see—we'll see! Here, Sambo, Quimbo, give this dog such a breakin' in as he won't get over this month!"

Source: Harriet Beecher Stowe, *Uncle Tom's Cabin; or, Life among the Lowly* (Boston: John P. Jewett, 1852), 197.

Although established only months before the fall 1854 elections, the Republican Party gained significant support in the Midwest, particularly in state and local campaigns. Meanwhile the American Party gained control of the Massachusetts legislature and nearly captured New York as well. These victories marked the demise of the Whigs as a national party. Although the American Party dissolved as a political force by 1856, the Republicans continued to gain strength. They replaced the Whig Party—which was built on a national constituency—with a party rooted solely in the North. Like Free-Soilers, the Republicans argued that slavery

12.4 Caroline Hentz | *The Planter's Northern Bride*, 1854

Soon, returning in grand march from the fields, came the negroes, poising on their heads immense baskets, brimming with the light and flaky cotton. . . . Eulalia . . . recollected all the horrible stories she had heard of negro insurrections, and thought what an awful thing it was to be at the mercy of so many slaves, on that lonely plantation. When she saw her husband going out among them, and they all closed round, shutting him in as with a thick cloud, she asked herself if he were really safe. Safe. . . . They gathered round him, eager to get within reach of his hand, the sound of his voice, the glance of his kind, protecting, yet commanding eye. More like a father welcomed by his children . . . he stood, the centre of that sable ring. . . . He appeared to her in a new character. She had known him as the fond, devoted bridegroom; now he was invested with the authority and responsibility of a master. And she must share that responsibility, assist him in his duties, and make the welfare, comfort, and happiness of these dependent beings the great object of her life. . . .

Never before had she made an elaborate comparison between the white and the black man. She had so often heard her father say that they were born equal . . . that she had believed it. . . . But as she

Illustration from *The Planter's Northern Bride*
Image courtesy of Documenting the American South, The University of North Carolina at Chapel Hill Libraries

looked at her husband, standing in their midst, the representative of the fair sons of Japheth [son of the biblical Noah], wearing on his brow the signet of a loftier, nobler destiny, every lineament and feature expressive of intellect and power, and then at each of that dark, lowly throng, she felt a conviction that freedom, in its broadest latitude, education, with its most exalted privileges, could never make them equal to him.

Source: Caroline Lee Hentz, *The Planter's Northern Bride* (Philadelphia: T. B. Peterson and Brothers, 1854), 331–33.

Interpret the Evidence

- What do these passages reveal about northern and southern opinions about slaves and slavery?
- Compare the attitudes of Simon Legree and Mr. Moreland toward their slaves. How might these characterizations have affected northern and southern readers?

Put It in Context

What do these different characterizations suggest about mid-nineteenth-century responses to the Fugitive Slave Act?

should not be extended into new territories. But the Republicans also advocated a program of commercial and industrial development and internal improvements. With this platform, the party attracted a broader base than did earlier antislavery political coalitions. The Republican Party included both ardent abolitionists and men whose only concern was keeping western territories open to free white men. This latter group was more than willing to accept slavery where it already existed and to exclude black migrants, who might compete for jobs and land, from western states and territories.

Bleeding Kansas and the Election of 1856

The 1854 congressional elections exacerbated sectional tensions by bringing representatives from a strictly northern party—the Republicans—into Congress, where Democrats and Southerners, by virtue of their seniority, controlled most of the powerful committee assignments. But the conflicts over slavery reached far beyond the nation's capital. After passage of the Kansas-Nebraska Act, advocates and opponents of slavery poured into Kansas in anticipation of a vote on whether the state would enter the Union slave or free. Southerners flooded in from Missouri, while emigrant aid societies in the North funded antislavery settlers willing to relocate to Kansas.

As Kansas prepared to hold its referendum, settlers continued to arrive daily, making it difficult to determine who was eligible to vote. In 1855 Southerners installed a proslavery government at Shawnee Mission, while abolitionists established a stronghold in Lawrence. Violence erupted when proslavery settlers invaded Lawrence, killing one resident, demolishing newspaper offices, and plundering shops and homes. Fearing that the southern settlers who had come to Kansas were better armed than the antislavery Northerners in the territory, eastern abolitionists raised funds to ship rifles to Kansas. The Reverend Henry Ward Beecher of Brooklyn, a popular preacher and leading abolitionist, advocated armed self-defense. As cases of Sharps rifles arrived in Kansas, they came to be known as Beecher's Bibles.

Longtime abolitionist John Brown took more direct action. He joined four of his sons already living in Kansas and, with two friends, kidnapped five proslavery advocates from their homes along Pottawatomie Creek and hacked them to death. The so-called Pottawatomie Massacre infuriated southern settlers; in response, they drew up the Lecompton Constitution, which declared Kansas a slave state. President Pierce made his support of the proslavery government clear, but Congress remained divided. While Congress deliberated, armed battles continued. In the first six months of 1856, another two hundred settlers were killed in what became known as **Bleeding Kansas**.

Fighting also broke out on the floor of Congress. Republican senator Charles Sumner of Massachusetts delivered an impassioned speech against the continued expansion of what he termed the Slave Power. He launched scathing verbal attacks on planter politicians like South Carolina senator Andrew Butler, who supported the admission of Kansas as a slave state. Butler's nephew, Preston Brooks, a Democratic member of the House of Representatives, felt compelled to redress his family's honor. He assaulted Sumner in the Senate chamber, beating him senseless with a cane. Sumner, who never fully recovered from his injuries, was considered a martyr in the North. Meanwhile Brooks was feted across the state of South Carolina.

Clarina Howard Nichols

An abolitionist, a journalist, and a women's rights advocate in Vermont, Clarina Howard Nichols joined the New England Emigrant Aid Society in 1854. The next year, she moved with her family to the Kansas Territory, where this photograph was taken. Nichols advocated women's legal rights through lectures and editorials and was the only woman to participate in the Kansas constitutional convention of 1859. Kansas State Historical Society

Explore

See Document 12.5 for one cartoonist's portrayal of the Kansas-Nebraska Act.

The presidential election of 1856 began amid an atmosphere poisoned by violence and recrimination. The Democratic Party nominated James Buchanan, a proslavery advocate and longtime party stalwart from Pennsylvania. The young Republican Party ticket was headed by John C. Frémont. The American Party, in its final presidential contest, selected former president Millard Fillmore as its candidate. The strength of nativism in politics was waning, however, and Fillmore won only the state of Maryland. Frémont attracted cheering throngs as he traveled across the nation. Large numbers of women turned out to see Jessie Frémont, the first national candidate's wife to play a

DOCUMENT 12.5

John Magee | Forcing Slavery down the Throat of a Freesoiler, 1856

The passage of the Kansas-Nebraska Act deepened the conflict over slavery. The act repealed the Missouri Compromise and allowed voters in Kansas and Nebraska to decide whether their territories would enter the Union as free or slave states. Advocates and opponents of slavery poured into Kansas, leading to open violence throughout the state. The following antislavery cartoon shows presidential candidate James Buchanan and Democratic senator Lewis Cass holding down a free-soiler while Franklin Pierce and Stephen Douglas force a black man down his throat.

Explore

Whom does Magee hold responsible for the violence in Kansas?

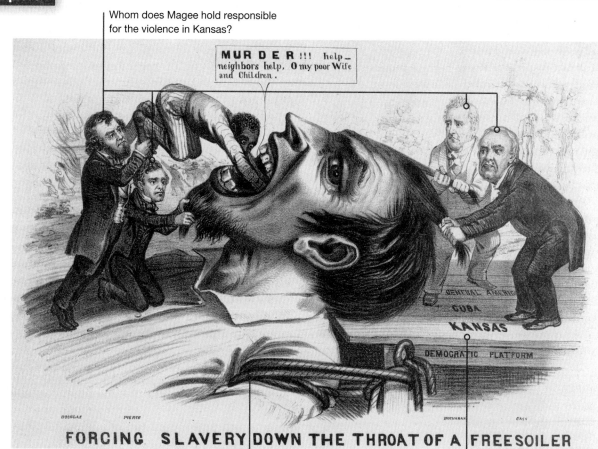

FORCING SLAVERY DOWN THE THROAT OF A FREESOILER

Library of Congress

What is the significance of binding the free-soiler to the Democratic Platform?

What argument is Magee making by putting Central America, Cuba, and Kansas on the Democratic Platform?

Put It in Context

What does this cartoon suggest about the role of northern Democratic Party leaders in the ongoing conflicts over the expansion of slavery?

significant role in a campaign. Frémont carried most of the North and the West, establishing the Republican Party's dominance in those regions. Buchanan, claiming that he alone could preserve the Union, captured the South along with Pennsylvania, Indiana, and Illinois. Although Buchanan won only 45.2 percent of the popular vote, he received a comfortable majority in the electoral college, securing his victory. But even as the nation was becoming increasingly divided along sectional lines, President Buchanan did little to resolve these differences.

The *Dred Scott* Decision

Just two days after Buchanan's inauguration, the Supreme Court finally announced its decision in the *Dred Scott* case. Led by Chief Justice Roger Taney, a proslavery Southerner, the majority ruled that a slave was not a citizen and therefore could not sue in court. Indeed, Taney claimed that black men had no rights that a white man was bound to respect. The ruling annulled Scott's suit and meant that he and his wife remained enslaved. But the ruling went further. The ***Dred Scott* decision** declared that Congress had no constitutional authority to exclude slavery from any territory, thereby nullifying the Missouri Compromise and any future effort to restrict slavery's expansion. Buchanan was happy to have the fate of slavery taken out of the hands of Congress, hoping it would alleviate sectional tensions. His hopes proved unfounded. Instead of quieting the debate over slavery, the ruling further outraged many Northerners, who were now convinced that a Slave Power conspiracy had taken hold of the federal government.

In 1858, when Stephen Douglas faced reelection to the U.S. Senate, the Republican Party nominated Abraham Lincoln to oppose him. The candidates participated in seven debates in which they explained their positions on slavery in the wake of the *Dred Scott* decision. Pointing to the landmark ruling, Lincoln asked Douglas how he could favor popular sovereignty, which allowed residents to keep slavery out of a territory, and yet support the *Dred Scott* decision, which protected slavery in all territories. Douglas devised a clever response, known as the Freeport Doctrine. He claimed that if residents did not adopt local legislation to protect slave-holders' property, they could thereby exclude slavery for all practical purposes. At the same time, he accused Lincoln of advocating "negro equality," a position that went well beyond his opponent's views. Lincoln did support economic opportunity for free blacks, but not political or social equality. Still, the Republican candidate did declare that "this government cannot endure permanently half slave and half free. . . . It will become all one thing or all the other."

The Lincoln-Douglas debates attracted national attention, but the Illinois legislature selected the state's senator. Narrowly controlled by Democrats, it returned Douglas to Washington. Although the senator retained his seat, he was chastened by how far the Democratic Party had tilted toward the South. So when President Buchanan tried to push the Lecompton Constitution through Congress, legitimating the proslavery government in Kansas, Douglas opposed him. The two struggled over control of the party, with Douglas winning a symbolic victory in January 1861 when Kansas was admitted as a free state. By then, however, the Democratic Party had split into southern and northern wings, and the nation was on the verge of civil war.

Dred and Harriet Scott

This illustration of Dred Scott and his wife Harriet appeared in the June 27, 1857, issue of *Frank Leslie's Illustrated Newspaper*, four months after the Supreme Court ruled that the Scotts were not legally entitled to their freedom. In the 1830s, Dred and Harriet had received permission from their owners to marry, and they had two children.
Library of Congress

What factors contributed to the spread of antislavery sentiment in the North beyond committed abolitionists?

How did the violence in Kansas in the mid-1850s reflect and intensify the growing sectional divide within the nation?

LEARNINGCurve bedfordstmartins.com/hewittlawson/LC

From Sectional Crisis to War

During the 1850s, a profusion of abolitionist lectures, conventions, and literature increased antislavery sentiment in the North. Mainstream as well as antislavery newspapers now covered rescues of fugitives, the *Dred Scott* case, and the bloody crisis in Kansas. Republican candidates in state and local elections also kept concerns about slavery's expansion and southern power alive. Nothing, however, riveted the nation's attention as much as John Brown's raid on the federal arsenal at Harpers Ferry, Virginia, in 1859. A year later, Republican Abraham Lincoln captured the White House. In the wake of his election, South Carolina seceded from the Union, agreeing with the president-elect that the nation could no longer exist half slave and half free.

John Brown's Raid

John Brown was committed not only to the abolition of slavery but also to complete equality between whites and blacks. A friend to many abolitionist leaders, Brown held views quite similar to those of David Walker, whose 1829 *Appeal* (see chapter 11) warned that slaves would eventually rise up and claim their freedom by force of arms. By 1859, following the bloody battles in Kansas, Brown believed strongly that direct action was the only answer. Deeply religious, he saw himself as the instrument of God's plan to liberate the enslaved.

Brown focused his efforts on the federal arsenal in **Harpers Ferry, Virginia**. With 18 followers—including 5 African Americans and 13 whites, including 3 of his sons—Brown planned to capture the arsenal and distribute the arms stored there to slaves in the surrounding area. He hoped this action would ignite a rebellion that would take down the plantation system. He tried to convince Frederick Douglass to join the venture, but Douglass, who admired Brown, considered it a foolhardy plan. However, the passionate rebel Brown did manage to persuade a small circle of white abolitionists to bankroll the effort.

On the night of October 16, 1859, Brown and his men successfully kidnapped some leading townsmen and seized the arsenal. Local residents were stunned but managed to alert authorities, and state militia swarmed into Harpers Ferry. The next day, federal troops arrived, led by Colonel Robert E. Lee. The rebels had failed to consider how they would alert slaves to the arsenal's capture so that slaves could gain access to the town and the weapons. With state and federal troops flooding into Harpers Ferry, Brown and his men were soon under siege, trapped in the arsenal. Fourteen rebels were killed, including two of Brown's sons. On October 18, Brown and three others were captured.

As word of the daring raid spread, Brown was hailed as a hero by devoted abolitionists and depicted as a madman by southern planters. Southern whites were sure he was part of a widespread conspiracy led by power-hungry abolitionists. Federal authorities moved quickly to quell slaveholders' fears and end the episode. Brown rejected his lawyer's advice to plead insanity, and a local jury found him guilty of murder, criminal conspiracy, and treason on October 31. He was hanged on December 2, 1859.

John Brown's execution unleashed a massive out-pouring of grief, anger, and uncertainty across the North. Abolitionists organized parades, demonstrations, bonfires, and tributes to the newest abolitionist martyr. Even many Quakers and other pacifists viewed John Brown as a hero for giving his life in the cause of emancipation. But most northern politicians and editors condemned the raid as a rash act that could only intensify sectional tensions. **See Document Project 12: Visions of John Brown, page 384.**

Among southern whites, fear and panic greeted the raid on Harpers Ferry, and the execution of John Brown did little to quiet the outrage they felt at having their peculiar institution once again threatened with violence. Southern intellectuals had developed a sophisticated proslavery argument that they believed demonstrated the benefits of bondage for African Americans and its superiority to the northern system of wage labor. Yet neither that argument nor any federal law or Supreme Court decision seemed able to deter antislavery activism. Not surprisingly, Americans on both sides of the sectional divide considered the 1860 presidential election critical to the nation's future.

The Election of 1860

Brown's hanging set the tone for the 1860 presidential campaign. The Republicans met in Chicago in May 1860 and made clear that they sought national prominence by distancing themselves from the more radical wing of the abolitionist movement. The party platform condemned

Republican Party Presidential Ticket, 1860

This campaign banner for the Republican ticket of Abraham Lincoln and Hannibal Hamlin highlighted Lincoln's backwoods origins by including rustic bentwood frames and a rail fence. The images of industrial growth and protection sought to appeal to laborers and manufacturers, while the motto "Free Speech, Free Homes, Free Territory" indicated the candidates' support for small farmers and their opposition to the extension of slavery. Library of Congress

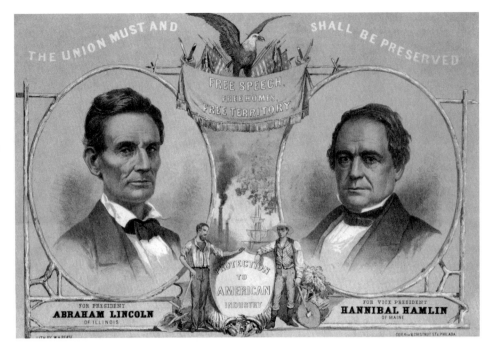

John Brown along with southern "Border Ruffians" who initiated the violence in Kansas. The platform accepted slavery where it already existed, but continued to advocate its exclusion from western territories. Finally, the party platform argued forcefully for internal improvements and protective tariffs. On the third ballot, Republicans nominated Abraham Lincoln as their candidate for president. Recognizing the impossibility of gaining significant votes in the South, the party focused instead on winning large majorities in the Northeast and Midwest.

The Democrats met in Charleston, South Carolina. Although Stephen Douglas was the leading candidate, he could not assuage southern delegates who were still angry that Kansas had been admitted as a free state. Mississippi senator Jefferson Davis then introduced a resolution to protect slavery in the territories, but Douglas's northern supporters rejected it. When President Buchanan came out against Douglas, the Democratic convention ended without choosing a candidate. Instead, various factions held their own conventions. A group of largely northern Democrats met in Baltimore and nominated Douglas. Southern or "cotton" Democrats selected John Breckinridge, the current vice president and a Kentucky slaveholder, on a platform that included the extension of slavery and the annexation of Cuba. The Constitutional Union Party, comprised mainly of former southern Whigs, advocated "no political principle other than the Constitution of the country, the union of the states, and the enforcement of the laws." Its members nominated Senator John Bell of Tennessee, a onetime Whig.

Although Lincoln won barely 40 percent of the popular vote, he carried a clear majority in the electoral college. With the admission of Minnesota and Oregon to the Union in 1858 and 1859, free states now outnumbered slave states eighteen to fifteen, and Lincoln won all but one

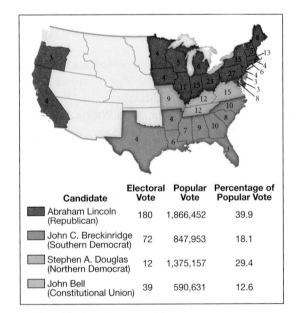

Candidate	Electoral Vote	Popular Vote	Percentage of Popular Vote
Abraham Lincoln (Republican)	180	1,866,452	39.9
John C. Breckinridge (Southern Democrat)	72	847,953	18.1
Stephen A. Douglas (Northern Democrat)	12	1,375,157	29.4
John Bell (Constitutional Union)	39	590,631	12.6

MAP 12.3 The Election of 1860

Four candidates vied for the presidency in 1860, and the voters split along clearly sectional lines. Although Stephen Douglas ran a vigorous campaign and gained votes in all regions of the country, he won a majority only in Missouri. Lincoln triumphed in the North and far West, and Breckinridge in most of the South.

of them. Moreover, free states in the Middle Atlantic and Midwest were among the most populous in the nation and therefore had a large number of electoral votes. Douglas ran second to Lincoln in the popular vote, but Bell and Breckinridge captured more electoral votes than Douglas did. Despite a deeply divided electorate, Lincoln became president (Map 12.3).

Although many abolitionists were wary of the Republicans' position on slavery, especially their willingness to leave slavery alone where it already existed, most were nonetheless relieved at Lincoln's victory and hoped he would become more sympathetic to their views once in office. Meanwhile, southern whites, especially those in the deep South, were furious that a Republican had won the White House without carrying a single southern state.

The Lower South Secedes

On December 20, 1860, six weeks after Lincoln's election, the legislature of South Carolina announced that because "a sectional party" had engineered "the election of a man to the high office of President of the United States whose opinions and purposes are hostile to slavery, [the people of South Carolina dissolve their union with] the other states of North America." The first southern state had seceded from the Union, and its leaders now worked to convince neighboring states to join them. In early 1861, Mississippi, Florida, Alabama, Georgia, Louisiana, and Texas followed suit. Representatives from these states met on February 8 in Montgomery, Alabama, where they adopted a provisional constitution, elected Mississippi senator and slaveholder

Jefferson Davis as their president, and established the **Confederate States of America** (Map 12.4).

Although President Buchanan was aware of developments in the South, he did nothing. His cabinet included three secessionists and two unionists, one of whom resigned in mid-December in frustration over Buchanan's failure to act. But Washington, D.C., was filled with southern sympathizers, who urged caution on an already timid president. Although some Northerners were shocked by the decision of South Carolina and its allies, many others supported their right to leave or believed they would return to the Union when they realized they could not survive economically on their own. Moreover, with Virginia, Maryland, and other Upper South slave states still part of the nation, the secession movement seemed both limited and unlikely to succeed.

Buchanan did urge Congress to find a compromise, and Kentucky senator John Crittenden proposed a plan that gained significant support. Indeed, Congress approved the first part of his plan, which called for a constitutional amendment to protect slavery from federal interference in any state where it already existed. But the second part of Crittenden's plan failed to pass after Republicans voiced their unanimous opposition. It would have extended the Missouri Compromise line (latitude 36°30′) to the California border and barred slavery north of that line. South of that line, however, slavery would be protected, including in any territories "acquired hereafter." Fearing that passage would encourage southern planters to once again seek territory in Cuba, Mexico, or Central America, Lincoln and the Republicans rejected the proposal. Despite the hopes of

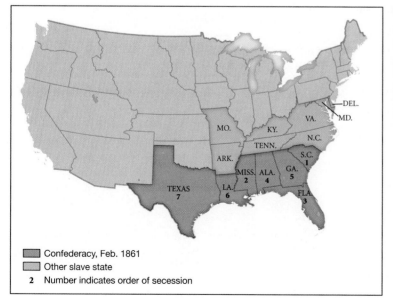

MAP 12.4   The Original Confederacy

Seven states in the Lower South seceded from the United States and formed the Confederate States of America in February 1861. While the original Confederacy was too limited in population and resources to defend itself against the U.S. government, its leaders hoped that other slave states would soon join them.

Confederacy, Feb. 1861
Other slave state
2   Number indicates order of secession

the Buchanan administration, it was becoming apparent that compromise was impossible. The Confederacy was not a fleeting disruption of the national order. It was the beginning of the Civil War.

REVIEW & RELATE

How and why did John Brown's raid on Harpers Ferry move the country closer to civil war?

Why did many in the South believe that the election of Abraham Lincoln was cause for secession?

✔ *LEARNINGCurve* bedfordstmartins.com/hewittlawson/LC

Conclusion: The Coming of the Civil War

Dred Scott did not live to see Abraham Lincoln take the oath of office in March 1861. Following the Supreme Court's 1857 ruling, Scott was returned to Irene Emerson, who had married abolitionist Calvin Chaffee while awaiting the Supreme Court ruling. When that ruling was announced, Chaffee found himself the owner of the most well-known slave in America. He quickly returned Dred Scott and his family to his original owners, the Blow family. On May 26, 1857, the Blows freed the Scotts, so Dred Scott spent the last year and a half of his life as a free man. His wife Harriet and his daughters survived to see Lincoln inaugurated, the Confederacy defeated, and slavery abolished throughout the nation. Although they had to face a brutal civil war, they could take comfort from the fact that the *Dred Scott* case had helped to solidify northern support for both Lincoln and abolition.

John C. Frémont, like almost all slavery opponents, was outraged at the *Dred Scott* decision. He had helped to open the far West to settlement and bring California into the Union as a free state. Yet these achievements led to the demise of large numbers of Indians and fueled the battle over slavery. Despite the efforts of the Comanche and other Indian nations to fend off white encroachment, the U.S. government and eastern settlers claimed more and more territory in the 1840s and 1850s. By 1860, however, most white Americans thought less and less about Indian policy as they focused more and more on slavery.

Some Confederate planters imagined a nation that included Cuba, Nicaragua, and other slave territories. Meanwhile Northerners proved they would fight back. Those outraged by the Fugitive Slave Act had launched rescues of fugitives, and those appalled by Bleeding Kansas applauded John Brown's raid. These more militant activists were joined by thousands of more moderate Northerners who voted for Lincoln in the fall of 1860. By the time Abraham Lincoln took office in March 1861, the ever-widening political chasm brought the United States face-to-face with civil war.

Yet even as war erupted, the issue of slavery remained unresolved. When Frémont was appointed major general in charge of the Department of the West in 1861, he faced a chaotic situation as proslavery forces tried to wrest Missouri from Union control. In response to a Confederate military victory in August 1861 at Wilson's Creek in southwest Missouri, Frémont issued a limited emancipation proclamation, freeing the slaves of Missourians who supported the Confederacy. But the order flew in the face of Lincoln's efforts to keep Missouri from joining the Confederacy and was soon rescinded. Southern states had seceded and were willing to wage war to maintain slavery. Was the North willing to face prolonged battles and high casualties to reunite the nation and abolish human bondage once and for all?

LEARNINGCurve
Check what you know.
bedfordstmartins.com/hewittlawson/LC

Chapter Review

Online Study Guide ▶ bedfordstmartins.com/hewittlawson

KEY TERMS

Oregon Trail (p. 363)
gold rush (p. 365)
Compromise of 1850 (p. 368)
Fugitive Slave Act of 1850 (p. 368)
Uncle Tom's Cabin (p. 372)
Kansas-Nebraska Act (p. 373)
Republican Party (p. 373)
Bleeding Kansas (p. 376)
Dred Scott decision (p. 378)
Harpers Ferry, Virginia (p. 379)
Confederate States of America (p. 381)

REVIEW AND RELATE

1. Why did Americans go west in the 1830s and 1840s, and what was the journey like?

2. What groups competed for land and resources in the West? How did competition lead to violence?

3. What steps did legislators take in the 1840s and early 1850s to resolve the issue of the expansion of slavery?

4. How were slavery and American imperialist ambitions intertwined in the 1840s and 1850s?

5. What factors contributed to the spread of antislavery sentiment in the North beyond committed abolitionists?

6. How did the violence in Kansas in the mid-1850s reflect and intensify the growing sectional divide within the nation?

7. How and why did John Brown's raid on Harpers Ferry move the country closer to civil war?

8. Why did many in the South believe that the election of Abraham Lincoln was cause for secession?

TIMELINE OF EVENTS

1842	John C. Frémont leads expedition along the Oregon Trail
1843	Marcus and Narcissa Whitman lead 1,000 Christian emigrants to the Oregon Territory
1845	Texas granted statehood
1846	Dred Scott and his family sue for their freedom
1848	Gold discovered at Sutter's Mill in California
1850	Compromise of 1850
	Fugitive Slave Act passed
1852	Harriet Beecher Stowe publishes *Uncle Tom's Cabin*
1854	U.S.-Japanese treaty allows for mutual trading
	Republican Party founded
May 1854	Fugitive slave Anthony Burns returned to his owner
	Kansas-Nebraska Act passed
1854–1858	Period of violence in Bleeding Kansas
1857	Supreme Court ruling in *Dred Scott* case
1858	Lincoln-Douglas debates
October 16, 1859	John Brown's raid on Harpers Ferry, Virginia
December 2, 1859	John Brown executed
November 1860	Abraham Lincoln elected president
December 20, 1860	South Carolina secedes from the Union
January 1861	Mississippi, Florida, Alabama, Georgia, Louisiana, and Texas secede
February 1861	Confederate States of America established
March 1861	Lincoln inaugurated as president

Visions of John Brown

On October 16, 1859, John Brown led a group of eighteen men on a raid on the federal arsenal at Harpers Ferry, Virginia. The plan failed, and Brown and his surviving accomplices were captured and put on trial. On December 2, a mere seven weeks after the raid began, Brown was executed by hanging.

The raid shocked the nation, not least because John Brown was a white man leading an uprising to free enslaved blacks. Brown's quick trial and execution were designed to calm southern fears and minimize northern support for his actions. Neither goal was accomplished. Although the northern press and political establishment denounced the raid, many tempered their observations with an equally powerful condemnation of slavery. Abolitionists held demonstrations, wrote tributes and poems to Brown, and organized a "Day of Mourning" to coincide with his execution (Documents 12.7 and 12.9). Southerners and some northern Democrats labeled Brown a terrorist and a traitor and believed he was part of a vast abolitionist conspiracy to violently overthrow their way of life (Documents 12.6 and 12.10). The raid on Harpers Ferry may have ended quickly, but it intensified the sectional dispute over slavery and gave both sides a focal point for their anger. The following sources highlight some of the varying attitudes about John Brown—painting him as a hero, a saint, a stooge, a brute, and a fanatic. In addition, a letter John Brown writes from prison captures his state of mind shortly after his capture, and an 1863 painting makes clear the continued importance of his legacy (Documents 12.8 and 12.11). The differing representations tell us as much about the authors of the sources as they do about Brown himself. As you examine them, consider what they reveal about America on the eve of the Civil War.

DOCUMENT 12.6

State Register (Springfield, Illinois) | The Irrepressible Conflict, 1859

While many Northerners shared Brown's antislavery beliefs, most disagreed with his violent approach to abolition. The following passage from an editorial in the *State Register* (Springfield, Illinois) reflects the outrage felt throughout the nation. The *State Register* was known as a supporter of the Democratic Party, and it blamed the Harpers Ferry raid on the Republican Party. The editorial singles out William Seward and Abraham Lincoln for condemnation because of earlier speeches in which they identified the differences between the North and South as, in Seward's words, an "irrepressible conflict."

The telegraphic dispatches yesterday morning startled the public with an account of one of the most monstrous villainies ever attempted in this country. It was no less than an effort on the part of a party of abolitionists and negroes to take possession of one of the national arsenals, at Harper's Ferry, with the military stores and the public money there deposited. Under the lead of the most infamous of the Kansas crew of black republican marauders, Ossawatomie Brown, the insurgents, to the number of five or six hundred, attacked and took possession of the whole town of Harper's Ferry, including the government buildings and stores, stopped the mails, imprisoned peaceable citizens, and, before they were dislodged, numbers were killed and wounded on both sides.

It was scarcely credible, when the first dispatch was received yesterday, that the object of the ruffians could be other than plunder, but late dispatches, including those we publish this morning, show, conclusively, that the movement was a most extensive one, having for its object the uprising of the negroes throughout the south, a servile war, and its consequences—murder, rapine, and robbery.

The leader chosen was just the man to initiate the work. Bankrupt in fortune and character, an outlaw and an outcast, he was just the man to commence the work which ultra Abolitionism, through its diligent Parkers and Garrisons, hope to reach the millennium of their traitorous designs. Their open-mouthed treason, which culminates in precisely such outrages as that at Harper's Ferry, is but the logical sequence of the teachings of Wm. H. Seward and Abraham Lincoln—the one boldly proclaiming an "irrepressible conflict" between certain states of the Union, because of their local institutions, and the other declaring from stump and hustings, the country round, that the Union cannot continue as the fathers made it—part slave and part free states. When such men, by specious demagogism, in the name of freedom and liberty, daily labor to weaken the bonds of our glorious governmental fabric, the work of sages and patriots, themselves the holders of black men as slaves, is it to be wondered at that ignorant, unprincipled, and reckless camp followers of the party for which these leaders speak, attempt, practically, to illustrate the doctrines which they preach, and in advocacy of which they seek to obtain control of the national government.

Brown, though a blood-stained ruffian, is a bold man. As a black republican he practices what his leaders preach. As it is urged by statesmen (save the mark!) of his party that there is an "irrepressible conflict," he wants it in tangible, material shape. He believes in blows, not words, and the Harper's Ferry villainy is the first in his line of performance.

Who is so blind as not to see the inevitable tendency of black republican teaching? Now we have a bloody, glaring, ghastly fact before us. The "conflict" by blows has commenced. The proofs of an extensive and ramified organization is disclosed, the object of which is to stir the southern slaves to bathe their hands in the blood of the whites of the south. Traitorous scoundrels, with white faces, but black hearts, lead them, and the country is stunned with their deeds of infamy, treason, and blood.

Such is the ripening of the black republican harvest. Can an intelligent people doubt that to such ends the maudlin philanthropy, the hypocritical cant, the blatant demagogism, of black republicanism, tends? "By their fruits shall ye know them." Disunion and bloody anarchy.

Source: "The 'Irrepressible Conflict' Fruits of the Lincoln-Seward Doctrine," *State Register* (Springfield, Illinois), October 20, 1859.

DOCUMENT 12.7

Henry David Thoreau | A Plea for Captain John Brown, 1859

Although most abolitionists were quick to condemn John Brown, Henry David Thoreau rushed to his defense. A prominent author, reformer, and transcendentalist, Thoreau had been introduced to Brown several years earlier by Franklin Sanborn, who helped finance the Harpers Ferry raid. A few weeks after the raid, Thoreau wrote an essay, "A Plea for Captain John Brown," and delivered it in front of a public gathering in Concord, Massachusetts. Thoreau's essay was widely circulated and helped establish Brown as a martyr for the abolitionist cause.

I do not wish to force my thoughts upon you, but I feel forced myself. Little as I know of Captain Brown, I would fain [willingly] do my part to correct the tone and the statements of the newspapers, and of my countrymen generally, respecting his character and actions. It costs us nothing to be just. We can at least express our sympathy with, and admiration of, him and his companions, and that is what I now propose to do. . . .

. . . He was a superior man. He did not value his bodily life in comparison with ideal things. He did not recognize unjust human laws, but resisted them as he was bid. For once we are lifted out of the trivialness and dust of politics into the region of truth and manhood. No man in America has ever stood up so persistently and effectively for the dignity of human nature, knowing himself for a man, and the equal of any and all governments. In that sense he was the most American of us all. He needed no babbling lawyer, making false issues, to defend him. He was more than a match for all the judges that American voters, or office-holders of whatever grade, can create. He could not have been tried by a jury of his peers, because his peers did not exist. When a man stands up serenely against the condemnation and vengeance of mankind, rising above them literally *by a whole body*—even though he were of late the vilest murderer, who has settled that matter with himself—the spectacle is a sublime one—didn't ye know it, ye Liberators, ye Tribunes, ye Republicans? [various newspapers]—and we become criminal in comparison. Do yourselves the honor to recognize him. He needs none of your respect. . . .

It was his peculiar doctrine that a man has a perfect right to interfere by force with the slaveholder, in order to rescue the slave. I agree with him. They who are continually shocked by slavery have some right to be shocked by the violent death of the slaveholder, but no others. Such will be more shocked by his life than by his death. I shall not be forward to think him mistaken in his method who quickest succeeds to liberate the slave. I speak for the slave when I say, that I prefer the philanthropy of Captain Brown to that philanthropy which neither shoots me nor liberates me. At any rate, I do not think it is quite sane for one to spend his whole life in talking or writing about this matter, unless he is continually inspired, and I have not done so. A man may have other affairs to attend to. I do not wish to kill nor to be killed, but I can foresee circumstances in which both these things would be by me unavoidable. We preserve the so-called peace of our community by deeds of petty violence every day. Look at the policeman's billy and handcuffs! Look at the jail! Look at the gallows! Look at the chaplain of the regiment! We are hoping only to live safely on the outskirts of *this* provisional army. So we defend ourselves and our hen-roosts, and maintain slavery. I know that the mass of my countrymen think that the only righteous use that can be made of Sharpe's rifles and revolvers is to fight duels with them, when we are insulted by other nations, or to hunt Indians, or shoot fugitive slaves with them, or the like. I think that for once the Sharpe's rifles and revolvers were employed in a righteous cause. The tools were in the hands of one who could use them.

The same indignation that is said to have cleared the temple once will clear it again. The question is not about the weapon, but the spirit in which you use it. No man has appeared in America, as yet, who loved his fellow-man so well, and treated him so tenderly. He lived for him. He took up his life and he laid it down for him. What sort of violence is that which is encouraged, not by soldiers but by peaceable citizens, not so much by laymen as by ministers of the gospel, not so much by the fighting sects as by the Quakers, and not so much by Quaker men as by Quaker women? . . .

I am here to plead his cause with you. I plead not for his life, but for his character—his immortal life; and so it becomes your cause wholly, and is not his in the least. Some eighteen hundred years ago Christ was crucified; this morning, perchance, Captain Brown was hung. These are the two ends of a chain which is not without its links. He is not Old Brown any longer; he is an angel of light.

I see now that it was necessary that the bravest and humanest man in all the country should be hung. Perhaps he saw it himself. I *almost fear* that I may yet hear of his deliverance, doubting if a prolonged life, if *any* life, can do as much good as his death.

"Misguided"! "Garrulous"! "Insane"! "Vindictive"! So ye write in your easy chairs, and thus he wounded responds from the floor of the Armory, clear as a cloudless sky, true as the voice of nature is: "No man sent me here; it was my own prompting and that of my Maker. I acknowledge no master in human form." . . .

I foresee the time when the painter will paint that scene, no longer going to Rome for a subject; the poet will sing it; the historian record it; and, with the Landing of the Pilgrims and the Declaration of Independence, it will be the ornament of some future national gallery, when at least the present form of Slavery shall be no more here. We shall then be at liberty to weep for Captain Brown. Then, and not till then, we will take our revenge.

Source: James Redpath, *Echoes of Harper's Ferry* (Boston: Thayer and Eldridge, 1860), 2, 30, 37–38, 41–42.

DOCUMENT 12.8

John Brown | Letter to E.B. from Jail, November 1, 1859

John Brown's actions raised especially difficult questions for Quaker abolitionists, who as pacifists did not support violence. A Quaker woman (E.B.) from Newport, Rhode Island, wrote Brown on October 27, expressing her admiration for his motives even though she opposed the means he employed. John Brown replied, offering a religious rationale for his raid. He also urged this letter writer, and many others, to worry less about him and more about his wife Mary, his daughters-in-law, and other widows of those who died during the raid. Although Brown's family received financial assistance, they found it difficult to escape the notoriety of Harpers Ferry and eventually resettled in California.

CHARLESTOWN, JEFFERSON COUNTY, VA., NOV. 1, 1859

My dear Friend E.B. of R.I.,

Your most cheering letter of the 27th of October is received; and may the Lord reward you a thousandfold for the kind feeling you express toward me; but more especially for your fidelity to the "poor that cry, and those that have no help." For this I am a prisoner in bonds. It is solely my own fault, in a military point of view, that we met with our disaster. I mean that I mingled with our prisoners and so far sympathized with them and their families that I neglected my duty in other respects. But God's will, not mine, be done.

You know that Christ once armed Peter. So also in my case I think he put a sword into my hand, and there continued it so long as he saw best, and then kindly took it from me. I mean when I first went to Kansas. I wish you could know with what cheerfulness I am now wielding the "sword of the Spirit" on the right hand and on the left. I bless God that it proves "mighty to the pulling down of strongholds." I always loved my Quaker friends, and I commend to their kind regard my poor bereaved widowed wife and my daughters and daughters-in-law, whose husbands fell at my side. One is a mother and the other likely to become so soon. They, as well as my own sorrow-stricken daughters, are left very poor, and have much greater need of sympathy than I, who, through Infinite Grace and the kindness of strangers, am "joyful in all my tribulations."

Dear sister, write them at North Elba, Essex County, N.Y., to comfort their sad hearts. Direct to Mary A. Brown, wife of John Brown. There is also another—a widow, wife of Thompson, who fell with my poor boys in the affair at Harper's Ferry—at the same place.

I do not feel conscious of guilt in taking up arms; and had it been in behalf of the rich and powerful, the intelligent, the great (as men count greatness), or those who form enactments to suit themselves and corrupt others, or some of their friends, that I interfered, suffered, sacrificed, and fell, it would have been doing very well. But enough of this. These light afflictions, which endure for a moment, shall but work for me "a far more exceeding and eternal weight of glory." I would be very grateful for another letter from you. My wounds are healing. Farewell. God will surely attend to his own cause in the best possible way and time, and he will not forget the work of his own hands.

Your friend,
John Brown

Source: F. B. Sanborn, *The Life and Letters of John Brown* (Boston: Roberts Brothers, 1891), 582–83.

DOCUMENT 12.9

Reverend J. Sella Martin | Day of Mourning Speech, December 2, 1859

On the day of John Brown's execution, abolitionists and African Americans around the country held a "Day of Mourning" in his honor. In Boston, four thousand people gathered at the Tremont Temple to celebrate Brown's life and to grieve over his passing. The Reverend J. Sella Martin, a former slave and the pastor of the Joy Street Baptist Church in Boston, addressed the crowd.

I KNOW THAT JOHN BROWN, in thus rebuking our public sin, in thus facing the monarch, has had to bear just what John the Baptist bore. His head today, by Virginia—that guilty maid of a more guilty mother, the American Government—has been cut off, and it has been presented to the ferocious and insatiable hunger, the terrible and inhuman appetite, of this corrupt government. Today, by the telegraph, we have received the intelligence that John Brown has forfeited his life—all this honesty, all this straight-forwardness, all this self-sacrifice, which has been manifested in Harper's Ferry. . . .

I know that there is some quibbling, some querulousness, some fear, in reference to an out-and-out endorsement of his course. Men of peace principles object to it, in consequence of their religious conviction; politicians in the North object to it, because they are afraid that it will injure their party; pro-slavery men in the South object to it, because it has touched their dearest idol; but I am prepared, my friends (and permit me to say, this is not the language of rage), I am prepared, in the light of all human history, to approve of the *means*; in the light of all Christian principle, to approve of the *end*. (Applause.) I say this is not the language of rage, because I remember that our Fourth-of-July orators sanction the same thing; because I remember that Concord, and Bunker Hill, and every historic battlefield in this country, and the celebration of those events, all go to approve the means that John Brown has used; the only difference being, that in our battles, in America, means have been used for *white* men and that John Brown has used his means for *black* men. (Applause.) And I say, that so far as principle is concerned, so far as the sanctions of the Gospel are concerned, I am prepared to endorse his end; and I endorse it because God Almighty has told us that we should feel with them that are in bonds as being bound with them. I endorse his end, because every single instinct of our nature rises and tells us that it is right. I find an endorsement of John Brown's course in the large assembly gathered here this evening; I find an endorsement of the principles that governed him in going to Virginia, in the presence of the men and women who have come here to listen to his eulogy, and sympathize with his suffering family. . . .

Now, I bring this question down to the simple test of the Gospel; and, agreeing with those men who say the sword should not be used, agreeing with them in that principle, and recognizing its binding obligation upon us all, yet I believe in that homeopathic principle which operates by mercury when mercury is in the system, and that that which is supported by the sword should be overthrown by the sword. I look at this question as a peace man. I say, in accordance with the principles of peace, that I do not believe the sword should be unsheathed. I do not believe the dagger should be drawn, until there is in the system to be assailed such terrible evidences of corruption, that it becomes the *dernier* [last] *resort*. And my friends, we are not to blame the application of the instrument, we are to blame the disease itself. When a physician cuts out a cancer from my face, I am not to blame the physician for the use of the knife; but the impure blood, the obstructed veins, the disordered system, that have caused the cancer, and rendered the use of the instrument necessary.

Source: *The Liberator*, December 9, 1859, in *Blacks on John Brown*, ed. Benjamin Quarles (Urbana: University of Illinois Press, 1972), 26–27.

A Southern Paper Reacts to Brown's Execution, December 3, 1859

The following article appeared in a North Carolina newspaper the day after Brown's execution. It predicts that the North will make Brown a martyr and ridicules the Day of Mourning held in his honor. The article singles out the celebration in Boston, at which J. Sella Martin gave a speech (Document 12.9), for particular condemnation and labels those who attended as treasonous.

The chances are ninety-nine in a hundred, that before this paper reaches our subscribers John Brown will have paid the penalty of his crimes on the gallows, and gone to render an account of his life to that Being who says "thou shalt do no murder."

While we have not the slightest fear that any attempt has been made to rescue Old Brown, we are not without painful apprehensions that among such a large body of inexperienced and excited soldiery, mischief has happened from the incautious use of fire arms.

It is to be hoped, with Brown's exit from the world, the excitement at the North will subside. But we must confess that this hope is but of the faintest character. Fanaticism at the North is rampant, and overrides every thing. On yesterday, the godly city of Boston, built up and sustained by the products of negro slave labor, went into mourning, fasting, and prayer, over the condign [deserved] punishment of a negro stealer, murderer, and traitor, and from fifty pulpits the Praise-God-Bare-bones belched forth volumes of blasphemy and treason.

In all the Noo England towns and villages, we may expect to hear that mock funerals have been celebrated, and all kinds of non-sensically lugubrious displays made. (It is a pity that they haven't a witch or two to drown or burn, by way of variety.) We hope that Gov. Wise [governor of Virginia] will have the gallows on which Brown was hung burned, and give notice of the fact. Our reasons for this wish is this: The Yankees have no objection to mingling money making with their grief, and they will, unless Brown's gallows is known to have been burned, set to work and make all kinds of jim-cracks and notions out of what they will call parts of Old John Brown's gallows and sell them. Let the rope which choked him, too, be burned and the fact advertised, or we shall see vast quantities of breast pins, lockets, and bracelets, containing bits of the "rope which hung Old Brown" for sale. [P. T.] Barnum is already in the market for Old Brown's old clothes, and hopes and expects to make [a good] speculation out of them.

Source: "Execution of John Brown," *Register* (Raleigh, North Carolina), December 3, 1859.

DOCUMENT 12.11

Currier and Ives | John Brown on His Way to Execution, 1863

In the weeks after Brown's death, newspapers were filled with accounts of his final days and execution. The *New York Tribune* published a story claiming that Brown had kissed a slave child he encountered on his way to the gallows. Although this story was untrue, it was widely repeated and became the subject of a painting by Louis Ransom. This 1863 Currier and Ives lithograph based on Ransom's painting further cemented the legend.

Library of Congress

Interpret the Evidence

1. How do these different sources describe Brown? What language and imagery do they use? How is religious imagery employed in the various documents?

2. In what ways do Brown's admirers, such as Henry David Thoreau (Document 12.7) and J. Sella Martin (Document 12.9), attempt to support Brown without praising the violence of his raid?

3. Those who condemned Brown often used his raid as a way to criticize the North and abolitionists. On what grounds did they make these more generalized claims of northern guilt (Documents 12.6 and 12.10)?

4. What is John Brown's state of mind after his conviction (Document 12.8)? How does he describe his actions?

5. What images and messages are used in the Currier and Ives illustration (Document 12.11) to portray Brown as a martyr?

Put It in Context

- How do the varied reactions to John Brown's 1859 raid on Harpers Ferry illuminate the conflicts that led to Abraham Lincoln's election as president in 1860 and South Carolina's secession in 1861?

background photos: page 387, Library of Congress; page 390, Peter Newark American Pictures/The Bridgeman Art Library

Library of Congress

Library of Congress

Confederate officer with wife and child.

Cabin interior with African American women and children, Spotsylvania Court House, Virginia, 1864.

13
Civil War
1861–1865

Library of Congress

● Union family in camp of Thirty-first Pennsylvania Infantry near Washington, D.C., 1862.

AMERICAN HISTORIES

Though born into slavery in 1818, by 1860 Frederick Douglass had become a celebrated orator, editor, and abolitionist. He ensured his fame in 1845 with publication of the *Narrative of the Life of Frederick Douglass*. In it, he described his experiences of slavery in Maryland, his defiance against his masters, and his eventual escape to New York in September 1838 with the help of Anna Murray, a free black servant.

Frederick and Anna married in New York and then moved to New Bedford, Massachusetts, and changed their last name to Douglass to avoid capture. But in 1841 Frederick began lecturing for the American Anti-Slavery Society, offering stirring accounts of his enslavement and escape. By publishing his *Narrative* four years later, Douglass made his capture even more likely, so in August 1845 he left for England, where wildly enthusiastic audiences attended his lectures and supporters raised funds to purchase his freedom. Douglass returned to Massachusetts in 1847, a truly free man.

A year later, Frederick moved to Rochester, New York, with Anna and their five children to launch his abolitionist paper, the *North Star*. Over the next decade, he became the most famous black abolitionist in the United States and an outspoken advocate of women's rights. He also broke with the Garrisonian branch of abolitionists by joining the Liberty Party and later the Free-Soil and Republican parties. He was thus well placed when war erupted in April 1861 to lobby President Lincoln to make emancipation a war aim and enlist African Americans in the Union army.

Douglass embraced electoral politics and the use of military force to end slavery. His greatest fear was that Lincoln was more committed to reconstituting the Union than to abolishing slavery. But after the president issued the Emancipation Proclamation in January 1863, Douglass spoke enthusiastically on its behalf. At the same time, he continued to believe that military service was essential for black men to demonstrate their patriotism. His stirring editorial "Men of Color, to Arms" was turned into a recruiting poster, and he urged his own sons to join the Massachusetts Fifty-fourth Colored Infantry, one of the first African American regiments. But Douglass also protested discrimination against black troops and lobbied for federal protections of black civil rights.

Like Douglass, Rose O'Neal was born on a Maryland plantation, but she was white and free. Her father was likely John O'Neal, a planter who was slain by a slave in 1817, when Rose was four years old. In early adolescence, she moved to Washington, D.C., with her older sister. They lived with an aunt who ran a fashionable boardinghouse near Capitol Hill. The boarders included John C. Calhoun, whose states' rights views Rose eagerly embraced. Intrigued by the lively political debates that marked the Jacksonian era, she was also schooled in the social graces. Charming and beautiful, Rose was welcomed into elite social circles, including invitations from Dolley Madison. In 1835 she married Robert Greenhow, a cultivated Virginian who worked for the State Department.

Rose O'Neal Greenhow quickly became a favorite Washington hostess. Like Dolley Madison, she entertained congressmen, cabinet ministers, and foreign diplomats with a wide range of views. In the midst of this social and political whirl, Rose gave birth to four daughters. Yet she also remained deeply invested in her husband's career. She assisted Robert in the 1840s as he researched U.S. land claims in the Pacific Northwest. Ardent proslavery expansionists, the Greenhows supported efforts to acquire Cuba, and in 1850 they traveled to Mexico City to study California land claims. When Robert died in 1854, Rose moved into a smaller house in Washington but continued to entertain political leaders and sustained friendships with powerful men like President James Buchanan.

In May 1861, just as the Civil War commenced, a U.S. army captain about to join the Confederate cause recruited Greenhow to head an espionage ring in Washington, D.C. With her close ties to southern sympathizers working in government offices and her extensive social network, Greenhow gathered important intelligence on Union political and military plans. Although she initially avoided suspicion, by August Greenhow was investigated and placed under house arrest. When she continued to smuggle out letters, embarrassing Union officials, she was sent to the Old Capitol Prison in January 1862. Once again, Greenhow managed to transmit information and riled up the other prisoners. In June, she was exiled to Richmond, where Confederate president Jefferson Davis hailed her as a hero and awarded her $2,500. ●

THE AMERICAN HISTORIES of Frederick Douglass and Rose O'Neal Greenhow were shaped by the sectional conflict over slavery that culminated in the Civil War. Both were born on Maryland plantations, one as a slave and the other a daughter of slave owners. Both honed their innate talents, one as an orator and a writer, the other as a hostess and gatherer of intelligence. And both embraced the Civil War as the last best hope for national salvation, one on the side of union and emancipation, the other on the side of secession and slavery. They were among hundreds of thousands of Americans—men and women, black and white, North and South—who saw the war as a means to achieve their goals: a free nation, a haven for slavery, or a reunited country.

The Nation Goes to War

When Abraham Lincoln took office, seven states in the Lower South had already formed the Confederate States of America, and the threat of more secessions remained. Lincoln had promised not to interfere with slavery where it already existed, but many southern whites were unconvinced by such assurances. By seceding, the southern slaveholding class also proclaimed its unwillingness to become a permanent minority in the nation. Still, not all slave states were yet willing to cut their ties to the nation, and Northerners, too, disagreed about the consequences of secession and the appropriate response to it. Once fighting erupted, however, preparations for war became the primary focus in both the North and the South.

The South Embraces Secession

Confederate president Davis joined other planters in arguing that Lincoln's victory jeopardized the future of slavery and that secession was, therefore, a necessity. Advocates of secession contended that the federal government had failed to implement fully the Fugitive Slave Act and the *Dred Scott* decision. With Republicans in power, they were convinced that the administration would do even less to support southern interests. White Southerners also feared that a Republican administration might inspire a massive uprising of slaves. In the aftermath of John Brown's raid on Harpers Ferry, one southern newspaper warned that the region was "slumbering over a volcano, whose smoldering fires may, at any quiet starry midnight, blacken the social sky with the smoke of desolation and death." Secession would allow whites to maintain greater control over the South's black population.

Slaveholders were also anxious about the loyalty of white Southerners who did not own slaves. "I mistrust our own people more than I fear all of the efforts of the Abolitionists," claimed a South Carolina politician in 1859. He went on to argue that by denouncing social and economic inequality, Republicans might recruit nonslaveholders to their party and thereby create a "contest for slavery . . . in the South between people of the South." Secession would effectively isolate southern yeomen from potential Republican allies.

When Lincoln was inaugurated, legislators in the Upper South still hoped a compromise could be reached. Although many Northerners believed that the secessionists needed to be punished, Lincoln sought to bring the Confederates back into the Union without using military force. Yet he also sought to demonstrate Union strength to curtail further secessions. He focused on **Fort Sumter** in South Carolina's Charleston harbor, where a small Union garrison was running low on food and medicine. On April 8, 1861, Lincoln dispatched ships to the fort but promised to use force only if the Confederates blocked his peaceful effort to send supplies.

Lincoln's action presented the Confederate government with a choice. It could attack the Union vessels and bear responsibility for starting a war, or it could permit a "foreign power" to maintain a fort in its territory. President Davis and his advisers chose the aggressive course, demanding the unconditional surrender of Fort Sumter before supplies arrived. The commanding officer refused, and on April 12 Confederate guns opened fire. Two days later, Fort Sumter surrendered. On April 15, Lincoln called for 75,000 volunteers to put down the southern insurrection.

The declaration of war led whites in the Upper South to reconsider secession. Some small farmers and landless whites in the region were drawn to Republican promises of free labor and free soil and remained suspicious of the goals and power of secessionist planters. Moreover, their land sat in the direct path of military engagement. Yet the vast majority of southern whites, rich and poor, defined their liberty in relation to black bondage. They feared that Republicans would free the slaves and introduce racial amalgamation in the South.

Explore

See Documents 13.1 and 13.2 for two sides of the secession debate in Georgia.

Fearing more secessions, Lincoln used the powers of his office to keep the border states that allowed slavery—Maryland, Delaware, Missouri, and Kentucky—in the Union. He waived the right of habeas corpus (which protects citizens against arbitrary arrest and detention), jailed secessionists, arrested state legislators, and limited freedom of the press. Despite these measures, four more slave states—North Carolina, Virginia, Tennessee, and Arkansas—seceded. Of these, Virginia was by far the most significant. It was strategically located near the nation's capital. Richmond was also home to the South's largest iron manufacturer, which could produce weapons and munitions. By June 1861, the Confederacy had moved its capital to Richmond in recognition of Virginia's importance.

DOCUMENTS 13.1 AND 13.2

Debating Secession in Georgia: Two Views

Immediately after Abraham Lincoln's election, several southern states began to discuss secession. Georgia called a special convention to debate the issue on November 13–14, 1860. Two of the principal speakers were Robert Toombs and Alexander Stephens, close friends who had met in Washington, D.C., as U.S. congressmen from Georgia. In the following selections from their speeches, Toombs argues in favor of secession, and Stephens urges a more cautious approach. In January 1861, Georgia became the fifth state to secede, two months before Lincoln took office. In February, Stephens was elected vice president of the Confederacy.

Explore

13.1 Robert Toombs | For Secession, 1860

The stern, steady march of events has brought us in conflict with our non-slaveholding confederates upon the fundamental principles of our compact of Union. We have not sought this conflict; we have sought too long to avoid it. . . . The door of conciliation and compromise is finally closed by our adversaries, and it remains only to us to meet the conflict with the dignity and firmness of men worthy of freedom. . . .

. . . The South at all times demanded nothing but equality in the common territories, equal enjoyment of them with their property, to that extended to Northern citizens and their property—nothing more. . . . In 1790 we had less than eight hundred thousand slaves. Under our mild and humane administration of the system they have increased above four millions. The country has expanded to meet this growing want, and Florida, Alabama, Mississippi, Louisiana, Texas, Arkansas, Kentucky, Tennessee, and Missouri have received this increasing tide of African labor; before the end of this century, at precisely the same rate of increase, the Africans among us in a subordinate condition will amount to eleven millions of persons. What shall be done with them? We must expand or perish. . . . The North understand it better—they have told us for twenty years that their object was to pen up slavery within its present limits—surround it with a border of free States, and like the scorpion surrounded with fire, they will make it sting itself to death.

Source: Frank Moore, ed., *The Rebellion Record: A Diary of American Events* (New York: G. P. Putnam and Henry Holt, 1864), 1:362–63, 365.

When the first seven states seceded, outrage and anxiety escalated in the North. Textile manufacturers feared the permanent loss of the southern cotton crop, and bankers worried whether Confederates would repay their loans. In northeastern cities, stock prices plummeted, banks shut their doors, factories laid off workers, and unsold goods piled up on docks. But the firing on Fort Sumter prompted many Northerners to line up behind Lincoln's call for war. Manufacturers and merchants, once intent upon maintaining economic links with the South, now rushed to support the president, while northern workers, including immigrants, responded to Lincoln's call for volunteers. They assumed that the Union, with its greater resources and manpower, could quickly set the nation right. New York editor Horace Greeley proclaimed, "Jeff Davis and Co. will be swingin' from the battlements at Washington at least by the 4th of July." A Philadelphia newspaper echoed, "This much-ado about nothing will end in a month." Greeley and his fellow journalists were sadly mistaken.

Both Sides Prepare for War

At the onset of the war, the Union held a decided advantage in resources and population. The Union states held more than 60 percent of the U.S. population, while the Confederate states held less than 40 percent. And the Confederacy included several million slaves who would not be armed for

13.2 Alexander Stephens | Against Secession, 1860

The first question that presents itself is, Shall the people of the South secede from the Union in consequence of the election of Mr. Lincoln to the Presidency of the United States? My countrymen, I tell you frankly, candidly, and earnestly, that I do not think they ought. . . . To make a point of resistance to the Government, to withdraw from it because a man has been constitutionally elected, puts us in the wrong. We are pledged to maintain the Constitution. Many of us have sworn to support it. Can we, therefore, for the mere election of a man to the Presidency, and that too in accordance with the prescribed forms of the Constitution, make a point of resistance to the Government, without becoming the breakers of that sacred instrument ourselves by withdrawing ourselves from it? Would we not be in the wrong? . . .

The Northern States, on entering into the Federal compact, pledged themselves [under the 1793 Fugitive Slave Law] to surrender such fugitives; and it is in disregard of their constitutional obligations that they have passed laws which even tend to hinder or inhibit the fulfillment of that obligation. . . . What ought we to do in view of this? . . . By the law of nations, you would have a right to demand the carrying out of this article of agreement, and I do not see that it should be otherwise with respect to the States of this Union; and in case it be not done, we would, by these principles, have the right to commit acts of reprisal on these faithless governments, and seize upon their property, or that of their citizens, wherever found. The States of this Union stand upon the same footing with foreign nations in this respect. But by the law of nations we are equally bound, before proceeding to violent measures, to set forth our grievances before the offending government, to give them an opportunity to redress the wrong. Has our State yet done this? I think not.

Source: Richard Malcolm Johnston and William Hand Browne, *Life of Alexander H. Stephens* (Philadelphia: J. B. Lippincott, 1878), 565–66, 575.

Interpret the Evidence

- What type of language does each man use to describe the North and the South?
- On what issues do they focus, and how do they describe the relationship of the South to the United States as a whole?

Put It in Context

Explain the importance of the issue of slavery to the arguments regarding secession that Toombs and Stephens make.

combat. The Union also outstripped the Confederacy in manufacturing and even led the South in agricultural production. The North's many miles of railroad track ensured greater ease in moving troops and supplies. And the Union could launch far more ships to blockade southern ports (Figure 13.1).

Yet Union forces were less prepared for war than were the Confederates, who had been organizing troops and gathering munitions for months. To match their efforts, Winfield Scott, general in chief of the U.S. army, told Lincoln he would need at least 300,000 men committed to serve for two or three years. But the president, who feared unnerving Northerners, asked for only 75,000 volunteers for three months. Recruits poured into state militias, and thousands more offered their services directly to the federal government. Yet rather than forming a powerful national army led by seasoned officers, Lincoln left recruitment, organization, and training largely to the states. The result was disorganization and the appointment of new officers based more on political connections than on military expertise.

Confederate leaders also initially relied on state militia units and volunteers, but they prepared for a prolonged war from the start. Before the firing on Fort Sumter, President Davis signed up 100,000 volunteers for a year's service. The labor provided by slaves allowed a large proportion of white working-age men to volunteer for military service. And Southerners knew they were likely to be fighting mainly on

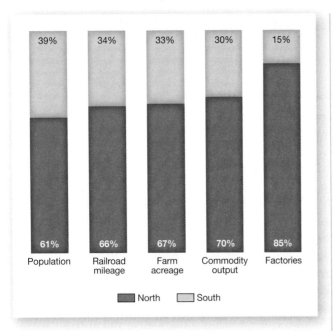

39%	34%	33%	30%	15%
61%	66%	67%	70%	85%
Population	Railroad mileage	Farm acreage	Commodity output	Factories

■ North □ South

FIGURE 13.1 Economies of the North and South, 1860

This figure provides graphic testimony to the enormous advantages in resources the North held on the eve of the Civil War. Perhaps most surprisingly, the North led the South in farm acreage as well as factories and commodity output. Over four years of war, the North's significantly larger population would also prove crucial. Source: Data from Stanley Engerman, "The Economic Impact of the Civil War," in *The Reinterpretation of American Economic History*, ed. Robert W. Fogel and Stanley Engerman (New York: Harper and Row).

home territory, where they had expert knowledge of the terrain. When the final four states joined the Confederacy, the southern army also gained important military leadership. It ultimately recruited 280 West Point graduates, including Robert E. Lee, Thomas "Stonewall" Jackson, James Longstreet, and others who had proved their mettle in the Mexican-American War.

The South's advantages were apparent in the first major battle of the war. But Confederate troops were also aided by information on Union plans sent by Rose Greenhow. Confederate forces were thus well prepared when 30,000 Union troops marched on northern Virginia on July 21, 1861. At the Battle of Bull Run (or Manassas), 22,000 Confederates repelled the Union attack. During the fighting, 800 men lost their lives, giving Americans their first taste of the carnage that lay ahead. Civilians from Washington who traveled to the battle site to view the combat had to flee for their lives to escape Confederate artillery.

Despite Union defeats at Bull Run and Wilson's Creek, Missouri, in August 1861, the Confederate army did not follow up with major strikes against Union forces. Meanwhile the Union navy began blockading the South's deepwater ports. When the armies settled into winter camps in 1861–1862, both sides recognized that the war was likely to be a long struggle demanding a far greater commitment of men and resources than anyone had imagined just months earlier.

Battle of Wilson's Creek

This illustration depicts the First Iowa Regiment, led by General Nathaniel Lyon, charging Confederate forces at the Battle of Wilson's Creek, near Springfield, Missouri, on August 10, 1861. Lyon was shot in the head and killed, becoming the first Union general to die in the war. The Confederates won the battle, marking their second victory together with Bull Run. Library of Congress

REVIEW & RELATE

What steps did Lincoln take to prevent war? Why were they ineffective?

What advantages and disadvantages did each side have at the onset of the war?

✔ *LEARNINGCurve* bedfordstmartins.com/hewittlawson/LC

Fighting for Union or against Slavery?

The Union and the Confederacy faced very different tasks in the war. The South had to defend its territory and force the federal government to halt military action. The North had to bring the Confederacy to its knees by invading the South and isolating it from potential allies abroad. While most northern leaders believed that the nation could be reunited without challenging the institution of slavery, enslaved Southerners immediately looked for ways to loosen their bonds. Meanwhile northern abolitionists worked to convince Lincoln and Congress that only emancipation could resolve the problems that had led to war.

Debating the Role of African Americans

The outbreak of war intensified debates over abolition. Some 225,000 African Americans lived in the free states, and many offered their services in the hopes that victory would lead to the emancipation of southern slaves. At a recruitment meeting in Cleveland, African American leaders proclaimed, "Today, as in the times of '76, we are ready to go forth and do battle in the common cause of our country." But Secretary of War Simon Cameron had no intention of calling up black soldiers, and some local officials prohibited African American recruitment meetings.

Northern optimism about a quick victory contributed to the rejection of black soldiers. Union leaders also feared that whites would not enlist if they had to serve alongside blacks. In addition, Lincoln and his advisers were initially wary of letting a war to preserve the Union become a war against slavery, and they feared that any further threat to slavery might drive the four slave states that remained in the Union into the Confederacy. African Americans and their supporters nevertheless believed that the war opened a door to freedom and that continued pressure might convince Union leaders to change their minds. As activist Amy Post proclaimed, "The abolitionists surely have a job to do now in influencing and directing the bloody struggle, that it may end in Emancipation."

For their part, southern slaves quickly realized that the presence of Union troops made freedom a distinct possibility. Enslaved workers living near battle sites circulated information on Union troop movements. Then, as slaveholders in Virginia began to send male slaves to more distant plantations for fear of losing them, some slaves chose to flee. Those who could headed to Union camps, where they provided labor as well as knowledge of the local terrain and the location of Confederate forces. Slave owners, in turn, followed fugitives into Union camps and demanded their return. Some Union commanders denied slaves entrance or returned them to their masters, but a few Union officers saw the value of embracing these fugitives.

On the night of May 23, 1861, for example, three Virginia slaves paddled upriver to the Union outpost at Fort Monroe, requesting sanctuary from General Benjamin Butler. Butler was no abolitionist, but he realized that slaves were valuable assets to the Union cause and so offered them military protection. He claimed fugitive slaves as **contraband** of war: property forfeited by the act of rebellion. As news of Butler's decision spread, more runaways sought refuge at Fort Monroe. Within four days, another sixty-seven slaves had arrived at "Freedom Fort."

Explore

See Document 13.3 for an account of life among freedpeople on the Sea Islands.

Lincoln endorsed Butler's policy as a legitimate tactic of war because it allowed the Union to strike at the institution of slavery without proclaiming a general emancipation that might prompt the border states with slaves to secede. Congress expanded Butler's policy. On August 6, 1861, it passed a confiscation act, proclaiming that any slave owner whose bondsmen were used by the Confederate army would lose all claim to those slaves. Although it was far from a clear-cut declaration of freedom, the act spurred the hopes of abolitionists.

Fighting for the Right to Fight

From the start, the Union army recruited a wide array of Americans. Indeed, nearly every ethnic and racial group served in Union ranks except African Americans. German and Irish immigrants; Catholic, Protestant, and Jewish Americans; native-born whites from the Northeast and Midwest; and Mexican American soldiers in the West all fought with the Union army. In an effort to eliminate this one exception, abolitionists had long argued that African Americans would make excellent soldiers, and Radical

DOCUMENT 13.3

Charlotte Forten | Life on the Sea Islands, 1864

As Union forces began receiving former slaves as "contraband," many were settled in the Sea Islands of South Carolina, which were controlled by the Union army. Northern abolitionists sent teachers to these camps to help educate the former slaves. Charlotte Forten, who came from a prominent free African American family in Philadelphia, was a well-known abolitionist and the first black teacher to arrive in the camps in 1864. Forten's impressions of the newly freed slaves appeared in an article she wrote for the *Atlantic Monthly*, a progressive literary and cultural magazine.

Explore

It was on the afternoon of a warm, murky day late in October that our steamer, the *United States*, touched the landing at Hilton Head. A motley assemblage had collected on the wharf—officers, soldiers, and "contrabands" of every size and hue: black was, however, the prevailing color. . . .

Little colored children of every hue were playing about the streets, looking as merry and happy as children ought to look—now that the evil shadow of Slavery no longer hangs over them. . . .

. . . The school was opened in September. Many of the children had, however, received instruction during the summer. It was evident that they had made very rapid improvement, and we noticed with pleasure how bright and eager to learn many of them seemed. . . .

These people are exceedingly polite in their manner towards each other, each new arrival bowing, scraping his feet, and shaking hands with the others, while there are constant greetings, such as, "Huddy? How's yer lady?" ("How d' ye do? How's your wife?"). The hand-shaking is performed with the greatest possible solemnity. There is never the faintest shadow of a smile on anybody's face during this performance. The children, too, are taught to be very polite to their elders, and it is the rarest thing to hear a disrespectful word from a child to his parent, or to any grown person. They have really what the New-Englanders call "beautiful manners." . . .

Daily the long-oppressed people of these islands are demonstrating their capacity for improvement in learning and labor. What they have accomplished in one short year exceeds our utmost expectations. . . . An old freedman said to me one day, "De Lord make me suffer long time. . . . But now we's free. He bring us all out right at las'."

Source: Charlotte Forten, "Life on the Sea Islands," *The Atlantic Monthly*, May–June 1864, 587, 589, 592, 676.

Interpret the Evidence

- How does Forten describe the former slaves? What aspects of their behavior seem to strike her most forcefully?
- How is Forten trying to shape northern opinion about former slaves in this article?

Put It in Context

What resources could northern abolitionists and teachers provide for newly freed slaves?

Republicans in Congress emphasized the military advantages of allowing black enlistment. As Massachusetts senator Charles Sumner explained, "You will observe that I propose no crusade for abolition. [Emancipation] is to be presented strictly as a measure of military necessity."

Meanwhile American Indians fought on both sides. The Comanches negotiated with both Union and Confederate agents while raiding the Texas frontier for horses and cattle. The Confederacy gained the greatest support from slaveholding Indians who had earlier been removed from the Southeast. The Cherokee general Stand Watie led a pan-Indian force that battled alongside white Confederate troops on the western frontier. However, most members of the Cherokee and other southeastern tribes, along with Osage, Delaware, and Seneca Indians, sided with the Union. Ely Parker, a Seneca sachem and engineer, rose to become a lieutenant colonel in the Union army, serving with General Ulysses S. Grant.

While some Indian regiments were rejected by state officials, African Americans were barred from enlisting by federal authority. In 1862, however, a series of military defeats helped transform northern attitudes. Although Union forces gained ground along the southern Mississippi River, they lost important battles farther north. In the spring of 1862, Confederate troops led by Stonewall Jackson won a series of stunning victories against three Union armies in Virginia's Shenandoah Valley. That June and July,

General Robert E. Lee fought General George B. McClellan to a standstill in the Seven Days Battle near Richmond. Then in August, Lee, Jackson, and General James Long-street joined forces to defeat Union troops at the Second Battle of Bull Run (Map 13.1).

As the war turned against the North, the North turned against slavery. In April 1862, Congress approved a measure to abolish slavery in the District of Columbia, symbolizing a significant shift in Union sentiment. During that bloody summer, Congress passed a second confiscation act, declaring that the slaves of anyone who supported the Confederacy should be "forever free of their servitude, and not again held as slaves." Finally, Congress passed a militia act that allowed

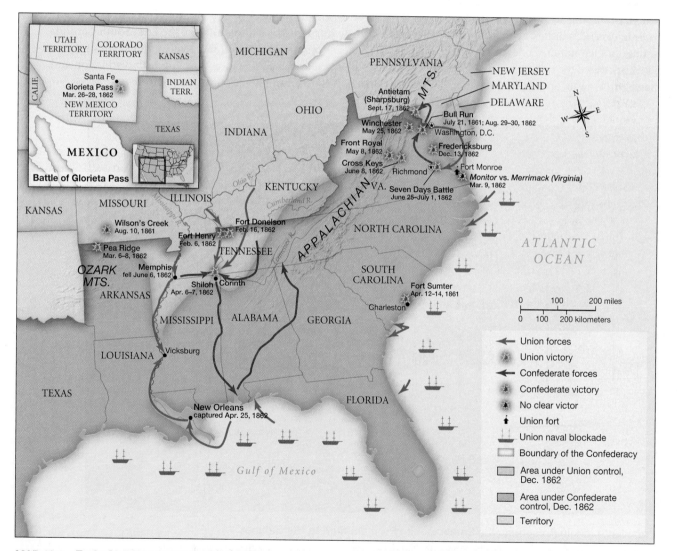

MAP 13.1 Early Civil War Battles, 1861–1862

In 1861 and 1862, the Confederate army stunned Union forces with a series of dramatic victories in Virginia and Missouri. However, the Union army won a crucial victory at Antietam (Sharpsburg); gained control of Confederate territory in Tennessee, Arkansas, and Mississippi; fended off Confederate efforts to gain New Mexico Territory; and established a successful naval blockade of Confederate ports.

"persons of African descent" to be employed in "any military or naval service for which they may be found competent." Lincoln quickly signed these acts into law.

Yet support for the 1862 militia act also built on Union victories. In April 1862, a Union blockade led to the capture of New Orleans, while the **Battle of Shiloh** in Tennessee provided the army entrée to the Mississippi valley. There Union troops came face-to-face with slavery. Few of these soldiers were abolitionists, but many were shocked by what they saw. At some captured plantations, soldiers discovered instruments used to torture slaves. One Union soldier reported he had seen "enough of the horror of slavery to make one an Abolitionist forever." Local blacks also provided valuable intelligence to Union officers.

The rising death toll also increased support for African American enlistment. The Battle of Shiloh was the bloodiest battle in American history up to that point. Earlier battles had resulted in a few hundred or even a few thousand casualties, but Shiloh raised the carnage to a new level. General Grant marveled, "I saw an open field . . . so covered with dead that it

would have been possible to walk across the clearing, in any direction, stepping only on dead bodies without a foot touching the ground." As the war continued, such deadly battles became routine. The Union army would need every available man to sustain its effort against the Confederates.

Amid the roller coaster of victory and defeat, African Americans gave practical force to the 1862 militia act. In October 1862, a group of African American soldiers in the First Kansas Colored Volunteers repulsed Confederates at a battle in Missouri. Early the next year, another black regiment—the Massachusetts Fifty-fourth—attracted recruits from across the North. Frederick Douglass helped recruit a hundred men from New York State, including his three sons—Charles, Lewis, and Frederick Jr. In the South, Colonel Thomas Wentworth Higginson and other abolitionist officers organized former slaves into units like the First South Carolina Volunteers. By late 1863, tens of thousands of African American soldiers were serving with distinction and contributing to key northern victories.

President Lincoln Presenting the Emancipation Proclamation to His Cabinet

In this engraving, based on a painting by Francis B. Carpenter, Lincoln reads the first draft of his Emancipation Proclamation to his cabinet on September 22, 1862. To the left of Lincoln are Secretary of War Edwin Stanton (seated) and Secretary of the Treasury Salmon P. Chase, the two strongest supporters of the Proclamation. To the right of Lincoln are Secretary of the Navy Gideon Welles (seated), Secretary of the Interior Caleb B. Smith, Secretary of State William Seward (seated), Postmaster General Montgomery Blair, and Attorney General Edward Bates (seated). Bates and Blair opposed the plan.   Library of Congress

Union Politicians Consider Emancipation

By the fall of 1862, African Americans and abolitionists had gained widespread support for emancipation as a necessary goal of the war. In making a final decision, Lincoln and his cabinet had to consider numerous factors. Embracing abolition as a war aim would likely prevent international recognition of southern independence, a significant advantage; but it might also arouse deep animosity in the slaveholding border states and drive them from the Union.

International recognition was critical to the Confederacy. Support from European nations might persuade the North to accept southern independence. More immediately, recognition would ensure markets for southern agriculture and access to manufactured goods and war materiel. Confederate officials were especially focused on Britain, the leading market for cotton and a potentially important supplier of industrial products. President Davis considered sending Rose Greenhow to England to promote the Confederate cause among British textile workers and government officials, who were concerned about disruptions to their economy caused by the Union blockade.

Fearing that the British might capitulate to Confederate pressure, abolitionist lecturers toured Britain, reminding residents of their early leadership in the antislavery cause. The abolitionists recognized that the Union's formal commitment to emancipation could give the North an edge in the battle for public opinion and prevent diplomatic recognition of the Confederacy. By the summer of 1862, Lincoln agreed. But he wanted to proclaim emancipation as a sign of Union strength, not weakness, so he waited for a victory before making a formal announcement.

A series of Union defeats in the summer of 1862 had allowed Lee to march his army into Union territory in Maryland. On September 17, Longstreet joined Lee in a fierce battle along Antietam Creek as Union troops brought the Confederate advance to a standstill near the town of Sharpsburg. Union forces suffered more than 12,000 casualties and the Confederates more than 10,000, the bloodiest single day in U.S. warfare. Yet because Lee and his army were forced to retreat, Lincoln claimed Antietam as a great victory. Five days later, the president announced his preliminary **Emancipation Proclamation** to the assembled cabinet. He held firm despite a bloody defeat at Fredericksburg, Virginia, that December, when Confederate troops inflicted nearly 13,000 Union casualties while suffering only 5,000 of their own.

On January 1, 1863, Lincoln signed the final edict, proclaiming that slaves in areas still in rebellion were "forever free" and inviting them to enlist in the Union army. In many ways, the proclamation was a conservative document, applying only to slaves largely beyond the reach of

federal power. Its provisions exempted from emancipation the 450,000 slaves in the loyal border states, 275,000 slaves in Union-occupied Tennessee, and tens of thousands more in Louisiana and Virginia. The proclamation also justified the abolition of southern slavery on military, not moral, grounds.

Despite its limits, the Emancipation Proclamation prompted joyous "Watch Meetings" as abolitionists and free blacks met to give thanks as the edict took effect. At black churches across the North, crowds sang "Glory Hallelujah," "John Brown's Body," and "Marching On." If the Union proved victorious, the Emancipation Proclamation promised a total transformation of southern society.

REVIEW & RELATE

What arguments did each side make in the debate over African American enlistment in the Union army?

How and why did the Civil War become a war to end slavery?

✓ *LEARNINGCurve* bedfordstmartins.com/hewittlawson/LC

War Transforms the North and the South

For soldiers caught in the midst of battle, for civilians caught between warring armies, and for ordinary families seeking to survive the upheaval, political pronouncements did little to alleviate the dangers they faced. The extraordinary death tolls in Civil War battles shocked Americans on both sides. On the home front, the war created labor shortages and severe inflation in both the North and the South. It initially disrupted industrial and agricultural production as men were called to service, but the North recovered fairly quickly by building on its prewar industrial base and technological know-how. In the South, manufacturing increased, with some enslaved laborers pressed into service as industrial workers. But pulling slaves away from agricultural work only created more problems on plantations, which were already suffering labor shortages. These changing circumstances required women to take on new responsibilities on the home front and the battlefront. But the dramatic transformations also inspired dissent and protest as rising death tolls and rising prices made the costs of war ever clearer.

Life and Death on the Battlefield

Few soldiers entered the conflict knowing what to expect. A young private wrote home that his idea of combat had

Civil War Soldiers

The Civil War was the first major war to be photographed extensively. Photographers recorded many images of the aftermath of battle and the daily lives of soldiers. Soldiers also had portraits taken to send to loved ones. These images of a black and a white soldier suggest the pride that these men felt in their uniforms and their weapons.   both photos: Library of Congress

been that the soldiers "would all be in line, all standing in a nice level field fighting, a number of ladies taking care of the wounded, etc., etc., but it isn't so." **See Document Project 13: Civil War Letters, page 417**. Even where traditional forms of engagement did occur, improved weaponry turned them into scenes of carnage. Although individual soldiers could fire only a few times a minute, their Enfield and Springfield rifles were murderously effective at a quarter-mile distance. New conical bullets that expanded to fit the grooves of rifles proved far more accurate and more deadly than older round bullets. Minié balls that exploded on impact also increased fatalities. By mid-1863, the rival armies relied on heavy fortifications, elaborate trenches, and distant mortar and artillery fire when they could, but the casualties continued to rise, especially since the trenches proved to be a breeding ground for disease.

The hardships and discomforts of war extended beyond combat itself. As General Lee complained before the fighting at Antietam, many soldiers went into battle in ragged uniforms and without shoes. In the First Battle of Bull Run, a Georgia major reported that more than one

hundred of his men were barefoot, "many of whom left bloody foot-prints among the thorns and briars through which they rushed." Rations, too, ran short. Food was dispensed sporadically and was often spoiled. Many Union troops survived primarily on an unleavened biscuit called hardtack as well as small amounts of meat and beans and enormous quantities of coffee. At least their diet improved over the course of the war as the Union supply system grew more efficient. Confederate troops, however, subsisted increasingly on cornmeal and fatty meat. As early as 1862, Confederate soldiers were gathering food from the haversacks of Union dead.

"There is more dies by sickness than gets killed," a recruit from New York complained in 1861. Indeed, for every soldier who died as a result of combat, three died of disease. Measles, dysentery, typhoid, and malaria killed thousands who drank contaminated water, ate tainted food, and were exposed to the elements. Prisoner-of-war camps were especially deadly locales. Debilitating fevers in a camp near Danville, Virginia, spread to the town, killing civilians as well as soldiers. In the fall of 1862, yellow fever and malaria killed nearly five hundred in

Wilmington, Delaware, as infected soldiers built fortifications along the beaches.

African American troops fared worst of all. The death rate from disease for black Union soldiers was nearly three times greater than that for white Union soldiers, reflecting their generally poorer health upon enlistment, the hard labor they performed, and the minimal medical care they received in the field. Those who began their army careers in contraband camps fared even worse, with a camp near Nashville losing a quarter of its residents to death in just three months in 1864.

Even for white soldiers, medical assistance was primitive. Antibiotics did not exist, antiseptics were still unknown, and a perennial shortage of anesthetics meant that amputations were frequently conducted without it. Union soldiers did gain some access to better medical care from the **U.S. Sanitary Commission**, which was established by the federal government in June 1861 to improve and coordinate the medical care of Union soldiers. Nonetheless, a commentator accurately described most field hospitals as "dirty dens of butchery and horror."

The need to bury the dead after battle was also a gruesome task. Early in the war, officers and enlisted men tried to recover and bury individual remains, but this practice proved unfeasible given the vast numbers killed. Instead, mass graves provided the final resting place for many soldiers on both sides. As the horrors of battle sank in and enlisted men discovered the inadequacies of food, sanitation, and medical care, large numbers of soldiers deserted. As the number of volunteers declined and the number of deserters rose, both the Confederate and the Union governments were eventually forced to institute conscription laws to draft men into service.

Explore

See Document 13.4 for an example of how photography brought the horrors of war home to civilians.

The Northern Economy Booms

As the war dragged on, the North's economic advantages became more apparent. The Union could provide more arms, food, and clothing to its troops and more of the necessities of life for families back home. Indeed, the Civil War quickened the industrial development of the North that had begun in the early nineteenth century. By 1860 manufacturing establishments in the region outnumbered those in the South six to one, with 1.3 million industrial workers in the North compared with only 110,000 in the South. Northern factories flourished as they turned out weapons, ammunition, blankets, clothing, and shoes, and shipyards built the fleets that blockaded southern ports.

Initially, the effects of the war on northern industry were little short of disastrous. Raw cotton for textiles was no longer available, southern planters stopped ordering shoes, and trade fell off precipitously in seaport cities. By 1863, however, the economic picture had improved dramatically. Coal mining and iron production boomed in Pennsylvania. In New England, woolen manufacturing replaced cotton, and the shoe industry thrived on orders from the army. Merchants dealing in war materiel made particularly handsome profits.

The economic boom was linked to a vast expansion in the federal government's activities. Direct orders from the War Office for blankets, firearms, boots, and other goods fueled the industrial surge. The government also granted large contracts to northern railroads to carry troops and supplies. With southern Democrats out of federal office, Congress increased the protection of northern industries by passing a steep tariff on imported manufactured goods. The government also hired thousands of "sewing women," who worked under contract in their homes (often in crowded tenements) to make uniforms for Union soldiers. Other women joined the federal labor force as clerical workers, who sustained the expanding bureaucracy by handling the increasing amounts of government-generated paperwork.

That paperwork multiplied exponentially when the federal government created a national currency and a national banking system. Before the Civil War, private banks (chartered by the states) issued their own banknotes, which were used in most economic transactions. During the war, Congress revolutionized this system, giving the federal government the power to create currency, issue federal charters to banks, and take on national debt (which totaled $2 billion by the war's end). The government used its new powers to flood the nation with treasury bills, commonly called **greenbacks**. The federal budget mushroomed as well—from $63 million in 1860 to nearly $1.3 billion in 1865. By the end of the war, the federal bureaucracy had grown to be the nation's largest single employer.

These federal initiatives provided a tremendous stimulus to industry, and northern manufacturers greeted them, on the whole, with enthusiasm. But they faced one daunting problem: a shortage of labor. Over half a million workers left their jobs to serve in the Union army, and others were hired by the expanding federal bureaucracy. Manufacturers dealt with the labor shortage primarily by mechanizing more tasks and by increasing the employment of native-born women and children and recently arrived immigrants. Mechanization advanced quickly in the clothing and shoe industries, allowing more jobs to be filled by unskilled or semiskilled workers. Industrialists also formed organizations such as the Boston Foreign

DOCUMENT 13.4

Timothy H. O'Sullivan | Burial of Federal Dead, Fredericksburg, Virginia, May 1864

As the first war to be photographed extensively, the Civil War offered civilians new perspectives on the horrors of battle. Exhibited in the studios of photographers such as Mathew Brady in New York City, urban residents could view the carnage of war in stunning detail. This image was taken by Timothy H. O'Sullivan, an Irish-born photographer who worked with Brady after serving in the Union army. It captures a Union burial team near Fredericksburg during a period of intense fighting in northern Virginia.

Explore

Why were black Union soldiers, like those pictured here, often assigned to bury the dead?

How does this photograph represent the boundary between the battlefront and the home front?

What does this image suggest about the different experiences of officers and enlisted men even after death?

Library of Congress

Put It in Context

How might images such as this one affect civilian attitudes toward the war?

Emigrant Aid Society to encourage European migration, which had fallen off sharply in the first two years of the war. By 1863 the number of immigrants—mostly Irish, German, and British—had reached pre-1860 levels and continued to increase. Combining the lower wages paid to women and immigrants with production speedups, manufacturers improved their profits while advancing the Union cause.

Urbanization and Industrialization in the South

Although Southerners had gone to war to protect an essentially rural lifestyle, several factors encouraged the growth of industry and cities during the war. The creation of a large governmental and military bureaucracy brought thousands of Southerners to the Confederate capital of Richmond. Refugees merely trickled into cities during the early years of the war, but by 1863 they were flooding Atlanta, Savannah, and Mobile.

Industrialization also contributed to urban growth. Military necessity spurred southern industrialization. At the beginning of the war, the South contained only 15 percent of the factories in the United States. But unable to buy industrial goods from the North and limited in its trade with Europe, the South was forced to industrialize. By January 1863, the huge Tredegar Iron Works in Richmond employed more than 2,500 men, black and white. A factory to produce cannons opened in Selma, Alabama, where more than 10,000 people worked in war industries. According to a local newspaper, clothing and shoe factories had "sprung up almost like magic" in Natchez and Jackson, Mississippi. War widows and orphans, enslaved blacks, and white men too old or injured to fight were recruited for industrial labor in many cities.

The vast expansion of the South's cities and industry enhanced class consciousness during the war. When Virginia legislators introduced a bill in the fall of 1863 to control food prices, Richmond workers hailed it by voicing their resentment toward the rich. "From the fact that he consumes all and produces nothing," they proclaimed, "we know that without [our] labor and production the man with money could not exist." Workers also criticized lavish balls hosted by the wives of wealthy industrialists, planters, and politicians during the war. Women like Mary Boykin Chesnut, a planter's wife, insisted that such events were necessary to maintain morale and demonstrate that the South was far from defeated. But the *Richmond Enquirer* captured the views of the laboring class, arguing that these events were "shameful displays of indifference to national calamity . . . a mockery of the misery and desolation that covers the land."

Women Aid the War Effort

Women of all classes contributed to the Union and Confederate war effort in numerous ways. Thousands filled jobs in agriculture, industry, and the government that were traditionally held by men. Others sought to assist the war effort more directly, by serving as nurses, spies, couriers, or soldiers; gathering supplies; and lobbying to influence government policies. Although Rose Greenhow and a few other women were recruited as spies early in the conflict, most military and political officials initially opposed women's direct engagement in the war. Yet so many women organized relief efforts early on that the federal government organized the U.S. Sanitary Commission to coordinate their efforts. By 1862 tens of thousands of women had volunteered funds and assistance through hundreds of local chapters across the North and Midwest. They hosted fund-raising fairs, coordinated sewing and knitting circles, rolled bandages, and sent supplies to the front lines. With critical shortages of medical staff, some female nurses and doctors eventually gained acceptance in northern hospitals and field camps. Led by such memorable figures as Clara Barton, Mary Ann "Mother" Bickerdyke, and Dr. Mary Walker, northern women almost entirely replaced men as military nurses by the end of the war.

In the South, too, much of the medical care was performed by women. But without a government-sanctioned body to coordinate efforts and lobby for resources, women were left largely to their own devices, and nursing was never recognized as a legitimate profession for them. As a result, a Confederate soldier's chances of dying from wounds or disease were even greater than those of his Union counterpart. Nonetheless, southern women worked tirelessly to supply soldiers with clothes, blankets, munitions, and food. But this work, too, was often performed locally and by individuals rather than as part of a coordinated Confederate effort. For example, Ann Cobb, the wife of a Georgia officer, went door-to-door among neighbors to gather provisions for her husband's eighty-man unit.

Some Union and Confederate women played even more unusual roles in the war. A few dozen women joined Greenhow in gathering information for military and political authorities. One of the most effective on the Union side was the former fugitive Harriet Tubman. She worked as a spy in South Carolina from 1862 to 1864 and regularly secured military intelligence from slaves living behind Confederate lines. Even more women served as couriers, carrying messages across battle lines to alert officers of critical changes in military orders or in the opponent's position. In addition, at least four hundred women disguised themselves as men and fought as soldiers; the identities of many were discovered only after they were wounded in battle.

Dr. Mary E. Walker

Dr. Mary E. Walker received her medical degree from Syracuse Medical College and became the first female army surgeon. Wearing bloomers (pants under a skirt), she assisted soldiers and civilians in numerous battlefield areas. Captured by Confederate troops in 1864, Walker soon returned to Union ranks. She was the first woman awarded the Medal of Honor for military service.   Library of Congress

Finally, abolitionist women sought to influence federal wartime policies. Following the Emancipation Proclamation, Elizabeth Cady Stanton, Susan B. Anthony, and Lucy Stone founded the **Women's National Loyal League** and launched a massive petition drive to broaden Lincoln's policy. Collecting 260,000 signatures, two-thirds of them from women, the League demanded a congressional act "emancipating all persons of African descent" everywhere in the nation.

Dissent and Protest in the Midst of War

While the Women's National Loyal League lobbied Congress for universal emancipation, other Northerners wondered whether defeating the Confederacy was worth the cost. Families were hard hit as wages fell and prices rose, and many Northerners cared more about the safe return of their husbands and sons than the fate of slavery. As the war dragged on, these concerns led to a rising tide of dissent and protest.

Despite the expanding economy, northern farmers and workers suffered tremendously during the war. Women, children, and old men took over much of the field labor in the Midwest, trying to feed their families and produce sufficient surplus to supply the army and pay their mortgages and other expenses. In the East, too, inflation eroded the earnings of factory workers, servants, and day laborers. As federal greenbacks flooded the market and military production took priority over consumer goods, prices climbed about 20 percent faster than wages. While industrialists garnered huge profits, railroad stocks leaped to unheard-of prices, and government contractors made huge gains, ordinary workers suffered. A group of Cincinnati seamstresses complained to President Lincoln in 1864 about employers "who fatten on their contracts by grinding immense profits out of the labor of their operatives." Although Republicans pledged to protect the rights of workers, employers successfully lobbied a number of state legislatures to pass laws prohibiting strikes. The federal government, too, proved a better friend to business than to labor. When workers at the Parrott arms factory in Cold Spring, New York, struck for higher wages in 1864, the government sent in troops, declared martial law, and arrested the strike leaders.

Discontent intensified when the Republican Congress passed a draft law in March 1863. The **Enrollment Act** provided for draftees to be selected by an impartial lottery, but a loophole allowed a person with $300 to pay the government in place of serving or to hire another man as a substitute. Many workers deeply resented the draft law's profound inequality. Some also opposed the emancipation of slaves who, they assumed, would compete for scarce jobs once the war ended.

Dissent turned to violence in July 1863 when the new draft law went into effect. Riots broke out in cities across the North. In New York City, where inflation caused tremendous suffering and a large immigrant population solidly supported the Democratic machine, implementation of the draft triggered four days of the worst rioting Americans had ever seen. Women and men—many of them Irish and German immigrants—attacked Protestant missionaries, Republican draft officials, and wealthy businessmen. Homes in wealthy neighborhoods were looted, but the free black community became the rioters' main target. Rioters lynched at least a dozen African Americans and looted and burned the city's Colored Orphan Asylum. The violence ended only when Union

New York City Draft Riots, July 1863

Between July 13 and 16, 1863, riots broke out in New York City against the Enrollment Act. Blaming African Americans for the war, working-class mobs lynched, beat, and mutilated dozens of black men. At least 120 civilians were killed and another 2,000 injured. This illustration shows the *New York Tribune*, an abolitionist newspaper, under attack from rioters. Federal troops were eventually called in to restore peace.   Private Collection/Peter Newark American Pictures/The Bridgeman Art Library

troops put down the riot by force. By then, more than one hundred New Yorkers lay dead.

A more prolonged battle raged in Missouri, where Confederate sympathizers never reconciled themselves to living in a Union state. From the beginning of this "inner civil war," prosouthern residents formed militias and staged guerrilla attacks on Union supporters. The militias, with the tacit support of Confederate officials, claimed thousands of lives and forced the Union army to station troops in the area. The militia members hoped that Midwesterners, weary of the conflicts, would elect peace Democrats and end the war.

Northern Democrats saw the widening unrest as a political opportunity. Although some Democratic leaders supported the war effort, many others—whom opponents called **Copperheads**, after the poisonous snake—rallied behind Ohio politician Clement L. Vallandigham in opposing the war. Presenting themselves as the "peace party," these Democrats enjoyed considerable success in eastern cities where inflation was rampant and immigrant workers were caught between low wages and military service. The party was also strong in parts of the Midwest where sympathy for the southern cause and antipathy to African Americans ran deep.

In the South, too, some whites expressed growing dissatisfaction with the war. In April 1862, Jefferson Davis had signed the first conscription act in U.S. history, inciting widespread opposition. The concept of a national draft undermined the southern tradition of states' rights. As in the North, men could hire a substitute if they had enough money, and an October 1862 law exempted men owning twenty or more slaves from military service. Although the exemption was supposedly a response to growing

unruliness among slaves in the absence of masters, in practice it meant that large planters, many of whom served in the Confederate legislature, had exempted themselves from fighting. As one Alabama farmer fumed, "All they want is to get you pumpt up and go to fight for their infernal negroes, and after you do their fighting you may kiss their hine parts for all they care."

Small farmers were also hard hit by policies that allowed the Confederate army to take whatever supplies it needed. The army's forced acquisition of farm produce intensified food shortages that had been building since early in the war. The southern economy was rooted in cash crops rather than foodstuffs. Quantities of grain and livestock were produced in South Carolina, central Virginia, and central Tennessee, but by 1863 the latter two areas had fallen under Union control. The Union blockade of port cities and the lack of an extensive railroad or canal system in the South limited the distribution of what food was available. Hungry residents of the Shenandoah Valley discovered that despite military victories there, food shortages worsened as Confederate troops ravaged the countryside.

Food shortages drove up prices on basic items like bread and corn, while the Union blockade and the focus on military needs dramatically increased the price of other consumer goods. As the Confederate government issued more and more treasury notes to finance the war, inflation soared 2,600 percent in less than three years. Food riots, often led by women, broke out in cities across the South, including the Confederate capital of Richmond.

Conscription, food shortages, and inflation took their toll on support for the Confederacy. The devastation of the war itself added to these grievances. Most battles were fought in the Upper South or along the Confederacy's western frontier, where small farmers saw their crops, animals, and fields destroyed. A phrase that had seemed cynical in 1862—"A rich man's war and a poor man's fight"—became the rallying cry of the southern peace movement in 1864. The Washington Constitutional Union, a secret peace society with a large following among farmers, elected several members to the Confederate Congress. Another secret organization centered in North Carolina took more drastic measures, providing Union forces with information on southern troop movements and encouraging desertion by Confederates. In mountainous regions of the South, draft evaders and deserters formed guerrilla groups that attacked draft officials and actively impeded the war effort. In western North Carolina, some women hid deserters, raided grain depots, and burned the property of Confederate officials.

When slaveholders led the South out of the Union in 1861, they had assumed the loyalty of yeomen farmers, the deference of southern ladies, and the privileges of the southern way of life. Far from preserving social harmony and social order, however, the war undermined ties between elite and poor Southerners, between planters and small farmers, and between women and men. Although most white Southerners still supported the Confederacy in 1864 and internal dissent alone did not lead to defeat, it did weaken the ties that bound soldiers to their posts in the final two years of the war.

REVIEW & RELATE

What were the short- and long-term economic effects of the war on the North?

How did the war change the southern economy? What social tensions did the war create in the South?

LEARNINGCurve bedfordstmartins.com/hewittlawson/LC

The Tide of War Turns

In the spring of 1863, Lee's army defeated a Union force twice its size at Chancellorsville, Virginia, setting the stage for a Confederate thrust into Pennsylvania. Yet Lee's decision to go on the offensive ultimately proved the Confederacy's undoing. Even as draft riots erupted across the North in July 1863, the Union won two decisive military victories: at Gettysburg, Pennsylvania, and Vicksburg, Mississippi. These victories improved northern morale while devastating Confederate hopes. At the same

time, the flood of African Americans, including former slaves, into the Union army transformed the very meaning of the war. In late 1864 and early 1865, the momentum favored the Union, and the South was forced to consider prospects for peace.

Key Victories for the Union

In mid-1863, Confederate commanders believed the tide was turning in their favor. Following victories at Fredericksburg and Chancellorsville, General Lee launched an invasion of northern territory. While the Union army maneuvered to protect Washington, D.C., from Lee's advance, General Joseph Hooker resigned as head of the Union army. When Lincoln appointed George A. Meade as the new Union commander, the general immediately faced a major engagement at **Gettysburg**, Pennsylvania. If Confederates won a victory there, European countries might finally recognize the southern nation and force the North to accept peace.

Neither Lee nor Meade set out to launch a battle in this small Pennsylvania town. But Lee was afraid of outrunning his supply lines, and Meade wanted to keep Confederates from gaining control of the roads that crossed at Gettysburg. So on July 1, fighting commenced, with Lee pushing Union forces to the south of town. The Union vanguard managed to hold the ground along Cemetery Ridge until more troops arrived the following day. Although Confederate troops suffered heavy losses on July 2, Lee believed that Union forces were spread thin and ordered General George Pickett to launch a frontal assault on July 3 (Map 13.2). But Pickett's men were mowed down as they crossed an open field. The battle was a disaster for the South: More than 4,700 Confederates were killed, including a large number of officers; another 18,000 were wounded, captured, or missing. Although the Union suffered similar casualties, it had more men to lose, and it could claim victory.

As a grieving Lee retreated to Virginia, the South suffered another devastating defeat. Troops under General Ulysses S. Grant had been pounding Vicksburg, Mississippi, for months. In May 1863, Grant sent his men in a wide arc around the city and attacked from the east, setting the stage for a six-week siege. Although civilians refused to leave and even hid out in caves to outlast the Union barrage, Confederate troops were forced to surrender the city on July 4. This victory was even more important strategically than Gettysburg (Map 13.2). Combined with a victory five days later at Port Hudson, Louisiana, the Union army now controlled the entire Mississippi valley, the richest plantation region in the South. This series of victories also effectively cut off the Confederacy from Louisiana, Arkansas, and Texas, ensuring Union control of the West. In

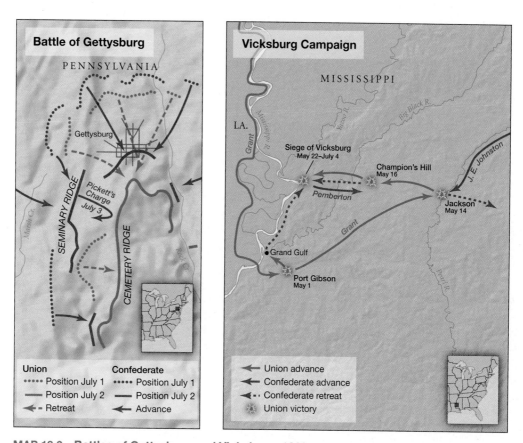

MAP 13.2 Battles of Gettysburg and Vicksburg, 1863

The three-day battle in Gettysburg and the six-week siege of Vicksburg led to critical victories for the Union. Together, these victories forced General Lee's troops back into Confederate territory and gave the Union control of the Mississippi River. Still, the war was far from over. Confederate troops controlled the southern heartland, and Northerners wearied of the ever-increasing casualties.

November 1863, Grant's troops achieved a major victory at Chattanooga, opening up much of the South's remaining territory to invasion. Thousands of slaves deserted their plantations, and many joined the Union war effort.

As 1864 dawned, the Union had twice as many forces in the field as the Confederacy, whose soldiers were suffering from low morale, high mortality, and dwindling supplies. Although some difficult battles still lay ahead, the war of attrition (in which the larger, better-supplied Union forces slowly wore down their Confederate opponents) had begun to pay dividends.

The changing Union fortunes increased support for Lincoln and his congressional allies. Union victories and the Emancipation Proclamation also convinced Great Britain not to recognize the Confederacy as an independent nation. And the heroics of African American soldiers, who in 1863 engaged in direct and often brutal combat against southern troops, encouraged wider support for emancipation. Republicans, who now fully embraced abolition as a war aim, were nearly assured the presidency and a congressional majority in the 1864 elections.

Northern Democrats still campaigned for peace and the readmission of Confederate states with slavery intact. They nominated George B. McClellan, the onetime Union commander, as their candidate for president. McClellan attracted working-class and immigrant voters who traditionally supported the Democrats and who bore the heaviest burdens of the war. But Democratic hopes for victory in November were crushed when Union general William Tecumseh Sherman captured Atlanta, Georgia, just two months before the election. Lincoln and the Republicans won easily, giving the party a clear mandate to continue the war to its conclusion.

African Americans Contribute to Victory

Lincoln's election secured the eventual downfall of slavery. Yet neither the president nor Congress eradicated human bondage on their own. From the fall of 1862 on, African Americans enlisted in the Union army and helped ensure that nothing short of universal emancipation would be the outcome of the war. By the spring of 1865, nearly 200,000

The 107th U.S. Colored Infantry Band

The 107th U.S. Colored Infantry Band was photographed at Fort Corcoran in Arlington, Virginia. These 20 African American soldiers with their musical instruments were among the nearly 200,000 black men who volunteered for military service and served as soldiers and sailors to prove their manhood and their worthiness for full citizenship. Some 37,000 black soldiers died during the Civil War. Library of Congress

African Americans were serving in the Union army and navy. Private Thomas Long, a former slave serving with the First South Carolina Volunteers, explained the connection between African American enlistment and emancipation: "If we hadn't become sojers, all might have gone back as it was before; our freedom might have slipped through de two houses of Congress and President Linkum's four years might have passed by and notin' been done for us. But now tings can neber go back, because we have showed our energy and our courage and our naturally manhood."

In the border states, which were exempt from the Emancipation Proclamation, enslaved men were adamant about enlisting since those who served in the Union army were granted their freedom. Because of this provision, slaveholders in the border states did everything in their power to prevent their slaves from joining the army, including assault and even murder. Despite these efforts, between 25 and 60 percent of military-age enslaved men in the four border states joined the Union army and quickly distinguished themselves in battle. By the end of the war, approximately 37,000 black soldiers had given their lives for freedom and the Union.

Yet despite their courage and commitment, black soldiers felt the sting of racism. They were segregated in camps, given the most menial jobs, and often treated as inferiors by white recruits and officers. Many blacks, for instance, were assigned the gruesome and exhausting task of burying the dead after grueling battles in which they had fought alongside whites. Particularly galling was the Union policy of paying black soldiers less than whites were paid. African American soldiers openly protested this discrimination even after a black sergeant who voiced his views was charged with mutiny and executed by firing squad in February 1864. An African American corporal wrote to Lincoln, describing the blood black troops had shed for the Union and asking, "We have done a Soldier's Duty. Why can't we have a Soldier's pay?" The War Department finally equalized wages in June 1864.

One of African American soldiers' primary concerns was to liberate slaves as Union armies moved deeper into the South. During 1863 and 1864, thousands more slaves headed for Union lines, joining the "contraband" who had escaped earlier in the war. Even those forced to remain on plantations realized that Union troops and freedom were headed their way. In areas close to Union lines, they talked openly of the advancing army. "Now they gradually threw off the mask," a slave remembered of this moment, "and were not afraid to let it be known that the 'freedom' in their songs meant freedom of the body in this world."

The Final Battles and the Promise of Peace

In the spring of 1864, the war entered its final stage. That March, Lincoln placed General Grant in charge of all Union forces, and he embarked on a strategy of **total war**, including attacks against civilian as well as military targets. Grant was willing to accept huge casualties in order to achieve victory. Over the next year, he led his troops overland through western Virginia in an effort to take Richmond. At the same time, he ordered General Sherman to head south through Georgia, destroying the remnants of the plantation system.

Grant's troops headed toward Richmond, where Lee's army controlled strong defensive positions. The Confederates won narrow victories in May 1864 at the Battles of the Wilderness and Spotsylvania Court House. In June, 7,000 Union soldiers were killed in one hour during a frontal assault at Cold Harbor, Virginia, where Confederates once again turned back the Union army. But Grant continued to push forward. Although Lee lost fewer men (31,000 casualties at Cold Harbor versus 55,000 for the Union), his army was melting away with each so-called victory.

The battles took a terrible toll on soldiers on both sides. Union troops and civilians called Grant "the butcher" for his seeming lack of regard for human life. Grant, however, was not deterred. He laid siege to Petersburg in June 1864, where both sides lived in trenches and tunnels for months on end. That August, Sherman also laid siege to Atlanta, but on September 2 he ordered his troops out of the trenches, swept around the city, and destroyed the roads and rails that connected it to the rest of the Confederacy. When General John B. Hood and his southern troops abandoned their posts, Sherman telegraphed Lincoln: "Atlanta is ours, and fairly won." The victory cut the South in two.

Sherman then led his troops on a 300-mile march to the Atlantic coast and north through the Carolinas. Embracing the strategy of total war, his troops cut a path of destruction 50 miles wide during their "March to the Sea," destroying crops, livestock, and houses before they reached Savannah in late December. Nearly 18,000 enslaved men, women, and children left the ruined plantations and sought to join Sherman's victorious troops. To the fleeing slaves' dismay, soldiers refused to take them along. Worse, some Union soldiers abused African American men, raped black women, or stole their few possessions. Angry Confederates captured many of those who were turned away, killing some and reenslaving others.

Richmond in Ruins, April 1865

This photograph captures the devastation the war brought to the Richmond and Petersburg Railroad Depot after General Grant drove General Lee's troops out of the Confederate capital in April 1865. This defining moment marked the end of the Civil War and the defeat of the South. During the next decade, the North and South struggled over reconfiguring the Union.   Library of Congress

Explore

See Document 13.5 for a description of the destruction of Columbia, South Carolina.

Sherman's callous actions caused a scandal in Washington. In January 1865, Lincoln dispatched Secretary of War Edwin Stanton to Georgia to investigate the charges. At an extraordinary meeting in Savannah, Stanton and Sherman met with black ministers to hear their complaints and to ask what newly emancipated African Americans wanted. The ministers spoke movingly of the war lifting "the yoke of bondage." Freed blacks, they argued, "could reap the fruit of their own labor" and, if given land, "take care of ourselves, and assist the Government in maintaining our freedom." In response, Sherman issued **Field Order Number 15**, setting aside more than 400,000 acres of captured Confederate land to be divided into small plots for former slaves. Although

Sherman's order proved highly controversial, it suggested that the Civil War might, in the end, be a revolutionary force for change.

As defeat loomed, even Confederate leaders began to talk of emancipating the slaves. Jefferson Davis called for recruiting slaves into the army, with their payment to include freedom for themselves and their families. The Confederate Congress passed such a law in early 1865, but it was too late to make any difference. Still, the very idea suggested that the Civil War had turned southern society upside down.

In early April 1865, with Sherman heading toward Raleigh, North Carolina, Grant captured Petersburg and then drove Lee and his forces out of Richmond. In one of the war's most dramatic moments, seasoned African American troops led the final assault on the city and were among the first Union soldiers to enter the Confederate capital. On April 9, after a brief engagement at

---

DOCUMENT 13.5

Eleanor Cohen Seixas | Journal Entry, February 1865

In February 1865, General Sherman and his men reached Columbia, South Carolina, intent on destroying as much property as possible. Thousands of residents fled the Columbia fires, including Philip and Cordelia Cohen and their daughter, Eleanor. Philip was a pharmacist, slave owner, and part of the state's small Jewish population. During the war, he moved his family to Columbia to find safety in the city. Eleanor recorded the trials of wartime and her hopes for southern victory in her journal. In this selection, she describes the arrival of Sherman's troops.

Explore

The fire raged fearfully all night, but on Saturday perfect quiet reigned. The vile Yankees took from us clothing, food, jewels, all our cows, horses, carriages, etc., and left us in a deplorable condition after stealing from us. Sherman, with great generosity, presented the citizens with 500 cattle, so poor they could hardly stand up. No words of mine can give any idea of the brutality of the ruffians. They swore, they cussed, plundered, and committed every excess. No age or sex was safe from them. Sometimes, after saving some valueless token, it was ruthlessly

snatched from our hands by some of their horde. Our noble women were insulted by words, and some, I have heard of, in deeds, but none came under my knowledge, for I myself, God be praised, I received no rude word from any of them. I did not speak . . . to them at all. The fire burned eighty-four squares, and nothing can tell the quantity of plunder they carried off as on Monday they left us, and though we feared starvation, yet we were glad to be rid of them.

Source: Jacob R. Marcus, ed., *Memoirs of American Jews, 1775–1885* (Philadelphia: Jewish Publication Society of America, 1955), 3:363.

Interpret the Evidence

- What does this journal entry reveal about how Southerners viewed the Union army?
- What insight does it provide into how Union soldiers felt about the South?

Put It in Context

What impact did Sherman's march have on Southerners' morale?

Appomattox Court House, Virginia, Lee surrendered to Grant with fewer than 30,000 soldiers remaining under his command. Within hours, his troops began heading home. Although Confederate soldiers continued to engage Union forces in North Carolina and west of the Mississippi, the Civil War, for all intents and purposes, had come to an end.

The legal abolition of slavery was initiated in Washington a few months before Lee's surrender. Following on the petitions submitted by the Women's National Loyal League, Congress passed the **Thirteenth Amendment** to the U.S. Constitution on January 31, 1865, prohibiting slavery and involuntary servitude anywhere in the United States. Although it still required approval by three-quarters of the states, wartime experiences made ratification likely. Some states and cities had already enacted laws to ease racial inequities. Ohio, California, and Illinois repealed statutes barring blacks from testifying in court and serving on juries. San Francisco, Cincinnati, Cleveland, and New York City desegregated their streetcars. In May 1865, Massachusetts passed the first comprehensive public-accommodations law in U.S. history, ensuring equal treatment in theaters, stores, schools, and other social spaces. With the final surrender of the Confederacy, many Northerners were hopeful that the nation reunited would be stronger and more just.

REVIEW & RELATE

- What role did African Americans play in the defeat of the South?
- How did the Union win the war? How did attitudes toward African Americans change in the final year of the war?

LEARNINGCurve bedfordstmartins.com/hewittlawson/LC

Conclusion: An Uncertain Future

Jubilation in the North did not last long. On April 14, less than a week after Lee's surrender, Abraham Lincoln was shot at Ford's Theatre by a Confederate fanatic named John Wilkes Booth. The president died the next day, leading to an outpouring of grief across the North and leaving the entire nation in shock.

Lincoln left behind an incredible legacy. He had led the Union to victory in a devastating civil war, promulgated the Emancipation Proclamation, and resolved the conflict between competing systems based on slavery and free labor. More than 600,000 Americans died in the war, but nearly 4 million Americans who had been born enslaved were now free. At the same time, northern and southern women had entered the labor force and the public arena in numbers never before imagined. Soldiers returned to their families, jobs, and communities with experiences and knowledge, but also with physical and emotional wounds that transformed their lives. And the federal government had extended its reach into more and more areas of daily life. The war had dramatically accelerated the pace of economic, political, and social change, transforming American society both during the war and afterward.

Still, the legacies of the war were far from certain in 1865. Defeated Southerners looked for heroes, and most considered Confederate generals the greatest representatives of the "Lost Cause." They honored Lee and his officers with statues, portraits, poems, and parades. Confederate women worked endlessly to preserve the memory of both military leaders and ordinary soldiers. They formed memorial associations to decorate cemeteries and promoted a southern perspective on the war in schools and history books. They also joined in paying tribute to heroines like Rose O'Neal Greenhow. Greenhow had traveled to England and France in 1863, promoting Confederate bond issues and publishing a book about her imprisonment under "abolition rule." On her return in August 1864, the British vessel she was on was pursued by federal ships blockading the harbor. Fearing capture, Greenhow insisted that she be rowed ashore carrying a bag of gold coins, the profits from her book. But the boat overturned in high seas, and Greenhow drowned. She was buried with full military honors in Wilmington, North Carolina.

Victorious Northerners had far more reason to celebrate, but they knew that much still needed to be done. Frederick Douglass was thrilled that slavery had been abolished, but he argued vehemently that "the work of Abolitionists is not done." He was deeply committed to the enfranchisement of African American men as the means to secure the rights of former slaves, for he had no illusions about the lengths to which many whites would go to protect their traditional privileges. Although Douglass considered the Republican Party the best hope for reconstructing the nation, not everyone shared his agenda. Some white abolitionists argued that their work was done; some women's rights advocates thought they were as entitled to voting rights as were black men; some militant blacks viewed the Republican Party as too moderate. Moreover, many northern whites were exhausted by four years of war and hoped to leave the problems of slavery and secession behind. Others wanted to rebuild the South quickly in order to ensure the nation's economic recovery. These competing visions—between Northerners and Southerners and within each group—would shape the promises of peace in ways few could imagine at the end of the war.

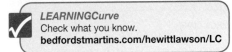

Chapter Review

Online Study Guide ▶ bedfordstmartins.com/hewittlawson

KEY TERMS

Fort Sumter (p. 395)
contraband (p. 399)
Battle of Shiloh (p. 402)
Emancipation Proclamation (p. 403)
U.S. Sanitary Commission (p. 405)
greenbacks (p. 405)
Women's National Loyal League (p. 408)
Enrollment Act (p. 408)
Copperheads (p. 409)
Gettysburg (p. 410)
total war (p. 413)
Field Order Number 15 (p. 414)
Thirteenth Amendment (p. 415)

REVIEW AND RELATE

1. What steps did Lincoln take to prevent war? Why were they ineffective?

2. What advantages and disadvantages did each side have at the onset of the war?

3. What arguments did each side make in the debate over African American enlistment in the Union army?

4. How and why did the Civil War become a war to end slavery?

5. What were the short- and long-term economic effects of the war on the North?

6. How did the war change the southern economy? What social tensions did the war create in the South?

7. What role did African Americans play in the defeat of the South?

8. How did the Union win the war? How did attitudes toward African Americans change in the final year of the war?

TIMELINE OF EVENTS

1845	Frederick Douglass publishes *Narrative of the Life of Frederick Douglass*
April 14, 1861	Fort Sumter surrenders to Confederate forces
May 23, 1861	General Benjamin Butler declares escaped slaves "contraband"
June 1861	U.S. Sanitary Commission established
July 21, 1861	First Battle of Bull Run (Manassas)
August 6, 1861	Confiscation Act passed
April 1862	Slavery abolished in the District of Columbia
	Battle of Shiloh
	Jefferson Davis signs conscription act
June 1862	Rose O'Neal Greenhow exiled to the South
September 1862	Battle of Antietam
	Lincoln issues preliminary Emancipation Proclamation
January 1, 1863	Lincoln signs Emancipation Proclamation
March 1863	Enrollment Act passed in North
July 1863	Draft riots in New York City
	Battle of Gettysburg
	Battle of Vicksburg
September 2, 1864	Atlanta falls; Sherman begins "March to the Sea"
1865	200,000 African Americans serving in the Union army and navy
January 1865	Sherman issues Field Order Number 15
January 31, 1865	Congress passes Thirteenth Amendment
April 9, 1865	General Lee surrenders to General Grant at Appomattox Court House
April 14, 1865	Assassination of President Abraham Lincoln

DOCUMENT PROJECT 13

Civil War Letters

Throughout the Civil War, many soldiers and their families kept in close touch by writing letters. The volume of wartime correspondence was immense, with ninety thousand letters a day processed in the Union alone. Letters from soldiers often described the boredom of encampments, the excitement or horrors of battle, and worries about their families back home (Document 13.7). Soldiers' letters also expressed their views on the causes of the war and sometimes their changing understandings of the war's meaning (Documents 13.6 and 13.10). Nurses provided another dramatic perspective on the war (Document 13.9), and letters from families revealed the experiences, as well as frustrations, of life on the home front. While many parents, spouses, and children of soldiers wrote letters to bolster the spirits of men at the front, they also expressed the heartbreak of separation and the problems experienced by families and local communities, including shortages of food and labor and spiraling inflation (Document 13.8). Regardless of the content, correspondence helped families maintain connections during soldiers' lengthy tours of duty. For historians, these letters are a unique window into the everyday lives of soldiers and their families during the Civil War.

The letters reprinted here, from both Northerners and Southerners, represent an array of experiences, including those of soldiers and civilians, women and men, blacks and whites. Written between April 1861 (Document 13.6) and November 1864 (Document 13.8), they also help us trace transformations in the North and South over the course of the war. As you read them, think about the usefulness of letters as primary sources. What common themes emerge in these letters? How do the letter writers feel about the larger significance of the Civil War? How do their feelings about the war change over time? What can we learn about the war from these letters?

DOCUMENT 13.6

Fred Spooner | Letter to His Brother Henry, April 30, 1861

At the start of the war, many Northerners expected a quick victory, as evidenced in this letter written by Fred Spooner to his older brother Henry. A native of Providence, Rhode Island, Fred believed the South was weakened by its reliance on slavery. Perhaps inspired by these same beliefs, Henry enlisted in the Union army in 1862. Henry later practiced law in Rhode Island and served in the U.S. House of Representatives.

Dear Henry,

Your letter was received, and I now sit down in my shirt sleeves (as it is warm) to write in return.

For the last few weeks there has been great excitement here, and nothing has been thought of scarcely except that one subject which now received the undivided attention of the whole loyal North—war.

And well may war, so hideous and disgusting in itself receive such attention when carried on for such noble and just principles as in the present case.

Traitors have begun the conflict, let us continue and end it. Let us settle it now, once and for all.

Let us settle it, even if the whole South has to be made one common graveyard, and their cotton soaked in blood. Let us do it *now* while the whole North is aroused from the inactivity and apparent laziness in which it has been so long.

There are plenty of men, an abundance of money, and a military enthusiasm never before known in the annals of history, all of which combined will do the work nice and clean, and if need be will wipe out that palmetto, pelican, rattlesnake region entirely. The holy cause in which our volunteers are enlisted will urge them on to almost super-human exertions. The South *may* be courageous but I doubt it, they can *gas* and *hag* [complain and bluster] first rate; they can lie and steal to perfection, but I really do believe that they cannot fight—"Barking dogs never bite." Southern senators can bluster, bully, and blackguard [verbally abuse], but I believe them to be cowards at heart. . . .

Besides the very nature of their country and their manner of living, have a tendency, I think, to make them otherwise than brave.

But granting them to be brave (which I don't believe can be proven) they have no chance to overturn this government. They haven't the resources, the "almighty dollar," that powerful ally, or formidable enemy—is against them. They have no money—their property has legs and will be continually disappearing.

They have prospered dealing in human flesh—let them now take the results of it.

They have had what *they* consider the *blessings* of slavery—let them now receive the *curses* of it.

They must be put down, conquered, and thoroughly subdued if need be. They have no earthly hope of overcoming this government. The fifteen weak states of the South can stand no chance against the nineteen powerful states of the North. . . .

When I began I did not intend to give a lecture or write a composition on the "crisis," and I had not as Mayor Knight [mayor of Providence] would say "made preparations for a speech," but unconsciously I got on the all-absorbing topic at the very commencement, and it was hard work to let go of it.

There hasn't been much studying lately, and it is very hard work to think or write concerning any other subject than that on which I've paused so long.

So therefore excuse my "crisis" beginning.

Source: Nina Silber and Mary Beth Sievens, eds., *Yankee Correspondence: Civil War Letters between New England Soldiers and the Home Front* (Charlottesville: University Press of Virginia, 1996), 55–56.

DOCUMENT 13.7

John Hines | Letter to His Parents, April 22, 1862

Confederate soldier John Hines describes the Battle of Shiloh in southwestern Tennessee in this letter written to his parents back home in Kentucky. The bloodiest battle up to that point in the war, Shiloh was also Hines's first combat experience. As was common for most soldiers on both sides of the conflict, Hines's early enthusiasm for the war and his opinion of the enemy changed with his first taste of battle.

Dear Ma and G. Pa

. . . I was in the battle of Shiloh from beginning to end. It is said to have been the hardest fought battle ever fought on this continent. Persons who were in the battles of Manassas and Ft. Donelson say they were skirmishes in comparison. . . .

Our squadron was ordered close to the federal lines on Saturday evening. We stopped close enough to hear their drums beating. We were very tired and hungry. Some of the men not having et [eaten] for 36 hours. I gave a teamster 50 cents for a biscuit. Tied my horse close to me and laid down without taking off boots or pistols and slept soundly until just at dawn the loud peal of some half dozen cannons aroused us. In a few moments we were in our saddles, overcoats and extra equipment lashed to our saddles. In our shirt sleeves, we sat on our horses examining our arms, ready for the coming fray, for we knew we would give the enemy battle if they would stand.

The increased roaring of artillery and an occasional ambulance bearing off wounded soldiers told that, as we say in camp, the ball was open. Before the sun was up we were marching to the scene of action, which was perhaps a mile off. We had not marched very far before we came upon our line of infantry. For three miles in one unbroken line stood our troops, their fixed bayonets glistening in the new sunbeams, for the sun was just coming over the top of a small elevation.

Almost every hill now on both sides looked like a volcano, for the deep mouthed cannon were roaring on every side. Soon the rattle of musketry announced that our vanguard had found the foe. The dark line of men now moved quickly in. After minutes more the volleys of musketry announced that they too had entered the bloody arena. It was really a grand scene now: you could not distinguish a musket shot now, it was one continual roar like the rushing of a storm. The thundering of the artillery at regular intervals alone disturbed the continual sounds. A shell or cannonball would tear some of your comrades to pieces and a person could not tell whose turn it might be next.

Being mounted and ordered to different places during the day, I had an opportunity to see everything that happened almost and I can assure you that a battlefield is far from being a pleasant place, laying aside the dangers of being hurt, because you can't get out of hearing the groans of the dying or out of sight of the dead. It seemed to me like my acquaintances were always lying in the most auspicious places. Turn what way we might I could find some ghastly looking face that perhaps an hour ago I had seen rushing to the contest with a smile on his face. I could not enumerate a hundredth part of the incidents of note that occurred during both days. . . .

We have again returned to camp which is now outside of the former federal [Union] lines and are resting quietly. I've a good slice of cheese and a can of oysters which I took out of a federal tent before setting fire to it. I have nothing to do but think over what has happened in the last few days. . . .

Your affectionate son,
J. H. Hines

Source: Rod Gragg, ed., *The Illustrated Confederate Reader* (New York: HarperCollins, 1989), 99–100.

DOCUMENT 13.8

Ginnie Ott | Letter to Enos Ott, November 21, 1864

The Ott family were longtime residents of Augusta County, Virginia. Union and Confederate forces had fought grueling battles in the region in 1862, but by the fall of 1864 the area was under firm Confederate control. However, the Confederate army regularly sent soldiers to confiscate crops, cattle, and other goods as the southern economy unraveled under the strain of war. In this letter, Ginnie Ott tells her husband Enos, stationed at Camp Lee in Richmond, about shortages in the area and encourages him to stay where he is rather than seek a transfer to a company closer to home.

Nov 21st 1864

My Dear Husband

I seat myself this morning to drop you a few lines, in answer to yours of the 15th. I was not at Pa's when they got the letter but they sent it to me the same day. I was glad to hear that you were well and hope when these few lines reach you, you may still be enjoying the best of health. Henry came home last night on a seven days furlough to gather up some provisions for the company he belongs to & to take down his cattle. Frank McNutt came with him. Henry has a bad cold & sore throat. Mag and Sister went to Staunton last Friday. I would have written and sent the letter by them but I sent with them for some things I was obliged to have and I thought I would not write until they would get back and see whether they could get the things or not. They got all I wanted except white flanel & I wish if you can get any in Richmond you would send me 4 or 5 yds. The calico you sent me came to hand all right; it is very pretty indeed. Mr. Row is at home now. He says he cannot make your boots without your measure. You will have to send it soon or he cannot make them atal [at all] as he expects to go to the army the ninth of next month. Mag went out last week to hunt the brandy & could not find it. She wishes to know where it is though I suppose she will say something about it in her letter. Sister wants to know what black calico is selling at down there. She wants to get a dress and there was but one peice in Staunton and it was very coarse. She says if [it] is not too dear she would [like] for you to get her a dress & she will pay you in silver if you wish it. There was three men here gathering the tithe corn [the 10 percent of crops requisitioned by the Confederate government] out of the field last week, and four men here yesterday trying to get wheat, and there are two wagons here now for the hay. I have not heard from Mr Newton yet whether he can let you have a hat or not. Pa will see about it and I will let you know. We will send you the things you wrote for as soon as we can. You spoke about getting before the board but I think if you have to stay in service you are as safe there as any place else. The men in the Valley have had some very hard marching to do lately. I believe I have no news to write. We are all well. Nothing more at present.

your affectionate Wife
Ginnie Ott

Source: Ginnie Ott to Enos Ott, November 21, 1864, The Valley of the Shadow: Augusta County, Virginia, Personal Papers, University of Virginia Library, http://valley.lib.virginia.edu/papers/A2909.

DOCUMENT 13.9

Katharine Prescott Wormeley | Letter to Her Mother, May 26, 1862

In 1861 the federal government created the U.S. Sanitary Commission to coordinate the efforts of female relief organizations and provide better medical care to Union soldiers. Throughout the North, women volunteered to collect and send money, medical supplies, and food to soldiers at the front. The commission also sent nurses to army camps, including volunteers such as British-born Katharine Prescott Wormeley, who lived in Rhode Island. In 1862 she worked as a nurse for the commission, transporting and caring for Union soldiers during the military campaign in Virginia. In this letter to her mother, she describes some of the difficulties of her work aboard hospital boats.

The boat had a little shelter-cabin. As we were laying mattresses on the floor, while the doctors were finding the men, the captain stopped us, refusing to let us put typhoid fever cases below the deck—on account of the crew, he said—and threatening to push off at once from the shore. Mrs. Griffin and I looked at him. I did the terrible, and she the pathetic; and he abandoned the contest. The return passage was rather an anxious one. The river is much obstructed with sunken ships and trees, and we had to feel our way, slackening speed every ten minutes. If we had been alone, it would not have mattered; but to have fifty men upon our hands unable to move was too heavy a responsibility not to make us anxious. The captain and pilot said the boat was leaking (we heard the water gurgling under our feet), and they remarked casually that the river was "four fathoms deep about there"; but we saw their motive, and were not scared. We were safe alongside the "Spaulding" by midnight; but Mr. Olmsted's tone of voice as he said, "You don't know how glad I am to see you," showed how much he had been worried. And yet it was the best thing we could have done, for three, perhaps five, of the men would have been dead before morning. We transferred the deck-men (who were not very ill) at once to the "Elm City," and kept the others on board the tug till the next morning (Sunday), when they were taken on board the "Spaulding," all living, and likely to live. Later in the day the "Spaulding" filled up to three hundred and fifty very sick men.

No one who has not shared them can form any idea of the hurry—unless it is kept down by extreme quiet of manner—and the solid hard work caused by this sudden influx of bad cases. Dr. Grymes taught me a valuable lesson the night I was at Yorktown on the "Webster." A man with a ghastly wound—the first I ever saw—asked for something; I turned hastily to get it, with some sort of exclamation. Dr. Grymes stopped me and said: "Never do that again; never be hurried or excited, or you are not fit to be here"; and I've thanked him for that lesson ever since. It is a piteous sight to see these men; no one knows what war is until they see this black side of it. We may all

(continued on page 422)

sentimentalize over its possibilities as we see the regiments go off, or when we hear of a battle; but it is as far from the reality as to read of pain is far from feeling it. We who are here, however, dare not let our minds, much less our imaginations, rest on suffering; while *you* must rely on your imagination to project you into the state of things here. . . .

I can give you *no* idea of the work thus accumulated into one day. But there were cheerful things in it after all. One thing I specially remember. A man very low with typhoid fever had been brought on board early in the afternoon, and begged me piteously to keep the bunk next him for his brother—his twin brother—from whom he had never been parted in his life, not even now in sickness; for his brother was sick too, and had come down on the same train. But, alas! in shipping the poor helpless fellows they had got separated. Of course I kept the next bunk empty, even taking out of it a man who had been put in during my absence; and all day long the painful look in the anxious eyes distressed me. Late at night, as the last men were coming off the "Elm City," and I was standing at the gangway by Dr. Draper, receiving his orders as he looked at the men when they came on board, I heard him read off the name of the brother! You may be sure I asked for that man; and the pleasure of putting him beside his brother cheered even that black night.

Source: Katharine Prescott Wormeley, *The Other Side of the War with the Army of the Potomac* (Boston: Ticknor, 1889), 75–80.

DOCUMENT 13.10

Thomas Freeman | Letter to His Brother-in-Law, March 26, 1864

The Massachusetts Fifty-fourth Colored Infantry, one of the Union's first black units, was regarded for its valor and heroism. The unit was also known for protesting the mistreatment of black soldiers, including a regiment-wide pay boycott to demand equal salaries for black and white soldiers. In this letter to his brother-in-law, Thomas Freeman of Worcester, Massachusetts, echoes black soldiers' discontent with discrimination and poor treatment.

Jacksonville, Florida
March 26, 1864

Dear William

    I will devote some spare moments I have in writing you a few lines which I hope may find you and all your family the same, also all of my many Friends in Worcester. Since the Regiment Departure from Morris Island I have enjoyed the best of health. The weather here is Beautiful; it is warm here as it is home in July. The Regiment in general are in Good Health but in Low Spirits and no reason why for they have all to a man done there duty as a soldier. It is 1 year the 1st Day of April since I enlisted and there is men here in the regiment that have been in Enlisted 13 Months and have never received one cent But there bounty and they more or less have family, and 2 thirds have never received any State Aid, and how do you think men can feel to do there duty as Soldiers, but let me say we are not Soldiers but Labourers working for Uncle Sam for nothing but our board and clothes. . . . We never can be Elevated in this country while such rascality is Performed. Slavery with all its horrorrs can not Equalise this for it is nothing but work from morning till night Building Batteries, Hauling Guns, Cleaning Bricks, clearing up land for other Regiments to settle on and if a Man Says he is sick it is the Doctors Priveledge to say yes or no. If you cannot work then you are sent to the Guard House Bucked Gagged and stay so till they see fit to relieve You and if you dont like that some white man will Give you a crack over the Head with his sword. Now do you call this Equality? If so God help such Equality. There is many things I could relate on this matter but I will say no more. I want You to consult some counsel in Relation to the Matter and see if a man could not sue for his Discharge and get his views on the Subject and let me know immiedeitely for I am tired of such treatment. Please answer as soon as you can and Oblidge Yours

T. D. Freeman

Source: Nina Silber and Mary Beth Sievens, eds., *Yankee Correspondence: Civil War Letters between New England Soldiers and the Home Front* (Charlottesville: University Press of Virginia, 1996), 47–48.

Interpret the Evidence

1. In reading these letters, what do you think accounts for the early popular support for the war in the North and the South?

2. Compare the letters from Fred Spooner (Document 13.6) and John Hines (Document 13.7). How did each view the enemy and the causes of the war?

3. In what ways do Ginnie Ott (Document 13.8) and Katharine Prescott Wormeley (Document 13.9) defy contemporary gender roles? In what ways do they affirm them?

4. What was life like for soldiers at the front (Documents 13.6, 13.7, and 13.10)? How would you compare the different war experiences revealed in these letters?

5. How did the war change the lives of each of these letter writers?

Put It in Context

• In what ways do the personal letters of soldiers and their families illuminate the standard political and military history of the Civil War?

Getty Images

Culver Pictures/The Art Archive at Art Resource, Inc.

Freed slaves in Richmond, Virginia, c. 1865.

Jack and Abby Landlord, freed slaves from Savannah, Georgia, 1875.

14
Emancipations and Reconstructions

1863–1877

Schlesinger Library, Radcliffe Institute, Harvard University/The Bridgeman Art Library

Women voting in Wyoming, 1870.

AMERICAN HISTORIES

Jefferson Franklin Long spent his life improving himself and his race. Born a slave in Alabama in 1836, Long showed great resourcefulness in taking advantage of the limited opportunities available to him under slavery. His master, a tailor who moved his family to Georgia, taught him the trade, but Long taught himself to read and write. When the Civil War ended, he opened a tailor shop in Macon, Georgia. The measure of financial security he earned allowed him to turn his attention to politics and participate in the Republican Party. Elected as Georgia's first black congressman in 1870, Long was committed to fighting for the political rights of freed slaves. In his first appearance on the House floor, he spoke out against a bill that would allow former Confederate officials to return to Congress. He questioned their loyalty to the Union from which they had recently rebelled and noted that many belonged to secret societies, such as the Ku Klux Klan, that intimidated black citizens. Despite his pleas, the measure passed, and Long decided not to run for reelection.

By the mid-1880s, Long had become disillusioned with the ability of black Georgians to achieve their objectives within the electoral system. Instead, he counseled African Americans to turn to institution building as the best hope for social and economic advancement. Advocating "Christianity, morality, education, and industry," Long helped found the Union Brotherhood Lodge, a black mutual aid society, with branches throughout central Georgia, that provided social and economic services for its members. He died in 1901, during a

**Jefferson Franklin Long
and Andrew Johnson**

time of political disfranchisement and racial segregation that swept through Georgia and the rest of the South. In fact, after Long, Georgia would not elect another black congressman for a hundred years.

Jefferson Long and Andrew Johnson shared many characteristics, but their views on race led them to support decidedly different programs following the Civil War. Whereas Long fought for the right of self-determination for African Americans, Johnson believed that whites alone could decide what was best for freedmen. Born in 1808 in Raleigh, North Carolina, Andrew Johnson grew up in poverty. At the age of thirteen or fourteen, Johnson became a tailor's apprentice, but he ran away before completing his contract. Johnson settled in Tennessee in 1826 and, like Long, opened a tailor shop. The following year, he married Eliza McCardle, who taught him how to write. He began to prosper, purchasing his own home, farm, and a small number of slaves.

As he made his mark in Greenville, Tennessee, Johnson moved into politics, following fellow Tennessean Andrew Jackson into the Democratic Party. Success followed success as he advanced to higher political positions, and by the time the Civil War broke out, he was a U.S. senator. During his early political career, Johnson, a social and political outsider, championed the rights of workers and small farmers against the power of the southern aristocracy.

At the onset of the Civil War, Johnson remained loyal to the Union even when Tennessee seceded in 1861. As a reward for his loyalty, President Abraham Lincoln appointed Johnson as military governor of Tennessee. In 1864 the Republican Lincoln chose the Democrat Johnson to run with him as vice president, thereby constructing a successful unity ticket. Less than six weeks after their inauguration in March 1865, Johnson became president upon Lincoln's assassination.

Fate placed Reconstruction in the hands of Andrew Johnson. After four years, the brutal Civil War between the rebellious southern states that seceded from the Union and the northern states that fought to preserve the nation had come to a close. Yet the hard work of reunion remained. Toward this end, President Johnson oversaw the reestablishment of state legislatures in the former Confederate states. These reconstituted governments agreed to the abolition of slavery, but they passed measures that restricted black civil and political rights. Johnson accepted these results and considered the southern states as having fulfilled their obligations for rejoining the Union. Most Northerners reached a different conclusion. Having won the bloody war, they suspected that they were now losing the peace to Johnson and the defeated South. •

both photos: Library of Congress

THE AMERICAN HISTORIES of Andrew Johnson and Jefferson Long intersected in Reconstruction, the hard-fought battle to determine the fate of the postwar South and the meaning of freedom for newly emancipated African Americans. Would the end of slavery be little more than a legal technicality, as Johnson and many other white Southerners hoped, or would Long's vision of a deeper economic and racial transformation prevail? From 1865 to 1877, the period of Reconstruction, Americans of all races and from all regions participated in the resolution of this question.

Prelude to Reconstruction

Even before Andrew Johnson became president in 1865 and emancipation freed Jefferson Long, Reconstruction had begun on a small scale. During the Civil War, blacks remaining in Union-occupied areas, such as the Sea Islands, located off the coast of South Carolina, had some experience with freedom. When Union troops arrived and most southern whites fled, the slaves chose to stay on the land. Some farmed for themselves, but most were employed by northern whites who moved south to demonstrate the profitability of newly freed black labor. The return of former plantation owners after the war generated conflicts. Rather than work for whites, freedpeople preferred to establish their own farms; but if forced to work for whites, they insisted on negotiating their wages instead of simply accepting what whites offered. Wives and mothers often refused to labor for whites at all in favor of caring for their own families. These conflicts reflected the priorities that would shape the actions of freedpeople across the South in the immediate aftermath of the war. For freedom to be meaningful, it had to include economic independence, the power to make family decisions, and the right to have some control over community issues.

African Americans Embrace Emancipation

When U.S. troops arrived in Richmond, Virginia, in April 1865, it signaled to the city's enslaved African American population that the war was over and that freedom was, finally, theirs. African American men, women, and children took to the streets and crowded into churches to celebrate. They gathered to dance, sing, pray, and shout. Four days after Union troops arrived, 1,500 African Americans, including a large number of soldiers, packed First African Baptist, the largest of the city's black churches. During the singing of the hymn "Jesus My All to Heaven Is Gone," they raised their voices at the line "This is the way I long have sought." Elsewhere in Virginia, black schoolchildren sang "Glory Hallelujah," and house slaves snuck out of the dinner service to shout for joy in the slave quarters. As the news of the Confederacy's defeat spread, newly freed African Americans across the South experienced similar emotions. However, the news did not reach some isolated plantations in Georgia, Louisiana, South Carolina, and Texas for months. David Harris, a South Carolina planter, claimed that he did not hear about the emancipation edict until June 1865. He did not mention it to the slaves on his plantation until August, when Union troops stationed nearby made it impossible for him to keep it from his workers any longer. Whenever they discovered their freedom, blacks recalled the moment vividly. Many years later, Houston H. Holloway, a Georgia slave who had been sold three times before he was twenty years old, recalled the day of emancipation. "I felt like a bird out a cage," he reported. "Amen. Amen, Amen. I could hardly ask to feel any better than I did that day."

For southern whites, however, the end of the war brought fear, humiliation, and uncertainty. From their point of view, the jubilation of their former slaves was salt in their wounds. In many areas, blacks celebrated their release from bondage under the protection of Union soldiers. When the army moved out, freedwomen and freedmen suffered deeply for their enthusiasm. When troops departed the area surrounding Columbia, South Carolina, for example, a plantation owner and his wife vented their anger and frustration on a former slave. The girl had assisted Union soldiers in finding silverware, money, and jewelry hidden by her master and mistress. Her former owners hanged the newly emancipated slave. Other whites beat, whipped, raped, slashed, and shot blacks who they felt had been too joyous in their freedom or too helpful to the Yankee invaders. As one North Carolina freedman testified, the Yankees "tol' us we were free," but once the army left, the planters "would get cruel to the slaves if they acted like they were free."

Newly freed slaves also faced less visible dangers. During the 1860s, disease swept through the South and through the contraband camps that housed many former slaves; widespread malnutrition and poor housing heightened the problem. A smallpox epidemic that spread south from Washington, D.C., killed more than sixty thousand freedpeople.

Despite the danger of acting free, southern blacks eagerly pursued emancipation. They moved; they married; they attended school; they demanded wages; they refused to work for whites; they gathered up their families; they created black churches and civic associations; they held political meetings. Sometimes, black women and men acted on their own, pooling their resources to advance their freedom. At other times, they called on government agencies for assistance and support. The most important of these agencies was the newly formed Bureau of Refugees, Freedmen, and Abandoned Lands, popularly known as the **Freedmen's Bureau**. Created by Congress in 1865 and signed into law by President Lincoln, the bureau provided ex-slaves with economic and legal resources. Private organizations—particularly northern missionary and educational associations, most staffed by former abolitionists, free blacks, and evangelical Christians—also aided African Americans in their efforts to give meaning to freedom.

Reuniting Families Torn Apart by Slavery

The first priority for many newly freed blacks was to reunite families torn apart by slavery. Men and women traveled across the South to find spouses, children, parents, siblings, aunts, and uncles. Well into the 1870s and 1880s, parents ran advertisements in newly established black newspapers, providing what information they knew about their children's whereabouts and asking for assistance in finding them. They sought help in their quests from government officials, ministers, and other African Americans. Milly Johnson wrote to the Freedmen's Bureau in March 1867, after failing to locate the five children she had lost under slavery. In the end, she was able to locate three of her children, but any chance of discovering the whereabouts of the other two was lost when the records of the slave trader who purchased them burned during the war. Although such difficulties were common, thousands of slave children were reunited with their parents in the aftermath of the Civil War.

Husbands and wives, or those who considered themselves as such despite the absence of legal marriage under slavery, also searched for each other. Those who lived on nearby plantations could now live together for the first time. Those whose husband or wife had been sold to distant plantation owners had a more difficult time. They wrote (or had letters written on their behalf) to relatives and friends who had been sold with their mate; sought assistance from government officials, churches, and even their former masters; and traveled to areas where they thought their spouse might reside.

Many such searches were complicated by long years of separation and the lack of any legal standing for slave marriages. In 1866 Philip Grey, a Virginia freedman, located his wife, Willie Ann, and their daughter Maria, who had been sold away to Kentucky years before. Willie Ann was eager to reunite with her husband, but in the years since being sold, she had remarried and borne three

children. Her second husband had joined the Union army and was killed in battle. When Willie Ann wrote to Philip in April 1866, explaining her new circumstances, she concluded: "If you love me you will love my children and you will have to promise me that you will provide for them all as well as if they were your own. . . . I know that I have lived with you and loved you then and love you still." Other spouses finally located their partner, only to discover that the husband or wife was happily married to someone else and refused to acknowledge the earlier relationship.

Despite these complications, most former slaves who found their spouse sought to legalize their relationship. Ministers, army chaplains, Freedmen's Bureau agents, and teachers were flooded with requests to perform marriage ceremonies. In one case, a Superintendent for Marriages for the Freedmen's Bureau in northern Virginia reported that he gave out seventy-nine marriage certificates on a single day in May 1866. In another, four couples went right from the fields to a local schoolhouse, still dressed in their work clothes, where the parson married them.

Of course, some former slaves hoped that freedom would allow them to leave an unhappy relationship. Having never been married under the law, couples could simply separate and move on. Complications arose, however, if they had children. In Lake City, Florida, in 1866, a Freedmen's Bureau agent asked for advice from his superiors on how to deal with Madison Day and Maria Richards. They refused to legalize the relationship forced on them under slavery, but both sought custody of their three children, the oldest only six years old. As with white couples in the mid-nineteenth century, the father eventually was granted custody on the assumption that he had the best chance of providing for the family financially.

Free to Learn

Reuniting families was only one of the many ways that southern blacks proclaimed their freedom. Learning to read and write was another. The desire to learn was all but universal. Writing of freedpeople during Reconstruction, Booker T. Washington, an educator and a former slave, noted, "It was a whole race trying to go to school. Few were too young, and none too old, to make the attempt to learn." A newly liberated father in Mississippi proclaimed, "If I nebber does nothing more while I live, I shall give my children a chance to go to school, for I considers education [the] next best ting to liberty."

A variety of organizations opened schools for former slaves during the 1860s and 1870s. By 1870 nearly a quarter million blacks were attending one of the 4,300 schools established by the Freedmen's Bureau. Black and white

Information Wanted.

INFORMATION is wanted of my mother, whom I left in Fauquier county. Va., in 1844, and I was sold in Richmond. Va., to Saml. Copeland. I formerly belonged to Robert Rogers. I am very anxious to hear from my mother, and any information in relation to her whereabouts will be very thankfully received. My mother's name was Betty, and was sold by Col. Briggs to James French.—Any information by letter, addressed to the Colored Tennessean. Box 1150, will be thankfully received.
THORNTON COPELAND.
sept16–3m

Reuniting Families

Thornton Copeland, a former slave, placed this advertisement in the *Colored Tennessean* in Nashville in October 1865. Like other freedpeople, he was looking for relatives, in this case his mother, from whom he had been forcibly separated. Courtesy of the Tennessee State Library and Archives

Wedding Day, 1866

A Freedmen's Bureau minister unites a black Union soldier and his bride in Vicksburg, Mississippi. Most postwar weddings of freedpeople were less formal, but *Harper's Weekly*, a political magazine published in New York City and an ally of the Republican Party, wanted to present black families as respectable.
Library of Congress

churches and missionary societies also launched schools. Even before the war ended, the American Missionary Association called on its northern members to take the freedpeople "by the hand, to guide, counsel and instruct them in their new life." This and similar organizations sent hundreds of teachers, black and white, women and men, into the South to open schools in former plantation areas. Their attitudes were often paternalistic and the schools were segregated, but the institutions they established offered important educational resources for African Americans.

The demand for education was so great that almost any kind of building was pressed into service as a schoolhouse. A mule stable in Helena, Arkansas; a billiard room on the Sea Islands; a courthouse in Lawrence, Kansas; and a former cotton shed on a St. Simon Island plantation all attracted eager students. In New Orleans, local blacks converted a former slave pen into a school and named it after the famous activist, orator, and ex-slave Frederick Douglass.

Parents worked hard to keep their children in school during the day. Children, as they gained the rudiments of education, passed on their knowledge to mothers, fathers, and older siblings whose work responsibilities prevented them from attending school. Still, many freedpeople, having worked all day in fields, homes, or shops, then walked long distances in order to get a bit of education for themselves. In New Bern, North Carolina, where many blacks labored until eight o'clock at night, a teacher reported that they still insisted on spending at least an hour "in earnest application to study."

Freedmen and freedwomen sought education for a variety of reasons. Some, like the Mississippi father noted above, viewed it as a sign of liberation. Others knew that they must be able to read the labor contracts they signed if they were ever to be free of exploitation by whites. Some men and women were eager to correspond with relatives far away, others to read the Bible. Growing numbers hoped to participate in politics, particularly the public meetings organized by freedpeople in cities across the South following the end of the war. These gatherings met to set an agenda for the future, and nearly everyone demanded that state

Freedmen's Bureau School

This photograph of a one-room Freedmen's Bureau school in North Carolina in the late 1860s shows the large number and diverse ages of students who sought to obtain an education following emancipation. The teachers included white and black northern women sent by missionary and reform organizations as well as southern black women who had already received some education.   The Granger Collection, New York

legislatures immediately establish public schools for African Americans. Most black delegates agreed with A. H. Ransier of South Carolina, who proclaimed that "in proportion to the education of the people so is their progress in civilization."

Despite the enthusiasm of blacks and the efforts of the federal government and private agencies, schooling remained severely limited throughout the South. A shortage of teachers and of funding kept enrollments low among blacks and whites alike. The isolation of black farm families and the difficulties in eking out a living limited the resources available for education. Only about a quarter of African Americans were literate by 1880.

Black Churches Take a Leadership Role

One of the constant concerns freedpeople expressed as they sought education was the desire to read the Bible and other religious material. Forced under slavery to listen to white preachers who claimed that God had placed Africans and their descendants in bondage, blacks sought to interpret the

Bible for themselves. Like many other churches, the African Methodist Episcopal Church, based in Philadelphia, sent missionaries and educators into the South. These church leaders were eager to open seminaries, such as Shaw University in Raleigh, North Carolina, to train southern black men for the ministry.

From the moment of emancipation, freedpeople gathered at churches to celebrate community events. Black Methodist and Baptist congregations spread rapidly across the South following the Civil War. In these churches, African Americans were no longer forced to sit in the back benches listening to white preachers claim that the Bible legitimated slavery. They were no longer punished by white church leaders for moral infractions defined by white masters. Now blacks filled the pews, hired black preachers, selected their own boards of deacons and elders, and invested community resources in purchasing land, building houses of worship, and furnishing them. Churches were the largest structures available to freedpeople in many communities and thus were used for a variety of purposes by a host of community organizations.

They often served as schools, with hymnals and Bibles used to teach reading. Churches also hosted picnics, dances, weddings, funerals, festivals, and other events that brought blacks together to celebrate their new sense of freedom, family, and community. Church leaders, especially ministers, often served as arbiters of community standards of morality.

One of the most important functions of black churches in the years immediately following the Civil War was as sites for political organizing. Some black ministers worried that political concerns would overwhelm spiritual devotions. Others agreed with the Reverend Charles H. Pearce of Florida, who declared, "A man in this State cannot do his whole duty as a minister except he looks out for the political interests of his people." Whatever the views of ministers, black churches were among the few places where African Americans could express their political views free from white interference.

REVIEW & RELATE

- What were freedpeople's highest priorities in the years immediately following the Civil War? Why?

- How did freedpeople define freedom? What steps did they take to make freedom real for themselves and their children?

✔ *LEARNINGCurve* bedfordstmartins.com/hewittlawson/LC

National Reconstructions

Presidents Abraham Lincoln and Andrew Johnson viewed Reconstruction as a process of national reconciliation. They sketched out terms by which the former Confederate states could reclaim their political representation in the nation without much difficulty. Southern whites, too, sought to return to the Union quickly and with as little change as possible. Congressional Republicans, however, had a more thoroughgoing reconstruction in mind. Like many African Americans, Republican congressional leaders expected the South to extend constitutional rights to the freedmen and to provide them with the political and economic resources to sustain their freedom. Over the next decade, these competing visions of Reconstruction played out in a hard-fought and tumultuous battle over the social, economic, and political implications of the South's defeat and of the abolition of slavery.

Abraham Lincoln Plans for Reunion

In December 1863, President Lincoln issued the **Proclamation of Amnesty and Reconstruction**. He believed that the southern states could not have constitutionally seceded from the Union and therefore only had to meet minimum standards before they regained their political and constitutional rights. Lincoln declared that defeated southern states would have to accept the abolition of slavery and that new governments could be formed when 10 percent of those eligible to vote in 1860 (which in practice meant white southern men but not blacks) swore an oath of allegiance to the United States. Lincoln's plan granted amnesty to all but the highest-ranking Confederate officials, and the restored voters in each state would elect members to a constitutional convention and representatives to take their seats in Congress. In the next year and a half, Arkansas, Louisiana, and Tennessee reestablished their governments under Lincoln's "Ten Percent Plan."

Republicans in Congress had other ideas. They argued that the Confederates had broken their contract with the Union when they seceded and should be treated as "conquered provinces" subject to congressional supervision. In 1864 Congress passed the Wade-Davis bill, which established much higher barriers for readmission to the Union than did Lincoln's plan. For instance, the Wade-Davis bill substituted 50 percent of voters for the president's 10 percent requirement. Lincoln put a stop to this harsher proposal by using a pocket veto—refusing to sign it within ten days of Congress's adjournment.

Although Lincoln and his fellow Republicans in Congress disagreed about many aspects of postwar policy, Lincoln was flexible, and his actions mirrored his desire both to heal the Union and to help southern blacks. For example, the president supported the **Thirteenth Amendment**, abolishing slavery, which passed Congress in January 1865 and was sent to the states for ratification. In March 1865, Lincoln signed the law to create the Freedmen's Bureau. That same month, the president also expressed his sincere wish for reconciliation between the North and the South. "With malice toward none, with charity for all," Lincoln declared in his second inaugural address, "let us strive on to finish the work . . . to bind up the nation's wounds." Lincoln would not, however, have the opportunity to shape Reconstruction with his balanced approach. When he was assassinated in April 1865, it fell to Andrew Johnson, a very different sort of politician, to lead the country through the process of national reintegration.

Andrew Johnson and Presidential Reconstruction

The nation needed a president who could transmit northern desires to the South with clarity and conviction and ensure that they were carried out. Instead, the nation got a president who substituted his own aims for those of the North, refused to engage in meaningful compromise even with sympathetic opponents, misled the South into believing that he could achieve restoration quickly, and subjected himself to political humiliation. Like his mentor, Andrew Jackson,

Andrew Johnson was a staunch Union man. He proved his loyalty by serving diligently as military governor of Union-occupied Tennessee from 1862 to 1864. In the 1864 election, Lincoln chose Johnson, a Democrat, as his running mate in a thinly veiled effort to attract border-state voters. The vice presidency was normally an inconsequential role, so it mattered little to Lincoln that Johnson, a southern Democrat, was out of step with many Republican Party positions.

As president, however, Johnson's views took on profound importance. Born into rural poverty, Johnson had no sympathy for the southern aristocracy. Johnson had been a slave owner himself for a time, so his political opposition to slavery was not rooted in moral convictions. Instead, it sprang from the belief that slavery gave plantation owners inordinate power and wealth, which came at the expense of the majority of white Southerners who owned no slaves. He saw emancipation as a means to "break down an odious and dangerous [planter] aristocracy," not to empower blacks. Consequently, he was unconcerned with the fate of African Americans in the postwar South. He saw no reason to punish the South or its leaders because he believed that the end of slavery would doom the southern aristocracy. He hoped to bring the South back into the Union as quickly as possible and then let Southerners take care of their own affairs.

Johnson's views, combined with a lack of political savvy and skill, left him unable to work constructively with congressional Republicans, even the moderates who constituted the majority, such as Senators Lyman Trumbull of Illinois, William Pitt Fessenden of Maine, and John Sherman of Ohio. Moderate Republicans shared the prevalent belief of their time that whites and blacks were not equal, but they argued that the federal government needed to protect newly emancipated slaves. Senator Trumbull warned that without national legislation, ex-slaves would "be tyrannized over, abused, and virtually reenslaved." They expected southern states, where 90 percent of African Americans lived, to extend basic civil rights to the freedpeople, including equal protection and due process of law, and the right to work and hold property.

Nearly all Republicans shared these positions. The Radical wing of the party, however, wanted to go still further. Led by Senator Charles Sumner of Massachusetts and Congressman Thaddeus Stevens of Pennsylvania, this small but influential group advocated suffrage, or voting rights, for African American men as well as the redistribution of southern plantation lands to freed slaves. Stevens called on the federal government to provide freedpeople "a homestead of forty acres of land," which would give them some measure of economic independence. Nonetheless, whatever disagreements the Radicals had with the moderates, all Republicans believed that Congress should have a strong voice in determining the fate of the former Confederate states. From May to December 1865,

with Congress out of session, they waited to see what Johnson's restoration plan would produce, ready to assert themselves if his policies deviated too much from their own.

At first, it seemed as if Johnson would proceed as they hoped. He appointed provisional governors to convene new state constitutional conventions and urged these conventions to ratify the Thirteenth Amendment abolishing slavery, revoke the states' ordinances of secession, and refuse to pay Confederate war debts, which the victorious North did not consider legitimate because repayment would benefit southern bondholders who financed the rebellion. He also allowed the majority of white Southerners to obtain amnesty and a pardon by swearing their loyalty to the U.S. Constitution, but he required those who had held more than $20,000 of taxable property—the members of the southern aristocracy—to petition him for a special pardon to restore their rights. Republicans expected him to be harsh in dealing with his former political foes. Instead, Johnson relished the reversal of roles that put members of the southern elite at his mercy. As the once prominent petitioners paraded before him, the president granted almost all of their requests for pardons.

By the time Congress convened in December 1865, Johnson was satisfied that the southern states had fulfilled his requirements for restoration. Moderate and Radical Republicans disagreed, seeing few signs of change or contrition in the South. As a result of Johnson's liberal pardon policy, many former leaders of the Confederacy won election to state constitutional conventions and to Congress. Indeed, Georgians elected Confederate vice president Alexander H. Stephens to the U.S. Senate. In addition, although most of the reconstituted state governments ratified the Thirteenth Amendment, South Carolina and Mississippi refused to repudiate the Confederate debt, and Mississippi rejected the Thirteenth Amendment.

Far from providing freedpeople with basic civil rights protection, the southern states passed a variety of **black codes** intended to reduce blacks to a condition as close to slavery as possible. Some laws prohibited blacks from bearing arms; others outlawed intermarriage and excluded blacks from serving on juries. Many of these laws were designed to ensure that white landowners had a supply of black labor now that slavery had ended. The codes made it difficult for blacks to leave plantations unless they proved they could support themselves. Many southern whites contended that they were acting no differently than their northern counterparts who used vagrancy laws to maintain control over workers.

Northerners viewed this situation with alarm. In their eyes, the postwar South looked very similar to the Old South, with a few cosmetic adjustments. If the black codes prevailed, one Republican proclaimed, "then I demand to know of what practical value is the amendment abolishing slavery?" Others wondered what their wartime sacrifices

Mourning at Stonewall Jackson's Gravesite, 1866

Many Northerners were concerned that the defeat of the Confederacy did not lessen white Southerners' devotion to the "Lost Cause" of a society based on the domination of African Americans. Women, who led the efforts to memorialize Confederate soldiers, are shown at the gravesite of General Stonewall Jackson in Lexington, Virginia.   Virginia Military Institute Archives

had been for if the South admitted no mistakes, was led by the same people, and continued to oppress its black inhabitants. The *Chicago Tribune* declared that Northerners would not allow the black codes to "disgrace one foot of soil in which the bones of our soldiers sleep and over which the flag of freedom waves." **See Document Project 14: Testing and Contesting Freedom, page 449.**

Johnson and Congressional Resistance

Faced with growing opposition in the North, Johnson stubbornly held his ground. He insisted that the southern states had followed his plan and were entitled to resume their representation in Congress. Republicans objected, and in December 1865 they barred the admission of southern lawmakers, an action that Johnson denounced as illegitimate. Up to this point, it was still possible for Johnson and Congress to work together, if Johnson had been willing to compromise. He was not. Instead, Johnson pushed moderates into the Radical camp with a series of legislative vetoes that challenged the fundamental tenets of Republican policies toward African Americans and the South. In January 1866, the president

refused to sign a bill passed by Congress to extend the life of the Freedmen's Bureau for another two years. A few months later, he vetoed the Civil Rights Act, which Congress had passed to protect freedpeople in the South from the restrictions placed on them by the black codes. These bills represented a consensus among moderate and Radical Republicans on the government's responsibility toward former slaves.

Explore

See Documents 14.1 and 14.2 for two perspectives on the Freedmen's Bureau.

Johnson justified his vetoes on both constitutional and personal grounds. Along with Democrats, he contended that so long as Congress refused to admit southern representatives, it could not legally pass laws affecting the South. The chief executive also condemned the Freedmen's Bureau bill because it infringed on the rights of states to handle their internal affairs concerning education and economic matters. Johnson's vetoes exposed his racism and his lifelong belief that the evil of slavery lay in the harm it did to poor white Southerners, not to enslaved blacks. Johnson

Debating the Freedmen's Bureau: Two Views

From the start, the Freedmen's Bureau generated controversy. To its Republican supporters, it helped southern blacks make the transition from slavery to freedom. For most white Southerners and many northern Democrats, however, the bureau was little more than an expensive social welfare program that rewarded idleness in blacks. Both points of view are represented in the following documents. In a report written to the Congressional Joint Committee on Reconstruction, Colonel Eliphalet Whittlesey, the assistant head of the Freedmen's Bureau in North Carolina, outlined the bureau's initial accomplishments. The anti-bureau cartoon reprinted here was created during the height of the conflict over Reconstruction between the Republican Congress and President Andrew Johnson; it was intended to support the election of a Democratic candidate for governor of Pennsylvania, an ally of Johnson.

Explore

14.1 Colonel Eliphalet Whittlesey | Report on the Freedmen's Bureau, 1865

All officers of the bureau are instructed—

To aid the destitute, yet in such a way as not to encourage dependence.

To protect freedmen from injustice.

To assist freedmen in obtaining employment and fair wages for their labor.

To encourage education, intellectual and moral. Under these four divisions the operations of the bureau can best be presented. . . .

The statistical reports prepared by Captain Almy, commissary of subsistence, forwarded herewith, will show a steady and healthy decrease of the number of dependents from month to month.

July there were issued 215,285 rations, valued at $44,994.56; August there were issued 156,289 rations, valued at $32,664.40; September there were issued 137,350 rations, valued at $28,706.15.

Should no unforeseen trouble arise, the number will be still further reduced. But we have in our camps at Roanoke island and Newbern, many women and children, families of soldiers who have died in the service, and refugees from the interior during the war, for whom permanent provision must be made. . . . The reports prepared by Surgeon Hogan will show the condition of freedmen hospitals. In the early part of the summer much suffering and mortality occurred for want of medical attendance and supplies. This evil is now being remedied by the employment of surgeons by contract. . . .

Contrary to the fears and predictions of many, the great mass of colored people have remained quietly at work upon the plantations of their former masters during the entire summer. The crowds seen about the towns in the early part of the season had followed in the wake of the Union army, to escape from slavery. After hostilities ceased these refugees returned to their homes, so that but few vagrants can now be found. In truth, a much larger amount of vagrancy exists among the whites than among the blacks. It is the almost uniform report of officers of the bureau that freedmen are industrious.

The report is confirmed by the fact that out of a colored population of nearly 350,000 in the State, only about 5,000 are now receiving support from the government. Probably some others are receiving aid from kind-hearted men who have enjoyed the benefit of their services from childhood. To the general quiet and industry of this people there can be no doubt that the efforts of the bureau have contributed greatly.

Source: *The Reports of the Committees of the House of Representatives Made during the First Session, Thirty-ninth Congress, 1865–1866* (Washington, D.C.: Government Printing Office, 1866), 186–87, 189.

Explore

14.2 Democratic Flier Opposing the Freedmen's Bureau Bill, 1866

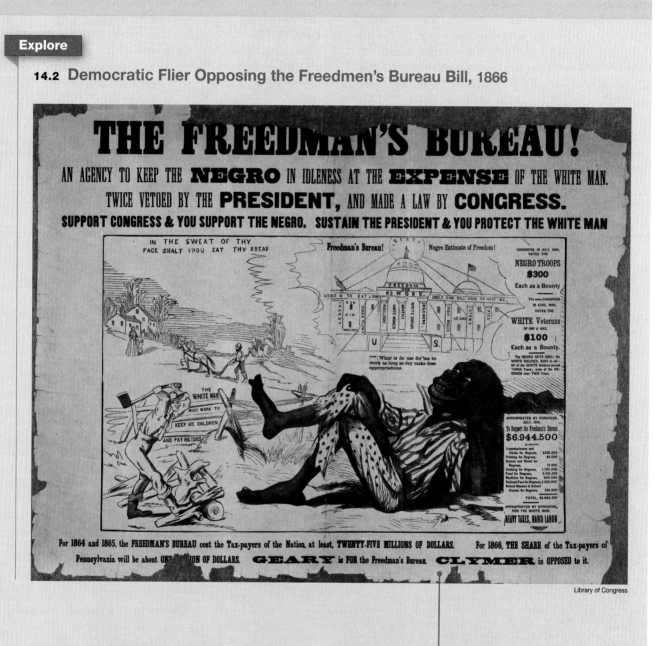

Library of Congress

Interpret the Evidence

- Why was there a need for the Freedmen's Bureau? How did Colonel Whittlesey measure its success?
- How is the Freedmen's Bureau portrayed in the poster? Why might its argument have appealed to some northern whites?

Put It in Context

How did prevailing racial assumptions shape both the cartoon and the report?

argued that these congressional bills discriminated against whites, who would receive no benefits under them, and put whites at a disadvantage with blacks who received government assistance. Johnson's private secretary recorded in his diary, "The president has at times exhibited a morbid distress and feeling against the Negroes," including those like Jefferson Long, who spoke out for their full civil rights.

Johnson's actions united moderates and Radicals against him. In April 1866, Congress repassed both the Freedmen's Bureau extension and Civil Rights Act over the president's vetoes. In June, lawmakers adopted the **Fourteenth Amendment**, which incorporated many of the provisions of the Civil Rights Act, and submitted it to the states for ratification (see Appendix). Reflecting its confrontational dealings with the president, Congress wanted to ensure more permanent protection for African Americans than simple legislation could provide. Lawmakers also wanted to act quickly, as the situation in the South seemed to be deteriorating rapidly. The previous month, a race riot had broken out in Memphis, Tennessee. For a day and a half, white mobs, egged on by local police, went on a rampage, during which they terrorized black residents of the city and burned their houses and churches. "The late riots in our city," the editor of a Memphis newspaper asserted, "have satisfied all of one thing, that the *southern man* will not be ruled by the *negro*."

The Fourteenth Amendment defined citizenship to include African Americans, thereby nullifying the ruling in the *Dred Scott* case of 1857, which declared that blacks were not citizens. It extended equal protection and due process of law to all persons and not only citizens. The amendment repudiated Confederate debts, which some state governments had refused to do, and it barred Confederate officeholders from holding elective office unless Congress removed this provision by a two-thirds vote. Although most Republicans were upset with Johnson's behavior, at this point they were not willing to embrace the Radical position entirely. Rather than granting the right to vote to black males at least twenty-one years of age, the Fourteenth Amendment gave the states the option of excluding blacks and accepting a reduction in congressional representation if they did so.

Johnson remained inflexible. Instead of counseling the southern states to accept the Fourteenth Amendment, which would have sped up their readmission to the Union,

Memphis Race Riot

A skirmish between white policemen and black Union veterans on May 1, 1866, resulted in three days of rioting by white mobs that attacked the black community of Memphis, Tennessee. Before federal troops restored peace, numerous women had been raped, and forty-six African Americans and two whites had been killed. This illustration from *Harper's Weekly* depicts the carnage.   Courtesy of the Tennessee State Library and Archives

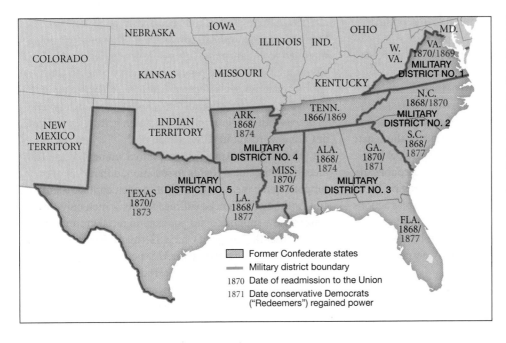

MAP 14.1   Reconstruction in the South

In 1867, Congress enacted legislation dividing the former Confederate states into five military districts. All the states were readmitted to the Union by 1870 and white, conservative Democrats (Redeemers) had replaced Republicans in most states by 1875. Only in Florida, Louisiana, and South Carolina did federal troops remain until 1877.

he encouraged them to reject it. Ironically, Johnson's home state of Tennessee ratified the amendment, but the other states refused. In the fall of 1866, Johnson decided to take his case directly to northern voters before the midterm congressional elections. Campaigning for candidates who shared his views, he embarked on a swing through the Midwest. Clearly out of touch with northern public opinion, Johnson attacked Republican lawmakers and engaged in shouting matches with audiences. On election day, Republicans increased their majorities in Congress and now controlled two-thirds of the seats, providing them with greater power to override presidential vetoes.

Congressional Reconstruction

When the Fortieth Congress convened in 1867, Republican lawmakers charted a new course for Reconstruction. With moderates and Radicals united against the president, Congress intended to force the former Confederate states not only to protect the basic civil rights of African Americans but also to grant them the vote. Moderates now agreed with Radicals that unless blacks had access to the ballot, they would not be able to sustain their freedom. Extending the suffrage to African Americans also aided the fortunes of the Republican Party in the South by adding significant numbers of new black voters. By the end of March, Congress enacted three Military Reconstruction Acts. Together they divided ten southern states into five military districts, each under the supervision of a Union general and his troops (Map 14.1). The male voters of each state, regardless of race, were to elect delegates to a constitutional convention; only former Confederate officials were disfranchised.

The conventions were required to draft constitutions that guaranteed black suffrage and ratified the Fourteenth Amendment. Within a year, North Carolina, South Carolina, Florida, Alabama, Louisiana, and Arkansas had fulfilled these obligations and reentered the Union.

Having ensured congressional Reconstruction in the South, Republican lawmakers turned their attention to disciplining the president. Johnson continued to resist congressional policy and used his power as commander in chief to order generals in the military districts to soften the intent of congressional Reconstruction. In response, Congress passed the Command of the Army Act in 1867, which required the president to issue all orders to army commanders in the field through the General of the Army in Washington, D.C., Ulysses S. Grant. The Radicals had won over Grant and knew they could count on him to carry out their policies. Even more threatening to presidential power, Congress passed the **Tenure of Office Act**, which prevented Johnson from firing cabinet officers sympathetic to congressional Reconstruction. This measure barred the chief executive from removing from office any appointee that the Senate had ratified previously without returning to the Senate for approval.

Johnson sincerely believed that the Tenure of Office Act violated his presidential prerogative to remove subordinates he considered disloyal or incompetent. He may have had a legitimate constitutional point. However, the quick-tempered Johnson chose to confront the Radical Republicans directly rather than find a way to maneuver around a congressional showdown. In February 1868, Johnson fired Secretary of War Edwin Stanton, a Lincoln appointee and a Radical sympathizer, without Senate approval. In response, congressional Radicals prepared articles of impeachment on eleven counts of misconduct, including willful violation of the Tenure of Office Act.

In late February, the House voted 126 to 47 to impeach Johnson, the first president ever to be impeached, or charged with unlawful activity. The case then went to trial in the Senate, where the chief justice of the Supreme Court presided and a two-thirds vote was necessary for conviction and removal from office. After a six-week hearing, the Senate fell one vote short of convicting Johnson. Most crucial for Johnson's fate were the votes of seven moderate Republicans who refused to find the president guilty of violating his oath to uphold the Constitution, convinced that Johnson's actions were insufficient to merit the enormously significant step of removing a president from office. Although Johnson narrowly remained in office, Congress effectively ended his power to shape Reconstruction policy.

Not only did the Republicans restrain Johnson but they also won the presidency in 1868. Ulysses S. Grant, the popular Civil War Union general, ran against Horatio Seymour, the Democratic governor of New York. Although an ally of the Radical Republicans, Grant called for reconciliation with the South. He easily defeated Seymour, winning nearly 53 percent of the popular vote and 73 percent of the electoral vote.

The Struggle for Universal Suffrage

In February 1869, Congress passed the **Fifteenth Amendment** to protect black suffrage, which had initially been guaranteed by the Military Reconstruction Acts. A compromise between moderate and Radical Republicans, the amendment prohibited voting discrimination based on race, but it did not deny states the power to impose qualifications based on literacy, payment of taxes, moral character, or any other standard that did not directly relate to race. Subsequently, the wording of the amendment provided loopholes for white leaders to disfranchise African Americans and any other "undesirable" elements. The amendment did, however, cover the entire nation, including the North, where several states, such as Connecticut, Kansas, Michigan, New York, Ohio, and Wisconsin, still excluded blacks from voting.

The Fifteenth Amendment sparked serious conflicts not only within the South but also among old abolitionist allies. The American Anti-Slavery Society disbanded with abolition, but many members believed that important work still remained to be done to guarantee the rights of freedpeople. They formed the **American Equal Rights Association** immediately following the war. Members of this group divided over the Fifteenth Amendment.

Women's rights advocates, such as Elizabeth Cady Stanton and Susan B. Anthony, had earlier objected to the Fourteenth Amendment because it inserted the word *male* into the Constitution for the first time when describing citizens. Although they had been ardent abolitionists before the war, Stanton and Anthony worried that postwar policies intended to enhance the rights of southern black men would further limit the rights of women. Some African American activists also voiced concern. At a meeting of the Equal Rights Association in 1867, Sojourner Truth noted, "There is quite a stir about colored men getting their rights, but not a word about colored women."

The Fifteenth Amendment ignored women. At the 1869 meeting of the Equal Rights Association, differences over supporting the measure erupted into open conflict. Stanton and Anthony denounced suffrage for black men only, and Stanton now supported her position on racial grounds. She claimed that the "dregs of China, Germany, England, Ireland, and Africa" were degrading the U.S. polity and argued that white, educated women should certainly have the same rights as immigrant and African American men. Black and white supporters of the Fifteenth Amendment, including Frances Ellen Watkins Harper, Wendell Phillips, Abby Kelley, and Frederick Douglass, denounced Stanton's bigotry. Believing that southern black men urgently needed suffrage to protect their newly won freedom, they argued that the ratification of black men's suffrage would speed progress toward the achievement of suffrage for black and white women.

> **Explore**
>
> See Document 14.3 for one activist's views on ratifying suffrage for black men.

This conflict led to the formation of competing organizations committed to women's suffrage. The **National Woman Suffrage Association**, established by Stanton and Anthony, allowed only women as members and opposed ratification of the Fifteenth Amendment. The **American Woman Suffrage Association**, which attracted the support of women and men, white and black, supported ratification. Less than a year later, in the spring of 1870, the Fifteenth Amendment was ratified and went into effect. However, the amendment did not grant the vote to either white or black women. As a result, women suffragists turned to the Fourteenth Amendment to achieve their goal. In 1875 Virginia Minor, who had been denied the ballot in Missouri, argued that the right to vote was one of the "privileges and immunities" granted to all citizens under the Fourteenth Amendment. In *Minor v. Happersatt*, the Supreme Court ruled against her.

REVIEW & RELATE

What was President Johnson's plan for reconstruction? How were his views out of step with those of most Republicans?

What characterized congressional Reconstruction? What priorities were reflected in congressional Reconstruction legislation?

Frances Ellen Watkins Harper | On Suffrage, 1869

Born a free person of color in Baltimore, Maryland, Frances Ellen Watkins Harper distinguished herself as a poet, a teacher, and an abolitionist. After the Civil War, she became a staunch advocate of women's suffrage and a supporter of the Fifteenth Amendment, which set her at odds with the suffragists Susan B. Anthony and Elizabeth Cady Stanton. In this discussion at the May 1869 American Equal Rights Association meeting, she argues for ratification of the Fifteenth Amendment.

Explore

When it was a question of race, she [black women] let the lesser question of sex go. But the white women all go for sex, letting race occupy a minor position. She liked the idea of working women, but she would like to know if it was broad enough to take colored women? . . . [When I] was at Boston there were sixty women who left work because one colored woman went to gain a livelihood in their midst. If the nation could only handle one question, I would not have the black women put a single straw in the way, if only the men of the race could obtain what they wanted.

Source: Susan B. Anthony, Elizabeth Cady Stanton, and Matilda Joslyn Gage, eds., *History of Women's Suffrage, 1861–1876* (Rochester, NY: Susan B. Anthony, 1882), 2:391–92.

Frances Ellen Watkins Harper　Image courtesy of Documenting the American South, The University of North Carolina at Chapel Hill Libraries

Interpret the Evidence

- According to Frances Harper, why do black and white women differ on support for black male suffrage?
- How does Harper's experience in Boston influence her opinion?

Put It in Context

Why was it important for black men to gain the right to vote even if it meant delaying women's suffrage?

Remaking the South

With President Johnson's power effectively curtailed, reconstruction of the South moved quickly. However, despite the fears of southern whites and their supporters in the North, the results were neither extreme nor revolutionary. Although African Americans for the first time participated extensively in electoral politics and made unprecedented gains, whites retained control of the majority of the region's wealth and political power. In contrast to revolutions and civil wars in other countries, only one rebel was executed for war crimes (the commandant of Andersonville Prison in Georgia); only one high-ranking official went to prison (Jefferson Davis); no official was forced into exile, though some fled voluntarily; very little land was confiscated and redistributed; and most rebels regained voting rights and the ability to hold office within seven years after the end of the rebellion.

Whites Reconstruct the South

During the first years of congressional Reconstruction, two groups of whites occupied the majority of elective offices in the South. A significant number of native-born Southerners joined Republicans in forming postwar constitutions and governments. Before the war, some had belonged to the Whig Party and opposed secession from the Union. Many mountain dwellers in Alabama, Georgia, North Carolina, and Tennessee had demonstrated a fiercely independent strain and had remained loyal to the Union. As a white resident of the Georgia mountains commented, "Now is the time for every man to come out and speak his principles publickly and vote for liberty as we have been in bondage long enough." Small merchants and farmers who detested large plantation owners also threw their lot in with the Republicans. Even a few ex-Confederates, such as General James A. Longstreet, decided that the South must change and allied with the Republicans. The majority of whites who continued to support the Democratic Party viewed these whites as traitors. They showed their distaste by calling them **scalawags**, an unflattering term meaning "scoundrels."

At the same time, northern whites came south to support Republican Reconstruction. They had varied reasons for making the journey, but most considered the South a new frontier to be conquered culturally, politically, and economically. Some had served in the Union army during the war, liked what they saw of the region, and decided to settle there. Some came to help provide education and assist the freedpeople in adjusting to a new way of

life. As a relatively underdeveloped area, the South also beckoned fortune seekers and adventurers who saw in the South an opportunity to get rich building railroads, establishing factories, and selling consumer goods. Southern Democrats denounced such northern interlopers as **carpetbaggers**, suggesting that they invaded the region with all their possessions in a satchel, seeking to plunder it and then leave. This characterization applied to some, but it did not accurately describe the motivations of most transplanted Northerners. While they did seek economic opportunity, they were acting as Americans always had in settling new frontiers and pursuing dreams of success. In dismissing them as carpetbaggers, their political enemies employed a double standard because they did not apply this demeaning label to those who traveled west—from both the North and the South—in search of economic opportunity at the expense of Indians and Mexicans settled there. Much of the negative feelings directed toward carpetbaggers resulted primarily from their attempts to ally with African Americans in reshaping the South.

Black Political Participation and Economic Opportunities

As much as the majority of southern whites detested scalawags and carpetbaggers, the primary targets of white hostility were African Americans who attempted to exercise their hard-won freedom. Blacks constituted a majority of voters in five states—Alabama, Florida, South Carolina, Mississippi, and Louisiana—while in Georgia, North Carolina, Texas, and Virginia they fell short of a majority. They did not use their ballots to impose black rule on the South as many white Southerners feared. Only in South Carolina did African Americans control the state legislature, and in no state did they manage to elect a governor. Nevertheless, for the first time in American history, blacks won a wide variety of elected positions. More than six hundred blacks served in state legislatures; another sixteen, including Jefferson F. Long, held seats in the U.S. House of Representatives; and two from Mississippi were chosen to serve in the U.S. Senate.

Officeholding alone does not indicate the enthusiasm that former slaves had for politics. African Americans considered politics a community responsibility, and in addition to casting ballots, they held rallies and mass meetings to discuss issues and choose candidates. Although they could not vote, women attended these gatherings and helped influence their outcome. Covering a Republican convention in Richmond in October 1867, held in the African First Baptist Church, the *New York Times* reported that "the entire colored population of Richmond" attended. Freedpeople also formed associations to promote education, economic advancement, and social welfare programs, all of which they saw as deeply intertwined with politics. These included organizations like Richmond's Mutual Benefit Society, a group formed by single mothers, and the Independent Order of St. Luke, a mutual aid society for black women and men. African American women led both.

The efforts of southern blacks to bolster their freedom included building alliances with sympathetic whites. The resulting interracial political coalitions produced considerable reform in the South. These coalitions created a public school system where none had existed before the war; provided funds for social services, such as poor relief and state hospitals; upgraded prisons; and rebuilt the South's transportation system by supporting railroads and construction projects. Moreover, the state constitutions that the Republicans wrote brought a greater measure of political democracy and equality to the South by extending the right to vote to poor white men as well as black men. Some states allowed married women greater control over their property and liberalized the criminal justice system. In effect, these Reconstruction governments brought the South into the nineteenth century.

Obtaining political representation was one way in which African Americans defined freedom. Economic independence constituted a second. Without government-sponsored land redistribution, however, the options for southern blacks remained limited. Lacking capital to start farms, they entered into various forms of tenant contracts with large landowners. **Sharecropping** proved the most common arrangement. Blacks and poor whites became sharecroppers for much the same economic reasons. They received tools and supplies from landowners and farmed their own plots of land on the plantation. In exchange, sharecroppers turned over a portion of their harvest to the owner and kept some for themselves. Crop divisions varied but were usually explained in detail on written agreements. To make this system profitable, sharecroppers concentrated on producing staple crops such as cotton and tobacco that they could sell for cash.

The benefits of sharecropping proved more valuable to black farmers in theory than in practice. To tide them over during the growing season, croppers had to purchase household provisions on credit from a local merchant, who was often also the farmers' landlord. At the mercy of store owners who kept the books and charged high interest rates, tenants usually found themselves in considerable debt at the end of the year. To satisfy the debt, merchants devised a crop lien system in which tenants pledged a portion of their yearly crop to satisfy what they owed. Most indebted tenants found themselves bound to the landlord because falling prices in agricultural staples during this period meant that they did not receive sufficient return on their produce to get out of debt. For many African Americans, sharecropping turned into a form of virtual slavery.

Explore

See Document 14.4 for an example of a sharecropping agreement.

The picture for black farmers was not all bleak, however. About 20 percent of black farmers managed to buy their own land. Through careful management and extremely hard work, black families planted gardens for household consumption and raised chickens for eggs and food. Despite its pitfalls, sharecropping provided a limited measure of labor independence and allowed some blacks to accumulate small amounts of cash.

Following the war's devastation, many of the South's white, small farmers known as yeomen also fell into sharecropping. Yet planters, too, had changed. Many sons of planters abandoned farming and became lawyers, bankers, and merchants. Despite these changes, one thing remained the same: White elites ruled over blacks and poor whites, and they kept these two economically exploited groups from uniting by fanning the flames of racial prejudice.

Economic hardship and racial bigotry drove many blacks to leave the South. In 1879 former slaves pooled their resources to create land companies and purchase property in Kansas on which to settle. They created black towns that attracted some 25,000 African American migrants from the South, known as **Exodusters**. Kansas was ruled by the Republican Party and had been home to the great antislavery martyr John Brown. As one hopeful freedman from Louisiana wrote to the Kansas governor in 1879, "I am anxious to reach your state . . . because of the sacredness of her soil washed in the blood of humanitarians for the cause of black freedom." Exodusters did not find the Promised Land, however, as poor-quality land and unpredictable weather made farming on the Great Plains a hard and often unrewarding experience. Nevertheless, for many African American migrants, the chance to own their own land and escape the oppression of the South was worth the hardships. In 1880 the census counted 40,000 blacks living in Kansas.

White Resistance to Congressional Reconstruction

Despite the Republican record of accomplishment during Reconstruction, white Southerners did not accept its legitimacy. They accused interracial governments of conducting a spending spree that raised taxes and encouraged corruption. Indeed, taxes did rise significantly, but mainly because of the need to provide new educational

DOCUMENT 14.4

Sharecropping Agreement, 1870

Because Congress did not generally provide freedpeople with land, African Americans lacked the capital to start their own farms. At the same time, plantation owners needed labor to plant and harvest their crops for market. Out of mutual necessity, white plantation owners entered into sharecropping contracts with blacks to work their farms in exchange for a portion of the crop, such as the following contract between Willis P. Bocock and several of his former slaves. Bocock owned Waldwick Plantation in Marengo County, Alabama.

Explore

What are the farmers' responsibilities?

Why would Bocock want to clarify that his laborers would work equally hard throughout the year?

How might putting a lien on crops for debts owed create difficulties for the black farmer?

Contract made the 3rd day of January in the year 1870 between us the free people who have signed this paper of one part, and our employer, Willis P. Bocock, of the other part. We agree to take charge of and cultivate for the year 1870, a portion of land, say [left blank] acres or thereabouts, to be laid off to us by our employer on his plantation, and to tend the same well in the usual crops, in such proportions as we and he may agree upon. We are to furnish the necessary labor, say an average hand to every 15 acres in the crops, making in all average hands; and are to have all proper work done, ditching, fencing, repairing, etc., as well as cultivating and saving the crops of all kinds, so as to put and keep the land we occupy and tend in good order for cropping, and to make a good crop ourselves; and to do our fair share of job work about the place. . . . We are to be responsible for the good conduct of ourselves, our hands, and families, and agree that all shall be respectful to employer, owners, and manager, honest, industrious, and careful about every thing, and shall not interrupt any thing about the place, working as industriously the last part of the year as the first; and then our employer agrees that he and his manager shall treat us kindly, and help us to study our interest and do our duty. If any hand or family proves to be of bad character, or dishonest, or lazy, or disobedient, or any way unsuitable our employer or manager has the right, and we have the right, to have such turned off. . . .

For the labor and services of ourselves and hands rendered as above stated, we are to have one third part of all the crops, or their net-proceeds, made and secured, or prepared for market by our force. . . .

We are to be furnished by our employer through his manager with provisions if we call for them: not over one peck of meal or corn, and $3\frac{1}{2}$ pounds of meat or its equivalent per week, for every 15 acres of land or average hand, to be charged to us at fair market prices.

And whatever may be due by us, or our hands to our employer for provisions or any thing else, during the year, is to be a lien on our share of the crops, and is to be retained by him out of the same before we receive our part.

Source: Waldwick Plantation Records, 1834–1971, LPR174, box 1, folder 9, Alabama Department of Archives and History.

Put It in Context

Why would free blacks and poor whites be willing to enter into such a contract?

Exodusters

This photograph of two black couples standing on their homestead was taken around 1880 in Nicodemus, Kansas. These settlers, known as Exodusters, had migrated to northwest Kansas following the end of Reconstruction. They sought economic opportunity free from the racial repression sweeping the South.   Library of Congress

and social services. Corruption, where building projects and railroad construction were concerned, was common during this time. Still, it is unfair to single out Reconstruction governments and especially black legislators as inherently depraved, as their Democratic opponents did. Economic scandals were part of American life after the Civil War. As enormous business opportunities arose and the pent-up energies that had gone into battles over slavery exploded into desires to accumulate wealth, many business leaders and politicians made unlawful deals to enrich themselves.

Most Reconstruction governments had only limited opportunities to transform the South. By the end of 1870, civilian rule had returned to all of the former Confederate states, and they had reentered the Union. Republican rule did not continue past 1870 in Virginia, North Carolina, and Tennessee and did not extend beyond 1871 in Georgia and 1873 in Texas. In 1874 Democrats deposed Republicans in Arkansas and Alabama; two years later, Democrats triumphed in Mississippi. In only three

states—Louisiana, Florida, and South Carolina—did Reconstruction last until 1877.

The Democrats who replaced Republicans trumpeted their victories as bringing "redemption" to the South. Of course, these so-called **Redeemers** were referring to the white South. For black Republicans and their white allies, redemption meant defeat, not resurrection. Democratic victories came at the ballot boxes, but violence, intimidation, and fraud usually paved the way. It was not enough for Democrats to attack Republican policies. They also used racist appeals to divide poor whites from blacks and backed them up with force. In 1865 in Pulaski, Tennessee, General Nathan Bedford Forrest organized Confederate veterans into a social club called the **Knights of the Ku Klux Klan (KKK)**. The name came from the Greek word *kuklos*, meaning "circle." Spreading throughout the South, the KKK did not function as an ordinary social association; its followers donned robes and masks to hide their identities and terrify their victims. Ku Kluxers wielded rifles and guns and rode on horseback to the homes and

Visit of the Ku Klux Klan

This 1872 wood engraving by the noted magazine illustrator Frank Bellew appeared at the height of Ku Klux Klan violence against freed blacks in the South. This image depicts a black family seemingly secure in their home in the evening while masked Klansmen stand in their doorway ready to attack with rifles.   Library of Congress

churches of black and white Republicans to keep them from voting. When threats did not work, they murdered their victims. In 1871, for example, 150 African Americans were killed in Jackson County in the Florida Panhandle. A black clergyman lamented, "That is where Satan has his seat." Here and elsewhere, many of the individuals targeted had managed to buy property, gain political leadership, or in other ways defy white stereotypes of African American inferiority. Local rifle clubs, hunting groups, and other white supremacist organizations joined the Klan in waging a reign of terror. During the 1875 election in Mississippi, which toppled the Republican government, armed terrorists killed hundreds of Republicans and scared many more away from the polls.

To combat the terror unleashed by the Klan and its allies, Congress passed three Force Acts in 1870 and 1871. These measures empowered the president to dispatch officials into the South to supervise elections and prevent voting interference. Directed specifically at the KKK, one law barred secret organizations from using force to violate equal protection of the laws. In 1872 Congress established a joint committee to probe Klan tactics, and its investigations produced thirteen volumes of vivid testimony about the horrors perpetrated by the Klan. Elias Hill, a freedman

from South Carolina who had become a Baptist preacher and teacher, was one of those who appeared before Congress. He and his brother lived next door to each other. The Klansmen went first to his brother's house, where, as Hill testified, they "broke open the door and attacked his wife, and I heard her screaming and mourning [moaning]. . . . At last I heard them have [rape] her in the yard. She was crying and the Ku-Klux were whipping her to make her tell where I lived." When Klansmen finally discovered Elias Hill, they dragged him out of his house, accused him of preaching against the Klan, beat and whipped him, and threatened to kill him. On the basis of such testimony, the federal government prosecuted some 3,000 Klansmen. Only 600 were convicted, however. As the Klan disbanded in the wake of federal prosecutions, other vigilante organizations arose to take its place.

REVIEW & RELATE

What role did black people play in remaking southern society during Reconstruction?

How did southern whites fight back against Reconstruction? What role did terrorism and political violence play in this effort?

The Unmaking of Reconstruction

The violence, intimidation, and fraud perpetrated by Redeemers against black and white Republicans in the South does not fully explain the unmaking of Reconstruction. Although Republicans in Congress enacted legislation combating the KKK and racial discrimination in public facilities, by the early 1870s white Northerners had grown weary of the struggle to protect the rights of freedpeople. In the minds of many, white Northerners had done more than enough for black Southerners, and it was time to focus on other issues. Growing economic problems intensified this feeling. More and more northern whites came to believe that any debt owed to black people for northern complicity in the sin of slavery had been wiped out by the blood shed during the Civil War. By the early 1870s, burying and memorializing the Civil War dead emerged as a common concern among white Americans, in both the North and the South. White America was once again united, if only in the shared belief that it was time to move on, consigning the issues of slavery and civil rights to history.

The Republican Retreat

Most northern whites shared the racial views of their counterparts in the South. Although they had supported protection of black civil rights and suffrage, they still believed that African Americans were inferior to whites, and social integration was no more tolerable to them than it was to white Southerners. They began to sympathize with racist complaints voiced from the South that blacks were not capable of governing honestly and effectively.

In 1872 a group calling themselves **Liberal Republicans** challenged the reelection of President Grant, the Civil War general who had won the presidency on the Republican ticket in 1868. Financial scandals had racked the Grant administration. This high-level corruption reflected the get-rich-quick schemes connected to economic speculation and development following the Civil War. Outraged by these misdeeds and the rising level of immoral behavior in government and business, Liberal Republicans nominated Horace Greeley, editor of the *New York Tribune*, to run against Grant. They linked government corruption to the expansion of federal power that accompanied Reconstruction, and called for the removal of troops from the South and amnesty for former Confederates. They also campaigned for civil service reform in order to establish a merit system for government employment and for abolition of the "spoils system"—in which the party in power rewarded loyal supporters with political

appointments—that had been in place since the administration of Andrew Jackson.

The Democratic Party believed that Liberal Republicans offered the best chance to defeat Grant, and it endorsed Greeley. Despite the scandals that surrounded him, Grant remained popular. Moreover, the main body of Republicans "waved the bloody shirt," reminding northern voters that a ballot cast for the opposition tarnished the memory of brave Union soldiers who had died during the war. With the newly created national cemeteries, particularly the one established in Arlington, Virginia, providing a vivid reminder of the hundreds of thousands of soldiers killed, the "bloody shirt" remained a potent symbol. The president won reelection with an even greater margin than he had four years earlier. Nevertheless, the attacks against Grant foreshadowed the Republican retreat on Reconstruction. Among the Democrats sniping at Grant was Andrew Johnson. Johnson had returned to Tennessee, and in 1874 the state legislature chose the former president to serve in the U.S. Senate. He continued to speak out against the presence of federal troops in the South until his death in 1875.

Congressional and Judicial Retreat

By the time Grant began his second term, Congress was already considering bills to restore officeholding rights to former Confederates who had not yet sworn allegiance to the Union. Black representatives, such as Georgia congressman Jefferson Long, as well as some white lawmakers, remained opposed to such measures, but in 1872 Congress removed the penalties placed on former Confederates by the Fourteenth Amendment and permitted nearly all rebel leaders the right to vote and hold office. Two years later, for the first time since the start of the Civil War, the Democrats gained a majority in the House of Representatives and prepared to remove the remaining troops from the South.

Economic concerns increasingly replaced racial considerations as the top priority for northern Republican leaders. Northerners and Southerners began calling more loudly for national unity and reconciliation. In 1873 a financial panic resulting from the collapse of the Northern Pacific Railroad triggered a severe economic depression lasting late into the decade. Tens of thousands of unemployed workers across the country worried more about finding jobs than they did about blacks in the South. Businessmen, too, were plagued with widespread bankruptcy. As workers looked to labor unions for support, business leaders looked to the federal government for assistance. When strikes erupted across the country in 1877, most notably the Great Railway Strike, employers asked the U.S. government to remove troops from the

South and dispatch them against strikers in the North and the West.

While Northerners sought a way to extricate themselves from Reconstruction, the Supreme Court weakened enforcement of the civil rights acts. In 1873 the *Slaughterhouse* cases defined the rights that African Americans were entitled to under the Fourteenth Amendment very narrowly. Reflecting the shift from moral to economic concerns, the justices interpreted the amendment as extending greater protection to corporations in conducting business than that extended to blacks. As a result, blacks had to depend on southern state governments to protect their civil rights, the same state authorities that had deprived them of their rights in the first place. In *United States v. Cruikshank* (1876), the high court narrowed the Fourteenth Amendment further, ruling that it protected blacks against abuses only by state officials and agencies, not by private groups such as the Ku Klux Klan. Seven years later, the Court struck down the Civil Rights Act of 1875, which had extended "full and equal treatment" in public accommodations for persons of all races.

The Presidential Compromise of 1876

The presidential election of 1876 set in motion events that officially brought Reconstruction to an end. The Republicans nominated Rutherford B. Hayes, a Civil War officer and governor of Ohio. A supporter of civil service reform, Hayes was chosen, in part, because he was untainted by the corruption that plagued the Grant administration. The Democrats selected their own crusader against bribery and graft, Governor Samuel J. Tilden of New York, who had prosecuted political corruption in New York City.

The outcome of the election depended on twenty disputed electoral votes, nineteen from the South and one from Oregon. Tilden won 51 percent of the popular vote, but Reconstruction political battles in Florida, Louisiana, and South Carolina put the election up for grabs. In each of these states, the outgoing Republican administration certified Hayes as the winner, while the incoming Democratic regime declared for Tilden.

The Constitution assigns Congress the task of counting and certifying the electoral votes submitted by the states. Normally, this is merely a formality, but 1876 was different. Democrats controlled the House, Republicans controlled the Senate, and neither branch would budge on which votes to count. Hayes needed all twenty for victory; Tilden needed only one. To break the logjam, Congress created a fifteen-member **Joint Electoral Commission**, composed of seven Democrats, seven Republicans, and one independent (five members of the House, five U.S. senators, and five Supreme Court justices). As it turned out, the independent commissioner, Justice David Davis,

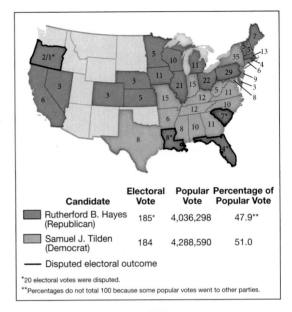

Candidate	Electoral Vote	Popular Vote	Percentage of Popular Vote
Rutherford B. Hayes (Republican)	185*	4,036,298	47.9**
Samuel J. Tilden (Democrat)	184	4,288,590	51.0
— Disputed electoral outcome			

*20 electoral votes were disputed.
**Percentages do not total 100 because some popular votes went to other parties.

MAP 14.2   The Election of 1876

The presidential election of 1876 got swept up in Reconstruction politics. Democrats defeated Republicans in Florida, Louisiana, and South Carolina, but both parties claimed the electoral votes for their candidates. A federal electoral commission set up to investigate the twenty disputed votes, including one from Oregon, awarded the votes and the election to the Republican, Rutherford B. Hayes.

resigned, and his replacement, Justice Joseph P. Bradley, voted with the Republicans to count all twenty votes for Hayes, making him president (Map 14.2).

Still, Congress had to ratify this count, and disgruntled southern Democrats in the Senate threatened a filibuster—unlimited debate—to block certification of Hayes. With the March 4, 1877, date for the presidential inauguration creeping perilously close and no winner officially declared, behind-the-scenes negotiations finally helped settle the controversy. A series of meetings between Hayes supporters and southern Democrats led to a bargain. According to the agreement, Democrats would support Hayes in exchange for the president appointing a Southerner to his cabinet, withdrawing the last federal troops from the South, and endorsing construction of a transcontinental railroad through the South. This **compromise of 1877** averted a crisis over presidential succession, underscored increased southern Democratic influence within Congress, and marked the end to strong federal protection for African Americans in the South.

REVIEW & RELATE

Why did northern interest in Reconstruction wane in the 1870s?

What common values and beliefs among white Americans were reflected in the compromise of 1877?

LEARNINGCurve bedfordstmartins.com/hewittlawson/LC

Conclusion: The Legacies of Reconstruction

Reconstruction was, in many ways, profoundly limited. African Americans did not receive the landownership that would have provided them with the economic independence to bolster their freedom from the racist assaults of white Southerners. The civil and political rights that the federal government conferred did not withstand Redeemers' efforts to disfranchise and deprive the freedpeople of equal rights. The Republican Party shifted its priorities elsewhere, and Democrats gained enough political power nationally to short-circuit federal intervention, while numerous problems remained unresolved in the South. Northern support for racial equality did not run very deep, so white Northerners, who shared many of the prejudices of white Southerners, were happy to extricate themselves from further intervention in southern racial matters. Nor was there sufficient support to give women, white and black, the right to vote. Finally, federal courts, with growing concerns over economic rather than social issues, sanctioned Northerners' retreat by providing constitutional legitimacy for abandoning black Southerners and rejecting women's suffrage in court decisions that narrowed the interpretation of the Fourteenth and Fifteenth Amendments.

Despite all of this, Reconstruction did transform the country. As a result of Reconstruction, slavery was abolished, and the legal basis for freedom was enshrined in the Constitution. Indeed, blacks exercised a measure of political and economic freedom during Reconstruction that never entirely disappeared over the decades to come. In many areas, freedpeople, as exemplified by Congressman Jefferson Franklin Long among many others, asserted what they could never have during slavery—control over their lives, their churches, their labor, and their families. What they could not practice during their own time because of racial discrimination, their descendants would one day revive through the promises codified in the Fourteenth and Fifteenth Amendments.

African Americans transformed not only themselves; they transformed the nation. The Constitution became much more democratic and egalitarian through inclusion of the Reconstruction amendments. Reconstruction lawmakers took an important step toward making the United States the "more perfect union" that the nation's Founders had pledged to create. Reconstruction established a model for expanding the power of the federal government to resolve domestic crises that lay beyond the abilities of states and ordinary citizens. It remained a powerful legacy for those elected officials in the future who dared to invoke it. And Reconstruction transformed the South to its everlasting benefit. It modernized state constitutions, expanded educational and social welfare systems, and unleashed the repressed potential for industrialization and economic development that the preservation of slavery had restrained. Ironically, Reconstruction did as much for white Southerners as it did for black Southerners in liberating them from the past.

LEARNINGCurve
Check what you know.
bedfordstmartins.com/hewittlawson/LC

Chapter Review　　Online Study Guide ▶ bedfordstmartins.com/hewittlawson

KEY TERMS

Freedmen's Bureau (p. 427)
Proclamation of Amnesty and Reconstruction
　(p. 431)
Thirteenth Amendment (p. 431)
black codes (p. 432)
Fourteenth Amendment (p. 436)
Tenure of Office Act (p. 437)
Fifteenth Amendment (p. 438)
American Equal Rights Association (p. 438)
National Woman Suffrage Association (p. 438)

American Woman Suffrage Association (p. 438)
scalawags (p. 440)
carpetbaggers (p. 440)
sharecropping (p. 441)
Exodusters (p. 441)
Redeemers (p. 443)
Knights of the Ku Klux Klan (KKK) (p. 443)
Liberal Republicans (p. 445)
Joint Electoral Commission (p. 446)
compromise of 1877 (p. 446)

REVIEW & RELATE

1. What were freedpeople's highest priorities in the years immediately following the Civil War? Why?

2. How did freedpeople define freedom? What steps did they take to make freedom real for themselves and their children?

3. What was President Johnson's plan for reconstruction? How were his views out of step with those of most Republicans?

4. What characterized congressional Reconstruction? What priorities were reflected in congressional Reconstruction legislation?

5. What role did black people play in remaking southern society during Reconstruction?

6. How did southern whites fight back against Reconstruction? What role did terrorism and political violence play in this effort?

7. Why did northern interest in Reconstruction wane in the 1870s?

8. What common values and beliefs among white Americans were reflected in the compromise of 1877?

TIMELINE OF EVENTS

1863	Lincoln issues Proclamation of Amnesty and Reconstruction
1865	Ku Klux Klan formed
	Freedmen's Bureau established
	Congress passes Thirteenth Amendment
April 1865	Lincoln assassinated; Andrew Johnson becomes president
May–December 1865	Presidential Reconstruction under Andrew Johnson
1866	Congress passes extension of Freedmen's Bureau and Civil Rights Act over Johnson's presidential veto
	Congress passes Fourteenth Amendment
1867	Military Reconstruction Acts divide the South into military districts
	Congress passes Command of the Army and Tenure of Office Acts
1868	Andrew Johnson impeached
1869	Congress passes Fifteenth Amendment
	Women's suffrage movement splits over support of Fifteenth Amendment
1870	250,000 blacks attend schools established by the Freedmen's Bureau
	Civilian rule reestablished in all former Confederate states
1870–1871	Jefferson Long serves as a Republican congressman from Georgia
1870–1872	Congress takes steps to curb KKK violence in the South
1872	Liberal Republicans challenge reelection of President Grant
1873	Financial panic sparks depression lasting until the late 1870s
1873–1883	Supreme Court limits rights of African Americans
1875	Congress passes Civil Rights Act outlawing discrimination in public accommodations, which the Supreme Court rules unconstitutional in 1883
1877	Republicans and southern Democrats reach compromise resulting in the election of Rutherford B. Hayes as president and the end of Reconstruction
1879	Black Exodusters migrate from South to Kansas

Testing and Contesting Freedom

Nine months after the Civil War ended in April 1865, twenty-seven states ratified the Thirteenth Amendment, abolishing slavery throughout the United States. Freedom, however, did not guarantee equal rights or the absence of racial discrimination. Immediately following the North's victory, white southern leaders enacted black codes, which aimed to prevent the former slaves from improving their social and economic status. Although Lincoln's successor, Andrew Johnson, himself a Southerner, did not support the codes, he did nothing to overturn them. An advocate of limited government, Johnson clashed repeatedly with Congress over Reconstruction, vetoing renewal of the Freedmen's Bureau bill and opposing ratification of the Fourteenth Amendment. In 1867 the Republican majority in Congress passed the Military Reconstruction Acts, which placed the South under military rule and forced it to extend equal political and civil rights to African Americans.

The Military Reconstruction Acts, followed by the ratification of the Fifteenth Amendment in 1870, extended suffrage to black men. In alliance with white Republicans, blacks won election to a variety of public offices, including seats on local and state governmental bodies. When these interracial legislatures provided funds for public education of blacks—for the first time in the South—and for black hospitals and other social services, their opponents attacked them for fraud, corruption, wasteful spending, and imposing "Black Rule." Opponents also created vigilante groups like the Ku Klux Klan to intimidate black and white Republicans through scare tactics backed up by violence and bloodshed. By 1877 the attempt of white southern Democrats, or Redeemers, had succeeded, leaving African Americans struggling to retain the freedom they had enjoyed during Reconstruction.

As you read the following documents, consider these general questions: How did blacks and whites view freedom? How essential was it for the federal government to supervise the movement from slavery to freedom? Why didn't southern whites accept the extension of civil rights for blacks, if only in a limited way? How did views about Reconstruction change over time?

DOCUMENT 14.5

Mississippi Black Code, 1865

Southern legislatures created black codes primarily to limit the rights of free blacks after emancipation and return them to a condition as close as possible to slavery. Mississippi was one of the first states to enact a black code. Although its laws did legalize marriage for blacks and allowed them to own property and testify in court, its primary intent was to limit freedpeople's mobility and economic opportunities. New vagrancy laws required blacks to provide written proof of residency and employment or else risk arrest, while other sections limited where they could live, restricted the terms of their employment, and banned intermarriage.

An Act to Confer Civil Rights on Freedmen, and for other Purposes

Section 1. All freedmen, free negroes and mulattoes may sue and be sued . . . in all the courts of law and equity of this State, and may acquire personal property, and choses in action [right to bring a lawsuit to recover chattels, money, or a debt], by descent or purchase, and may dispose of the same in the same manner and to the same extent that white persons may: Provided, That the provisions of this section shall not be so construed as to allow any freedman, free negro or mulatto to rent or lease any lands or tenements except in incorporated cities or towns, in which places the corporate authorities shall control the same.

Section 2. All freedmen, free negroes and mulattoes may intermarry with each other, in the same manner and under the same regulations that are provided by law for white persons: Provided, that the clerk of probate shall keep separate records of the same.

Section 3. All freedmen, free negroes or mulattoes who do now and have herebefore lived and cohabited together as husband and wife shall be taken and held in law as legally married, and the issue shall be taken and held as legitimate for all purposes; and it shall not be lawful for any freedman, free negro or mulatto to intermarry with any white person; nor for any person to intermarry with any freedman, free negro or mulatto; and any person who shall so intermarry shall be deemed guilty of felony, and on conviction thereof shall be confined in the State penitentiary for life; and those shall be deemed freedmen, free negroes and mulattoes who are of pure negro blood, and those descended from a negro to the third generation, inclusive, though one ancestor in each generation may have been a white person.

Section 4. In addition to cases in which freedmen, free negroes and mulattoes are now by law competent witnesses, freedmen, free negroes or mulattoes shall be competent in civil cases, when a party or parties to the suit, either plaintiff or plaintiffs, defendant or defendants; also in cases where freedmen, free negroes and mulattoes is or are either plaintiff or plaintiffs, defendant or defendants. They shall also be competent witnesses in all criminal prosecutions where the crime charged is alleged to have been committed by a white person upon or against the person or property of a freedman, free negro or mulatto. . . .

Section 5. Every freedman, free negro and mulatto shall, on the second Monday of January, one thousand eight hundred and sixty-six, and annually thereafter, have a lawful home or employment, and shall have written evidence thereof as follows, to wit: if living in any incorporated city, town, or village, a license from that mayor thereof; and if living outside of an incorporated city, town, or village, from the member of the board of police of his beat, authorizing him or her to do irregular and job work; or a written contract, as provided in Section 6 in this act; which license may be revoked for cause at any time by the authority granting the same.

SECTION 6. All contracts for labor made with freedmen, free negroes and mulattoes for a longer period than one month shall be in writing, and a duplicate, attested and read to said freedman, free negro or mulatto by a beat, city or county officer, or two disinterested white persons of the county in which the labor is to [be] performed, of which each party shall have one: and said contracts shall be taken and held as entire contracts, and if the laborer shall quit the service of the employer before the expiration of his term of service, without good cause, he shall forfeit his wages for that year up to the time of quitting. . . .

An Act to Amend the Vagrant Laws of the State . . .

SECTION 2. All freedmen, free negroes and mulattoes in this State, over the age of eighteen years, found on the second Monday in January, 1866, or thereafter, with no lawful employment or business, or found unlawful[ly] assembling themselves together, either in the day or night time, and all white persons assembling themselves with freedmen, free negroes or mulattoes, or usually associating with freedmen, free negroes or mulattoes, on terms of equality, or living in adultery or fornication with a freed woman, freed negro or mulatto, shall be deemed vagrants, and on conviction thereof shall be fined in a sum not exceeding, in the case of a freedman, free negro or mulatto, fifty dollars, and a white man two hundred dollars, and imprisonment at the discretion of the court, the free negro not exceeding ten days, and the white man not exceeding six months. . . .

SECTION 6. The same duties and liabilities existing among white persons of this State shall attach to freedmen, free negroes or mulattoes, to support their indigent families and all colored paupers; and that in order to secure a support for such indigent freedmen, free negroes, or mulattoes, it shall be lawful, and is hereby made the duty of the county police of each county in this State, to levy a poll or capitation tax on each and every freedman, free negro, or mulatto, between the ages of eighteen and sixty years, not to exceed the sum of one dollar annually to each person so taxed, which tax, when collected, shall be paid into the county treasurer's hands, and constitute a fund to be called the Freedman's Pauper Fund, which shall be applied by the commissioners of the poor for the maintenance of the poor of the freedmen, free negroes and mulattoes of this State, under such regulations as may be established by the boards of county police in the respective counties of this State.

Source: *Laws of the State of Mississippi, Passed at a Regular Session of the Mississippi Legislature, Held in the City of Jackson, October, November, and December, 1865* (Jackson, MS, 1866), 82–86, 165–67.

DOCUMENT 14.6

Richard H. Cain | Federal Aid for Land Purchase, 1868

Richard H. Cain, a free black minister raised in Ohio, went to South Carolina after the war and served as a Republican member of the U.S. House of Representatives for two terms in the 1870s. The following excerpt comes from a speech Cain made in 1868 as a representative to the South Carolina constitutional convention. Cain proposed that the convention petition Congress for a $1 million loan to purchase land that could be resold to freedmen at a reasonable price.

BELIEVE THE BEST MEASURE to be adopted is to bring capital to the State, and instead of causing revenge and unpleasantness, I am for even-handed justice. I am for allowing the parties who own lands to bring them into the market and sell them upon such terms as will be satisfactory to both sides. I believe a measure of this kind has a double effect: first, it brings capital, what the people want; second, it puts the people to work; it gives homesteads, what we need; it relieves the Government and takes away its responsibility of feeding the people; it inspires every man with a noble manfulness, and by the thought that he is the possessor of something in the State; it adds also to the revenue of the country. By these means men become interested in the country as they never were before. It was said that five and one-seventh acres were not enough to live on. If South Carolina, in its sovereign power, can devise any plan for the purchase of the large plantations in this State now lying idle, divide and sell them out at a reasonable price, it will give so many people work. I will guarantee to find persons to work every five acres. I will also guarantee that after one year's time, the Freedman's Bureau will not have to give any man having one acre of land anything to eat. This country has a genial clime, rich soil, and can be worked to advantage. The man who can not earn a living on five acres, will not do so on twenty-five.

I regret that another position taken by gentlemen in the opposition, is that they do not believe that we will get what we ask for. I believe that the party now in power in the Congress of the United States, will do whatever they can for the welfare of the people of this State and of the South. I believe that the noble men who have maintained the rights of the freedmen before and since their liberation, will continue to do everything possible to forward these great interests. I am exceedingly anxious, if possible, to allay all unpleasant feeling—I would not have any unpleasant feeling among ourselves.

I would not have any unpleasant feelings between the races. If we give each family in the State an opportunity of purchasing a home, I think they will all be better satisfied.

But it is also said that it will disturb all the agricultural operations in the State. I do not believe if the Congress of the United States shall advance one million of dollars to make purchase of lands, the laborers will abandon their engagement and run off. I have more confidence in the people I represent. I believe all who have made contracts will fulfill those contracts, and when their contracts have expired, they will go on their own lands, as all freemen ought to go.

Source: *Proceedings of the South Carolina Constitutional Convention of 1868* (Charleston, SC, 1868), 420–21.

DOCUMENT 14.7

Ellen Parton | Testimony on Klan Violence, 1871

In March 1871, white mobs killed some thirty African Americans in Meridian, Mississippi. Later that month, a joint committee of the Mississippi legislature held hearings on the violence, which included the following testimony by Ellen Parton of Mississippi, a former slave and domestic worker. The Klan suspected that Parton's husband was involved in the Union League, a southern affiliate of the Republican Party. Congress also conducted hearings on the vigilante violence against blacks throughout the South.

Ellen Parton, being sworn, states:

I reside in Meridian; have resided here nine years; occupation, washing and ironing and scouring; Wednesday night was the last night they came to my house; by "they" I mean bodies or companies of men; they came on Monday, Tuesday, and Wednesday. On Monday night they said that they came to do us no harm. On Tuesday night they said they came for the arms; I told them there was none, and they said they would take my word for it. On Wednesday night they came and broke open the wardrobe and trunks, and committed rape upon me; there were eight of them in the house; I do not know how many there were outside; they were white men; there was a light in the house; I was living in Marshal Ware's house; there were three lights burning. Mr. Ware has been one of the policemen of this town. He was concealed at the time they came; they took the claw hammer and broke open the pantry where he was lying; he was concealed in the pantry under some plunder, covered up well; I guess he covered himself up. A man said "here is Marshal's hat, where is Marshal?" I told him "I did not know"; they went then into everything in the house, and broke open the wardrobe; I called upon Mr. Mike Slamon, who was one of the crowd, for protection; I said to him "please protect me tonight, you have known me for a long time." This man covered up his head then; he had a hold of me at this time; Mr. Slamon had an oil-cloth and put it before his face, trying to conceal himself, and the man that had hold of me told me not to call Mr. Slamon's name any more. He then took me in the dining room, and told me that I had to do just what he said: I told him I could do nothing of that sort; that was not my way, and he replied "by God, you have got to," and then threw me down. This man had a black eye, where some one had beaten him; he had a black velvet cap on. After he got through with me he came through the house, and said that he was after the Union Leagues; I yielded to him because he had a pistol drawn; when he took me down he hurt me of course; I yielded to him on that account.

Source: *Report of the Joint Select Committee [of Congress] to Inquire into the Condition of Affairs in the Late Insurrectionary States, Mississippi* (Washington, D.C.: Government Printing Office, 1872), 1:38–39.

DOCUMENT 14.8

The Force Act, 1871

As testimony of antiblack violence mounted, Congress passed the Force Act (also known as the Ku Klux Klan Act) in April 1871. A federal response to stop the terror and intimidation of southern black and white Republicans by their opponents, the act provided both civil relief for damages and criminal penalties. It was rooted in the Fourteenth Amendment's guarantees of the rights and privileges of U.S. citizenship. The federal government dispatched troops to enforce the law and prosecuted hundreds of Klan members, often before predominantly black juries, resulting in the breakup of the Klan within a few years.

Be it enacted . . . That any person who, under color of any law, statute, ordinance, regulation, custom, or usage of any State, shall subject, or cause to be subjected, any person within the jurisdiction of the United States to the deprivation of any rights, privileges, or immunities secured by the Constitution of the United States, shall, any such law, statute, ordinance, regulation, custom, or usage of the State to the contrary notwithstanding, be liable to the party injured in any action at law, suit in equity, or other proper proceeding for redress; such proceeding to be prosecuted in the several district or circuit courts of the United States, with and subject to the same rights of appeal, review upon error, and other remedies provided in like cases in such courts, under the provisions of the [Civil Rights Act of 1866], and the other remedial laws of the United States which are in their nature applicable in such cases. . . .

SEC. 3. That in all cases where insurrection, domestic violence, unlawful combinations, or conspiracies in any State shall so obstruct or hinder the execution of the laws thereof, and of the United States, as to deprive any portion or class of the people of such State of any of the rights, privileges, or immunities, or protection, named in the Constitution and secured by this act, and the constituted authorities of such State shall either be unable to protect, or shall, from any cause, fail in or refuse protection of the people in such rights, such facts shall be deemed a denial by such State of the equal protection of the laws to which they are entitled under the Constitution of the United States; and in all such cases, or whenever any such insurrection, violence, unlawful combination, or conspiracy shall oppose or obstruct the laws of the United States or the due execution thereof, or impede or obstruct the due course of justice under the same, it shall be lawful for the President, and it shall be his duty to take such measures, by the employment of the militia or the land and naval forces of the United States, or of either, or by other means, as he may deem necessary for the suppression of such insurrection, domestic violence, or combinations. . . .

SEC. 6. That any person or persons, having knowledge that any of the wrongs conspired to be done and mentioned in the second section of this act are about to be committed, and having power to prevent or aid in preventing the same, shall neglect or refuse to do so, and such wrongful act shall be committed, such person or persons shall be liable to the person injured, or his legal representatives, for all damages caused by any such wrongful act which such first-named person or persons by reasonable diligence could have prevented.

Source: George P. Sanger, ed., *Statutes at Large and Proclamations of the United States of America from March 1871 to March 1873* (Boston: Little, Brown, 1873), 13–15.

DOCUMENT 14.9

Thomas Nast | Colored Rule in a Reconstructed (?) State, 1874

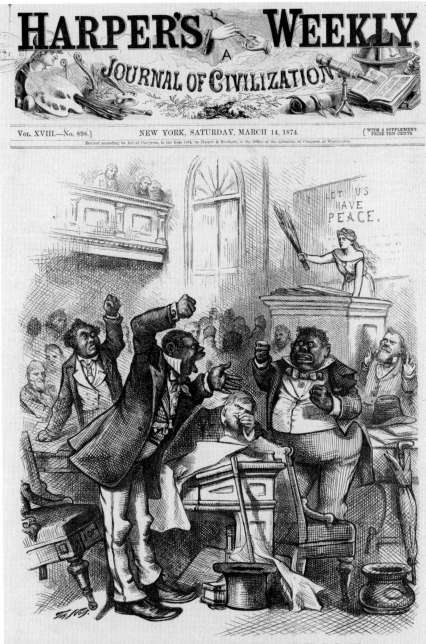

Thomas Nast began drawing for the popular magazine *Harper's Weekly* in 1859. Nast initially used his illustrations to rouse northern public sentiment for the plight of blacks in the South after the Civil War. By 1874, however, many Northerners had become disillusioned with federal efforts to enforce Reconstruction. Like them, Nash accepted the white southern point of view that "Black Reconstruction" was a recipe for corruption and immorality. This cartoon imagines a raucous scene in the South Carolina legislature, where black legislators have taken over the floor and call each other "thieves, liars, rascals, and cowards." Note the figure of Columbia (at the top right), who represents the nation, chastising black lawmakers with a switch. Nast highlights Columbia's message in the caption: "You are Aping the lowest Whites. If you disgrace your Race in this way you had better take Back Seats."

DOCUMENT 14.10

What the Centennial Ought to Accomplish, 1875

The following editorial appeared in the northern periodical *Scribner's Journal*. A year before the celebration of the nation's centennial, Northerners as well as Southerners were calling for national unity and reconciliation, and thus a true end to Reconstruction. Rather than dwelling on the "Lost Cause," the magazine's editors remind southern readers of the glories of the old nation as celebrated by former Confederate president Jefferson Davis in recalling the national unity during the victorious Mexican-American War.

W E ARE TO HAVE grand doings next year. There is to be an Exposition. There are to be speeches, and songs, and processions, and elaborate ceremonies and general rejoicings. Cannon are to be fired, flags are to be floated, and the eagle is expected to scream while he dips the tip of either pinion in the Atlantic and the Pacific, and sprinkles the land with a new baptism of freedom. . . .

. . . Before we begin our celebration of this event, would it not be well for us to inquire whether we have a nation? In a large number of the States of this country there exists not only a belief that the United States do not constitute a nation, but a theory of State rights which forbids that they ever shall become one. We hear about the perturbed condition of the Southern mind. We hear it said that multitudes there are just as disloyal as they were during the civil war. This, we believe, we are justified in denying. . . . They are not actively in rebellion, and they do not propose to be. They do not hope for the re-establishment of slavery. They fought bravely and well to establish their theory, but the majority was against them; and if the result of the war emphasized any fact, it was that *en masse* the people of the United States constitute a nation—indivisible in constituents, in interest, in destiny. The result of the war was without significance, if it did not mean that the United States constitute a nation which cannot be divided; which will not permit itself to be divided; which is integral, indissoluble, indestructible. . . . The great point with them is to recognize the fact that, for richer or poorer, in sickness and health, until death do us part, these United States constitute a nation; that we are to live, grow, prosper, and suffer together, united by bands that cannot be sundered.

Unless this fact is fully recognized throughout the Union, our Centennial will be but a hollow mockery. If we are to celebrate anything worth celebrating, it is the birth of a nation. If we are to celebrate anything worth celebrating, it should be by the whole heart and united voice of the nation. If we can make the Centennial an occasion for emphasizing the great lesson of the war, and universally assenting to the results of the war, it will, indeed, be worth all the money expended upon and the time devoted to it. . . .

A few weeks ago, Mr. Jefferson Davis, the ex-President of the Confederacy, was reported to have exhorted an audience to which he was speaking to be as loyal to the old flag of the Union now as they were during the Mexican War. If the South could know what music there was in these words to Northern ears—how grateful we were to their old chief for them—it would appreciate the strength of our longing for a complete restoration of the national feeling that existed when Northern and Southern blood mingled in common sacrifice on Mexican soil. This national feeling, this national pride, this brotherly sympathy *must be restored*; and accursed be any Northern or Southern man, whether in power or out of power, whether politician, theorizer, carpet-bagger, president-maker, or plunderer, who puts obstacles in the way of such a restoration. Men of the South, we want you. Men of the South, we long for the restoration of your peace and your prosperity. We would see your cities thriving, your homes happy, your plantations teeming with plenteous harvests, your schools overflowing, your wisest statesmen leading you, and all causes and all memories of discord wiped out forever. You do not believe this? Then you do not know the heart of the North. Have you cause of complaint against the politicians? Alas! so have we. Help us, as loving and loyal American citizens, to make our politicians better. Only remember and believe that there is nothing that the North wants so much to-day, as your recognition of the fact that the old relations between you and us are forever restored—that your hope, your pride, your policy, and your destiny are one with ours. Our children will grow up to despise our childishness, if we cannot do away with our personal hates so far, that in the cause of an established nationality we may join hands under the old flag.

To bring about this reunion of the two sections of the country in the old fellowship, should be the leading object of the approaching Centennial. A celebration of the national birth, begun, carried on, and finished by a section, would be a mockery and a shame. The nations of the world might well point at it the finger of scorn. The money expended upon it were better sunk in the sea, or devoted to repairing the waste places of the war. Men of the South, it is for you to say whether your magnanimity is equal to your valor—whether you are as reasonable as you are brave, and whether, like your old chief, you accept that definite and irreversible result of the war which makes you and yours forever members of the great American nation with us. Let us see to it, North and South, that the Centennial heals all the old wounds, reconciles all the old differences, and furnishes the occasion for such a reunion of the great American nationality, as shall make our celebration an expression of fraternal good-will among all sections and all States, and a corner-stone over which shall be reared a new temple to national freedom, concord, peace, and prosperity.

Source: "What the Centennial Ought to Accomplish," *Scribner's Monthly*, August 1875, 509–10.

Interpret the Evidence

1. How did the black codes (Document 14.5) attempt to reimpose bondage on former slaves?

2. Why did African Americans consider property holding a fundamental right (see Document 14.6)?

3. Under what circumstances did the Force Act (Document 14.8) authorize federal prosecutions?

4. Contrast the image of South Carolina's black politicians as presented in Richard Cain's speech (Document 14.6) and Thomas Nast's cartoon (Document 14.9).

5. Despite Ku Klux Klan intimidation and the fear it produced in African Americans, what does the testimony of Ellen Parton (Document 14.7) reveal about black attempts to resist it?

6. What sources of unity existed between the North and the South that would bring Reconstruction to an end (see Document 14.10)?

Put It in Context

- How much did Reconstruction transform the South and the nation? What were its limitations?

The Declaration of Independence

In Congress, July 4, 1776.

The unanimous Declaration of the thirteen united States of America,

When in the course of human events, it becomes necessary for one people to dissolve the political bands which have connected them with another, and to assume, among the powers of the earth, the separate and equal station to which the laws of nature and of nature's God entitle them, a decent respect to the opinions of mankind requires that they should declare the causes which impel them to the separation.

We hold these truths to be self-evident, that all men are created equal; that they are endowed by their Creator with certain unalienable rights; that among these, are life, liberty, and the pursuit of happiness. That, to secure these rights, governments are instituted among men, deriving their just powers from the consent of the governed; that, whenever any form of government becomes destructive of these ends, it is the right of the people to alter or to abolish it, and to institute a new government, laying its foundation on such principles, and organizing its powers in such form, as to them shall seem most likely to effect their safety and happiness. Prudence, indeed, will dictate that governments long established, should not be changed for light and transient causes; and, accordingly, all experience hath shown, that mankind are more disposed to suffer, while evils are sufferable, than to right themselves by abolishing the forms to which they are accustomed. But, when a long train of abuses and usurpations, pursuing invariably the same object, evinces a design to reduce them under absolute despotism, it is their right, it is their duty, to throw off such government and to provide new guards for their future security. Such has been the patient sufferance of these colonies, and such is now the necessity which constrains them to alter their former systems of government. The history of the present King of Great Britain is a history of repeated injuries and usurpations, all having, in direct object, the establishment of an absolute tyranny over these States. To prove this, let facts be submitted to a candid world: He has refused his assent to laws the most wholesome and necessary for the public good.

He has forbidden his governors to pass laws of immediate and pressing importance, unless suspended in their operation till his assent should be obtained; and, when so suspended, he has utterly neglected to attend to them.

He has refused to pass other laws for the accommodation of large districts of people, unless those people would relinquish the right of representation in the legislature; a right inestimable to them, and formidable to tyrants only.

He has called together legislative bodies at places unusual, uncomfortable, and distant from the depository of their public records, for the sole purpose of fatiguing them into compliance with his measures.

He has dissolved representative houses repeatedly for opposing, with manly firmness, his invasions on the rights of the people.

He has refused, for a long time after such dissolutions, to cause others to be elected; whereby the legislative powers, incapable of annihilation, have returned to the people at large for their exercise; the state remaining in the meantime exposed to all the danger of invasion from without, and convulsions within.

He has endeavoured to prevent the population of these States; for that purpose, obstructing the laws for naturalization of foreigners, refusing to pass others to encourage their migration hither, and raising the conditions of new appropriations of lands.

He has obstructed the administration of justice, by refusing his assent to laws for establishing judiciary powers.

He has made judges dependent on his will alone, for the tenure of their offices, and the amount and payment of their salaries.

He has erected a multitude of new offices, and sent hither swarms of officers to harass our people, and eat out their substance.

He has kept among us, in times of peace, standing armies, without the consent of our legislature.

He has affected to render the military independent of, and superior to, the civil power.

He has combined, with others, to subject us to a jurisdiction foreign to our Constitution, and unacknowledged by our laws; giving his assent to their acts of pretended legislation:

For quartering large bodies of armed troops among us:

For protecting them by a mock trial, from punishment, for any murders which they should commit on the inhabitants of these States:

For cutting off our trade with all parts of the world:

For imposing taxes on us without our consent:

For depriving us, in many cases, of the benefit of trial by jury:

For transporting us beyond seas to be tried for pretended offences:

For abolishing the free system of English laws in a neighboring province, establishing therein an arbitrary government, and enlarging its boundaries, so as to render it at once an example and fit instrument for introducing the same absolute rule into these colonies:

For taking away our charters, abolishing our most valuable laws, and altering, fundamentally, the powers of our governments:

For suspending our own legislatures, and declaring themselves invested with power to legislate for us in all cases whatsoever.

He has abdicated government here, by declaring us out of his protection, and waging war against us.

He has plundered our seas, ravaged our coasts, burnt our towns, and destroyed the lives of our people.

He is, at this time, transporting large armies of foreign mercenaries to complete the works of death, desolation, and tyranny, already begun, with circumstances of cruelty and perfidy scarcely paralleled in the most barbarous ages, and totally unworthy the head of a civilized nation.

He has constrained our fellow citizens, taken captive on the high seas, to bear arms against their country, to become the executioners of their friends, and brethren, or to fall themselves by their hands.

He has excited domestic insurrections amongst us, and has endeavored to bring on the inhabitants of our frontiers, the merciless Indian savages, whose known rule of warfare is an undistinguished destruction of all ages, sexes, and conditions.

In every stage of these oppressions, we have petitioned for redress; in the most humble terms; our repeated petitions have been answered only by repeated injury. A prince, whose character is thus marked by every act which may define a tyrant, is unfit to be the ruler of a free people.

Nor have we been wanting in attention to our British brethren. We have warned them, from time to time, of attempts made by their legislature to extend an unwarrantable jurisdiction over us. We have reminded them of the circumstances of our emigration and settlement here. We have appealed to their native justice and magnanimity, and we have conjured them, by the ties of our common kindred, to disavow these usurpations, which would inevitably interrupt our connections and correspondence. They, too, have been deaf to the voice of justice and consanguinity. We must, therefore, acquiesce in the necessity which denounces our separation, and hold them as we hold the rest of mankind, enemies in war, in peace, friends.

We, therefore, the representatives of the United States of America, in general Congress assembled, appealing to the Supreme Judge of the world for the rectitude of our intentions, do, in the name, and by authority of the good people of these colonies, solemnly publish and declare, that these united colonies are, and of right ought to be, free and independent states: that they are absolved from all allegiance to the British Crown, and that all political connection between them and the state of Great Britain is, and ought to be, totally dissolved; and that, as free and independent states, they have full power to levy war, conclude peace, contract alliances, establish commerce, and to do all other acts and things which independent states may of right do. And, for the support of this declaration, with a firm reliance on the protection of Divine Providence, we mutually pledge to each other our lives, our fortunes, and our sacred honor.

The foregoing Declaration was, by order of Congress, engrossed, and signed by the following members:

JOHN HANCOCK

New Hampshire
Josiah Bartlett
William Whipple
Matthew Thornton

Massachusetts Bay
Samuel Adams
John Adams
Robert Treat Paine
Elbridge Gerry

Rhode Island
Stephen Hopkins
William Ellery

Connecticut
Roger Sherman
Samuel Huntington
William Williams
Oliver Wolcott

New York
William Floyd
Phillip Livingston
Francis Lewis
Lewis Morris

New Jersey
Richard Stockton
John Witherspoon
Francis Hopkinson
John Hart
Abraham Clark

Pennsylvania
Robert Morris
Benjamin Rush
Benjamin Franklin
John Morton
George Clymer
James Smith
George Taylor
James Wilson
George Ross
Caesar Rodney
George Read
Thomas M'Kean

Maryland
Samuel Chase
William Paca
Thomas Stone
Charles Carroll, of Carrollton

North Carolina
William Hooper
Joseph Hewes
John Penn

South Carolina
Edward Rutledge
Thomas Heyward, Jr.
Thomas Lynch, Jr.
Arthur Middleton

Virginia
George Wythe
Richard Henry Lee
Thomas Jefferson
Benjamin Harrison
Thomas Nelson, Jr.
Francis Lightfoot Lee
Carter Braxton

Georgia
Button Gwinnett
Lyman Hall
George Walton

Resolved, That copies of the Declaration be sent to the several assemblies, conventions, and committees, or councils of safety, and to the several commanding officers of the continental troops; that it be proclaimed in each of the United States, at the head of the army.

The Articles of Confederation and Perpetual Union

Agreed to in Congress, November 15, 1777.
Ratified March 1781.

Between the states of New Hampshire, Massachusetts Bay, Rhode Island and Providence Plantations, Connecticut, New York, New Jersey, Pennsylvania, Delaware, Maryland, Virginia, North Carolina, South Carolina, Georgia.*

Article 1
The stile of this confederacy shall be "The United States of America."

Article 2
Each State retains its sovereignty, freedom and independence, and every power, jurisdiction, and right, which is not by this confederation expressly delegated to the United States, in Congress assembled.

Article 3
The said states hereby severally enter into a firm league of friendship with each other for their common defence, the security of their liberties and their mutual and general welfare; binding themselves to assist each other against all force offered to, or attacks made upon them, or any of them, on account of religion, sovereignty, trade, or any other pretence whatever.

Article 4
The better to secure and perpetuate mutual friendship and intercourse among the people of the different states in this union, the free inhabitants of each of these states, paupers, vagabonds, and fugitives from justice excepted, shall be entitled to all privileges and immunities of free citizens in the several states; and the people of each State shall have free ingress and regress to and from any other State, and shall enjoy therein all the privileges of trade and commerce, subject to the same duties, impositions, and restrictions, as the inhabitants thereof respectively; provided, that such restrictions shall not extend so far as to prevent the removal of property, imported into any State, to any other State of which the owner is an inhabitant; provided also, that no imposition, duties, or restriction, shall be laid by any State on the property of the United States, or either of them. If any person guilty of, or charged with treason, felony, or other high misdemeanor in any State, shall flee from justice and be found in any of the United States, he shall, upon demand of the governor or executive power of the State from which he fled, be delivered up and removed to the State having jurisdiction of his offence. Full faith and credit shall be given in each of these states to the records, acts, and judicial proceedings of the courts and magistrates of every other State.

Article 5
For the more convenient management of the general interests of the United States, delegates shall be annually appointed, in such manner as the legislature of each State shall direct, to meet in Congress, on the 1st Monday in November in every year, with a power reserved to each State to recall its delegates, or any of them, at any time within the year, and to send others in their stead for the remainder of the year.

No State shall be represented in Congress by less than two, nor by more than seven members; and no person shall be capable of being a delegate for more than three years in

*This copy of the final draft of the Articles of Confederation is taken from the Journals, 9:907–925, November 15, 1777.

any term of six years; nor shall any person, being a delegate, be capable of holding any office under the United States, for which he, or any other for his benefit, receives any salary, fees, or emolument of any kind.

Each State shall maintain its own delegates in a meeting of the states, and while they act as members of the committee of the states.

In determining questions in the United States, in Congress assembled, each State shall have one vote.

Freedom of speech and debate in Congress shall not be impeached or questioned in any court or place out of Congress: and the members of Congress shall be protected in their persons from arrests and imprisonments, during the time of their going to and from, and attendance on Congress, except for treason, felony, or breach of the peace.

Article 6

No State, without the consent of the United States, in Congress assembled, shall send any embassy to, or receive any embassy from, or enter into any conference, agreement, alliance, or treaty with any king, prince, or state; nor shall any person, holding any office of profit or trust under the United States, or any of them, accept of any present, emolument, office or title, of any kind whatever, from any king, prince, or foreign state; nor shall the United States, in Congress assembled, or any of them, grant any title of nobility.

No two or more states shall enter into any treaty, confederation, or alliance, whatever, between them, without the consent of the United States, in Congress assembled, specifying accurately the purposes for which the same is to be entered into, and how long it shall continue.

No state shall lay any imposts or duties which may interfere with any stipulations in treaties entered into by the United States, in Congress assembled, with any king, prince, or state, in pursuance of any treaties already proposed by Congress to the courts of France and Spain.

No vessels of war shall be kept up in time of peace by any State, except such number only as shall be deemed necessary by the United States, in Congress assembled, for the defence of such State or its trade; nor shall any body of forces be kept up by any State, in time of peace, except such number only as, in the judgment of the United States, in Congress assembled, shall be deemed requisite to garrison the forts necessary for the defence of such State; but every State shall always keep up a well regulated and disciplined militia, sufficiently armed and accoutred, and shall provide, and constantly have ready for use, in public stores, a due number of field pieces and tents, and a proper quantity of arms, ammunition and camp equipage.

No State shall engage in any war without the consent of the United States, in Congress assembled, unless such State be actually invaded by enemies, or shall have received certain advice of a resolution being formed by some nation of Indians to invade such State, and the danger is so imminent as not to admit of a delay till the United States, in Congress assembled, can be consulted; nor shall any State grant commissions to any ships or vessels of war, nor letters of marque or reprisal, except it be after a declaration of war by the United States, in Congress assembled, and then only against the kingdom or state, and the subjects thereof, against which war has been so declared, and under such regulations as shall be established by the United States, in Congress assembled, unless such State be infested by pirates, in which case vessels of war may be fitted out for that occasion, and kept so long as the danger shall continue, or until the United States, in Congress assembled, shall determine otherwise.

Article 7

When land forces are raised by any State for the common defence, all officers of or under the rank of colonel, shall be appointed by the legislature of each State respectively, by whom such forces shall be raised, or in such manner as such State shall direct; and all vacancies shall be filled up by the State which first made the appointment.

Article 8

All charges of war and all other expences, that shall be incurred for the common defence or general welfare, and allowed by the United States, in Congress assembled, shall be defrayed out of a common treasury, which shall be supplied by the several states, in proportion to the value of all land within each State, granted to or surveyed for any person, as such land and the buildings and improvements thereon shall be estimated according to such mode as the United States, in Congress assembled, shall, from time to time, direct and appoint.

The taxes for paying that proportion shall be laid and levied by the authority and direction of the legislatures of the several states, within the time agreed upon by the United States, in Congress assembled.

Article 9

The United States, in Congress assembled, shall have the sole and exclusive right and power of determining on peace and war, except in the cases mentioned in the 6th article; of sending and receiving ambassadors; entering into treaties and alliances, provided that no treaty of commerce shall be made, whereby the legislative power of the respective states shall be restrained from imposing such imposts and duties on foreigners as their own people are subjected to, or from prohibiting the exportation or importation of any species of goods or commodities whatsoever; of establishing rules for deciding, in all cases, what captures on land or water shall be legal, and in what manner prizes, taken by land or naval forces in the service of the United States, shall be divided or appropriated; of granting letters of marque and reprisal in times of peace; appointing courts for the trial of piracies and felonies committed on the high seas, and establishing courts for receiving and determining, finally, appeals in all cases of captures; provided, that no member of Congress shall be appointed a judge of any of the said courts.

The United States, in Congress assembled, shall also be the last resort on appeal in all disputes and differences now subsisting, or that hereafter may arise between two or more states concerning boundary, jurisdiction or any other cause whatever; which authority shall always be exercised in the manner following: whenever the legislative or executive authority, or lawful agent of any State, in controversy with another, shall present a petition to Congress, stating the matter in question, and praying for a hearing, notice thereof shall be given, by order of Congress, to the legislative or executive authority of the other State in controversy, and a day assigned for the appearance of the parties by their lawful agents, who shall then be directed to appoint, by joint consent, commissioners or judges to constitute a court for hearing and determining the matter in question; but, if they cannot agree, Congress shall name three persons out of each of the United States, and from the list of such persons each party shall alternately strike out one, the petitioners beginning, until the number shall be reduced to thirteen; and from that number not less than seven, nor more than nine names, as Congress shall direct, shall, in the presence of Congress, be drawn out by lot; and the persons whose names shall be so drawn, or any five of them, shall be commissioners or judges to hear and finally determine the controversy, so always as a major part of the judges who shall hear the cause shall agree in the determination; and if either party shall neglect to attend at the day appointed, without shewing reasons which Congress shall judge sufficient, or, being present, shall refuse to strike, the Congress shall proceed to nominate three persons out of each State, and the secretary of Congress shall strike in behalf of such party absent or refusing; and the judgment and sentence of the court to be appointed, in the manner before prescribed, shall be final and conclusive; and if any of the parties shall refuse to submit to the authority of such court, or to appear or defend their claim or cause, the court shall nevertheless proceed to pronounce sentence or judgment, which shall, in like manner, be final and decisive, the judgment or sentence and other proceedings begin, in either case, transmitted to Congress, and lodged among the acts of Congress for the security of the parties concerned: provided, that every commissioner, before he sits in

judgment, shall take an oath, to be administered by one of the judges of the supreme or superior court of the State where the cause shall be tried, "well and truly to hear and determine the matter in question, according to the best of his judgment, without favour, affection, or hope of reward:" provided, also, that no State shall be deprived of territory for the benefit of the United States.

All controversies concerning the private right of soil, claimed under different grants of two or more states, whose jurisdictions, as they may respect such lands and the states which passed such grants, are adjusted, the said grants, or either of them, being at the same time claimed to have originated antecedent to such settlement of jurisdiction, shall, on the petition of either party to the Congress of the United States, be finally determined, as near as may be, in the same manner as is before prescribed for deciding disputes respecting territorial jurisdiction between different states.

The United States, in Congress assembled, shall also have the sole and exclusive right and power of regulating the alloy and value of coin struck by their own authority, or by that of the respective states; fixing the standard of weights and measures throughout the United States; regulating the trade and managing all affairs with the Indians not members of any of the states; provided that the legislative right of any State within its own limits be not infringed or violated; establishing and regulating post offices from one State to another throughout all the United States, and exacting such postage on the papers passing through the same as may be requisite to defray the expences of the said office; appointing all officers of the land forces in the service of the United States, excepting regimental officers; appointing all the officers of the naval forces, and commissioning all officers whatever in the service of the United States; making rules for the government and regulation of the said land and naval forces, and directing their operations.

The United States, in Congress assembled, shall have authority to appoint a committee to sit in the recess of Congress, to be denominated "a Committee of the States," and to consist of one delegate from each State, and to appoint such other committees and civil officers as may be necessary for managing the general affairs of the United States, under their direction; to appoint one of their number to preside; provided that no person be allowed to serve in the office of president more than one year in any term of three years; to ascertain the necessary sums of money to be raised for the service of the United States, and to appropriate and apply the same for defraying the public expences; to borrow money or emit bills on the credit of the United States, transmitting, every half year, to the respective states, an account of the sums of money so borrowed or emitted; to build and equip a navy; to agree upon the number of land forces, and to make requisitions from each State for its quota, in proportion to the number of white inhabitants in such State; which requisitions shall be binding; and thereupon, the legislature of each State shall appoint the regimental officers, raise the men, and cloathe, arm, and equip them in a soldier-like manner, at the expence of the United States; and the officers and men so cloathed, armed, and equipped, shall march to the place appointed and within the time agreed on by the United States, in Congress assembled; but if the United States, in Congress assembled, shall, on consideration of circum-stances, judge proper that any State should not raise men, or should raise a smaller number than its quota, and that any other State should raise a greater number of men than the quota thereof, such extra number shall be raised, officered, cloathed, armed, and equipped in the same manner as the quota of such State, unless the legislature of such State shall judge that such extra number cannot be safely spared out of the same, in which case they shall raise, officer, cloathe, arm, and equip as many of such extra number as they judge can be safely spared. And the officers and men so cloathed, armed, and equipped, shall march to the place appointed and within the time agreed on by the United States, in Congress assembled.

The United States, in Congress assembled, shall never engage in a war, nor grant letters of marque and reprisal in time of peace, nor enter into any treaties or alliances, nor coin money, nor regulate the value thereof, nor ascertain the sums and expences necessary for the defence and welfare of the United States, or any of them: nor emit bills, nor borrow money on the credit of the United States, nor appropriate money, nor agree upon the number of vessels of war to be built or purchased, or the number of land or sea forces to be raised, nor appoint a commander in chief of the army or navy, unless nine states assent to the same; nor shall a question on any other point, except for adjourning from day to day, be determined, unless by the votes of a majority of the United States, in Congress assembled.

The Congress of the United States shall have power to adjourn to any time within the year, and to any place within the United States, so that no period of adjournment be for a longer duration than the space of six months, and shall publish the journal of their proceedings monthly, except such parts thereof, relating to treaties, alliances or military operations, as, in their judgment, require secrecy; and the yeas and nays of the delegates of each State on any question shall be entered on the journal, when it is desired by any

delegate; and the delegates of a State, or any of them, at his, or their request, shall be furnished with a transcript of the said journal, except such parts as are above excepted, to lay before the legislatures of the several states.

Article 10
The committee of the states, or any nine of them, shall be authorized to execute, in the recess of Congress, such of the powers of Congress as the United States, in Congress assembled, by the consent of nine states, shall, from time to time, think expedient to vest them with; provided, that no power be delegated to the said committee, for the exercise of which, by the articles of confederation, the voice of nine states, in the Congress of the United States assembled, is requisite.

Article 11
Canada acceding to this confederation, and joining in the measures of the United States, shall be admitted into and entitled to all the advantages of this union; but no other colony shall be admitted into the same, unless such admission be agreed to by nine states.

Article 12
All bills of credit emitted, monies borrowed and debts contracted by, or under the authority of Congress before the assembling of the United States, in pursuance of the present confederation, shall be deemed and considered as a charge against the United States, for payment and satisfaction whereof the said United States and the public faith are hereby solemnly pledged.

Article 13
Every State shall abide by the determinations of the United States, in Congress assembled, on all questions which, by this confederation, are submitted to them. And the articles of this confederation shall be inviolably observed by every State, and the union shall be perpetual; nor shall any alteration at any time hereafter be made in any of them, unless such alteration be agreed to in a Congress of the United States, and be afterwards confirmed by the legisla-tures of every State.

These articles shall be proposed to the legislatures of all the United States, to be considered, and if approved of by them, they are advised to authorize their delegates to ratify the same in the Congress of the United States; which being done, the same shall become conclusive.

The Constitution of the United States*

Agreed to by Philadelphia Convention, September 17, 1787. Implemented March 4, 1789.

Preamble

We the people of the United States, in order to form a more perfect union, establish justice, insure domestic tranquility, provide for the common defense, promote the general welfare, and secure the blessings of liberty to ourselves and our posterity, do ordain and establish this Constitution for the United States of America.

Article I

Section 1. All legislative powers herein granted shall be vested in a Congress of the United States, which shall consist of a Senate and a House of Representatives.

Section 2. The House of Representatives shall be composed of members chosen every second year by the people of the several States, and the electors in each State shall have the qualifications requisite for electors of the most numerous branch of the State Legislature.

No person shall be a Representative who shall not have attained to the age of twenty-five years, and been seven years a citizen of the United States, and who shall not, when elected, be an inhabitant of that State in which he shall be chosen.

Representatives and direct taxes shall be apportioned among the several States which may be included within this Union, according to their respective numbers, *which shall be determined by adding to the whole number of free persons, including those bound to service for a term of years and excluding Indians not taxed, three-fifths of all other persons.* The actual enumeration shall be made within three years after the first meeting of the Congress of the United States, and within every subsequent term of ten years, in such manner as they shall by law direct. The number of Representatives shall not exceed one for every thirty thousand, but each State shall have at least one Representative; and until such enumeration shall be made, *the State of New Hampshire shall be entitled to choose three, Massachusetts eight, Rhode Island and Providence Plantations one, Connecticut five, New York six, New Jersey four, Pennsylvania eight, Delaware one, Maryland six, Virginia ten, North Carolina five, South Carolina five, and Georgia three.*

When vacancies happen in the representation from any State, the Executive authority thereof shall issue writs of election to fill such vacancies.

The House of Representatives shall choose their Speaker and other officers; and shall have the sole power of impeachment.

Section 3. The Senate of the United States shall be composed of two Senators from each State, *chosen by the legislature thereof,* for six years; and each Senator shall have one vote.

Immediately after they shall be assembled in consequence of the first election, they shall be divided as equally as may be into three classes. The seats of the Senators of the first class shall be vacated at the expiration of the second year, of the second class at the expiration of the fourth year, and of the third class at the expiration of the sixth year, so that one-third may be chosen every second year; and if vacancies happen by resignation or otherwise, during the recess of the legislature of any State, the Executive thereof may make temporary appointments until the next meeting of the legislature, which shall then fill such vacancies.

No person shall be a Senator who shall not have attained to the age of thirty years, and been nine years a citizen of the United States, and who shall not, when elected, be an inhabitant of that State for which he shall be chosen.

The Vice-President of the United States shall be President of the Senate, but shall have no vote, unless they be equally divided.

The Senate shall choose their other officers, and also a President pro tempore, in the absence of the Vice-President, or when he shall exercise the office of President of the United States.

The Senate shall have the sole power to try all impeachments. When sitting for that purpose, they shall be on oath or affirmation. When the President of the United States is tried, the Chief Justice shall preside: and no person shall be convicted without the concurrence of two-thirds of the members present.

Judgment in cases of impeachment shall not extend further than to removal from the office, and disqualification to hold and enjoy any office of honor, trust or profit under the United States: but the party convicted shall nevertheless be liable and subject to indictment, trial, judgment and punishment, according to law.

Section 4. The times, places and manner of holding elections for Senators and Representatives shall be prescribed in each State by the legislature thereof; but the Congress may at any time by law make or alter such regulations, except as to the places of choosing Senators.

*Passages no longer in effect are in italic type.

The Congress shall assemble at least once in every year, and such meeting *shall be on the first Monday in December, unless they shall by law appoint a different day.*

Section 5. Each house shall be the judge of the elections, returns and qualifications of its own members, and a majority of each shall constitute a quorum to do business; but a smaller number may adjourn from day to day, and may be authorized to compel the attendance of absent members, in such manner, and under such penalties, as each house may provide.

Each house may determine the rules of its proceedings, punish its members for disorderly behavior, and with the concurrence of two-thirds, expel a member.

Each house shall keep a journal of its proceedings, and from time to time publish the same, excepting such parts as may in their judgment require secrecy; and the yeas and nays of the members of either house on any question shall, at the desire of one fifth of those present, be entered on the journal.

Neither house, during the session of Congress, shall, without the consent of the other, adjourn for more than three days, nor to any other place than that in which the two houses shall be sitting.

Section 6. The Senators and Representatives shall receive a compensation for their services, to be ascertained by law and paid out of the treasury of the United States. They shall in all cases except treason, felony and breach of the peace, be privileged from arrest during their attendance at the session of their respective houses, and in going to and returning from the same; and for any speech or debate in either house, they shall not be questioned in any other place.

No Senator or Representative shall, during the time for which he was elected, be appointed to any civil office under the authority of the United States, which shall have been created, or the emoluments whereof shall have been increased, during such time; and no person holding any office under the United States shall be a member of either house during his continuance in office.

Section 7. All bills for raising revenue shall originate in the House of Representatives; but the Senate may propose or concur with amendments as on other bills.

Every bill which shall have passed the House of Representatives and the Senate, shall, before it become a law, be presented to the President of the United States; if he approve he shall sign it, but if not he shall return it with objections to that house in which it shall have originated, who shall enter the objections at large on their journal, and proceed to reconsider it. If after such reconsideration two-thirds of that house shall agree to pass the bill, it shall be sent, together with the objections, to the other house, by which it shall likewise be reconsidered, and, if approved by two-thirds of that house, it shall become a law. But in all such cases the votes of both houses shall be determined by yeas and nays, and the names of the persons voting for and against the bill shall be entered on the journal of each house respectively. If any bill shall not be returned by the President within ten days (Sundays excepted) after it shall have been presented to him, the same shall be a law, in like manner as if he had signed it, unless the Congress by their adjournment prevent its return, in which case it shall not be a law.

Every order, resolution, or vote to which the concurrence of the Senate and House of Representatives may be necessary (except on a question of adjournment) shall be presented to the President of the United States; and before the same shall take effect, shall be approved by him, or being disapproved by him, shall be repassed by two-thirds of the Senate and House of Representatives, according to the rules and limitations prescribed in the case of a bill.

Section 8. The Congress shall have power
To lay and collect taxes, duties, imposts, and excises, to pay the debts and provide for the common defense and general welfare of the United States; but all duties, imposts and excises shall be uniform throughout the United States;

To borrow money on the credit of the United States;

To regulate commerce with foreign nations, and among the several States, and with the Indian tribes;

To establish an uniform rule of naturalization, and uniform laws on the subject of bankruptcies throughout the United States;

To coin money, regulate the value thereof, and of foreign coin, and fix the standard of weights and measures;

To provide for the punishment of counterfeiting the securities and current coin of the United States;

To establish post offices and post roads;

To promote the progress of science and useful arts by securing for limited times to authors and inventors the exclusive right to their respective writings and discoveries;

To constitute tribunals inferior to the Supreme Court;

To define and punish piracies and felonies committed on the high seas and offences against the law of nations;

To declare war, grant letters of marque and reprisal, and make rules concerning captures on land and water;

To raise and support armies, but no appropriation of money to that use shall be for a longer term than two years;

To provide and maintain a navy;

To make rules for the government and regulation of the land and naval forces;

To provide for calling forth the militia to execute the laws of the Union, suppress insurrections and repel invasions;

To provide for organizing, arming, and disciplining the militia, and for governing such part of them as may be employed in the service of the United States, reserving to the States respectively the appointment of the officers, and the authority of training the militia according to the discipline prescribed by Congress;

To exercise exclusive legislation in all cases whatsoever, over such district (not exceeding ten miles square) as may, by cession of particular States, and the acceptance of Congress, become the seat of the government of the United States, and to exercise like authority over all places purchased by the consent of the legislature of the State, in which the same shall be, for erection of forts, magazines, arsenals, dock-yards, and other needful buildings;—and

To make all laws which shall be necessary and proper for carrying into execution the foregoing powers, and all other powers vested by this Constitution in the government of the United States, or in any department or officer thereof.

Section 9. *The migration or importation of such persons as any of the States now existing shall think proper to admit shall not be prohibited by the Congress prior to the year one thousand eight hundred and eight; but a tax or duty may be imposed on such importation, not exceeding ten dollars for each person.*

The privilege of the writ of habeas corpus shall not be suspended, unless when in cases of rebellion or invasion the public safety may require it.

No bill of attainder or ex post facto law shall be passed.

No capitation, or other direct, tax shall be laid, unless in proportion to the census or enumeration herein before directed to be taken.

No tax or duty shall be laid on articles exported from any State.

No preference shall be given by any regulation of commerce or revenue to the ports of one State over those of another; nor shall vessels bound to, or from, one State be obliged to enter, clear, or pay duties in another.

No money shall be drawn from the treasury, but in consequence of appropriations made by law; and a regular statement and account of the receipts and expenditures of all public money shall be published from time to time.

No title of nobility shall be granted by the United States: and no person holding any office of profit or trust under them, shall, without the consent of the Congress, accept of any present, emolument, office, or title, of any kind whatever, from any king, prince, or foreign state.

Section 10. No State shall enter into any treaty, alliance, or confederation; grant letters of marque and reprisal; coin money; emit bills of credit; make anything but gold and silver coin a tender in payment of debts; pass any bill of attainder, ex post facto law, or law impairing the obligation of contracts, or grant any title of nobility.

No State shall, without the consent of Congress, lay any imposts or duties on imports or exports, except what may be absolutely necessary for executing its inspection laws: and the net produce of all duties and imposts, laid by any State on imports or exports, shall be for the use of the treasury of the United States; and all such laws shall be subject to the revision and control of the Congress.

No State shall, without the consent of Congress, lay any duty of tonnage, keep troops, or ships of war in time of peace, enter into any agreement or compact with another State, or with a foreign power, or engage in war, unless actually invaded, or in such imminent danger as will not admit of delay.

Article II

Section 1. The executive power shall be vested in a President of the United States of America. He shall hold his office during the term of four years, and, together with the Vice-President, chosen for the same term, be elected as follows:

Each State shall appoint, in such manner as the legislature thereof may direct, a number of electors, equal to the whole number of Senators and Representatives to which the State may be entitled in the Congress; but no Senator or Representative, or person holding an office of trust or profit under the United States, shall be appointed an elector.

The electors shall meet in their respective States, and vote by ballot for two persons, of whom one at least shall not be an inhabitant of the same State with themselves. And they shall make a list of all the persons voted for, and of the number of votes for each; which list they shall sign and certify, and transmit sealed to the seat of government of the United States, directed to the President of the Senate. The President of the Senate shall, in the presence of the Senate and House of Representatives, open all the certificates, and the votes shall then be counted. The person having the greatest number of votes shall be the President, if such number be a majority of the whole number of electors appointed; and if there be more than one who have such majority, and have an equal number of votes, then the House of Representatives shall immediately choose by ballot one of them for President; and if no person have a majority, then from the five highest on the list said house shall in like manner choose the President. But in choosing the President the votes shall be taken by States, the representation from each State having one vote; a quorum for this purpose shall consist of a member or members from two-thirds of the States, and a majority of all the States shall be necessary to a choice. In every case, after the choice of the President, the person having the greatest number of votes of the electors shall be the Vice-President. But if there should remain two or more who have equal votes, the Senate shall choose from them by ballot the Vice-President.

The Congress may determine the time of choosing the electors, and the day on which they shall give their votes; which day shall be the same throughout the United States.

No person except a natural-born citizen, *or a citizen of the United States at the time of the adoption of this Constitution,* shall be eligible to the office of President; neither shall any person be eligible to that office who shall not have attained to the age of thirty-five years, and been fourteen years a resident within the United States.

In cases of the removal of the President from office or of his death, resignation, or inability to discharge the powers and duties of the said office, the same shall devolve on the Vice-President, and the Congress may by law provide for the case of removal, death, resignation, or inability, both of the President and Vice-President, declaring what officer shall then act as President, and such officer shall act accordingly, until the disability be removed, or a President shall be elected.

The President shall, at stated times, receive for his services a compensation, which shall neither be increased nor diminished during the period for which he shall have been elected, and he shall not receive within that period any other emolument from the United States, or any of them.

Before he enter on the execution of his office, he shall take the following oath or affirmation:—"I do solemnly swear (or affirm) that I will faithfully execute the office of the President of the United States, and will to the best of my ability preserve, protect and defend the Constitution of the United States."

Section 2. The President shall be commander in chief of the army and navy of the United States, and of the militia of the several States, when called into the actual service of the United States; he may require the opinion, in writing, of the principal officer in each of the executive departments, upon any subject relating to the duties of their respective offices, and he shall have power to grant reprieves and pardons for offenses against the United States, except in cases of impeachment.

He shall have power, by and with the advice and consent of the Senate, to make treaties, provided two-thirds of the Senators present concur; and he shall nominate, and by and with the advice and consent of the Senate, shall appoint ambassadors, other public ministers and consuls, judges of the Supreme Court, and all other officers of the United States, whose appointments are not herein otherwise provided for, and which shall be established by law: but Congress may by law vest the appointment of such inferior officers, as they think proper, in the President alone, in the courts of law, or in the heads of departments.

The President shall have power to fill up all vacancies that may happen during the recess of the Senate, by granting commissions which shall expire at the end of their next session.

Section 3. He shall from time to time give to the Congress information of the state of the Union, and recommend to their consideration such measures as he shall judge necessary and expedient; he may, on extraordinary occasions, convene both houses, or either of them, and in case of disagreement between them, with respect to the time of adjournment, he may adjourn them to such time as he shall think proper; he shall receive ambassadors and other public ministers; he shall take care that the laws be faithfully executed, and shall commission all the officers of the United States.

Section 4. The President, Vice-President and all civil officers of the United States shall be removed from office on impeachment for, and on conviction of, treason, bribery, or other high crimes and misdemeanors.

Article III

Section 1. The judicial power of the United States shall be vested in one Supreme Court, and in such inferior courts as the Congress may from time to time ordain and establish. The judges, both of the Supreme and inferior courts, shall hold their offices during good behavior, and shall, at stated times, receive for their services a compensation which shall not be diminished during their continuance in office.

Section 2. The judicial power shall extend to all cases, in law and equity, arising under this Constitution, the laws of the United States, and treaties made, or which shall be made, under their authority;—to all cases affecting ambassadors, other public ministers and consuls;—to all cases of admiralty and maritime jurisdiction;—to controversies to which the United States shall be a party;—to controversies between two or more States;—between a State and citizens of another State;—between citizens of different States;—between citizens of the same State claiming lands under grants of different States, and between a State, or the citizens thereof, and foreign states, citizens or subjects.

In all cases affecting ambassadors, other public ministers and consuls, and those in which a State shall be party, the Supreme Court shall have original jurisdiction. In all the other cases before mentioned, the Supreme Court shall have appellate jurisdiction, both as to law and fact, with such exceptions, and under such regulations, as the Congress shall make.

The trial of all crimes, except in cases of impeachment, shall be by jury; and such trial shall be held in the State where said crimes shall have been committed; but when not committed within any State, the trial shall be at such place or places as the Congress may by Law have directed.

Section 3. Treason against the United States shall consist only in levying war against them, or in adhering to their enemies, giving them aid and comfort. No person shall be convicted of treason unless on the testimony of two witnesses to the same overt act, or on confession in open court.

The Congress shall have power to declare the punishment of treason, but no attainder of treason shall work corruption of blood, or forfeiture except during the life of the person attainted.

Article IV

Section 1. Full faith and credit shall be given in each State to the public acts, records, and judicial proceedings of every other State. And the Congress may by general laws prescribe the manner in which such acts, records, and proceedings shall be proved, and the effect thereof.

Section 2. The citizens of each State shall be entitled to all privileges and immunities of citizens in the several States.

A person charged in any State with treason, felony, or other crime, who shall flee from justice, and be found in another State, shall on demand of the executive authority of the State from which he fled, be delivered up, to be removed to the State having jurisdiction of the crime.

No Person held to service or labor in one State, under the laws thereof, escaping into another, shall, in consequence of any law or regulation therein, be discharged from such service or labor, but shall be delivered up on claim of the party to whom such service or labor may be due.

Section 3. New States may be admitted by the Congress into this Union; but no new State shall be formed or erected within the jurisdiction of any other State; nor any State be formed by the junction of two or more States, or parts of States, without the consent of the legislatures of the States concerned as well as of the Congress.

The Congress shall have power to dispose of and make all needful rules and regulations respecting the territory or other property belonging to the United States; and nothing in this Constitution shall be so construed as to prejudice any claims of the United States, or of any particular State.

Section 4. The United States shall guarantee to every State in this Union a republican form of government, and shall protect each of them against invasion; and on application of the legislature, or of the executive (when the legislature cannot be convened), against domestic violence.

Article V

The Congress, whenever two-thirds of both houses shall deem it necessary, shall propose amendments to this Constitution, or, on the application of the legislatures of two-thirds of the several States, shall call a convention for proposing amendments, which, in either case, shall be valid to all intents and purposes, as part of this Constitution, when ratified by the legislatures of three-fourths of the several States, or by conventions in three-fourths thereof, as the one or the other mode of ratification may be proposed by the Congress; *provided that no amendments which may be made prior to the year one thousand eight hundred and eight shall in any manner affect the first and fourth clauses in the ninth section of the first article;* and that no State, without its consent, shall be deprived of its equal suffrage in the Senate.

Article VI

All debts contracted and engagements entered into, before the adoption of this Constitution, shall be as valid against the United States under this Constitution, as under the Confederation.

This Constitution, and the laws of the United States which shall be made in pursuance thereof; and all treaties made, or which shall be made, under the authority of the United States, shall be the supreme law of the land; and the judges in every State shall be bound thereby, anything in the Constitution or laws of any State to the contrary notwithstanding.

The Senators and Representatives before mentioned, and the members of the several State legislatures, and all executive and judicial officers, both of the United States and of the several States, shall be bound by oath or affirmation to support this Constitution; but no religious test shall ever be required as a qualification to any office or public trust under the United States.

Article VII

The ratification of the conventions of nine States shall be sufficient for the establishment of this Constitution between the States so ratifying the same.

Done in convention by the unanimous consent of the States present, the seventeenth day of September in the year of our Lord one thousand seven hundred and eighty-seven and of the Independence of the United States of America the twelfth. In witness whereof we have hereunto subscribed our names.

GEORGE WASHINGTON, President and Deputy from Virginia

New Hampshire
John Langdon
Nicholas Gilman

Massachusetts
Nathaniel Gorham
Rufus King

Connecticut
William Samuel
  Johnson
Roger Sherman

New York
Alexander Hamilton

New Jersey
William Livingston
David Brearley
William Paterson
Jonathan Dayton

Pennsylvania
Benjamin Franklin
Thomas Mifflin
Robert Morris
George Clymer
Thomas FitzSimons
Jared Ingersoll
James Wilson
Gouverneur Morris

Delaware
George Read
Gunning Bedford, Jr.
John Dickinson
Richard Bassett
Jacob Broom

Maryland
James McHenry
Daniel of St. Thomas Jenifer
Daniel Carroll

Virginia
John Blair
James Madison, Jr.

North Carolina
William Blount
Richard Dobbs Spaight
Hugh Williamson

South Carolina
John Rutledge
Charles Cotesworth Pinckney
Charles Pinckney
Pierce Butler

Georgia
William Few
Abraham Baldwin

Amendments to the Constitution
(including six unratified amendments)

Amendment I
[Ratified 1791]

Congress shall make no law respecting an establishment of religion, or prohibiting the free exercise thereof; or abridging the freedom of speech, or of the press; or the right of the people peaceably to assemble, and to petition the government for a redress of grievances.

Amendment II
[Ratified 1791]

A well-regulated militia being necessary to the security of a free State, the right of the people to keep and bear arms shall not be infringed.

Amendment III
[Ratified 1791]

No soldier shall, in time of peace, be quartered in any house without the consent of the owner, nor in time of war, but in a manner to be prescribed by law.

Amendment IV
[Ratified 1791]

The right of the people to be secure in their persons, houses, papers, and effects, against unreasonable searches and seizures, shall not be violated, and no warrants shall issue but upon probable cause, supported by oath or affirmation, and particularly describing the place to be searched, and the persons or things to be seized.

Amendment V
[Ratified 1791]

No person shall be held to answer for a capital, or otherwise infamous crime, unless on a presentment or indictment of a grand jury, except in cases arising in the land or naval forces, or in the militia, when in actual service in time of war or public danger; nor shall any person be subject for the same offence to be twice put in jeopardy of life or limb; nor shall be compelled in any criminal case to be a witness against himself, nor be deprived of life, liberty, or property, without due process of law; nor shall private property be taken for public use without just compensation.

Amendment VI
[Ratified 1791]

In all criminal prosecutions, the accused shall enjoy the right to a speedy and public trial, by an impartial jury of the State and district wherein the crime shall have been committed, which district shall have been previously ascertained by law, and to be informed of the nature and cause of the accusation; to be confronted with the witnesses against him; to have compulsory process for obtaining witnesses in his favor, and to have the assistance of counsel for his defence.

Amendment VII
[Ratified 1791]

In suits at common law, where the value in controversy shall exceed twenty dollars, the right of trial by jury shall be preserved, and no fact tried by a jury shall be otherwise reexamined in any court of the United States, than according to the rules of the common law.

Amendment VIII
[Ratified 1791]

Excessive bail shall not be required, nor excessive fines imposed, nor cruel and unusual punishments inflicted.

Amendment IX
[Ratified 1791]

The enumeration in the Constitution, of certain rights, shall not be construed to deny or disparage others retained by the people.

Amendment X
[Ratified 1791]

The powers not delegated to the United States by the Constitution, nor prohibited by it to the States, are reserved to the States respectively, or to the people.

Unratified Amendment
[Reapportionment Amendment (proposed by Congress September 25, 1789, along with the Bill of Rights)]

After the first enumeration required by the first article of the Constitution, there shall be one Representative for every thirty thousand, until the number shall amount to one hundred, after which the proportion shall be so regulated by Congress, that there shall be not less than one hundred Representatives, nor less than one Representative for every forty thousand persons, until the number of Representatives shall amount to two hundred; after which the proportion shall be so regulated by Congress, that there shall not be less than two hundred Representatives, nor more than one Representative for every fifty thousand persons.

Amendment XI
[Ratified 1798]

The judicial power of the United States shall not be construed to extend to any suit in law or equity, commenced or prosecuted against one of the United States by citizens of another State, or by citizens or subjects of any foreign state.

Amendment XII
[Ratified 1804]

The electors shall meet in their respective States, and vote by ballot for President and Vice-President, one of whom, at least, shall not be an inhabitant of the same State with themselves; they shall name in their ballots the person voted for as President, and in distinct ballots the person voted for as Vice-President, and they shall make distinct lists of all persons voted for as President, and of all persons voted for as Vice-President, and of the number of votes for each, which lists they shall sign and certify, and transmit sealed to the seat of government of the United States, directed to the President of the Senate;—the President of the Senate shall, in the presence of the Senate and House of Representatives, open all the certificates and the votes shall then be counted;—the person having the greatest number of votes for President shall be the President, if such number be a majority of the whole number of electors appointed; and if no person have such majority, then from the persons having the highest numbers not exceeding three on the list of those voted for as President, the House of Representatives shall choose immediately, by ballot, the President. But in choosing the President, the votes shall be taken by States, the representation from each State having one vote; a quorum for this purpose shall consist of a member or members from two-thirds of the States, and a majority of all the States shall be necessary to a choice. And if the House of Representatives shall not choose a President whenever the right of choice shall devolve upon them, before *the fourth day of March* next following, then the Vice-President shall act as President, as in the case of the death or other constitutional disability of the President.

The person having the greatest number of votes as Vice-President shall be the Vice-President, if such number be a majority of the whole number of electors appointed; and if no person have a majority, then from the two highest numbers on the list the Senate shall choose the Vice-President; a quorum for the purpose shall consist of two-thirds of the whole number of Senators, and a majority of the whole number shall be necessary to a choice. But no person constitutionally ineligible to the office of President shall be eligible to that of Vice-President of the United States.

Unratified Amendment
[Titles of Nobility Amendment (proposed by Congress May 1, 1810)]

If any citizen of the United States shall accept, claim, receive or retain any title of nobility or honor or shall, without the consent of Congress, accept and retain any present, pension, office or emolument of any kind whatever, from any emperor, king, prince or foreign power, such person shall cease to be a citizen of the United States, and shall be incapable of holding any office of trust or profit under them or either of them.

Unratified Amendment

[Corwin Amendment (proposed by Congress March 2, 1861)]

No amendment shall be made to the Constitution which will authorize or give to Congress the power to abolish or interfere, within any State, with the domestic institutions thereof, including that of persons held to labor or service by the laws of said State.

Amendment XIII

[Ratified 1865]

Section 1. Neither slavery nor involuntary servitude, except as a punishment for crime whereof the party shall have been duly convicted, shall exist within the United States, or any place subject to their jurisdiction.

Section 2. Congress shall have power to enforce this article by appropriate legislation.

Amendment XIV

[Ratified 1868]

Section 1. All persons born or naturalized in the United States, and subject to the jurisdiction thereof, are citizens of the United States and of the State wherein they reside. No State shall make or enforce any law which shall abridge the privileges or immunities of citizens of the United States; nor shall any State deprive any person of life, liberty, or property, without due process of law; nor deny to any person within its jurisdiction the equal protection of the laws.

Section 2. Representatives shall be appointed among the several States according to their respective numbers, counting the whole number of persons in each State, excluding Indians not taxed. But when the right to vote at any election for the choice of Electors for President and Vice-President of the United States, Representatives in Congress, the executive and judicial officers of a State, or the members of the legislature thereof, is denied to any of the *male* inhabitants of such State, being *twenty-one* years of age and citizens of the United States, or in any way abridged, except for participation in rebellion, or other crime, the basis of representation therein shall be reduced in the proportion which the number of such male citizens shall bear to the whole number of *male* citizens *twenty-one* years of age in such State.

Section 3. No person shall be a Senator or Representative in Congress, or Elector of President and Vice-President, or hold any office, civil or military, under the United States, or under any State, who, having previously taken an oath, as a member of Congress, or as an officer of the United States, or as a member of any State legislature, or as an executive or judicial officer of any State, to support the Constitution of the United States, shall have engaged in insurrection or rebellion against the same, or given aid or comfort to the enemies thereof. Congress may, by a vote of two-thirds of each house, remove such disability.

Section 4. The validity of the public debt of the United States, authorized by law, including debts incurred for payment of pensions and bounties for services in suppressing insurrection or rebellion, shall not be questioned. But neither the United States nor any State shall assume or pay any debt or obligation incurred in aid of insurrection or rebellion against the United States, or any claim for the loss or emancipation of any slave; but all such debts, obligations, and claims shall be held illegal and void.

Section 5. The Congress shall have power to enforce, by appropriate legislation, the provisions of this article.

Amendment XV

[Ratified 1870]

Section 1. The right of citizens of the United States to vote shall not be denied or abridged by the United States or by any State on account of race, color, or previous condition of servitude.

Section 2. The Congress shall have power to enforce this article by appropriate legislation.

Amendment XVI

[Ratified 1913]

The Congress shall have power to lay and collect taxes on incomes, from whatever source derived, without apportionment among the several States, and without regard to any census or enumeration.

Amendment XVII

[Ratified 1913]

Section 1. The Senate of the United States shall be composed of two Senators from each State, elected by the people thereof, for six years; and each Senator shall have one vote. The electors in each State shall have the qualifications requisite for electors of [voters for] the most numerous branch of the State legislatures.

Section 2. When vacancies happen in the representation of any State in the Senate, the executive authority of such State shall issue writs of election to fill such vacancies: Provided, that the Legislature of any State may empower the executive thereof to make temporary appointments until the people fill the vacancies by election as the Legislature may direct.

Section 3. *This amendment shall not be so construed as to affect the election or term of any Senator chosen before it becomes valid as part of the Constitution.*

Amendment XVIII
[Ratified 1919; repealed 1933 by Amendment XXI]

Section 1. *After one year from the ratification of this article the manufacture, sale, or transportation of intoxicating liquors within, the importation thereof into, or the exportation thereof from the United States and all territory subject to the jurisdiction thereof, for beverage purposes, is hereby prohibited.*

Section 2. *The Congress and the several States shall have concurrent power to enforce this article by appropriate legislation.*

Section 3. *This article shall be inoperative unless it shall have been ratified as an amendment to the Constitution by the legislatures of the several States, as provided by the Constitution, within seven years from the date of the submission thereof to the States by the Congress.*

Amendment XIX
[Ratified 1920]

Section 1. The right of citizens of the United States to vote shall not be denied or abridged by the United States or by any State on account of sex.

Section 2. Congress shall have the power to enforce this article by appropriate legislation.

Unratified Amendment
[Child Labor Amendment (proposed by Congress June 2, 1924)]

Section 1. *The Congress shall have power to limit, regulate, and prohibit the labor of persons under eighteen years of age.*

Section 2. *The power of the several States is unimpaired by this article except that the operation of State laws shall be suspended to the extent necessary to give effect to legislation enacted by Congress.*

Amendment XX
[Ratified 1933]

Section 1. The terms of the President and Vice-President shall end at noon on the 20th day of January, and the terms of Senators and Representatives at noon on the 3rd day of January, of the years in which such terms would have ended if this article had not been ratified; and the terms of their successors shall then begin.

Section 2. The Congress shall assemble at least once in every year, and such meeting shall begin at noon on the 3rd day of January, unless they shall by law appoint a different day.

Section 3. If, at the time fixed for the beginning of the term of the President, the President-elect shall have died, the Vice-President-elect shall become President. If a President shall not have been chosen before the time fixed for the beginning of his term, or if the President-elect shall have failed to qualify, then the Vice-President-elect shall act as President until a President shall have qualified; and the Congress may by law provide for the case wherein neither a President-elect nor a Vice-President-elect shall have qualified, declaring who shall then act as President, or the manner in which one who is to act shall be selected, and such person shall act accordingly until a President or Vice-President shall have qualified.

Section 4. The Congress may by law provide for the case of the death of any of the persons from whom the House of Representatives may choose a President whenever the right of choice shall have devolved upon them, and for the case of the death of any of the persons from whom the Senate may choose a Vice-President whenever the right of choice shall have devolved upon them.

Section 5. Sections 1 and 2 shall take effect on the 15th day of October following the ratification of this article.

Section 6. This article shall be inoperative unless it shall have been ratified as an amendment to the Constitution by the Legislatures of three-fourths of the several States within seven years from the date of its submission.

Amendment XXI
[Ratified 1933]

Section 1. The eighteenth article of amendment to the Constitution of the United States is hereby repealed.

Section 2. The transportation or importation into any State, Territory, or Possession of the United States for delivery or use therein of intoxicating liquors, in violation of the laws thereof, is hereby prohibited.

Section 3. This article shall be inoperative unless it shall have been ratified as an amendment to the Constitution by conventions in the several States, as provided in the Constitution, within seven years from the date of the submission thereof to the States by the Congress.

Amendment XXII
[Ratified 1951]

Section 1. No person shall be elected to the office of the President more than twice, and no person who has held the office of President, or acted as President, for more than two years of a term to which some other person was elected President shall be elected to the office of President more than once. But this article shall not apply to any person holding the office of President when this Article was proposed by the Congress, and shall not prevent any person who may be holding the office of President, or acting as President, during the term within which this Article becomes operative from holding the office of President or acting as President during the remainder of such term.

Section 2. This article shall be inoperative unless it shall have been ratified as an amendment to the Constitution by the legislatures of three-fourths of the several States within seven years from the date of its submission to the States by the Congress.

Amendment XXIII
[Ratified 1961]

Section 1. The District constituting the seat of Government of the United States shall appoint in such manner as the Congress may direct: A number of electors of President and Vice-President equal to the whole number of Senators and Representatives in Congress to which the District would be entitled if it were a State, but in no event more than the least populous State; they shall be in addition to those appointed by the States, but they shall be considered for the purposes of the election of President and Vice-President, to be electors appointed by a State; and they shall meet in the District and perform such duties as provided by the twelfth article of amendment.

Section 2. The Congress shall have the power to enforce this article by appropriate legislation.

Amendment XXIV
[Ratified 1964]

Section 1. The right of citizens of the United States to vote in any primary or other election for President or Vice-President, for electors for President or Vice-President, or for Senator or Representative in Congress, shall not be denied or abridged by the United States or any State by reason of failure to pay any poll tax or other tax.

Section 2. The Congress shall have the power to enforce this article by appropriate legislation.

Amendment XXV
[Ratified 1967]

Section 1. In case of the removal of the President from office or of his death or resignation, the Vice-President shall become President.

Section 2. Whenever there is a vacancy in the office of the Vice-President, the President shall nominate a Vice-President who shall take office upon confirmation by a majority vote of both Houses of Congress.

Section 3. Whenever the President transmits to the President pro tempore of the Senate and the Speaker of the House of Representatives his written declaration that he is unable to discharge the powers and duties of his office, and until he transmits to them a written declaration to the contrary, such powers and duties shall be discharged by the Vice-President as Acting President.

Section 4. Whenever the Vice-President and a majority of either the principal officers of the executive departments or of such other body as Congress may by law provide, transmit to the President pro tempore of the Senate and the Speaker of the House of Representatives their written declaration that the President is unable to discharge the powers and duties of his office, the Vice-President shall immediately assume the powers and duties of the office as Acting President.

Thereafter, when the President transmits to the President pro tempore of the Senate and the Speaker of the House of Representatives his written declaration that no inability exists, he shall resume the powers and duties of his office unless the Vice-President and a majority of either the principal officers of the executive department[s] or of such other body as Congress may by law provide, transmit within four days to the President pro tempore of the Senate and the Speaker of the House of Representatives their written declaration that the President is unable to discharge the powers and duties of his office. Thereupon Congress shall decide the issue, assembling within forty-eight hours for that purpose if not in session. If the Congress, within twenty-one days after receipt of the latter written declaration, or, if Congress is not in session, within twenty-one days after Congress is required to assemble, determines by two-thirds vote of both Houses that the President is unable to discharge the powers and duties of his office, the Vice-President shall continue to discharge the same as Acting President; otherwise, the President shall resume the powers and duties of his office.

[Ratified 1971]

Section 1. The right of citizens of the United States, who are eighteen years of age or older, to vote shall not be denied or abridged by the United States or by any State on account of age.

Section 2. The Congress shall have power to enforce this article by appropriate legislation.

[Equal Rights Amendment (proposed by Congress March 22, 1972; seven-year deadline for ratification extended to June 30, 1982)]

Section 1. *Equality of rights under the law shall not be denied or abridged by the United States or by any State on account of sex.*

Section 2. *The Congress shall have the power to enforce, by appropriate legislation, the provisions of this article.*

Section 3. *This amendment shall take effect two years after the date of ratification.*

[D.C. Statehood Amendment (proposed by Congress August 22, 1978)]

Section 1. *For purposes of representation in the Congress, election of the President and Vice-President, and article V of this Constitution, the District constituting the seat of government of the United States shall be treated as though it were a State.*

Section 2. *The exercise of the rights and powers conferred under this article shall be by the people of the District constituting the seat of government, and as shall be provided by Congress.*

Section 3. *The twenty-third article of amendment to the Constitution of the United States is hereby repealed.*

Section 4. *This article shall be inoperative, unless it shall have been ratified as an amendment to the Constitution by the legislatures of three-fourths of the several states within seven years from the date of its submission.*

[Ratified 1992]

No law, varying the compensation for the services of the Senators and Representatives, shall take effect, until an election of Representatives shall have intervened.

Admission of States to the Union

State	Year of Admission	State	Year of Admission
Delaware	1787	Michigan	1837
Pennsylvania	1787	Florida	1845
New Jersey	1787	Texas	1845
Georgia	1788	Iowa	1846
Connecticut	1788	Wisconsin	1848
Massachusetts	1788	California	1850
Maryland	1788	Minnesota	1858
South Carolina	1788	Oregon	1859
New Hampshire	1788	Kansas	1861
Virginia	1788	West Virginia	1863
New York	1788	Nevada	1864
North Carolina	1789	Nebraska	1867
Rhode Island	1790	Colorado	1876
Vermont	1791	North Dakota	1889
Kentucky	1792	South Dakota	1889
Tennessee	1796	Montana	1889
Ohio	1803	Washington	1889
Louisiana	1812	Idaho	1890
Indiana	1816	Wyoming	1890
Mississippi	1817	Utah	1896
Illinois	1818	Oklahoma	1907
Alabama	1819	New Mexico	1912
Maine	1820	Arizona	1912
Missouri	1821	Alaska	1959
Arkansas	1836	Hawaii	1959

Presidents of the United States

President	Term	President	Term
George Washington	1789–1797	Benjamin Harrison	1889–1893
John Adams	1797–1801	Grover Cleveland	1893–1897
Thomas Jefferson	1801–1809	William McKinley	1897–1901
James Madison	1809–1817	Theodore Roosevelt	1901–1909
James Monroe	1817–1825	William H. Taft	1909–1913
John Quincy Adams	1825–1829	Woodrow Wilson	1913–1921
Andrew Jackson	1829–1837	Warren G. Harding	1921–1923
Martin Van Buren	1837–1841	Calvin Coolidge	1923–1929
William H. Harrison	1841	Herbert Hoover	1929–1933
John Tyler	1841–1845	Franklin D. Roosevelt	1933–1945
James K. Polk	1845–1849	Harry S. Truman	1945–1953
Zachary Taylor	1849–1850	Dwight D. Eisenhower	1953–1961
Millard Fillmore	1850–1853	John F. Kennedy	1961–1963
Franklin Pierce	1853–1857	Lyndon B. Johnson	1963–1969
James Buchanan	1857–1861	Richard M. Nixon	1969–1974
Abraham Lincoln	1861–1865	Gerald R. Ford	1974–1977
Andrew Johnson	1865–1869	Jimmy Carter	1977–1981
Ulysses S. Grant	1869–1877	Ronald Reagan	1981–1989
Rutherford B. Hayes	1877–1881	George H. W. Bush	1989–1993
James A. Garfield	1881	Bill Clinton	1993–2001
Chester A. Arthur	1881–1885	George W. Bush	2001–2009
Grover Cleveland	1885–1889	Barack Obama	2009–

Glossary of Key Terms

Alamo Texas fort captured by General Santa Anna on March 6, 1836, from rebel defenders. Sensationalist accounts of the siege of the Alamo increased popular support in the United States for Texas independence. (p. 310)

Albany Congress June 1754 meeting in Albany, New York, of Iroquois and colonial representatives meant to facilitate better relations between Britain and the Iroquois Confederacy. Benjamin Franklin also put forward a plan for colonial union that was never implemented. (p. 131)

Alien and Sedition Acts 1798 security acts passed by the Federalist-controlled Congress. The Alien Act allowed the president to imprison or deport noncitizens; the Sedition Act placed significant restrictions on political speech. (p. 213)

American Anti-Slavery Society (AASS) Abolitionist society founded by William Lloyd Garrison in 1833 that became the most important northern abolitionist organization of the period. (p. 346)

American Colonization Society (ACS) Organization formed in 1817 to establish colonies of freed slaves and freeborn blacks in Africa. The ACS was led by a group of white elites whose primary goal was to rid the nation of African Americans. (p. 233)

American Equal Rights Association Group of black and white women and men formed in 1866 to promote gender and racial equality. The organization split in 1869 over support for the Fifteenth Amendment. (p. 438)

American System Plan proposed by Henry Clay to promote the U.S. economy by combining federally funded internal improvements to aid farmers with federal tariffs to protect U.S. manufacturing and a national bank to oversee economic development. (p. 265)

American system of manufacturing Production system focused on water-powered machinery, division of labor, and the use of interchangeable parts. The introduction of the American system in the early nineteenth century greatly increased the productivity of American manufacturing. (p. 244)

American Woman Suffrage Association Organization founded in 1869 to support ratification of the Fifteenth Amendment and campaign for women's suffrage. (p. 438)

Antifederalists Opponents of ratification of the Constitution. Antifederalists were generally more rural and less wealthy than the Federalists. (p. 206)

Appeal . . . to the Colored Citizens Radical abolitionist pamphlet published by David Walker in 1829. Walker's work inspired some white abolitionists to take a more radical stance on slavery. (p. 346)

Articles of Confederation Plan for national government proposed by the Continental Congress in 1777 and ratified in March 1781. The Articles of Confederation gave the national government limited powers, reflecting widespread fear of centralized authority. (p. 174)

Aztecs Spanish term for the Mexica, an indigenous people who built an empire in present-day Mexico in the centuries before the arrival of the Spaniards. The Aztecs built their empire through conquest. (p. 5)

Bacon's Rebellion 1676 uprising in Virginia led by Nathaniel Bacon. Bacon and his followers, many of whom were former servants, were upset by the Virginia governor's unwillingness to send troops to intervene in conflicts between settlers and Indians and by the lack of representation of western settlers in the House of Burgesses. (p. 47)

Battle of Saratoga Site of key Revolutionary War battle. The patriot victory at Saratoga in October 1777 provided hope that the colonists could prevail and increased the chances that the French would formally join the patriot side. (p. 173)

Battle of Shiloh April 1862 battle in Tennessee that provided the Union entrance to the Mississippi valley. Shiloh was the bloodiest battle in American history to that point. (p. 402)

benign neglect British colonial policy from about 1700 to 1760 that relaxed supervision of internal colonial affairs as long as the North American colonies produced sufficient raw materials and revenue; also known as *salutary neglect*. (p. 140)

Beringia Land bridge that linked Siberia and Alaska during the Wisconsin period. Migrants from northeast Asia used this bridge to travel to North America. (p. 5)

Bill of Rights The first ten amendments to the Constitution. These ten amendments helped reassure Americans who feared that the federal government established under the Constitution would infringe on the rights of individuals and states. (p. 207)

black codes Racial laws passed in the immediate aftermath of the Civil War by southern legislatures. The black codes were intended to reduce free African Americans to a condition as close to slavery as possible. (p. 432)

Black Death The epidemic of bubonic plague that swept through Europe beginning in the mid-fourteenth century and wiped out roughly half of Europe's population. (p. 10)

Bleeding Kansas The Kansas Territory during a period of violent conflicts over the fate of slavery in the mid-1850s. The violence in Kansas intensified the sectional division over slavery. (p. 376)

Boston Massacre 1770 clash between colonial protesters and British soldiers in Boston that led to the death of five colonists. The bloody conflict was used to promote the patriot cause. (p. 146)

carpetbaggers Derogatory term for white Northerners who moved to the South in the years following the Civil War. Many white Southerners believed that such migrants were intent on exploiting their suffering. (p. 440)

Church of England National church established by Henry VIII after he split with the Catholic Church. (p. 37)

Coercive Acts (Intolerable Acts) 1774 act of Parliament passed in response to the Boston Tea Party. The Coercive Acts were meant to force the colonists into submission, but they only resulted in increased resistance. Colonial patriots called them the Intolerable Acts. (p. 149)

Columbian exchange The biological exchange between the Americas and the rest of the world. Although the initial impact of the Columbian exchange was strongest in the Americas and Europe, it was soon felt all over the world. (p. 18)

committee of correspondence Type of committee first established in Massachusetts to circulate concerns and reports of protests and other events to leaders in other colonies in the aftermath of the Sugar Act. (p. 141)

Common Sense Pamphlet arguing in favor of independence written by Thomas Paine and published in 1776. *Common Sense* was widely read and had an important impact on the debate over declaring independence from Britain. (p. 165)

Compromise of 1850 Series of acts following California's application for admission as a free state. Meant to quell sectional tensions over slavery, the act was intended to provide something for all sides but ended up fueling more conflicts. (p. 368)

Compromise of 1877 Compromise between Republicans and southern Democrats that resulted in the election of Rutherford B. Hayes. Southern Democrats agreed to support Hayes in the disputed presidential election in exchange for his promise to end Reconstruction. (p. 446)

Confederate States of America Nation established in 1861 by the eleven slave states that seceded between December 1860 and April 1861. (p. 381)

conquistadors Spanish soldiers who were central to the conquest of the civilizations of the Americas. Once conquest was complete, conquistadors often extracted wealth from the people and lands they now ruled. (p. 20)

Continental Congress Congress convened in Philadelphia in 1774 in response to the Coercive Acts. The delegates hoped to reestablish the freedoms colonists had enjoyed in earlier times. (p. 149)

contraband Designation assigned to escaped slaves by Union general Benjamin Butler in May 1861. By designating slaves as property forfeited by the act of rebellion, the Union was able to strike at slavery without proclaiming a general emancipation. (p. 399)

Copperheads Northern Democrats who did not support the Union war effort. Such Democrats enjoyed considerable support in eastern cities and parts of the Midwest. (p. 409)

Corps of Discovery Expedition organized by the U.S. government to explore the Louisiana Territory. Led by Meriwether Lewis and William Clark, the expedition set out in May 1804 and journeyed to the Pacific coast and back by 1806 with the aid of interpreters like Sacagawea. (p. 237)

cotton gin Machine invented by Eli Whitney in 1793 to deseed short-staple cotton. The cotton gin dramatically reduced the time and labor involved in deseeding, facilitating the expansion of cotton production in the South and West. (p. 243)

Crusades Eleventh- and twelfth-century campaigns to reclaim the Holy Land for the Roman Catholic Church. The Crusades were, on the whole, a military failure, but they did stimulate trade and inspire Europeans to seek better connections with the larger world. (p. 9)

Declaration of Independence Document declaring the independence of the colonies from Great Britain. Drafted by Thomas Jefferson and then debated and revised by the Continental Congress, the Declaration was made public on July 4, 1776. (p. 166)

Declaration of Sentiments Call for women's rights in marriage, family, religion, politics, and law issued at the 1848 Seneca Falls convention. It was signed by 100 of the 300 participants. (p. 348)

Democratic-Republican Party Political party that emerged out of opposition to Federalist policies in the 1790s. The Democratic-Republicans chose Thomas Jefferson as their presidential candidate in 1796, 1800, and 1804. (p. 211)

Democrats and National Republicans Two parties that resulted from the split of the Democratic-Republicans in the early 1820s. Andrew Jackson emerged as the leader of the Democrats. (p. 275)

deskilling The replacement of skilled labor with unskilled labor and machines. (p. 333)

***Dred Scott* decision** 1857 Supreme Court case centered on the status of Dred Scott and his family. In its ruling, the Court denied the claim that black men had any rights and blocked Congress from excluding slavery from any territory. (p. 378)

Dunmore's Proclamation 1775 proclamation issued by the British commander Lord Dunmore that offered freedom to all enslaved African Americans who joined the British army. The proclamation heightened concerns among some patriots about the consequences of independence. (p. 165)

Emancipation Proclamation January 1, 1863, proclamation that declared all slaves in areas still in rebellion "forever free." While stopping short of abolishing slavery, the Emancipation Proclamation was, nonetheless, seen by blacks and abolitionists as a great victory. (p. 403)

Embargo Act 1807 act that prohibited American ships from leaving their home ports until Britain and France repealed restrictions on U.S. trade. The act had a devastating impact on American commerce. (p. 239)

encomiendas System first established by Columbus by which Spanish leaders in the Americas received land and the labor of all Indians residing on it. From the Indian point of view, the encomienda system amounted to little more than enslavement. (p. 14)

Enlightenment European cultural movement that emphasized rational and scientific thinking over traditional religion and superstition. Enlightenment thought appealed to many colonial elites. (p. 112)

Enrollment Act March 1863 Union draft law that provided for draftees to be selected by an impartial lottery. A loophole in the law that allowed wealthy Americans to escape service by paying $300 or hiring a substitute created widespread resentment. (p. 408)

Enterprise of the Indies Columbus's proposal to sail west across the Atlantic to Japan and China. In 1492 Columbus gained support for the venture from Ferdinand and Isabella of Spain. (p. 14)

Erie Canal Canal built in the early 1820s that made water transport from the Great Lakes to New York City possible. The success of the Erie Canal inspired many similar projects and ensured New York City's place as the premier international port in the United States. (p. 265)

Exodusters Blacks who migrated from the South to Kansas in 1879 seeking land and a better way of life. (p. 441)

Federalists Supporters of ratification of the Constitution, many of whom came from urban and commercial backgrounds. (p. 206)

Field Order Number 15 Order issued by General Sherman in January 1865 setting aside more than 400,000 acres of Confederate land to be divided into plots for former slaves. Sherman's order came in response to pressure from African American leaders. (p. 414)

Fifteenth Amendment Amendment to the Constitution prohibiting the abridgment of a citizen's right to vote on the basis of "race, color, or previous condition of servitude." From the 1870s on, southern states devised numerous strategies for circumventing the Fifteenth Amendment. (p. 438)

Fort Sumter Union fort that guarded the harbor in Charleston, South Carolina. The Confederacy's decision to fire on the fort and block resupply in April 1861 marked the beginning of the Civil War. (p. 395)

Fourteenth Amendment Amendment to the Constitution defining citizenship and protecting individual civil and political rights from abridgment by the states. Adopted during Reconstruction, the Fourteenth Amendment overturned the *Dred Scott* decision. (p. 436)

Freedmen's Bureau Federal agency created in 1865 to provide ex-slaves with economic and legal resources. The Freedmen's Bureau played an active role in shaping black life in the postwar South. (p. 427)

Fugitive Slave Act of 1850 Act strengthening earlier fugitive slave laws, passed as part of the Compromise of 1850. The Fugitive Slave Act provoked widespread anger in the North and intensified sectional tensions. (p. 368)

gag rule Rule passed by the House of Representatives in 1836 to table, or postpone action on, all antislavery petitions without hearing them read in order to stifle debate over slavery. It was renewed annually until it was rescinded in 1844. (p. 311)

Gettysburg Key July 1863 battle that helped turn the tide for the Union. Union victory at Gettysburg, combined with a victory at Vicksburg that same month, positioned the Union to push farther into the South. (p. 410)

Glorious Revolution 1688 rebellion that forced James II from the English throne and replaced him with William and Mary. The Glorious Revolution led to greater political and commercial autonomy for the British colonies. (p. 67)

gold rush The rapid influx of migrants into California after the discovery of gold in 1848. Migrants came from all over the world seeking riches. (p. 365)

Great Awakening Series of religious revivals in colonial America that began in 1720 and lasted to about 1750. (p. 114)

greenbacks U.S. treasury notes issued by the federal government during the Civil War. Using its new control over the currency and banking systems, the federal government issued large quantities of greenbacks during the war, contributing to inflation. (p. 405)

Haitian Revolution Revolt against French rule by free and enslaved blacks in the 1790s on the island of Saint Domingue. The revolution led in 1803 to the establishment of Haiti, the first independent black-led nation in the Americas. (p. 236)

Harpers Ferry, Virginia Site of the federal arsenal that was the target of John Brown's 1859 raid. Brown hoped to rouse the region's slave population to a violent uprising. (p. 379)

Hartford Convention 1814 convention of Federalists opposed to the War of 1812. Delegates to the convention considered a number of constitutional amendments, as well as the possibility of secession. (p. 262)

Hopewell people Indian people who established a thriving culture near the Mississippi River in the early centuries C.E. (p. 7)

horticulture A form of agriculture in which people work small plots of land with simple tools. (p. 5)

House of Burgesses Local governing body in Virginia established by the English crown in 1619. (p. 44)

import duty Tax imposed on goods imported into the colonies, paid by the importer rather than directly by the consumer; also known as a *tariff*. (p. 140)

impressment The forced enlistment of civilians into the army or navy. The impressment of residents of colonial seaports into the British navy was a major source of complaint in the eighteenth century. (p. 118)

Incas Andean people who built an empire in the centuries before the arrival of the Spaniards. At the height of their power in the fifteenth century, the Incas controlled some sixteen million people. (p. 7)

indentured servants Servants contracted to work for a set period of time without pay. Many early migrants to the English colonies indentured themselves in exchange for the price of passage to North America. (p. 44)

Indian Removal Act 1830 act by which Indian peoples in the East were forced to exchange their lands for territory west of the Mississippi River. Andrew Jackson was an ardent supporter of Indian removal. (p. 281)

Intolerable Acts *See* Coercive Acts.

Jamestown The first successful English colony in North America. Settled in 1607, Jamestown was founded by soldiers and adventurers under the leadership of Captain John Smith. (p. 42)

Jay Treaty 1796 treaty that required British forces to withdraw from U.S. soil, required American repayment of debts to British firms, and limited U.S. trade with the British West Indies. (p. 212)

Joint Electoral Commission Commission created by Congress to resolve the disputed presidential election of 1876. The commission consisted of five senators, five House members, and five Supreme Court justices—seven Republicans, seven Democrats, and one independent. The commission sided with the Republican presidential candidate, Rutherford B. Hayes. (p. 446)

Judiciary Act of 1801 Act passed by the Federalist-controlled Congress to expand the federal court system by creating sixteen circuit (regional) courts, with new judges appointed for each, just before Democratic-Republicans took control of the presidency and Congress. (p. 239)

Kansas-Nebraska Act 1854 act creating the territories of Kansas and Nebraska out of what was then Indian land. The act stipulated that the issue of slavery would be settled by a popular referendum in each territory. (p. 373)

King Philip's War 1675–1676 conflict between New England settlers and the region's Indians. The settlers were the eventual victors, but fighting was fierce and casualties on both sides were high. (p. 55)

King William's War 1689–1697 war that began as a conflict over competing French and English interests on the European continent but soon spread to the American frontier. Both sides pulled Indian allies into the war. (p. 71)

Knights of the Ku Klux Klan (KKK) Organization formed in 1865 by General Nathan Bedford Forrest to enforce prewar racial norms. Members of the KKK used threats and violence to intimidate blacks and white Republicans. (p. 443)

Liberal Republicans Political group organized to challenge the reelection of President Grant in 1872. The Liberal Republicans called for an end to federal efforts at Reconstruction in the South. (p. 445)

Liberator Radical abolitionist newspaper launched by William Lloyd Garrison in 1831. Through the *Liberator*, Garrison called for immediate, uncompensated emancipation of slaves. (p. 346)

Liberty Party Antislavery political party formed in 1840. The Liberty Party, along with the Free-Soil Party, helped place slavery at the center of national political debates. (p. 349)

Louisiana Territory Vast territory stretching from the Mississippi River to the Rocky Mountains and from New Orleans to present-day Montana that the United States purchased from France in 1803, doubling the size of the nation. (p. 236)

loyalist A colonial supporter of the British during the Revolutionary War. Loyalists came from all economic backgrounds and had a variety of motives for siding with the British. (p. 169)

manifest destiny Term coined by John L. O'Sullivan in 1845 to describe what he saw as the nation's God-given right to expand its borders. Throughout the nineteenth century, the concept of manifest destiny was used to justify U.S. expansion. (p. 313)

Marbury v. Madison 1803 Supreme Court decision that established the authority of the Supreme Court to rule on the constitutionality of federal laws. (p. 239)

Maya People who established large cities in the Yucatán peninsula. Mayan civilization was strongest between 300 and 800 C.E. (p. 7)

Mayflower Compact Written constitution created by the Pilgrims upon their arrival in Plymouth. The Mayflower Compact was the first written constitution adopted in North America. (p. 49)

McCulloch v. Maryland 1819 Supreme Court decision that reinforced the federal government's ability to employ an expansive understanding of the implied powers clause of the Constitution. (p. 239)

mercantilism Economic system centered on the maintenance of a favorable balance of trade for the home country, with more gold and silver flowing into that country than flowed out. Seventeenth- and eighteenth-century British colonial policy was heavily shaped by mercantilism. (p. 76)

Middle Passage The brutal voyage of slave ships laden with human cargo from Africa to the Americas. The voyage was the middle segment in a triangular journey that began in Europe, went first to Africa, then to the Americas, and finally back to Europe. (p. 77)

Missouri Compromise 1820 act that allowed Missouri to enter the Union as a slave state and Maine to enter as a free state and established the southern border of Missouri as the boundary between slave and free states throughout the Louisiana Territory. (p. 272)

Monroe Doctrine Assertion by President James Monroe in 1823 that the Western Hemisphere was part of the U.S. sphere of influence. Although the United States lacked the power to back up this claim, it signaled an intention to challenge Europeans for authority in the Atlantic world. (p. 267)

multiplier effect The diverse changes spurred by a single invention, including other inventions it spawns and the broader economic, social, and political transformations it fuels. (p. 242)

Nat Turner's rebellion 1831 slave uprising in Virginia led by Nat Turner. Turner's rebellion instilled panic among white Southerners, leading to tighter control of African Americans and reconsideration of the institution of slavery. (p. 302)

National Republicans *See* Democrats and National Republicans.

National Road Road constructed using federal funds that ran from western Maryland through southwestern Pennsylvania to Wheeling, West Virginia; also called the Cumberland Road.

Completed in 1818, the road was part of a larger push to improve the nation's infrastructure. (p. 242)

National Woman Suffrage Association Organization founded in 1869 to support women's voting rights. Founders Susan B. Anthony and Elizabeth Cady Stanton objected to the Fifteenth Amendment because it did not provide suffrage for women. (p. 438)

nativists Anti-immigrant Americans who launched public campaigns against foreigners in the 1840s. Nativism emerged as a response to increased immigration to the United States in the 1830s and 1840s, particularly the large influx of Catholic immigrants. (p. 337)

Navigation Acts Acts passed by Parliament in the 1650s and 1660s that prohibited smuggling, established guidelines for legal commerce, and set duties on trade items. In the 1760s, British authorities sought to fully enforce these laws, leading to resistance by colonists. (p. 140)

Neutrality Act 1793 act prohibiting ships of belligerent nations—including France and Great Britain—from using American ports. The act was meant to help keep America out of the conflict between France and Great Britain and to enhance U.S. commerce. (p. 210)

New Light clergy Colonial clergy who called for religious revivals and emphasized the emotional aspects of spiritual commitment. The New Lights were leaders in the Great Awakening. (p. 112)

Non-Intercourse Act Act passed by Congress in 1809 allowing Americans to trade with every nation except France and Britain. The act failed to stop the seizure of American ships or improve the economy. (p. 261)

Northwest Land Ordinance (1785 and 1787) Act of the confederation congress that provided for the survey, sale, and eventual division into states of the Northwest Territory. The 1787 act clarified the process by which territories could become states. (p. 198)

nullification The doctrine that individual states have the right to declare federal laws unconstitutional and, therefore, void within their borders. South Carolina attempted to invoke the doctrine of nullification in response to the tariff of 1832. (p. 278)

Old Light clergy Colonial clergy from established churches who supported the religious status quo in the early eighteenth century. (p. 112)

Oregon Trail The route west from the Missouri River to the Oregon Territory. By 1860, some 350,000 Americans had made the three- to six-month journey along the trail. (p. 363)

panic of 1819 The nation's first severe recession. The panic of 1819 lasted four years and resulted from irresponsible banking practices and the declining demand for American goods, including cotton, abroad. (p. 268)

panic of 1837 Severe economic recession that began shortly after Martin Van Buren's presidential inauguration. The panic of 1837 started in the South and was rooted in the changing fortunes of American cotton in Great Britain. (p. 311)

patriarchal family Model of the family in which fathers have absolute authority over wives, children, and servants. Most colonial Americans accepted the patriarchal model of the family, at least as an ideal. (p. 102)

Peace of Paris 1763 peace treaty that brought the Seven Years' War to a close. Under the terms of the treaty, Britain gained control of North America east of the Mississippi River and of present-day Canada. (p. 133)

Pequot War 1636–1637 conflict between New England settlers, their Narragansett allies, and the Pequots. The English saw the Pequots as both a threat and an obstacle to further English expansion. (p. 53)

Petticoat Affair 1829 political conflict over Jackson's appointment of John Eaton as secretary of war. Eaton was married to a woman of allegedly questionable character, and the wives of many prominent Washington politicians organized a campaign to snub her. (p. 278)

Pietists German Protestants who decried the power of established churches and urged individuals to follow their heart rather than their head in spiritual matters. Pietism had a profound influence on the leaders of the Great Awakening. (p. 112)

Pilgrims Group of English religious dissenters who established a settlement at Plymouth, Massachusetts, in 1620. Unlike more mainstream Protestants, the Pilgrims were Separatists who aimed to sever all connections with the Church of England. (p. 49)

Pinckney Treaty 1796 treaty that defined the boundary between U.S. and Spanish territory in the South and opened the Mississippi River and New Orleans to U.S. shipping. (p. 212)

Powhatan Confederacy Large and powerful Indian confederation in Virginia. The Jamestown settlers had a complicated and contentious relationship with the leaders of the Powhatan Confederacy. (p. 43)

Proclamation Line of 1763 Act of Parliament that restricted colonial settlement west of the Appalachian Mountains. The Proclamation Line sparked protests from rich and poor colonists alike. (p. 135)

Proclamation of Amnesty and Reconstruction 1863 proclamation that established the basic parameters of President Lincoln's approach to Reconstruction. Lincoln's plan would have readmitted the South to the Union on relatively lenient terms. (p. 431)

proprietary colonies Colonies granted to individuals, rather than held directly by the crown or given to chartered companies. Proprietors of such colonies, such as William Penn of Pennsylvania, had considerable leeway to distribute land and govern as they pleased. (p. 67)

Protestantism Religious movement initiated in the early sixteenth century that resulted in a permanent division within European Christianity. Protestants differed with Catholics over the nature of salvation, the role of priests, and the organization of the church. (p. 37)

Pueblo revolt 1680 uprising of Pueblo Indians against Spanish forces in New Mexico that led to the Spaniards' temporary retreat from the area. The uprising was sparked by mistreatment and the suppression of Indian culture and religion. (p. 70)

Puritans Radical English Protestants who hoped to reform the Church of England. The first Puritan settlers in the Americas arrived in Massachusetts in 1630. (p. 50)

Redeemers White, conservative Democrats who challenged and overthrew Republican rule in the South during Reconstruction. (p. 443)

redemptioners Immigrants who borrowed money from shipping agents to cover the costs of transport to America, loans that were repaid, or "redeemed," by colonial employers. Redemptioners worked for their "redeemers" for a set number of years. (p. 81)

Regulators Local organizations formed in North and South Carolina to protest and resist unpopular policies. After first seeking redress through official institutions, Regulators went on to establish militias and other institutions of self-governance. (p. 137)

Renaissance The cultural and intellectual flowering that began in Italy in the fifteenth century and then spread north. The Renaissance occurred at the same time that European rulers were pushing for greater political unification of their states. (p. 10)

Republican Party Party formed in 1854 that was committed to stopping the expansion of slavery and advocated economic development and internal improvements. Although their appeal was limited to the North, the Republicans quickly became a major political force. (p. 373)

scalawags Derisive term for white Southerners who supported Reconstruction. (p. 440)

seasoning The period of time in which newly arrived slaves regained their strength, adapted to their new environments, and were absorbed into American slave culture. (p. 78)

Second Continental Congress Assembly of colonial representatives that served as a national government during the Revolutionary War. Despite limited formal powers, the Continental Congress coordinated the war effort and conducted negotiations with outside powers. (p. 164)

Second Great Awakening Evangelical revival movement that began in the South in the early nineteenth century and then spread to the North. The social and economic changes of the first half of the nineteenth century were a major spur to religious revivals, which in turn spurred social reform movements. (p. 339)

Second Seminole War 1835–1842 war between the Seminoles, including fugitive slaves who had joined the tribe, and the U.S. government over whether the Seminoles would be forced to leave Florida and settle west of the Mississippi River. Despite substantial investments of men, money, and resources, it took seven years for the United States to achieve victory. (p. 307)

separate spheres The notion that men and women should occupy separate social, economic, and political spheres. According to this middle-class ideal, men were best suited for the public world of business and politics, while women were meant to manage the home. (p. 331)

sharecropping A system that emerged as the dominant mode of agricultural production in the South in the years after the Civil War. Under the sharecropping system, sharecroppers received tools and supplies from landowners in exchange for a share of the eventual harvest. (p. 441)

Shays's Rebellion 1786 rebellion by western Massachusetts farmers caused primarily by economic turmoil in the aftermath of the Revolutionary War. (p. 203)

Sons of Liberty Boston organization first formed to protest the Stamp Act. The Sons of Liberty spread to other colonies and played an important role in the unrest leading to the American Revolution. (p. 142)

spectral evidence Evidence given by spirits acting through possessed individuals. A number of the accused in the 1692 Salem witch trials were convicted on the basis of spectral evidence. (p. 99)

spoils system Patronage system introduced by Andrew Jackson in which federal offices were awarded on the basis of political loyalty. The system remained in place until the late nineteenth century. (p. 278)

Stamp Act 1765 act of Parliament that imposed a duty on all transactions involving paper items. The Stamp Act prompted widespread, coordinated protests and was eventually repealed. (p. 141)

Stono rebellion 1739 uprising by African American slaves in South Carolina. In the aftermath of the uprising, white fear of slave revolts intensified. (p. 87)

Sugar Act 1764 act of Parliament that imposed an import tax on sugar, coffee, wines, and other luxury items. The Sugar Act sparked colonial protests that would escalate over time as new revenue measures were enacted. (p. 140)

syncretic culture A hybrid culture that combines elements of previously distinct cultures. Enslaved African Americans created a syncretic culture by combining elements of African, West Indian, and European cultures. (p. 301)

Tejanos Mexican residents of Texas. Although some Tejano elites allied themselves with American settlers, most American settlers resisted the adoption of Tejano culture. (p. 310)

temperance The movement to moderate and then ban the sale and consumption of alcohol. The American temperance movement emerged in the early nineteenth century as part of the larger push for improving society from the 1820s to the 1850s. (p. 340)

Tenure of Office Act Law passed by Congress in 1867 to prevent President Andrew Johnson from removing cabinet members sympathetic to the Republican Party's approach to congressional Reconstruction without Senate approval. Johnson was impeached, but not convicted, for violating the act. (p. 437)

Thirteenth Amendment Amendment to the Constitution abolishing slavery. The Thirteenth Amendment was passed in January 1865 and sent to the states for ratification. (pp. 415, 431)

three-fifths compromise Compromise between northern and southern delegates to the 1787 Constitutional Convention to count enslaved persons as three-fifths of a free person in apportioning representation in the House of Representatives and taxation by the federal government. (p. 205)

total war The strategy of attacking civilian as well as military targets. Engaging in a war of attrition to wear down the Confederacy, General Grant and his commanders used this strategy in 1864 and 1865. (p. 413)

Townshend Act 1767 act of Parliament that instituted an import tax on a range of items including glass, lead, paint, paper, and tea. The Townshend Act prompted a boycott of British goods and contributed to violence between British soldiers and colonists. (p. 143)

Trail of Tears The forced march of some 15,000 Cherokees from Georgia to Indian Territory. Inadequate planning, food, water, sanitation, and medicine led to the deaths of thousands of Cherokees. (p. 309)

transcendentalism A movement founded by Ralph Waldo Emerson in the 1830s that proposed that individuals look inside themselves and to nature for spiritual and moral guidance rather than to the dogmas of formal religion. Transcendentalism attracted a number of important American writers and artists to its vision. (p. 341)

Treaty of Guadalupe Hidalgo 1848 treaty ending the Mexican-American War. By the terms of the treaty, the United States acquired control over Texas north and east of the Rio Grande plus the New Mexico territory, which included present-day Arizona and New Mexico and parts of Utah, Nevada, and Colorado. The treaty also ceded Alta California, which had declared itself an independent republic during the war, to the United States. (p. 316)

Treaty of New Echota 1836 treaty in which a group of Cherokee men agreed to exchange their land in the Southeast for money and land in Indian Territory. Despite the fact that the treaty was obtained without tribal sanction, it was approved by the U.S. Congress. (p. 308)

Treaty of Paris 1783 treaty that formally ended the conflict between Britain and its North American colonies. The newly established United States gained benefits from the treaty. (p. 182)

U.S. Sanitary Commission Federal organization established in June 1861 to improve and coordinate the medical care of Union soldiers. Northern women played a key role in the commission. (p. 405)

Uncle Tom's Cabin Novel published in 1852 by Harriet Beecher Stowe. Meant to publicize the evils of slavery, the novel struck an emotional chord in the North and was an international best seller. (p. 372)

underground railroad A series of routes from southern plantation areas to northern free states and Canada along which abolitionist supporters, known as conductors, provided hiding places and transportation for runaway slaves seeking freedom. (p. 346)

utopian societies Communities formed in the first half of the nineteenth century to embody alternative social and economic visions and to create models for society at large to follow. (p. 344)

Valley Forge Site of Continental Army winter encampment in 1777-1778. Despite the harsh conditions, the Continental Army emerged from its encampment at Valley Forge as a more effective fighting force. (p. 173)

Virginia Plan Plan put forth at the beginning of the 1787 Constitutional Convention that introduced the ideas of a strong central government, a bicameral legislature, and a system of representation based on population. (p. 204)

Walking Purchase 1737 treaty that allowed Pennsylvania to expand its boundaries at the expense of the Delaware Indians. The treaty, quite possibly a forgery, allowed the British to add territory that could be walked off in a day and a half. (p. 111)

War of the Spanish Succession 1702-1713 war over control of Spain and its colonies; also called Queen Anne's War. Although the Treaty of Utrecht that ended the war in 1713 was intended to bring peace through the establishment of a balance of power, imperial conflict continued to escalate. (p. 71)

Whig Party Political party formed in the 1830s to challenge the power of the Democratic Party. The Whigs attempted to forge a diverse coalition from around the country by promoting commercial interests and moral reforms. (p. 307)

Whiskey Rebellion Uprising by western Pennsylvania farmers who led protests against the excise tax on whiskey in the early 1790s. (p. 211)

Wilmot Proviso 1846 proposal by Democratic congressman David Wilmot of Pennsylvania to outlaw slavery in all territory acquired from Mexico. The proposal was defeated, but the fight over its adoption foreshadowed the sectional conflicts of the 1850s. (p. 316)

Women's National Loyal League Organization founded by abolitionist women during the Civil War to press Lincoln and Congress to enact universal emancipation. (p. 408)

XYZ affair 1798 incident in which French agents demanded bribes before meeting with American diplomatic representatives. (p. 213)

yeoman farmers Southern independent landowners who did not own slaves. Although yeomen farmers had connections to the South's plantation economy, many realized that their interests were not always identical to those of the planter elite. (p. 303)

Yorktown Site of decisive patriot victory. The surrender of British forces on October 19, 1781, at Yorktown, Virginia, effectively sealed the patriot victory in the Revolutionary War. (p. 181)

Chapter 2

Document 2.1: From *Word from New France: The Selected Letters of Marie de L'Incarnation*, translated and edited by Joyce Marshall. Copyright © Oxford University Press Canada 1967. Reprinted by permission of the publisher.

Map 2.1: "Jamestown, c. 1615" from *Pocahontas and Powhatan's Dilemma*, page viii, by Camilla Townsend.

Document 2.9: From *Encounters in the New World: A History in Documents* by Jill Lepore. Reprinted by permission of Oxford University Press, Inc.

Chapter 3

Figure 3.2: From *Time on the Cross: The Economics of American Negro Slavery* by Robert William Fogel and Stanley L. Engerman. Copyright © 1974 by Robert William Fogel and Stanley L. Engerman. Used by permission of W. W. Norton & Company, Inc.

Chapter 4

Table 4.2: From *Rape and Sexual Power in Early America* by Sharon Block. Copyright © 2006 by the University of North Carolina Press. Published for the Omohundro Institute of Early American History and Culture. Used by permission of the publisher, www.uncpress.unc.edu.

Map 4.1: From *At the Crossroads: Indians & Empires on a Mid-Atlantic Frontier, 1700–1763* by Jane T. Merritt. Copyright © 2003 by the University of North Carolina Press. Used by permission of the publisher, www.uncpress.unc.edu.

Chapter 11

Map 11.1: Reprinted from Whitney R. Cross, *The Burned-Over District: The Social and Intellectual History of Enthusiastic Religion in Western New York, 1800–1850*. Copyright © 1950 by Cornell University. Used by permission of the publisher, Cornell University Press.

Chapter 13

Document 13.6: Fred Spooner, Letter to Henry Joshua Spooner, April 30, 1861, Henry Joshua Spooner Papers, MSS 732, Box 1, Folder 6, the Rhode Island Historical Society. Used by permission.

Document 13.7: "Letter to His Parents," April 22, 1862, by John Hines. Hines Family Collection, MSS 91, Library Special Collections, Western Kentucky University, Bowling Green. Courtesy of Kentucky Library and Museum, Western Kentucky University.

Document 13.8: Ginnie Ott to Enos Ott, November 21, 1864, The Valley of the Shadow: Augusta County, Virginia, Personal Papers, University of Virginia Library (http://valley.lib.virginia.edu/papers/A2909). Used by permission of Gail Ott.

A Note about the Index: Names of individuals appear in boldface. Letters in parentheses following page numbers refer to documents (*d*), figures (*f*), illustrations (*i*), maps (*m*), and tables (*t*).

THE CONTEMPORARY WORLD

CANADA

Alaska
(U.S.)

Greenland
(Den.)

ICELAND

UNITED
KINGDOM

IRELAND

FRANCE

SPAIN

PORTUGAL

UNITED STATES

ATLANTIC
OCEAN

Azores
(Port.)

Bermuda (U.K.)

MOROCCO

Canary Is.
(Sp.)

Western Sahara
(Mor.)

MEXICO

BAHAMAS

DOMINICAN
REPUBLIC

HAITI

Puerto Rico (U.S.)

CUBA

ST. KITTS AND NEVIS

MAURITANIA

JAMAICA

ANTIGUA AND BARBUDA

CAPE
VERDE

BELIZE

Guadeloupe (Fr.)

DOMINICA

HONDURAS

Martinique (Fr.)

ST. VINCENT AND THE GRENADINES

SENEGAL

MALI

GUATEMALA

ST. LUCIA

BARBADOS

GAMBIA

EL SALVADOR

NICARAGUA

GRENADA

GUINEA-BISSAU

TRINIDAD AND TOBAGO

COSTA RICA

GUYANA

GUINEA

VENEZUELA

SURINAME

SIERRA LEONE

PANAMA

French Guiana (Fr.)

LIBERIA

COLOMBIA

CÔTE D'IVOIRE

Hawaii (U.S.)

BURKINA FASO

GHANA

PACIFIC OCEAN

Galápagos Is.
(Ec.)

ECUADOR

Equator

PERU

BRAZIL

SAMOA

BOLIVIA

TONGA

PARAGUAY

Easter I.
(Chile)

CHILE

ATLANTIC
OCEAN

URUGUAY

ARGENTINA

0   1,500   3,000 miles
0   1,500   3,000 kilometers

Falkland Is.
(U.K.)

80°N

60°N

40°N

20°N

0°

20°S

40°S

60°S

80°S

160°W   140°W   120°W   100°W   80°W   60°W   40°W   20°W

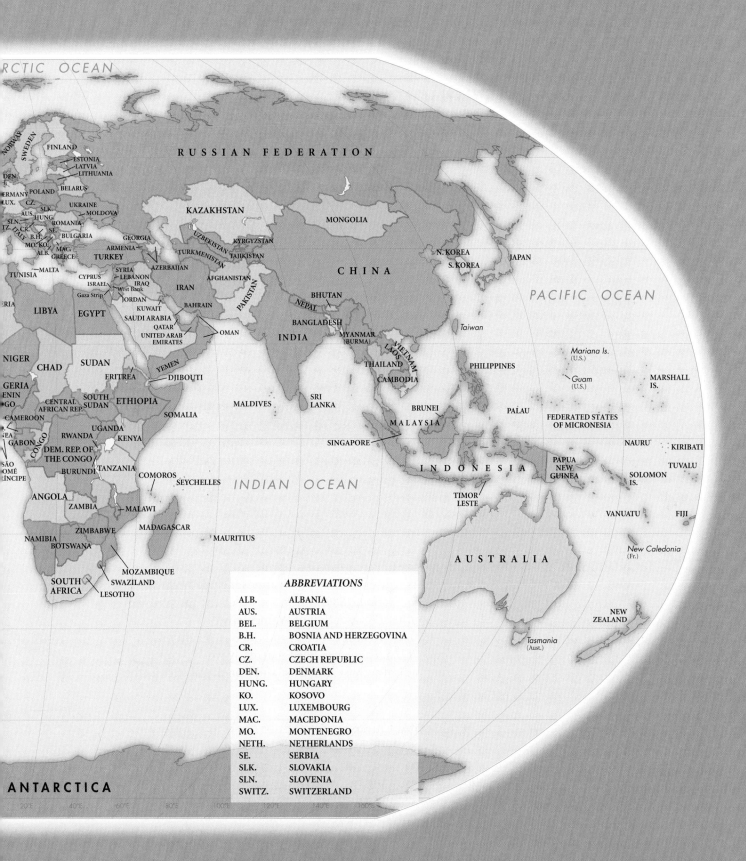

ARCTIC OCEAN

RUSSIAN FEDERATION

NORWAY
SWEDEN
FINLAND
ESTONIA
LATVIA
LITHUANIA
DEN.
GERMANY POLAND
BELARUS
LUX.
CZ.
SLK.
UKRAINE
MOLDOVA
AUS.
SLN.
HUNG.
ROMANIA
CR.
SE.
IZ.
B.H.
BULGARIA
ITALY
MO. KO.
MAC.
ALB.
GREECE
MALTA
TUNISIA

KAZAKHSTAN

MONGOLIA

GEORGIA
ARMENIA
TURKEY
AZERBAIJAN
CYPRUS
SYRIA
LEBANON
ISRAEL
West Bank
Gaza Strip
JORDAN
UZBEKISTAN
KYRGYZSTAN
TURKMENISTAN
TAJIKISTAN
IRAN
AFGHANISTAN
PAKISTAN

N. KOREA
S. KOREA
JAPAN

CHINA

PACIFIC OCEAN

ERIA
LIBYA
EGYPT
KUWAIT
SAUDI ARABIA
QATAR
UNITED ARAB
EMIRATES
BAHRAIN
OMAN
YEMEN
DJIBOUTI

BHUTAN
NEPAL
INDIA
BANGLADESH
MYANMAR
(BURMA)
LAOS
VIETNAM
THAILAND
CAMBODIA

Taiwan

Mariana Is.
(U.S.)
Guam
(U.S.)
MARSHALL
IS.

NIGER
CHAD
SUDAN
ERITREA
GERIA
BENIN
GO
CENTRAL
AFRICAN REP.
SOUTH
SUDAN
ETHIOPIA
SOMALIA
CAMEROON
EA
GABON
CONGO
UGANDA
RWANDA
KENYA
DEM. REP. OF
THE CONGO
BURUNDI
TANZANIA
SÃO
OMÉ
ÍNCIPE
ANGOLA
ZAMBIA
MALAWI
COMOROS
SEYCHELLES
MALDIVES
SRI
LANKA
PHILIPPINES
BRUNEI
MALAYSIA
PALAU
FEDERATED STATES
OF MICRONESIA
NAURU
KIRIBATI
SINGAPORE
INDONESIA
PAPUA
NEW
GUINEA
SOLOMON
IS.
TUVALU

INDIAN OCEAN

NAMIBIA
BOTSWANA
ZIMBABWE
MADAGASCAR
MAURITIUS
MOZAMBIQUE
SWAZILAND
SOUTH
AFRICA
LESOTHO

TIMOR
LESTE
VANUATU
FIJI

AUSTRALIA

New Caledonia
(Fr.)

NEW
ZEALAND

Tasmania
(Aust.)

ANTARCTICA

20°E   40°E   60°E   80°E   100°E   120°E   140°E   160°E

ABBREVIATIONS	
ALB.	ALBANIA
AUS.	AUSTRIA
BEL.	BELGIUM
B.H.	BOSNIA AND HERZEGOVINA
CR.	CROATIA
CZ.	CZECH REPUBLIC
DEN.	DENMARK
HUNG.	HUNGARY
KO.	KOSOVO
LUX.	LUXEMBOURG
MAC.	MACEDONIA
MO.	MONTENEGRO
NETH.	NETHERLANDS
SE.	SERBIA
SLK.	SLOVAKIA
SLN.	SLOVENIA
SWITZ.	SWITZERLAND

About the authors

Authors Steven F. Lawson and Nancy A. Hewitt outside the couple's home with their trusty consultant, Scooter.

Nancy A. Hewitt (Ph.D., University of Pennsylvania) is professor of history and of Women's and Gender Studies at Rutgers University. Her publications include *Southern Discomfort: Women's Activism in Tampa, Florida, 1880s–1920s,* for which she received the Julia Cherry Spruill Prize from the Southern Association of Women Historians; *Women's Activism and Social Change: Rochester, New York, 1822–1872*; and the edited volume *No Permanent Waves: Recasting Histories of U.S. Feminism.* She is currently working on a biography of the nineteenth-century radical activist Amy Post and a book that recasts the U.S. woman suffrage movement.

Steven F. Lawson (Ph.D., Columbia University) is professor emeritus of history at Rutgers University. His research interests include U.S. politics since 1945 and the history of the civil rights movement, with a particular focus on black politics and the interplay between civil rights and political culture in the mid-twentieth century. He is the author of many works, including *Running for Freedom: Civil Rights and Black Politics in America since 1941*; *Black Ballots: Voting Rights in the South, 1944–1969*; and *In Pursuit of Power: Southern Blacks and Electoral Politics, 1965–1982.*